CATALOGUE

OF THE

Books Manuscripts and Engravings

BELONGING TO

WILLIAM MENZIES

OF

NEW YORK

PREPARED BY JOSEPH SABIN

NEW YORK

1875

PRESS OF JOEL MUNSELL.
ALBANY, N. Y.

NOTICE.

THE intelligent and diligent book-buyer will need but little incentive to a perusal of this catalogue, for the reputation of Mr. William Menzies as a collector, who, to a ripened judgment unites a fastidious taste, is so extensive, that it is almost superfluous to attempt a description of his grand and probably unrivalled collection of books. It is much more than a collection, it is a library in every sense of the term; for in the departments to which it is devoted it is replete with the best editions of the best authors, in the very best condition, selected and purchased from time to time, without regard to cost, during a period of nearly forty years.

It has been at once our occupation and privilege, during the last five and twenty years, to compile many catalogues, some of which, from the nature and extent of the libraries catalogued, possess considerable bibliographical interest, but we have never, until now, had the pleasure of preparing a catalogue in which almost every book possesses special importance, and we might with propriety terminate this notice by remarking, that where all the books are good, it seems invidious to make a selection, but, as this catalogue will circulate among many buyers whose engagements are numerous, and whose time is limited, we have thought it worth while to group in a succinct preliminary notice some of the leading specialities.[1]

The department of Early Printed Books merits attention as containing some fine specimens by the inventors of Printing. Lots 74 and 167 being respectively the work of John Gutenberg, and Fust & Schoiffer; lot 75 is from the press of Peter Schoiffer; and there are several other examples, dated and undated, printed by the fathers of the art between the years 1460 and 1472; while English Printing is illustrated by a beautiful specimen of William Caxton's work, viz., lot 926 Higden's Polycronycon; and three examples of Wynkyn de Worde, one of which, lot 2132, is the earliest example of the use of Italian type in England.

The specimens of American Typography include some of the rarest of the books in this catalogue. Among them lot 665 Eliot's Bible, which, in addition to its claim as the first Bible printed in America, is worthy of distinction as being one of the finest copies in existence. Lot 514 besid

[1] The alphabetical list of the rare books which follows this notice was prepared for another pu but is reprinted for its convenience as to their order in the catalogue.

being an early specimen of printing in Massachusetts, 1663, is remarkable as the only known copy which has occurred for sale in 40 years. Lot 1511, by John Norton, 1664, is almost equally rare and interesting. Lot 1219 is conspicuous as the first book printed in Pennsylvania and is believed to be *unique*. Lot 1250 is the first book printed in New York, and the only known copy. Lot 990 is the first book printed in Boston. Lot 452 is the first book printed in Connecticut.

Of books printed by William Bradford, the first printer in the middle colonies, there are nearly 50 titles, many of which are properly included in the following list of rare books. Benjamin Franklin, *the printer*, is represented by upward of 20 titles, including an uncut copy of his *chef d'œuvre*, Cicero's Cato Major, and others equally rare. Chris. Sower, of Germantown battle-ground renown, is represented by several titles, so also is John P. Zenger, the successor to William Bradford.

Of Printing on Vellum, we have specimens of two of the only three works known to have been so printed in the United States; several Heures on vellum, printed in Paris, are here worthy of mention, as also is lot 2002 Turnbull's Birds of Pennsylvania, which is one of the most beautiful specimens of modern printing on vellum that we have ever seen.

It is scarcely necessary to remark that the zealous collector is always desirous of obtaining uncut copies of his favorite works, particularly of such as have generally fallen victims to the bookbinder's plough, in this special field Mr. Menzies has been more than ordinarily successful, for the library abounds in uncut copies many of which may be regarded as almost *unique*, and none of them as common. We content ourselves with a brief enumeration of some of their titles, viz., Smith's New Jersey, Heath's Memoirs, Peters' Connecticut, Franklin's Cato Major, Hutchinson's Massachusetts Bay and Papers, Backus' Church History, Burk's Virginia, Sanderson's Signers on large paper, Calef's More Wonders, Mather's Invisible World, Mather's Further Trials, Mante's American War, Bullock's Virginia, M'Call's Georgia, Thomas' History of Printing, Proud's Pennsylvania, Smith's Canada, and Donck's New Netherland.

Of books which relate to America, and possess the attraction of much rarity, the alphabetical list appended to this notice contains short titles of the principal portion, but we call special attention to a remarkably fine series of De Bry's, and of Hakluyt's Voyages, Purchas' Pilgrimes, Smith's Virginia, True Travels, and New-England, Mourt's Relation, Symmes' Piggwacket Fight, Denton's, Wolley's, and Smith's New York, the last on large paper and the only known copy, Hamor's, Bullock's and Jones' Virginia, Thomas' and Budd's Pennsylvania, Colden's Indian Nations, st edition, Cook's Sot-Weed Factor, Gorges' America Painted to the Life, e's North West Fox, Mather's Magnalia on large paper, and many other s by the Mathers, Romans' Florida, Anne Bradstreet's Poems, Colden's

Action in Matter, Hale on Witchcraft, Jefferson's Notes on Virginia, first edition, Trials of Gens. St. Clair and Lee, Linschoten's Voyages, Haywood's Tennessee, André's Cow Chace, Horsmanden's Negro Plot, three editions, and Campanius' New Sweden.

Among the more modern, but almost equally rare works, is a series of the books printed by Mr. George Wymberley-Jones, at Wormsloe. A set of Munsell's Historical Series on large paper, the only one ever offered for sale. The collections relative to Burke, Burr, Cobbett, Howe, Burgoyne, Wesley, Whitefield, Dr. Johnson, Paine, Wilkinson, Bancroft, &c., are unusually complete, and of much interest.

Mr. Menzies' predilection for the literature of Scotland will be conspicuously apparent in the editions of Burns. We are acquainted with no other catalogue in which may be found the Kilmarnock, the first Edinburgh, the first London, and the first two American editions; while the set of Scott's Novels is exceptionally fine, and *unique*.

The department of Bibliography, though not extensive, is nevertheless replete with the best English, French and American authors. The series of works by Thomas Frognal Dibdin is simply magnificent; in order to make it so, in some instances, not less than three copies of a work have been used in order to complete one without spot or blemish. Fine sets of Watt, Brydges, Beloe, Clarke, Horne, Lowndes, and Brunet, the last three on large paper, and the Bibliotheca Grenvilliana, also on large paper, are embraced in the series of English and French Bibliography. American Bibliography includes, among others, the works of Rich, Stevens, Asher, Ludewig, Faribault, Kennett, Ternaux, Harrisse, and Sabin, the last four of which are on large paper.

The collection of Illustrated Books includes so much that is excellent, that we should exhaust our list of adjectives in any attempt to do it justice. Preëminent and unapproachable, both as to extent and character, is the *piece de resistance* of the sale—Irving's Life of Washington extended to 10 vols., 4to. It is a set of books worthy of a much more expanded description than it has received in the catalogue, and, like many other works in this library, it must be seen and examined to be appreciated. It is the noblest tribute to the memory of the "father of his country" that Bibliomania has ever offered, and no amount of money could now produce its like. In regard to the illustrated books in general, we would call attention to the statement that they contain upward of Ten Thousand Choice Engravings, all, with scarce an exception, fine, strong, and choice impressions, a very large proportion of which are proofs, India proofs, etc., of the finest character, and highest class. The necessary inlaying has been done in the best manner, by Mr. Geo. Trent. In addition to the plates, nearly Three Hundred Autograph Letters are inserted, many of which strictly pertain to the works in which they are inserted, while all of them will be found to be in the most satisfactory condition. The reader is referred to the following lots viz.: 14 Adams' Works. 104 Bailey's Records of Patriotism. 150 Beloe's Sexagenarian. 190 Boaden's Shakespeare Portraits. 432 Colden's Life of Fulton. 504 Custis' Recollections of Washington. 579, 580, 587, 591, 592 and 593 Dibdin's Works. 623 Drake's History of Boston. 643 and 644 Dunlap's Works. 739 Francis' Old New York. 749 and 750 Franklin's Works. 767 Froissart's Chronicles. 794 Garden's American Anecdotes. 974 Hosack's Life of Clinton. 1042 and 1043 Irving's Works and Life. 1562 Parton's Life of Jackson. 1670 Randall's Life of Jefferson. 1693 Riedesel's Memoirs. 1752 Sanderson's Lives of the Signers. 1759 Sargent's Life of André. 1740 Blennerhassett Papers. 1767 Schroeder's Life of Washington. 1776 Scott's Novels. 1802 Knight's Shakspere. 2030 Walpole's Painters. 2048 Warren's American Revolution.

Of Manuscripts the number is not large, but the importance of lot 2051 can scarcely be over-estimated; it is Washington's Correspondence with General Reed during the American Revolution; and includes Fifty-four original Autograph Letters of Washington, which form the subject of an extended notice in the catalogue to which the reader is referred. We take occasion to remark that the library is unusually rich in works pertaining to General Washington, there being nearly two hundred Eulogies and Orations relative to his memory, all in the finest condition and mostly uncut, all the editions of the Washingtoniana, &c., and a few books from his library. Second only in interest to lot 2051, is lot 2095 General Wayne's MS. Orderly Book. Lot 95 is a Collection of Autograph Letters of the Presidents of the United States. Lot 1573 is Original Autograph Letters written by the Friends and Relatives of Washington, on the Portrait painted by Rembrandt Peale. Lot 1824 is a remarkably fine series of Autograph Letters of the Signers to the Constitution of the U. S. Lot 96 is a series of Autographs of Distinguished Americans. There are also Autograph Chapters from Irving's Washington, Bancroft's History, and Dawson's Battles of the U. S., Major Rogers' Original MS. Diary of the Siege of Detroit, Dr. Franklin's own annotated copy of the Second Protest, Autographs for Freedom, and, though last not least, A Poem by Robert Burns in his own hand-writing. In addition to these, some of the volumes are enriched by inserted autograph letters and signatures; Proud's Pennsylvania, Smith's New Jersey, and Greene's Life of Genl. Greene, are examples. There are also two fine and richly illuminated MSS. written on vellum during the fourteenth and fifteenth centuries respectively.

There are three books enumerated in the catalogue, of which one copy only has been printed in the style described, viz., Laurens' Letters, Pouchot's Memoir, and the Poetry of New Netherland.

The attention of the American collector may perhaps be arrested by the fact, that the most extensive, as well as the most important of the specialities which distinguish this remarkable collection, will be found in the assemblage of the books which relate to America — particularly to the British North American Colonies. We have elsewhere referred to some of the rarer and more curious works in which that department abounds, and would now remark, that there is scarcely an important work in English, claiming a place among the rare Americana, which may not be found in this fine library. Briefly, the collection of Americana has not been excelled in attractiveness or importance, by that of any other collection ever sold.

The condition of the books throughout, is all that the most exacting and tasteful collector can desire; the slightest blemish was always a cause for rejection; and as very nearly all of them are bound by the best English, French and American binders, including the names of Roger Payne, Bedford, Mackenzie, Hayday, Pratt, Lortic, Henderson & Bissett, David, Matthews, Bradstreet, and Smith, their state, internal and external, is unsurpassed by that of any other similar collection which has ever passed under our notice, or, of which we have any knowledge. This is high praise, but we know whereof we speak, and desire to create no impression concerning the books which will not be most amply borne out by the books themselves. The reader need be under no apprehension as to a too frequent use of the words scarce, rare, and most rare, &c., they have not been lightly considered, but express, according to the best of our knowledge and belief, the exact bibliographical status of the various works which are so described.

We cannot terminate this notice without expressing our acknowledgments to Mr. Menzies for his valuable assistance without which the catalogue would have fallen far short of its present completeness; neither can we forbear to direct attention to its typographical beauty. Mr. Munsell has printed it from entirely new type, and the result, typographically speaking, is a catalogue which in point of taste as to style, and accuracy as to composition, has rarely been excelled by any production of a similar character. As to the other characteristics of the catalogue they must speak for themselves. For reasons which do not concern the public, Mr. Menzies has directed the collection to be sold at auction, at a time and place to be hereafter announced. As nothing short of an actual inspection can convey an adequate idea of its beauty of condition, and general desirability, it will be on view (*by cards only*), one week previous to the sale.

JOSEPH SABIN.

LIST

OF SOME OF THE UNCOMMON, SCARCE, RARE AND VALUABLE BOOKS CONTAINED IN THIS CATALOGUE.

4 Acosta. Historie of the East and West Indies. *Lond.* 1604.
5 Acrelius. Christian Subjects. *Franklin & Hall. Phil.* 1756.
6 Acugna. Voyages and Discoveries in South America. *Lond.* 1698.
19 Adams. God's Eye on the Contrite. *Bost.* 1685.
20 Ady. A Candle in the Dark. *Lond.* 1756.
22 Aitken. (John the Painter.) Trial of. [*n.p.*] 1777.
23 Aitken. Short Account of the Motives of. Uncut. *Lond.* 1777.
29 Allen. Narrative of his Captivity. Orig. Ed. *Phil.* 1779.
32 Allen. Life of Philidor. Printed on Vellum. *Phil.* 1863.
42 Almon. The Remembrancer. 22 vols. *Lond.* [*v.d.*]
57 Analectic Press Series. 5 vols. Uncut. *N. Y.* 1872–73.
61 André. The Cow Chace. Orig. Ed. Uncut. *N. Y.* 1780.
63 André. Trial of. Orig. Ed. *Phil.* 1780.
74 Aquinas. Summa de Articulis &c. [*John Gutenberg. Mog.* 1460.]
75 Aquinas. Prima Pars Secunde. *Peter Schoiffer. Mog.* 1471.
76 Argensola. Molucco and Philippine Islands. *Lond.* 1708.
82 Ash and Rathband. Letter of Many Ministers. *Lond.* 1643.
83 Ash. Present State of Carolina. *Lond.* 1682.
89 Audubon. Birds. 7 vols. First 8vo Ed. *N. Y.* 1844.
90 Audubon. Quadrupeds. 3 vols. First 8vo Ed. Uncut. *N. Y.* 1854.
91 Augustinus. De Anima Et Spiritu. [*n.p.*] 1472.
94 Autographic Writings of Eminent Men. [*N. Y.* 1864.]
95 Autograph Letters of the Presidents of the United States.
96 Autographs of Distinguished Americans.
100 Backus. Hist. of New England. 3 vols. Uncut. *Bost.* 1777–96.
101 Backus. Church History of New England. *Bost.* 1804.
111 Bancroft. History of the U. S. 8 vols. L. P. Uncut. *Bost.* 1861.
120 Barbour. Life and Acts of Robert Bruce. *Edin.* 1758.
145 Beatty. Journal of a Tour. Orig. Ed. Uncut. *Lond.* 1768.
150 Beloe. The Sexagenarian. 2 vols. Uncut. Illustrated. *Lond.* 1817.
152 Benson. Vindication of the Captors of André. Uncut. *N. Y.* 1817.
163 Beverley. History of Virginia. *Lond.* 1722.
165 Bible. The Souldiers Pocket Bible. L. P. Uncut. *Camb.* 1861.
166 Bible. The Souldiers Pocket Bible. Printed on Vellum. *Lond.* 1862.
167 Bible. A Fragment. *Fust & Schoiffer. Mog.* 1462.
178 Bishop. New-England Judged. 3 Pts. Orig. Ed. *Lond.* 1661–67.

179 Bishop. New England Judged. *Lond.* 1703.
186 Bleecker. Works of Ann Eliza Bleecker. *N. Y.* 1793.
188 Blome. Present State of America. *Lond.* 1687.
193 Bond. Public Tryal of the Quakers. *Bost.* 1682.
198 Boston. Narrative of the Boston Massacre. Uncut. *Bost.* 1770.
199 Boston. Narrative of the Boston Massacre. *Lond.* 1770.
201 Boston. Account of the late Disturbance. Uncut. *Lond.* 1770.
223 Bradford Club. Publications. 11 vols. Uncut. *N. Y.* [*v.d.*]
225 Bradstreet. The Tenth Muse. *Lond.* 1650.
240 Brown. Bibliotheca Americana. 4 vols. Uncut. *Prov.* 1865–71.
243 Brunet. Manuel du Libraire. 12 vols. L. P. Uncut. *Paris.* 1860–65.
244 Bry. Grand Collection of Voyages. 9 vols. *Frank.* 1590–1602.
249 Brydges. Restituta. 4 vols. Uncut. *Lond.* 1814.
250 Brydges. Censura Literaria. 10 vols. Uncut. *Lond.* 1815.
257 Budd. Good Order Established in Pensilvania. *Lond.* 1685.
260 Bullock. Virginia Impartially Examined. Uncut. *Lond.* 1649.
261 Bulwer. Anthropometamorphosis. Bd. by Roger Payne. *Lond.* 1653.
262 Burder. The Welsh Indians. *Lond.* 1797.
276 Burk. History of Virginia. 4 vols. Uncut. *Petersb.* 1804–16.
282 Burns. Poems. First, or, Kilmarnock Ed. *Kilmar.* 1786.
283 Burns. Poems. First Edinburgh Ed. Uncut. *Edin.* 1787.
284 Burns. Poems. First London Ed. Uncut. *Lond.* 1787.
285 Burns. Poems. First New York Ed. *N. Y.* 1788.
286 Burns. Poems. First Philadelphia Ed. *Phil.* 1788.
289 Burns. Poems. 2 vols. Uncut. Illustrated. *Glas.* 1852.
294 Burnyeat. The Truth Exalted. *Lond.* 1691.
295 Burr. Burriana. 19 vols. *N. Y.* [*v.d.*]
300 Burrough. Persecution of the Quakers. *Lond.* 1660.
313 Byfield. The Late Revolution in New-England. *Lond.* 1689.
315 Cabeça de Vaca. Narrative of. L. P. Uncut. *Wash.* 1851.
319 Calef. Wonders of the Invisible World. Uncut. *Lond.* 1700.
320 Calef. Wonders of the Invisible World. Second Ed. *Salem.* 1796.
326 Callender. Hist. Discourse of Rhode Island. Orig. Ed. *Bost.* 1739.
327 Campanius. Description of New Sweden. *Stock.* 1702.
334 Carolina. Brief Description of the Province of. *Lond.* 1666.
339 Carter. A Genuine Detail &c. *Lond.* 1784.
344 Casas. Regionum Indicarum per Hispanos &c. *Heidelb.* 1564.
345 Casas. Popery Truly Displayed in its Bloody Colours. *Lond.* 1689.
346 Casas. First Voyages and Discoveries of the Spaniards. *Lond.* 1699.
347 Case. The Angelical Guide. Bound by Roger Payne. *Lond.* 1697.
351 Castell. A Short Discoverie of America. *Lond.* 1644.
352 Castleman. Description of Pennsylvania. *Lond.* 1726.
356 Catlin. North American Indians. 2 vols. Col. Plates. *Lond.* 1857.
362 Chalkley. Works of. *Franklin & Hall. Phil.* 1749.
364 Chalmers. Political Annals. Uncut. *Lond.* 1780.
368 Champlain. Voyages and Discoveries. *Paris.* 1613.
377 Charlevoix. New France. 6 vols. L. P. Uncut. *N. Y.* 1866–72.
383 Chauncy. Seasonable Thoughts. Uncut. *Bost.* 1743.

385 Chrysostomi. Liber beati Joannis Chrisostomi. [*Colon.* 1467.]
389 Cicero. Cato Major. Uncut. *B. Franklin. Phil.* 1744.
390 Cieça de Leon. Travels through Peru. *Lond.* 1709.
392 Clark. Ill Newes from New-England. Uncut. *Lond.* 1652.
395 Clarke. Narrative of the Battle of Bunker's Hill. Uncut. *Lond.* 1775.
397 Clarke. Repertorium Bibliographicum. Uncut. Illust. *Lond.* 1819.
398 Clayton. Account of Observables in Virginia. *Lond.* 1708.
422 Coddington. Demonstration of True Love. *Lond.* 1674.
428 Colden. First Causes of Action in Matter. Uncut. *N. Y.* 1745.
429 Colden. Hist. of the Indian Nations. Map. *W. Bradford. N. Y.* 1727.
442 Columbus. De Insulis Nuper Inuentis. *Basle.* 1494.
449 Condie. Life of George Washington. Orig. Ed. *Phil.* 1800.
451 Confession of Faith. *Bost.* 1680.
452 Confession of Faith. *New-Lond.* 1710.
455 Cook. The Sot-weed Factor. *Lond.* 1708.
464 Copie de deux Lettres envoiées de la Nouvelle France. *Alb.* 1835.
465 Corbin. Sermon preached at King's Town. *W. Bradford. N. Y.* 1703.
470 Corry. Life of George Washington. Orig. Ed. *Lond.* 1800.
479 Cotton. Abstract of the Lawes of New-England. *Lond.* 1641.
480 Cotton. Way of the Churches of Christ in New-England. *Lond.* 1645.
481 Cotton. The Bloudy Tenent Washed. *Lond.* 1647.
497 Currer. Catalogue of the Library at Eshton Hall. Uncut. *Lond.* 1820.
498 Currer. Catalogue of Miss Currer's Library. Uncut. *Lond.* 1833.
514 Davenport. A Discourse about Civil Government. *Camb.* 1663.
533 Dawson. The Gazette Series. 4 vols. Uncut. *Yonk.* 1866.
543 Deane. Address to the Citizens of the U. S. *Hart.* 1784.
545 Deane. Paris Papers. Uncut. *N. Y.* 1782.
549 DeBrahm. History of Georgia. L. P. Uncut. *Wormsloe.* 1849.
558 Denton. Brief Description of New-York. *Lond.* 1670.
566–594 Dibdin. Works. 53 vols. Uncut. *Lond.* [*v.d.*]
595 Dickinson. God's Protecting Providence. *Lond.* [*n.d.*]
609 Donck. Description of the New Netherlands. Uncut. *Amster.* 1656.
623 Drake. Hist. of Boston. 2 vols. L. P. Uncut. Illust. *Bost.* 1857.
628 Drayton. Northern and Eastern Tour. Uncut. *Char.* 1794.
630 Dring. Recollections of the Jersey Prison-Ship. *Prov.* 1829.
631 Dring. Recollections of the Jersey Prison-Ship. *N. Y.* 1831.
642 Dunlap. André. A Tragedy. *Lond.* 1799.
643 Dunlap. Hist. of the Am. Theatre. 4 vols. Uncut. Illust. *Lond.* 1833.
644 Dunlap. The Arts of Design. 6 vols. Uncut. Illust. *N. Y.* 1834.
655 Eccleston. Epistle to Friends. Uncut. *W. Bradford. N. Y.* 1732.
665 Eliot. Indian Bible. *Camb.* 1663.
666 Eliot. Communion of Churches. Uncut. *Camb.* 1665.
667 Eliot and Mayhew. Tears of Repentance. *Lond.* 1653.
679 Elmer. On the Character of Washington. Uncut. *Trenton.* 1800.
698 Exquemelin. Bucaniers of America. *Lond.* 1684.
699 Exquemelin. Bucaniers of America. 2 vols. *Lond.* 1771.
701 Fanning. Narrative of Col. D. Fanning. Uncut. *Rich.* 1861.
702 Faribault. Catalogue d'ouvrages. Uncut. *Queb.* 1837.

704 Federalist. 2 vols. Orig. Ed. Uncut. *N. Y.* 1788.
710 Ferriar. The Bibliomania. L. P. Uncut. *Lond.* 1809.
719 Filson. Discovery and Settlement of Kentucke. *Wil.* 1784.
721 Findley. History of the Insurrection. Uncut. *Phil.* 1796.
730 Force. Tracts relating to North America. Uncut. *Wash.* 1836.
737 Fox and Burnyeat. A N. E. Fire-Brand Quenched. [*n.p.*] 1679.
738 Foxe. North West Fox. Map. *Lond.* 1635.
739 Francis. Old New York. 4 vols. Uncut. Illustrated. *N. Y.* 1865.
740 Franklin. Proceedings *vs.* Mr. Hemphill. *B. Franklin. Phil.* 1735.
741 Franklin. Theophilus and Eugenio. *B. Franklin. Phil.* 1747.
743 Franklin. Account of the Penn. Hos. *Franklin & Hall. Phil.* 1754.
745 Franklin. The Second Protest. *Paris.* 1766.
749 Franklin. Works. 10 vols. L. P. Uncut. Illust. *Bost.* 1836–40.
751 Franklin. Tracts. *Franklin & Hall, and Sower. Phil.* 1759.
756 Freneau. Poems of Philip Freneau. *Phil.* 1786.
757 Freneau. Journey from Philadelphia to New York. *Phil.* 1787.
758 Freneau. Miscellaneous Works. *Phil.* 1788.
759 Freneau. Poems Written between the Years 1768–94. *Mon.* 1795.
760 Freneau. Letters on Interesting and Important Subjects. *Phil.* 1799.
761 Freneau. Poems Written during the Rev. War. 2 vols. *Phil.* 1809.
762 Freneau. Poems on American Affairs. 2 vols. Uncut. *N. Y.* 1815.
767 Froissart. Chronicles. 2 vols. Uncut. Illuminated. *Lond.* 1844.
773 Fulton. Treatise on Canal Navigation. L. P. *Lond.* 1796.
774 Furman. Notes on Brooklyn. Orig. Ed. Uncut. *Brook.* 1824.
778 Fyssher. Penytencyall Psalmes. *Wynkyn de Worde. Lond.* 1509.
779 Gage. The English-American. Best Ed. *Lond.* 1648.
799 Georgia. Late Political Observations. Uncut. *Wormsloe.* 1847.
814 Gomara. Historie of the Conquest of the Weast India. *Lond.* 1578.
816 Gorges. America Painted to the Life. *Lond.* 1659.
817 Gospel Order Revived. *W. Bradford. N. Y.* 1700.
823 Graves. Two Letters from W. Graves. Orig. Ed. *Lond.* 1782.
835 Gregorius. Liber Regule Pastoral &c. *Fust & Schoiffer. Mog.* [1465.]
836 Grenville. Bib. Grenvilliana. 4 vols. L. P. Uncut. *Lond.* 1842–72.
843 Groom. A Glass for the People of New-England. [*n.p.*] 1676.
848 Hacke. Collection of Original Voyages. *Lond.* 1699.
849 Haeghoort. Keten der Goddelyke &c. *J. P. Zenger. N. Y.* 1738.
850 Hakluyt. Voyages and Discoveries. *Lond.* 1589.
851 Hakluyt. Voyages and Discoveries. 3 vols. *Lond.* 1599–1600.
852 Hakluyt. Voyages and Discoveries. 5 vols. Uncut. *Lond.* 1809–12.
854 Hale. Enquiry into the Nature of Witchcraft. *Bost.* 1702.
870 Hamiltoniad. Papers Relating to the late Duel. Uncut. *Phil.* 1804.
871 Hamor. A True Discourse of Virginia. Orig. Ed. *Lond.* 1615.
876 Hanger. An Address to the Army. Uncut. *Lond.* 1789.
891 Harrisse. Biblio. Americana Vetus. L. P. Uncut. *N. Y.* 1866.
893 Harrisse. Early History of Printing in America. *N. Y.* 1866.
894 Harrisse. Notes on Columbus. *N. Y.* 1866.
900 Hartlib. The Reformed Virginian Silk-Worm. *Lond.* 1655.
906 Haywood. Civil Hist. of Tennessee. *Knox.* 1823.

909 Heath. Memoirs of Major-Gen. Heath. Uncut. *Bost.* 1798.

915 Hennepin. New Discovery in America. *Lond.* 1698.

916 Hennepin. New Discovery in America. *Lond.* 1699.

922 Heures a l' Usaige de Rome. Printed on Vellum. *Paris.* [1518.]

925 Hieronymi. Expositio Symboli Apostolorum. [*Cologne.* 1460.]

926 Higden. Polycronycon. *William Caxton. Lond.* 1482.

927 Higginson. New-England's Plantation. *Lond.* 1630.

928 Higginson. Cause of God in New England. *Camb.* 1663.

934 History of the War in America. 3 vols. Uncut. *Bost.* 1780.

937 Hoar. The Sting of Death, and Death Unstung. *Bost.* 1680.

942 Holbrook. N. American Herpetology. 5 vols. Uncut. *Phil.* 1842.

945 Holland. Herωologia Anglica. *Arnhem.* [1620.]

957 Hooke. New Englands Teares &c. *Lond.* 1641.

965 Hore Beate Marie Virginis. Printed on Vellum. *Paris.* 1500.

966 Hore Intemerate Virginis. Printed on Vellum. *Paris.* [1508.]

969 Horologium Devotionis. [*May.* 1480.]

971 Horsmanden. Detection of the Negro Conspiracy. *N. Y.* 1744.

972 Horsmanden. Detection &c. Uncut. *Lond.* 1747.

973 Horsmanden. History of the Negro Plot. Uncut. *N. Y.* 1810.

974 Hosack. Memoir of Clinton. 2 vols. Uncut. Illust. *N. Y.* 1829.

988 Howgill. The Deceiver of the Nations Discovered. *Lond.* 1600.

990 Hubbard. Narrative of the Indian Wars. *Bost.* 1677.

991 Hubbard. Narrative of the Indian Wars. *Bost.* 1775.

994 Hubley. Hist. of the American Revolution. Uncut. *North.* 1805.

1001 Humble Petition and Address. *Lond.* 1660.

1002 Humble Address to which King you please. *Lond.* 1691.

1020 Hutchins. Description of Virginia &c. Uncut. *Bost.* 1787.

1021 Hutchinson. Essay Concerning Witchcraft. Uncut. *Lond.* 1720.

1022 Hutchinson. Hist. of Mass. 3 vols. Uncut. *Lond.* 1760–1828.

1023 Hutchinson. Collection of Original Papers. Uncut. *Bost.* 1769.

1029 Impartial Hist. of the War. Uncut. *Lond.* 1780.

1031 Indian Treaty at Lancaster. Uncut. *B. Franklin. Phil.* 1744.

1032 Indian Conferences with Sir W. Johnson. *Lond.* 1756.

1033 Ingersoll. The War of 1812. 4 vols. Uncut. *Phil.* 1845–52.

1041 Irving. Washington. 12 vols. Uncut. L. P. Illust. *N. Y.* 1855–59.

1042 Irving. Works. 16 vols. L. P. Uncut. Illust. *N. Y.* 1860–63.

1043 Irving. Life of. 4 vols. L. P. Uncut. Illust. *N. Y.* 1862–64.

1053 Jacob. Life of Captain Cresap. Orig. Ed. *Cumb.* 1826.

1061 James. Life of Marion. Uncut. *Char.* 1821.

1067 Jefferson. Notes on Virginia. Orig. Ed. *Paris.* 1782.

1077 Jésuites. Relations des Jésuites. 3 vols. Uncut. *Queb.* 1858.

1080 Johnson. General History of the Pyrates. *Lond.* 1724.

1085 Johnson. Ethica. *Franklin & Hall. Phil.* 1752.

1086 Johnson. Noetica. *Franklin & Hall. Phil.* 1752.

1100 Jones. Present State of Virginia. *Lond.* 1725.

1104 Josselyn. New-Englands Rarities Discovered. *Lond.* 1672.

1105 Josselyn. Two Voyages to New-England. *Lond.* 1674.

1107 Journal of the Siege of Quebec, 1775–6. *Lond.* 1824.

1110 Joutel. Journal of the Last Voyage of De la Sale. *Lond.* 1714.
1120 Kay. Series of Original Portraits. 2 Vols. L. P. *Edin.* 1837–38.
1122 Keith. Visible Churches in N. England. *W. Bradford. Phil.* 1689.
1123 Keith. The Pretended Antidote. *W. Bradford. Phil.* 1690.
1124 Keith. A Serious Appeal. *W. Bradford. Phil.* 1692.
1129 Keith. Christian Faith of the Quakers. *W. Bradford. Phil.* 1692.
1134 Keith. Heresie and Hatred. *W. Bradford. Phil.* 1693.
1135 Keith. New England's Spirit &c. [*W. Bradford. n.p.* 1694.]
1136 Keith. Tryals of Boss, Keith, Budd, and Bradford. *Lond.* 1693.
1138 Keith. Reply to Increase Mather. *W. Bradford. N. Y.* 1703.
1139 Keith. The Spirit of Railing Shimei. *W. Bradford. N. Y.* 1703.
1142 Keith. The Notes of the True Church. *W. Bradford. N. Y.* 1704.
1143 Keith. Necessity of the Sacraments. *W. Bradford. N. Y.* 1704.
1144 Keith. Answer to Samuell Willard. *W. Bradford. N. Y.* 1704.
1146 Keith. Travels from New-Hampshire to Caratuck. *Lond.* 1706.
1148 Keith. Hist. of the British Plantations in America. *Lond.* 1738.
1153 Kennett. Bibliotheca Americanæ Primordia. L. P. *Lond.* 1713.
1155 Kidd. Proceedings in Relation to Captain Kidd. *Lond.* 1701.
1175 Knox. Campaigns in North-America. Uncut. *Lond.* 1769.
1181 Lallemant. Lettres Envoiées de la Nouvelle France. *Paris.* 1660.
1184 Landais. Memorial to Justify his Conduct. Uncut. *N. Y.* [1787.]
1196 Lawson. Christ's Fidelity against Satan's Malignity. *Lond.* 1704.
1200 Lawson. History of Carolina. Map and Plate. *Lond.* 1714.
1202 Lechford. Plain Dealing. *Lond.* 1642.
1205 Lee. Trial of Major Gen. Charles Lee. Orig. Ed. *Phil.* 1778.
1219 Leeds. The Temple of Wisdom. *W. Bradford. Phil.* 1688.
1220 Leeds. The Rebuker Rebuked. *W. Bradford. N. Y.* 1703.
1222 Leeds. Am. Almanack. 8 vols. *W. Bradford. N. Y.* 1731–43.
1223 Legendæ Catholicæ. Uncut. *Edin.* 1840.
1230 Leslie. Short and Easie Method with the Deists. *Bost.* 1738.
1233 Letchworth. A Descant on the Times. *Franklin & Hall. Phil.* 1766.
1238 Letters of Valens. Uncut. *Lond.* 1777.
1240 Letters Relating to Pennsylvania. Uncut. *Phil.* 1855.
1243 Lewis. Life of Mayster Wyllyam Caxton. L. P. *Lond.* 1737.
1250 Letter of Advice to a Young Gentleman. *W. Bradford. N. Y.* 1696.
1254 Linschoten. Voyages into ye Easte and West Indies. *Lond.* [1598.]
1255 Linschoten. Another Copy. Illustrations. *Lond.* [1598.]
1261 Livingston. Military Operations in North America. *Lond.* 1757.
1262 Livingston. Military Operations in North America. *Dub.* 1757.
1264 Long. Voyages and Travels. Uncut. *Lond.* 1791.
1283 Lucas. Journal and Letters of Eliza Lucas. Uncut. *Wormsloe.* 1850.
1285 Ludewig. American Local Hist. with Supplement. *N. Y.* 1846.
1288 M'Afee. Hist. of the War in the West. Uncut. *Lex.* 1816.
1290 M'Call. History of Georgia. 2 vols. Uncut. *Sav.* 1811–16.
1300 McIan. Clans of the Scottish Highlands. 2 vols. *Lond.* 1845.
1306 Mackenzie. Strictures on Tarleton's History. Uncut. *Lond.* 1787.
1307 M'Kinney. The Indian Tribes. 3 vols. Uncut. *Phil.* 1838–44.
1315 Madison. Selections from his Private Correspondence. *Wash.* 1859.

1322 Mante. History of the late War. Uncut. *Lond.* 1772.
1323 Manuscript. Hore Beate Marie Virginis. [*Sæc.* xv.]
1324 Marquette. Recit des Voyages, 1674–75. Uncut. [*Alb.* 1855.]
1329 Martin. Privately Printed Books. L. P. Uncut. *Lond.* 1834.
1332 Martyr. History of the West and East Indies. *Lond.* 1577.
1333 Martyr. Historie of the West Indies. *Lond.* [1597.]
1334 Martyr. The Famovs Historie of the Indies. *Lond.* 1628.
1338 Mason. Brief History of the Pequot War. *Bost.* 1736.
1342 Massachusetts. Comfort to a Melancholy Country. *Bost.* 1721.
1343 Massachusetts. Coll. of the Mass. Hist. Soc. 41 vols. Uncut. *Bost.* 1792–1871.
1350 Mather. Memorable Providences. *Lond.* 1691.
1351 Mather. Wonders of the Invisible World. Uncut. *Lond.* 1693.
1352 Mather. The Bostonian Ebenezer. *Bost.* 1698.
1353 Mather. Magnalia Christi Americana. L. P. *Lond.* 1702.
1354 Mather. Psalterium Americanum. *Bost.* 1718.
1355 Mather. India Christiana. *Bost.* 1721.
1356 Mather. The Christian Philosopher. *Lond.* 1721.
1357 Mather. Parentator. Memoirs &c. *Bost.* 1724.
1358 Mather. Memoirs of Rev. Increase Mather. *Lond.* 1725.
1359 Mather. Hist. of the War with the Indians. *Lond.* 1676.
1360 Mather. Discourse Concerning Comets. *Bost.* 1683.
1361 Mather. Illustrious Providences. *Bost.* 1684.
1362 Mather. Tryals of the N. E. Witches. Uncut. *Lond.* 1693.
1363 Mather. De Successu Evangelii. *Ultrajecti.* 1699.
1366 Mather. Church-Government Discussed. *Lond.* 1643.
1367 Mather. Modest and Brotherly Answer. *Lond.* 1644.
1368 Mather. The Life of Cotton Mather. *Bost.* 1729.
1369 Mather. America Known to the Ancients. *Bost.* 1773.
1376 Mayhew. The Snare Broken. *Bost.* 1766.
1377 Mayhew. Conquests and Triumphs of Grace. Uncut. *Lond.* 1695.
1379 Mein. Sagittarius's Letters. *Bost.* 1775.
1380 Mémoire Contenant le Précis des Faits. *Paris.* 1756.
1381 Memorial Containing a Summary View of Facts. *N. Y.* 1757.
1386 Metcalf. Narratives of Indian Warfare. Uncut. *Lex.* 1821.
1387 Michaux & Nuttall. Am. Sylva. 6 vols. Uncut. *Phil.* 1852–53.
1399 Indian Conferences. Uncut. *Franklin & Hall. Phil.* 1763.
1400 Minutes of the Trial of Certain Persons for Conspiracy. *Lond.* 1786.
1401 Missale Romanum. A MS. of the Fourteenth Century.
1402 Mitchel. Nehemiah on the Wall. *Camb.* 1671.
1404 Mocquet. Travels and Voyages into America. *Lond.* 1696.
1405 Mohawk. Book of Common Prayer. *Lond.* 1787.
1406 Monardes. Ioyfull Newes. *Lond.* 1596.
1409 Montanus. Die Unbekante Neue Welt. *Amster.* 1673.
1410 Montcalm. Letters from the Marquis de Montcalm. *Lond.* 1777.
1412 Moody. Narrative of his Exertions and Sufferings. *Lond.* 1783.
1415 Moore. A Voyage to Georgia. 1735. *Lond.* 1744.
1427 Morgan. Anti-Paedo-Rantism. *B. Franklin. Phil.* 1747.

1438 Morton. New-England's Memorial. *Bost.* 1721.
1440 Morton. New English Canaan. *Amster.* 1637.
1447 Mourt. Relation of Plimoth Plantation. *Lond.* 1622.
1454 Munsell. Historical Series. 10 vols. L. P. Uncut. *Alb.* 1857-61.
1456 Munsell. Local Hist. Series. 9 vols. L. P. Uncut. *Alb.* 1863-68.
1463 Murray. Impartial Hist. of the War. 3 vols. *Newcastle.* [*n. d.*]
1466 Nantucket. Papers Relating to Nantucket. Uncut. *Alb.* 1856.
1469 Narrative of the Miseries of New-England. *Lond.* 1689.
1475 New Englands First Fruits. *Lond.* 1643.
1476 New England. Brief Relation of the State of. *Lond.* 1689.
1477 New England. The Revolution in N. E. Justified. *Bost.* 1691.
1480 New-Netherland. Beschryvinge Van N. Nederlandt. *Aemstel.* 1656.
1481 New-Netherland. Vertoogh, &c. Uncut. *N. Y.* 1854.
1483 New-York. Laws of the Colony of. *W. Bradford. N. Y.* 1719.
1490 New-York. Journal of the Gen. Assembly. 1766-76. *Alb.* 1820.
1493 New-York. Natural Hist. 19 vols. Col. Plates. *Alb.* 1842-67.
1502 Nichols. Literary Anecdotes. 17 vols. Uncut. *Lond.* 1812-58.
1507 Noah's Dove. *W. Bradford. N. Y.* 1704.
1508 North American Review. 84 vols. *Bost.* 1815-56.
1510 Norton. Life and Death of John Cotton. *Lond.* 1658.
1511 Norton. Three Choice and Profitable Sermons. *Camb.* 1664.
1518 Oglethorpe. Account of South-Carolina and Georgia. *Lond.* 1732.
1519 Old England for Ever, or Spanish Cruelty display'd. *Lond.* 1740.
1531 Lex Parliamentaria. *W. Bradford. N. Y.* 1716.
1573 Peale. Washington Album. *Phil.* [1854.]
1577 Penn. Letter from William Penn. *Lond.* 1683.
1578 Penn. Information for Persons Inclined to America. [*Lond.* 1684.]
1580 Pennsylvania. Brief State of the Province of. Uncut. *Lond.* 1755.
1581 Pennsylvania. Answer to A Brief State. Uncut. *Lond.* 1755.
1582 Pennsylvania. Sequel to A Brief State. Uncut. *Lond.* 1756.
1583 Pennsylvania. True and Impartial State of. *Lond.* 1759.
1590 Peters. General History of Connecticut. Uncut. *Lond.* 1781.
1594 Philadelphia. Charter, Laws, &c., of the Phil. Lib.
Franklin & Hall. Phil. 1764.
1603 Pietas et Gratulatio. *Bost.* 1761.
1606 Plymouth. First Plymouth Patent. Printed on Vellum. *Camb.* 1854.
1612 Political Magazine. *Autographs of Washington.* *Lond.* 1783.
1619 Post. Second Journal of Christian Frederick Post. *Lond.* 1759.
1635 Prince. Chronological History of New England. *Bost.* 1736.
1645 Proud. Hist. of Pennsylvania. 2 vols. Uncut. *Phil.* 1797.
1646 Psalms. The Whole Book of Psalmes. Uncut. *Camb.* 1862.
1649 Purchas. Voyages and Discoveries. 5 vols. *Lond.* 1625-26.
1675 Reed and Cadwallader Controversy. 2 vols. *Phil.* 1783.
1681 Relation of Jesuit Missions in New France. *Alb.* 1854.
1686 Retrospective Review. 18 vols. Uncut. *Lond.* 1820-53.
1690 Rich. Bibliographical Works. 3 vols. Uncut. *Lond.* 1832-46.
1707 Robin. Travels in N. America. Orig. Ed. Uncut. *Phil.* 1783.
1712 Rochambeau. Memoirs of. Uncut. *Paris.* 1838.

1715 Rogers. MS. Diary of the Siege of Detroit. [1763-65.]
1718 Rogers. Ponteach: or the Savages of America. *Lond.* 1766.
1722 Romans. Concise History of Florida. *N. Y.* 1775.
1729 Ruskin. Modern Painters. &c. 7 vols. Uncut. *Lond.* 1849-60.
1733-4 Rutgers vs. Waddington. *N. Y.* 1784.
1736 Rutty. Liberty of the Spirit. *Franklin & Hall. Phil.* 1759.
1741 St. Clair. Trial of Major General St. Clair. *Phil.* 1778.
1744 St. Memin. Collection of Portraits. Uncut. *N. Y.* 1862.
1748 Sampson. The Female Review. Orig. Ed. *Ded.* 1797.
1750 Sanders. History of the Indian Wars. *Mont.* 1812.
1751 Sanderson. Bio. of the Signers. 9 vols. L. P. Un. *Phil.* 1820-27.
1752 Sanderson. Another Copy. S. P. Uncut. Illust. *Phil.* 1820-27.
1753 Sargent. Diary of St. Clair's Campaign. Uncut. *Wormsloe.* 1851.
1757 Sargent. Loyalist Poetry. Uncut. *Phil.* 1857.
1759 Sargent. Life of André. L. P. Uncut. Illustrated. *Bost.* 1861.
1765 Schoolcraft. Indian Tribes. 6 vols. L. P. Uncut. *Phil.* 1851-57.
1767 Schroeder. Washington. 4 vols. Uncut. Illust. *N. Y.* 1857-59.
1776 Scott. Novels. Abb. Ed. 24 vols. Uncut. Illust. *Lond.* 1844-47.
1794 Sewall. Phænomena quædam Apocalyptica. *Bost.* 1727.
1802 Shakspere. Works. 9 vols. Uncut. Illust. *Lond.* 1838-43.
1806 Shakespeare. Works. 12 vols. L. P. Uncut. *Bost.* 1857-66.
1809 Sharp. Sermon on Lady Cornbury. *W. Bradford. N. Y.* 1706.
1811 Shea. Jesuit Relations. 21 vols. L. P. Uncut. *N. Y.* 1858-66.
1815 Shepard. The Day Breaking. *Lond.* 1647.
1816 Shepard. The Clear Sunshine of the Gospel. *Lond.* 1648.
1817 Shepard. Eye-Salve. *Camb.* 1673.
1824 Signers of the Constitution of the U. S. [1787.]
1825 Simcoe. Military Journal. Orig. Ed. *Exeter.* [1787.]
1834 Simple Cobbler of Clerkenwell. Uncut. [*Lond.*] 1776.
1841 Smith. The American War. 1775-1783. *N. Y.* 1797.
1848 Smith. General Historie of Virginia. *Lond.* 1627.
1849 Smith. True Travels, Adventures, &c. *Lond.* 1630.
1851 Smith. General Historie of Virginia. *Lond.* 1632.
1859 Smith. History of New-Jersey. Uncut. *Bur.* 1765.
1863 Smith. History of the Province of New-York. L. P. *Lond.* 1757.
1864 Smith. Another Copy. S. P. *Lond.* 1757.
1867 Smith. Account of Bouquet's Expedition. *Phil.* 1765.
1868 Smith. Account of Bouquet's Expedition. Uncut. *Lond.* 1766.
1871 Smith. History of Canada. 2 vols. Uncut. *Queb.* 1815.
1882 South Carolina Documents. *Lond.* 1856.
1897 Stedman. Hist. of the American War. 2 vols. Uncut. *Lond.* 1794.
1903 Stephenson. A Call from Death to Life. *Lond.* 1660.
1916 Stith. History of Virginia. *Will.* 1747.
1918 Stokes. Narrative of his Official Conduct. *Lond.* [1784.]
1939 Syllacius. De Insulis Meridiani &c. *N. Y.* 1859.
1940 Symmes. Memoir of Piggwacket Fight. Orig. Ed. *Bost.* 1725.
1942 Tailfer. Narrative of the Colony of Georgia. *Char.* 1741.

1957 Thomas. Account of Pennsylvania &c. *Lond.* 1698.
1971 Thorowgood. Jews in America. *Lond.* 1650.
1972 Thorowgood. Jews in America. *Lond.* 1660.
1977 Timberlake. Memoirs. Uncut. *Lond.* 1765.
1982 Torrey. An Exhortation unto Reformation. *Camb.* 1674.
1983 Toulmin. Description of Kentucky. *Lond.* 1792.
1987 Trial of the British Soldiers. Orig. Ed. Uncut. *Bost.* 1770.
2002 Turnbull. Birds of Pennsylvania. Printed on Vellum. *Glas.* 1869.
2008 Van Driessen. Sermons. *J. P. Zenger. Alb.* 1726.
2013 Varnum. Trevett against Weeden. *Prov.* 1787.
2014 Vaughan. The Golden Fleece. Map. *Lond.* 1626.
2017 Vespuctius. Von der new gefundē Region &c. Uncut. *Paris.* [1861.]
2023 Voragine. Legenda Aurea. *Wynkyn de Worde. Lond.* 1527.
2030 Walpole. Anecdotes. 5 vols. Uncut. Illustrated. *Lond.* 1828.
2038 Ward. Simple Cobbler. First Edition. *Lond.* 1647.
2039 Ward. Simple Cobbler. Second Edition. *Lond.* 1647.
2048 Warren. The Am. Revol. 3 vols. Uncut. Illust. *Bost.* 1805.
2050 Washington. Journal of Major Geo. Washington. *Lond.* 1756.
2051 Washington. MS. Correspondence with Joseph Reed. 1775–82.
2075 Washington. Writings. 12 vols. L. P. Un't. Illust. *Bost.* 1837.
2095 Wayne. Original MS. Valley Forge Orderly Book. 1778.
2097–8 Webster. Works. 8 vols. L. P. Uncut. Illust. *Bost.* 1851–57.
2105 Welde. Short Story of the Antinomians. *Lond.* 1692.
2106 Wells. Life of Samuel Adams. 3 vols. L. P. Uncut. *Bost.* 1866.
2109 Wesleyiana. 13 vols. [*Lond. v.d.*]
2114 Wheatley. Poems on Various Subjects. Uncut. *Bost.* 1773.
2118 Whitbourne. Discourse of New-Found-Land. *Lond.* 1622.
2120 Whitefield. Journals &c. 7 vols. *Lond.* [*v.d.*]
2121 Whitefield. Marks of the New Birth. *W. Bradford. N.Y.* 1739.
2122 Whitefield. Answer to the Bishop. *W. Bradford. N. Y.* 1739.
2123 Whitefield. Three Letters from. *B. Franklin. Phil.* 1740.
2124 Whitfield. The Light Appearing. *Lond.* 1651.
2125 Whitfield. Strength out of Weakness. *Lond.* 1652.
2132 Whytinton. Tullyes Offyces. *Wynkyn de Worde. Lond.* 1534.
2137 Wilkinsoniana. 10 vols. Uncut. [*v.p. v.d.*]
2141 Willett Narr. of Marinus Willett. Uncut. Illust. *N. Y.* 1831.
2143 Williams. Virginia's Discovery of Silke-Wormes. *Lond.* 1650.
2145 Williams. Discourse concerning the Com. Prayer. *Lond.* 1694.
2152 Williams. The Bloudy Tenent. *Lond.* 1644.
2168 Wilson. An Account of Carolina. *Lond.* 1682.
2177 Wise. The Churches Quarrel Espoused. *Bost.* 1715.
2181 Wolley. A Two Years Journal in New York. *Lond.* 1701.
2187 Wood. New Englands Prospect. *Lond.* 1635.
2188 Wood. New England's Prospect. Third Ed. *Bost.* 1764.
2202 Zenger. Trial of John Peter Zenger. *Lond.* 1738.
2204 Zinzendorf. Remarks, &c. *B. Franklin. Phil.* 1742.

Catalogue.

1 ABBOT (A.) An Eulogy on the Illustrious Life and Character of George Washington; delivered before the Inhabitants of the Town of Haverhill, on his Birth Day, 1800. ... By Abiel Abbot. *Haverhill: Seth H. Moore.* [1800.]

8vo, pp. 27, 21. UNCUT. Includes a reprint of Washington's Farewell Address. *Presentation copy from the author.*

2 ABBOTT (J. J.) A Description of Harper's Printing Establishment. By John Jacob Abbott. Embellished with Numerous Engravings. *New York: Harper & Brothers.* [1855.]

Sq. 8vo, pp. 160. *Half purple morocco, gilt top,* UNCUT.

3 ABBOTT (J. S. C.) The History of Napoleon Bonaparte. By John S. C. Abbott. With Maps and Illustrations. *New York: Harper & Brothers.* 1855.

2 *vols., roy. 8vo, pp.* 611; 666. 2 *Portraits,* 251 *Engravings and* 37 *Maps. Half green levant morocco, gilt top,* UNCUT. Plate of LA BELLE ALLIANCE *inserted.*

This historical romance may be read with advantage as a counterpoise to Sir Walter Scott's Life of Napoleon, for though the facts are distorted the style is attractive.

4 ACOSTA (J.) The | Naturall | and Morall Historie of the | East and West | Indies. | Intreating of the remarkeable things of Heaven, of the | Elements, Mettalls, Plants and Beasts which are pro- | per to that Country: Together with the Manners, | Ceremonies, Lawes, Governments, and Warres of the Indians. | Written in Spanish by Joseph Acosta, and translated | into English by E. G. | *London | Printed by Val. Sims for Edward Blount and William | Aspley.* 1604.

Sm. 4to, pp. (6), 590, (14). *Gray calf, paneled sides, carmine edges.* A beautiful copy. RARE.

The best evidence of the merits of this work is, that it has been translated into almost every language in Europe. Sabin's Dictionary enumerates 22 editions.

Acosta composed part of his work in Peru, and the remainder on his return to Europe. The translator was Edward Grimstone.

"Replete with details of the Aborigines, before their peculiar customs had become modified by contact with the whites. Although he was one of the earliest, yet he was one of the most curious and accurate observers of the customs and peculiarities of the Aborigines who have attempted to describe them."— *Field.*

5 ACRELIUS (I.) A | Sermon, | Explaining | The Duties of Christian Subjects | to their Sovereign ; | Preached in | Christiana Church, | in Newcastle County and Christiana Hun- | dred, upon Delaware, on the Twenty-fourth | Sunday after Trinity, | in the year 1755. | By Israel Acrelius, M. A. | Commissary of the Swedish Congregations upon | Delaware, and Missionary at Christiana. | *Philadelphia :* | *Printed and Sold by* B. FRANKLIN | *and* D. HALL, *at the New Printing-* | *Office, in Market street,* MDCCLVI.

Sm. 8vo, pp. 23. *Half gray calf, carmine edges. Fine copy.*

Acrelius had charge of the Swedish churches in this country from 1749 to 1756, when he returned to Sweden. We have never seen another copy of this VERY RARE BOOK.

6 ACUGNA (C. de) Voyages and Discoveries in South America. The first up the River of Amazons to Quito in Peru, and back again to Brazil, ... By Christopher d'Acvgna. The Second up the River of Plata, and thence by Land to the Mines of Potosi, By Mons. Acarete. The Third from Cayenne into Guiana, in search of the Lake of Parima, reputed the richest place in the world, By M. Grillet and Bechamel. Done into English from the Originals, being the only accounts of those Parts hitherto extant.
London : S. Buckley. 1698.

8vo, pp. viii., 190, (2), 79, (4), 68. 2 *Maps. Polished calf, yellow edges, by* W. MATTHEWS. An elegant copy. SCARCE.

"Chapters XXVI. to XLIII., of Acugna's Relation, and almost all of that of Fathers Grillet and Bechamel are devoted to descriptions of the peculiarities of the Indian tribes they encountered. Their narratives possess a greater interest from being made by the first Europeans, who traversed these regions, and penetrated to the territories of the Indian nations, the Arragoues and Nouragones."—*Field.*

7 ADAIR (J.) The History of the American Indians ; particularly those Nations adjoining to the Mississippi, East and West Florida, Georgia, South and North Carolina, and Virginia : Containing An Account of their Origin, Language, Manners, Religious and Civil Customs, Form of Government, Punishments, Conduct in War and Domestic Life, their Habits, Diet, Agriculture, Manufactures, Diseases and Method of Cure, and other Particulars, sufficient to render it A Complete Indian System... . By James Adair, Esquire.
London : Charles Dilly. MDCCLXXV.

4to, pp. (10), 464. *Map. Half crushed blue levant morocco, gilt top,* UNCUT, *by* W. MATTHEWS. Fresh and clean as when issued.

"Mr. Adair points out various customs of the Indians, having a striking resemblance to those of the Jews ; and the great object of his work appears to be to prove that the aborigines of America are descended from that race."—*Allen's Bio. Dict.* See also *Rich,* and *Field.*

8 ADAMS [(Abigail.)] Journal and Correspondence of Miss Adams, Daughter of John Adams. Edited by her Daughter.
New York : Wiley and Putnam. 1841.

2 *vols., 12mo, pp. xii.,* 247 ; *xiii.,* 218. *Portraits and Plates. Half calf.*

9 ADAMS (A.) A Concise Historical View of the Difficulties, Hardships, and Perils, which attended the Planting and Progressive Improvements of New England. With a particular Account of its long and Destructive Wars, Expensive Expeditions, &c. By Amos Adams, A.M. Pastor of the First Church in Roxbury. ...
London: Edward and Charles Dilley. MDCCLXX.

8vo, pp. (4), 68. *Half morocco, gilt top,* UNCUT. *Very scarce in this condition.*

For an account of this rare work, see *Collections of the Mass. Historical Society.* XXVII. 280. Also *M. R.* XLII. 156.

10 ADAMS (H.) A Summary History of New-England, from the First Settlement at Plymouth, to the Acceptance of the Federal Constitution. Comprehending a General Sketch of the American War. By Hannah Adams. *Dedham: Printed for the Author.* 1799.

8vo. pp. 513, (3). *Half blue morocco.* PORTRAIT *inserted.*

11 ADAMS. A Memoir of Mrs. Hannah Adams, written by Herself. With Additional Notices by a Friend. *Boston: Gray and Bowen.* 1832.

12mo, pp. iv., 110. *Portrait. Half red morocco,* UNCUT.

12 ADAMS (J.) Letters of John Adams, addressed to his Wife. Edited by his Grandson, Charles Francis Adams.
Boston: Little and Brown. 1841.

2 *vols., 12mo, pp. xxxii.,* 286; *xx.,* 282. *Portrait. Half calf.* Uniform with No. 8.

13 ADAMS (*Mrs.* J.) Letters of Mrs. Adams, the Wife of John Adams. ... Edited by Charles F. Adams. *Boston: Little and Brown.* 1841.

2 *vols., 12mo, pp. xcv.,* 208; *xi.,* 282. *Portrait and Facsimile. Half calf.* Uniform with the preceding No.

14 ADAMS (J.) The Works of John Adams, Second President of the United States: With a Life of the Author, Notes and Illustrations, by his Grandson, Charles Francis Adams.
Boston: Little, Brown and Company. 1850–56.

10 *vols., imp. 8vo, half olive morocco, gilt top,* UNCUT. LARGE PAPER. *Two hundred copies printed.* Upwards of Two HUNDRED ILLUSTRATIONS, chiefly PORTRAITS, *inserted.* A BEAUTIFUL COPY. Uniform in size with the writings of *Washington, Franklin, Webster,* &c.

15 ADAMS. *and* [Leonard (Daniel.)] Novanglus, and Massachusettensis; or Political Essays, published in the years 1774 and 1775, on the Principal Points of Controversy, between Great Britain and Her Colonies. The former by John Adams, late President of the United States, the latter by Jonathan Sewall, then King's Attorney General of the province of Massachusetts Bay. To which are added a number of Letters, lately written by President Adams to the Honourable William Tudor; Some of which were never before published.
Boston: Hews & Goss. 1819.

8vo, pp. 312. *Half green morocco, gilt top,* UNCUT. *Portrait of* JOHN ADAMS *inserted.*

Notwithstanding the positive statement on the title, it is satisfactorily settled that Daniel Leonard was the author of "Massachusettensis."

16 ADAMS (J. Q.) Dermot Mac Morrogh, or the Conquest of Ireland. An Historical Tale of the Twelfth Century. In Four Cantos. By John Quincy Adams. *Boston: Carter, Hendee and Co.* 1832.

8vo, pp, 108. *Half green morocco, gilt top.* PORTRAIT *inserted.*

17 ADAMS. The Jubilee of the Constitution. A Discourse delivered ... in the City of New York, on ... the 30th of April, 1839; being the Fiftieth Anniversary of the Inauguration of George Washington as President of the United States. ... By John Quincy Adams. *New York:* M DCCC XXXIX.

8vo, pp. 136. *Half green morocco.* PORTRAIT of the AUTHOR, and a fine impression of the RARE PORTRAIT of WASHINGTON, engraved by CHAPMAN, *inserted.*

Abounding in valuable minute points of historical information which are not, elsewhere, to be met with.

18 ADAMS (S.) An Oration delivered at the State House, in Philadelphia, to a very numerous Audience, on Thursday, the 1st of August, 1776; by Samuel Adams, Member of the ******* ******* General Congress of the ****** ****** of America. *Philadelphia: Printed. London: Reprinted.* MDCCLXXVI.

8vo, pp. (2), 42. *Half claret morocco,* UNCUT. *Scarce.*

An undelivered oration. See Wells' *Life of Adams.* Vol. II. p. 439; Vol. III. p. 403. There is no Philadelphia edition.

"Mr. Adams the American Cicero, declaims with warmth and energy against kingly government and hereditary succession."—*M. R.* LV. p. 397.

19 ADAMS (W.) God's Eye | on the | Contrite | or a | Discourse | shewing | That True Poverty and Contrition of Spirit and Trembling at God's | Word is the Infallible and only way for the Obtaining and Retaining | of Divine Acceptation. | As it was made in the Audience of the General Assembly of the | Massachusetts Colony at Boston in New-England; | May 27. 1685. being the Day of Election there. | By Mr. William Adams. | *Boston in New-England,* | *Printed by Richard Pierce for Samuel Sewall.* 1685.

Sm. 4to, pp. (2), 41. *Crimson morocco, gilt edges, by* F. BEDFORD. FINE COPY of a PARTICULARLY RARE BOOK. One of the EARLIEST Boston imprints.

Priced in the "Nuggets" at £3.3.0.

20 ADY (T.) A | Candle in the Dark: | or, | A Treatise | Concerning the Nature of | Witches and Witchcraft: | Being | Advice to Judges, Sheriffes, Justices of the | Peace, and Grand-Jury-men what to do, be- | fore they passe Sentence on such as are Arraigned | for their lives, as Witches. | By Thomas Ady M.A. | *London,* | *Printed for R. I. to be sold by Tho. Newberry at the three Lions* | *in Cornhill by the Exchange.* 1756.

4to, pp. (6), 172. *Polished calf, carmine edges.* FINE COPY. VERY RARE.

"Of the three Books, into which this RARE VOLUME is divided, the first states that Witches are in the Scriptures; the second, how grossly they have been misinterpreted by Anti-Christ; and the third, the errors of some English writers upon the same subject."—*F. Wrangham.*

See Calef's *More Wonders.* p. 119. Also Drake's *Witchcraft Delusion.* Vol. III. p. 74.

21 ÆSOP. The Fables of Æsop. With a Life of the Author; and Embellished with One Hundred & Twelve Plates.

London: John Stockdale. 1793.

2 *vols., imp. 8vo, half calf antique.* A fine copy of Stockdale's magnificent edition, printed in large type, with 112 BEAUTIFUL ENGRAVINGS by Blake, Stothard, Landseer, etc., *fine and early impressions; scarce.*

The Prince copy brought £8 at Sotheby's in Nov. '63.

22 AITKEN (J.) The Trial at Large of James Hill, otherwise James Hind, otherwise James Aitken, commonly known by the name of John the Painter, who was tried and convicted at the Assizes held at Winchester, on Thursday March 6, 1777, and Executed and Hung in Chains, at Portsmouth, on Monday March 10, for Setting Fire to the Rope-house in his Majesty's Dock-yard at Portsmouth, on Saturday the 7th of December, 1776. Together with the Confession he made before Magistrates, and to Commissioner Gambier; and an Account of his Behaviour at the time of his Execution. Also, the Particulars of his Life, previous to his Setting Fire to the Dock-yard, which he gave to Mr. White, Keeper of the Goal at Winchester. The Second Edition. Copper Plate portrait of John the Painter, and figure of the machine by which he set Fire to the Rope-house.

[*London:*] 1777.

Sm. 8vo, pp. 94. *Half morocco.* EXCEEDINGLY RARE.

Aitken was a native of Scotland. He was condemned, executed, and hung in chains, for setting fire to the Royal Dock-yard and shipping at Portsmouth, in December, 1776. With the privity of Silas Deane, whom he met and conferred with at Paris, the attempt to destroy the government property, stores, and shipping at Portsmouth, was determined on, which, notwithstanding its apparently desperate and impracticable character, partially succeeded. From Deane, who supplied him with a royal passport, and a sum of money in advance, he had assurances of a reward proportioned to the services he should render to the American cause. The Counsel for the crown on the trial, publicly accused Benjamin Franklin and Silas Deane of complicity in the enterprise, and expressed a hope that they might be called to account for it. The affair, says Gordon, created much confusion, apprehension, and suspicion throughout England at the time of its occurrence.

23 AITKEN. A Short Account of the Motives which determined the man, called John the Painter; and a Justification of his Conduct; written by Himself, and sent to his Friend, Mr. A. Tomkins, with a request to publish it after his Execution. *London:* 1777.

4to, pp. 15. *Half morocco, gilt top,* UNCUT, *by* BRADSTREET. PORTRAIT of JOHN THE PAINTER *inserted.* A beautiful copy, VERY RARE.

"They think it monstrous and terrible, and I do not know what, to attempt to burn the Dock Yard at Portsmouth. Not considering how many docks, and towns, and ships of ours, have been burned by their soldiers in America." — P. 11.

24 ALDEN (T.) A Collection of American Epitaphs and Inscriptions, with Occasional Notes. By Rev. Timothy Alden, A.M. ... .

New York: 1814.

5 *vols.,* 16*mo, half morocco, gilt top,* UNCUT. *Clean* and *fine* as when issued. VERY RARE in such condition.

The only extensive series of American Epitaphs.

25 ALDEN (T. Jun.) A Sermon delivered ... in Portsmouth, January 5th, 1800. Occasioned by the Death of George Washington. By Timothy Alden, Jun. *Portsmouth:* 1800.

8vo, pp. 24. UNCUT.

26 ALEXANDER (C.) A Sermon; Occasioned by the Death of His Excellency George Washington, ... who departed this life, December 14, 1799, ÆT. 68 ... . By Caleb Alexander, A.M. Pastor of the Church in Mendon. *Boston:* 1800.

8vo, pp. 23.

27 ALLAN (J.) A Catalogue of the Books, Autographs, Engravings, and Miscellaneous Articles, belonging to the Estate of the late John Allan. *New York:* 1864.

Roy. 8vo, half green morocco, gilt top, UNCUT. LARGE PAPER. 100 *copies only printed. A Fine Unlettered India Proof* PORTRAIT *of* MR. ALLAN *inserted.*

"Sometime before the owner's death he would have sold his remarkable collection for fifteen thousand dollars, while it realized by the auction process about thirty-nine thousand. Taking the whole collection, it was the most extensive and valuable ever sold in America."—*W. Gowans.*

28 ALLAN. Catalogue of the Library and Antiquarian Collection of John Allan, Esq., with the Names of Purchasers and the price each article sold for, preceded by a few Introductory Remarks. [By William Gowans.] *New York: William Gowans.* 1865.

Roy. 8vo, half green morocco, gilt top, UNCUT. LARGE PAPER. 100 *copies only printed.* Contains list of purchasers' names and prices *only.*

29 ALLEN (E.) A Narrative of Colonel Ethan Allen's Captivity, From the Time of his being taken by the British, near Montreal, on the 25th Day of September, in the Year 1775, to the Time of his Exchange on the 6th day of May, 1778, Containing, His Voyages and Travels, With the most remarkable Occurrences respecting himself, and many other Continental Prisoners of different Ranks and Characters, which fell under his Observation, in the Course of the same; particularly the Destruction of the Prisoners at New York, by General Sir William Howe, in the Years 1776 and 1777. Interspersed with some Political Observations. Written by Himself, and now Published for the Information of the Curious of all Nations. [Motto.] Price Ten Paper Dollars. *Philadelphia, Printed and Sold by Robert Bell. In Third Street,* M.DCC.LXXIX.

8vo, pp. 46. *Brown morocco, gilt edges.* A *fine copy* of the ORIGINAL EDITION. A volume of the highest historical interest, and of the GREATEST RARITY.

Bought at the sale of Mr. Fisher's collection for fifty-six dollars.

30 ALLEN. [Title as above.] To which are now Added a considerable number of Explanatory and Occasional Notes, together with an Index of Reference to the most remarkable Occurrences in the Narrative. *Walpole, N. H.: Thomas and Thomas.* 1807.

12mo, pp. 158, (1). *Half green morocco.* PORTRAIT *inserted.*

This edition, which is VERY SCARCE, contains a list of the subscribers to the work.

31 ALLEN. Ethan Allen's Narrative of the Capture of Ticonderoga, and of His Captivity and Treatment by the British. Written by Himself. Fifth Edition, with Notes. *Burlington: C. Goodrich.* 1849.

8vo, pp. 50. *Half morocco, gilt top,* UNCUT, *by* BRADSTREET.
This edition contains much that is not in any other.

32 ALLEN (G.) The Life of Philidor, Musician and Chess-Player. By George Allen. *Philadelphia: E. H. Butler & Co.* 1863.

LARGEST SIZE. ONE OF TWO COPIES ONLY PRINTED ON VELLUM.
THE FIRST BOOK PRINTING EXECUTED ON VELLUM IN AMERICA.

Roy. 8vo, pp. (4), *xii.,* 156. *Elegantly bound in light green gros grained crushed levant morocco, richly ornamented back, paneled and gilt sides after Roger Payne's manner, gilt top,* UNCUT, *vellum end leaves, in a crimson morocco pull-off case.* A BEAUTIFUL EXAMPLE of the bookbinder's art as executed by MR. F. BEDFORD of London.

Contains the two additional leaves subsequently PRINTED ON VELLUM of which TWO COPIES ONLY were struck off, embracing an extra title page and a statement, on the part of the printer, relative to the difficulty between himself and the Author. Inserted are also the original note of invitation to the present owner requesting his presence at the PULLING OF THE FIRST VELLUM SHEET PRINTED IN AMERICA, and two newspaper cuttings, inlaid by TRENT, giving an account of the ceremonies observed on that interesting occasion.

See Plymouth. No. 1606.

33 ALLEN. Life of Philidor. [Another copy.] *Philadelphia: E. H. Butler & Co.* 1863.

8vo, pp. (4), *xii.,* 156. *Half green morocco, gilt top,* UNCUT. LARGE DUTCH LAID PAPER, *a few copies only printed, and very scarce.*

Contains the two additional leaves *subsequently printed,* embracing an extra title page and an account of the difficulty between the author and the printer.

34 ALLEN. Novena of Nine Tuesdays in Honor of St. Antony of Padua. *Philadelphia: H. McGrath.* 1859.

Sm. 8vo, pp. viii., 24. *Half calf, gilt top,* UNCUT. PRIVATELY PRINTED and VERY RARE.

35 ALLEN (I.) The Natural and Political History of the State of Vermont, one of the United States of America. To which is added, An Appendix, containing Answers to Sundry Queries, addressed to the Author. By Ira Allen, Esquire, Major-General of the Militia in the State of Vermont. *London: Printed by J. W. Myers for W. West.* 1798.

8vo, pp. vii., 300. *Map. Half green levant morocco, gilt top,* UNCUT, *by* W. MATTHEWS. A fine copy and RARE in *uncut* condition.

See *M. R. New Series.* XXIX. p. 260.

36 ALLEN (J.) An Oration on the Character of the late Gen. George Washington: Pronounced Before the Inhabitants of the Town of Western, on Saturday the 22d of February, 1800. By Joseph Allen, Junr. .... *Brookfield, Mass.: March.* 1800.

Sm. 4to, pp. 12. UNCUT. SCARCE.

37 ALLEN (P.) History of the Expedition under the Command of Captains Lewis and Clark, to the Sources of the Missouri, thence across

the Rocky Mountains and down the River Columbia to the Pacific Ocean, Performed during the years 1804-5-6. ...Prepared for the press by Paul Allen, Esquire. *Philadelphia: Bradford and Inskeep.* 1814.

2 vols., 8vo, pp. xxviii., 470; ix., 522. 6 Maps. Half red morocco, gilt top, UNCUT, *by* BRADSTREET. *A Beautiful copy.*

"This work was commenced by Captain Lewis himself, who was on his route to Philadelphia to engage in its completion, when the derangement seized him, under the influence of which he committed suicide at St. Louis. It was then undertaken by Mr. Nicholas Biddle, who in conjunction with Captain Clarke, arranged the numerous notes, and copious diaries and journals, kept by each of the principal explorers, and enlarged the skeleton of many incidents from the recollections of the survivor." — *Field.*

38 ALLEN (P.) A History of the American Revolution; comprehending all the Principal Events, both in the Field and in the Cabinet. To which are added the most Important Resolutions of the Continental Congress, and many of the most Important Letters of General Washington. By Paul Allen, Esq.
Baltimore: John Hopkins. 1819.

2 vols., 8vo, pp. xi., 592; xiii., 510. Half morocco, gilt top, UNCUT. AN ELEGANT COPY with scarce *inserted* PORTRAITS of Generals WASHINGTON and WAYNE.

"Although the name of Paul Allen is on the title, this work was written by John Neal and Mr. Watkins." — *Allen's Biog. Dict.*

39 ALLEN (W.) The American Biographical Dictionary: containing an Account of the Lives, Characters, and Writings of the most Eminent Persons, deceased in North America, from its First Settlement. By William Allen. Third Edition.
Boston: John P. Jewett and Company. 1857.

Roy. 8vo, pp. ix., 905. Half green morocco, gilt top, UNCUT.

The edition of 1809 was the first work of its kind issued in the United States.

40 ALLIBONE (S. A.) A Critical Dictionary of English Literature, and British and American Authors, Living and Deceased, from the Earliest Accounts to the Middle of the Nineteenth Century. Containing Thirty Thousand Biographies and Literary Notices, with Forty Indexes of Subjects. By S. Austin Allibone.
Philadelphia: J. B. Lippincott & Co. 1871.

3 vols., imp. 8vo, half red levant morocco, gilt top, UNCUT, *by* W. MATTHEWS. A SPLENDID COPY, with an *autograph note of the* AUTHOR *inserted.*

"It is not only the most extensive BIBLIOGRAPHICAL DICTIONARY extant, but the most comprehensive 'Classified Record of Works,' by English and American Authors, ever compiled. What gives a great and novel charm to the work is the introduction of Criticisms on the various authors, which are selected from the best authorities. The article on Shakspeare alone occupies 49 pages, in which 1,040 printed volumes and tracts are named." — *B. Quaritch.*

41 ALLISON (P.) A Discourse Delivered in the Presbyterian Church, in the City of Baltimore, the 22d February, 1800, the Day Dedicated to the Memory of Gen. George Washington. By the Reverend Patrick Allison, D.D. *Baltimore:* [1800.]

8vo, pp. 24. EXCEEDINGLY RARE.

42 [ALMON (John.)] The Remembrancer; or, Impartial Repository of Public Events. [17 vols.] *London: J. Almon, [and J. Debrett.]* MDCCLXXV to 1784.— A Collection of Interesting, Authentic Papers, relative to the Dispute between Great Britain and America: shewing the Causes and Progress of that Misunderstanding, from 1764 to 1775. *London: J. Almon.* MDCCLXXVII.— Journal of the Proceedings of Congress, Held at Philadelphia, from September 5, 1775, to April 30, 1776. *London: J. Almon.* MDCCLXXVIII.— The Remembrancer; ... Vol. I. The Third Edition. *London: J. Almon.* MDCCLXXV.— [And:] A Collection of the most Interesting Tracts, lately published in England and America, on the subjects of Taxing the American Colonies, and Regulating their Trade. [2 vols.] *London: J. Almon.* MDCCLXVI.

Together 22 vols., 8vo, calf, sprinkled edges, by CLYDE *of London. A remarkably fine* and *unusually complete* set of this EXTREMELY SCARCE work.

The two volumes of Tracts are VERY SCARCE, and are seldom found with the work, to which, however, they form an important addition. The later editions of the first volume of the Remembrancer are in royal octavo, and contain a "Map of the Invirons of Boston in 1775," together with several Important Papers not included in the first edition.

43 [ALMON.] The Remembrancer. *London:* 1775—81.

16 vols., 8vo, boards, UNCUT.

An incomplete set, consisting of The Journal of Congress May 10th, 1775.— The Journal of Congress September 5th, 1775.— The Prior Documents.— The Remembrancer, Vol. I., first edition, wanting signature T.— Vol. I., fourth edition, and Vols. II. to XII. Requiring the acquisition of the five latest vols. only, to complete an *uncut* set which would form a prominent feature in *any collection.*

"The American War gave rise to this Work in 1775. Every authentic paper relative to that war, as also with France and Spain, whether published in England or America, by the British Ministry or the American Congress, are all carefully inserted, also the letters of the several Commanding Officers, Addresses and Resolutions of the various Committees, Conventions, &c. To these have been prefixed a collection of authentic papers on the various subjects of dispute, from the resolutions which gave rise to the Stamp Act, in 1764, to the Battle of Lexington, in 1775." The above is the Publisher's account of this work, and may give some idea of its importance. COMPLETE SETS ARE NOW OF THE GREATEST RARITY.

44 ALSOP (G.) A Character of the Province of Maryland. Described in Four Distinct Parts. Also a Small Treatise on the Wild and Naked Indians (or Susquehanokes) of Maryland, their Customs, Manners, Absurdities, and Religion. ... By George Alsop. A New Edition with an Introduction and Copious Historical Notes. By John Gilmary Shea, LL.D. ... *New York: William Gowans.* 1869.

4to, pp. 125. *Portrait and Map. Catalogue, pp.* 40. *Half calf, gilt top,* UNCUT. LARGE PAPER; *sixty-four copies only printed.*

Forms part V. of Gowans' "Bibliotheca Americana." For the remainder of the series, *see* Nos. 258, 559, 1391, and 2182.

45 ALSOP (R.) A Poem; Sacred to the Memory of George Washington, Late President of the United States. Adapted to the 22d of Feb. 1800. By Richard Alsop. ... *Hartford:* 1800.

8vo, pp. 23. UNCUT.

46 AMBROSE (I.) Deaths Arrest. | A | Sermon | Preached | at Preston in Lancashire in Great- | Britain. | ... | By Isaac Ambrose, Minister of | Christ. | *New-York :* | *Re-printed and sold by* WILLIAM BRADFORD *in* | *the Year* 1733.

12*mo, pp.* 64. *Polished calf, gilt edges,* by F. BEDFORD. ONE OF THE RAREST OF BRADFORD'S IMPRINTS.

47 AMERICAN ANTIQUARIAN SOCIETY. Proceedings of, at the annual meeting held in Worcester, October 21, 1864. *Boston :* 1864.

8*vo, pp.* 80. *Half morocco, gilt top,* UNCUT. One of 25 *copies only printed on fine paper.*

48 AMERICAN HISTORICAL RECORD. Edited by Benson J. Lossing. *Philadelphia :* 1872–73.

Sm. 4*to, vols. I. and II., in parts as published.*

49 AMERICAN NOTES AND QUERIES. Nos. 1, to 4. [*Philadelphia: W. Brotherhead.* 1857.]

8*vo, pp.* 160. *Half calf,* UNCUT. An *Autograph letter* from the *publisher* announcing the failure of the work, and setting forth the causes thereof *inserted.*

Contains articles on " Book Illustrators," an account of the sale of " E. B. Corwin's Library," reprints of rare Autograph Letters, etc.

50 AMERICAN PIONEER. (The) A Monthly Periodical, Devoted to the objects of the Logan Historical Society ; or to Collecting and Publishing Sketches Relative to the Early Settlement and Successive Improvement of the Country. ...

Cincinnati : John S. Williams. 1842–3.

2 *vols., roy.* 8*vo, pp.* 448 ; 480. *Numerous Engravings. Half red morocco, gilt top,* UNCUT. A SPLENDID COPY. Very difficult to find Complete. PLATES and FACSIMILES of ANTIQUITIES, OLD HISTORICAL BUILDINGS, RELICS, &c.

Edited by John S. Williams.

" The great mass of historic material in these volumes is composed of Journals of Campaigns against the Indians, Narratives of Captivity, Incidents of Border Warfare, Biographical Sketches of Frontiersmen, Indian Warriors, and White Scouts."—*Field.*

51 AMERICA'S | APPEAL | to | The Impartial World. | Wherein the Rights of the Americans, as | Men, British Subjects, and as Colo- | nists ; the Equity of the Demand, and of the Man- | ner in which it is made upon them by Great Britain, | are stated and considered. And, | The Opposition made by the Colonies to Acts of Parlia- | ment, their resorting to Arms in their necessary | Defence, against the Military Armaments, | employed to enforce them, Vindicated. | *Hartford,* | *Printed by Ebenezer Watson.* 1775.

8*vo, pp.* 72. *Half morocco.*

A VERY RARE TRACT *not mentioned by* RICH. *We have never sold a copy.*

52 AMES (F.) An Oration on the Sublime Virtues of General George Washington, Pronounced at the Old South Meeting-House in Boston ... on Saturday the 8th of February, 1800. By Fisher Ames. *Boston : Young & Minns.* [1800.]

8*vo, pp.* 31. UNCUT. First Edition. RARE.

53 AMES. An Oration. [Another Edition.] *Philadelphia:* 1800.

8vo, pp. 51.

54 AMES. An Oration. [Another Edition.] *New York:* 1800.

55 AMES. Works of Fisher Ames. Compiled by a Number of his Friends. To which are prefixed, Notices of his Life and Character. [By J. T. Kirkland.] *Boston: T. B. Wait & Co.* 1809.

8vo, pp. xxxi., (6), 519. *Portrait. Half red morocco, gilt top,* UNCUT.

"American Principles" a Review of the above, by John Quincy Adams, 8vo, pp. 56, is bound in at the end of the volume. This, in its turn, was answered by John Lowell.

56 AMORY (T. C.) The Military Services and Public Life of Major General Sullivan, of the American Revolutionary Army. By Thomas C. Amory. *Boston: Wiggin and Lunt.* 1868.

8vo, pp. 320. *Portrait. Half green morocco, gilt top,* UNCUT.

57 ANALECTIC PRESS SERIES. [The following works are Printed exclusively for Private Distribution, and have never before occurred for sale.]

The series consists of:

I. American Chronology Illustrated by Quotations from Shakspeare. [By John B. Moreau.] *New York:* 1872.

pp. (3), 60. *Sixty copies only printed.*

II. A Collection of One Hundred and Fifty Engravings, Executed on Wood by Alexander Anderson, after his Ninetieth Year. With an Introductory Notice by Evart A. Duyckinck. *New York:* 1873.

pp. 8, (72). *Fifty copies only printed.*

III. Illustrations of Mother Goose's Melodies. Designed and Engraved on Wood by Alexander Anderson, M.D. With an Introductory Notice by Evart A. Duyckinck. *New York:* 1873.

pp. 10, (36). *Ten copies only printed.*

IV. Poems hitherto Uncollected, by the Rev. Francis L. Hawks, D.D. With a Preface by Evart A. Duyckinck. *New York:* 1873.

pp. 27. *Ten copies only printed. India proof* PORTRAIT *of the* AUTHOR *inserted.*

Extra No. Journal of a Cruise in the Fall of 1780 in the Private-Sloop of War, Hope. By Solomon Drowne, M.D., of Providence, R. I. With Notes by Henry T. Drowne. *New York:* 1872.

pp. 27. *Twenty-five copies only printed. The only copy with a half-title.* PORTRAIT *of one of the printers inserted.*

Together 5 vols., roy. 8vo, half light green crushed levant morocco, gilt top, UNCUT, *by* W. MATTHEWS.

Beautifully printed on one side only by MASTER CHARLES L. MOREAU, a youthful amateur printer, on his own private hand-press, exclusively for presents. In the production of the Extra No. Master Moreau was assisted by MASTER H. R. DROWNE.

AN ELEGANT, RARE AND MOST DESIRABLE SET OF VOLUMES.

58 [ANBURY (Thomas.)] Travels through the Interior Parts of America. In a Series of Letters. By an Officer. ... *London: William Lane.* MDCCLXXXIX.

2 *vols., 8vo, pp. vii.*, (21), 467; 558. *Map and 7 Plates. Half gray calf. Fine copy of* the FIRST EDITION, with the *Facsimiles of Continental Money*, not included in the Second.

59 [ANBURY.] Travels through the Interior Parts of America; in a Series of Letters. By an Officer. A New Edition.
London: William Lane. MDCCXCI.

2 vols., 8vo, half blue morocco, gilt top, UNCUT. *Map and* 6 *Plates. Very fine Copy.*

The Author was an officer under General Burgoyne, for whose unfortunate campaign these volumes were intended as a vindication.

60 ANDERSON [(Thomas.)] The History of the Life and Adventures of Mr. Anderson, containing his strange varieties of Fortune in Europe and America. Compiled from his own Papers. *London: Owen.* 1754.

12mo, pp. 263. *Half calf.*

The author was kidnapped in London, taken to America, and sold to a planter at Senupexen Inlet, Md., for £10, and afterwards joined the Virginia Rangers against the French Indians, &c. *See* M. R. x. 147.

61 ANDRÉ (*Major* John.) The Cow Chace. [As Originally published in Three Numbers of RIVINGTON'S ROYAL GAZETTE.]
New York: 1780.

Folio, half olive morocco, gilt top, UNCUT.

The VERITABLE FIRST EDITION of the COW CHACE, of which we are unable to trace the sale of any other copy.

62 ANDRÉ. The Cow Chace, A Poem in Three Cantos. By Major John André, Adjutant General to the British Army in New York, in 1780. *Albany: J. Munsell.* 1866.

Sm. 4to, pp. 69. *Half blue morocco, gilt top,* UNCUT. *Thirty Copies only printed. India proof* PORTRAIT of MAJOR ANDRÉ *inserted.*

Edited by Franklin B. Hough.

63 ANDRÉ. Proceedings of a Board of General Officers, Held by Order of His Excellency Gen. Washington, Commander in Chief of the Army of the United States of America. Respecting Major John André, Adjutant General of the British Army. September 29, 1780.
Philadelphia: Printed by Francis Bailey. M.DCC.LXXX.

Sm. 8vo, pp. (2), 21. *Crimson morocco, gilt top, nearly uncut.* AN Elegant Copy of the ORIGINAL EDITION. VERY RARE.

64 ANDRÉ. Proceedings of a Board of General Officers Respecting Major John André. *New York: Privately Printed.* 1867.

Roy. 8vo, pp. (2), 21. *Half green morocco, gilt top,* UNCUT. *Forty-nine Copies only printed* in EXACT FACSIMILE of the *rare original edition,* with the print of "THE UNFORTUNATE DEATH OF MAJOR ANDRÉ."

65 ANDRÉ. Minutes of a Court of Inquiry, upon the case of Major John André, with Accompanying Documents. ... With an Additional Appendix containing Copies of the Papers found upon Major André when arrested. *Albany: J. Munsell.* 1865.

Sm. 4to, pp. iv., 66. *Portrait. Half red morocco, gilt top,* UNCUT. *One hundred copies only privately reprinted* for Mr. John F. McCoy.

66 ANDRÉANA. Containing the Trial, Execution and Various Matters connected with the History of Major John André Adjutant General of the British Army in America, A.D., 1780.
Philadelphia: Horace W. Smith. 1865.

4to, pp. (4), 67, (4). *Half red morocco, gilt top,* UNCUT. *Fifty Copies only printed on this paper.*

The engravings published with the volume have been replaced with *finer* and *better* impressions. *Eight* fine PORTRAITS are *inserted*, mostly INDIA PROOFS and PROOFS BEFORE LETTERS, among which are the RARE PORTRAIT of ANDRÉ drawn by himself, and engraved by SHERWIN; and that of SIR H. CLINTON, engraved by BARTOLOZZI, and printed in tint.

67 [ANDREWS (Charles.)] The Prisoners' Memoirs; or Dartmoor Prison; Containing a Complete and Impartial History of the entire Captivity of the Americans in England, ... Also a Particular Detail of ... that Horrid Massacre at Dartmoor, on the Fatal Evening of the 6th of April, 1815. *New York: Printed for the Author.* 1815.

12mo, pp. 283. *Plate. Half olive morocco, gilt top,* UNCUT. The folded "View of Dartmoor Prison," is frequently wanting.

68 ANDREWS (E. W.) An Address before the Washington Benevolent Society, in Newburyport, on the 22d of Feb., 1816. By Edward W. Andrews, A.M. ... [In Verse.]
Newburyport: William B. Allen & Co. 1816.

8vo, pp. 15. *Half green morocco, gilt top,* UNCUT, *by* BRADSTREET. *India proof* PORTRAIT *of* WASHINGTON *inserted.*

69 ANDREWS (J.) History of the War with America, France, Spain, and Holland; commencing in 1775 and ending in 1783. By John Andrews, LL.D. With Portraits, Maps, and Charts.
London: MDCCLXXXVI.

4 *vols., 8vo, pp. ii.,* 448; 449; 445; 416, (60), *xiv.* 24 *Portraits and* 7 *Maps. Half olive morocco, gilt top,* UNCUT. FINE COPY.

Highly commended by Dr. Boucher. Includes portraits of Gens. Washington, Greene, Clinton, Burgoyne, Cornwallis, Lafayette, De Grasse, Count D'Estaing, and Captain Asgill.

70 ANDREWS (J.) An Eulogy on General George Washington. ... Delivered ... in Newburyport, February 22d, 1800. By John Andrews, A.M. ... *Newburyport:* [1800.]

8vo, pp. 21. UNCUT.

71 ANDROS (T.) The Old Jersey Captive: or a Narrative of the Captivity of Thomas Andros, ... on board the Old Jersey Prison-Ship at New York, 1781. In a series of Letters to a Friend. ...
Boston: William Peirce. 1833.

12mo, pp. 80. *Half crimson morocco.*

72 ANNUAL REGISTER. (The) Or a View of the History, Politicks, and Literature of the Years 1758 to 1792. *London: Dodsley.* 1759–92.

35 *vols., Index* 2 *vols., together* 37 *vols., 8vo, calf.*

These volumes cover the entire period of the American Revolution; for the history of which they are acknowledged to be the best and most profuse authority.

73 ANTIQUITY, HONOR, AND DIGNITY OF TRADE, particularly as connected with the City of London; Written by a Peer of England, and Addressed to his Youngest Son, as an Inducement to follow a Mercantile Concern. *Westminster: Machell Stace.* 1813.

Roy. 8vo, pp. (2), 65. *Paneled calf.* Printed on writing paper. EXCEEDINGLY SCARCE. SIXTY PORTRAITS *inserted;* many of which are SCARCE and CURIOUS and some VERY RARE.

From the De La Forrest collection, at the sale of which the late Mr. John Allan was an eager competitor and always coveted the work, which he never was able to obtain.

74 **Aquinas (Thomas.) Summa de Articulis Fidei et Ecclesiæ Sacramentis.** [*Moguntiæ: typis Joh. Guttenberg. Circa.* 1460.]

Sm. 4to, Gothic Letter, rubricated capitals, 13 *leaves,* 34 *lines to a page. Not in* BRUNET. *Olive morocco, richly tooled and gilt sides after an elegant Grolier pattern, inside lined with polished crimson morocco beautifully tooled and gilt, morocco joints, gilt edges.*

IN THE FINEST STATE OF PRESERVATION.

"One of the scarcest books in the world, consisting only of 12 leaves according to Santander; Panzer says 13, and Laire, Ind. II. p. 260, gives it 14. Panzer is most correct: it ends in the following manner:

'Explicit summa de articulis et ecclesie sacramentis, edita a fratre Thoma de Aquino ordinis fratrum predicatorum DEO GRATIAS.'

The types exactly resemble those used in the celebrated Catholicon of Joh. de Balbis in 1460; it is printed in long lines, of which there are 34 in a page. No mark of punctuation but the period, no initial letters, catchword, signature, &c. The paper thick, white, and good."—Beloe's *Anecdotes of Scarce Books.* Vol. IV. page 138.

The following occurs on the fly leaf: "With the exception of a perfect copy of the Mazarine Bible, belonging to Mr. Lenox, and the fragment of the same work in my collection, this little tract is believed to be the earliest specimen of typography in this country."—G(EORGE) L(IVERMORE.)

75 **Aquinas. Incipit Prima Pars Secunde Edita a Fratre Thoma De Aquino.** (Colophon.) *Alma in vrbe moguntina. ... p petrū Schoiffer de gernshem. Anno dn̄i millesimo quadringentesimo Septuagesimo p̄mo.* [1471] *Octaua die nouembris.*

Folio, Gothic Letter, rubricated capitals, 175 *double column leaves,* 61 *lines to a column.*

Half old morocco. A VERY LARGE COPY.

Notwithstanding that a worm has pierced a few leaves, and that some others are slightly water-stained; this volume forms a most desirable specimen of the "divine art" in its infant state. The precision and regularity of its register are not excelled by the best typographical examples of the present day. Books with a date so early as 1471 are of very rare occurrence, and especially so, when from the press of PETER SCHOIFFER the veritable inventor of movable types.

76 ARGENSOLA (B. L.) The Discovery and Conquest of the Molucco and Philippine Islands. Containing, their History, Ancient and Modern, National and Political. Their Description, Product, Religion, Government, Laws, Languages, Customs, Manners, Habits, Shape, and Inclination of the Natives. With an Account of many other adjacent Islands, and several remarkable Voyages through the Streights of Magellan, and in other Parts. Written in Spanish by Bartholomew Leonardo de Argensola. Now translated into English and Illustrated with a Map &c. *London: Printed in the year* 1708.

Sm. 4to, pp. (4), 260, (8). *Map and 3 Plates. Half blue morocco, gilt edges.* FINE COPY.

77 ARMISTEAD (W.) Memoirs of James Logan; a Distinguished Scholar and Christian Legislator; Founder of the Loganian Library at Philadelphia, and for Two Years Governor of the Province .... By Wilson Armistead. *London: Charles Gilpin.* MDCCCLI.

12mo, pp. 192. *Portrait and Plate. Half olive morocco, gilt top,* UNCUT.

78 ARMSTRONG (J.) Notices of the War of 1812. By John Armstrong, late a Major-General in the Army of the United States, and Secretary of War. *New York: Wiley & Putnam.* 1840.

2 *vols., 12mo, pp.* 260; *iv.,* 244. *Half blue calf.*

79 ARNETT (J. A.) Bibliopegia: or the Art of Bookbinding in all its branches. Illustrated with Engravings. By John Andrews Arnett. *London: Richard Groombridge.* 1835.

Sm. 12mo, pp. iv., 212. *Half calf,* UNCUT. *Scarce.*

80 ARNETT. An Inquiry into the Nature and Form of the Books of the Ancients; with a History of the Art of Bookbinding, from the times of the Greeks and Romans to the Present Day. Interspersed with Bibliographical References to Men and Books of all Ages and Countries. Illustrated with Numerous Engravings. By John Andrews Arnett. *London: Richard Groombridge.* 1837.

12mo, pp. iv., 212. *Half morocco, gilt top,* UNCUT. *Scarce.*

81 ARNOLD (Benedict.) Proceedings of a General Court Martial for the Trial of Major General Arnold, with an Introduction, Notes and Index. *New York: Privately Printed.* 1865.

Roy. 8vo, pp. xxix., 182. *Portrait. Half blue morocco, gilt top,* UNCUT. 100 *copies only printed.* The Portrait in this copy is an UNLETTERED INDIA PROOF. An Elegant Volume.

82 ASH (S.) *and* RATHBAND (W.) A Letter of | Many Ministers | in Old | England, | Requesting | The judgement of their Reverend | Brethren in New England con- | cerning Nine Positions. | Written Anno Dom. 1637. | Together with their Answer thereunto returned, | Anno 1639. | And the Reply made unto the said Answer, and sent over | unto them, Anno 1640. | Now published ... | upon the desire of many | godly and faithfull Ministers in and about the City | of London, who love and seeke | the truth. | By Simeon Ash, and William Rathband. | ... | *London,* | *Printed for Thomas Vnderhill, at the signe of the Bible in* | *great Woodstreet.* 1643.

Sm. 4to, pp. (10), 90. *Crushed blue levant morocco, gilt edges, by* F. BEDFORD. *Fine Copy.* VERY SCARCE.

83 A[SH] (T[homas.)] Carolina; | or a | Description | of the Present State of that | Country, | and | The Natural Excellencies thereof, viz. The | Healthfulness of the Air, Pleasantness of the Place, | Advantage and Usefulness of those Rich Commo- | dities there plentifully abound-

ing, which much | encrease and flourish by the Industry of the Plan- | ters that daily enlarge that Colony. | Published by T. A. Gent. | Clerk on Board his Majesties Ship the Richmond, which was | sent out in the year 1680. With particular Instructions to | enquire into the State of that Country, by his Majesties | Special Command, and Return'd this Present Year, 1682. | *London,* | *Printed for W. C. and to be Sold by Mrs. Grover in Pelican* | *Court in Little Britain.* 1682.

Sm. 4to, pp. (2), 40. *Crushed blue levant morocco, gilt top, by* F. BEDFORD. A LARGE and FINE copy. VERY RARE.

One of the EARLIEST BOOKS relating to CAROLINA.

84 ASHER (G. M.) A Bibliographical and Historical Essay on the Dutch Books and Pamphlets relating to New Netherland and to the Dutch West India Company, and to its possessions in Brazil, Angola, etc. ... By G. M. Asher. *Amsterdam: Frederick Muller.* 1854–67.

Sm. 4to, half crimson levant morocco, gilt top, UNCUT, *by* W. MATTHEWS.

Indispensable to the collector of books relating to New York. The titles are given in Dutch with an English translation. The notes are numerous, and in some instances, extend to great length.

85 ASHER. Henry Hudson the Navigator. The Original Documents in which his Career is Recorded, Collected, Partly Translated, and Annotated, with An Introduction, by G. M. Asher, LL.D. *London: Printed for the Hakluyt Society.* M,DCCC,LX.

8vo, pp. (12), *ccxviii.,* 292. 2 *Maps. Half purple morocco, gilt top,* UNCUT.

"The relations of his three voyages to the coast of America by the eminent and unfortunate discoverer, afford us the first authentic information regarding the Indians of New York, and of the Esquimaux of Labrador. The editor asserts what we do not recollect to have seen elsewhere stated: 'Verrazano seems to have been the pilot [of the *Samson* and *Mary*] and to have lost his life in an encounter with the North American Indians.'"—*Field.*

86 ASPINWALL [(Thomas.)] Catalogue of Books relating to America, in the collection of Colonel Aspinwall, Consul of the United States of America at London. [*Paris:* 1832 ?]

8vo, pp. (4), 66. *Half red morocco, gilt top,* UNCUT.

The collection of which this was the Catalogue, was sold entire to Mr. S. L. M. Barlow of New York, but a large portion of the books, of the least value however, was destroyed by fire. The catalogue was *privately printed* and is VERY RARE.

87 ATHERTON (C. H.) Eulogy on Gen. George Washington ... delivered at Amherst, N. H. ... on the 22d day of February, 1800 .... By Charles Humphrey Atherton. *Amherst:* 1800.

8vo, pp. 23. VERY SCARCE.

88 ATWELL (A. M.) An Address delivered before Mount Vernon Lodge, on their Anniversary Election of Officers, February 22, 5800. By Amos Maine Atwell, A.M. *Providence:* 5800.

8vo, pp. 18. UNCUT. EXCEEDINGLY RARE. Not in Hough's "Bibliographical List."

89 AUDUBON (J. J.) The Birds of America, from Drawings made in the United States and their Territories. By John James Audubon. ...
New York: J. J. Audubon. 1840–44.

7 vols., roy. 8vo, half green levant morocco, gilt edges. A fine clean copy with a *photographic* PORTRAIT of the AUTHOR *inserted.*

The ORIGINAL EDITION in this form, which, for the beauty and perfection of its plates, is beyond any comparison with the more modern issues.

See Cassin (J.) No. 350.

90 AUDUBON *and* BACHMAN (J.) The Quadrupeds of North America, by J. J. Audubon ... and the Rev. John Bachman, D.D.
New York: J. J. Audubon. 1846–54.

3 vols., imp. 8vo, half green morocco, gilt top, UNCUT. Bound from *selected* numbers as originally issued. PORTRAIT of AUDUBON *inserted.*

An elegant copy of the genuine first octavo edition, in which the plates are incomparably superior to those in Lockwood's re-issue.

" A most beautiful and interesting work, the Engravings exhibiting in most instances two or more figures (male and female,) in the most life-like attitudes, with their young, prey, &c., the entire plate coloured, with views of their favourite haunts and localities."

91 AUGUSTINUS (SANCTUS.) De Anima et Spiritu — De Ebrietate — De Vanitatibus Sæculi — De Vita Christiana — Ad Virgines de Sobrietate et Ebrietate — De quatuor virtutibus caritatis — De contricione cordis. [Colophon] *Anno ab incarnacōe dn̄ica millesimo quadringentesimo septuagesimo sēdo.* [1472] *qn̄to idus novēbris.*

Sm. 4to, Gothic Letter, *rubricated capitals, 74 leaves, 24 lines to a page. Fine clean copy, beautifully bound in brown morocco super extra, gilt edges, by* LORTIC.

Of this VERY RARE specimen of early typography (which is by Panzer attributed to one of the Italian presses,) Brunet is unable to cite more than one complete copy, which was sold at Sir Mark Sykes's sale for *8l. 18s. 6d.*

92 AUSTIN (J. T.) The Life of Elbridge Gerry. With Contemporary Letters to the Close of the American Revolution. By James T. Austin. *Boston: Wells and Lilly.* 1828.

2 vols., 8vo, pp. xvi., 520; vii., 408. Portrait and Facsimile. Half maroon morocco, gilt top, UNCUT. PORTRAIT, and AUTOGRAPH LETTER written and signed by Mr. GERRY *inserted.*

93 AUTHENTIC (An) NARRATIVE of Facts relating to the Exchange of Prisoners taken at the Cedars; supported by the Testimonies and Depositions of His Majesty's Officers, with Several Original Letters and Papers. Together with Remarks upon the Report and Resolves of the American Congress on that Subject.
London: T. Cadell. MDCCLXXVII.

8vo, pp. 50. Half blue morocco. Fine copy of an EXTREMELY RARE and interesting Revolutionary tract.

94 [AUTOGRAPHIC WRITINGS BY EMINENT MEN. Consisting of Original Autographs and Characteristic Original Writings, of the

following Eminent men, viz.: President LINCOLN, Vice-President HAMLIN, WILLIAM H. SEWARD, SCHUYLER COLFAX, J. P. UPSHER, GIDEON WELLES, E. W. BATES, JOSIAH QUINCY, JARED SPARKS, EDWARD EVERETT, WM. C. BRYANT, HENRY W. LONGFELLOW, R. WALDO EMERSON, RICHARD H. DANA, WM. LLOYD GARRISON, OLIVER WENDELL HOLMES, FRANCIS LIEBER, GEO. BANCROFT, Chief Justice CHASE, HENRY WARD BEECHER, Gen. WINFIELD SCOTT, L. E. AGASSIZ, J. R. LOWELL, and WENDELL PHILLIPS. *New York:* 1864.]

Imp. 8vo, crimson levant morocco, paneled and gilt sides, broad inside borders on polished crimson morocco, watered silk linings, morocco joints, gilt edges, by W. MATTHEWS.

This UNIQUE and BEAUTIFUL volume was prepared for the Sanitary Fair, held at New York in 1865, and was sold for the benefit of the Sanitary Commission.

95 [AUTOGRAPHS. FIFTEEN ORIGINAL AUTOGRAPH LETTERS of the PRESIDENTS of the UNITED STATES from WASHINGTON to LINCOLN inclusive. With PORTRAITS of the respective WRITERS. *Philadelphia:* 1864.]

4to, half calf, gilt top.

This UNIQUE and MOST DESIRABLE volume was prepared by FERDINAND J. DREER, Esq. and by him presented to the Sanitary Fair, at Philadelphia, in 1864. The BEAUTIFULLY EXECUTED MS. TITLE PAGE was written by one of his sons. The letters are uniformly in the FINEST STATE OF PRESERVATION. It is hardly necessary to observe that a series of this description is of the highest interest and of the GREATEST RARITY.

96 AUTOGRAPHS OF DISTINGUISHED AMERICANS. A Collection of ONE HUNDRED ORIGINAL SIGNATURES &c. with many PORTRAITS of the WRITERS. Collected and Arranged by T. H. Morrell. [*New York:* 1859.]

4to, blue morocco, paneled sides, broad outside and inside gilt borders, gilt edges.

A UNIQUE volume comprising Original AUTOGRAPH SIGNATURES, LETTERS and NOTES, of the persons designated in the neatly prepared manuscript index appended to the collection, which embraces a complete set of the signatures of the PRESIDENTS of the UNITED STATES from WASHINGTON to BUCHANAN; many of the GENERALS and STATESMEN of the AMERICAN REVOLUTION; and a numerous assemblage of those of Americans eminent in the walks of Science, Literature and Art. The in-laying in this BEAUTIFUL and MOST INTERESTING volume was executed by MR. TRENT, and is in his best manner.

97 [AYSCOUGH (Samuel.)] Remarks on the Letters from an American Farmer; or a Detection of the Errors of M. J. Hector St. John; pointing out the Pernicious Tendency of these Letters to Great Britain. *London: John Fielding.* 1783.

8vo, pp. 26. Half red morocco, gilt top, UNCUT. RARE.

"The writer of this pamphlet is of opinion that M. St. John's design in publishing his letters, was to diffuse a spirit of migrating to America. He accuses him also of a palpable falsehood, in describing himself as a native American, descended from Scotch parents, it being a fact, according to this writer, well known, that he is a native of Normandy, and that his chief residence while in America was at New York."—*M. R.* LXVIII. 537.

"The author was the Rev. Samuel Ayscough."—*Nichols' Anecdotes.* IX. 55.

98 AYTOUN (W. E.) Ballads of Scotland. Edited by William Edmondstone Aytoun, D.C.L. Second Edition. Revised and Augmented. *London : Blackwood.* 1859.

2 *vols., sm. 8vo, pp. xcv.,* 296; *viii.,* 403. *Brown morocco, gilt edges, by* HENDERSON & BISSETT.

99 [BACHE (Benjamin Franklin.)] Remarks occasioned by the late Conduct of Mr. Washington, as President of the United States. MDCCXCVI. *Philadelphia : Printed for Benjamin Franklin Bache.* 1797.

8vo, pp. vi., 84. *Half morocco, gilt top.* PORTRAIT *of* WASHINGTON *inserted.*

100 BACKUS (J.) A History of New England, With particular Reference to the Denomination of Christians called Baptists. Containing The first principles and settlements of the Country ; The rise and increase of the Baptist Churches therein ; The intrusion of Arbitrary Power under the cloak of Religion ; The Christian Testimonies of the Baptists and others against the same, with their Sufferings under it, from the Beginning to the present Time. Collected from most Authentic Records and Writings, both Ancient and Modern. By Isaac Backus, Pastor of the first Baptist Church in Midleborough. *Boston, and Providence :* 1777–1796.

3 *vols., 8vo, crushed green levant morocco, paneled and gilt sides, gilt top,* UNCUT, *by* F. BEDFORD. A MATCHLESS COPY of this VERY RARE work, the *third* volume of which is generally deficient. Green's copy of vols. I. and II. only, sold for $75.

Mr. Bancroft remarks that this history, as to its facts, is "more to be depended on than any of the early histories of New England."

See *Rich.* I. 253. Also *Bartlett's Biblio. of R. I.* p. 22.

101 BACKUS. Church History of New England, from 1602 to 1804, abridged, with a concise History of the Baptists in the Southern parts of America. By Isaac Backus. *Boston : Printed for the Author.* 1804.

8vo, pp. 271. *Half green levant morocco, gilt top by* F. BEDFORD. Uniform with the preceding No. A FINE COPY. VERY RARE. Contains a Chronological Index to the history of New England.

102 BACON (F.) The Works of Francis Bacon ... Lord High Chancellor of England. Collected and edited by James Spedding, M.A. ... Robert Leslie Ellis, M.A. ... and Douglas Devon Heath .... *Cambridge : Printed at the Riverside Press.* 1863.

15 *vols., 8vo, half blue morocco, gilt top,* UNCUT. LARGE PAPER : 100 *copies only printed, and now* SCARCE.

The finest production of this celebrated Press, and the most beautiful example of American typography. It is a reprint of the best London edition, with corrections and some additions by the senior editor, Mr. Spedding. The Indexes are much more copious than those in the English edition.

"The intellectual chart by him is the only one of which modern philosophy has yet to boast; the united talents of Diderot and of D'Alembert, aided by all the lights of the eighteenth century, have been able to add little to what he has performed." — *Dugald Stewart.*

See Dixon (W. H.) No. 607.

103 [BACON *and* INGRAM.] The History of Bacon and Ingram's Rebellion in Virginia, in 1675 and 1676.
Cambridge: John Wilson and Son. 1867.

8vo, pp. 50. *Half blue morocco, gilt top,* UNCUT. 200 *copies only* printed in this form from the "Proceedings of the Mass. Hist. Soc.," for 1866-67.

Copied from a contemporary MS., written by an unknown author.

104 BAILEY (W.) Records of Patriotism and Love of Country. By William Bailey. *Washington:* 1826.

2 *vols., 8vo, pp. xiii.,* (2), 114; 115–216. *Half green morocco, gilt top,* UNCUT. One volume *extended* to TWO, by the *insertion* of SEVENTY-FOUR fine engravings, mostly PORTRAITS, many of which are now *scarce,* and some *rare;* with RUBRICATED TITLE PAGES printed expressly for the set. A UNIQUE and BEAUTIFUL work.

105 BALDWIN (T.) A Sermon delivered to the Second Baptist Society in Boston ... December 29, 1799. Occasioned by the Death of General George Washington. ... By Thomas Baldwin, A.M. ...
Boston: [1800.]

8vo, pp. 28. UNCUT.

106 BALMANNO [(Mary.)] Pen and Pencil. By Mrs. Balmanno.
New York: D. Appleton & Co. 1858.

4to, pp. xi., 299. *Numerous Engravings and Facsimiles. Half green morocco, gilt top,* UNCUT. *Scarce. Two Autograph Letters* of MR. BALMANNO, and one of MRS. BALMANNO *inserted.*

107 BANCROFT (A.) An Eulogy on the Character of the late Gen. George Washington; delivered ... at Worcester, on the 22d of February 1800. By Aaron Bancroft. *Worcester:* 1800.

8vo, pp. 21. UNCUT.

108 BANCROFT. Life of George Washington, Commander in Chief of the American Army through the Revolutionary War, and the First President of the United States. By Aaron Bancroft.
London: John Stockdale. 1808.

8vo, pp. xii., 560. *Half green morocco, gilt top,* UNCUT. *Two* PORTRAITS of WASHINGTON *inserted;* one, a fine *original* impression from the plate engraved by Savage in 1792.

109 BANCROFT (G.) The History of the American Revolution. By George Bancroft. *Boston:* 1858–66.

3 *vols., 8vo, half green morocco, gilt top,* UNCUT, *by* BRADSTREET. Photographic PORTRAIT of the AUTHOR; Swett's "Defence of Timothy Pickering;" a leaf of the Author's MS. of the work; and Ellis' "Reply to Bancroft's Memorandum," *inserted.* One of the few sets with RUBRICATED title pages.

110 BANCROFT. The American Revolution. By George Bancroft. Chap. XLVI. Vol. II. in the AUTHOR'S MANUSCRIPT.

4to, 36 *leaves*. *Half green morocco, gilt top by* BRADSTREET. An *unlettered* INDIA PROOF PORTRAIT of the AUTHOR and a RUBRICATED TITLE printed expressly for the volume *inserted*.

Examples of Mr. Bancroft's method of composition are exceedingly difficult to obtain, great care being taken to ensure their destruction when once in type.

111 BANCROFT. History of the United States, from the Discovery of the American Continent. By George Bancroft. *Boston: Little, Brown & Co.* 1861.

8 *vols., imp. 8vo, half green morocco, gilt top*, UNCUT. LARGE PAPER: 50 *copies only printed*. Uniform in size with the works of *Washington, Franklin, Adams*, &c.

112 BANCROFT. Memorial Address on the Life and Character of Abraham Lincoln, delivered, at the Request of both Houses of the Congress of America, before them, in the House of Representatives at Washington, on the 12th of February, 1866. By George Bancroft. *Washington: Government Printing Office.* 1866.

4to, pp. 80. *Portrait. Half green morocco, gilt top*, UNCUT. SCARCE. LARGE PAPER: 50 *copies only printed*; with an addition to the Appendix (pp. 71–80,) "Correspondence relating to the Memorial Address," and the *bordered* PORTRAIT engraved and printed at the Treasury Department.

113 BANCROFT. POEMS: by George Bancroft. *Cambridge: Hilliard and Metcalf.* 1823.

12mo, pp. (2), 77. *Green morocco, paneled sides, gilt top*, UNCUT. A beautiful copy.

These early effusions of the historian are of the GREATEST RARITY. Davis' copy sold for $41.00.

114 BANCROFTIANA.

[The following works form a Complete Series of the Controversial Tracts which grew out of the publication of the Ninth Volume of Bancroft's History of the United States.]

The series consists of the following works.

I. An Examination of some Statements concerning Major-General Greene, in the Ninth Volume of Bancroft's History. ... By George Washington Greene. *Boston:* 1866.

pp. 86. PORTRAIT *of* GEN. GREENE: Mr. Bancroft's Reply to Mr. Greene: *pp.* 14; and Mr. Greene's Rejoinder: *pp.* 20; *inserted*.

II. President Reed of Pennsylvania. A Reply to Mr. George Bancroft and Others. Second Edition. *Philadelphia:* 1867.

pp. 132. PORTRAIT of GEN. REED, on India paper, *inserted*.

III. A Criticism on Mr. Wm. B. Reed's Aspersions on the Character of Dr. Benjamin Rush, and an Incidental Consideration of Gen. Joseph Reed's Character. By a Member of the Philadelphia Bar. [John G. Johnson.] *Philadelphia:* 1867.

pp. 61. PORTRAIT *of* DR. RUSH *inserted*.

IV. Correspondence and Remarks upon Bancroft's History of the Northern Campaign of 1777, and the Character of Major General Philip Schuyler. By George L. Schuyler. *New York:* 1867.

pp. 47. PORTRAIT *of* GEN. SCHUYLER *inserted*.

V. William B. Reed, of Chestnut Hill, Expert in the Art of Exhumation of the Dead. [By Benjamin Rush.] Reprinted from the London Edition. [*n.p. n.d.*]

pp. 15. PORTRAIT *of* BENJAMIN RUSH *inserted.*

VI. Joseph Reed: A Historical Essay. By George Bancroft. *New York:* 1867.

pp. 64. PORTRAIT *of the* AUTHOR *inserted.*

VII. A Rejoinder to Mr. Bancroft's Historical Essay on President Reed. By Wm. B. Reed. *Philadelphia:* 1867.

pp. 114. *Scarce* PORTRAIT *of* GEN. REED *inserted.*

VIII. General John Sullivan. A Vindication of his Character. ... By Thomas C. Amory. *Morrisania:* 1867.

pp. 52. *India proof* PORTRAIT *of* GEN. SULLIVAN *inserted.*

8 *vols.*, 8*vo*, *half green morocco, gilt top*, UNCUT, *by* BRADSTREET. Uniform in size and binding with No. 109. COMPLETE SETS, like this, are VERY SCARCE.

115 [BARBÉ-MARBOIS.] Complot d'Arnold et de Sir Henry Clinton contre les Etats-Unis d'Amérique et contre le Général Washington. September 1780. ... *Paris:* MDCCCXVI.

Sm. 8*vo*, *pp. xliv.*, 184. 2 *Portraits and Plan. Half blue morocco, gilt top.*

116 [BARBÉ-MARBOIS.] Complot d'Arnold etc. [Translated into English by R. Walsh.] *Philadelphia:* 1817.

8*vo*, *pp.* 63. *Half crimson morocco, gilt top*, UNCUT. *Rare contemporary* PORTRAIT *of* ARNOLD, and *other illustrations inserted.*

Extracted from the "American Register," 1817.

117 BARBÉ-MARBOIS. The History of Louisiana, particularly of the Cession of that Colony to the United States of America; with An Introductory Essay on the Constitution and Government of the United States. By Barbé-Marbois. ... Translated from the French by an American Citizen. [Wm. B. Lawrence.] *Philadelphia: Carey & Lea.* 1830.

8*vo*, *pp. xviii.*, 15–455, (1). *Half red levant morocco, gilt top*, UNCUT, *by* W MATTHEWS. FIVE ILLUSTRATIONS *inserted.* SCARCE in *uncut* condition.

See N. A. R. XXVIII. 389: XXX. 551.

118 BARBER (J. W.) Historical, Poetical and Pictorial American Scenes; ... Being a Selection of interesting Incidents in American History: to which is added a Historical Sketch, of each of the States. By John W. Barber. *New Haven, Ct.: J. H. Bradley.* [1850.]

12*mo*, *pp.* 226. *Map and many Engravings. Half blue morocco, gilt top*, UNCUT. SCARCE.

119 BARBER (J. W.) *and* HOWE (H.) Historical Collections of the State of New York; containing a General Collection of the most Interesting Facts, Traditions, Biographical Sketches, Anecdotes, &c., relating to its History and Antiquities, with Geographical Descriptions of every Township in the State. Illustrated by Two Hundred and Thirty Engravings. By J. W. Barber and Henry Howe. *New York:* 1845.

8*vo*, *pp.* 616. *Map and Engravings. Half gray calf antique.*

120 [BARBOUR (John.)] The Life and Acts of the Most Victorious Conqueror Robert Bruce, King of Scotland. Wherein also are contained the Martial Deeds of the Valiant Princes Edward Bruce, Sir James Douglass, Earl Thomas Randell, Walter Stewart, and sundry others. *Edinburgh: Printed by James Watson, Printer to the King's Most Excellent Majesty.* 1758.

Black Letter. *4to, pp.* 443. *Calf antique, gauffered edges.* Uniform with the "Acts and Deeds of Sir William Wallace," No. 2029. A volume of EXTREME RARITY. We are unable to record the sale of a copy in the United States.

121 BARBOUR. The Bruce; or, the History of Robert I. King of Scotland. Written in Scottish Verse by John Barbour. The First Genuine Edition, published from a MS. dated 1489; with Notes and a Glossary by J. Pinkerton. *London: G. Nicbol.* 1790.

3 *vols., sm. 8vo, pp. xxiv.,* 208; 198; 179, (28). 4 *Plates and Facsimile. Old calf.* VERY SCARCE.

"The Bruce is a work not only remarkable for a copious circumstantial detail of the exploits of that illustrious prince and his brave companions in arms, but also for the beauty of the style, which is not inferior to Chaucer."

122 BARLOW (J.) The Vision of Columbus; A Poem in Nine Books. By Joel Barlow, Esquire.
Hartford: Printed for the Author. M.DCC.LXXXVII.

Sm. 8vo, pp. 248, (12). *Half morocco.* ORIGINAL EDITION. VERY SCARCE.

The subscribers' names include His Most Christian Majesty [Louis XVI,] 25 copies; His Excellency George Washington, Esq., 20 copies; Maj.-Gen. le Marquis de la Fayette, 10 copies; etc. Afterwards amplified into "The Columbiad."

123 BARLOW. The Columbiad. A Poem. By Joel Barlow.
Philadelphia: C. and A. Conrad and Co. 1807.

4to, pp. xvi., 454. 11 *Plates. Purple morocco, paneled sides, broad gilt borders, gilt edges.* LARGE and FINE COPY.

The earliest attempt at an American Epic. It was printed at the expense of Robert Fulton, to whom it was dedicated. It is a new edition, with great alterations of the "Vision of Columbus," beautifully printed, and illustrated with eleven fine engravings from Smirke's designs.

124 BARLOW. The Columbiad. [Second Edition.]
Philadelphia: C. and A. Conrad and Co. 1809.

2 *vols., 12mo, pp. xiv.,* 258; 218. *Half green morocco, gilt top,* UNCUT.

125 BARNARD (T.) A Sermon preached December 29, 1799, in ... Salem, the Lord's Day after the Melancholy Tidings were received of the Death of General George Washington ... . By Thomas Barnard, D.D. ... *Salem:* [1800.]

8vo, pp. 27. UNCUT.

126 BARNES (D.) Discourse delivered ... in Scituate, February 22, 1800. The day ... to mourn the Decease ... of General George Washington. By David Barnes, D.D. *Boston:* [1800.]

8vo, pp. 16. VERY SCARCE.

127 BARNEY (M.) A Biographical Memoir of the Late Commodore Joshua Barney: from Autographical Notes and Journals. ... Edited by Mary Barney. *Boston: Gray and Bowen.* 1832.

8vo, pp. xvi., 328. *Portrait. Half morocco, gilt top,* UNCUT. PRIVATELY PRINTED for circulation among friends.

128 BARNUM (H. L.) The Spy Unmasked; or, Memoirs of Enoch Crosby, alias Harvey Birch, the Hero of Mr. Cooper's Tale of the Neutral Ground; being an Authentic Account of the Scout Services which he rendered his country during the Revolutionary War. (Taken from his own lips in short-hand.) Comprising many Interesting Facts and Anecdotes, never before published. By H. L. Barnum. *New York: J. and J. Harper.* 1828.

8vo, pp. 206. 6 *Plates. Half olive morocco, gilt top,* UNCUT, *by* BRADSTREET. SIX ILLUSTRATIONS *inserted. Original* and *Best Edition.* VERY SCARCE.

129 BARNUM. The Spy Unmasked; or, Memoirs of Enoch Crosby, alias Harvey Birch, the Hero of the "Spy, a Tale of the Neutral Ground," by Mr. Cooper. By H. L. Barnum. *London: A. K. Newman and Co.* 1829.

12mo, 2 vols. in one, pp. 234; 222. *Half gray calf, red edges.* FOUR ILLUSTRATIONS *inserted.* A VERY SCARCE EDITION.

130 BARTLETT (E.) Memorial of Edwin Bartlett. Died at Annandale, N. Y., September 10, 1867. [*Philadelphia*: 1868.]

Imp. 8vo, pp. 127. *Portrait. Cloth extra, gilt top,* UNCUT. *A few copies only* PRIVATELY PRINTED.

Mr. Bartlett was one of the founders of the Panama Railroad Co.

131 BARTLETT (J. R.) Dictionary of Americanisms. A Glossary of Words and Phrases usually regarded as peculiar to the United States. By John Russell Bartlett. Second Edition. ... *Boston: Little, Brown and Company.* 1859.

8vo, pp. xxxii., 524. *Half blue morocco, gilt top,* UNCUT.

132 BARTLETT. A History of the Destruction of His Britannic Majesty's Schooner Gaspee, in Narragansett Bay, on the 10th June, 1772; accompanied by the Correspondence connected therewith; ... and the Official Journal of the Proceedings of the Commission of Inquiry appointed by King George the Third on the same. By John Russell Bartlett. *Providence:* 1861.

Sm. folio, pp. 140. *Half crimson morocco, gilt top,* UNCUT. Plate of the "Destruction of the Gaspee," *inserted.* One hundred and twenty-five copies *printed for private distribution.*

133 BARTLETT. Bibliography of Rhode Island. A Catalogue of Books and other Publications relating to the State of Rhode Island, with Notes, Historical, Biographical, and Critical. By John Russell Bartlett. ... *Providence:* 1864.

Imp. 8vo, pp. 287. *Half red morocco, gilt top,* UNCUT, *by* BRADSTREET. *One hundred and fifty* copies printed.

134 BARTLETT. A Report of the Pre-Historic Man and his Associates. ... By John Russell Bartlett. ... *Worcester*: 1868.

8vo, half morocco, gilt top, UNCUT. FIFTY COPIES *only printed for private circulation.*

135 BARTLETT (W. H.) American Scenery; or, Land, Lake, and River Illustrations of Transatlantic Nature. From Drawings by W. H. Bartlett ... the Literary Department by N. P. Willis, Esq. *London: George Virtue.* M.DCCC.XL.

2 vols., 4to, russia, gilt edges. ORIGINAL EDITION with *fine impressions* of the ONE HUNDRED AND TWENTY PLATES.

136 BARTLETT. The Pilgrim Fathers; or, The Founders of New England in the Reign of James the First. By W. H. Bartlett. ... *London:* 1854.

Roy. 8vo, pp. 240. 28 *Steel Engravings* and 31 *Wood-cuts. Half green morocco, gilt top,* UNCUT. *Two* PORTRAITS *inserted.*

Contains some very important particulars of these personages, and their connections, previous to their leaving England and Holland, which were entirely unknown to former writers.

137 BARTON (B. S.) A Memoir concerning the Fascinating Faculty which has been ascribed to the Rattle-Snake, and other American Serpents. By Benjamin Smith Barton, M.D. ... *Philadelphia: the Author.* 1796.

8vo, pp. 70. *Half blue morocco, gilt top,* UNCUT. PRIVATELY PRINTED and VERY RARE.

138 BARTON (W.) Memoirs of the Life of David Rittenhouse, LL.D. ... Late President of the American Philosophical Society, &c. Interspersed with various Notices of Many Distinguished Men; with an Appendix. ... By William Barton, M.A. *Philadelphia: Edward Parker.* 1813.

8vo, pp. 614. *Portrait and Facsimile. Half morocco, gilt top,* UNCUT. PORTRAIT of RITTENHOUSE *inserted.*

139 BARTRAM (J.) *and* KALM (P.) Observations on the Inhabitants, Climate, Soil, Rivers, Productions, Animals, and other matters worthy of Notice. Made by Mr. John Bartram, in his Travels from Pensilvania to Onondago, Oswego, and the Lake Ontario, in Canada. To which is annex'd a curious Account of the Cataracts at Niagara. By Mr. Peter Kalm, a Swedish Gentleman who travelled there. *London: J. Whiston and B. White.* 1751.

8vo, pp. 94. *Plan. Half crushed red levant morocco, gilt top,* UNCUT, *by* W. MATTHEWS. *Fine copy.* RARE in *uncut* condition.

John Bartram's Journal among the New York Indians is becoming a work of more and more interest, and Mr. Kalm's appendage is a good continuation of the subject. The Editor claims that Mr. Kalm's scientific description of the Falls of Niagara is the first that appeared in our language.

140 BARTRAM (W.) Travels through North and South Carolina, Georgia, East & West Florida, the Cherokee Country, the Extensive

4

Territories of the Muscogulges or Creek Confederacy, and the Country of the Chactaws, containing an account of the soil and Natural Productions of those Regions; together with Observations on the Manners of the Indians. Embellished with Copper Plates. By William Bartram. *London: J. Johnson.* 1792.

8vo, pp. xxiv., 520, (12). *Portrait, Map and 7 Plates. Half blue morocco, gilt top*, UNCUT. *An elegant copy.*

Unequalled for the vivid picturesqueness of its descriptions of nature, scenery, and productions. "It is written in the spirit of the old travellers."— *Coleridge.*

141 BASCOM (J.) An Oration, delivered February 22, 1800. The Day of Public Mourning For the Death of General George Washington. By Rev. Jonathan Bascom, of Orleans.... *Boston:* 1800.

8vo, pp. 15. UNCUT.

142 BAYARD (S.) A Funeral Oration, Occasioned by the Death of Gen. George Washington; and Delivered on the First of January, 1800, ... at New-Rochelle, in the State of New York. By Samuel Bayard, Esq. *New Brunswick:* 1800.

8vo, pp. 24.

143 BEAMISH (N. L.) The Discovery of America by the Northmen, In the Tenth Century, with Notices of the Early Settlements of the Irish in the Western Hemisphere. By North Ludlow Beamish.... *London: T. & W. Boone.* 1841.

8vo, pp. (16), 239, (12). 2 *Maps and Plate. Half red morocco, gilt top*, UNCUT, by BRADSTREET.

The author attempts to prove that as Irish ecclesiastics were constantly passing between Iceland and Ireland, it is more than probable that America was first discovered by men of Hibernian birth.

144 BEATTIE (W.) Scotland Illustrated in a Series of Views taken Expressly for this Work by Messrs. T. Allom, W. H. Bartlett, and H. McCulloch. By William Beattie, M.D. *London: George Virtue.* 1838.

2 *vols.*, 4*to, half blue morocco, gilt edges.* FIRST EDITION, with *fine impressions* of the ONE HUNDRED AND TWENTY PLATES.

145 BEATTY (C.) The Journal of a Two Months Tour; with a view of Promoting Religion among the Frontier Inhabitants of Pennsylvania, and of Introducing Christianity among the Indians to the Westward of the Alegh-geny Mountains. To which are added, Remarks on the Language and Customs of some particular Tribes among the Indians. ... By Charles Beatty, A.M.... *London:* MDCCLXVIII.

8vo, pp. 110. *Half red levant morocco, gilt top*, UNCUT, by W. MATTHEWS. ORIGINAL EDITION. VERY RARE.

This journal is enlivened with many agreeable notes and circumstances relating to the manners and customs of the Delaware Indians, who, from certain similar customs and some traditions among them, the author conjectures to be the descendants of the ten tribes of Israel.

146 BEERS (W. P.) An Oration on the Death of General Washington; pronounced Before the Citizens of Albany, ... January 9th, 1800. By William P. Beers, Esquire. *Albany:* [1800.]

4to, pp. 17. UNCUT. VERY SCARCE.

147 BELKNAP (J.) A Discourse, intended to Commemorate the Discovery of America by Christopher Columbus; Delivered ... on the 23d day of October, 1792, being the Completion of the Third Century since that Memorable Event. ... By Jeremy Belknap, D.D. *Boston: Belknap & Hall.* MDCCXCII.

8vo, pp. 132. *Half crushed red levant morocco, gilt top,* UNCUT, *by* F. BEDFORD. PORTRAIT of COLUMBUS *inserted.* SCARCE in such fine condition.

148 BELKNAP. The History of New-Hampshire. Comprehending the Events of one complete Century from the Discovery of the River Piscataqua. By Jeremy Belknap, A.M. Containing also a Geographical Description of the State, etc. *Dover, N. H.: O. Crosby and J. Varney.* 1812.

3 *vols., 8vo, pp.* 351; 377; 354. *Map. Half purple morocco, gilt top,* UNCUT. *Three* PORTRAITS, and *Two Autograph Notes* of the AUTHOR *inserted.*

This work has long ranked as one of the best of our local state histories.

149 BELOE (W.) Anecdotes of Literature and Scarce Books. By the Rev. William Beloe. *London:* 1808–14.

6 *vols., 8vo, calf extra, marbled edges. A fine copy.*

Contains much valuable and interesting bibliographical information in general, besides many copious extracts from rare and curious old English books, in prose and verse.

150 BELOE. The Sexagenarian, or Recollections of a Literary Life. By the Rev. William Beloe. *London: Rivingtons.* 1817.

2 *vols., 8vo, pp. viii.,* 436; 386. *Half crimson levant morocco, gilt top,* UNCUT, by W. MATTHEWS.

A UNIQUE COPY of the FIRST and UNCASTRATED EDITION containing all the virulent and defamatory passages subsequently suppressed. Nearly all the blanks have been neatly filled in with pencil, and EIGHTY ILLUSTRATIONS, mostly FINE CONTEMPORARY PORTRAITS, *inserted.*

151 BENSON (E.) Memoir read before the Historical Society of the State of New York, 31st December, 1816; by Egbert Benson. *New York: T. and W. Mercein.* 1817.

8vo, pp. 72. *Half calf,* UNCUT. One of a few copies enriched with numerous and lengthy notes, upon separate leaves, in *the Author's handwriting;* one of which gives a detailed account of his misunderstanding with the New York His. Soc., in consequence of its having recalled the vote of thanks which was passed when this work was read at one of its meetings.

152 [BENSON.] Vindication of the Captors of Major André. *New York: Kirke and Mercein.* 1817.

12mo, pp. 99. *Half red morocco, gilt top,* UNCUT. PORTRAIT of ANDRÉ *inserted.* VERY SCARCE.

Fisher's copy sold in March, 1866, for $41.

153 BENSON. Vindication of the Captors of Major André, By Egbert Benson, LL.D. With Introduction and Appendix. [By C. I. Bushnell.] *New York: Privately Printed, [for Francis S. Hoffman.]* 1865.

8vo, pp. ix., 134. *Half blue morocco, gilt top,* UNCUT. *Scarce full length* PORTRAIT of ANDRÉ, and one of MAJOR TALLMADGE *inserted.* Edition 115 copies, of which 35 are on large paper.

154 [BENTALOU (Paul.)] Pulaski Vindicated from an Unsupported Charge, Inconsiderately or Malignantly introduced in Judge Johnson's Sketches of the Life and Correspondence of Major Gen. Nathaniel Greene. *Baltimore:* 1824.

8vo, pp. 34, *iii. Half green morocco, gilt top,* UNCUT. VERY SCARCE.

155 BENTALOU. A Reply to Judge Johnson's Remarks on an Article in the North American Review, relating to Count Pulaski. By Paul Bentalou. ... *Baltimore:* 1826.

8vo, pp. 41. *Half green morocco, gilt top,* UNCUT. Uniform with the preceding No. VERY SCARCE.

156 BENTLEY (W.) An Oration in Commemoration of the Birthday of Washington, delivered at Salem, Massachusetts, February 22d, 1793. By William Bentley, D.D. *Morrisania:* 1870.

Imp. 8vo, pp. (8), 19. *Half green morocco, gilt top,* UNCUT, by BRADSTREET. *Thirty copies* only printed for *Private Circulation.* A UNIQUE COPY, with two fine PORTRAITS of WASHINGTON *inserted;* INDIA PROOF *and* INDIA PROOF BEFORE LETTERS, *both from* PRIVATE PLATES.

157 BENZONI (G.) History of the New World, by Girolamo Benzoni, of Milan. Showing his Travels in America, from A.D. 1541 to 1556; with some particulars of the Island of Canary. Now First Translated and Edited by Rear-Admiral W. H. Smyth.
London: printed for the Hakluyt Society. MDCCCLVII.

8vo, pp. (6), *iv.,* (6), 280. 18 *Engravings. Half purple morocco, gilt top,* UNCUT.

"The narrative of Girolamo Benzoni is one of the most interesting of all the early travellers in America, for the minute details of the life and habits of the Aborigines more than three centuries ago."—*Field.*

158 [BERESFORD (James.)] Bibliosophia; or Book Wisdom, Containing some Account of the Pride, Pleasure, and Privileges of that Glorious Vocation, Book-Collecting. By an Aspirant.
London: William Miller. 1810.

12mo, pp. vii., 126. *Half morocco,* SCARCE.

159 BERNARD (Francis.) Letters to the Ministry, from Governor Bernard, General Gage, and Commodore Hood. And also Memorials to the Lords of the Treasury, from the Commissioners of the Customs. With sundry Letters and Papers annexed to the said Memorials.
Boston: Edes & Gill. 1769.

[Also:] An Appeal to the World; or a Vindication of the Town of Boston, from Many false and malicious Aspersions contain'd in certain Letters and Memorials, written by Governor Bernard, General Gage, Commodore Hood, the Commissioners of the American Board of Customs, and others, and by them respectively transmitted to the British Ministry. Published by order of the Town.

Boston: Edes & Gill. 1769.

8vo, 2 vols. in one, pp. 108; 37. *Half blue morocco, gilt top,* UNCUT. VERY SCARCE.

"Copies of the 'Appeal' were ordered at a town meeting, to be sent to Col. Isaac Barre, Governor Pownal, Doctor Franklin, William Bollan, Dennys de Berdt, and Alderman Trecothick."—*Rich.* Often attributed to William Cooper, but really by Samuel Adams.

160 BERNARD. Letters to the Ministry from Governor Bernard, General Gage, and Commodore Hood. And also Memorials to the Lords of the Treasury, from the Commissioners of the Customs. With Sundry Letters and Papers annexed to the said Memorials.

London: J. Wilkie. [1769.]

8vo, pp. 146. *Half blue morocco.* LARGE *and* FINE *copy.* SCARCE.

161 BERNARD. Letters to the Right Honourable the Earl of Hillsborough, from Governor Bernard, General Gage, and the Honourable His Majesty's Council for the Province of Massachusetts Bay. With an Appendix, containing Divers Proceedings referred to in the said Letters. *London: J. Almon.* [1769.]

8vo, pp. 165. *Half blue morocco. Fine Copy.* SCARCE.

"This, and the preceding collection of letters were first printed in Boston. They commence in January, 1768, and reach to July, 1769. So that the two contain a complete view of the political contests and dissensions in the colony of Massachusetts Bay during that period. The copies were obtained and sent to Boston by William Bollan, at the time agent for the Council of Massachusetts."—*Rich.*

162 [BERTIE (Willoughby.)] Thoughts on the Letter of Edmund Burke, Esq.; to the Sheriffs of Bristol, on the Affairs of America. By the Earl of Abingdon. The Second Edition.

Oxford: W. Jackson. [1777.]

8vo, pp. 64. *Half red morocco, gilt top.*

Concerning this *see* Sabin's Dictionary. Vol. I. No. 61.

See Chalmers (George.) No. 363.

163 [BEVERLEY (Robert.)] The History of Virginia, In Four Parts. I. The History of the First Settlement of Virginia, and the Government thereof, to the Year 1706. II. The natural Productions and Conveniences of the Country, suited to Trade and Improvement. III. The Native Indians, their Religion, Laws, and Customs, in War and Peace. IV. The Present State of the Country, as to the Polity of the Government, and the Improvements of the Land, the 10th of June 1720. By a Native and Inhabitant of the Place. The Second Edition revis'd and enlarg'd by the Author.

London: F. Fayram and J. Clarke. 1722.

8vo, pp. (6), 284, (24). 14 *Plates. Half crimson levant morocco, gilt top,* by W. MATTHEWS. An Elegant Copy. VERY SCARCE.

"This work appeared anonymously in two English and one French edition, but is known to have been written by Robert Beverley. The plates by Gribelin are reduced copies of those in Hariot's Virginia, drawn and engraved by the brothers De Bry."—*Field.*

164 BEYARD (N.) *and* LODOWICK (C.) Journal of the Late Actions of the French at Canada, by Col. Nicholas Beyard, and Lieut. Col. Charles Lodowick. *New York:* 1868.

4*to*, *pp.* 56. *Half red morocco, gilt top,* UNCUT, by BRADSTREET. 150 *copies only printed.*

165 BIBLE. The Souldiers Pocket Bible: Containing the most (if not all) those places contained in holy Scripture, which doe shew the qualifications of his inner man, that is a fit Souldier to fight the Lord's Battels, both before the fight, in the fight, and after the fight; Which Scriptures are reduced to severall heads, and fitly applyed to the Souldiers severall occasions, and so may supply the want of the whole Bible, which a Souldier cannot conveniently carry about him: And may bee also usefull for any Christian to meditate upon, now in this miserable time of Warre. Imprimatur, Edm. Calamy. ...
Printed at London by G. B. and R. W. for G. C. 1643. *Cambridge: Reprinted.* 1861.

8*vo*, *pp. vi.*, (2), 16. *French blue morocco, paneled and gilt sides, gilt top,* UNCUT. LARGE PAPER. *Twenty-five copies only* PRIVATELY PRINTED for MR. LIVERMORE, for distribution among his friends.

An *exact reprint* of the *original edition*, only two copies of which are now known; one in the British Museum, the other in the collection of the late Mr. George Livermore. It does not appear to have been known to Watt, Lowndes, or Dibdin, nor is it described or mentioned by any bibliographer.

"Trust in the Lord, and keep the Powder dry."— *Title.*

166 BIBLE. The Souldiers Pocket Bible printed at London by G. B. and R. W. for G. C. 1643. Reproduced in Fac-simile with an Introduction by Francis Fry, F.S.A. *London: Willis and Sotheran.* 1862.

Sm. 8*vo*, *pp. viii.*, 16. *Purple morocco, blank tooled sides, broad inside gilt borders, gilt edges, vellum fly leaves.* An elegant volume, and one of FIVE COPIES ONLY PRINTED ON VELLUM.

"This reproduction of the only known copy in this kingdom, is a faithful representation of the original recently discovered in the British Museum. That every soldier in Cromwell's army was furnished with a pocket Bible of some sort is an undoubted tradition. But it has never been satisfactorily determined what edition was so used, although some curious conjectures have been made on the subject. The curious tract now copied solves the difficulty."— *Introduction.*

167 **Biblia Sacra Latina.**
Mogunt: per Fust et Schoiffer. MCCCCLXII.

Two leaves from the FIRST EDITION of the LATIN BIBLE with a Date; in fine preservation; loose in a cover. A desirable specimen of early typographical art, and very difficult to obtain.

168 BIBLIA PAUPERUM. Reproduced in Facsimile, from a copy in the British Museum. With an Historical and Bibliographical Introduction. By J. Ph. Berjeau. *London: John Russell Smith.* 1859.

Roy. 4*to*, *half morocco*, UNCUT.

A literary curiosity of great interest, being a faithful reproduction of one of the very first Essays towards the Art of Printing by Letters and Figures cut out in blocks of wood before the invention of movable types.

169 BIBLIOMANE. (Le) [Two numbers only, all that were published.] *London: Trübner & Co.* 1861.

Roy. 8vo, pp. 42. *Cuts. Half blue morocco, gilt top,* UNCUT.

170 BIBLIOPHILE FRANÇAIS. (Le) Gazette Illustrée des Amateurs de Livres, d'Estampes et de haute curiosité. *Paris: Bachelin-Deflorenne.* 1868–70.

[Also:] Armorial des Bibliophiles, ou Recueil général de tous les Ex-Libris ou Blasons des Bibliophiles célèbres anciens et modernes, avec une Notice sur leurs Bibliothèques, par M. J. Guigard. Parts I and II. [All published.] *Paris: Bachelin-Deflorenne.* 1870–71.

5 *vols., imp. 8vo,* boards, UNCUT. The 28 portraits are selected INDIA PROOF IMPRESSIONS, imported expressly for this set.

"A more splendid Journal of Bibliophily has never been published in Europe. It was interrupted in consequence of the war, and will not be resumed at present. The 5th volume will be completed by the *Armorial des Bibliophiles.*"—*Pub. Note.*

171 BIBLIOTHECA AMERICANA; or, a Chronological Catalogue of the most Curious and Interesting Books, Pamphlets, State Papers, &c., upon the Subject of North and South America, from the Earliest Period to the Present, in Print and Manuscript; for which research has been made in the British Musæum, and the most Celebrated Public and Private Libraries. ... *London: J. Debrett.* 1789.

4to, pp. (2), 271. *Half green morocco, gilt top,* UNCUT.

With an introductory discourse "On the Present State of Literature in those Countries," which has many curious particulars, and is evidently written by some one who had visited the United States. Though the name of the author is not known, it has been variously ascribed to Dalrymple, Homer, Long, and with more probability, by Homer himself, to Reid.

172 BIDDLE (N.) An Ode to Bogle. By Nicholas Biddle, July 16, 1829. *Philadelphia: Privately printed for Ferdinand J. Dreer.* 1865.

4to, pp. 8. *Half green morocco, gilt top,* UNCUT. LARGE PAPER. 25 copies only printed. *Portrait* of the AUTHOR and an UNCANCELLED U. S. Bank BOND for ONE THOUSAND POUNDS STERLING (with coupons) signed by him *inserted.*

173 [BIDDLE (Richard.)] A Memoir of Sebastian Cabot, with a Review of the History of Maritime Discovery. Illustrated by Documents from the Rolls, now first published. *London: Hurst, Chance & Co.* 1831.

8vo, pp. viii., 333. *Half green morocco, gilt top,* UNCUT, by BRADSTREET.

174 BIGELOW (T.) An Eulogy on the Life, Character and Services of Brother George Washington, Deceased. Pronounced before the fraternity of ... Masons, by Request of the Grand Lodge, ... at Boston, Feb. 11, 1800. By Brother Timothy Bigelow. *Boston:* [1800.]

8vo, pp. 26. UNCUT.

175 [BINNEY (Horace.)] An Inquiry into the Formation of Washington's Farewell Address. ... *Philadelphia:* 1859.

8vo, pp. 250. *Half green morocco, gilt top,* UNCUT. SCARCE in this condition. *Four* PORTRAITS *inserted.*

176 BIOGRAPHICAL Memoirs of the Illustrious General George Washington, Late President of the United States of America, and Commander in Chief of their Armies, during the Revolutionary War. Dedicated to the Youth of America.
From Sidney's Press For I. Cooke & Co. ... New Haven. 1811.

18*mo, pp.* 144. *Calf extra, by* F. BEDFORD. VERY SCARCE.

177 BISHOP (S. G.) An Eulogium on the Death of Gen. George Washington, ... pronounced at Pittsfield, February 22d. 1800 ... By Samuel G. Bishop. ... *Gilmanton: The Author.* 1800.
Roxbury: Privately Re-printed. 1866.

Imp. 8vo, pp. iv., 15. *Half green morocco, gilt top,* UNCUT. PORTRAIT *inserted.* Sixty-six copies only printed.

178 BISHOPE (G.) New England Judg d, | Not by Man's, but the Spirit of the Lord: And | The Summe sealed up of New-England's | Persecutions. | Being | A Brief Relation of the Sufferings of the People called Quakers in | those Parts of America, from the beginning of the Fifth | Moneth 1656. (the time of their first Arrival at Boston from | England) to the later End of the Tenth Moneth, 1660. | Wherein | The Cruel Whippings and Scourgings, Bonds and Imprisonments, Beat- | ings and Chainings, Starvings and Huntings, Fines, and Confiscati- | on of Estates, Burning in the Hand and Cutting of Ears, Orders of Sale | for Bond-men, and Bond-Women, Banishment upon pain of | Death, and Putting to Death of those People, are Shortly touched; | With a Relation of the Manner, and Some of the Other most Ma- | terial Proceedings; and a Judgement thereupon | In Answer | To a Certain Printed Paper, intituled, A Declaration | of the General Court of the Massachusets holden at Boston, the | 18 October, 1658. Apologizing for the same. | By George Bishope. | ... | *London: Printed for Robert Wilson, in Martins le Grand.* 1661. | [Followed by] An | Appendex | to the Book, Entituled, | New England Judged: | being | Certain Writings, (never yet Printed) | of those Persons which were there | Executed. | Together | with a short Relation, of the Tryal, | Sentence, and Execution, | of William Leddra. | Written by them in the time of their Imprisonment, in the | Bloody Town of Boston. | *London,* | *Printed for Robert Wilson, at the sign of the Black-spread-* | *Eagle and Windmil, in Martins Le Grand.* | 1661. | [Also:] New England | Judged. | The Second Part. | Being, | A Relation of the cruel and Bloody Sufferings of the People | called | Quakers, in the Jurisdiction chiefly of the Massa- | chusets; Beginning with the Sufferings of William Ledra, | whom they murthered, and hung upon

a Tree at Boston, the | 14th of the first month, 166$\frac{0}{1}$. barely for being such a one as | is called a Quaker, and coming within their Jurisdiction ; | And ending with the Sufferings of Edward Wharton, the 3d | month, 1665. And the remarkable Judgements of God | in the Death of John Endicot Governour, John Norton, | High Priest, and Humphrey Adderton, Major General. | By George Bishope. | *London*, *Printed in the Year*, 1667.

Sm. 4to, pp. 206, 147. *Crushed red levant morocco, gilt edges by* F. BEDFORD.

These THREE WORKS together form a complete book, and a copy equal to this is of the HIGHEST DEGREE OF RARITY. It is unnecessary to dilate upon the great historical importance of this volume. The following is an abbreviation :

179 BISHOPE. New-England Judged, | by the | Spirit of the Lord. | In Two Parts. | First, Containing a Brief Relation of the Sufferings | of the People call'd Quakers in New-England, from the | Time of their first Arrival there, in the Year 1656, to | the Year 1660. Wherein their Merciless Whippings, | Chainings, Finings, Imprisonings, Starvings, Burning in | the Hand, Cutting off Ears, and Putting to Death, with | divers other Cruelties, inflicted upon the Bodies of In- | nocent Men and Women, only for Conscience sake, are | briefly described. In Answe.,to the Declara ;ion of their | Persecutors Apologizing for the same, MDCLIX. | Second Part, Being a farther Relation of the Cruel and | Bloody Sufferings of the People call'd Quakers in New-England, Continued from anno 1660, to anno 1665. Be- | ginning with the Sufferings of William Leddra, whom | they put to Death. | Formerly Published by George Bishop, and now | somewhat Abreviated. | With an Appendix, | Containing the Writings of several of the Sufferers ; with | some Notes, showing the Accomplishment of their Pro- | phecies ; and a Postscript of the Judgements of God that | have befallen divers of their Prosecutors. | Also, | An Answer to Cotton Mather's Abuses of the said People, | in his late History of New-England, Printed anno 1702. | The whole being at this time Published in the said Peoples | Vindication, as a Reply to all his Slanderous Calumnies. | ... | ... | *London*, *printed and Sold by T. Sowle, in White-* | *Hart-Court in Gracious-Street.* 1703.

8vo, pp. (6), 498. Followed by John Whiting's "*Truth and Innocency Defended.*" *pp.* 212, 12. *Brown morocco, carmine edges.* A *large* and *beautiful copy* with all *seven title pages*. VERY SCARCE.

180 [BLACKBURNE (Francis.)] Memoirs of Thomas Hollis, Esq. F. R., and A.S.S. *London :* MDCCLXXX.

2 vols., imp. 4to, half russia, gilt top, UNCUT. PRIVATELY PRINTED.

This elegant copy contains *all the additional engravings* including the beautiful mezzotint portrait of Isaac Newton. There are in all 36 *engravings* by CIPRIANA, BARTOLOZZI, and BASIRE. It also has the Index which did not appear until 25 years after the publication of the work, and is rarely found in any copy. It further contains, *all* the suppressed or Star pages in which most copies are more or less deficient. These Star pages, as they are usually called, come in between pages 522 and 523 in the second volume in this order, 533* to 580*, followed by 577* to 584*, and embrace 52 *pages*. *Most copies contain from* 42 *to* 48 *pages* only.

Mr. Hollis was well known for his devotion to the cause of liberty, and for his munificent benefactions to Harvard College, and other Literary Institutions in America. The work abounds with the letters of his American correspondents; in Vol. 1, at p. 371, is a fine portrait of Dr. Jonathan Mayhew, of Boston.

181 BLADENSBURGH RACES. (The) Written shortly after the Capture of Washington City, August 24, 1814. [Probably it is not generally known, that the flight of Mahomet, the flight of John Gilpin, and the flight of Bladensburgh, all occurred on the twenty-fourth of August.] [*n. p.*] *Printed for the Purchaser.* 1816.

16mo, half green morocco, gilt top, UNCUT.

A satirical poem on Madison, and his administration, in imitation of John Gilpin.

182 BLADES (W.) The Life and Typography of William Caxton, England's First Printer, with Evidence of His Typographical Connection with Colard Mansion, the Printer at Bruges. Compiled from Original Sources by William Blades. *London: Joseph Lilly.* 1861.

2 vols., 4to, pp. xv., 298; *lx.,* 310, (1). 65 *Plates. Half purple levant morocco, gilt top*, UNCUT.

Besides copious quotations from original documents, illustrative of the life and times of Caxton, derived from hitherto unexplored sources, it includes the whole of his prologues and epilogues attached to the various books printed by him; also his own historical work, entitled "Policronicon Liber Ultimus," and is illustrated with more than 60 FACSIMILE PLATES, executed by Tupper in the most careful manner.

The second volume is devoted to a bibliographical and literary account of all the works printed by, or ascribed to, the press of Caxton, including many books undescribed by Dr. Dibdin and other bibliographers, accompanied with most careful collations, and a list of copies of books printed by Caxton, in number, more than four hundred and fifty, now in the public and private libraries of Great Britain. Published by subscription; only 250 copies printed, and now *very scarce.*

183 BLAKE (G.) A Masonic Eulogy, on the Life of the Illustrious Brother George Washington, pronounced before the Brethren of St. John's Lodge, on the Evening of the 4th Feb. 5800. ... By Brother Geo. Blake. *Boston:* 5800.

8vo, pp. 23. UNCUT.

184 BLAKE (G.) A Masonic Eulogy. Second Edition. *Boston:* 5800.

8vo, pp. 23. UNCUT.

185 BLAND PAPERS. (The) Being a Selection from the Manuscripts of Colonel Theodorick Bland, Jr. of Prince George County, Virginia. To which are prefixed an Introduction, and a Memoir of Colonel Bland. ... Edited by Charles Campbell. *Petersburg:* 1840–43.

2 vols., 8vo, in one, pp. xxxi., 160; (2), 9, 130. *Half calf. Two* PORTRAITS *inserted. Large* and *fine* copy.

This collection of papers relating to the Revolution is now SCARCE.

186 BLEECKER (A. E.) Posthumous Works of Ann Eliza Bleecker, in Prose and Verse. To which is added, A Collection of Essays, Prose and Poetical, by Margaretta V. Faugeres. *New York: T. & J. Swords.* 1793.

12mo, pp. (12), *xviii.,* 375. PORTRAIT. *Green morocco, gilt edges. A fine* LARGE *copy.*

The Memoirs of Mrs. Bleecker and her poems, were published many years ago; but I have sought in vain among the libraries, and the Bleeckers to obtain a copy."— W. L. STONE'S "Life of Brant," Vol. 1, p. 207.

187 BLEEKER (L.) The Order Book of Capt. Leonard Bleeker, Major of Brigade in the early part of the Expedition under Gen. James Clinton, against the Indian Settlements of Western New York, in the Campaign of 1779. [Edited by Franklin B. Hough.] *New York: Joseph Sabin.* 1865.

4to, pp. 138. *Half purple morocco, gilt top,* UNCUT. LARGE PAPER. *Fifty copies only printed.* AN INDIA PROOF PORTRAIT of GEN. JAMES CLINTON *inserted.*

188 [BLOME (R.)] The Present State Of His Majesties Isles and Territories in America, viz. Jamaica, Barbadoes, S. Christophers, Mevis, Antego, S. Vincent, Dominica, New-Jersey, Pensilvania, Monserat, Anguilla, Bermudas, Carolina, Virginia, New-England, Tobago, New-Found-Land, Mary-Land, New-York. With New Maps of every Place. Together with Astronomical Tables, Which will serve as a constant Diary or Calendar, for the Use of the English Inhabitants in those Islands; from the Year, 1686, to 1700. Also a Table by which, at any time of the Day or Night here in England, you may know what Hour it is in any of those parts. And how to make Sun-Dials fitting for all those Places. Licens'd, July 20, 1686. Roger L'Estrange. *London: Dorman Newman.* 1687.

8vo, pp. (8), 262, (36). *Portrait, Plate and 7 Maps. Polished calf, yellow edges, by* W. MATTHEWS. A beautiful copy of a VERY RARE edition.

189 BLUE LAWS (The) of New Haven Colony, usually called Blue Laws of Connecticut; Quaker Laws of Plymouth and Massachusetts; Blue Laws of New York, Maryland, Virginia and South Carolina. First Record of Connecticut; Interesting Extracts from Connecticut Records; Cases of Salem Witchcraft; Charges and Banishment of Roger Williams, &c.; and other Interesting and Instructive Antiquities. Compiled By an Antiquarian. [Royal R. Hinman.] *Hartford:* 1838.

12mo, pp. 336. *Half roan.*

190 BOADEN (J.) Inquiry into the Authenticity of various Pictures and Prints, which, from the Decease of the Poet to our own Times, have been offered to the Public as Portraits of Shakespeare. ... Illustrated by Accurate and Finished Engravings by the ablest artists, from such Originals as were of Undisputable Authority. By James Boaden. *London: Robert Triphook.* 1824.

8vo, pp. v., (5), 206. 5 *Portraits. Half red morocco, gilt top* UNCUT. A beautiful and UNIQUE copy with an AUTOGRAPH letter and PORTRAIT of the AUTHOR, and SIX fine and scarce PORTRAITS (some *India proofs before letters*) of SHAKSPERE *inserted.*

191 BODDILY (J.) A Sermon delivered at Newburyport, on the 22d of February, 1800. By Rev. John Boddily, ... [On the Death of George Washington.] *Newburyport:* 1800.

8vo, pp. 15, UNCUT and RARE.

192 BOLTON (R.) A History of the County of Westchester, from its First Settlement to the Present Time. By Robert Bolton.
New York: 1848.

2 *vols.*, 8*vo*, *pp. xxxii.*, 559; (2), 582. 2 *Maps and numerous Engravings. Half morocco.* A fine copy. *Very Scarce.* PORTRAIT *inserted.*

193 BOND (S.) A | Publick Tryal | of the | Quakers | in Barmudas | Upon the first Day of May, 1678. | First, The Charge against them was openly read, containing | the Particulars: as | 1. That a Quakers pretended Saviour within him, is not the true Christ, | but the False Christ, the Devil. | 2. That the main end of the Quakers Meetings in these Islands, is to make | the Lord's Christ, His Holy Spirit, His Angels, and Apostles, all Lyars | and False Witnesses of God. | 3. That the Prim-Principles of a Quaker, are the same Held and Pro- | fessed by the Beasts, which Paul fought with at Ephesus. | Secondly, the Charge being Proved by the Testimony | of the Holy Scriptures: was found by the Sheriffe, and | Justices of Peace, a true and just Charge. | Thirdly, Being found Guilty, they are here Sentenced, and | brought forth unto the deserved Execution of the Presse. | By Samson Bond late Preacher of the Gospel in | Barmudas. | *Boston in New-England*: | *Printed by Samuel Green, upon Assignment of Samuel Sewall*: | 1682.

4*to*, *pp.* (4), 100. *Crimson morocco, gilt edges.* FINE COPY. VERY RARE. One of the *earliest* of Boston imprints, and PRESQUE UNIQUE.

"This insuing Discourse had been Printed sooner, had not Mr. John Foster (the Printer) been disenabled by a tedious sickness of which he Died.—*Preface.*

194 BOOK OF COMMON PRAYER, and Administration of the Sacraments and other Rites and Ceremonies of the Church ... in the Confederate States of America; together with the Psalter. ...
Richmond, [*Virginia*:] *J. W. Randolph.* MDCCCLXIII.

16*mo*, *purple morocco, gilt edges.*

In this edition, really printed by Eyre & Spottiswoode, London, the prayers for the President of the United States are altered to "The President of the *Confederate States.*" But, by a curious omission, the prayer to be used at sea remains unchanged, and the Almighty is asked to be a safeguard unto the *United States.* The greater part of the edition was captured from the Anglo-Rebel blockade-runner Minna, by the Government dispatch ship Circassian, off Wilmington, Dec. 6, 1863.

195 BOOK OF BALLADS. (The) Edited by Bon Gaultier and Illustrated by Doyle, Leech, and Crowquil. Sixth Edition.
Edinburgh: Blackwoods. 1859.

Sq. 8*vo*, *calf antique, carmine edges.*

196 BOOK WORM. (The) A Literary and Bibliographical Review, edited and illustrated by J. P. Bearjeu. *London*: 1866–1870.

5 *vols.*, *imp.* 8*vo*, *half olive levant morocco, gilt top*, UNCUT, by W. MATTHEWS. AN ELEGANT SET of which *only* 250 *copies* were printed for subscribers.

"This curious review, which forms a splendid set of volumes, illustrated by hundreds of original and facsimilie engravings, contains much interesting matter. For librarians and collectors of old books it is invaluable, as it gives full descriptions of the books which have been sold for ten pounds and upwards by public auction.

"Bibliomaniacs, bibliographers, and others interested in old books, woodcuts, ancient printers, their lives, works and marks, may be served by our quaint and wonderfully erudite, but exceedingly whimsical contemporary."— *Athenæum.*

197 BOOTH (M.L.) History of the City of New York, from its Earliest Settlement to the Present Time. By Mary L. Booth. ... *New York: W. R. C. Clark & Meeker.* MDCCCLIX.

8vo, pp. 846. 101 *Engravings, half morocco, gilt top,* UNCUT.

198 BOSTON. A Short Narrative of the Horrid Massacre in Boston, perpetrated In the Evening of the Fifth Day of March, 1770. By Soldiers of the XXIXth Regiment; which with the XIVth Regiment were then Quartered there: With some Observations on the State of Things prior to that Catastrophe. *Printed by Order of the Town of Boston, And sold by Edes and Gill.* ... 1770.

8vo, pp. 48, 87. *Half crimson morocco, gilt top,* UNCUT. Fine copy. EXCEEDINGLY RARE.

One of the rare copies containing the subsequently printed "*Additional Observations to a Short Narrative,*" following the Narrative, and continuously paged therewith; respecting which see Sabin's Dictionary, ii., 329, No. 6741.

199 BOSTON. A Short Narrative of the Horrid Massacre in Boston, perpetrated in the Evening of the Fifth Day of March 1770. By Soldiers of the XXIXth Regiment, which with the XIVth Regiment were then quartered there: with some Observations on the State of Things prior to that Catastrophe. To which is added an Appendix, containing the several Depositions referred to in the preceding Narrative; and also other Depositions relative to the Subject of it. *Boston: Printed. London Re-printed for W. Bingley.* MDCCLXX.

8vo, pp. 38, 83. *Plate. Half blue morocco. Fine, large, clean copy;* with the *large folded plate* often wanting.

200 BOSTON. A Short Narrative. [Another Edition.] Re-published with Notes and Illustrations, by John Doggett, Jr. *New York:* 1849.

8vo, pp. 122. *Plate, and Plan. Half green morocco, gilt top,* UNCUT. *View* of the *Massacre inserted,* and a *facsimile copy* of the "Boston Gazette," for Monday, March 12th, 1770, giving an account of the affair, laid loose in the Volume.

This edition contains the rare "*Additional Observations,*" printed from "*the original in the Library of Harvard University.*"

201 BOSTON. A Fair Account of the late Unhappy Disturbance at Boston in New England; extracted From the Depositions that have been made concerning it by Persons of all Parties. With an Appendix, Containing Some Affidavits and other Evidences relating to this Affair, not mentioned in the Narrative of it that has been published at Boston. *London: B. White.* MDCCLXX.

8vo, pp. 28, 31. *Half red morocco, gilt top,* UNCUT. *Beautiful Copy.* VERY RARE.

"A defence of the massacre at Boston. The author is a zealous advocate for the soldiers, and endeavours to prove that their firing upon their assailants was, if not wholly unavoidable, at least highly excusable; that they were provoked to it by the most unsufferable insults, and that the people were entirely the aggressors. He supports his representations by the affidavits of twenty-nine persons; most of whom, however, it will be observed, are officers in the army."—*M. R.* XLIII, 68.

202 BOSTON. The Votes and Proceedings of the Freeholders and other Inhabitants of the Town of Boston, in Town Meeting assembled, according to Law. [Published by Order of the Town.] To which is prefixed, as Introductory, An attested Copy of a Vote of the Town at a preceding Meeting. The whole containing a particular Enumeration of those Grievances that have given Rise to the present alarming Discontents in America.
Dublin: George Faulkner. M,DCC,LXXIII.

8vo, pp. viii., 32. *Half morocco.* A VERY RARE EDITION *of which we have never seen another copy.*

203 BOTTA (C.) History of the War of the Independence of the United States of America. Written by Charles Botta. Translated ... by George Alexander Otis. ...
Philadelphia: Printed for the Translator. 1820.

3 *vols., 8vo, pp.* 448; *v.,* 567; *xii.,* 503. *Half red levant morocco, gilt top,* UNCUT, by W. MATTHEWS. A fine PORTRAIT of the AUTHOR, an *autograph letter* of THOMAS JEFFERSON to MR. VAUGHAN expressing a desire to transmit a copy of the translation to MR. BOTTA, and *other illustrations inserted.*

UNIQUE and ELEGANT copy of the *best edition.* VERY SCARCE.

One of the most impartial of all the histories of the American Revolution.

204 BOUCHER (J.) A View of the Causes and Consequences of the American Revolution, in Thirteen Discourses, Preached in North America, between the Years 1763 and 1775: with an Historical Preface. By Jonathan Boucher ... .
London: G. C. & A. J. Robinson. M.DCC.XCVII.

8vo, pp. (8), *xciv.,* (1), 596. *Half crimson morocco, gilt top, uncut.* PORTRAIT of the AUTHOR, and two other scarce PORTRAITS *inserted.* Fine copy.

"Dedicated to Washington. The author was a refugee, who returned to England, on account of his political principles, in 1775, and died there, in 1804. In the preface, he passes in review the different histories of the American Revolution, all of which are censured as partial and defective."—*M. R.,* XXIX, 369.

205 BOUDINOT (E.) A Star in the West; or, A Humble Attempt to discover the long lost Ten Tribes of Israel, preparatory to their Return to their Beloved City Jerusalem. By Elias Boudinot.
Trenton: N. J. 1816.

8vo, pp. iv., 312. *Half green morocco.* SCARCE.

Not in Mr. Field's Bibliography. Pages 89–107 are devoted to an enquiry into the language of the American Indians.

206 BOWDITCH (N. J.) Suffolk Surnames. By N. J. Bowditch. Second Edition Enlarged. *Boston: Ticknor and Fields.* 1858.

8vo, pp. xv., 383. *Half green morocco, gilt top.*

207 BOWERS (B.) An Alarm Sounded to Prepare the Inhabitants of the World to Meet the Lord in the Way of his Judgements. By Bath Bowers. [*New York: William Bradford.* 1709.]

Sm. 4to, pp. 23. *Calf, gilt edges, by* HAYDAY.

Dated at the end, *Philadelphia*, July 17, 1709, but evidently printed by W. BRADFORD, at *New York.*

208 BOWNAS (S.) An Account of the Life, Travels, and Christian Experiences in the Work of the Ministry of Samuel Bownas. The Second Edition. *London: Luke Hind.* 1761.

8vo, pp. viii., 199. *Half calf.* A remarkably fine copy. SCARCE.

Bownas landed in Maryland, 1702. Soon after he arrived he held a public dispute with George Keith; also with William Bradford, and suffered imprisonment for his belief. His account of the *Labadies*, a community resembling the Shakers, is very amusing.

209 [BOWYER (W.)] The Origin of Printing. In two Essays; I. The Substance of Dr. Middleton's Dissertation on the Origin of Printing in England. II. Mr. Meerman's Account of the Invention of the Art at Harleim, and its Progress to Mentz. With Occasional Remarks; and an Appendix. The Second Edition: with some Improvements. *London: W. Bowyer and J. Nichols.* 1776.

8vo, pp. xvi., 300. *Half morocco.* VERY SCARCE.

210 BOYER (*Lieut.*) A Journal of Wayne's Campaign; ... against the North-western Indians; ... 1794. ... By Lieutenant Boyer. *Cincinnati: William Dodge.* 1866.

4to, pp. 23. *Half purple morocco, gilt top*, UNCUT.

211 BOYNTON (E. C.) History of West Point, and its Military Importance during the American Revolution: and the Origin and Progress of the United States Military Academy. By Captain Edward C. Boynton, A. M. *New York: D. Van Nostrand.* 1864.

Imp. 8vo, *pp. xviii.*, (2), 9–408. 7 *Maps and* 29 *Plates. Half purple levant morocco, gilt top*, UNCUT. LARGE PAPER, *one hundred copies* only printed. SIXTEEN ENGRAVINGS, mostly fine INDIA PROOFS, some BEFORE LETTERS, *inserted.*

212 BRACKENRIDGE (H. H.) Modern Chivalry: containing the Adventures of a Captain, and Teague O'Regan, his Servant. By H. H. Brackenridge. *Richmond: Jacob Johnson.* 1803–7.

2 *vols.*, 12*mo, pp., vi.*, 210, 178; *ix.*, 175, 163. *Half calf. Fine copy.* VERY SCARCE.

One of the earliest works of humour by an American Author.

213 BRACKENRIDGE. Incidents of the Insurrection in the Western Parts of Pennsylvania, in the Year 1794. By Hugh H. Brackenridge. *Philadelphia: John McCulloch.* 1795.

8vo, half green morocco, gilt top, UNCUT. VERY SCARCE in *uncut* condition.

A scarce book, in defence of the author and the subject. "It was at first intended to publish this work in three vols., with an appendix to each vol., &c. ... But this plan was relinquished, and it was judged best to publish the whole in one vol." This accounts for the three paginations; that the second and third begin with page 5 is, perhaps, owing to title-pages, etc., being dropped.

For other works relating to this subejct, *see* the following No.; also, Nos. 483, 720, 765, and 1641.

214 BRACKENRIDGE (H. M.) History of the Western Insurrection in Western Pennsylvania, commonly called the Whiskey Insurrection. 1794. By H. M. Brackenridge, ... *Pittsburgh: W. S. Haven.* 1859.

8vo, pp. 336. *Half green morocco, gilt top,* UNCUT, *by* BRADSTREET.

The only *uncut* copy we have ever seen. Now scarce, as most of the copies were destroyed by fire.

The author's father defended the insurgents; in this work, the father is defended. *See* "Hist. Mag.," III, 377.

215 BRADFORD (A.) An Eulogy in Commemoration of the Sublime Virtues of Gen. George Washington, ... Pronounced in Wiscasset, February 22, 1800. ... By Alden Bradford. *Wiscasset:* 1800.

8vo, pp. 16. UNCUT.

216 BRADFORD. History of Massachusetts, From 1764, to July 1775: when General Washington took Command of the American Army. By Alden Bradford, ... *Boston: Richardson and Lord.* 1822.

8vo, pp. 414. *Half green morocco, gilt top,* UNCUT. PORTRAIT *inserted.*

217 BRADFORD. History of Massachusetts, from July, 1775, when General Washington took Command of the American Army at Cambridge, to the Year 1789, (Inclusive,) When the Federal Government was established under the Present Constitution. By Alden Bradford ... *Boston: Wells and Sibley.* 1825.

8vo, pp. 376. *Half green morocco, gilt top,* UNCUT. PORTRAIT *inserted.* Uniform with the preceding No.

218 BRADFORD. History of Massachusetts, from the Year 1790 to 1820. By Alden Bradford. *Boston: The Author.* 1829.

8vo, pp. 327. *Half green morocco, gilt top,* UNCUT. PORTRAIT *inserted.* Uniform with the preceding No.

"The work of a gentleman, with whom New England History has been the study of a life, and who, from the official relation which he long sustained, as Secretary of the Commonwealth, enjoyed peculiar advantages for its prosecution."— *N. Am. Rev.*

219 BRADFORD (A. W.) American Antiquities and Researches into the Origin and History of the Red Race. By Alexander W. Bradford. *New York: Wiley and Putnam.* 1843.

8vo, pp. 435. *Half crushed red levant morocco, gilt top,* UNCUT, *by* BRADSTREET.

Contains a *resumé* of the discoveries of American antiquities, with a description of their size, character, and location, and is a very excellent collection of the material facts relating to them.— *Field.*

220 BRADFORD (W.) History of Plymouth Plantation. By William Bradford, the Second Governor of the Colony. Now First Printed

from the Original Manuscript. ... Edited, with Notes, by Charles Deane. *Boston: Little, Brown, and Company.* 1856.

8vo, pp. xix., (1), 477. *Half crimson morocco, gilt top,* UNCUT. *Fifty copies only reprinted,* from the Massachusetts His. Society's Collections.

221 [BRADFORD (W.)] Report of the Committee of the Historical Society of Pennsylvania, on their Visit to New York, May 20, 1863, at the Celebration of the Two Hundredth Birth-Day of William Bradford, who Introduced the Art of Printing into the Middle Colonies of British America. By Horatio Gates Jones. *Philadelphia:* 1863.

8vo, green morocco, gilt top, UNCUT. Engraving of BRADFORD'S TOMB-STONE *inserted.* The *interleaved, large type,* and *emphacized* copy of the Address delivered by MR. WALLACE on the above occasion, bound in after the Report, is the *identical copy* from which he read at the Cooper Institute.

222 [BRADFORD.] Some Account of "The Book of Common Prayer," printed A.D., 1710. By William Bradford, under the Auspices of Trinity Church, New York. The First Edition of that Book ever printed on the American Continent.
Privately printed for Horatio Gates Jones. 1870.

Sm. 8vo. A few copies only printed. Accompanied with an *autograph letter* from JOHN H. HICKCOX, Assistant Librarian of the N. Y. State Library, describing the earliest known example of Bradford's printing in New York, now in that institution.

223 BRADFORD CLUB. [A Complete Set of the Publications of "THE CLUB," so called, and of the "BRADFORD CLUB."] *New York:* [*v. d.*]

11 *vols., royal 8vo, half crimson morocco, gilt top,* UNCUT, *except* Melvin's Journal *which is gilt edged.*

The Series consists of:

I. A Journal of the Expedition to Quebec, in the Year 1775, under the Command of Colonel Benedict Arnold. By James Melvin. *New York:* 1857.

pp. 30. *No.* 3, *of* 102 *copies only printed, strictly for* PRIVATE DISTRIBUTION. *Fine unlettered proof* PORTRAIT *of* ARNOLD *inserted.*

II. Diary of Washington; from the first day of October, 1789, to the tenth day of March, 1790. From the Original Manuscript, now First Printed. *New York:* 1858.

pp. 89. *No.* 1, *of* 110 *copies only printed,* for PRIVATE DISTRIBUTION. *Fine unlettered proof* PORTRAIT *of* WASHINGTON *inserted.*

After the publication of this work the BRADFORD CLUB was organized and issued the following:

I. Papers Concerning the Attack upon Hatfield and Deerfield by a party of Indians from Canada September 19, 1677. [Edited by F. B. Hough.] *New York:* 1859.

pp. 82. *Map.* 110 *copies printed.* CLUB COPY *No.* 4. *India proof* PORTRAIT *of the* EDITOR *inserted.*

II. The Croakers, by Joseph Rodman Drake and Fitz-Greene Halleck. First Complete Edition. *New York:* MDCCCLX.

pp. viii., 191. PORTRAITS *of* HALLECK *and* DRAKE *in* TWO *states, lettered and unlettered India proofs. A fine unlettered India proof* PORTRAIT *of* HALLECK, *from a different plate inserted.* 257 *copies printed.* CLUB COPY *No.* 3.

III. The Operations of the French Fleet under Count de Grasse in 1781–2. As described in Two Contemporaneous Journals. [Edited by J. G. Shea.] *New York:* 1864.

pp. 216. *India proof* PORTRAIT *of* LORD RODNEY *inserted.* 165 *copies printed.* CLUB COPY *No.* 2.

6

IV. Anthology of New Netherland or Translations from the Early Dutch Poets of New York with Memoirs of their Lives by Henry C. Murphy. *New York:* 1865.

pp. 209. PORTRAIT *in* THREE *different tints. The leaf of* " Additions and Corrections," *and the corrected impression of the* Facsimile, *laid in at the end, are not to be found in all copies.* 200 *copies printed.* CLUB COPY No. 4.

V. Narratives of the Career of Hernando de Soto in the Conquest of Florida. ... Translated by Buckingham Smith. *New York:* 1866.

pp. xxviii., 324. PORTRAIT *of* DE SOTO *in* FIVE, *and the engraving of* BRADFORD'S TOMB-STONE, *in* THREE *different states.* 203 *copies printed.* CLUB COPY *No.* 1.

VI. The Northern Invasion of Oct., 1780, a Series of Papers Relating to the Expeditions from Canada under Sir John Johnson and Others against the Frontiers of New York, which were supposed to have Connection with Arnold's Treason. With an Introduction and Notes by Franklin B. Hough. *New York:* MDCCCLXVI.

pp. 224, *Map.* PORTRAIT *inserted.* 155 *copies printed.* CLUB COPY *No.* 1.

VII. The Army Correspondence of Colonel John Laurens in the Years 1777–8, now First Printed from the Original Letters addressed to his Father Henry Laurens President of Congress. With a Memoir by William Gilmore Simms. *New York:* 1867.

pp. 250. PORTRAIT *in* FOUR *different states. Of that opposite the title page* TWELVE *impressions only were taken. Proof, and India proof* PORTRAITS *of the* EDITOR, *and of* HENRY LAWRENS *inserted.* 131 *copies printed.* CLUB COPY *No.* 1.

Extra No. Memorial of John Allan. [By Evart A. Duyckinck.] *New York:* 1864.

pp. 39. PORTRAIT *of* MR. ALLAN *in* THREE *different states; his* PHOTOGRAPH, *and an* AUTOGRAPH *note* WRITTEN *and* SIGNED *by him; a* PHOTOGRAPH *of his* RESIDENCE *during the time of his funeral service; and an interesting autograph letter of the late* GEORGE LIVERMORE *respecting* MR. ALLAN *inserted. No.* 1, *of* 260 *copies printed,* ALL FOR PRESENTATION.

Private No. Memorial of John Allan. [By Evart A. Duyckinck.] *New York:* 1864

pp. 39. *The* PORTRAIT *in* THREE *different states.* UNPUBLISHED; *and* FIVE COPIES *only printed on* WHITE PAPER *for the Members of the Bradford Club. This copy is No.* 1.

An UNRIVALLED SET, and very difficult to obtain, as there are but FIVE COMPLETE SETS, like the present, in existence.

224 BRADFORD CLUB. [A Complete Set of the Regular Series, 8 *vols.*, together with a set of the Publications of " THE CLUB" so called, 2 *vols.*] *New York:* 1857–64.

Forming 10 *vols., roy.* 8*vo, boards and paper,* UNCUT; Melvin's Journal *excepted, none of which were left uncut.*

225 [BRADSTREET (*Mrs.* Anne.)] The | Tenth Muse | Lately sprung up in America. | Or | Severall Poems, compiled | with great variety of VVit | and Learning, full of delight. | Wherein especially is contained a com- | pleat discourse and description of | The Four | Elements, | Constitutions, | Ages of Man, | Seasons of the Year. | Together with an Exact Epitomie of | the four Monarchies, viz. | The | Assyrian, | Persian, Grecian, | Roman. | Also a Dialogue between Old England and | New, concerning the late troubles. | With divers other pleasant and serious Poems. | By a Gentlewoman in those parts. | *Printed at London for Stephen Bowtell at the signe of the* | *Bible in Popes Head-Alley.* 1650. |

Small 8*vo, pp.* (14), 207. *Red morocco, gilt edges.* EXCESSIVELY RARE. *We are unable to trace the sale of* more than ONE COPY *in this country.*

Cotton Mather, in his " Magnalia," remarks, " these poems, divers times printed, have afforded a grateful entertainment unto the ingenious, and a monument for her memory beyond the stateliest marbles," which is higher praise than we can accord them. Ward, author of the "Simple Cobler of Agawam," says, "The Authoress was a right Du Bartas girle." Some extensive selections from this writer are included in Duyckinck's "Cycl.," 1, pp. 47, 52.

226 BRADSTREET. The Works of Anne Bradstreet, in Prose and Verse. Edited by John Harvard Ellis. *Charlestown: A. E. Cutter.* 1867.

Imp. 8vo, pp. lxxvi., 434. Facsimile, Portrait, and Plate. Half green levant morocco, gilt top, UNCUT *by* BRADSTREET. *One Hundred and Fifty copiec printed.* The fine full page wood engraving of The BRADSTREET HOUSE is in duplicate; on plain, and on *India Paper.* Of the last, *five impressions only* were taken.

227 BRAINARD (J. G.) An Oration Commemorative of ... General George Washington; spoken in the ... City of New London, February 22d, 1800. By J. G. Brainard, Esq. *New London:* 1800.

8vo, pp. 14. VERY RARE.

228 BRENT (J. C.) Biographical Sketches of the most Reverend John Carroll, first Archbishop of Baltimore, with Select Portions of his Writings. Edited by John Caroll Brent. *Baltimore: J. Murphy.* 1843.

12mo, pp. 321. *Portrait. Half morocco, gilt top.* SIX ILLUSTRATIONS *inserted.*

Bishop Carroll was sent by Congress, in 1786, with Dr. Franklin and others, on a mission to Canada.

229 BRESSANI (F. J.) Relation abrégée de quelques missions des S. pères de la Compagnie de Jésus, dans la Nouvelle-France. Par le R. P. F.-J. Bressany ... Traduit de l'Italien et augmenté d'un avant-propos, de la biographie de l'auteur, et d'un grand nombre de notes et de gravures, par le R. P. F. Martin.
Montreal: des presses de John Lovell. 1852.

8vo, pp. 336. *2 Maps, 33 Engravings. Sheep. Fine Copy.* VERY SCARCE.

230 BRIEF (A) REVIEW of the Rise and Progress, Services and Sufferings, of New England, especially the Province of Massachusetts-Bay. Humbly submitted to the Consideration of both Houses of Parliament. *London: J. Buckland.* MDCCLXXIV.

8vo, pp. 32. *Half morocco.* VERY SCARCE.

"A very fair and impartial statement of facts."—*M. R.*

231 BRIEF (A) and True Narrative of the Hostile Conduct of the Barbarous Natives Towards the Dutch Nation. Translated by E. B. O'Callaghan from the original Dutch MS.
Albany: J. Munsell. MDCCCLXIII.

8vo, pp. 48. *Half orange morocco, gilt top,* UNCUT. *Only* 50 *copies printed.*

"As late as 1655, the Indians of New York were revenging the murderous slaughter of four hundred of their countrymen at Pavonia, by that sanguinary coward, Governor Kieft. The petition shows that three hundred of the Dutch colony had been slain, and one hundred carried away captives. So audacious had the fierce Indians become, that several of the Dutch had been killed on the island of Manhattan; and on one occasion sixty-four canoes loaded with the savages had landed on the shore of the North River, and before daylight, had filled the streets of New Amsterdam. The first objects upon which the eyes of the astonished Dutchmen rested in the morning, were the crowds of savages to whose forbearance alone they owed their lives." — *Field.*

232 BRISSOT DE WARVILLE (J. P.) A Critical Examination of the Marquis de Chastellux's Travels in North America, in a Letter addressed to the Marquis; Principally intended as a Refutation of his Opinions Concerning the Quakers, the Negroes, the People, and Mankind. Translated from the French of J. P. Brissot de Warville, with Additions and Corrections of the Author.
Philadelphia: Printed by Joseph James. M,DCC,LXXXVIII.

8vo, pp. 89. *Half red morocco, carmine edges*. A VERY RARE pamphlet.
See Chastellux (Francis Jean Marquis de.) No. 378.

233 BRISSOT DE WARVILLE. New Travels in the United States of America, performed in M,DCC,LXXXVIII. ... By J. P. Brissot de Warville. *London: J. S. Jordan.* 1794.

8vo, half calf; large clean copy.

The author came to the United States just before the French Revolution, for the purpose of selecting a suitable place for establishing a colony of respectable persons, who had determined to abandon the then despotic government of France, and seek an asylum under the mild and equal government of the United States. A second volume was subsequently published.

234 BRODHEAD (J. R.) The History of the State of New York. First [and Second] Periods. By John Romeyn Brodhead.
New York: Harper & Brothers. 1859–71.

2 *vols., 8vo, half blue levant morocco, gilt top,* UNCUT, by W. MATTHEWS. Two PORTRAITS *inserted.* A *splendid* copy.

235 BRODHEAD. Oration on the Conquest of New Netherland. Delivered before the New York Historical Society, Oct. 12, 1864. By John Romeyn Brodhead. *New York.* 1864.

Imp. 8vo, pp. 87. *Portrait and Map. Half orange morocco, gilt top,* UNCUT.

236 BROOKS (J.) An Eulogy, on General Washington; delivered before the Inhabitants of the Town of Medford, ... the 13th of January, 1800. By John Brooks, A.M. ... *Boston:* 1800.

8vo, pp. 15. UNCUT.

237 BROOKLYN. The Battle of Brooklyn a Farce in two acts as it was performed on Long Island on Tuesday the 27th day of August, 1776. By the Representatives of the Tyrants of America Assembled at Philadelphia. *New York: Printed for J. Rivington, in the Year of the Rebellion.* 1776. [*Brooklyn: Reprinted.* 1873.]

8vo, pp. 45. *Half red morocco, gilt top,* UNCUT, *by* BRADSTREET.

Only a few copies of this curious work have been reprinted for private distribution."—*Preface.*

238 BROTHERHEAD (W.) Autographi Holographiani.
Philadelphia: 1857.

Imp. 4to, pp. 10. *Half calf.* Twenty-five copies *privately printed* from the "American Notes and Queries," for which, see No. 49 *supra.*

239 BROUGHAM (H.) Lives of Men of Letters and Science, who flourished in the Time of George III. By Henry Lord Brougham. With Portraits engraved on Steel.
London: Charles Knight and Co. 1845–1846.

2 *vols., royal 8vo, half red morocco, gilt top,* UNCUT. *Selected impressions* of the fifteen portraits, which are much finer than those usually found in the work.

240 BROWN (J. C.) Bibliotheca Americana. A Catalogue of Books relating to North and South America in the Library of John Carter Brown of Providence Rhode Island. With Notes by John Russell Bartlett. *Providence:* 1865–71.

4 *vols., imp. 8vo, half crushed red levant morocco, gilt top,* UNCUT, by WM. MATTHEWS. FIFTY COPIES ONLY PRINTED FOR PRIVATE DISTRIBUTION, AND EXCESSIVELY SCARCE.

"A catalogue of Mr. Brown's library, prepared by John R. Bartlett, with copious notes, was printed a few years ago in four imperial octavos. This superb catalogue, of which only fifty copies were printed, was never offered for sale, but was presented to collectors of books relating to America, and to a few of the public libraries of the United States and Europe. Six of these copies are owned by well known collectors in New York and Brooklyn, and a seventh is in the library of the New York Historical Society.

Volume I. includes 300 titles of books printed between 1493 and 1600. Volume II., between 1601 and 1700, 1160 titles; Volumes III. and IV., between 1701 and 1800, 4173 titles, making 5635, in all." Sabin's "*American Bibliopolist.*"

241 BROWNE (J.) History of the Highlands, and of the Highland Clans; with an Extensive Selection from the hitherto Inedited Stuart Papers; By James Browne. Illustrated by Sixty-Six Engravings and numerous woodcuts. *Edinburgh:* 1852.

4 *vols., roy. 8vo.* LARGE PAPER. *Half green levant morocco, gilt top,* UNCUT. The PLATES of the CLAN TARTANS are beautifully and accurately COLOURED in the *Large Paper* copies.

This complete and comprehensive work contains most interesting and authentic accounts of the aboriginal Highland Tribes, their Pictish and Scoto-Irish Kings, Antiquities, Poetry, Superstitions, &c., together with an exciting History of the Feuds, Battles, Revolts, and Proceedings in the Highlands through the Roman, Pictish, and Scottish Periods, including full accounts of their rising under Montrose, Hamilton, Argyle, in the Rebellions of Charles I., the two Pretenders, &c.

242 [BRUCE (D.)] Poems chiefly in the Scottish Dialect, originally written under the signature of the Scots-Irishman, by a Native of Scotland. [D. Bruce.] With Notes and Illustrations.
Washington: [Penn.] 1801.

12*mo, pp.* xii., 126, (11). *Half purple morocco.*

Relating entirely to American subjects, and VERY SCARCE.

243 BRUNET (Jacques Charles.) Manuel du Libraire et de l'amateur de livres contenant un nouveau Dictionnaire Bibliographique, et une table en forme de Catalogue Raisonné. ... Cinquième édition originale, entièrement refondue, et augmentée d'un tiers par l'auteur.
Paris: Didot. 1860–65.

12 *vols., imp. 8vo, half crimson levant morocco, gilt top,* UNCUT, by W. MATTHEWS. A GRAND SET, printed on LARGE HOLLAND PAPER, of which ONLY 100 COPIES were issued, *all for subscribers.*

It is illustrated with NUMEROUS FACSIMILES of the DEVICES *of the* EARLY PRINTERS, is altogether a most superb book, and one of the most correct Bibliographical Dictionaries extant. Now out of print and VERY SCARCE.

244 BRY (Theodore de.) Collectiones Peregrinationum in Indiam Occidentalem, IX. Partibus comprehensæ a Theodoro, Joan-Theodoro de Bry, publicatæ. *Francofurti ad Mœnum.* 1590–1602.

9 vols., folio. Superbly bound in blue gros grained morocco, elegant. Filleted and gilt backs, rich inside borders, paneled sides, corner ornaments, double silk head bands, gilt edges, by F. BEDFORD.

The Nine Parts which form this set are all ORIGINAL IMPRESSIONS, but *vary in numerous particulars* from the collation of Brunet. *See* the following copy of the translation of Brunet's article, made for Mr. Sabin's Dictionary, *in which the* VARIATIONS, and NUMEROUS IMPORTANT ADDITIONS &c. are *fully* and *carefully noted.*

This is a series of what is known as the "Grands Voyages" and contains all of the Latin version which was published during the life time of the elder De Bry, and as the title of Part IX bears the words "*Postrema Pars,*" it is evident that it was intended to stop there, but the success of the enterprise induced its continuation. It would be easy to expatiate on the beauty, desirability, utility, and value of this GRAND SERIES of works but we content ourselves by referring the reader to the descriptions of the work in *Brunet's* Manual, or, the mere English Reader to the translation of the same in "Sabin's Dictionary of Books relating to America" article Bry (T. de) a few copies of which were printed separately for the owner of this set and are described below.

"No such expensive efforts were ever after made by any Expedition or Colony to collect such vivid and picturesque material of the New World, its inhabitants, and natural products."—Stevens' "*Bibliotheca Historica.*"

245 BRY. A Bibliographical Description of the Collection of "Grands Voyages" of De Bry. Translated from Brunet's "Manual du Librarie," by Charles A. Cutter. *New York: Privately Printed.* 1869.

Imp. 8vo, pp. 61. *Half red morocco, gilt top,* UNCUT, *by* BRADSTREET. No. 3 of 25 *copies only,* reproduced from Sabin's "*Dictionary of Books relating to America.*"

In this copy there has been neatly written, an EXACT COLLATION of the preceding nine parts of the "Grands Voyages," showing all the *differences, variations, additions to,* and *peculiarities* of those nine parts, and should accompany them.

246 BRY. [Another Copy.]

No. 1. *Half red morocco, gilt top,* UNCUT, *by* BRADSTREET.

247 BRY. [Another Copy.]

Paper, UNCUT.

248 BRYANT (William C.) Bryant Festival. (The) At "THE CENTURY." Illustrated Edition.
New York: Published by the Century Association. 1865.

4to, pp. 88. *Half green morocco, gilt top,* UNCUT. LARGE PAPER. 150 Copies only printed. The photographs published with the work have been *remounted* and *inlaid* by TRENT. An AUTOGRAPH STANZA *written and signed by* MR. BRYANT, and *twelve* other ILLUSTRATIONS, all of which are PROOFS, and INDIA PROOFS, some BEFORE LETTERS *inserted.* The *prints* of the Homes of the Authors have been thrown out, and INDIA PROOF impressions inserted instead.

A BEAUTIFUL VOLUME.

249 BRYDGES (E.) RESTITUTA, or Titles, Extracts, and Characters of old Books in English Literature revived. By Sir Egerton Brydges.
London: Longman. 1814.

4 vols., 8vo, half blue morocco, gilt top, UNCUT. Uniform with the "CENSURA." EXTREMELY SCARCE in *uncut* Condition. PORTRAIT of the AUTHOR *inserted.*

See Vol. II, p. 202, for a reprint from the excessively scarce original of "A True Report of the Laste Voyage into the West and Northwest Regions, etc., 1577, worthily atchieved by Captaine Frobisher, etc." It is a valuable work, with copious extracts of the rarest and most curious books in early English literature; 250 copies only were printed, which were published at £6 6*s*., in numbers.

250 BRYDGES. CENSURA LITERARIA. Containing Titles, Abstracts, and Opinions of Old English Books, with Original Disquisitions, Articles of Biography, and other Literary Antiquities. By Sir Egerton Brydges, Bart. ... Second Edition. With the Articles classed in Chronological Order under their Separate Heads. *London: Longman.* 1815.

10 *vols.*, 8*vo*, *half blue morocco, gilt top*, UNCUT. Uniform with "RESTITUTA." An appropriate *frontispiece inserted* in each volume, embracing *three fine* and *scarce* PORTRAITS of the AUTHOR, and an *autograph note* written and signed by him. A BEAUTIFUL COPY.

Of this SECOND and BEST Edition one hundred copies only were printed, and it is of *so much rarity* that *we are unable to quote the price of* ANY COPY publicly sold in this country. Mr. Quaritch of London, priced a copy in a recent catalogue at 18 guineas.

251 BRYDGES. The Autobiography, Times, Opinions, and Contemporaries of of Sir Egerton Brydges, Bart. ... *London: Cochrane and M'Crone.* 1834.

2 *vols.*, 8*vo*, *pp.* *xxvii.*, 424, *xxiv.*, 431, 2 *Portraits. Half crimson morocco, gilt top*, UNCUT.

252 BUCKINGHAM (J. T.) Specimens of Newspaper Literature: with Personal Memoirs, Anecdotes, and Reminiscences. By Joseph T. Buckingham. *Boston: Little & Brown.* 1850.

2 *vols.*, 8*vo*, *half calf, gilt top*, UNCUT. *Portraits.*

Contains many interesting literary anecdotes connected with the early history of this country.

253 BUCKMINSTER (J.) Discourse delivered in ... Portsmouth, December 14, 1800, the Anniversary of the Death of George Washington. ... By Joseph Buckminster, A.M. *Portsmouth, New Hampshire:* 1800.

8*vo*, *pp.* 21. *Scarce.*

254 BUCKMINSTER. A Sermon, delivered in the First Church in Portsmouth, on the Lord's Day after the Melancholy Tidings of The Death of George Washington, the Father, Guardian and Ornament of His country. By Joseph Buckminister, A.M. *Portsmouth:* 1800.

8*vo*, *pp.* 17.

The two following sermons form part of the same vol.: A Sermon, delivered in the First Church in Portsmouth, January 5th, 1800. The house being dressed in mourning in token of respect to the memory of General Washington. 8*vo*, *pp.* 19–29. A Second Sermon, delivered Lord's day, January 5, 1800. 8*vo*, *pp.* 31–45.

255 BUCKMINISTER. Religion and Righteousness the Basis of National Honor and Prosperity. A Sermon Preached to the North and South Parishes in Portsmouth, Fraternally united in Observance of the 22d February, 1800; The day appointed by Congress to pay tributary respect to the Memory of General Washington. By Joseph Buckminster, A.M. *Portsmouth, New Hampshire: Charles Peirce.* 1800.

8*vo*, *pp.* 28.

256 BUCKTAIL BARDS. (The) The State Triumvirate, a Political Tale; and The Epistles of Brevet Major Pindar Puff. *New York: The Author.* 1819.

12mo, pp. 215. *Half green morocco, gilt top,* UNCUT. SCARCE.

An amusing satire on Dewitt Clinton, Dr. John W. Francis, Dr. Samuel L. Mitchell, Gulian C. Verplanck, and other literary and political celebrities of the period.

257 BUDD (T.) Good Order Established | in | Pennsilvania & New-Jersey | in | America, | Being a true Account of the Country; | With its Produce and Commodities there made. | And the great Improvements that may be made by | means of Publick Store-houses for Hemp, Flax, and | Linnen-Cloth; also the Advantages of a Publick- | School, the Profits of a Publick-Bank, and the Proba- | bility of its arising, if those directions here laid down are | followed. With the advantages of publick Granaries. | Likewise, several other things needful to be understood by | those that are or do intend to be concerned in planting in | the said Countries. | All which is laid down very plain, in this small Treatise; it | being easie to be understood by any ordinary Capacity. To | which the Reader is referred for his further satisfaction. | By Thomas Budd. | [*London:*] *Printed in the Year* 1685. |

Sm. 4to, pp. 40. *Red levant morocco, gilt edges, by* W. PRATT. A FINE COPY, from the Rice Collection, of one of the RAREST of books relating to Pennsylvania.

See the following reprint for an extended account of the Author.

258 BUDD. Good Order Established in Pennsylvania and New Jersey, in America, being a True Account of the Country; with its Produce and Commodities there made in the year 1685. By Thomas Budd. A new Edition, with Introduction and Notes by Edward Armstrong. *New York: W. Gowans.* 1865.

4to, pp. 111, *half calf, gilt top,* UNCUT. Sixty copies only printed on LARGE PAPER. Forms No. 4 of Gowans' "*Bibliotheca Americana.*"

259 [BUDD (Thomas.)] A True Copy of Three Judgments given forth by a Party of Men, called Quakers at Philadelphia, against George Keith and his Friends. With two answers to the said Judgments. [*Philadelphia: Printed by William Bradford.* 1692.]

Sm. 4to, half blue morocco.

On the verso of the last leaf of this VERY RARE and curious book is a list of the "Books to be sold by William Bradford, in Philadelphia, 1692," with the prices; and at the bottom of the page is the following note: "And whereas it is reported that the printer being a favorer of G. K., he will not print for any other, which is the reason that the other party appear not in print as well as G. K. These are to signifie that the printer hath not yet refused to print anything for either party; and also signifies that he doth not refuse, but is willing and ready to print anything for the future that G. K.'s opposers shall bring to him."

The following notice of WILLIAM BRADFORD is from Joseph Smith's Catalogue of "*Friends' Books,*" and is here introduced on account of the interest which attaches to his name, as well as on account of the numerous books, contained in this library, which were printed by him. "William Bradford was born in Leicester, about the year 1659. He was placed as an apprentice to learn the printing business with Andrew Sowle in London. Whilst in this situation, he appears to have been convinced of Friends' principles, and was admitted into membership among them. Shortly after he was of age he married Elizabeth Sowle, a daughter of his late master, and then went over to America. This was in 1682 or 1683. A Certificate of Devonshire House Monthly Meeting, recommending William Bradford and Elizabeth his wife, as members of the Society of Friends, was read in Philadelphia Monthly Meeting, held the 4th of the 11th month, 1685, and accepted. They were not, however, settled in Philadelphia, but in Oxford township; and belonged to Oxford Monthly Meeting. His press was probably at Burlington, or at Chester, or at Kensington. Having received his printing materials from England, William Bradford was now ready to carry on business. The first work that he printed appears to have been 'An Epistle of John Burnyeat's, in 1686.' In the year 1687, he issued a prospectus for publishing by subscription a folio Bible with notes, but not receiving sufficient encouragement, the work was relinquished. In the year 1691, he joined with George Keith in his controversy with the Society, and in 1692 wished to be discharged from the engagement as Friends' printer. He removed to New York with his press in 1693, and was appointed printer to the government. There he continued to reside until 5th month 23rd, 1752, when he suddenly deceased, aged 94 years. He signed many books and papers during the Keithian controversy. It is scarcely necessary to add, that Bradford being the first printer in the Middle Colonies, books printed by him are eagerly sought for by the American collector; many of them are printed without a separate title-page, but their completeness is ascertained by the paging and signatures." For a list of books printed by Bradford, *see* J. W. Wallace's "Address." No. 2026.

260 BULLOCK (W.) Virginia | Impartially examined, and left | to publick view, to be considered by all Judi- | cious and honest men. | Under which Title, is compre- | hended the Degrees from 34 to 39, wherein | lyes the rich and healthfull Countries of Roanock, | the now Plantations of Virginia | and Mary-land. | Looke not upon this Booke, as | those that are set out by private men, for private | ends; for being read, you'l find, the publick | good is the Authors onely aime. | For this Piece is no other then the Adventurers | or Planters faithfull Steward, disposing the Ad- | venture for the best advantage, advising | people of all degrees, from the highest | Master, to the meanest Servant, | how suddenly to raise their | fortunes. | Peruse the Table, and you shall finde the | way plainely layd downe. | By William Bvllock, Gent. | 19 April, 1649. Imprimatur, Hen: Whaley. | *London: Printed by John Hammond, and are to be sold at his house | over-against S. Andrews Church in Holborne.* 1649.

Small 4to, pp. (12), 66. *Blue levant morocco, paneled and gilt sides, corner ornaments, gilt top,* UNCUT, *by* F. BEDFORD.

An ELEGANT and PRESQUE UNIQUE copy, notwithstanding one leaf is in most accurate facsimile, and 4 leaves remargined by VIGNE of Paris.

This EXTREMELY RARE book is dedicated to "the Earle of Arundell and Surrey, and the Lord Baltimore." Concerning the work *see* Ternaux, No. 685, and Rich No. 271.

261 [BULWER (John.)] ANTHROPOMETAMORPHOSIS: Man Transformed: or the Artificial Changling historically presented, on the mad and cruell Gallantry, foolish Bravery, ridiculous Beauty, filthy Fineness, and loathsome Loveliness of most Nations, fashioning and attiring their Bodies from the mould intended by Nature; with figures of those Transfigurations. To which Artificiall and Affected Deformations are added, all the Native and National Monstrosities that have appeared to disfigure the Humane Fabrick. With a Vindication of the Regular Beauty and Honesty of Nature. And an

Appendix of the Pedigree of the English Gallant. Scripsit I. B. Cognomento Chirosophus, M.D.
London: Printed by William Hunt. 1653.

4to, pp. (52), 559, (28), *russia, gilt edges.* Bound by ROGER PAYNE, for Dr. Mosely, with Payne's *long, interesting, and very curious bill* for binding the volume *inserted.*

An excellent copy of the *best edition* of this no less curious than RARE volume, with a PORTRAIT by FAITHORNE, a frontispiece by CROSS, and *numerous woodcuts.* It is a most entertaining book relative to the customs of the seventeenth century, especially the fashions of dress and adornment of the body.

262 BURDER (G.) The Welch Indians; or, a Collection of Papers, respecting a people whose Ancestors emigrated from Wales to America, in the year 1170, with Prince Madoc, (three hundred years before the First Voyage of Columbus), and who are said now to inhabit a beautiful Country on the West Side of the Mississippi. Dedicated to the Missionary Society by George Burder.
London: T. Chapman. [1797.]

8vo, pp. 35. *Half red morocco, carmine edges.*

A VERY RARE piece not included in Mr. Field's Bibliography.

See Williams (J.) No. 2149.

263 BURGES (T.) Battle of Lake Erie, with Notices of Commodore Elliot's Conduct in that Engagement. By Hon. Tristam Burges.
Boston: B. B. Mussey. 1839.

12mo, pp. xv., 117. *Diagrams. Calf.*

264 [BURGOYNE (John.)] The Substance of General Burgoyne's Speeches, on Mr. Vyner's Motion, on the 26th of May; and upon Mr. Hartley's Motion, on the 28th of May, 1778. With an Appendix, containing General Washington's Letter to General Burgoyne, etc. *London: J. Almon.* 1778.

8vo, pp. 42, (6). *Half morocco, gilt top,* UNCUT. Fine copy.

265 [BURGOYNE.] A Brief Examination of the Plan and Conduct of the Northern Expedition in America, in 1777. And of the Surrender of the Army under the Command of Lieutenant-General Burgoyne.
London: M DCC LXXIX.

8vo, pp. 52. *Half morocco.*

Concerning this, *See M. R. First Series,* LIX. 320.

266 BURGOYNE. A Letter from Lieut. Gen. Burgoyne to his Constituents, upon his late Resignation; with the Correspondences between the Secretaries of War and him, relative to his return to America. *London: J. Almon.* MDCCLXXIX.

8vo, pp. 37. *Half morocco, gilt top,* UNCUT.

After General Burgoyne's surrender, he was allowed to return to England on *parole.* Thinking himself ill-treated by the Government, and having been elected member of Parliament for Preston, he joined the opposition; whereupon an official order was sent to him, signifying that it was the King's pleasure that he should return to America and rejoin his captive army. He remonstrated and was again ordered, and in consequence resigned all his civil and military employments. In this letter he gives an explanation of his conduct.

267 [BURGOYNE.] A Letter to Lieut. Gen. Burgoyne, on his Letter to his Constituents. *London: T. Becket.* 1779.

8vo, pp. 35. *Half morocco, gilt top,* UNCUT.

Instead of the liberal manner of a gentleman, this writer attacks Mr. Burgoyne with the ferocity of one of his own savages, reeking and hot from the murder of poor Miss McRay" [*sic*].—*Monthly Review*, LXI., 389.

268 [BURGOYNE.] A Reply to Lieutenant General Burgoyne's Letter to his Constituents. ... *London: J. Wilkie.* MDCCLXXIX.

8vo, pp. (4), 46. *Half morocco.*

"This writer merits commendation for the decent and candid strain in which he writes. He does not, like the general's antagonist above mentioned, assail with a blunted tomahawk. He cuts up like a skillful surgeon, and dissects his subject with the dexterity of an able anatomist."—*M. R.* LXI. 389. Attributed to Sir John Dalrymple, but with more probability to George Germaine, Lord Sackville; who was colonial secretary during the American Revolution.

269 BURGOYNE. A State of the Expedition from Canada, as laid before the House of Commons, by Lieutenant-General Burgoyne, and verified by Evidence; with a Collection of Authentic Documents, and an Addition of many Circumstances which were prevented from appearing before the House. ... Written and Collected by Himself. *London: J. Almon.* MDCCLXXX.

4to, pp. viii., 140, *lxii.*, (1). 6 *Folded Plans. Half purple levant morocco, gilt top,* UNCUT. *A beautiful copy,* with a FINE and EXTREMELY RARE PORTRAIT of BURGOYNE *inserted.*

"General Burgoyne writes well; his very interesting story is told in a masterly manner, and the materials of which it is composed will be held in great estimation by the historian who shall record the events of the unhappy war to which they owe their birth."—*Monthly Review*, LXII. 247.

270 BURGOYNE. A Supplement to the State of the Expedition from Canada, containing General Burgoyne's Orders, respecting the Principal Movements, and Operations of the Army to the Raising of the Siege of Ticonderoga. *New York: Privately Reprinted [for F. S. Hoffman.]* 1865.

4to, pp. 26. *Half purple morocco, gilt top,* UNCUT. An INDIA PROOF PORTRAIT of BURGOYNE; and "*The Lamentations of Gen. Burgoyne after he became a prisoner to the Rebels.*" *18mo, pp.* 18, *inserted.*

The New York edition of which 75 copies were issued was printed mostly for presentation. The work was originally published without Gen. Burgoyne's authority. *See M. R.*, XLII. 492.

271 [BURGOYNE.] A Letter to Lieut. Gen. Burgoyne, occasioned by a Second Edition of his State of the Expedition from Canada. *London: G. Kearsley.* 1780.

8vo, pp. 32. *Half morocco, gilt top,* UNCUT.

"The great object of this letter is to defend Lord G. Germaine, and Government in general, from the charges brought against them, in the prefatory speech to the state of the expedition. The general is attacked with great severity, and Sir William Howe comes in for a share of the author's keen animadversion."—RICH, I. 285.

272 [BURGOYNE.] An Enquiry into, and Remarks upon the Conduct of Lieutenant General Burgoyne. The Plan of Operation for the Campaign of 1777, the Instructions from the Secretary of State, and the Circumstances that led to the Loss of the Northern Army. *London: J. Matthews.* 1780.

8vo, pp. 50. *Half morocco.*

273 [BURGOYNE.] Essay on Modern Martyrs: with a Letter to General Burgoyne. *London: Payne.* 1780.

8vo, pp. 52. *Half morocco.*

Supposed to be written by a Mr. Dallas.

274 [BURGOYNE.] Condolence; | An | Elegiac Epistle | from | Lieut. Gen. B-rg-yne, | Captured at Saratoga, Oct. 17, 1777, | To | Lieut. Gen. Earl. C-rnw-ll-s, | Captured at York-Town, Oct. 17, 1781. | With | Notes by the Editor. | *London: T. Evans.* MDCCLXXXII.

4to, pp. 32. *Half morocco, gilt top,* UNCUT. VERY SCARCE.

275 BURGOYNE. The Dramatic and Poetical Works of the Late Lieut.-Gen. J. Burgoyne; to which is prefixed Memoirs of the Author. Embellished with Copper Plates. *London: C. Whittingham.* 1808.

2vols., 8vo, LARGE PAPER. *Half morocco, gilt top,* UNCUT. VERY SCARCE in this size.

The Memoirs include a sketch of the author's campaign in America. *See M. R.* LVII, 99.

276 BURK (J.) The History of Virginia, from its First Settlement to the Present Day. By John Burk. *Petersburg, Virginia: the Author.* 1804–1805 [3 vols.] The History of Virginia, commenced by John Burk, and continued by Skelton Jones, and Louis Hue Girardin; Vol. IV. *Petersburg, Virginia: Printed by M. W. Dunnavant, for the Proprietors.* 1816.

4 *vols., 8vo, purple morocco, paneled sides, broad inside gilt borders, gilt top,* UNCUT; except the fourth volume; which is *never found uncut,* but is bound to range with the set.

It is perhaps THE FINEST SET ever offered for sale. The fourth volume is the most rare, a large portion of the edition having been destroyed by fire. This SPLENDID COPY contains a fine impression of the *original engraving* of CAPT. JOHN SMITH from the map in his "*History of Virginia.*" *London.* 1627; and a COLOURED photograph of L. H. GIRARDIN who aided in the completion of the work. An account of the duel, which terminated in the author's death, in the hand-writing of MR. INGRAHAM, is also inserted.

277 BURKE (E.) Speech of Edmund Burke, Esq., on American Taxation, April 19, 1774. *London: J. Dodsley.* MDCCLXXV.

8vo, pp. 96. *Half red morocco, gilt top.* PORTRAIT of MR. BURKE *inserted.*

278 [BURKE.] An Answer to the letter of Edmund Burke, Esq. one of the Representatives of the City of Bristol, to the Sheriffs of that City. *London:* M. DCC. LXXVII.

8vo, pp. (4), 60. *Half morocco, gilt top.*

Perhaps by Dr. Shebbeare. *See M. R.* LVII. 85.

279 BURKE. A Letter from Edmund Burke, Esq; One of the Representatives in Parliament for the City of Bristol, to John Farr, and John Harris, Esqrs. Sheriffs of that City, On the Affairs of America. The Second Edition. *London: J. Dodsley.* M DCC LXXVII.

8vo, pp. 79. Half red morocco, gilt top.

Some of Burke's best writings and most eloquent orations, are in defence of the measures taken by the American Colonists.

280 BURNABY (A.) Travels through the Middle Settlements in North America, in the Years 1759 and 1760: With Observations upon the State of the Colonies. By the Rev. Andrew Burnaby, A.M. Edition the Third: revised, corrected, and greatly enlarged, by the Author. *London: T. Payne.* 1798.

4to, pp. xix., 209. Engraving of Passaic Falls. Map. Half calf, UNCUT.

Valuable as exhibiting a view of the colonies before the Revolutionary War. *See M. R.,* LV. 401, and "*Biog. Universelle.*"

281 BURNETT (G.) Specimens of English Prose Writers, from the Earliest Times to the Close of the Seventeenth Century, with Sketches, Biographical and Literary; including an account of Books as well as of their Authors, with Occasional Criticisms. By George Burnett. Second Edition. *London: John Bumpus.* 1813.

3 vols., crown 8vo, half calf. LARGE and FINE COPY.

"An elegant and judicious compilation, forming a companion to Ellis's Specimens."—*Lowndes.*

282 BURNS (R.) Poems, Chiefly in the Scottish Dialect. By Robert Burns. *Kilmarnock: Printed by John Wilson.* 1786.

8vo, pp. 240. Green morocco extra, broad outside and inside gilt borders, gilt edges, by GRIEVE *of* Edinburgh.

A BEAUTIFUL, LARGE, and CLEAN copy of the EXCESSIVELY RARE FIRST OR KILMARNOCK EDITION, now almost unobtainable at any price. Indeed a first folio Shakespeare, or the first edition of Milton's Paradise Lost, are much less rare. Mr. Allan's copy, much inferior to this, sold for $106.

283 BURNS. Poems, chiefly in the Scottish Dialect. By Robert Burns. *Edinburgh: Printed for the Author, and sold by William Creech.* 1787.

8vo, pp. xlviii., 9–368. Portrait. Green morocco, paneled and gilt sides, gilt top, UNCUT. A SPLENDID COPY, *fresh* and *clean* as when published, with a *beautiful impression* of the PORTRAIT after NASMYTH.

THE FIRST EDINBURGH EDITION AND VERY RARE; dedicated to the Members of the Caledonian Hunt. The portrait is said to be the best extant of the poet; he having sat for it, to both painter and engraver.

284 BURNS. Poems, chiefly in the Scottish Dialect. By Robert Burns. The Third Edition.

London: Printed for A. Strahan; T. Cadel in the Strand; and W. Creech, Edinburgh. 1787.

8vo, pp. xlviii., 13–372. Portrait. Half red morocco, UNCUT. A FINE COPY of the FIRST LONDON EDITION. VERY RARE in *uncut* condition.

It has been conjectured that this is a re-issue of the *first Edinburgh edition*, of same date, with a different title page, but a very casual examination will suffice to show that it was printed from an *entirely different* and *re-composed form*. Besides; the second edition was *printed for the author* at Edinburgh, whereas *this* was printed for Strahan at London. The second has an "Addenda" to the List of Subscribers, which addenda is incorporated in one alphabet in this. The Edinburgh edition has 368 pages, this has 372.

285 BURNS. Poems, chiefly in the Scottish Dialect. By Robert Burns. To which are added, Scots Poems, Selected from the works of Robert Ferguson.

New York: printed by J. and A. M'Lean, Franklin's Head, No. 41, Hanover-Square. 1788.

Sm. 8vo, pp. 306. *Portrait engraved by* SCOTT. *Green levant morocco, paneled and gilt sides, gilt edges, by* F. BEDFORD.

A BEAUTIFUL and MOST RARE VOLUME. The identical copy referred to in the quaint notice below, and which Mr. Gowans persistently refused to part with, on any consideration, during the lifetime of the late Mr. John Allan. The owner never saw another copy.

"No doubt THE FIRST AMERICAN EDITION."— M'Kie's "*Burnsiana.*"

"The New York edition of the works of Robert Burns, 1788, may so far be pronounced unique. No copy with the exception of the one named has been seen by the most sharp hawk-eyed book hunter, or the keenest bibliographer, nor by any of the living generation so far as known. I used to banter the Nestor of Vandewater Street (John Allan, who was very anxious to possess this book) that I would exchange my copy of the first American edition for his Kilmarnock, the first Scotch edition, providing he would add a fifty dollar bill by way of inducing me to part with such a rarity. He declined to comply with this generous offer and so never had the pleasure of being possessed of what he long had set his affections on. He lived in the hopes of some day procuring a copy, but before that day arrived he had "passed that bourne from whence no traveller returns."—"WESTERN MEMORABILIA," [i. e. *Wm. Gowans.*]

286 BURNS. Poems, Chiefly in the Scottish Dialect. By Robert Burns.

Philadelphia: Printed for, and sold by Peter Stewart and George Hyde. 1788.

12mo, pp. 304. *Green morocco, paneled sides, gilt edges.* In *fine preservation* and EXTREMELY RARE.

Not in "*Burnsiana.*"

It is a reprint, of Burns' second edition of his Poems, with the Dedication "to the Noblemen and Gentlemen of the Caledonian Hunt," but leaving out the List of Subscribers, occupying 38 pages in the original.—The late William Gowans remarks: "It is difficult at this time to determine, whether this or the New York edition bearing the same date, was the first of Burns's works published in America. It may, however, be presumed that the Philadelphia edition was the first perhaps by a month or two. The quaker city was then the capital of the lately enfranchised Colonies, and as a matter of course communication with Europe was much more frequent and direct than [with] any other port on the Atlantic coast."

287 BURNS. Poems, Chiefly in the Scottish Dialect. The Second [Edinburgh] Edition considerably enlarged.

Edinburgh: William Creech. 1793.

2 vols., sm. 8vo, pp. xi., 237; (4), 283. PORTRAIT. *Half green morocco, gilt top,* UNCUT. PORTRAIT of BURNS *engraved* by TIEBOUT *inserted.* A BEAUTIFUL COPY of the SECOND EDINBURGH EDITION. VERY SCARCE.

Unnoticed by Mr. M'Kie.

This was the REV. COOPER WILLYAMS' copy with his *Autograph* on the fly leaf of each Volume. Mr. Willyams served as Chaplain on the English frigate, "SWIFTSURE" at the battle of the Nile, and a note in his hand-writing, at one time in this volume, but now lost or abstracted, intimated that this copy of Burns, then and there, formed a part of his Sea Library.

288 BURNS. The Works of Robert Burns; with an Account of his Life and Writings. By James Currie. *London:* 1817–20.

5 *vols.*, 8*vo*, *calf*. *Numerous Engravings on Steel.* AN ELEGANT SET of the best library edition to which is added, Cromek's "Reliques of Burns," comprising original poems, letters, and illustrations.

289 BURNS. The works of Robert Burns; with a Complete Life of the Poet, and an Essay on his Genius and Character, by Professor Wilson. Also numerous Notes, Annotations, and Appendices. Embellished by Eighty-one Portraits and Landscape Illustrations. *Glasgow: Blackie and Son.* 1852.

2 *vols.*, *imp.* 8*vo*, *green morocco*, *paneled and gilt sides*, *gilt top*, UNCUT.

A UNIQUE and most beautiful copy with a genuine AUTOGRAPH MANUSCRIPT by BURNS inserted. It is the earliest issue of the best and most comprehensive work on Burns extant, with fine impressions of the Eighty-two beautiful PORTRAIT and LANDSCAPE ILLUSTRATIONS from the DRAWINGS of D. O. HILL, S.A. The volumes are further ILLUSTRATED by the *insertion* of upwards of ONE HUNDRED PORTRAITS, VIEWS, &c., including a fine PROOF SET of STORER and GREIG'S VIEWS; a set in similar state of the ILLUSTRATIONS to CURRIE'S BURNS; numerous INDIA PROOF VIGNETTE tail pieces mounted by TRENT; the ORIGINAL MS. of the "*Elegy on the year* 1788," in the HAND WRITING of the AUTHOR, preceding the title in Vol. I.; and an Autograph letter signed of DR. CURRIE, at p. cxxxvi, Vol. I, both from the collection of ALLAN CUNNINGHAM. Also, an occasional short poetic effusion WRITTEN and SIGNED by AGNES MCLEHOSE, the "*Clarinda*" of Burns, from the same collection, at p. 301 Vol. II.; and a characteristic Autograph note of ALLAN CUNNINGHAM at p. ccxli. Vol. I. Mr. M'Kie in his "*Bibliotheca Burnsiana*," says "it is certainly the most magnificent edition of the entire works of the Ayrshire Bard that has ever appeared."

290 BURNS. Facsimile of Burns' Celebrated Poem entitled the Jolly Beggars. From the Original Manuscript. *Glasgow: James Lumsden & Son.* 1823.

4*to*, *half green morocco*, *gilt top*, UNCUT. PORTRAIT of BURNS *inserted.* VERY SCARCE.

291 BURNS. The Land of Burns, a Series of Landscapes and Portraits, illustrative of the Life and Writings of the Scottish Poet. The Landscapes from Paintings made expressly for the Work, by D. O. Hill, R.S.A. The Literary Department, by Professor Wilson, and Robert Chambers, Esq. *Glasgow: Blackie and Son.* 1840.

2 *vols.*, 4*to*, *in one*, *half green morocco*, *gilt edges.* An *original subscriber's copy*, with brilliant impressions of the *eighty-two fine plates.*

292 [BURNS.] The Contemporaries of Burns, and the more Recent Poets of Ayrshire. With Selections from their Writings. *Edinburgh: Hugh Paton.* 1840.

8*vo*, *pp.* 416, 24. 6 *Plates.* *Half calf.* *Fine copy.* VERY SCARCE.

293 [BURNS.] BIBLIOTHECA BURNSIANA. Title pages and imprints of the various Editions of Burns in the Private Library of James M'Kie, Kilmarnock, Prior to 1866. [With an Addenda, containing List of Editions not in his Possession.] *Kilmarnock.* 1866.

8vo, boards. Describes 443 editions and works.

294 BURNYEAT. The Truth Exalted in the Writings of that Eminent and Faithful Servant of Christ John Burnyeat, collected Into this Ensuing Volume as a Memorial to his Faithful Labours in and for the Truth. ... *London: Printed for Thomas Northcott.* 1691.

Small 4to, 4l., pp. 264. *Green morocco, gilt edges. Very fine copy.* RARE.

Contains an account of his travels and labors in various parts of America, and sundry epistles addressed to the Friends in Barbadoes, Maryland, New Jersey, etc., in company with George Fox. *See* Smith's "*Catalogue of Friends' Books,*" I. 348–9.

295 BURR (Aaron.) [BURRIANA.] [*v. p. v. d.*]

The following is perhaps the most interesting and extensive series of books ever collected relating to the extraordinary career of this extraordinary man. It consists of 19 *vols., 8vo, uniformly bound in half dark olive morocco,* and would form a most desirable acquisition in its entirety, but as many collectors, no doubt, already possess some of the series, it has been decided to offer them in detail. Many of the volumes are *scarce,* and some *extremely rare.*

I. Letter from Alexander Hamilton, concerning the Public Conduct and Character of John Adams, Esq., President of the United States. *New York: John Lang.* 1800.

pp. 54. *Gilt top,* UNCUT. *Passed through no less than six editions.*

II. An Answer to Alexander Hamilton's Letter, concerning the Public Conduct and Character of John Adams, Esq. President of the United States. By a Citizen of New York. *New York: P. R. Johnson & J. Stryker.* 1800.

pp. 32. *Gilt top,* UNCUT.

III. A Letter to Major-General Hamilton containing Observations on his Letter, concerning the Public Conduct and Character of John Adams, Esq. President of the United States. By a Citizen of these States. *New York: Printed by G. F. Hopkins.* 1800.

pp. 32. *Gilt top,* UNCUT.

IV. A Letter to Thomas Jefferson, President of the United States. By Junius Philænus. *New York: P. R. Johnson.* 1802.

pp. 64.

V. Letters to Alexander Hamilton, King of the Feds, Ci-devant Secretary of the Treasury of the United States of America, Inspector-General of the Standing Armies thereof, Counsellor of Law, &c. &c. &c. Being intended as a reply to a Scandalous Pamphlet lately published under the sanction, as it is presumed, of Mr. Hamilton, and signed with the signature of Junius Philænus. By Tom Callender, Esq., Citizen of the World. *New York: Printed by Richard Reynolds.* 1802.

pp. 64. *Gilt top,* UNCUT. *A copy of the* "HAMILTONIAD" *by* ANTHONY PASQUIN, [*i.e. John Williams*] *is bound in with this.*

VI. A Narrative of the Suppression by Col. Burr, of the History of the Administration of John Adams, late President of the United States, written by John Wood. To which is added a Biography of Thomas Jefferson, President of the United States; and of General Hamilton; with strictures on the Conduct of John Adams, and on the Character of General C. C. Pinckney. By a Citizen of New York. [i. e. James Cheetham.] *New York: Denniston and Cheetham.* 1802.

pp. 72. *Gilt top,* UNCUT.

See Wood (John.) 2189.

VII. A View of the Political Conduct of Aaron Burr, Esq. Vice President of the United States. By the Author of the "Narrative." [i. e. James Cheetham.]
New York: Printed by Denniston & Cheetham. 1802.
pp. 120. *Gilt top,* UNCUT.

VIII. A Correct Statement of the Various Sources from which the History of the Administration of John Adams was compiled, and the Motives for its Suppression, by Col. Burr. With some Observations on a Narrative, by a Citizen of New York. By John Wood, Author of the Said History. *New York: G. F. Hopkins.* 1802.
pp. 49.
See Wood (John.) 2183.

IX. An Antidote to John Wood's Poison. By Warren.
New York: Printed by Southwick and Crooker. 1802.
pp. 63. *Gilt top.*
"WARREN" *is the pseudonym* of JAMES CHEETHAM.

X. Nine Letters on the Subject of Aaron Burr's Political Defection, with An Appendix. By James Cheetham. *New York: Denniston & Cheetham.* 1803.
pp. 139. *Gilt top,* UNCUT.

XI. A Letter to a Friend on the Conduct of the Adherents to Mr. Burr. By James Cheetham. *New York: Printed by James Cheetham.* 1803.
pp. 72. *Gilt top,* UNCUT.

XII. The Speeches at full length of Mr. Van Ness, Mr. Caines, the Attorney-General, Mr. Harrison, and General Hamilton, in the Great Cause of the People, against Harry Croswell, on an Indictment for a Libel on Thomas Jefferson, President of the United States. *New York: G. & R. Waite.* 1804.
pp. 78. *Gilt top,* UNCUT.

XIII. An Examination of the various Charges exhibited against Aaron Burr, Esq., Vice-President of the United States; and a Development of the Characters and Views of his Political Opponents. A New Edition, Revised and Corrected with Additions. By Aristides. [*New York.*] *Printed for the Author.* 1804.
pp. (4), 116.
"ARISTIDES" *is the pseudonym of* WILLIAM P. VAN NESS.

XIV. An Oration Commemorative of the Late Major-General Alexander Hamilton; pronounced before the New York State Society of the Cincinnati, on Tuesday the 31st of July, 1804. By J. M. Mason, D.D. *New York: G. F. Hopkins.* 1804.
pp. 40. *Gilt top,* UNCUT.

XV. A Letter to Aaron Burr, Vice-President of the United States of America, on the Barbarous Origin, the Criminal Nature and the Baneful Effects of Duels; occasioned by his late fatal interview with the deceased and much lamented General Alexander Hamilton. By Philanthropos. *New York: Printed for the Author.* 1804.
pp. 32. *Gilt top,* UNCUT.

XVI. A Full Statement of the Trial and Acquittal of Aaron Burr, Containing, all the Proceedings and Debates that took place before the Federal Court at Frankfort, Kentucky, November 26, 1806. By John Wood, Editor of the "Western World" who attended at the Trial. *Alexandria: Cottom and Stewart.* 1807.

pp. 36. *Gilt top,* UNCUT. CADWALLADER D. COLDEN'S *Copy with his Book Plate, and an interesting note in his handwriting.* "Two Opinions on the Case of John Fries" *inserted.*

XVII. The Examination of Col. Aaron Burr, before the Chief Justice of the United States upon the Charges of a High Misdemeanor, and of Treason against the United States; together with the Arguments of Counsel and Opinion of the Judge. To which is added An Appendix, containing the opinion of the Supreme Court, delivered by Chief Justice Marshall, in the case of Bollman and Swartwout.
Richmond: S. Grantland. 1807.

pp. 46. *Gilt top,* UNCUT.

XVIII. Letters of Marcus and Philo-Cato, addressed to DeWitt Clinton, Esq., Mayor of the City of New York. A New Edition, containing one letter of Marcus, and several numbers of Philo-Cato, never published before. *New York:* 1810.

pp. 86. *Gilt top,* UNCUT.

A caustic, and sometimes comical, *exposé* of the political quarrels arising out of the Burr Union, etc., formed about the year 1806, between the Clintonians and Burrites, by Matthew L. Davis.

XIX. A Narrative of the Celebrated Dyde Supper. By the Editor and Proprietor of the New-York Morning Post and Morning Star.

New York: Printed for the Author. 1811.

pp. (6), 61. *Gilt top,* UNCUT.

296 BURR. Reports of the Trials of Colonel Aaron Burr (late Vice-President of the United States), for Treason and for a Misdemeanor, in preparing the means of a Military Expedition against Mexico, a Territory of the King of Spain, with whom the United States were at Peace. ... By David Robertson.

Philadelphia: Hopkins and Earle. 1808.

2 vols., 8vo, half red morocco, gilt top, UNCUT. RARE.

297 BURR. Memoirs of Aaron Burr. With Miscellaneous Selections from His Correspondence by Matthew L. Davis.

New York: Harper and Brothers. 1836.

2 vols., 8vo, pp. 436; 449. *2 Portraits and Facsimile. Half green morocco.*

UNIQUE copy with an *Autograph Letter Signed,* of AARON BURR; PORTRAIT of ANDRÉ; copy of a Letter from ANDRÉ to MRS. ARNOLD; an Article from the N. A. Review, and interesting mounted newspaper cuttings, *inserted* in Vol. I. An *Autograph Letter Signed,* of AARON BURR; a Review of the work; a Vindication of Colonel Duane; and mounted newspaper cuttings, *inserted* in Vol. II.

298 BURR. The Private Journal of Aaron Burr, during his Residence of Four Years in Europe; with Selections from his Correspondence. Edited by Matthew L. Davis. ...

New York: Harper & Brothers. 1838.

2 vols., 8vo, pp. 451; 9–453. *Half green morocco.*

Contains a curious and interesting AUTOGRAPH LETTER SIGNED of SAMUEL SWARTWOUT proposing to BURR to engage in smuggling cotton bagging into the United States. It was published in "American Notes and Queries." Phil. 1857; also in Parton's "Life of Burr," from this original.

The later editions of this work are printed on thinner paper.

299 BURRILL (G. R.) An Oration pronounced at ... Providence ... the Seventh of January, 1800, at the Funeral Ceremony on the Death of Gen. George Washington. By Col. George R. Burrill.

Providence: [1800.]

8vo, pp. 15. UNCUT and RARE.

300 [BURROUGH (E.)] A | Declaration Of the Sad and Great | Persecution and Martyrdom | Of the People of God, called | Quakers, in New-England, | for the Worshipping of God. | Whereof | 22 have been Banished upon pain of Death. | 03 have been Martyred. | 03

have had their Right-Ears cut. | 01 hath been burned in the Hand with the letter H. | 31 Persons have received 650 Stripes. | 01 was beat while his Body was like a jelly. | Several were beat with Pitched Ropes. | Five Appeals made to England, were denied | by the Rulers of Boston. | One thousand forty-four pounds worth of Goods hath | been taken from them (being poor men) for meeting | together in the fear of the Lord, and for keeping the | Commands of Christ. | One now lyeth in Iron-fetters, condemned to dye. | Also, | Some Considerations, presented to the King, which is | in Answer to a Petition and Address, which was presented | unto Him by the General Court at Boston: Subscribed by | J. Endicot, the chief Persecutor there; thinking thereby to | cover themselves from the Blood of the Innocent. ... [By Edward Burrough] | *London: Printed for Robert Wilson, in Martins Le Grand.* | [1660.]

Small 4to, pp. 32. *Polished calf extra, gilt edges, by* F. BEDFORD. *Rubricated Title. A Fine Copy.* VERY RARE.

Contains the first printed account of the execution of Mary Dyer, and others, of Boston. *See* "Hist. Mag." II. 119; Sewell's "Hist. of the Quakers;" Hazard's Collections, ii. 594; Hutchinson Papers, 325–9; Smith's Catalogue, I. 351.

301 [BURT (Edward.)] Letters from a Gentleman in the North of Scotland, to his Friend in London: containing the Description of a Capital Town in that Northern Country, with an account of some uncommon Customs of the Inhabitants; likewise an Account of the Highlands, with the Customs and Manners of the Highlanders. ... *London: S. Birt.* 1754.

2 *vols.,* 8*vo, pp. x.,* 344; 368. 9 *Plates. Polished calf.* VERY SCARCE.

ORIGINAL and BEST EDITION of this very curious work which was written by Capt. Burt, when stationed at Inverness about 1730, and gives the most minute and characteristic account of Scotland at that time, for which it is constantly quoted by Sir Walter Scott. The Plates (naturally) gave great offence, and were omitted in subsequent editions.

302 BURTON (J. H.) The Book-Hunter. By John Hill Burton. *William Blackwood & Sons, Edinburgh.* 1862.

Crown 4*to, pp. viii.,* 384. LARGE PAPER, *half olive morocco, gilt top,* UNCUT. TWENTY-FIVE COPIES *only printed.* PORTRAIT *inserted.*

303 BURTON. The Book-Hunter etc. By John Hill Burton. With additional Notes by Richard Grant White. *New York: Sheldon and Company.* 1863.

Post 8*vo. Half olive morocco, gilt top,* UNCUT. *Two* PORTRAITS *inserted.*

304 BURTON (R.) The English Empire in America: Or a Prospect of His Majesties Dominions in the West-Indies. Namely, New-foundland, New-England, New-York, Pensilvania, New-Jersey, Maryland, Virginia, Carolina, Bermudas Berbuda, Anguilla, Monserrat, Dominica, St. Vincent, Antego, Mevis, or Nevis, St. Christophers, Barbadoes, Jamaica. With an account of the Discovery, Situation, Product, and other Excellencies and Rarieties of these Countries. To

which is prefixed, a Relation of the first Discovery of the New World called America by the Spaniards. And of the remarkable Voyages of several Englishmen to divers places therein. Illustrated with Maps and Pictures. By Robert Burton. The Sixth Edition.

London: A. Betteswortb. 1723.

12mo, pp. 192. 2 *Maps, and* 3 *Plates. Polished calf, gilt edges, by* W. PRATT.

"Robert Burton is a name placed in the title-pages of a number of books by Nath'l Crouch, a bookseller, who is supposed to have written them himself."—*Watt.*

305 [BURTON (Robert.)] Anatomy of Melancholy what it is, with all the Kinds, Causes, Symptoms, Prognostics, and several Cures of it. In Three Partitions. ... By Democritus Junior. ... A New Edition. Corrected and Enriched by Translations of the numerous Classical Extracts. *Cambridge: Printed at the Riverside Press.* 1861.

3 *vols.,* 8*vo, half morocco, gilt top,* UNCUT. LARGE PAPER; *Seventy-five copies printed:* one of FIFTEEN COPIES ONLY *with duplicate title in each volume, having the coat-of-arms of Burton finished in* COLORS *and* GOLD.

306 BUSHNELL (C. I.) Crumbs for Antiquarians: [Containing Early New York Business Tokens, Memoirs of Samuel Smith, Journal of Solomon Nash, Memoirs of Tarleton Brown, Narrative of Levi Hanford, Journal of R. J. Meigs during the Expedition against Quebec. With the Narratives of Leggett, Moody, Blatchford, and Fletcher.] By Charles I. Bushnell.

New York: Privately Printed. 1864–66.

2 *vols.,* 8*vo, half blue morocco, gilt top,* UNCUT. PRIVATELY PRINTED, and FIFTY COMPLETE SETS only. VERY SCARCE.

A Series of Revolutionary Memoirs, Journals, and Narratives written or edited by Mr. Bushnell. The numerous portraits, &c., were mostly engraved by Dr. Anderson, when in his eighty-eighth year. Mr. Bushnell's notes are both copious and minute, and, in some cases, exceed in volume the original text.

307 BUSHNELL. The Adventures of Christopher Hawkins, containing Details of his Captivity, a first and second time on the High Seas, in the Revolutionary War, by the British, and his consequent sufferings, and escape from the Jersey Prison Ship, then lying in the Harbour of New York, by swimming. Now first printed from the original Manuscript. Written by Himself. With an Introduction and Notes by Charles I. Bushnell. *New York: Privately Printed.* 1864.

8*vo, pp.* 316. 8 *Plates. Half blue morocco, gilt top,* UNCUT. SEVENTY-FIVE COPIES ONLY PRIVATELY PRINTED. *Uniform with the preceding No.*

308 [BUTLER (George B.)] The Case of Great-Britain and America, addressed to the King, and both Houses of Parliament.

Philadelphia: William and Thomas Bradford. 1769.

8*vo, pp.* 16. *Half red morocco.*

In the catalogue of the Bodleian Library, this work is attributed to Gervase Parker Bushe.

309 [BUTLER.] The Case of Great Britain and America. The Second Edition. *London:* MDCCLXIX.

8*vo, pp.* (1), 43. *Half blue morocco, carmine edges.*

"A well connected and clear statement of our disputes with the colonies concerning taxation, reduced into short compass; and one of the best tracts on the subject."—*Monthly Review.*

310 BUTLER (M.) A History of the Commonwealth of Kentucky, from the Exploration and Settlement by the Whites, to the Close of the Northwestern Campaign in 1813. With an Introduction, exhibiting the Settlement of Western Virginia. ... By Mann Butler. Second Edition, revised and enlarged by the Author.
Cincinnati: J. A. James and Co. 1836.

12mo, pp. lxxii., 551. Half olive morocco, gilt top, UNCUT. PORTRAIT *inserted.*

311 [BUTLER (William A.)] Memorial of Charles H. Marshall.
New York: D. Appleton and Company. 1867.

8vo, pp. 96. Portrait. Cloth, gilt edges. Privately Printed.

312 [BYERLEY (Thomas.)] Relics of Literature. By Stephen Collet.
London: Thomas Boys. 1823.

8vo, green morocco; back and sides inlaid, tooled and gilt; gilt top, UNCUT. An ELEGANT COPY; tastefully ILLUSTRATED, by MR. T. H. MORRELL, with *thirty-six engravings.*

Collet was a "*nom de plume*" of the late Thomas Byerley, who was also the *Reuben Percy* of the "Percy Anecdotes."

"Contains upwards of 200 very amusing articles, many of them notices of RARE and CURIOUS BOOKS. Also the Praise of Kissing, by various Authors; Eccentric Advertisements; Ancient Value of Books; Voltaire and the Booksellers; Book Destroyers; Singular Surnames; Epitaphs, Mottoes, Epigrams, Window Gleanings, &c."

313 BYFIELD (N.) An | Account | of the | Late Revolution | in | New-England. | Together with the | Declaration | of the | Gentlemen, Merchants, and Inhabitants of Boston, | and the Country adjacent. April 18, 1689. | Written by Mr. Nathaniel Byfield, | a Merchant of Bristol in New-England, to his Friends | in London. | Licensed, June 27, 1689. J. Fraser. | *London: Printed for Ric. Chiswell, at the Rose and Crown in | St. Paul's Church-Yard.* M DC LXXXIX.

4to, pp. 20. Polished calf, gilt edges, by W. MATTHEWS.

FINE COPY of the *Original Edition* of a RARE and highly interesting New England historical tract.

See New-England. No. 1476.

314 BYRD (W.) The Westover Manuscripts; containing the History of the Dividing Line betwixt Virginia and North Carolina; a Journey to the Land of Eden, A.D., 1733: and a Progress to the Mines, written from 1728 to 1736, and now first published. By William Byrd, of Westover. *Petersburgh:* 1841.

Rl. 8vo, pp. iv., 144. Half blue morocco, gilt top, UNCUT. A very *fine copy* of the *original* edition.

It includes a Journal of the Survey of the line between Virginia and North Carolina, through the Dismal Swamp, in 1728, with many amusing incidents connected therewith.

315 CABEÇA DE VACA. The Narrative of Alvar Nuñez Cabeça de Vaca. Translated by Buckingham Smith. *Washington:* 1851.

Folio, pp. 138. 8 *Maps. Half blue levant morocco, gilt top,* UNCUT, by W. MATTHEWS. A *Splendid Copy.* EXCESSIVELY RARE. STRICTLY PRIVATELY PRINTED, and one of TEN COPIES only on LARGE PARCHMENT PAPER, *Five* of which were distributed in the United States, and the remainder in England.

"This Narrative was privately printed for Mr. G. W. Riggs of Washington, entirely for presentation to societies and personal friends. It is the earliest relation of Florida, and the territory from the Atlantic coast across the Mississippi to the Pacific which we possess.

The narration of the unfortunate expedition of Cabeça de Vaca across the territory now occupied by the Southern States from Florida to Texas in the year 1527, nearly three and a half centuries ago, is full of the most melancholy yet absorbing interest. Nine years of wanderings and captivity among the Indians elapsed before this ill-fated member of a still more unfortunate band escaped almost alone of all who set out so joyously with him."— *T. W. Field.*

316 CABEÇA DE VACA. The Narrative of Alvar Nuñez Cabeça de Vaca. Translated by Buckingham Smith. *New York:* 1871.

Imp. 8vo, half crimson levant morocco, gilt top, UNCUT, *by* W. MATTHEWS. Edition *one hundred copies only.* A fine UNLETTERED INDIA PROOF PORTRAIT of DE SOTO, and an *interesting* A. L. S. of MR. SMITH, respecting the work *inserted.*

This is a new edition; with many important additions, of the preceding No. A Memoir of Cabeça de Vaca by T. W. Field, occupies pp. 233 to 254. A Preface by Hon. H. C. Murphy, precedes the Relation. A Memoir of the translator, written by Mr. J. G. Shea, fills pp. 255 to 263.

317 CALDWELL (C.) An Elegiac Poem on the Death of General Washington. By Charles Caldwell, A.M. M.D. *Philadelphia:* 1800.

8vo, pp. (4), 12. RARE.

318 CALDWELL. Memoirs of the Life and Campaigns of the Hon. Nathaniel Greene, Major General in the Army of the United States, and Commander of the Southern Department, in the War of the Revolution. By Charles Caldwell, M.D. ...
Philadelphia: Robert Desilver. 1819.

8vo, pp. xxiii., (1), 452. *Portrait and 2 Facsimiles. Half green morocco, gilt top,* UNCUT. A *beautiful copy.* PORTRAIT of GEN. GREENE *inserted.*

319 CALEF (R.) More | Wonders | of the | Invisible World: | Or, The Wonders of the | Invisible World, | Display'd in Five Parts. | Part I. An Account of the Sufferings of Margaret Rule, Written by | the Reverend Mr. C. M. | P. II. Several Letters to the Author, &c. And his Reply relating | to Witchcraft. | P. III. The Differences between the Inhabitants of Salem-Village, and | Mr. Parris, their Minister in New-England. | P. IV. Letters of a Gentleman uninterested, En-

deavouring to prove | the received Opinions about Witchcraft to be Orthodox. With short | Essays to their Answers. | P. v. A short Historical Accout [*sic*] of Matters of Fact in that Affair. | To which is added, A Postscript relating to a Book intitled, The | Life of Sir William Phips. | Collected by Robert Calef, Merchant, of Boston in New-England. | Licensed and Entered according to Order. | *London: Printed for Nath. Hiller, at the Princes-Arms, in Leaden-Hall-street, | over against St. Mary-Ax, and Joseph Collyer, at the Golden-Bible, | on London-Bridge.* 1700.

Sm. 4to, 6l., pp. 156. *Polished calf, gilt edges, by* F. BEDFORD. EXTREMELY RARE, *and probably as* LARGE *and* FINE *a copy as exists,* the fore edges being barely cut, the bottom entirely uncut.

"The author gave great offence by opposing the then popular belief concerning witches. In his discussion with Cotton Mather, he is as superior to him in reasoning as he was in good sense and courage." — *N. A. R.* III. 316.

This was Woodward's copy, which was sold in 1869, for $130.

320 CALEF. More Wonders of the Invisible World. [Same title as the preceding No. Second Edition.]
Salem, Massachusetts: William Carlton. 1796.

12mo, pp. 318. *Half calf antique, gilt back.* A FINE COPY. Almost as RARE as the first edition.

321 [CALLENDER (J. T.)] The American Annual Register; or, Historical Memoirs of the United States, for the Year 1796.
Philadelphia: 1797.

8vo, pp. vii., 288. *Half calf,* UNCUT. All ever published. SCARCE.

322 [CALLENDER.] The History of the United States for 1796; including a Variety of Interesting Particulars Relative to the Federal Government previous to that Period.
Philadelphia: Press of Snowden & McCorkle. 1797.

8vo, pp. viii., 312. *Half calf, gilt top,* UNCUT. An excellent impression of the *very scarce* PORTRAIT of HAMILTON painted by ROBERTSON, and engraved by GRAHAM for JAMES RIVINGTON *inserted.*

First published in numbers, as a kind of continuation, though a separate work, of the American Annual Register for 1796. Chapters VI. and VII. contain those famous charges of peculation against Alexander Hamilton, which finally induced that distinguished Statesman to saw a leg off to cure a corn.

See Hamilton (A.) No. 864.

323 CALLENDER. Segdwick & Co. or A Key to the Six Per Cent Cabinet. By James Thomson Callender.
Philadelphia: the Author. 1798.

8vo, pp. 88. *Half calf, gilt top,* UNCUT. *Very Scarce.*

324 CALLENDER. Sketches of the History of America. By James Thomson Callender. *Philadelphia: Snowden & M'Corkle.* 1798.

8vo, pp. 263. *Half calf, gilt top,* UNCUT. *Fine copy. Scarce.*

325 [CALLENDER.] The Prospect Before Us. ...
Richmond, Virginia : the Author. 1800.

8vo, 2 vols. in one, pp. 184; 152. *Half calf.* VERY SCARCE.

Sold by the author in the jail at Richmond, and the most difficult to obtain complete of any of his racy productions. This copy wants Part II. of the second volume.

326 CALLENDER (J.) An | Historical Discourse | on the | Civil and Religious Affairs | of the Colony of | Rhode Island | and Providence Plantations | in New-England | in America, | From the first Settlement 1838, to the End of [the] First Century. | By John Callender, A.M. | *Boston : Printed and Sold by S. Kneeland and T. Green | in Queen Street.* MDCCXXXIX.

8vo, pp. 14, 120, (1). *Red levant morocco, gilt edges, by* F. BEDFORD. A *beautiful copy of* the *first edition.* VERY SCARCE and important.

327 CAMPANIUS (T.) Kort Beskrifning | Om | Provincien | Nya Swerige uti | America, | Som nu förtjden af the Engelske Kallas | Pensylvania. | Af lärde och trowärdige Mäns skrifter och berättelser ihopaletad och sammanstrefwen, samt med äthskillige Figurer | utzirad af | Thomas Campanius Holm. | *Stockholm Tryckt uti Kongl. Boktr. hos Sal. Wankijfs | Ankia med egen bekostnad, af J. H. Werner Ahr.* MDCCII.

4to, Engraved and Printed Titles, 7l., pp. 190, *Errata 1l.* 7 *Maps and Plates. Green levant morocco, paneled sides, gilt edges, by* W. PRATT. A LARGE and ELEGANT COPY. VERY RARE.

The engraved title reads: "Novæ Sueciæ, seu Pensylvaniæ in America descriptio." "The author was never in America. His work is made up from verbal accounts received from his father, and notes left by his grandfather, to which he has added facts obtained from the manuscripts of Peter Lindström, an engineer."—*Duponceau.* "A very scarce work relating to the establishment of the Swedes in New Sweden, afterwards Pennsylvania."—*Rich.*

The following is a translation.

328 CAMPANIUS. Description of the Province of New Sweden. Now called, by the English, Pennsylvania, in America. Compiled from the Relations and Writings of Persons worthy of credit, and adorned with Maps and Plates. By Thomas Campanius Holm. Translated from the Swedish, for the Historical Society of Pennsylvania. With Notes. By Peter S. Du Ponceau, LL.D. ...
Philadelphia: McCarty & Davis. 1834.

8vo, pp. vi., v—166. 5 *Maps and Plates. Half green morocco, gilt top,* UNCUT. Frontispiece *inserted.* Scarce in *uncut* condition.

Often improperly catalogued under the name of Holm.

329 CAMPBELL (C.) Some Materials to serve for a Brief Memoir of John Daly Burk, Author of a History of Virginia. With a Sketch of the Life and Character of ... Judge John Junius Burk. Edited by Charles Campbell. *Albany, N. Y. : Joel Munsell.* 1868.

8vo, pp. 123. *Half levant morocco, gilt top,* UNCUT. *Scarce full length* PORTRAIT of JOHN RANDOLPH *inserted.*

330 CAMPBELL (W. W.) Annals of Tryon County; or, The Border Warfare of New-York during the Revolution. By William W. Campbell. ... *New York: J. & J. Harper.* 1831.

8vo, pp. 191, 78. *Map. Half calf.* Fine large copy.

331 CAREY (M.) A Short Account of the Malignant Fever, lately Prevalent in Philadelphia: With a Statement of the Proceedings that took place on the Subject in Different Parts of the United States. By Mathew Carey. *Philadelphia: Printed by the Author.* 1793.

8vo, pp. 103. *Half green morocco, gilt top,* UNCUT, *by* BRADSTREET. SCARCE.

Contains lists of the Names of all the persons buried in the several grave yards of Philadelphia from August 1st, to November 9th, 1793.

"This pamphlet is a historical account of the circumstances attending the visitation of the yellow fever, which proved so fatal in Philadelphia, in the year 1793, and in which Mr. Carey has presented his fellow-citizens with a collection of facts and observations well calculated for the satisfaction of their anxious curiosity."—*M. R.*, xiv., 187.

332 CAREY. The Olive Branch; or Faults on both sides, Federal and Democratic. A Serious Appeal on the necessity of Mutual Forgiveness and Harmony. ... By M. Carey. Sixth Edition, enlarged. *Philadelphia: The Author.* 1815.

8vo, *calf.*

333 CAREY. Autobiographical Sketches. In a Series of Letters addressed to a Friend. Vol. I. Containing a view of the Rise and Progress of the American System: The Efforts made to secure its Establishment: the Causes which prevented its Complete Success, &c. By M. Carey. *Philadelphia: John Clarke.* [1829.]

12mo, pp. xvi., 156. *Half blue morocco, gilt top,* UNCUT. An AUTOGRAPH LETTER *of the* AUTHOR *inserted.* All ever published, and VERY SCARCE.

Contains curious particulars respecting Mr. Carey's numerous publications.

334 CAROLINA. A Brief Description | of | The Province | of | Carolina | On the Coasts of Floreda. | And | More Perticularly of a New-Plantation | begun by the English at Cape Feare, | on that River now by them called Charles-River, | the 29 of May. 1664. | Wherein is set forth | The Healthfulness of the Air; | the Fertility of | the Earth, and Waters; | and the great Pleasure and | Profit will accrue to those that shall go thither to enjoy | the same. | Also, | Directions and advice to such as shall go thither whether | on their own accompts, or to serve under another. | Together with | A most accurate Map of the whole Province. | *Printed at London for Robert Horne.* 1666.

Sm. 4to, pp. (2), 10. *Map. Red levant morocco, gilt edges, by* F. BEDFORD. BEAUTIFUL and VERY LARGE COPY of the RARE FIRST PRINTED DESCRIPTION of Carolina.

335 [CARPENTER (Stephen C.)] Memoirs of the Hon. Thomas Jefferson, Secretary of State, Vice-President, and President of the United States of America; containing a Concise History of those States from the Acknowledgment of their Independence. With a view of the

Rise and Progress of French Influence and French Principles in that Country. ... *Printed for the Purchasers.* 1809.

2 *vols.*, 8*vo*, *pp.* *iv.*, 404; (2), 434. *Half green morocco, gilt top*, UNCUT. A fine copy. *Very Scarce.* PORTRAIT of MR. JEFFERSON *inserted.*

"The history of this memoir is somewhat curious, and is probably known to very few persons. It bears on the title page, 'Printed for the purchasers, 1809,' and was copyrighted by 'Thomas Hall;' but contains no name of either author or publishers. In fact, the work never was published. After printing a considerable edition the printers became alarmed, in view of the stringency of the law of libel at the time, and bethought themselves to take advice. A small number of copies — I think twenty — were bound, and one of them was brought to the late Samuel M. Hopkins, then a young lawyer in Auburn, N. Y., for his opinion. Mr. Hopkins dipped into the book; read some twenty or thirty pages here and there; and informed the printer that 'he found, on the average, a libel to every page.' On this the memoir was suppressed."

336 CARROLL (C.) Journal of Charles Carroll of Carrollton, during his Visit to Canada in 1776, as One of the Commissioners from Congress; ... With a Memoir and Notes by Brantz Mayer. ... *Baltimore: John Murphy.* 1845.

8*vo*, *pp.* 84. *Half blue morocco.* THIRTY-THREE PLATES, PORTRAITS, VIEWS, ETC., *inserted. Large and fine copy.* Published by the Maryland Historical Society.

337 [CARROLL (John.)] An Address from the Roman Catholics of America, to George Washington, President of the United States. *London: Printed by J. P. Coghlan.* 1790.

Folio. *Half green morocco, gilt top*, UNCUT; *Privately Reprinted* in Facsimile, for Dr. J. G. Shea, with portraits, facsimile of Washington's reply, etc. [*New York.* 1857.] *All for presentation.*

338 CARROLL. A Discourse on General Washington. Delivered in the Catholic Church of St. Peter, in Baltimore, Feb. 22d, 1800. By the Right Rev. Bishop Carroll. *Baltimore:* [1800.]

8*vo*, *pp.* 24. Very Scarce.

339 CARTER (W.) A Genuine Detail | of the Several | Engagements, Positions, | and Movements | of the | Royal and American Armies, | during the Years 1775 and 1776; | with an | Accurate Account | of the | Blockade of Boston, | and a | Plan of the Works on Bunker's Hill, | at the time it was abandoned by his Majesty's | Forces on the 17th of March, 1776. | In a Series of Letters to a Friend. | By William Carter, | Late a Lieutenant of the 40th Regiment of Foot. | *London: G. Kearsley.* 1784.

4*to*, *pp.* 50. *Plan. Polished calf, gilt edges, by* F. BEDFORD. Splendid copy. VERY SCARCE.

340 [CARTWRIGHT (John.)] American Independence the Interest and Glory of Great Britain; or, Arguments to prove, that not only in Taxation, but in Trade, Manufactures, and Government, the Colonies are entitled to an entire Independency on the British Legislature. ... In a Series of Letters to the Legislature. To which are added copious Notes; containing Reflections on the Boston and

Quebec Acts; and a full Justification of the People of Boston, for destroying the British-taxed Tea; submitted to the Judgment, not of those who have none but borrowed Party-opinions, but of the candid and honest.

London: Printed for the Author by H. S. Woodfall. M. DCC. LXXIV.

8vo, pp. xvi, iv, 72. Half morocco. Very Scarce.

Speaking of this publication, the author's biographer says, "at a time when no Member of Parliament had sufficient decision of mind to propose the Independence of America, Major Cartwright suggested the expediency of an Union between Great Britain and her Colonies under separate Legislatures." *See also M. R.*, LVIII, 238.

341 CARUTHERS (E. W.) A Sketch of the Life and Character of the Rev. David Caldwell, D.D., near Sixty Years Pastor of the Churches of Buffalo and Alamance. Including Two of his Sermons; Some Account of the Regulation, Together with the Revolutionary Transactions and Incidents in which he was Concerned; and a very brief notice of the Ecclesiastical and Moral Condition of North-Carolina while in its Colonial State. By the Rev. E. W. Caruthers, A.M.

Greensborough, N. C.: Swain & Sherwood. 1842.

8vo, pp. 302. Index, 1 l. Half red levant morocco, gilt top, by W. MATTHEWS. *An elegant copy.* RARE.

"This rare Revolutionary Biography is replete with incidents of interest associated with the campaigns of Cornwallis, Tarleton, &c., in the South, and it is curious that no copy—either owing to its scarcity, or to the fact of its historical value being unknown—appeared in the libraries devoted to Americana, viz: those of Rice, Roche, Wight, Fisher, Davis, Morrell, and others."

342 CARVER (J.) Travels through the Interior Parts of North America, in the Years 1766, 1767, and 1768. By J. Carver, Esq., Captain of a Company of Provincial Troops during the late War with France. Illustrated with Copper Plates.

London: Printed for the Author. MDCCLXXVIII.

Rl. 8vo, pp. (20), *xvi.*, 544. 2 *Maps*, 4 *Plates. Half crimson morocco extra, gilt top*, UNCUT. An unusually LARGE and CLEAN COPY.

"Carver came to England soon after he returned from his travels, with the intention of publishing his account of them; but when he had already sold the MS. to a bookseller he was ordered by the government to deliver up all his maps and journals; and it was not until nearly ten years after, that he obtained permission to publish the work."— *M. R.*, LX., 90.

343 CARVER. Travels through the Interior Parts of North America, in the Years 1766, 1767, and 1768. By J. Carver, Esq., Captain of a Company of Provincial Troops, during the late War with France. Illustrated with Copper Plates. The Third Edition. To which is added, Some Account of the Author, and a copious Index.

London: C. Dilly. ... M DCC LXXXI.

8vo, pp. (22), 543, (21). 2 *Maps, Portrait, and* 4 *plates. Half red levant morocco, gilt top*, UNCUT, *by* W. MATTHEWS. An ELEGANT COPY of this SCARCE EDITION with three plates COLORED, and *rarely found uncut.*

To this third and best edition, a biography of the author, and an Index, are added by John Coakley Lettsom, M.D., who had become the proprietor of the work, and whose preface is dated March 30, 1781.

344 CASAS (B. de) Regionvm | Indicarum per | Hispanos olim devastatarum | accuratissima descriptio, insertis Fi- | guris æneis ad vivum fabrefactis, | Authore | Bartholomæo de las Casas | Episcopo Hispano | Editio nova Priori longè cor- | rectior. *Heidelbergae,* | *Typis Gvilielmi Walteri* | *Acad. Typogr.* A.S. MDCLXIV. |

4to, pp. (2), 112. *Title and seventeen plates engraved by* DE BRY. *Half green morocco, gilt edges.* MR. FURMAN's copy, with four leaves in his hand-writing describing the work. Some copies have a second title page which is wanting in this.

FINE COPY, and RARE in any condition.

345 CASAS. Popery | Truly Display'd in its | Bloody Colours: | Or, a Faithful | Narrative | Of The | Horrid and Unexampled Massacres, But- | cheries, and all manner of Cruelties, that Hell and | Malice could invent, Committed by the Popish Spanish | Party on the Inhabitants of West-India: Together | With the Devastations of several Kingdoms in America | by Fire and Sword, for the space of Forty and Two | Years, from the time of its first Discovery by them. | Composed first in Spanish by Bartholemew de las Casas, a Bishop | there, and an Eye-Witness of most of these Barbarous Cruelties: | afterward Translated by him into Latin, then by other hands, into | High-Dutch, Low-Dutch, French, and now Taught to speak | Modern English. | *London: Printed for R. Hewson at the Crown in Cornhil,* | *near the Stocks-Market.* 1689.

4to, 4l., pp. 80. *Half crimson morocco, gilt edges.* VERY LARGE and FINE COPY. RARE.

346 CASAS. A | Relation | of the First | Voyages and Discoveries | Made by the Spaniards in America. | With An Account of their unparallel'd Cruelties | on the Indians, in the destruction of a- | bove Forty Millions of People. | Together with the Propositions offer'd to the | King of Spain, to prevent the further Ruin | of the West Indies. | By Don Bartholomew de las Casas, Bishop of Chiapa, | who was an Eye-witness of their Cruelties. | Illustrated with Cuts. | To which is added, | The Art of Travelling, showing how a Man may | dispose his Travels to the best Advantage. | *London:* | *Printed for Daniel Brown at the Black Swan and Bible* | *without Temple-Bar, and Andrew Bell at the Cross-* | *Keys and Bible in Cornhil near Stocks Market.* | 1699.

8vo, pp. (8), 248, 40. *Two folded plates. Polished calf, gilt edges by* F. BEDFORD. A LARGE and FINE COPY. RARE.

"This edition is not noticed in Mr. Sabin's Dictionary, nor in his Monograph of Las Casas' Works. The work professes to be a translation of the French book entitled "*Tyrannies et Cruautez des Espagnols.*"—*Field.*

See "Old England for Ever." No. 1518.

347 CASE (J.) The Angelical Guide: Shewing Men and Women their Lott or Chance, in this Elementary Life. In Four Books. I. Of the Creation of the World. II. The Centre or Circle of the Life of Man: or, the Human Egg of Generation. III. The Angelical Guide, or the Lott of Man: shewing all the Chances and

Contingencies in this present World. IV. Experimental Knowledge of several Examples; proving the Truth and Certainty of these our Angelical Lotts. By John Case, M.D. *London: I. Dawks.* 1697.

Sm. 8vo, Title, 9l., pp. 287. *Portrait engraved by* VAN HOVE; 8 *folded Diagrams. Russia extra, symbolically gilt sides, gilt edges, by* ROGER PAYNE, with his curious bill for the work, covering one side of a sheet of paper eleven inches square. The following is an extract. "Binding in the very best Manner in Russia Leather of the true Russia Colour as imported sewed in the very best manner with Silk round every Band no false Bands very neat morocco Joints very neat Boards Boards Strong and not clumsy the Back lined with Russia Leather under the Cover great care hath been taken of the Margins in Refolding and placing them True in Line. Finished in the highest Venetian Taste with Scientific Insignia of small Tools a great deal of Lettering very correct Fine Drawing paper Inside to suit ye original Colour of the Book."

"One of the most profound astrological pieces that the world ever saw. The diagrams would probably have puzzled Euclid, though he had studied astrology. A copy of the work is in the British Museum."—*Lowndes.*

We are unable to record the sale of ANY COPY *in the United States.*

348 CASE (W.) Revolutionary Memorials, embracing Poems by the Rev. Wheeler Case, Published in 1778, and An Appendix containing General Burgoyne's Proclamation (in burlesque). ... A late Authentic Account of the Death of Miss Jane McCrea, &c. ... Edited by the Rev. Stephen Dodd. *New York: M. W. Dodd.* 1852.

12*mo, pp.* 69. *Half crimson morocco.*

349 CASE (The) and Claim of the American Loyalists Impartially Stated and Considered.

[*London:*] *Printed by Order of their Agents.* [1783.]

Small 8vo, pp. (2), 38. *Half morocco.* Very scarce.

For other works on this subject, *see* Nos. 789, 799, 1738, and 2160.

350 CASSIN (J.) Illustrations of the Birds of California, Texas, Oregon, British and Russian America. Intended to contain Descriptions and Figures of all North American Birds not given by Former American Authors, and a General Synopsis of North American Ornithology. By John Cassin.

Philadelphia: J. B. Lippincott & Co. 1865.

8*vo, pp. viii.,* 298. *Half green morocco, gilt tops,* UNCUT. Uniform with Audubon's Birds, to which it forms an important and necessary addition. It contains FIFTY BEAUTIFULLY COLORED PLATES of new or unfigured Birds inhabiting the United States, which have not been given by former American authors, in connection with whose works it continues, as far as possible, to the present time, the pictorial representation of all *North American Birds.*

See Audubon (J. J.) No. 89.

351 CASTELL (W.) A Short | Discoverie | Of the Coasts and Continent of | America, | From the Equinoctiall Northward, and | of the adjacent Isles. | By William Castell, Minister of the Gospell at | Courtenhall in Northamptonshire. | Whereunto is prefixed the Author's Petition to this pre- | sent Parliament, for the propagation of the Gospell | in America, attested by many eminent English | and Scottish Divines. | And a late Ordinance of Parliament for that | purpose, and for the better government of the | English Plantations there. | Together

with Sir Benjamin Ruyder's Speech, in Parliament, 21 Jan., concerning America. | *London: Printed in the yeer* 1644.

4to, pp. (4), 48, 54. *Polished calf, gilt edges, by* W. PRATT. Although the title page, (and perhaps the leaf following) is an exact fac-simile, by Harris, and the upper margins of 4 leaves restored, this is a FINE COPY of a book of MUCH RARITY.

A copy was priced in a recent English catalogue at £45.

352 CASTLEMAN (R.) The Voyage, Shipwrack, and Miraculous Escape of Richard Castleman, Gent. With a Description of Pensylvania, and the City of Philadelphia, &c.
[*London:*] *Printed in the Year.* MDCCXXVI.

8vo, pp. 333–374. *Engraved Frontispiece. Polished calf, gilt edges, by* F. BEDFORD. AN ELEGANT COPY. Extracted from "Boyles Voyages."

Castleman's narrative bears marks of authenticity. His visit to Philadelphia took place in 1710.

353 CATALOGUE of a Valuable Collection of Curious, Rare & Interesting Books, being Purchase-Duplicates from the Bodleian Library, Oxford. Sold by Auction, 1865. *London:* [1865.]

8vo, cloth, UNCUT. Ruled; with *names* and *prices.*

354 CATALOGUE of an Extraordinary Collection of Works relating to America. [Known as the Bruce Collection.] *New York:* 1868.

8vo, half green morocco, gilt top, UNCUT, *by* BRADSTREET. Neatly ruled, and *priced.*

355 CATALOGUE of the Antiquities, Works of Art and Historical Scottish Relics exhibited in the Museum of the Archaeological Institute of Great Britain and Ireland during their Annual Meeting, held in Edinburgh, July, 1856. ... Comprising Notices of the Portraits of Mary Queen of Scots, Collected on that Occasion, etc.
Edinburgh: Thomas Constable & Co. 1859.

8vo, pp. xxxiv., 233. *Half orange morocco, gilt top,* UNCUT.

Contains 32 beautiful full page plates embracing FOUR FINE PORTRAITS of MARY QUEEN of SCOTS, besides 112 engravings printed in the text. The FINE and interesting plate of the DARNLEY JEWELLS, ILLUMINATED in GOLD and COLOURS, *inserted* at page 163, was published separately at half a guinea.

AN ELEGANT VOLUME.

356 CATLIN (G.) Illustrations of the Manners, Customs, and Condition of the North American Indians: in a Series of Letters and Notes written during Eight Years of Travel and Adventure among the Wildest and most Remarkable Tribes now Existing. With Three Hundred and Sixty Engravings from the Author's Original Paintings. By Geo. Catlin. Ninth Edition.
London: Henry G. Bohn. MDCCCLVII.

2 *vols., roy. 8vo, pp. viii.,* 264; *viii.,* 266. 360 COLOURED PLATES. *Half red morocco, gilt edges.* A FINE SET, and one of TWELVE COPIES ONLY COLOURED in this manner. VERY SCARCE.

"Mr. Catlin is the Historian of the Red Races of mankind; of a world fast fading away, and leaving hardly a trace or a wreck behind. With his pen and pencil he has brought the existence of these wild and uncivilized beings so vividly before our eyes, that we seem to have accompanied him in his wanderings, seen them, mixed with them, and impressed the recollection of their forms and features, their costume, strange customs, feasts, ceremonies, religious rites, wars, dances, sports, and other modes of life, distinctly upon our minds."—*Literary Gazette.*

357 CATLIN. O-Kee-Pa: A Religious Ceremony: and other Customs of the Mandans. By George Catlin.
Philadelphia: J. B. Lippincott and Company. 1867.

Imp. 8vo, half morocco, gilt edges; by BRADSTREET. 13 COLORED ILLUSTRATIONS. Uniform with the preceding No.

"In the latter part of 1866 one of the numbers of Trübner's monthly catalogue contained a notice of a pamphlet purporting to be written by Mr. Catlin upon the secret customs of the Mandans, said to be indescribably lascivious. This excited the indignant denial by Mr. Catlin, of his authorship of the essay, of which, as only fifty copies were printed, little was known. The next year, as a more effectual disproval of his association with what he deemed a disreputable performance, Mr. Catlin produced O-KEE-PA."—*Field.*

358 CATS (J.) *and* Farlie (R.) Moral Emblems, with Aphorisms, Adages, and Proverbs of all Ages and Nations. From Jacob Cats and Robert Farlie. With Illustrations freely rendered, from Designs found in their Works, by John Leighton, F.S.A. ...
New York: [i. e. London.] 1860.

4to, purple morocco, gilt back and sides, gilt edges. Contains upwards of 120 beautiful engravings by the most eminent English artists, after the original designs of ADRIAN VAN DE VENNE. A SPLENDID COPY from the ALLAN Collection.

The Emblems and other works of Cats have for two centuries been household books in Holland, both for their moral doctrine, and for the ingenious designs with which Adrian Van de Venne symbolized their teachings. The Tail pieces are from Farlie's "Lights, or Moral Emblems."

359 CAVENDISH (G.) The Life of Cardinal Wolsey. By George Cavendish, his Gentleman Usher. From the Original Autograph Manuscript. With Notes and other Illustrations, by Samuel Weller Singer, F. S. A. Second Edition. *London: Harding and Lepard.* 1827.

8vo, pp. xxix., 542. 8 Plates and Facsimile. Half olive morocco, gilt top, UNCUT.

"One of the most interesting and valuable specimens of biography in the English Language."—*Lowndes.*

360 **Caxton, (W.)** The Game of the Chesse. By William Caxton.
[Reprinted, London: 1855.]

4to, Calf antique. EIGHTY COPIES *only printed.*

Frequently as we read of the Works of Caxton and the early English Printers, and of their **Black Letter** Books, very few persons ever had the opportunity of seeing any of these productions, and forming a proper estimate of the ingenuity and skill of those who first practiced the "Noble Art of Printing." This Fac-Simile reproduction of the FIRST WORK PRINTED BY CAXTON at Westminster, containing 23 woodcuts, is intended in some measure to supply this deficiency, and bring the present age into somewhat greater intimacy with the Father of English Printers.

361 **Caxton.** Here begynneth a lityll treatise shorte and abredged spekynge of the arte or crafte to knowe well to dye translated oute of frenshe in to englysshe by Willm. Caxton. 1490.
[Reprinted, London: 1852.]

Sm. folio, green morocco, carmine edges. RARE. An *exact* facsimile reprint of the UNIQUE ORIGINAL in the British Museum. SIX COPIES ONLY were *privately reprinted* for the late MR. THOMAS RODD.

362 CHALKLEY (T.) A Collection of the Works of Thomas Chalkley. In Two Parts.
Philadelphia: Printed by B. FRANKLIN *and* D. HALL. MDCCXLIX.

2 vols., sm. 8vo, pp. xiii., (2), 326; 329–590. Half gray calf, by BRADSTREET. *A fine copy.*

Chalkley was a Quaker preacher, who came to America in the year 1700, and settled at Philadelphia. He travelled and preached in all the British Colonies from New England to North Carolina. He also visited the West India Islands, and the Bermudas. "Some of the New England priests," he says, "were so bitter against Friends, that, instead of being humbled, under the mighty hand of God upon them in suffering the Indians to destroy them, they express'd their enmity against the poor Quakers."

363 [CHALMERS (George.)] Second Thoughts: or, Observations upon Lord Abingdon's Thoughts on the Letter of Edmund Burke, Esq., to the Sheriffs of Bristol. By the Author of the Answer to Mr. Burke's Letter. *London: T. Cadell.* 1777.

8vo, pp. 74, half morocco, gilt top.

See Bertie (Willoughby.) No. 162.

364 CHALMERS. Political Annals of the Present United Colonies, from their Settlement to the Peace of 1763: Compiled chiefly from Records, and authorized often by the Insertion of State Papers. ... By George Chalmers, Esq. Book I.
London: Printed for the Author · and Sold by G. Bowen. M.DCC.LXXX.

4to, pp. (8), 695. Half purple levant morocco, gilt top, UNCUT. Clean and fine as when issued. RARE in this state. PROOF PORTRAIT of the AUTHOR *inserted.*

The seeond part was never published. "Chalmers was a strenuous supporter of the right of the mother country to tax the colonies, and, throughout his narrative, every fact which would admit of it was studiously applied to support this principle."

365 CHALMERS. An Introduction to the History of the Revolt of the American Colonies; being a Comprehensive View of its Origin, derived from the State Papers contained in the Public Offices of Great Britain. By George Chalmers.
Boston: James Monroe and Company. 1845.

2 vols., 8vo, half calf, gilt top, UNCUT. An *elegant* copy.

The author carefully suppressed the original edition, either "owing to the separation of the colonies, which happened just at the season for publication, namely, December, 1782, or the prior cause in April precedent, the dismission of a Tory administration." This Boston edition was printed from the author's MS.

366 CHAMBERS (R.) Scottish Songs and Ballads; Collected and Illustrated. By Robert Chambers. ... *Edinburgh: William Tait.* 1829.

3 vols., post 8vo, half green morocco, gilt top, UNCUT.

A tasteful selection. One of the earliest of its editor's works. *Now Scarce.*

367 CHAMBERS. Popular Rhymes of Scotland. Third Edition with

Additions, [and] Original Poems. By Robert Chambers. *Edinburgh : W. & R. Chambers.* 1847.

Sm. 8vo, Engraved Title, pp. 357. *Half calf.*

Probably the scarcest of all the numerous productions of Robert Chambers.

368 CHAMPLAIN. Les Voyages | dv Sievr de Champlain | Xaintongeois, Capitaine | ordinaire pour le Roy, | en la marine. | Divisez en Devx Livres. | ou, | Iovrnal tres-fidele des Observa- | tions faites és descouuertures de la Nouuelle France: tant en la descri- | ptiô des terres, costes, riuieres, ports, haures, leurs hauteurs, & plusieurs | declinaisons de la guide-aymant; qu' eñ la creâce des peuples, leur super- | stition, façon de viure & de guerroyer: enrichi de quantité de figures. | Ensemble deux cartes geografiques: la premiere seruant à la na- | uigation, dressée selon les compas qui nordestent, sur lesquels | les mariniers nauigent: l'autre en son vray Meridien, auec ses | longitudes & latitudes: à laquelle est adiousté le voyage du | destroict qu'ont trouué les Anglois, au dessus de Labrador, | depuis le 53e degré de latitude, iusques au 63e en l'an 1612. | cerchans vn chemin par le Nord, pour aller à la Chine. | *A Paris*, | *Chez Iean Berjon*, *rue S. Iean de Beauuais*, *au Cheual* | *volant*, *& en sa boutique au Palais*, *à la gallerie* | *des prisonniers.* | M.DC.XIII. Avec Privilege dv Roy.

4to, 10*l. pp.* 325, (5), Quatriesme Voyage, *pp.* 1–52. 8 *Maps and* 3 *Plates, several Plates in the Text. Half gray calf, carmine edges.* LARGE and FINE COPY, with *all* the MAPS and PLATES, but the Map of QUEBEC at page 176, which is wanting in many copies, in this, has been replaced with an exact facsimile by the Photo Lithographic process.

The copies of this edition vary in the maps. Mr. Lenox's copy differs from that in the New York Historical Society. Sometimes in one map there are more references than in the other, and the spelling of the references varies. The large map to this edition is usually in two parts, and is very often wanting or defective.

"The volume contains an account of Champlain's first voyage in 1604, his second in 1610, and his third in 1611. At the end of the book is an account of his fourth voyage in 1613, apparently printed separately, after the first three were published."—*Rich.*

"Copies of any of the editions of Champlain in perfect condition are exceedingly rare, and have, within a few years, risen to almost fabulous prices. $150 each has been paid for the editions of 1613, 1618, 1620, 1627, and 1632."—*Field.*

369 CHAMPLAIN. Narrative of a Voyage to the West Indies and Mexico in the Years 1599–1602, with Maps and Illustrations. By Samuel Champlain. Translated from the Original and Unpublished Manuscript, with a Biographical Notice and Notes by Alice Wilmere. Edited by Norton Shaw.
London : Printed for the Hakluyt Society. M.DCCC,LVII.

8vo, pp. 3*l.*, *xcix.*, 48. 10 *Plates, and Map. Half purple morocco, gilt top,* UNCUT.

"This Narrative of Champlain's First Voyage to the New World, is of great value to us in establishing, by an unimpeachable authority, the story of the awful cruelties which were inflicted upon the Indians of the West Indies by the Spaniards. Fac-simile lithographs of Champlain's drawings are given; among which are representations of Indian feasts, flogging Indians to church, and burning groups of the natives at the stake. The biography gives an interesting narration of Champlain's dealings with the Indians of New France."—*Field.*

370 CHANDLER (P. W.) American Criminal Trials. By Peleg W. Chandler. *Boston: Charles C. Little and James Brown.* MDCCCXLI.

2 vols., 12mo, half calf. Large and fine copy. Vol. II is *scarce.*

Includes an account of the New York Negro Plot, Boston Massacre, and the trials of Zenger, Leisler, Major André, and Joshua Hett Smith.

371 CHAPMAN (I. A.) A Sketch of the History of Wyoming. By Isaac Chapman, Esq. To which is added an Appendix, containing a Statistical Account of the Valley and Adjacent Country. By a Gentleman of Wilkesbarre. *Wilkesbarre, Pa.: Sharp D. Lewis.* 1830.

12mo, pp. 209. Half calf. SCARCE.

372 CHARACTERS. Containing an Impartial Review of the Public Conduct and Abilities of the most Eminent Personages in the Parliament of Great Britain: considered as Statesmen, Senators, and Public Speakers. Revised and Corrected by the Author. ...
London: J. Bew. 1777.

8vo, pp. xv., 152. Half crimson morocco. RARE.

Nineteen characters are held up to public view in this interesting volume, viz: Lords Mansfield, Camden, Lyttelton, Chatham, Germain, Hillsborough, Suffolk, Shelburne, Sandwich and North; Dukes of Grafton and Richmond; and Messrs. Thurloe, Burke, Barré, Wedderburne, Fox, Ellis, and Dunning, besides many others incidentally. A large portion pertains to American affairs.

373 CHARLESTON. The Siege of Charleston, by the British Fleet and Army under the Command of Admiral Arbuthnot and Sir Henry Clinton, which terminated with the Surrender of that place on the 12th of May 1870. *Albany: J. Munsell.* 1867.

4to, pp. 224. Half red morocco, gilt top UNCUT. *125 copies only printed.* Edited by Franklin B. Hough.

374 CHARLESTOWN. Proceedings of the Town of Charlestown, in the County of Middlesex, and Commonwealth of Massachusetts; in Respectful Testimony of the Distinguished Talents and Pre-eminent Virtues of the late George Washington.
[*Charlestown.*] *January,* M.DCCC.

8vo, pp. 46, 36. UNCUT.

Contains Morse's "Prayer and Sermon," which was reprinted in London. The account of the proceedings was written by Josiah Bartlett, Esq.

375 CHARLEVOIX. (F. X. de) Letters to the Duchess of Lesdiguieres; giving an Account of a Voyage to Canada, and Travels through that vast Country, and Louisiana, to the Gulf of Mexico. Undertaken by Order of the present King of France. By Father Charlevoix. ...
London: Printed for R. Goadby. 1763.

8vo, pp. xiv., (2), 384. Half crushed red levant morocco, gilt top, UNCUT, *by* W. MATTHEWS. A *beautiful copy* of a RARE EDITION, differing from the work of Charlevoix, in two volumes.

376 CHARLEVOIX. Journal of a Voyage to North America. Undertaken by Order of the French King. Containing The Geographical Description and Natural History of that Country, particularly Canada. Together with An Account of the Customs, Characters, Religion, Manners and Traditions of the original Inhabitants. In a Series of Letters to the Duchess of Lesdiguieres. Translated from the French of P. de Charlevoix. ... *London: R. and J. Dodsley.* M DCC LXI.

2 vols., 8vo, pp. viii., 382; viii., 380, (22). Map. Half calf antique. Fine copy.

"The most important work on what were then the immense French Possessions in America. The author is the most eminent among Missionary travellers; he made what may be called the grand tour of interior America, proceeding up the St. Lawrence, through the lakes and down the Mississippi, to New Orleans, collecting materials for the best published account of the country, and the institutions and characters of the Indian Tribes."—*Murray.*

377 CHARLEVOIX. History and General Description of New France. By the Rev. P. F. X. de Charlevoix, S.J. Translated, with Notes, by John Gilmary Shea. *New York: John Gilmary Shea.* 1866–72.

6 vols., roy. 4to, half crushed red levant morocco extra, gilt top, UNCUT, *by* W. MATTHEWS. LARGE PAPER, 25 *copies only printed.* A SPLENDID SET, with *all* the MAPS and PLATES complete.

This is the first translation into English of Charlevoix's celebrated and important work. Dr. Shea has added notes, corrected references, and improved the bibliography, at the same time retaining Charlevoix's text in all its originality.

378 CHASTELLUX (*Marquis.* de) Travels in North America, in the years 1780, 1781, and 1782. By the Marquis de Chastellux. ... Major General in the French Army, serving under the Count De Rochambeau. Translated from the French by an English Gentleman, who resided in America at that Period. With Notes by the Translator. [J. Kent.] *London: Robinson.* M DCC LXXXVII.

2 vols., 8vo, pp. xv., 462; xii., 432. 2 Maps and 3 Plates. Half blue morocco, gilt top, UNCUT.

"Nothing escapes the eager eye and minute attention of this lively traveller, and we owe to him the most graphic account of the private life of the Revolutionary era."

See Brissot de Warville (J. P.) No. 232.

379 [CHASTELLUX.] Remarks on the Travels of the Marquis de Chastellux in North America. *London: G. and T. Wilkie.* MDCCLXXXVII.

8vo, pp. (4), 86. Half red morocco. VERY SCARCE.

Attributed to GENERAL ARNOLD. See *Sargent's André. p.* 457. Also *Hist. Mag.* I. 90.

380 CHAUDRON (S.) Oraison Funèbre, du Frère George Washington Prononcée le premier Janvier 1800, dans la Loge Française l'Aménité: par Le F:. Simon Chaudron, Orateur de la Loge. *Philadelphie: Thomas and William Bradford.* 1801.

8vo, pp. 35.

381 CHAUDRON. Funeral Oration on Brother Geo. Washington, delivered January 1st, 1800, before the French Lodge L'Aménité. By

Brother Simon Chaudron. Translated from the French by Samuel T. Bradford. *Philadelphia:* 1800.

8vo, pp. 26. EXCEEDINGLY RARE. The *only copy* noticed by Dr. Hough.

382 [CHAUDRON.] Lettres ecrites à la Loge l'Aménité No. 73, à l'Occasion de l'Oraison Funèbre du F:. George Washington. Imprimé par ordre de la Loge. *Philadelphie:* 1801.

8vo, pp. 16. UNCUT. COLOURED photographic PORTRAIT of CHAUDRON *inserted.* VERY RARE. Unnoticed by Dr. Hough.

Contains correspondence relative to Chaudron's Oration, embracing letters from Theo. Sedgwick, John Adams, Thomas Jefferson, and others.

383 CHAUNCY (C.) Seasonable Thoughts on the State of Religion in New-England, A Treatise in five Parts. ... With a Preface, Giving an Account of the Antinomians, Familists, and Libertines, who infected these Churches, above an hundred Years ago: Very needful for these Days; the like Spirit and Errors, prevailing now as did then. The whole being intended, and calculated, to serve the Interest of Christ's Kingdom. By Charles Chauncy, D.D. Pastor of the First Church of Christ in Boston.
Boston: Printed by Rogers & Fowle, for Samuel Eliot. 1743.

8vo, pp. xxx., 18, 424. *Half red levant morocco, gilt top,* UNCUT, by W. MATTHEWS. A FINE COPY and RARE in *uncut* condition. Contains a list of six hundred subscribers.

An important volume for the history, civil as well as religious, of New England.

384 CHITTENDEN (L. E.) The Capture of Ticonderoga. Annual Address before the Vermont Historical Society delivered at Montpelier, Vt. ... October 8, 1872. By Hon. Lucius E. Chittenden.
Rutland: 1872.

8vo, pp. 127. *Half red morocco, gilt top,* UNCUT, by BRADSTREET. *One hundred copies only left uncut.* INDIA PROOF PORTRAIT of MONTCALM, of which, *fifty impressions only* were taken from a PRIVATE PLATE, *inserted.*

385 **Chrysostomi (J.) Incipit Liber beati Joannis Chrisostomi de eo quod nemo leditur ab alio nisi a semetipso fuerit Iesus quem in exilio constitutus confidenter scripsit.** [*Coloniæ: Typis Ulrici Zell.* 1467.]

Sm. 4to, 21 leaves, 27 lines to a page; gothic letter, rubricated capitals, VERY FINE COPY *in claret morocco, richly tooled in the old style, gilt edges, with* "Sti. Chrysostomi Tractatus 1467." *in letters of gold on the side.* OF THE GREATEST RARITY.

A most beautiful specimen of Early Typography, in the finest possible state. ULRIC ZELL was the first Cologne Printer and a workman for Schoiffer, one of the first printers. To English Collectors his productions are still more interesting from his having been in all probability the chief instructor of WILLIAM CAXTON, whose residence at Cologne is attested by himself in several of his interesting prefaces and colophons, many critics have also considered that he was the actual printer of the celebrated Trojan Histories. It is certain that Caxton used the same types at Cologne, probably after a course of instructions in the office of Zell, and with them printed his celebrated Playe of the Chesse.— *See Humphrey's Hist. of Printing.*

386 [CHURCH (Benjamin.)] The Times: a Poem. By an American. [*Boston*: 1765.]

4to, pp. 16. *Half morocco, gilt top,* UNCUT.

A satire upon and against the Stamp Act. Severe on Jared Ingersol, the Stamp Distributer, and others of that class. VERY RARE.

387 CHURCH (B.) An Oration delivered March Fifth, 1773, at the Request of the Inhabitants of the Town of Boston; to Commemorate the Bloody Tragedy of the Fifth of March, 1770. By Dr. Benjamin Church.
Boston: Printed and Sold at the New Printing Office. M,DCC,LXXIII.

4to, pp. 20. *Half green morocco, gilt top.* Fine copy. RARE.

388 CHURCHILL (S.) A Sermon, occasioned by the Death of Gen. Washington. ... Delivered at Lebanon, in the Town of Canaan, February 22d, 1800. By Silas Churchill, A.M. ... *Albany:* M,DCCC.

12mo, pp. 31. UNCUT. VERY RARE.

389 CICERO (M. T.) Cicero's | Cato Major, | or his | Discourse | of | Old-Age: | with explanatory Notes. | *Philadelphia:* | *Printed & Sold by B. Franklin.* MDCCXLIV.

4to, pp. viii., 159. *Green levant morocco, back and sides elegantly blank tooled, broad inside borders richly tooled and gilt, morocco joints, gilt top,* UNCUT, *by* W. MATTHEWS. Fine head of MARCUS TULLIUS CICERO, a *proof on India paper*, engraved by BARTOCINI, *inserted.* A SPLENDID COPY; clean, fresh and crisp as it came from the press, and altogether such a one as cannot be excelled.

The finest production of Franklin's press, and really a splendid specimen of the art. The title page is rubricated. The translator was Judge James Logan; and Franklin, in his address, "The Printer to the Reader," calls it, "this first translation of a classic in this Western World," which is not strictly correct. Sandys' translation of Ovid was made in Virginia about ninety years earlier, but printed and published in London; and Franklin himself had printed Cato's "Moral Distiches," Englished in couplets, in 1739, which translation is attributed to James Logan. It is, doubtless, the second classic author translated and *printed* in North America, and is eagerly sought after by American collectors. UNCUT copies are among the RAREST of RARE BOOKS. We know of but *four copies* — the one mentioned above, one belonging to Mr. C. E. Mann, and one in each of the collections of Mr. C. H. Kalbfleisch, and Mr. E. G. Asay.

390 CIEÇA DE LEON (P.) The | Seventeen Years Travels | of | Peter de Cieza, | Through the Mighty Kingdom of | Peru, | and | The large Provinces of | Cartagena and Popayan | in | South America: | From the city of Panama, on the Isthmus, | to the Frontiers of Chili. | Now first Translated from the Spanish, and Illustrated | with a Map, and several Cuts. | *London:* | *Printed in the Year* MDCCIX.

4to, 3*l.*, *pp.* 244, 6*l.* *Plan and* 5 *Plates. Red morocco, gilt edges.* A LARGE and FINE copy of this VERY SCARCE work, but wanting the Map.

391 CLAIBORNE (N. H.) Notes on the War in the South; with Biographical Sketches of the Lives of Montgomery, Jackson, Sevier, the late Gov. Claiborne, and others. By Nathaniel Herbert Claiborne. ... *Richmond: William Ramsay.* 1819.

12mo, pp. 112. *Half calf. A fine copy.* VERY SCARCE.

392 CLARK (J.) Ill | Newes | from | New-England : | or | A Narrative of New-Englands | Persecution. | Wherein is declared | That while old England is becoming new, | New-England is becoming Old. | Also four Proposals to the Honoured Parliament and Councel of State, | touching the way to Propagate the Gospel of Christ (with small | charge and great safety) both in Old England and New. | Also four conclusions touching the faith and order of the Gospel of | Christ out of his last Will and Testament, confirmed and justified. | By John Clark Physician, of Rode Island in America. | *London : | Printed by Henry Hills living in Fleet-Yard, next door to the Rose | and Crown, in the year* 1652.

4to, pp. (20), 76. *Red levant morocco, paneled and gilt sides, corner ornaments, inside lined with polished green levant morocco richly tooled and gilt after an elegant design, gilt top,* UNCUT, by F. BEDFORD. A SPLENDID COPY and EXTREMELY RARE.

Dr. John Clark was the founder of the first Baptist Church at Newport, in 1644.

393 [CLARK (McDonald.)] The Elixir of Moonshine; being a Collection of Prose and Poetry, by the Mad Poet. A Great Proportion of which has never before been Published. *Gotham : A. M.* 5822.

12mo, pp. 150. *Half morocco, gilt top,* UNCUT.

394 CLARKE (A. L.) A Discourse occasioned by the Death of General George Washington at Mount-Vernon, Dec. 14, 1799. Delivered... in Providence, on Saturday, the 22d of February A.L. 5800. By Abraham L. Clark, A.M. ... *Providence :* 1800.

8vo, pp. 26. UNCUT. VERY RARE.

395 CLARKE (J.) An | Impartial and Authentic | Narrative | of the Battle | Fought on the 17th of June, 1775, | between | His Britannic Majesty's Troops | and the | American Provincial Army, | on | Bunker's Hill, near Charles Town, in New-England. | With | A True and Faithful Account of the Officers | who were killed and wounded in that memorable | Battle. | To which are added, | Some particular Remarks and Anecdotes which | have not yet transpired. | The whole being collected and written on the Spot. | The Second Edition, | With Extracts from Three Letters lately received from | America; | And all the Promotions in the Army and Marines | since the said Battle. | By John Clarke, | First Lieutenant of Marines. | *London : | Printed for the Author : and Sold by J. Millar, Whitehall ; | J. Bew, in Paternoster Row ; and — Sewel, in Cornhill.* | MDCCLXXV.

8vo, title, pp. 36. *Polished calf, gilt top,* UNCUT, *by* F. BEDFORD. This interesting contemporary report of that famous battle is a VOLUME OF MUCH RARITY, and especially so in UNCUT condition.

396 CLARKE. An Impartial and Authentic Narrative, &c. [*New York :* 1868.]

8vo, pp. 36. *Half crimson morocco, gilt top,* UNCUT, by W. MATTHEWS. *Ninety-nine copies* PRIVATELY REPRINTED from the preceding work.

397 [CLARKE (William.)] Repertorium Bibliographicum; or, Some Account of the Most Celebrated British Libraries.
London: William Clark. M DCCC XIX.

Roy. 8vo, half purple morocco, gilt top, UNCUT.

This ELEGANT COPY has the unpaged leaf between pages vi. and vii. referring to "RARE DOINGS AT ROXBURGH HALL," &c. It also has "THE DIALOGUE IN THE SHADES," and "RARE DOINGS AT ROXBURGH HALL" in at the end; preceded by the unpaged leaf signed W. W. A FINE PROOF impression, of which *twelve copies only* were taken before CLARK's face was altered, of the plate at the head of the "DIALOGUE," and upwards of FORTY appropriate illustrations *inserted.*

The late Mr. Beckford assisted in the compilation of this work, particularly in the description of his own library at Fonthill.

398 CLAYTON (J.) A Letter from Mr. John Clayton, Rector or Crofton, at Wakefield in Yorkshire, to the Royal Society, May 12, 1688, giving an Account of Several Observables in Virginia, and in his Voyage thither, more particularly concerning the Air.
London: 1708.

Sm. 8vo, pp. (1), 281–355. *Engraved Frontispiece. Polished calf, gilt edges, by* F. BEDFORD. A fine copy of the ORIGINAL EDITION, extracted from "Miscellanea Curiosa." With he engraved frontispiece, title, and contents. VERY SCARCE.

399 CLEAVELAND (M.) An Oration Commemorative of the Life and Death of General George Washington, delivered at Windham (Connecticut,) On the 22d day of February, 1800. ... By Moses Cleveland. ... *Windham:* 1800.

8vo, pp. 15. RARE.

400 [CLINTON (DeWitt.)] An Account of Abimelech Coody and other Celebrated Writers of New York: In a Letter from a Traveller, to his Friend in South Carolina: January, 1815.
[*New York: Reprinted.* 1864.]

Roy. 8vo, pp, 22. *Half green morocco, gilt top, uncut.*

First printed in 1815. Abimelech Coody was a pseudonym adopted by the late Gulian C. Verplanck. This rare satirical pamphlet refers to the "Trinity Church" affair in which Verplanck, Maxwell and others were concerned. Of this edition THIRTY-FIVE COPIES only were PRIVATELY PRINTED.

401 CLINTON (H.) Correspondence between His Excellency General Sir Henry Clinton and Lieutenant General Earl Cornwallis.
[*New York:* 1781.]

8vo, pp. 76, *and an unpaged leaf between pages* 54 *and* 55. *Half red morocco.* VERY RARE. *Not in Sabin's Dictionary.*

402 CLINTON. The Narrative of Lieutenant-General Sir Henry Clinton, K.B. relative to his Conduct during part of his Command of the King's Troops in North America; Particularly to that which respects the unfortunate Issue of the Campaign in 1781, with An Appendix, ... Sixth Edition. *London: J. Debrett.* 1783.

[*Followed by*] An Answer to that Part of the Narrative of Lieutenant-General Sir Henry Clinton, K.B. which relates to the Conduct of Lieutenant-General Earl Cornwallis, during the Campaign in North-America in the Year 1781. By Earl Cornwallis.
London: J. Debrett. M.DCC.LXXXIII.

[*Replied to by*] Observations on some Parts of the Answer of Earl Cornwallis to Sir Henry Clinton's Narrative. By Lieutenant-General Sir Henry Clinton, K.B. To which is added an Appendix containing Extracts of Letters and other Papers, to which Reference is necessary.
London: J. Debrett. M.DCC.LXXXIII.

3 *vols., 8vo, in one, half green morocco, gilt top,* UNCUT. FINE COPIES. *Scarce* PORTRAIT *of* SIR HENRY CLINTON *inserted.*

"In these details Sir Henry Clinton acquits himself of all share in Lord Cornwallis' misfortune; leaving that general to answer for misconceptions of the orders sent him, and for the choice of the post he was reduced to surrender. Cornwallis' answer consists of the chain of correspondence between the two commanders during the campaign referred to, for the purpose of proving that 'the conduct and opinions of the author were not the cause of the catastrophe which terminated the campaign of 1781.'" *See "M. Rev.,"* LXVIII. 266.

403 CLINTON. A Letter from Lieut. Gen. Sir Henry Clinton, K.B., to the Commissioners of Public Accounts, relative to Some Observations in their Seventh Report, Which may be judged to imply Censure on the late Commanders in Chief of His Majesty's Army in North America. *London: J. Debrett.* M,DCC,LXXXIV.

8vo, pp. 31. *Half morocco.*
See "M. Rev.," LXXI. 152.

404 CLINTON. Observations on Mr. Stedman's History of the American War. By Lieutenant-General Sir Henry Clinton, K.B.
London: 1794. *Privately Reprinted.* [*New York:* 1864.]

4to, pp. 34. *Half blue morocco, gilt top,* UNCUT. *No.* 49 *of fifty copies* PRIVATELY PRINTED. Beautiful PORTRAIT of SIR HENRY CLINTON. VERY SCARCE.

General CLINTON, referring to his services in America, says: "I conceive myself called upon by a recent publication, which has misstated material facts, whether from error or a desire of courting a late Governor General of India, I will not pretend to determine; but at a time when my services were actually called for, and these more than insinuations may make an impression on the public, it is my duty to refute them."— *Preface.*

See Stedman (C.) No. 1896.

405 CLOQUET (J.) Recollections of the Private Life of General Lafayette. By M. Jules Cloquet, M.D. Embellished with numerous Engravings, as in the original Paris Edition. *London:* 1835.

8vo, half calf. AUTOGRAPH LETTER of LAFAYETTE *inserted.*

"Written at the request of Mr. Isaiah Townsend, of Albany, and translated by him and published in the New York 'Evening Star;' afterwards published simultaneously in London, Paris, and New York."

406 [COBBETT (William.)] The Political Censor; or, Monthly Review of Political Occurrences relative to the United States of Ame-

rica. By Peter Porcupine. [March, April and May, 1796.] The Third Edition. *Philadelphia: William Cobbett.* 1796.

pp. 37–240. *Portrait.*

[Followed by] The Scare Crow; being an Infamous Letter, sent to Mr. John Olden, Threatening Destruction to his House, and Violence to the Person of his Tenant, William Cobbett. By Peter Porcupine. The Second Edition. *Philadelphia: William Cobbett.* 1796.

pp. 23.

The Life and Adventures of Peter Porcupine, with a Full and Fair Account of all his Authorising Transactions; being a Sure and Infallible Guide for all Young Men who wish to Make a Fortune by Writing Pamphlets. By Peter Porcupine Himself. Second Edition. *Philadelphia: William Cobbett.* 1796.

pp. 56.

Porcupine's Political Censor, for September, 1796. Containing the Life of Tom Paine, interspersed with Remarks on "A Roaster for Peter Porcupine." "The Blue Shop." "Porcupine, a Print." "History of a Porcupine." &c. *Philadelphia: William Cobbett.* [1796.]

pp. 79.

Porcupine's Political Censor for November, 1796. Containing Observations on the Insolent and Seditious Notes, Communicated to the People of the United States, by the late French Minister Adet. *Philadelphia: ... William Cobbett. Nov.* 1796.

pp. 78.

Porcupine's Political Censor For December, 1796. Containing Remarks on the Debates in Congress, Particularly on the Timidity of the Language held towards France. Also; A Letter to the Infamous Tom Paine, In answer to his brutal attack on the Federal Constitution, and on the conduct and character of General Washington. *Philadelphia: William Cobbett.* [1796.]

pp. 47.

8vo, half calf antique. 8 *pieces in one vol.*, with separate title for each, and a general title and table of contents for the volume.

407 [COBBETT.] The Bloody Buoy, thrown out as a Warning to the Political Pilots of America; or, a Faithful Relation of a Multitude of Acts of Horrid Barbarity, such as the Eye never witnessed, the Tongue never expressed, or the Imagination conceived, until the Commencement of the French Revolution. Illustrated with Four Striking Copper-Plates. The Second Edition. ... By Peter Porcupine. *Philadelphia: Benjamin Davies.* 1796.

16*mo, pp. xii.,* 15–362. 4 *Plates. Old calf rebacked.*

"It appears, then, that these bloody revolutionists, who stiled themselves the Friends of Freedom and of Mankind, destroyed in one city of France a population equal to that of the United States."— *Extract.*

408 [COBBETT.] A Bone to Gnaw for the Democrats. By Peter Porcupine. ... To which is prefixed A Rod for the Backs of the Critics; containing an Historical Sketch of the present State of Political Criticism in Great Britain; as exemplified in the Conduct of the Monthly, Critical, and Analytical Reviews. Interspersed with Anecdotes. By Humphrey Hedgehog. *London: J. Wright.* 1797.

Sm. 8vo, pp. xcv., 175. Half green morocco, gilt top, UNCUT.

409 [COBBETT.] A Letter To the Infamous Tom Paine, in Answer to his Letter to General Washington, By Peter Porcupine. *London: Reprinted for David Ogilvy and Son.* 1797.

8vo, pp. 23. Half green morocco, gilt top.

Some years later Cobbett made a pilgrimage to the United States, from whence he took the bones of "The Infamous Tom Paine" to England.

See Paine (Thomas.) Nos. 1540 and 1541.

410 [COBBETT.] Porcupine's Political Tracts, of 1794 and 1795. Containing: First: Observations on the Emigration of Dr. Priestley, commonly called the Fire Brand Philosopher.—Second and Third: A Bone to Knaw for the Democrats. Parts I. and II.—Fourth: A Kick for a Bite.—Fifth: A little plain English; or a Defense of the British Treaty against Franklin.—Sixth: A New Year's Gift for the Democrats.—Seventh: A Prospect from the Congress Gallery. *Philadelphia: William Cobbett.* 1797.

8vo, half calf antique. 7 pieces in one vol., with a separate title and imprint to each, and a general title to the volume.

411 [COBBETT.] Porcupine's Political Censor for the months of January, and March, 1797. Containing Remarks on the Proceedings in Congress. Mr. Pickering's Letter. Attack on the same by the sansculotte Bache. The Festival of Fools. Noah Webster's Attack on Porcupine. Porcupine's Two Letters to Webster. Porcupine's Last Will and Testament. &c. *Philadelphia: William Cobbett.* [1797.]

8vo, pp. 115, (9). Half calf antique. With separate title for each month. There was no Censor issued for February of this year.

412 [COBBETT.] The Republican Judge; or the American Liberty of the Press, as Exhibited, Explained, and Exposed, in the base and partial Prosecution of William Cobbett for a pretended Libel against the King of Spain and his Embassador, before the Supreme Court of Pennsylvania. ... By Peter Porcupine. *London: J. Wright.* 1798.

8vo, pp. 96. Half calf antique.

The Republican Judge was Gov. M'Kean; the Spanish Ambassador, the Marquis of Casa Irujo, who married Gov. M'Kean's daughter.

413 [COBBETT.] The American Rush-Light; by the help of which Wayward and Disaffected Britons may see a complete specimen of the

Baseness, Dishonesty, Ingratitude, and Perfidy of Republicans, and of the Profligacy, Injustice, and Tyranny of Republican Governments. By Peter Porcupine. *London: Published For the Author.* 1800.

8vo, pp. 192, 209–309. *Half calf antique.* PORTRAITS of COBBETT and RUSH and an AUTOGRAPH LETTER SIGNED of RUSH *inserted.* All the SIX PARTS *perfect* and *complete.* VERY SCARCE.

"This highly spiced and Cobbetty publication comprising six numbers, begun in Philadelphia and finished in London, fills 309 pages, and is perhaps the most difficult of all Cobbett's many personal squibs, to find complete. It grew out of a lawsuit with Dr. Benj. Rush 'the noted bleeding Physician,' of Philadelphia, in which Cobbett was mulcted in $5,000 damages for slander. He took it out in spice." — *Stevens.*

414 COBBETT. Porcupine's Works, containing various Writings and Selections, exhibiting a Faithful Picture of the United States of America; of their Governments, Laws, Politics, and Resources; of the Characters of their Presidents, Governors, Legislators, Magistrates, and Military Men: and of the Customs, Manners, Morals, Religion, Virtues and Vices of the People: comprising also a Complete Series of Historical Documents and Remarks, from the End of the War, in 1783, to the Election of the President, in March, 1801. By William Cobbett. ... *London: Cobbett and Morgan. May,* 1801.

12 *vols., 8vo, half green morocco, gilt top,* UNCUT.

"Cobbett in these volumes has left a picture of the politics and leading politicians of the United States, from 1783 to 1801, which must be studied by all who would understand the party questions which then agitated the community, and the violence with which they were discussed." — *Prest. King.*

"As an author, he stands very high Southey declared that there never was a better or a more forcible English writer. The nervous simplicity of his style, as well as the great amount of information they contain, make his books so extremely useful, that they are continually sought after." — *Penny Cyclop.*

415 COBBETT. The Pride of Britannia Humbled; or, the Queen of the Ocean Unqueen'd, "By the American Cock Boats," Or, "The Fir built Things, with bits of Striped Bunting at their Mast Heads." (As the Right Hon. Mr. Canning, in the British parliament, called our American Frigates.) ... By William Cobbett, Esq. Including a number of his most Important Letters, and Arguments, in Defence of the American Republic. To which is added, A Glimpse of the American Victories, on Land, on the Lakes, and on the Ocean. A New Edition. *Philadelphia: William Reynolds.* 1815.

12mo, pp. 215, (1). *Plate. Half crimson morocco.* VERY SCARCE.

This work was edited by Thomas Branagan, whose name sometimes appears as the author.

416 COBBETT. Letters on the Late War between the United States and Great Britain: together with other Miscellaneous Writings, on the same subject. By William Cobbett, Esq.
New-York: J. Belden and Co. 1815.

8vo, pp. 407. *Half calf,* UNCUT. An AUTOGRAPH NOTE signed of COBBETT, dated from Newgate prison, *inserted.*

417 [Cobbett.] A Rub from Snub; or a Cursory Analytical Epistle: addressed to Peter Porcupine. ... Containing Glad Tidings for the Democrats, and a Word of Comfort to Mrs. S. Rowson. Wherein the said Porcupine's Moral, Political, Critical and Literary Character is fully illustrated. *Philadelphia: printed for the Purchasers.* 1795.

8vo, pp. 80. *Half calf antique.* Uncut.

418 [Cobbett.] A Congratulatory Epistle to the Redoubtable "Peter Porcupine," on his "Complete Triumph over the Once towering but fallen and despicable faction in the United States." A Poem, By Peter Grievous, Junr. To which is annexed The Vision, A Dialogue between Marat and Peter Porcupine in the Infernal Regions. *Philadelphia: From the Free and Independent Political & Literary Press of Thomas Bradford.* 1796.

8vo, pp. 44. *Half calf antique.* Uncut.

419 [Cobbett.] A Pill for Porcupine: Being a Specific for an Obstinate Itching which that Hireling has long contracted for Lying and Calumny, containing, A Vindication of the American, French, and Irish Characters, Against his Scurrilities, by A Friend to Political Equality. ... *Philadelphia: Printed for the Author. September* 1, 1796.

[Followed by] The Porcupiniad: a Hudibrastic Poem, in Four Cantos. Addressed to William Cobbett, by Mathew Carey. [Canto I.] *Philadelphia: Printed for the Author.* 1799.

8vo, pp. 83; 52. *Plate.* 2 *pieces in one vol., half calf antique.*

420 [Cobbett.] The Imposter Detected, or A Review of Some of the Writings of "Peter Porcupine." By Timothy Tickletoby. ... To which is annexed A Refreshment for the Memory of William Cobbet [*sic*], by Samuel F. Bradford. *Philadelphia: Thomas Bradford.* 1796.

[Also:] A Plumb Pudding for the Humane, Chaste, Valiant, Enlightened Peter Porcupine. By his Obliged Friend, Mathew Carey. ... *Philadelphia: Printed for the Author.* [1799.]

8vo, pp. 51, 23; 48. 2 *tracts in one vol., half calf antique.* A curious contemporary and *very pithy* "Advertisement" is inserted in the Plumb Pudding.

421 [Cockings (George.)] The American War, A Poem; In Six Books. In which the Names of the Officers who have Distinguished themselves, During the War, are Introduced. *London: Printed for the Author.* MDCCLXXXI.

8vo, pp. (4), 181. *Plan of Bunkerhill. Half green morocco, gilt top, by* Bradstreet. A large and fine copy with the very scarce portrait of the Author *inserted.*

"A very remarkable specimen of poetry." *See M. Rev.* lxv. 469.

422 CODDINGTON (W.) A | Demonstration | of | True Love | unto | You the Rulers of the Colony of the | Massachusets | in | Nevv-England ; | Shewing | to you that are now in Authority the unjust | Paths that your Predecessors walked in, and of the | Lord's Dealings with them in his severe Judgments, for | persecuting his Saints and Children. | Which may be a Warning unto you, that you walk not in | the same Steps, lest you come under the same Condemnation. | Written by one who was once in Authority with them ; but al- | ways testified against their persecuting Spirit, who am call'd | William Coddington of Road-Island. | [*London :*] *Printed in the Year* 1674.

4to, pp. 20. *Crimson levant morocco, gilt edges, by* F. BEDFORD. VERY RARE.

A very interesting and rare tract concerning the persecution of the Quakers by the Puritans of Massachusetts. "The author was one of the first who agreed to form a 'bodie politic' in Rhode Island." *See* Bartlett's *Bib. R. I.* p. 80.

423 CODE (The) of 1650, being a Compilation of the earliest Laws and Orders of the General Court of Connecticut. Also, the Constitution or Compact, entered into and adopted by the towns of Windsor, Hartford and Weathersfield, in 1638–9. To which is added, some Extracts from the Laws and Judicial Proceedings of New-Haven Colony, commonly called the Blue Laws.
Hartford: Silas Andrus. 1822.

12mo, pp. 119. *Half blue morocco.*

On page 96 may be read, "It is ordered by the authority of this Courte, that no person under the age of 21 years, nor any other that hath not already accustomed himselfe to the use thereof, shall take any tobacko, untill hee hath brought a certificate under the hands of some who are approved for knowledge and skill in phisick, that it is usefull for him, and allso, that hee hath received a lycense from the Courte for the same."

424 COFFIN (E.) A Sermon delivered February 22d, 1800, the day of National Mourning, Recommended by the Government of The United States, for the Death of General George Washington. ... By the Rev. Ebenezer Coffin, A.B., Pastor of a Church in Brunswick.
Portland: 1800.

8vo, pp. 16. EXCEEDINGLY RARE. The *only copy* seen by Dr. Hough.

425 COFFIN (C.) History of the Battle of Breed's Hill, by Major-Generals William Heath, Henry Lee, James Wilkinson and Henry Dearborn. Compiled by Charles Coffin. *Portland:* 1835.

8vo, pp. 36. *Half crimson morocco, gilt top.* PLATE *inserted.*

426 COGHLAN [(Margaret.)] Memoirs of Mrs. Coghlan, (daughter of the late Major Moncrieffe). Written by herself, and Dedicated to the British Nation; being interspersed with Anecdotes of the late American and present French War, with Remarks, Moral and Political. *London : Printed for the Author.* MDCCXCIV.

Sm. 8vo, 2 vols. in one, pp. (8), *xx.*, 152; (2), 172. *Red morocco, gilt top,* UNCUT, by F. BEDFORD. A BEAUTIFUL COPY of the ORIGINAL and BEST EDITION. VERY SCARCE.

427 COGHLAN. Memoirs. [Another Edition.]
New York: T. & J. Swords. 1795.

12mo, pp. xix., 194. *Half calf. A fine clean copy.* The New York edition contains a preface which is not in the English one.

428 [COLDEN (Cadwallader.)] An | Explication | of the | First Causes | of | Action In Matter, | And, | Of the | Cause of Gravitation. | *New-York: Printed by James Parker.* 1745.

Sm. 8vo, pp. vi., 43, (1). *Half calf, gilt top,* UNCUT. A work of the GREATEST RARITY. *We have never seen another copy.*

The dedication to James Alexander, Esq., at New York, is dated, "Coldingham, in the Province of New York, Dec. 10, 1745," and signed Cadwallader Colden. The work seems to have become scarce as early as 1786, for in January of that year Mr. Jefferson, writing to Francis Hopkinson, observes:—"Many, many years ago, Cadwallader Colden wrote a very small pamphlet on the subjects of Attraction and Impulsion, a copy of which he sent to Monsieur de Buffon. He was so charmed with it that he put it into the hands of a friend to translate, who lost it. It has ever since weighed upon his mind, and he has made repeated trials to have it found in England. But in vain. He applied to me. I am in hopes if you write a line to the booksellers of Philadelphia to rummage their shops, that some of them will find it. Or perhaps some of the careful old people of Philadelphia or New Jersey may have preserved a copy." Whether Hopkinson was successful does not appear.

429 COLDEN (C.) The | History | of the | Five Indian Nations | Depending on the Province | of | New-York | In America. | By Cadwallader Colden. | *Printed and Sold by* WILLIAM BRADFORD, *in* | *New-York.* 1727.

12mo, Title, pp. xviii., 119. *Crushed red levant morocco, paneled and gilt sides, gilt edges, by* F. BEDFORD. A BEAUTIFUL COPY with a fine impression of the EXCEEDINGLY RARE CONTEMPORARY MAP *inserted,* which, alone, commands from forty to fifty dollars. It is a volume of the GREATEST RARITY not more than SIX COPIES being known in the United States, and, with the *Map,* forms one of the *desiderata* of this collection.

430 COLDEN. The History of the Five Indian Nations of Canada, which are ... the Barrier between the English and French, in that part of the World. With Accounts of their Religion, Manners, Customs, Laws, and Forms of Government; their several Battles and Treaties with the European Nations; ... their several Wars with the other Indians; And a true Account of the present State of our Trade with them. ... By the Honorable Cadwallader Colden, Esq. ... To which are added: Accounts of the several other Nations of Indians in North-America, their Numbers, Strength &c., and the Treaties which have been lately made with them. ...
London: T. Osborne. 1747.

8vo, pp. 20, 204, 283. *Map. Half calf antique.* A very fine copy.

"The three London editions differ from one another only in the titles, but in all of them are some differences from the New York edition, which drew forth a protest from the author."—*Stevens.*

431 COLDEN. The History of the Five Indian Nations depending on the Province of New-York. By Cadwallader Colden. Reprinted

exactly from Bradford's New York edition, (1727). With an Introduction and Notes, by John Gilmary Shea.

New York: T. H. Morrell. 1866.

Imp. 8vo, pp. xi., xviii., 141. *Half blue morocco, gilt top,* UNCUT. LARGE PAPER. *Thirty copies only printed.*

"This fourth edition is a reprint of the first. Dr. Shea gives in his introduction, a valuable bibliographical notice of the editions, with collations of their contents, and an analysis, noting the changes made by the English editors or publishers. His notes, are characterized by the fullness, research, and exactness, with which this writer always invests every subject he illustrates."—*Field.*

432 COLDEN (C. D.) The Life of Robert Fulton, by his Friend Cadwallader D. Colden. ... Comprising some Account of the Invention, Progress, and Establishment of Steam-Boats; of Improvements on the Construction and Navigation of Canals, and other objects of Public Utility. With an Appendix.

New York: Kirk & Mercein. 1817.

8vo, pp. vi., 371. *Portrait. Half green morocco, gilt top,* UNCUT. A *large* and *fine* copy with an interesting AUTOGRAPH LETTER of FULTON giving directions respecting the construction of a steamboat, and upwards of FORTY ENGRAVINGS *inserted.*

433 COLDEN. A Vindication by Cadwallader D. Colden, of the Steam Boat Right granted by the State of New York: In the form of an Answer to the Letter of Mr. Duer, addressed to Mr. Colden.

Albany: Websters & Skinners. 1818.

8vo. pp. 178. *Half calf.*

See Duer (W. A.) No. 638.

434 [COLDEN.] An Examination of Cadwallader D. Colden's Book entitled A Life of Robert Fulton. By a Friend of John Fitch, deceased. [*n. p.*] 1818.

8vo, pp. 38. *Half green morocco, gilt top,* UNCUT.

435 COLDEN. Memoir, Prepared at the Request of a Committee of the Common Council of the City of New York, and Presented to the Mayor of the City, at the Celebration of the Completion of the New York Canals. By Cadwallader D. Colden.

Printed by Order of the Corporation of New York, by W. A. Davis. 1825.

4to, pp. (8), 408, (2). *Half purple morocco, gilt top,* UNCUT. An unusually fine and clean copy, and VERY SCARCE in *uncut* condition. Contains portraits of Colden, Philip Hone, S. L. Mitchill, etc., engraved by Durand. The narrative was written by the late W. L. Stone, of whom a PORTRAIT is *inserted.*

436 COLE (J.) Bibliographical and Descriptive Tour from Scarborough, to the Library of a Philobiblist in its Neighbourhood. By John Cole.

Scarborough: John Cole. 1821.

8vo, pp. iv., 92. *Half olive morocco, gilt top,* UNCUT, by W. MATTHEWS. LARGE PAPER. *Fifty copies only printed;* with views of Scarborough on the title, and at the end, (not in the small paper copies) and WOODCUTS by BEWICK. An ELEGANT COPY, with an unlettered India proof PORTRAIT of the "PHILOBIBLIST" (Archdeacon Wrangham) *inserted.*

437 [COLEMAN (William.)] A Collection of the Facts and Documents, relative to the Death of Major-General Alexander Hamilton; with Comments; together with the Various Orations, Sermons, and Eulogies, that have been published or written on his Life and Character. *New York: J. Riley & Co.* 1804.

8vo, Title, pp. (1), 238. *Half green morocco, gilt top.* An *interesting* and UNIQUE copy with TWENTY-FIVE ENGRAVINGS *inserted;* also, 28 pages of matter cut from the newspapers of the period and mounted by TRENT, giving an account of the origin of the duel; the death of HAMILTON; BURR's flight; and subsequent events.

438 COLLIER (J. P.) A Book of Roxburghe Ballads. Edited by John Payne Collier. *London: Longman.* 1847.

4to, pp. xxvi., 340. *Half blue morocco, gilt top,* UNCUT, by W. MATTHEWS.

Nearly all the ballads contained in this interesting collection are unique. They are printed from the extraordinary collection which belonged successively to the Duke of Roxburghe, and Mr. Bright. At the sale of Mr. Bright's library, in 1845, they produced £535.

439 COLUMBUS (C.) Lettera in lingua Spagnuola diretta da Cristoforo Colombo a Luis de Santangel (15 Febbrajo 14 Marzo 1493) riprodotta a fac-simile ed illustrata per cura di Gerolamo d'Adda dall' unico esemplare a stampa sinora conosciuto che si conserva nella Bibliotheca Ambrosiana. *Milano: Teodora Laengner.* M.DCCC.LXVI.

4to, pp. xxxii., 8 *leaves in Facsimile. Half red morocco, gilt top,* UNCUT, *by* BRADSTREET. *One Hundred and fifty copies* printed for PRIVATE DISTRIBUTION. VERY SCARCE.

"While still on board his caravel, February 15th, off the island of St. Mary, Columbus wrote two official accounts of his voyage, one of which was addressed to Raphael or Gabriel Sanchez or Sanxis, the Crown Treasurer. No copy, either in print or in manuscript, of the Spanish original, has yet been found, but the discovery made a few years ago, in the Ambrosian Library, of a printed copy of the letter addressed to Luis de Santangel, warrants the belief that not only it may have been printed, but that it is not irretrievably lost. As to the original itself, notwithstanding the diligent searches instituted by Muñoz in Simancas, and Navarrete in the *Lonja* at Seville, where, after the establishment of the General Archives, of the Indies, in 1792, all documents relating to the Western World had been transferred, no traces of it have ever been discovered. The Spanish text of the letter to Santangel had been made known through Navarrette, who possessed a transcript from the original, which, in 1818, was still deposited among the archives at Simancas. It was not known then, or even suspected, that this important document had been printed before. This *rarissime plaquette* is printed in a kind of semi-gothic type, of the roughest character, resembling none of the incunabula which we have been able to examine. The fact alone that the text is in the Spanish language authorizes the belief that it was printed in Spain. The text of the Ambrosian plaquette was first published three years ago. It is also in two late American publications. The Marquis D'Adda has lately reproduced the entire letter in facsimile." — *Harrisse.* pp. 6, 24, 25, and 27.

440 COLUMBUS. Letter of Columbus to Luis de Santangel, 1493. [*New York:* 1864.]

8vo, Title, Facsimile, 1 *p., pp.* 12. *Half morocco, gilt top,* UNCUT.

A facsimile of the Spanish letter of Columbus, published in 1493, from the only known copy in the Ambrosian Library, Milan, with a literary and bibliographical description by Mr. James Lenox. A FEW COPIES ONLY *printed for presentation.*

441 **Columbus. De Insulis inuentis** | Epistola Cristoferi Colom (cui etas nostra | multū debet: de Insulis in mari Indico nup |

inuētis. Ad quas perquirendas octauo antea | mense: auspicijs et ere Inuictissimi Fernandi | Hispaniarum Regis missus fuerat) ad. Mag- | nificum dñm Raphaelez Sanxis: eiusdē sere- | nissimi Regis Thesaurariū missa. quam nobi | lis ac litteratus vir Aliander d'Cosco: ab His- | pano ydeomate in latinū conuertit: tercio kl's | Maij. M.cccc.xciij. Pontificatus Alexandri | Sexti Anno Primo.

Sm. 8vo, 10 leaves of 27 lines to a full page. Half green levant morocco, gilt top, UNCUT.

One of TWENTY COPIES ONLY, reproduced in Paris by Pelinski about 1858. After it was issued it was discovered that it had been facsimilied from an *imperfect* copy, and wanted the first and last leaves. In *this* copy they are reproduced. Mr. Lenox possesses the only known *perfect copy* of the *original edition.* Two other copies, both wanting the tenth leaf, are known, one in the British Museum, and one which is said to have been stolen from the Ambrosian Library at Milan.

442 VERARDUS-COLUMBUS. In LAUDEM Serenissimi Ferdinandi Hispaniarum regis Bethicæ et regni Granatæ obsidio victoria et triumphus. Et de Insulis in mari Indico nuper Inuentis. (*On the recto of the second leaf:*) CAROLI VERARDI Cæsenatis Cubicularii Pontificii in historium Bæticam ad R. P. Raphælem Riarium S. Georgii Diaconum Cardinalem. (*Colophon on the recto of the 29th leaf:*) Acta Ludis Romanis Innocentio octauo in solio Petri Sedente Anno a Natali Saluatoris MCCCC.XCII. Vndecimo Kalendis Maii. . 1. 4. 9. 4. Nihil sine causa .I B. (*Basle: Bergman de Olpe.*) (*On the verso of the 29th leaf:*) De Insulas nuper in mari Indico repertis. (*On the recto of the 30th leaf:*) **De Insulis Nuper Inuentis** Epistola Christopheri Colom (cui etas nostra multum debet: de Insulis in mari Indico nuper inuentis: ad quas perquirendas octauo antea mense: auspiciis & ere inuictissimi Fernandi Hispaniarū Regis missus fuerat) ad Magnificū dominū Raphælem Sanxis: eiusdem serenissimi Regis Thesaurarium missa: quam nobilis ac litteratus vir Aliander de Cosco: ab Hispano idiomate: in latinum conuertit: tercio Kalendis Maii M.CCCC.XCIII. Pontificatus Alexandri Sexti Anno Primo.

8vo, 36 unnumbered leaves; the Letter of Columbus filling only the last seven and a half; 6 woodcuts. Citron morocco, paneled sides, gilt edges, by W. MATTHEWS.

Of the seven early editions known of the Cosco translation of this celebrated Letter of COLUMBUS, only two bear a date. The first part of the work is simply a drama on the capture of Granada from the Moors by Ferdinand. From that portion of the volume signature bb is wanting. In all other respects it is a most superior copy, and a volume OF EXTREME RARITY.

Washington Irving, in his life of Columbus, is very eloquent in praise of the language used in this first document ever printed relative to the discovery of America, and he considers it, on the whole, as far more authentic and valuable than the subsequent works of other authors, who, for the most part, wrote of things they never saw, and who recorded as facts, circumstances and deeds which were entirely fictitious, and existed only in their own imaginations. All other writers, since the discovery of these precious gems, unite in admiration and the warmest eulogiums of their merit and extraordinary rarity. Dr. Robertson, notwithstanding his research, was totally unacquainted with their existence.

443 COLUMBUS. Memorials of Columbus; or a Collection of Authentic Documents of that Celebrated Navigator, now first published

from the Original Manuscripts, by order of the Decurions of Genoa; preceded by a Memoir of his Life and Discoveries. Translated from the Spanish and Italian. *London: Treuttel and Wurtz.* 1823.

8vo, pp. (4), *clix., Facsimile,* (1), 255. *Portrait. Half blue morocco, gilt top,* UNCUT. A very uncommon PORTRAIT of COLUMBUS *inserted.*

444 COLUMBUS. The Discovery of America by Christopher Columbus. *Dublin:* 1824.

12mo, pp. 177, (1). *Half red morocco, gilt top,* UNCUT, *by* BRADSTREET.

445 COLUMBUS. Personal Narrative of the First Voyage of Columbus to America. From a Manuscript recently discovered in Spain. Translated from the Spanish. [By Samuel Kettell.] *Boston: Thomas B. Wait and Son.* 1827.

8vo, pp. 303. *Half maroon morocco, gilt top,* UNCUT. A *Fine* PROOF PORTRAIT of COLUMBUS *inserted.*

The personal narrative of the great discoverer affords us many views of the savages as they appeared to one of the fairest, most unprejudiced minds that ever existed, and before their manners or habits of thought were colored by the influences of civilization.

446 COLUMBUS. Select Letters of Christopher Columbus, with other Original Documents, relating to his Four Voyages to the New World. Translated and Edited by R. H. Major. ... *London: Printed for the Hakluyt Society.* M.DCCC.XLVII.

8vo, 4l., pp. xc., (1), 240. *Half purple morocco, gilt top,* UNCUT.

"The translated documents are seven in number. Four are letters from the hand of Columbus, describing his four voyages; another, describing the second voyage, is by Dr. Chanca, physician to the fleet; the seventh, an extract from the will of Diego Montez, one of Columbus's officers during the fourth voyage."— *Preface.*

447 COMMODITIES (THE) of the Iland called Manati ore Long Ile which is in the Continent of Virginia. *Imprinted by J. M. for J. G. S. and for sale at the sign of the Two Storks.* [*Albany.* 1862.]

8vo, pp. 16. *Map. Half red morocco, gilt top,* UNCUT, by BRADSTREET. Fifty copies only PRIVATELY PRINTED, of which but a few have the MAP. SCARCE.

448 CONDICT (I.) A Funeral Discourse, delivered in the Presbyterian Church of New-Brunswick, on the 31st of December, 1799; the Day set Apart by the Citizens for paying Solemn Honors to the Memory of Gen. George Washington. By the Rev. Ira Condict, A.M. ... *New-Brunswick, New-Jersey: Printed by Abraham Blauvelt.* 1800.

8vo, pp. 23. *Half calf.* EXCEEDINGLY RARE.

449 [CONDIE (Thomas.)] Biographical Memoirs of the Illustrious Gen. Geo. Washington, late President of the United States of America. ... Containing, A History of the principal Events of his Life,

with Extracts from his Journals, Speeches to Congress, and Public Addresses: Also, A Sketch of his Private Life.
Philadelphia: Printed by Charless & Ralston. 1800.

12mo, pp. 243. *Blue levant morocco, gilt edges.* EXCESSIVELY RARE.

450 [CONDIE.] Biographical Memoirs of the Illustrious Gen. George Washington. ... Also, A Sketch of his Private Life.
Brattleborough: Published by William Fessenden. 1814.

12mo, pp. 287. *Polished calf, gilt edges,* by BEDFORD. *Very rare* PORTRAIT of WASHINGTON, engraved by BOLT in 1796, *inserted.* Edited by the publisher, and VERY SCARCE.

451 A | CONFESSION | OF | FAITH | Owned and consented unto by the | Elders and Messengers | of the Churches | Assembled at Boston in New-England, | May 12, 1680. | Being the second | Session of that | Synod. | *Boston: | Printed by John Foster.* 1680. |

pp. 2 *l.*, (4), 65.

[Also:] A | Platform | Of | Church Discipline | Gathered out of | The Word Of God, | And Agreed upon by the | Elders and Messengers | of the Churches Assembled in the | Synod. | At Cambridge in N. E. | To be presented to the Churches and General Court | for their Consideration and Acceptance in | the Lord, the 8th. Moneth, Anno. 1649. | *Boston: Printed by John Foster.* 1680.

pp. (24), 64. *Contents* 2 *l.*

2 *vols., sm.* 8*vo, in one. Blue morocco, gilt edges; in the finest condition.* One of the EARLIEST BOSTON IMPRINTS, and EXTREMELY RARE.

452 A | CONFESSION | OF FAITH | Owned and Consented to by the | Elders and Messengers | Of the Churches | In the Colony of Connecticut in | New-England, | Assembled by Delegation at Say-Brook | September 9th, 1708. | *New-London in N. E.* | *Printed by Thomas Short.* | 1710.

Sm. 8*vo, Title, pp.* 116. *Red levant morocco extra, gilt edges by* F. BEDFORD. A BEAUTIFUL COPY of THE FIRST BOOK PRINTED IN CONNECTICUT, and so RARE that *we are unable to record the public sale of a copy.*

In "Memoirs of Pious Females." New Haven, 1733, it is stated that James Pierpont was the author of this work.

See Thomas, *Hist. of Printing*, I., 406.

453 CONSTITUTIONS (The) of the several Independent States of America; the Declaration of Independence; the Articles of Confederation between the said States; the Treaties between His Most Christian Majesty and the United States of America. Published by Order of Congress. *Philadelphia: F. Bailey.* M.DCC.LXXXI.

Sm. 8*vo, pp.* 226. *Purple morocco, paneled sides, gilt top,* UNCUT. An elegant copy of the FIRST EDITION, of which *only* 200 *copies were printed.* EXCESSIVELY RARE.

This was Governor Bloomfield's copy, and contains his AUTOGRAPH and PORTRAIT.

The following notice, from page 2, will attest its historical and political interest, as the *first authoritative* and *original printed text* of these important documents:

"In Congress, December 29, 1780. Resolved, That a Committee of three be appointed to collect and cause to be published *two hundred correct copies* of the Declaration of Independence, etc. [as in title above], to be bound together in boards, etc.

CHARLES THOMSON, Secretary."

"Extract from the Minutes."

There are other and later editions which contain this notice, but this is a *genuine* original copy of the Government edition.

454 COLLECTION (A) of the Constitutions of The Thirteen United States of North-America. ... Published by Order of Congress. *Philadelphia: Printed. Glasgow: Re-printed by John Bryce.* M,DCC,LXXXIII.

Sm. 8vo, pp. (1), 257. *Polished calf extra, by* F. BEDFORD.

455 COOK (E.) The | Sot-weed | Factor: | Or, a Voyage to | Maryland. | A | Satyr. | In which is describ'd | The Laws, Government, Courts and | Constitutions of the Country; and also the | Buildings, Feasts, Frolicks, Entertainments | and Drunken Humours of the Inhabitants of | that Part of America. | In Burlesque Verse. | By Eben. Cook, Gent. | *London: Printed and Sold by B. Bragg, at the Raven in Pater- | Noster-Row.* 1708.

4to, Title, pp. 21. *Red levant morocco, paneled sides, corner ornaments, gilt edges, by* F. BEDFORD. A BEAUTIFUL COPY *of the* EXCESSIVELY RARE, ORIGINAL EDITION.

This was General B. Mayer's copy, and the *only one* of which we can find any record as having been for sale in the United States.

456 COOK. The Sot-weed Factor. [Another Edition.] [*New York: Reprinted.* 1865.]

4to, pp. vi., 26, (1). *Half red levant morocco, gilt top,* UNCUT, *by* W. MATTHEWS. LARGE PAPER; *only* 30 *copies printed.* Now entirely out of print.

Forms No. II. of Shea's "*Early Southern Tracts.*"

Edited by Brantz Mayer, who "thinks it extremely probable that the author really was 'Eben. Cook, Gent.' or some other equally afflicted gentleman assuming that name, who

'Condemned by Fate to wayward Curse,
Of Friends unkind and empty purse,'—

fled from his native land to become a Sot-Weed factor in America."

457 COOKE (W. D.) Revolutionary History of North Carolina, in Three Lectures, by Rev. Francis L. Hawks. ... Hon. David L. Swain ... and Hon. Wm. A. Graham: ... . To which is prefixed a Preliminary Sketch of the Battle of the Alamance. Compiled by William D. Cooke, A.M. Illustrated by Darley and Lossing. *Raleigh: William D. Cooke. New York: George P. Putnam.* 1853.

12mo, pp. 236. *Woodcuts. Half blue morocco.* FOUR PORTRAITS *inserted.*

458 COOPER (J. F.) The History of the Navy of the United States of America. By J. Fenimore Cooper, Esq. *London: Richard Bentley.* 1839.

2 *vols.*, 8*vo. Half green morocco, gilt top,* UNCUT, *by* BRADSTREET. FOURTEEN PORTRAITS *inserted.* AN ELEGANT COPY.

459 COOPER. The Battle of Lake Erie, or Answers to Messrs. Burges, Duer, and Mackenzie. By J. Fenimore Cooper.

Cooperstown: H. & E. Phinney. 1843.

12mo, pp. 117, (1). *Half red morocco.*

460 [COOPER (Myles.)] A Friendly Address to all Reasonable Americans, on The Subject of our Political Confusions: in which The Necessary Consequences of Violently opposing the King's Troops, and of A General Non-Importation are fairly stated. ...

America: Printed for the Purchasers. 1774.

8vo, pp. 55. *Half green morocco.*

Ascribed to Dr. Myles Cooper, President of Kings (Columbia) College, who was soon after obliged to leave New York on account of his Tory principles.

For a Reply *see* "The Other Side of the Question" No. 1528.

461 [COOPER.] What think ye of the Congress now? Or, an Enquiry how far the Americans are bound to abide by and execute the Decisions of the Late Continental Congress. With a Plan, by Samuel Galloway, Esq., for a Proposed Union between Great Britain and the Colonies. To which is added, an Alarm to the Legislature of the Province of New York, occasioned by the Present Political Disturbances. Addressed to the Representatives in General Assembly convened. *London: Richardson & Urquhart.* 1775.

8vo, pp. 90. *Half blue morocco.*

"Intended to dissuade the people of New York from concurring with their sister colonies in adhering to the association, etc., of the congress."—*M. Rev.* "The first appearance of this Congress," the writer says, "raised our curiosity, but excited no terror. But it was not long before it turned out to be a perfect monster — a mad, blind monster!"

462 COOPER (S.) A Sermon Preached before His Excellency Thomas Pownall, Esq.; Captain-General and Governor in Chief ... Of the Province of Massachusetts-Bay in New-England, October 16th, 1759. Upon Occasion of the Success of His Majesty's Arms in the Reduction of Quebec. By Samuel Cooper ... .

Boston: Green & Russell. [1759.]

8vo, pp. 53. *Half morocco.*

463 COOPER (T.) Some Information respecting America. Collected by Thomas Cooper. ... The Second Edition.

London: J. Johnson. 1795.

8vo, pp. iv., 240. *Map. Half red morocco, gilt top,* UNCUT, *by* BRADSTREET. With the large *folded Map* often wanting.

One of the most interesting and instructive works relating to the period of which it treats.

464 COPIE DE DEVX | LETTRES Envoie'es de la | Novvelle France, | Au Pere Procureur des Missions | de la compagnie de Iesvs en ces con-

trées. | *A Paris*, | *chez Sebastien Cramoisy*, | *Imprimeur ordinaire du Roy* | *et Gabriel Cramoisy.* | *rüe S. Iacques aux Cicognes.* | M. DC. LVI. | *Auec priuilege du Roy.* | [*Albany*; 1835.]

12*mo*, *pp.* 28, (1). *Brown morocco, gilt edges. A few copies only reprinted* by Weed and Parsons, for Mr. James Lenox, in 1835. One perfect copy only, of the Original Work, is known to exist. *Presentation copy* from Mr. Lenox to the Baron Sobolewski.

465 CORBIN (W.) A | Sermon | preached at | King's Town in Jamaica | Upon the 7th of June, | Being the Anniversary Fast for that Dreadful | Earth-Quake which happened there in the | year 1692. | By William Corbin, T.B. | *Printed and Sold by* WILLIAM BRADFORD, *at the Bible* | *in New York.* 1703.

4*to*, *pp.* (4), 16. *Calf extra, by* HAYDAY. EXCESSIVELY RARE. The ONLY COPY within our knowledge.

466 CORNEY (B.). Curiosities of Literature, by I. D'Israeli, Esq. ... Illustrated by Bolton Corney, Esq., ...
GREENWICH: *Printed by Especial Command.* 1837.

Small 8*vo*, *pp.* (6), 160. *Half red morocco, gilt top,* UNCUT, *by* BRADSTREET. RARE PRIVATELY PRINTED EDITION of this trenchant attack on the historical accuracy of D'Israeli's "*Curiosities of Literature.*"

Presentation copy from the author.

467 CORNEY. Curiosities of Literature. ... Second Edition, Revised and Acuminated. To which are added, Ideas on Controversy: Deduced from the practice of a Veteran; and adapted to the meanest capacity.
London: Bentley. 1838.

Small 8*vo*, *pp.* *xi.*, 256. *Half blue morocco.* VERY SCARCE.

"One of the most learned and acute contributions to literary history that has appeared in our day."—*Edin. Rev.*

468 CORNWALLIS (*Earl.*) Examination of Lieutenant General The Earl Cornwallis before a Committee of the House of Commons, upon Sir William Howe's Papers. *London: J. Robson.* MDCCLXXIX.

8*vo*, *pp.* 60. *Half red morocco.* With numerous marked passages and notes throughout the whole tract, seemingly in the handwriting of CORNWALLIS HIMSELF. We find no trace of this VERY SCARCE work in any of our public Libraries.

469 CORNWALLIS. As great a Man as Nelson! ... The Life of the most Noble, The Marquis Cornwallis, That Great Friend to his Country! Who has been engaged in the Service of it ever since the year 1776, up to 1805, In the American and Indian War. Who has proved himself a bold and valiant warrior — a Peace Maker — a good Statesman — a Man for the People; a Friend. To which is added the Riddle, Shot from the Camp, with an Explanation. *London:* [*n. d.*]

12*mo*, *pp.* 36. *Portrait. Half red morocco, gilt top,* UNCUT. VERY RARE. This, the ONLY COPY we have ever seen, was formerly in the Wight Collection.

470 CORRY (J.) The Life of George Washington, late President, and Commander-in-Chief of the Armies of the United States of Ame-

rica; Interspersed with Biographical Anecdotes of the most Eminent Men who effected the American Revolution. ... By John Corry. *London: G. Kearsley.* 1800.

12mo, pp. 228, (3). *Half green morocco.* FIRST EDITION. *A fine copy.* VERY RARE.

471 CORRY. [Same title.] *Dublin: P. Wogan.* 1801.

12mo, pp. 228, (3). *Polished calf, gilt edges, by* F. BEDFORD. PORTRAIT *inserted.* Even RARER than the former No.

472 CORRY. The Life of George Washington, late President and Commander-in-Chief of the Armies of the United States of America. By John Corry. ... A New Edition. [*London:*] *B. Crosby & Co.* 1802.

Sm. 8vo, pp. 57, 2. *Portrait. Half green morocco, gilt top,* UNCUT, *by* BRADSTREET.
Reprinted in New York with the following title:

473 CORRY. The Life of George Washington, Commander in Chief of the Armies, and late President of the United States of America. By John Corry, ... Including the Declaration of Independence, and the Constitution of the United States. First American Edition, from the Second London Edition, with Corrections, Additions and Improvements. ... *New York: J. Low.* 1807.

12mo, pp. 349, *vii., Portrait. Green levant morocco, paneled sides, gilt edges, by* W. SMITH. VERY SCARCE.
The list of subscribers occupies seven pages.

474 [CORRY.] Biographical Memoirs of the Illustrious General Washington, Late President of the United States. Containing a History of the Principal Events of his Life, with his Speeches to Congress, and Public Addresses: to which is added, an Oration upon his Death, by the Rev. Samuel Stanhope Smith. ... A New Edition Improved. *Trenton: James Oram.* 1811.

12mo, *Portrait. Half green morocco.* A VERY SCARCE *edition.*

475 CORTES (H.) The Despatches of Hernando Cortes, the Conqueror of Mexico, addressed to the Emperor Charles V. Written during the Conquest, and containing a Narrative of its events. Now first translated into English from the original Spanish, with an Introduction and Notes, By George Folsom... . *New York: Wiley & Putnam.* 1843.

Roy. 8vo, pp. xii., 431. *Half maroon morocco, gilt top,* UNCUT. Two PORTRAITS of CORTES; one a RARE INDIA PROOF, *inserted.* LARGE PAPER. VERY SCARCE.
First appearance of the three collected dispatches in English, being a translation from Lorenzana, including a portion of his notes. *See N. Am. Rev.,* LVII. 459.

476 CORTES. The Fifth Letter of Hernan Cortes to the Emperor Charles V, containing an Account of his Expedition to Hon-

duras. Translated from the Original Spanish by Don Pascual de Gayangos.... *London: Printed for the Hakluyt Society.* M.DCCC.LXVIII.

8vo, pp. xvi., 156. *Half purple morocco, gilt top,* UNCUT.

The Spanish text was first printed in the "Documentos Inéditos," and this is the first English translation.

477 CORWIN (E. B.) ... Catalogue of the ... Books, ... &c., of the late Mr. E. B. Corwin, ... relating to America, ... &c. ... sold ... November 10th, 1856, ... [Prepared by Joseph Sabin.] [*New York.* 1856.]

Roy. 8vo, pp. vii., 263. *Half morocco, gilt top,* UNCUT. LARGE PAPER. 100 *copies only printed. Priced.*

478 COTTON (H.) The Typographical Gazetteer, attempted by the Rev. Henry Cotton. ... Second Edition, corrected and much enlarged. *Oxford:* MDCCCXXXI. Second Series. *Oxford:* MDCCC.LXVI.

2 *vols., 8vo, pp. xviii.*, 393; *xvi.*, 376, (1). *Half red morocco, gilt top,* UNCUT, *by* BRADSTREET.

The number of American places cited in the Second Series is very large, and pp. 243–308 are devoted to a monograph on the newspaper press in the United States.

479 [COTTON (John.)] An Abstract of the Lawes of New England, as they are now Established. *London: F. Coles & W. Ley.* 1641.

Sm. 4to, pp. 15, 2. *Red morocco, gilt edges, by* HAYDAY. Cut rather close, but otherwise a fine copy. VERY RARE.

The first printed collection of the Laws of New England. The Laws are very concise, and each is based upon some passage from the Holy Scriptures, to which, reference is made in the margin.

480 COTTON (J.) The | Way of the Churches | of Christ | in New England. | Or, | the VVay of Churches | walking in Brotherly equalitie, or co- | ordination, without Subjection of | one Church to another. | Measured and examined by the | Golden Reed of the Sanctuary. | Containing a full Declaration of the Church- | way in all Particulars. | By Mr. J. Cotton, Teacher of the | Church at Boston in New-England. | Published according to Order. | *London: | Printed by Matthew Simmons in Aldersgate-street.* | 1645.

4to, pp. (8), 116, 4. *Green levant morocco, paneled sides, gilt edges, by* F. BEDFORD. *A Fine Copy.* VERY RARE.

481 COTTON. The | Bloudy Tenent, | washed, | And made white in the bloud of the | Lambe: being discussed and discharged of | bloud-guiltinesse by just Defence. | Wherein | The great Questions of this present time are | handled, viz. How farre Liberty of Conscience | ought to be given to those that truly feare God? And how farre | restrained to turbulent and pestilent persons, that not one- | ly raze the foundation of Godliness, but disturb the Civill | Peace where they live? Also how farre the Magistrate may pro- | ceed in the duties of the first Table? And that all the Magistrates | ought to study the

word and will of God, that they may frame | their Government according to it. | Discussed | As they are alledged from divers Scriptures, out of | the Old and New Testament. Wherein also the practise of | Princes is debated, together with the Judgement of the An- | cient and late Writers of most precious esteeme. | Whereunto is added a Reply to Mr. [Roger] Williams | Answer, to Mr. Cottons Letter. | By John Cotton Batchelor in Divinity, and | Teacher of the Church of Christ at Boston in New-England. | *London*, | *Printed by Matthew Symmons for Hannah Allen, at the Crowne in* | *Popes-Head-Alley*. 1647.

4to, Title, pp. 195, 144. *Olive morocco, gilt edges.* A LARGE AND FINE COPY. EXCESSIVELY RARE.

The foregoing works of John Cotton are of a more historical character than their titles would seem to indicate. They relate to important events in the Ecclesiastical History of New England, and are of the GREATEST RARITY.

482 COXE (T.) A View of the United States of America, in a Series of Papers, written at various Times between ... 1787 and 1794, by Tench Coxe, of Philadelphia; interspersed with Authentic Documents: the Whole tending to exhibit the Progress and Present State of Civil and Religious Liberty, Population, Agriculture, Exports, Imports, Fisheries, Navigation, Ship-Building, Manufactures, and General Improvement. *London: Re-printed for J. Johnson.* 1795.

8vo, half calf. PORTRAIT and AUTOGRAPH LETTER of the AUTHOR *inserted.*

483 CRAIG (N. B.) Exposure of a Few of the many Misstatements in H. M. Brackenridge's History of the Whiskey Insurrection. By Neville B. Craig. *Pittsburgh: John S. Davidson.* 1859.

18mo, pp. 79. *Half morocco.*

484 CRANTZ (D.) The History of Greenland: containing a Description of the Country, and its Inhabitants: And Particularly, A Relation of the Mission, carried on for above these Thirty Years by the Unitas Fratrum, At New Herrnhuth and Lichtenfels, in that Country. By David Crantz. Translated from the High-Dutch, and illustrated with Maps and other Copper-plates. *London:* MDCCLXVII.

2 vols., 8vo, pp. lix., 405; 498. *2 Maps and 7 Plates. Half calf.* A *fine clean copy.* SCARCE.

The first English, and a literal translation of the German edition.

485 CRANTZ. The History of Greenland: Including an Account of the Mission Carried on by the United Brethren in that Country. From the German of David Crantz. With a Continuation to the Present Time; Illustrative Notes; and an Appendix, Containing a Sketch of the Mission of the Brethren in Labrador. *London: Longman.* 1820.

2 vols., 8vo, pp. ix., 359; *vi.,* 323. *2 Maps and 7 Plates. Half green morocco, gilt top, by* BRADSTREET.

486 CRESPEL (E.) Travels in North America, By Emanuel Crespel, with a Narrative of His Shipwreck, and Extraordinary Hardships and Sufferings on the Island of Anticosti; and an Account of that Island, and of the Shipwreck of his Majesty's Ship Active and others. *London: Sampson Low.* 1797.

12mo, pp. xxviii., 187. Half morocco, gilt top, UNCUT. *Scarce.*

487 CREVECŒUR (J. H. St. John. de) Letters from an American Farmer; Describing Certain Provincial Situations, Manners, and Customs, not generally known; and conveying some Idea of the late and present Interior Circumstances of the British Colonies in North America. Written for the Information of a Friend in England. By J. Hector St. John, a Farmer in Pennsylvania. *London: Thomas Davies.* M DCC LXXXII.

8vo, half red morocco, gilt top, UNCUT. A beautiful copy.

488 CROCKETT (D.) Sketches and Eccentricities of Col. David Crockett, of West Tennessee. ... New Edition. *New-York: J. & J. Harper.* 1833.

12mo, half olive morocco, gilt top, UNCUT.

489 CROCKETT. A Narrative of the Life of David Crockett of the State of Tennessee. ... Written by Himself. *Philadelphia: Carey and Hart.* 1834.

12mo, half olive morocco, gilt top, UNCUT. A CHARACTERISTIC AUTOGRAPH LETTER from the AUTHOR to the publisher respecting the work, *inserted.*

490 CROES (J.) A Discourse delivered at Woodbury, in New Jersey, on the Twenty-Second of February, Eighteen Hundred. Before the Citizens of Gloucester County, assembled to pay Funeral Honours to the memory of General George Washington. ... By John Croes, A.M. Rector of Trinity Church at Swedesborough. ... *Philadelphia:* 1800.

8vo, pp. 32. VERY RARE.

491 CROMEK (R. H.) Select Scottish Songs, Ancient and Modern; with Critical Observations and Biographical Notices, by Robert Burns. Edited by R. H. Cromek, F.S.A. *London: Cadel and Davis.* 1810.

2 *vols., 8vo, in one. Half green morocco, gilt top,* UNCUT. Printed on INDIA PAPER, and MOST RARE.

492 CROWNINSHIELD (E. A.) Catalogue of the Library of the late Edward A. Crowninshield, embracing ... Early Voyages and Travels, the Bay Psalm Book, Eliot's Indian Bible, &c. To be sold by auction, November 1st., 1856. *Boston:* 1859.

8vo, half green morocco, gilt top. One of a few copies only *printed on tinted paper.*

This sale did not take place. The collection was withdrawn from public sale in consequence of its purchase by Henry Stevens Esq. for $9500, who, after disposing of a portion of it, sold the residue, with some additions, at auction in London in the following year. No. 878, the Bay Psalm Book, was sold by Mr. Stevens to the British Museum for £157. 10*s.*

493 CROWNINSHIELD. Catalogue of the singularly Interesting, Fine and Rare Books, from the Library of Edward A. Crowninshield, Esq. Sold by auction July, 1860. *London:* 1860.

8vo, half green morocco, gilt top, UNCUT. With "GUESSES BY A YANKEE" *inserted.* RARE.

The "GUESSES" consist of eleven pages printed on India paper, giving the lot numbers of the catalogue in one column, and the price which each lot was *expected to bring*, in an opposite one.

For an interesting account of this collection, written by Mr. Stevens, see *Allibone.* III. 2248.

494 CUNDALL (J.) On Ornamental Art applied to Ancient and Modern Bookbinding. Illustrated with Specimens of various Dates and Countries. ... By Joseph Cundall. *London:* 1848.

4to, pp. 15. 21 *Plates. Half blue morocco, gilt top,* UNCUT. A full length PORTRAIT of ROGER PAYNE at work in his dilapidated bindery *inserted.* SIX COPIES only were taken, and the *negative then destroyed.*

495 CUNNINGHAM (A.) Songs of Scotland, Ancient and Modern; with an Introduction and Notes, Historical and Critical, and Characters of the most Eminent Lyric Poets of Scotland. By Allan Cunningham. *London:* 1825.

4 *vols., crown 8vo, calf. A fine copy.*

One of the best collections of Scottish Songs extant, and now scarce. Copies have been sold at auction for $40.

496 CUNNINGHAM (W.) An Eulogy delivered at Lunenburg, on the 22d of February, 1800. The Day recommended by Congress to commemorate the ... Services of Gen. George Washington. ... By William Cunningham, Jun. ... *Worcester:* 1800.

8vo, pp. 16. UNCUT.

497 [CURRER (*Miss* Richardson.)] Catalogue of the Library at Eshton Hall, in the County of York. *London: By Robert Triphook.* 1820.

8vo, pp. xi., 308. *Half olive morocco, gilt top,* UNCUT. A FINE COPY. EXCEEDINGLY RARE. FORTY COPIES ONLY PRIVATELY PRINTED. Presentation copy to William Upcott, with his AUTOGRAPH on the fly-leaf. A cancelled title page; an AUTOGRAPH NOTE of MISS CURRER; VIEW of "Eshton Hall;" and VIEW of the "Interior of the Library," *inserted.*

The catalogue was compiled by MR. TRIPHOOK.

498 CURRER. Catalogue of the Library collected by Miss Richardson Currer, at Eshton Hall, Craven, Yorkshire, By C. J. Stewart, Bookseller. *London: Printed for Private Circulation only.* 1833.

Roy. 8vo, pp. xii., 501. *Half olive morocco, gilt top,* UNCUT. A presentation copy, with MISS CURRER'S *inscription.*

This catalogue contains much more than that by Triphook, and has the FOUR FINE ENGRAVINGS from DRAWINGS by the compiler, namely, "View of Eshton Hall," two "Interiors of the Library," and "Landscape fronting the House," all on INDIA PAPER. *See* "Notes and Queries." Second Series. XII, 77.

A BEAUTIFUL COPY AND EXCESSIVELY RARE.

499 CURWEN (S.) The Journal and Letters of Samuel Curwen, an American in England, from 1775 to 1783; with an Appendix of Biographical Sketches. By George Atkinson Ward. Fourth Edition. *Boston: Little, Brown, and Company.* 1864.

8vo, pp. xxiv., 678. Portrait. Half brown morocco, gilt top, UNCUT.

500 CUSHING (A.) Historical Letters on the First Charter of Massachusetts Government. By Abel Cushing. *Boston: J. W. Bang, Printer.* 1839.

18mo, title, pp. 11–204. *Half green morocco, gilt top,* UNCUT, *by* BRADSTREET. SCARCE. PORTRAIT of INCREASE MATHER *inserted.*

501 CUSHMAN (R.) "A Sermon preached at Plimmoth in New-England, December 9, 1621." By Robert Cushman. Supposed to be the Earliest Printed Sermon delivered in the English Colonies in America. With a Historical and Bibliographical Preface [by Charles Deane.] *Boston: [J. K. Wiggin.]* 1870.

4to, half green morocco, gilt top, UNCUT, *by* BRADSTREET. LARGE HOLLAND PAPER. THIRTEEN COPIES ONLY PRINTED. Contains a photo-lithographic facsimile of the whole of the original edition.

502 CUSICK (D.) History of the Six Nations. David Cusick's Sketches of the Ancient History of the Six Nations: — comprising — First — a Tale of the Foundation of the Great Island, (now North America,) the Two Infants Born, and the Creation of the Universe. Second — A Real Account of the Early Settlers of North America, and their Dissentions. Third — Origin of the Kingdom of the Five Nations, which was called a Long House: the Wars, Fierce Animals, &c. *Lockport:* 1848.

8vo, pp. 35. 4 *Plates. Half calf.*

"The production of a pure blooded North American Indian, belonging to one of the Tribes of the Five Nations, whose scanty remnants now inhabit Western New York and Canada." — *Western Memorabilia.*

503 CUSTIS (G. W. P.) Recollections and Private Memoirs of Washington, by George Washington Parke Custis, of Arlington. Compiled from Files of the National Intelligencer, Printed at Washington, D. C. *Washington, D.C.:* 1859.

8vo, pp. 104, (1). *Half green morocco, gilt top,* UNCUT. VERY SCARCE. PORTRAITS of the AUTHOR, and of GEN. WASHINGTON *inserted.*

504 CUSTIS. Recollections and Private Memoirs of Washington, by his adopted son, George Washington Parke Custis, with a Memoir of the Author, by his Daughter; and ... Notes by Benson J. Lossing. ... With Illustrations. *New York: Derby & Jackson.* 1860.

8vo, pp. 644. 3 *Plates and* 2 *Facsimiles. Half green morocco, gilt top,* UNCUT. One volume extended to TWO, and ILLUSTRATED by the *insertion* of nearly NINETY FINE ENGRAVINGS, with RUBRICATED TITLES printed expressly for this copy.

A CHOICE AND ELEGANT SET.

505 CUTTER (W.) The Life of Israel Putnam, Major-General in the Army of the American Revolution. Compiled from the best Authors. By William Cutter. *New-York: Geo. F. Cooledge & Bro.* 1847.

12mo, pp. 383. *Numerous Engravings. Half calf.*

506 [DALRYMPLE (*Sir* John.)] The Address of the People of Great Britain to the Inhabitants of America. *London: T. Cadell.* MDCCLXXV.

[Also:] Considerations addressed to all Persons of Property in Great Britain concerning the Present Disposition of the Americans towards this Country. *London: W. Owen.* 1777.

8vo, 2 Tracts in one vol., pp. 60; 17. *Half blue morocco.*

"This address is said to have been written by Sir John Dalrymple, and printed at the public expense, to be distributed in America, where the greatest part of a large impression has been sent, apparently to coöperate with a late conciliatory resolution of the House of Commons."—*Monthly Review.*

507 [DALRYMPLE.] The Rights of great Britain Asserted against the Claims of America: being an Answer to the Declaration of the General Congress. The Ninth Edition. To which is now added, a Further Refutation of Dr. Price's State of the National Debt. *London: T. Cadell.* M DCC LXXVI.

8vo, pp. (2), 131. *Half crimson morocco, gilt top,* UNCUT, *by* BRADSTREET.

"This celebrated performance is said to have been written, printed, and liberally distributed both in Great Britain and America, at the instance and expense of government; but whether this be true or not, the work itself, we are afraid, will answer no other purpose than to exasperate the people of Great Britain against their brethren of America. *M. R.*

See Declaration (The). No. 551.

508 DANA (D.) A Discourse on the Character and Virtues of General George Washington: delivered on the Twenty-second of February, 1800 ... . By Daniel Dana ... of ... Newburyport. ... *Newburyport:* [1800.]

8vo, pp. 31. UNCUT.

509 DANA (J.) A Discourse on the Character and Death of General George Washington, ... delivered at Ipswich on the 22d February, 1800. By Josiah Dana. ... *Newburyport:* 1800.

8vo, pp. 28, (1).

510 DANA (R. H. Jr.) An Address upon the Life and Services of Edward Everett; delivered before the Municipal Authorities and Citizens of Cambridge, February 22, 1865, by Richard H. Dana, Jr. *Cambridge:* 1865.

4to, half green morocco, gilt top, UNCUT. LARGE PAPER. 50 *copies only* PRIVATELY PRINTED. TWO PORTRAITS of MR. EVERETT *inserted.* One an INDIA PROOF from a PRIVATE PLATE, the other an UNLETTERED INDIA PROOF.

511 DANIEL (G.) Catalogue of the most Valuable, Interesting and Highly Important Library of the Late George Daniel, Esq. of Cannonbury, together with his Collection of Original Drawings and Engraved Portraits ... Beautiful Water Colour Drawings, ... and other Fine Examples of Art and Vertu. ... Sold by auction, July, 1864. [*London:* 1864.]

Roy. 8vo, cloth, UNCUT. With *Names* and *Prices.* VERY SCARCE.

This interesting Catalogue, with its still more interesting notes, was compiled by the late John Bryant, of the firm of Messrs. Sotheby, Wilkinson, and Hodge, and assistant editor of the new Lowndes' Bibliographer's Manual. The Shakespeare folios and quartos sold for upward of £5,000. Miss Burdett Coutts paid £616. 2*s.* for the folio of 1623. The sale produced nearly £16,000 for only 2,278 lots

512 DANKERS (J.) *and* SLUYTER (P.) Journal of a Voyage to New York and a Tour in several of the American Colonies in 1679–80, by Jasper Dankers and Peter Sluyter of Wiewerd in Friesland. Translated from the Original Manuscript in Dutch for the Long Island Historical Society, and Edited by Henry C. Murphy. ... *Brooklyn:* 1867.

Imp. 8vo, pp. xlvii., 440. 12 *Plates. Half morocco, gilt top,* UNCUT. LARGE PAPER. 100 *copies only printed.*

"Long Island Hist. Soc. Publications," Vol. I.

513 DARNELL (E.) A Journal containing an Accurate and Interesting Account of the Hardships, Sufferings, Battles, Defeat, and Captivity of those Heroic Kentucky Volunteers and Regulars, commanded by General Winchester, in the Years 1812–13. Also, Two Narratives, by men that were wounded in the Battles on the River Raisin, and taken Captive by the Indians. By Elias Darnell. *Philadelphia: Lippincott, Grambo, and Co.* 1854.

18*mo, pp.* 98, (1). *Half blue morocco, gilt top,* UNCUT.

514 [DAVENPORT (John.)] A | Discourse | about | Civil Government | in a | New Plantation | Whose Design is | Religion. | Written many years since, | By that Reverend and Worthy Minister of the Gospel, | John Cotton, B.D. | and now Published by some Undertakers of | a new Plantation, for General Direction | and Information. | *Cambridge:* | *Printed by Samuel Green and Marmaduke Johnson.* | MDCLXIII.

Sm. 4to, pp. 24. *Half red morocco, gilt top, by* BRADSTREET. VERY RARE. Purchased at the Corwin sale in 1856, *since which time we have not seen another copy.* Two leaves are a little stained, and there is a MS. note in a contemporary hand, at the bottom of p. 6.

This discourse was written by John Davenport, of New Haven Colony, the name of John Cotton having been inserted in the title page by mistake. Its great influence in shaping our institutions is universally admitted. It is also interesting as ONE OF THE EARLIEST BOOKS PRINTED IN THIS COUNTRY. There was no printing press in New York until thirty years after this date — 1663.

This copy was sold by Royal Gurley, in 1847, for $14.50; was re-sold by Bangs, in 1852, purchased by Mr. Corwin, and sold with his collection, in 1856, for $25, and would now (1871) command at least three times that amount.— See *Sabin's Dictionary.*

515 DAVIDS (T.) History of Ink, including its Etymology, Chemistry, and Bibliography. By Thaddeus Davids. *New York:* [1860.]

12mo, cloth, gilt edges. PLATES.

516 [DAVIES (Charles A.)] Letters of J. Downing, Major, Downingville Militia, Second Brigade, to his Old Friend, Mr. Dwight. ... *New York: Harper & Brothers.* 1834.

16mo, pp. x., 367. Half calf. Scarce.

It is not generally known that two different authors assumed the name of Jack Downing, but such is the fact. The one, Seba Smith, the other a Mr. Davies, the former a down-easter, the latter a Knickerbocker.

517 DAVIES (S.) Religion and Patriotism the Constituents of a Good Soldier. A Sermon preached to Captain Overton's Independent Company of Volunteers, raised in Hanover County, Virginia, August 17, 1755. By Samuel Davies, A.M., Minister of the Gospel there. *London: J. Buckland, J. Ward, and T. Field.* 1756.

8vo, pp. 38. Calf, gilt edges, by W. MATTHEWS. A fine copy. VERY SCARCE.

This remarkable sermon contains the following prophetic note on page 12: "As a remarkable instance of this, I may point out to the public that heroic youth, Col. Washington, whom I cannot but hope Providence has hitherto preserved in so signal a manner, for some important service to his country."

518 DAVIS (J.) Travels of Four Years and a Half in the United States of America; During 1798, 1799, 1800, 1801, and 1802. Dedicated by Permission to Thomas Jefferson, Esq. President of the United States. By John Davis. ... *London: T. Ostell.* 1803.

8vo, pp. viii., 454. Half blue morocco, gilt top, UNCUT, *by* W. MATTHEWS. PORTRAIT of MR. JEFFERSON *inserted.* SCARCE.

Davis came to the United States in search of literary employment, and had much intercourse with Col. Burr, Jefferson, and others, concerning whom he gives many new facts. *See Rich,* II. 13, for a long note; *also* "*Edinb. Rev.*," II. 443; and "*M. Rev.*," XLIV. 387.

519 DAVIS (J.) An Eulogy, on General George Washington, pronounced at Boston, on Wednesday, February XIX, MDCCC. before the American Academy of Arts and Sciences. ... By John Davis ... . *Boston:* MDCCC.

4to, pp. 24. UNCUT.

520 DAVIS (J.) A Narrative of Joshua Davis, an American Citizen who was Pressed and Served on board Six Ships of the British Navy. He was in Seven Engagements, Once Wounded, Five Times confined in Irons, and obtained his Liberty by Desertion. The whole being an Interesting and Faithful Narrative of the Discipline, Various Practices and Treatment of Pressed Seamen in the British Navy, and Containing Information that never was before presented to the American People. *Boston: Printed by B. True.* 1811.

12mo, pp. 72. Half calf, gilt top, UNCUT, *by* F. BEDFORD. SCARCE.

Davis was born in Boston in 1760. In June, 1779, he embarked in the privateer Jason, and was soon after taken by the enemy. He returned to Boston in 1787, but did not publish his Narrative till 1811.

521 DAVIS (W.) An Olio of Bibliographical and Literary Anecdotes and Memoranda, Original and Selected. ... By William Davis. *London: J. Rodwell.* 1814.

12mo, pp. vi., 126. Half olive morocco, gilt top, UNCUT.

522 DAVIS. A Journey Round the Library of a Bibliomaniac; or, Cento of Notes and Reminiscences concerning Rare, Curious, and Valuable Books. [Also:] A Second Journey Round the Library of a Bibliomaniac. *London: William Davis.* 1821–24.

2 vols., 8vo, in 1. pp. viii., 96; 120. Half olive levant morocco, gilt top, UNCUT, *by* W. MATTHEWS. LARGE PAPER of which 50 *copies only* were printed.

Contains interesting particulars regarding many curious books, including keys to works written with feigned names and initials, collations of books, and other particulars.

523 DAVIS (W. J.) Catalogue of the Entire Private Library of the Late Mr. William J. Davis. [Also:] In Memoriam. Prepared by Henry B. Dawson. *New York:* 1865.

4to, half blue morocco, gilt top, UNCUT. *Portrait.*

The catalogue is ruled and priced. 70 copies only printed in this size.

524 [DAVIS (J.)] The American Mariners, or the Atlantic Voyage. A Moral Poem. Prefixed is a vindication of the American Character from the Aspersions of the Quarterly Reviewers. To which are added Naval Annals; or an Impartial Summary of the actions fought, during the late War, at Sea, and on the Lakes, between the ships of Great Britain and those of the United States of America. Copious Notes and Illustrations. *Salisbury: Brodie & Downing.* [1822.]

Sm. 8vo, pp. xii., 384. Half blue morocco, gilt top, UNCUT.

Full of incident, anecdote and facts, respecting the War of 1812.

525 [DAWSON (Henry B.)] The Life and Times of Anne Hutchinson. *New York:* [*n. d.*]

4to, half brown morocco, gilt top, UNCUT. RARE.

Published in the "Baptist Chronicle," from which it was cut, and mounted upon 21 double column ruled leaves, with a composite title page prepared by TRENT. It is an exhaustive and interesting memoir, which, we believe, cannot be obtained in any other form.

526 DAWSON (H. B.) Battles of the United States, by Sea and Land: embracing those of the Revolutionary and Indian Wars, the War of 1812, and the Mexican War; with Important Official Documents, ... By Henry B. Dawson, ... Illustrated with ... Engravings. *New York:* [1858.]

2 vols., 4to, pp. 746; 530. 41 *Plates. Half maroon morocco, gilt top,* UNCUT. Bound from carefully *selected* numbers. Many of the PLATES are PROOFS ON INDIA PAPER.

527 DAWSON. [The Battle of Monmouth. Being Chapter XXXVII. of the "Battles of the United States," in the MANUSCRIPT of the AUTHOR. *New York:* 1858.]

4to, half crimson morocco, gilt top, UNCUT.

528 DAWSON. The Sons of Liberty in New York. A Paper read before the New York Historical Society, May 3d, 1859. By Henry B. Dawson. *Printed, as Manuscript, for Private Circulation.* 1859.

8vo, pp. 118. *Half red morocco, gilt top,* UNCUT. THREE PORTRAITS *inserted. A few copies only printed.*

529 DAWSON. Major-General Israel Putnam. A Correspondence on this Subject, with the Editor of the "Hartford Daily Post." By "Selah," of that city, and Henry B. Dawson, of White Plains, N. Y. *Morrisania: N. Y.* 1860.

Roy. 8vo, pp. 169. *Half red morocco, gilt top,* UNCUT. TEN ILLUSTRATIONS *inserted.* VERY SCARCE. Two hundred and fifty copies privately printed, 117 of which were destroyed by fire.

Forms Part VI. of Dawson's "Gleanings from the Harvest-field of American History."

530 DAWSON. The Assault on Stony Point, by General Anthony Wayne, July 16, 1779. Prepared for the New York Historical Society, and read at its Regular Monthly Meeting, April 1, 1862, with a Map, Fac-similes, and Illustrative Notes. By Henry B. Dawson. *Morrisania: N. Y.* 1863.

Roy. 8vo, pp. viii., 156. *Map and* 17 *Facsimiles. Half red morocco, gilt top,* UNCUT. EIGHT PORTRAITS *inserted.* 250 copies only printed.

Forms Part XI. of Dawson's "Gleanings, etc."

531 DAWSON. Current Fictions tested by Uncurrent Facts, &c. A Correspondence between John Jáy and Henry B. Dawson, and between James A. Hamilton and Henry B. Dawson, concerning the Fœderalist. *New York: J. M. Bradstreet & Son.* 1864.

4to, half red morocco, gilt top, UNCUT, *by* BRADSTREET. PORTRAIT *inserted.* LARGE PAPER. 25 copies printed.

532 DAWSON. Correspondence between John Jáy and Henry B. Dawson, and between James A. Hamilton and Henry B. Dawson, concerning the Fœderalist. *New York:* 1864.

8vo, half red morocco, gilt top, UNCUT, *by* BRADSTREET.

533 DAWSON. THE GAZETTE SERIES. Vol. I. Papers Concerning the Capture and Detention of Major André. Collected by Henry B. Dawson.—Vol. II. Papers Concerning the Town and Village of Yonkers, Westchester County. A Fragment. By Henry B. Dawson.—Vol. III. Papers Concerning the Boundary between the States of New York and New Jersey. Written by Several Hands.—Vol.

IV. Rambles in Westchester County, New York. A Fragment. By Henry B. Dawson. *Yonkers: N. Y.* 1866.

4 *vols., roy. 8vo, pp.* (8), 247; (8), 45; (8), 293; (8), 43. *Blue morocco extra, gilt top,* UNCUT, *by* W. MATTHEWS. An ELEGANT COPY with a *frontispiece inserted* in each volume. TWENTY-SIX COPIES PRINTED, FOR PRIVATE CIRCULATION ONLY. VERY RARE. Made up from the columns of the "Westchester Gazette," hence the name of the series, sets of which have sold for $100.

534 DAWSON. The Park and its Vicinity, in the City of New York. By Henry B. Dawson. *Morrisania: N. Y.* 1867.

Roy. 8vo, pp. viii., 95. Half red morocco, gilt top, UNCUT.

Forms Part I. of "Gleanings, etc.," and is an amplification of the following No.

535 [DAWSON *and* DAVIS (William J.)] Reminiscences of the Park and its Vicinity. *New York:* 1855.

12mo, half orange morocco, gilt top, UNCUT. NINETEEN ILLUSTRATIONS and *six leaves of cuttings,* mounted and inlaid by TRENT, *inserted.* TWENTY-FIVE COPIES only *privately printed.* EXCESSIVELY SCARCE.

536 DAWSON (*Editor.*) Diary of David How, a Private in Colonel Paul Dudley Sargent's Regiment of the Massachusetts Line, in the Army of the American Revolution. From the original Manuscript. With a Biographical Sketch of the Author by George Wingate Chase, and Illustrative Notes by Henry B. Dawson. *Morrisania: N. Y.* 1865.

Imp. 8vo, pp. xv., 51. Half red morocco, gilt top, UNCUT. 250 copies only printed.

Forms Part IV. of Dawson's "Gleanings, etc."

537 DEAN (J. W.) A Memoir of the Rev. Nathaniel Ward, A.M., Author of the Simple Cobler of Aggawam in America. With Notices of his Family. By John Ward Dean. *Albany: J. Munsell.* 1868.

8vo, pp. 213. Half green levant morocco, gilt top, UNCUT. PORTRAIT *of* GOV. WINTHROP *inserted.*

538 DEANE (C.) A Bibliographical Essay on Governor Hutchinson's Historical Publications. By Charles Deane. *Boston: Privately Printed.* 1857.

Sq. 8vo, pp. 39. Half green morocco, gilt top, UNCUT, *by* BRADSTREET. VERY SCARCE. 50 *copies only* PRIVATELY PRINTED.

539 [DEANE.] Bibliographical Tracts. Number One. Spurious Reprints of Early Books. [By Charles Deane.] *Boston:* 1865.

Roy. 8vo, half crimson morocco, gilt top, UNCUT. SCARCE. 131 copies only printed.

"From the Boston Daily Advertiser of March 24, 1865." This reprint was not made for Mr. Deane. It is a caustic and deserved critique of "Salem Witchcraft by Robert Calef, and Cotton Mather ... with Notes by Samuel P. Fowler." No. II. has not yet appeared.

See Salem Witchcraft. No. 1746.

540 DEANE. Communication [to the Mass. Hist. Soc.] respecting the Seal of the "Council for New England." By Charles Deane. [*Cambridge: Mass.* 1867.]

8vo, half green morocco, gilt top, UNCUT, *by* BRADSTREET. *Thirty copies only* PRIVATELY REPRINTED from the "Proceedings of the Massachusetts Hist. Soc. for 1866–67."

541 [DEANE.] Remarks on Sebastian Cabot's Mappe-Monde. From the Proceedings of the American Antiquarian Society, for April, 1867. [By Charles Deane.] *Cambridge:* 1867.

8vo, half red morocco, gilt top, UNCUT, *by* BRADSTREET. *Fifty copies only* PRIVATELY REPRINTED.

542 DEANE. Memoir of George Livermore. Prepared agreeably to a Resolution of the Massachusetts Historical Society. By Charles Deane. *Cambridge: Press of John Wilson and Son.* 1869.

4to, pp. 60. *Half green levant morocco, gilt top,* UNCUT, *by* W. MATTHEWS. LARGE PAPER; a limited number only printed for PRIVATE DISTRIBUTION. THIRTEEN FINE ILLUSTRATIONS *inserted*, embracing an excellent photograph of MR. LIVERMORE, and TWELVE PORTRAITS of his friends; all PROOFS, AND PROOFS BEFORE LETTERS, ON INDIA PAPER.

543 DEANE (Silas.) An Address to the Free and Independent Citizens of the United States of North-America. By Silas Deane, Esquire. *Hartford: Printed by Hudson & Goodwin.* MDCCLXXXIV.

Sm. 8vo, pp. 30. *Half roan,* UNCUT. VERY SCARCE.

Charges of fraud and peculation in the management of the public moneys, and of engaging himself in the interest of the enemies of his country, etc., led to this publication, which is so SCARCE that we are unable to record ANY OTHER copy.

See Lee (Arthur.) No. 1204.

544 DEANE. An Address to the United States of North America. To which is added, A Letter to the Hon. Robert Morris, Esq., with Notes and Observations. By Silas Deane, Esq. Late one of the Commissioners Plenipotentiary from the United States, to the Court of Versailles. *London: J. Debrett.* 1784.

8vo, pp. (4), 95. *Half morocco.* RARE.

The author's vindication of himself from a charge of mismanagement of the public money. It was reprinted at New London, but both this and the reprint are equally "TRES RARE."

545 DEANE. Paris Papers; or Mr. Silas Deane's late intercepted Letters, to his Brothers, and other intimate Friends, in America. To which are annexed for Comparison, the Congressional Declaration of Independency in July, 1776, and that now inculating [*sic*] among the revolted Provinces, with the never-to-be-forgotten Orders of the Rebel General in August, 1776, for preventing a Pacification. *New-York: James Rivington.* [1782.]

Sm. 8vo, pp. xii., 141, *xxxii.,* 24, (36). *Half olive morocco, gilt top,* UNCUT. A FINE COPY. VERY RARE. The two Declarations are printed face to face, numbering eleven pages each.

Mr. Gowans, from whom this volume was purchased, assured its present owner that *he had never seen another copy*, and the compiler of this catalogue knows of *only one other*; that at the Boston Athenæum.

Mr. Deane declared that the letters were intercepted and published by the enemy with a view to ruin him in the eyes of his countrymen.

546 DEARBORN (Henry.) An Account of the Battle of Bunker Hill. Written for the Portfolio, at the request of the Editor. By H. Dearborn, Maj.-Gen. U. S. A. Illustrated by a Map, drawn by Henry de Berniere, 10th Royal British Infantry, and corrected by Gen. Dearborn. *Philadelphia:* 1818.

8vo, pp. 16. *Map. Half crimson morocco, gilt top.* The *Map*, mounted on linen, is laid in only. Two ENGRAVINGS *inserted.*

547 [DEARBORN.] Enquiry into the Conduct of Gen. Putnam in relation to the Battle of Bunker Hill, and Remarks on S. Swett's Sketch of that Battle. *Boston:* 1819.

8vo, pp. 58. *Half crimson morocco, gilt top, uncut.* PORTRAIT *inserted.*

548 DEARBORN (H. A. S.) Sketch of the Life of the Apostle Eliot, prefatory to a Subscription for erecting a Monument to his Memory. By H. A. S. Dearborn. *Roxbury: Norfolk Co. Journal Press.* 1850.

8vo, pp. 32. *Plate. Half green morocco, gilt top,* UNCUT, *by* BRADSTREET.

Contains not only the history of the translating of the Bible into the Indian language, but also of the printing of it.

549 DE BRAHM (J. G. W.) History of the Province of Georgia: with Maps of Original Surveys. By John Gerar William de Brahm, His Majesty's Surveyor-General for the Southern district of North America. Now first Printed. *Wormsloe.* MDCCCXLIX.

4to, pp. 55, (1). 6 *Plates. Half morocco, gilt top,* UNCUT: *Forty-nine copies* PRIVATELY PRINTED; FIVE ON PLATE PAPER, of which this is one.

Printed from a manuscript in the Library of Harvard College, for the editor, George Wymberley-Jones. It is so RARE that we have seen *only one* ordinary paper copy sold; that at the Ingraham sale in 1851, where it brought $49.00.

550 DE BURY (R.) Philobiblion. A Treatise on the Love of Books. By Richard De Bury, Bishop of Durham, and Lord Chancellor of England. First American Edition, with the Literal English Translation of John B. Inglis. Collated and Corrected with Notes, by Samuel Hand. *Albany: Joel Munsell.* MDCCCLXI.

8vo, half olive morocco, gilt top, UNCUT. LARGE PAPER. *Thirty copies only printed.* VERY SCARCE.

The first treatise on bibliography by an English writer; it relates the measures he took, the difficulties he encountered, and all the art he exerted to gratify his favorite passion. When Chancellor and Treasurer of England, A. D., 1340, he took his perquisites and new-year's gifts in books.

551 DECLARATION (The) by the Representatives of the United Colonies of North America, now met in General Congress at Philadelphia, setting forth the Causes and Necessity of taking up Arms. The Letter of the Twelve United Colonies by their Delegates in Congress to the Inhabitants of Great Britain, their Humble Petition to his Majesty, and their Address to the People of Ireland. Collected

together for the Use of Serious Thinking Men. By Lovers of Peace. *London: Printed in the Year*, MDCCLXXV.

8vo, pp. 32. *Half roan*, UNCUT.

See [Dalrymple (John.)] No. 507.

552 DE COSTA (B. F.) A Narrative of Events at Lake George, from the Early Colonial Times to the close of the Revolution. By B. F. DeCosta. *New York:* 1868.

Imp. 8vo, pp. 74. *Plate. Half red morocco, gilt top*, UNCUT, *by* BRADSTREET. *Seventy-five copies only* PRIVATELY PRINTED. Fine INDIA PROOF VIEW of Lake George *inserted.*

553 DE COSTA. The Pre-Columbian Discovery of America by the Northmen, illustrated by Translations from the Icelandic Sagas, edited with Notes and a General Introduction, by B. F. DeCosta. With a Map of Cape Cod, as it appeared at the beginning of the Seventeenth Century. *Albany: Joel Munsell.* 1868.

8vo, Map. Half green levant morocco, gilt top, UNCUT, *by* W. SMITH.

554 DE COSTA. The Northmen in Maine; a Critical Examination of the Views expressed in connection with the Subject, by Dr. J. H. Kohl, in Volume I of the New Series of the Maine Historical Society. To which are added, Criticisms on other Portions of the Work, and a Chapter on the Discovery of Massachusetts Bay. By the Rev. B. F. DeCosta .... *Albany: Joel Munsell.* 1870.

8vo, pp. 146. *Cloth.* Now out of print, and SCARCE.

555 DE HASS (W.) History of the Early Settlement and Indian Wars of Western Virginia; embracing an Account of the Various Expeditions in the West, previous to 1795. Also, Biographical Sketches of Col. Ebenezer Zane, Major Samuel McColloch, Lewis Wetzel, Genl. Andrew Lewis, Genl. Daniel Brodhead, Capt. Samuel Brady, Col. Wm. Crawford; and other Distinguished Actors in our Border Wars. By Willis De Hass . ... Illustrated by Numerous Engravings. *Wheeling: H. Hoblitzell.* 1851.

8vo, pp. 416. *Cuts. Half green morocco, gilt top.* LARGE *and* FINE COPY of this SCARCE WORK.

556 DEHON (T.) A Discourse, delivered in Newport, Rhode-Island; before the Congregation of Trinity Church. ... The Sunday following the intelligence of the Death of General George Washington. By Theodore Dehon, A.M. *Newport:* M,DCCC.

4to, pp. 17. (2), UNCUT.

557 DELAPLAINE (Joseph.) Delaplaine's Repository of the Lives and Portraits of Distinguished American Characters. *Philadelphia:* 1815–18.

4to, 3 parts in I *vol., half levant morocco, gilt top*, UNCUT. A FINE CLEAN COPY, with SELECTED impressions of every plate, *all* the ENGRAVED TITLES and FRONTISPIECES, and the

RARE *unpublished* PORTRAITS of WILLIAM H. HARRISON, and THOMAS C. JAMES, M.D., laid in at the end of the volume. SCARCE in such fine condition.

558 DENTON (D.) A | Brief Description | of | New-York: | Formerly Called | New-Netherlands. | With the Places thereunto Adjoyning. | Together with the | Manner of its Scituation, Fertility of the Soyle, | Healthfulness of the Climate, and the | Commodities thence produced. | Also | Some Directions and Advice to such as shall go | thither: An Account of what Commodities they Shall | take with them; The Profit and Pleasure that | may accrew to them thereby. | Likewise | A Brief Relation of the Customs of the | Indians there. | By Daniel Denton. | *London: | Printed for John Hancock, at the first Shop in Popes-Head-Alley in | Cornhil at the three Bibles, and William Bradley at the three Bibles | in the Minories.* 1670.

Sm. 8vo, 2 l. pp. 21. Crushed red levant morocco, gilt edges, by F. BEDFORD. A LARGE and BEAUTIFUL COPY of the FIRST ACCOUNT OF NEW YORK printed in English, and EXCESSIVELY RARE. The title page having been printed on paper larger than the rest of the volume, the date is often found to have been cut off by the binder. In this copy it has been restored in *most exact facsimile* by MR. HARRIS of London.

The compiler of this catalogue has sold but *one copy* of this work, for which he obtained $275.00, and for which its present owner has since refused an offer of $400.00.

The following is a reprint.

559 DENTON. A Brief Description of New York, formerly called New Netherlands, with the Places Thereunto Adjoining. Likewise a Brief Relation of the Customs of the Indians there. A New Edition, with an Introduction and Copious Historical Notes. By Gabriel Furman. *New York: William Gowans.* 1845.

4to, half calf, gilt top, UNCUT. LARGE PAPER. *One hundred copies only printed.*

The introduction contains interesting bibliographical notes respecting the original work.

Forms No. 1, of Gowans' "*Bibliotheca Americana.*"

560 DETAIL (The) and Conduct of the American War, under Generals Gage, Howe, Burgoyne, and Vice Admiral Lord Howe. With a very Full and Correct State of the whole of the Evidence, as given before a committee of the House of Commons; and the Celebrated Fugitive Pieces, which are said to have given Rise to that Important Inquiry. The whole exhibiting a Circumstantial, Connected and Complete History of the Real Causes, Rise, Progress and Present State of the American Rebellion. The Third Edition. *London: Richardson & Urquhart.* M,DCC,LXXX.

8vo, pp. 190. *Half calf.* FINE COPY. BEST EDITION. SCARCE.

"Praise is due to the editor of this publication for the care and attention which he has manifested in digesting the very important materials of which it is composed, especially the letters from Boston, New York, &c. This is a much enlarged and improved edition of 'A View of the Evidence,' etc."— *Monthly Review,* LXII. 84. *See also* Rich, I. 285.

561 DETAIL (A) of some Particular Services performed in America, during the years 1776, 1777, 1778, and 1779. Compiled from

Journals and Original Papers, supposed to be chiefly taken from the Journal kept on board of the Ship Rainbow, commanded by Sir George Collier, while on the American Station during that period: giving a minute account of many important attacks on towns and places, expeditions sent up rivers, skirmishes, negociations, etc., some of which are nowhere else correctly represented, and many others not as minutely described in the histories of that period. Printed for Ithiel Town from a manuscript obtained by him while in London, in the summer of 1830.

New York: [*Privately Printed.*] 1835.

12mo, pp. ix., 117. *Half brown morocco, gilt top,* UNCUT. VERY SCARCE. The greater part of the edition was destroyed by fire.

562 DEUX-PONTS (W. de) My Campaigns in America: a Journal kept by Count William de Deux-Ponts, 1780–81. Translated from the French Manuscript, With an Introduction and Notes, by Samuel Abbott Green. *Boston:* 1868.

8vo, pp. xvi., (1), 176. *Half red levant morocco, gilt top,* UNCUT, *by* W. SMITH. PORTRAIT of GEN. ROCHAMBEAU *inserted.*

563 DEWITT (T.) A Discourse delivered in the North Reformed Dutch Church, in the City of New York, on the last Sabbath in August, 1856. By Thomas Dewitt, D.D. *New York:* 1857.

8vo, pp. 100. 9 *Plates. Half green morocco, gilt top,* UNCUT, *by* BRADSTREET. INDIA PROOF PORTRAIT of GOV. STUYVESANT *inserted.*

"Not a mere sermon, but rather a history of this church from its building in 1731; the appendix contains a list of all the ministers of the Reformed Dutch Church in New-York, from 1633 to 1849, and also of all the ministers of that religious body in North-America from 1633 to 1800, with historical notes etc. A facsimile view of the edifice in the year 1731, a view of New Amsterdam in 1656, etc., are added." — *F. Muller.*

564 DEXTER (E.) Theory of Existence: Part I. Devoted to the Enunciation of the Laws which determine the Motions that result from the Collision of Ponderable Bodies. By Elias Dexter.

New York: Edward Dexter. 1869.

8vo, pp. 155. 6 *Plates. Half red morocco, gilt top,* UNCUT. *A few copies only printed for private circulation.*

565 DIAZ DEL CASTILLO (B.) The Memoirs of the Conquistador Bernal Diaz del Castillo written by himself containing a True and Full Account of the Discovery and Conquest of Mexico and New Spain. Translated from the Original Spanish by John Ingram Lockhart, F.R.A.S. ... *London: J. Hatchard and Son.* MDCCCXLIV.

2 *vols., 8vo, half red morocco, gilt top,* UNCUT. PORTRAIT *of* BERNAL DIAZ *inserted.*

AN UNEQUALLED COLLECTION
OF
DIBDIN'S BIBLIOGRAPHICAL WORKS
WITH UPWARDS OF
ONE THOUSAND HIGH CLASS INSERTED ILLUSTRATIONS.

The following, beautiful, very complete, and extraordinary assemblage of Dibdin's Bibliographical Works has been made at a large cost of time and money, and is the result of many years of diligent and discriminative collecting. We venture to remark, that it would be difficult, if indeed it were possible, to produce another such set ; a conclusion at which the intelligent collector will speedily arrive on a careful perusal of the notes to the respective works. It is unnecessary to attempt to add to the superlative praises which have been lavished upon the works of Mr. Dibdin by the most intelligent critics, and the most refined admirers of the productions of art. An English Reviewer remarks, "we are decidedly of opinion that no bibliographical collection can be complete without Mr. Dibdin's volumes, which are, independent of the solid information they contain, frequently enlivened by literary anecdotes, and rendered generally interesting by great variety of observation, and acuteness of remark."

Mr. Allibone observes, "Now of all Englishmen who have ever lived, there never was a man better suited to make a dry study attractive, and a learned subject plain, than Dr. Dibdin of Roxburghe memory. This magician could with his pen dress up a begrimed, uncouth-looking volume, in more attractive style than could Grolier's binder with his most cunning tools. He could convert 'Belindas' and 'Almasas' into BIBLIOMANIACS, and make a dry catalogue of old English poetry more attractive than the last novel. It was but necessary for him to apply the epithets 'excessively rare,' or 'exceedingly curious,' and the neglected Caxton in your garret would buy you a year's clothing for your household, and the old family Bible would defray your Christmas festivities."

The set here noted is especially remarkable for the strength and beauty of the impressions of the plates, the spotless purity of the paper, its large and uncut margins, the appropriate chasteness of its binding, and the extraordinary character of the numerous added illustrations. As the several works of Dibdin greatly vary in size, an attempt has been made, in the present instance, to obtain all the uniformity of range possible. This can only be accomplished by selecting large paper copies of some of the works, and small paper copies of others, which method has been adopted by the owner of this set, with very considerable success. The collection is uniformly bound in *half crushed rich olive brown levant morocco, gilt top*, UNCUT, *by* W. MATTHEWS ; Mr. Utterson's copy of the "Bibliomania," and "Book Rarities," excepted, which are gilt edged.

The tools used in its ornamentation were cut expressly for the set, and each volume has had the same care and attention in its forwarding and finishing, as if it were in full binding; the present style having been adopted in order that perfect freedom might be exercised in the use of the volumes for reference or examination. In fine, we do not hesitate to state, that, taking the collection volume for volume, leaf for leaf, and plate for plate, its purity and beauty of condition cannot be excelled, if indeed equalled, by any other, either in, or out of, the United States. It may here be remarked that no part of the set has been subjected to the process of washing, as the crisp and firm texture of each and every leaf, throughout, will sufficiently testify.

The several works are here, with two or three exceptions, arranged in chronological order.

566 DIBDIN (T. F.) Poems. By T. F. Dibdin.
London: Printed for the Author. 1797.

8*vo*. VERY RARE.

"In the first edition of the Bibliomania is a curious note respecting these poems, from which it appears that 500 copies were printed, the major part of which were destroyed. 'My only consolation (says Dibdin) is that the volume is exceedingly rare!'"

567 [DIBDIN.] The Director. A Weekly Literary Journal, containing Essays on Subjects of Literature, the Fine Arts and Manners, Bibliographiana, &c. *London: Longman.* 1807

2 *vols.*, 8*vo*. An *unlettered India proof* PORTRAIT *inserted* in front of each volume.

Contains essays on literature and the fine arts, bibliographiana, accounts of rare and curious books and book sales, sketches of modern writers, eminent ancient artists, &c.

568 DIBDIN. Specimen Bibliothecæ Britannicæ. Specimen of a Digested Catalogue of Rare, Curious, and Useful Books in the English Language, or appertaining to British Literature and Antiquities. By the Rev. T. F. Dibdin. *London:* 1808.

4*to*, LARGE PAPER. EXCESSIVELY RARE.

"The present impression is on large paper of which only eight copies were printed. The plate opposite page 14 is not attached to the small paper copies."— *T. F. D.* (*Manuscript note by Dibdin.*) Of ordinary copies 40 only were PRIVATELY PRINTED, not published.

569 DIBDIN. ... Utopia; written in Latin by the Right Worthy and Famous Sir Thomas More, Knight, and translated into English by Raphe Robinson, A.D. 1551. A New Edition; With copious Notes ... by the Rev. T. F. Dibdin, F.S.A.
London: William Miller. 1808.

4*to*. LARGE PAPER. *Forty copies only printed;* with the PRIVATE PLATE of "The Family of Sir Thomas More," which is not in the small paper copies. A fine *unlettered India proof* PORTRAIT of MR. DIBDIN engraved by MEYER, *with the border*; and FOUR different *unlettered India proof* PORTRAITS of SIR THOMAS MORE *inserted.*

570 DIBDIN. The Bibliomania; or Book Madness; containing some account of the History, Symptoms, and Cure of this Fatal Disease.

In an epistle addressed to Richard Heber, Esq. By the Rev. Thomas Frognall Dibdin, F.S.A. *London: Longman.* 1809.

8vo. FIRST EDITION. VERY RARE. PORTRAIT of SIR JOHN HARRINGTON *inserted.* *See* Ferriar (J.) No. 710.

571 DIBDIN. Typographical Antiquities: or the History of Printing in England, Ireland, and Scotland, Containing Memoirs of our Ancient Printers, and a Register of the Books Printed by them. Begun by the late Joseph Ames. Considerably augmented by William Herbert, of Cheshunt, Herts; And now greatly enlarged, with Copious Notes, and illustrated with appropriate Engravings; Comprehending the History of English Literature, and a View of the Progress of the Art of Engraving, in Great Britain. By the Rev. Thomas Frognall Dibdin. *London:* 1810–19.

4 *vols.*, 4*to.*

Many of the plates in this copy are *selected impressions* from the unused stock in the hands of a London bookseller, and are consequently *much finer* than those usually found in the work. The rare Index [pp. 32.] to the early English books, subsequently printed for S. R. Maitland, is *inserted* at the end of the second volume. An extra PORTRAIT of AMES is also *inserted.*

572 DIBDIN. Bibliomania; or Book Madness: A Bibliographical Romance, in Six Parts. Illustrated with Cuts. By the Rev. Thomas Frognall Dibdin. *London: Printed for the Author.* 1811.

8vo, wrinkled red morocco, square flexible back, morocco joints, silk linings, gilt edges. A choice specimen of CHARLES LEWIS' *binding.*

This was MR. UTTERSON'S COPY, and has his Arms in gold on the sides. The EXCESSIVELY RARE PORTRAIT of the AUTHOR "in Canonicals," of which *twenty-five impressions only* were taken, and the plate then destroyed, is *inserted* in *three different states.* (*See* the "Reminiscences," p. 325, for some account of this *most rare* plate.) This copy is one of those thus referred to at p. 289, of the "Reminiscences." "Some few dozen copies of the small paper were struck off with the word 'Bibliomania' in the title page printed in red ink. Those are now classed among the *Libri Rarissimi.*" A *trial proof* of the title page vignette, is also *inserted.*

573 DIBDIN. Bibliomania. [Another copy.] *London:* 1811.

2 *vols.*, 8*vo.* VERY RARE. A fine impression of the FULL LENGTH PORTRAIT of THOMAS BRITTON, the Musical Small Coal-Man, *inserted.* We have never seen another copy of this work *in two volumes.*

"Abounds with anecdotes of Books and Book Collectors, an account of the rarer articles in their collections, and the prices at which they were sold. It will be always consulted as a first authority."

574 DIBDIN. Book Rarities; or a Descriptive Catalogue of some of the most Curious, Rare, and Valuable Books of Early Date; Chiefly in the Collection of the Right Honourable George John Earl Spencer, K.G. &c., &c., &c. By the Rev. T. F. Dibdin. *London: printed by W. Bulmer and Co.* 1811.

8vo, gilt edges. VERY RARE. *Thirty-six copies* only printed. Not published.

"The Foundation Stone of the 'Bibliotheca Spenceriana.'"—*Dibdin.*

575 [DIBDIN.] Bibliography, a Poem, in Six Books. With Preface and Notes. *London:* 1812.

8vo. VERY RARE. *Fifty copies only* PRIVATELY PRINTED, not published, the greater part of which were destroyed by the author.

"There is no title-page to this effusion from the pen of Dr. Dibdin."—*Martin.*

576 DIBDIN. Bibliotheca Spenceriana; or a Descriptive Catalogue of the Books printed in the Fifteenth Century, and of many Valuable First Editions, in the Library of George John Earl Spencer, K.G., etc. etc. etc. By the Reverend Thomas Frognall Dibdin. *London: Printed for the Author.* 1814–15.

4 *vols. imp. 8vo.*

AN AUTOGRAPH LETTER of the AUTHOR announcing the presentation of a copy of the work from EARL SPENCER to MR. THOMAS SHARPE at Coventry; EARL SPENCER'S presentation to MR. SHARPE and MR. SHARPE'S book plate, inlaid on one leaf; and an *open letter proof* PORTRAIT of EARL SPENCER, are inserted.

The duplicate of p. 509, Vol. III. containing the beautifully engraved figure of HESIOD, printed after the volume was issued, and wanting in many copies, is in its place in this.

"This catalogue contains only the works printed in the fifteenth century and the Editiones Principes. It is compiled with the greatest care and industry, and those who have had occasion to consult its pages, can testify to its accuracy and great utility. The collection is the finest private one in Europe; the catalogue will ever be regarded as of the first importance to the theologian, the historian, and the critic, and as a perfect model for the bibliographer."—*Lowndes.*

577 DIBDIN. Ædes Althorpianæ; or an Account of the Mansion, Books, and Pictures, at Althorp; the Residence of George John Earl Spencer, K.G. To which is added a Supplement to the Bibliotheca Spenceriana. By the Rev. Thomas Frognall Dibdin. *London: Payne & Foss.* 1822.

2 *vols., imp. 8vo.*

Besides the numerous beautiful ENGRAVINGS which accompany and adorn this work, there have been *inserted* FORTY additional ILLUSTRATIONS of the *finest character*, and, three excepted, all either *proofs; artist's proofs before letters; India proofs;* or *India proofs before letters;* two of which are impressions from PRIVATE PLATES, and of EXCESSIVE RARITY, viz: The Medallion Head of EARL SPENCER from a bust by CHANTREY; and a splendid impression of the celebrated large portrait of DIANE DE POICTIERS, engraved by THOMSON for EARL SPENCER, of which *Fifty* impressions only were printed, and the plate then destroyed. Copies of this portrait, when to be had, are worth ten guineas in London. The portrait of SIR JOHN SPENCER is duplicated with an engraver's *proof before letters.* That of ROBERT SPENCER is triplicated with two *engraver's proofs*, on different papers, and *before any letters.* That of HENRY EARL of SUNDERLAND is triplicated by impressions from the plate in *different states*, before any lettering. GEORGE JOHN EARL SPENCER is duplicated by an *India proof before letters.*

See the author's Reminiscences, II. 557–94, for an interesting account of the publication of this work, where it appears that the cost of engraving the portraits was upwards of £2000. It was designed as a Supplement to the "Bibliotheca Spenceriana" and contains accounts of the ancestors of Earl Spencer; of the Mansion at Althorp; of the gallery, with engravings of the most important pictures; and of editions of the Scriptures, Aldine Editions, and books printed in the fifteenth century, not contained in the former volumes.

578 DIBDIN. A Descriptive Catalogue of the Books printed in the Fifteenth Century, lately forming Part of the Library of the Duke Di Cassano Serra, and now the Property of George John Earl Spencer, K.G. With a General Index of Authors and Editions

contained in the Present Volume, and in the Bibliotheca Spenceriana and Ædes Althorpianæ. By the Rev. Thomas Frognall Dibdin.
London: Printed for the Author. 1823.

Imp. 8vo. Fine PORTRAIT of EARL SPENCER *inserted.*

Forms another supplemental volume to the "Bibliotheca Spenceriana," with an index to the seven volumes, and completes the work.

579 DIBDIN. The Bibliographical Decameron; or, Ten Days Pleasant Discourse upon Illuminated Manuscripts, and Subjects connected with Early Engravings, Typography, and Bibliography. By the Rev. T. F. Dibdin. *London: Printed for the Author.* 1817.

3 *vols., imp. 8vo.*

These beautiful volumes contain nearly SEVENTY *inserted* PORTRAITS of persons alluded to in their pages, FIFTY-FIVE of which consist of PROOFS, INDIA PROOFS, and INDIA PROOFS BEFORE LETTERS; including nearly *thirty* impressions from PRIVATE PLATES, of which the following is a partial list. The AUTHOR; *India proof*, painted and etched by WYATT, 1844.— WILLIAM ALEXANDER; *India proof*, VERY RARE.— JOHN BROSTER, the auctioneer; *India proof*, VERY RARE.— THOMAS BAKER; "Quisquilius." *India proof before letters*, RARE.— SIR HENRY ENGLEFIELD; *proof*, *drawn* and *etched* by SIR FRANCIS CHANTREY.— LORD GRENVILLE; *proof before letters*, A GEM, of EXCESSIVE RARITY.— CHARLES LEWIS, the bookbinder; a *star proof* on *India paper*.— MR. LANG; "Meliades." *India proof*, VERY RARE.—MARY QUEEN of SCOTS; A GEM, *twenty-five copies only struck off*, EXCESSIVELY RARE.— SIR M. M. SYKES; two impressions, *India proofs*, *before* and *after letters*.— EARL SPENCER; *proof before letters*, RARE. EARL SPENCER; *India proof*, engraved by BARTOLOZZI 1792. VERY RARE.— E. V. UTTERSON; *India proof before letters*.— MRS. UTTERSON; *India proof before letters*.— And others. In addition to which, there are also inserted; a *beautiful India proof impression* of the VERY RARE and costly engraving of "THE PRESENTATION IN THE TEMPLE;" drawn and engraved by LEWIS, after the original by VERONESI.— An impression on *India paper* and *probably* UNIQUE, of the missing woodcut designed for the work, but *not found in any copy*, respecting which see a "Tale of Woe," in Vol. II. p. 259. An elegant and highly finished COLOURED CHALK DRAWING of CHRISTOPHER PLANTIN, the celebrated printer; by the CHEVALIER VAN BRÉE, from the original by RUBENS.— Duplicate impressions, *artist's unlettered proofs*, of the PORTRAITS of FROBEN, and CHRACHERODE;—and an *original Prospectus* of the Decameron, June 6th, 1815. 2 leaves.

The "beautiful specimen" of printing in gold, "glittering like the sun," missing in many copies, will be found in its place in Vol. II.

"This work may be considered as a continuation of the Bibliomania, the same characters being introduced in the dialogues. From the information which it contains, and the splendor of the decorations and printing, it will ever be considered as a model of excellence and good taste in typography and the arts. Both the copper-plates and the wood-cuts which embellished the work have been destroyed."— *Lowndes.*

580 DIBDIN. A Bibliographical Antiquarian and Picturesque Tour in France and Germany. By the Rev. Tho. Frognall Dibdin.
London: Printed for the Author. 1821.

4 *vols., imp. 8vo.*

Three volumes *extended* to FOUR, with an extra title page, in exact fac-simile, for the fourth volume: and containing in addition to the numerous engravings whieh accompany the work, nearly ONE HUNDRED FINE *inserted* ILLUSTRATIONS; all but two of which are either *proofs*, *India proofs*, or *proofs before letters;* comprising among others, a fine subscription set of "Lewis's Groups," genuine *proofs* on *India paper* obtained from the parts as originally issued; together with the ENTIRE TEXT of the work, including the very scarce and exceedingly tart eight page "Advertisement," subsequently suppressed, respecting the "little unpleasantness" between MR. LEWIS and the AUTHOR of the Tour. A complete *India proof set* of the TEN FINE PLATES engraved for the second edition of the Tour, none of which were issued with the first. The portrait of COMPTE DE BRIENNE, one of the set, is in duplicate in two states. Complete sets are of EXCESSIVE RARITY in any condition; and perhaps unfindable on *India paper*, and genuine *proofs*, as this set is guaranteed to be. There are also inserted THE PRATER AT VIENNA. — DIANE DE POICTIERS. — M. LAMOUROUX; etched by COTMAN.— The very fine and scarce PORTRAIT, from a PRIVATE PLATE, of DOM. ARTARIA.— The RARE and very beautiful PORTRAIT, also from a PRIVATE PLATE, of The ABBÉ DE LA RUE.— And an exact and artistic copy, in WATER COLOUR, from the DRAWING of DIANE DE POICTIERS the original of which was sold in London for 25 guineas.— The *large print* of the "HALT OF THE PILGRIMS," missing in many copies will be found in its place.— The "View of the Interior of the Public Library at Rouen," is in *duplicate*, in two states. The sixty-three engravings in the text are all upon *India paper*.— The large full length duplicate PORTRAIT of the COMPTE DE BRIENNE, is of EXCESSIVE RARITY; a copy was recently priced by Mr. Quaritch at four guineas.

"A work calculated to have as intoxicating an effect on the imagination of literary antiquaries, as the adventures of the heroes of the Round Table on all true knights, or the tales of the early American voyagers on the ardent spirits of their age. It has not passed, however, without some hostile (though unfounded) remarks from the printers, binders, and librarians of France."— *Wrangham.*

581 DIBDIN. [First Thoughts. Corrected Proof Sheets of the Tour in France and Germany.]

Imp. 8vo.

Nearly one hundred and forty proof pages of the "Tour in France and Germany." Covered with MR. DIBDIN'S corrections, alterations, and additions in his own hand writing. An interesting example of the elaborate process attendant upon the production of his beautiful books.

"It is very curious, consisting of a number of proof sheets of the Foreign Bibliographical Tour, with numerous alterations, remarks, &c. &c. These sheets are called First Thoughts, because the text in the published work varies considerably therefrom."

582 [DIBDIN.] Lettre Neuvième relatif à la Bibliothèque de Rouen, traduite de l'Anglais, avec des Notes par T. Licquet, Conservateur de cette Bibliothèque. *Paris:* 1821.

Imp. 8vo. ONLY ONE HUNDRED COPIES of this RARE TRACT were printed. It seldom occurs for sale.

583 [DIBDIN.] Lettre Trentième concernant l'Imprimerie et la Librairie de Paris, traduite de l'Anglais, avec des notes, par G. A. Crapelet. *Paris.* 1821.

Imp. 8vo. Only ONE HUNDRED COPIES printed; the Notes and Preface which contain much that is "silly" and "scurrilous," drew from Dr. Dibdin the following reply.

584 DIBDIN. A Roland for an Oliver; or, Brief Remarks upon the Preface and Notes of G. A. Crapelet, attached to his Translation of the Thirtieth Letter of the Bibliographical, Antiquarian, and Picturesque Tour. By the Author of that Tour. *London:* 1821.

Imp. 8vo. Of this EXCESSIVELY RARE morceau, the RAREST perhaps of all Dr. Dibdin's works, ONLY THIRTY-SIX COPIES were PRIVATELY PRINTED.

585 [DIBDIN.] Lettre d'un Relieur Français a un Bibliographe Anglais, par Lesné, Relieur, a Paris. *Paris:* 1822.

Imp. 8vo. LARGE PAPER. ONE HUNDRED COPIES *only printed.* VERY RARE.

586 [DIBDIN.] A Series of Groups, Illustrating the Physiognomy, Manners, and Character of the People of France and Germany. By George Lewis. Containing Sixty Plates suitable to Illustrate the Original Edition of the Tour in France and Germany. *London:* 1823.

4to, LARGEST PAPER. GENUINE INDIA PROOF IMPRESSIONS. VERY SCARCE in this size.

587 DIBDIN. The Library Companion; or the Young Man's Guide, and the Old Man's Comfort, in the Choice of a Library. By the Rev. T. F. Dibdin. *London:* 1824.

2 vols., roy. 8vo. LARGE PAPER. VERY SCARCE.

EIGHTY ILLUSTRATIONS *inserted:* comprising *twenty-five* beautiful INDIA PROOFS, and nearly FIFTY INDIA PROOFS BEFORE LETTERS, of the *very finest character.* The RARE PORTRAIT of the AUTHOR, from a PRIVATE PLATE *etched* by MRS. DAWSON TURNER, is also *inserted.* The volumes have been neatly and tastefully *ruled in red ink*, around the text, throughout.

From an anecdote recorded at page 394 of this edition, concerning "certain buckskins," and which is omitted in the subsequent ones, it has acquired the title of the "*Breeches Edition.*"

"It contains much curious and important bibliographical information not elsewhere to be found, and will at all times be consulted, as a work of reference, by the Bibliographer, Biographer, and Historian."—*Lowndes.*

588 DIBDIN. An Introduction to the Knowledge of Rare and Valuable Editions of the Greek and Latin Classics. Together with an Account of Polyglot Bibles, Polyglot Psalters, Hebrew Bibles, Greek Bibles and Greek Testaments; the Greek Fathers, and the Latin Fathers. By the Rev. Thomas Frognall Dibdin, D.D. Fourth Edition; greatly Enlarged and Corrected. *London:* 1827.

2 vols., Imp. 8vo. LARGE PAPER.

BEST EDITION, entirely re-written, and only *fifty copies* printed in this size to range with the "Bibliotheca Spenceriana."

589 DIBDIN. A Bibliographical, Antiquarian and Picturesque Tour in France and Germany. By the Reverend Thomas Frognall Dibdin. D.D. The Second Edition. *London: R. Jennings.* 1829.

3 vols., 8vo. TWENTY illustrations *inserted; twelve* of which are *India proofs*, and *one* a PRIVATE PLATE. Several of the plates which belong in the work are on *India paper.*

This edition omits some of the plates contained in the first, but has others which are not in that. It is esteemed for its preface, 28 pp., in whieh the author summarily disposes of CRAPELET, LICQUET, and LESNÉ.

590 [DIBDIN.] Bibliophobia. Remarks on the Present Languid and Depressed State of Literature and the Book Trade. In a Letter addressed to the Author of the Bibliomania. By Mercurius Rusticus. With Notes by Cato Parvus. *London:* 1832.

Imp. 8vo. LARGE PAPER. *One hundred copies* only printed for "Those whom it may concern." SIXTEEN fine ILLUSTRATIONS *inserted, twelve* of which are either *India proofs, proofs before letters*, or *India proofs before letters.* The beautiful plate of ARCHBISHOP PARKER'S SALT CELLAR which belongs in the work, but was issued separately, and is wanting in many copies; in this, is a fine *unlettered India proof* impression.

"Fear is the order of the day. To those very natural and long established fears of Bailiffs and Tax Gatherers, must now be added the fear of Reform, of Cholera, and of Books." P. 6.

591 DIBDIN. Reminiscences of a Literary Life; By the Reverend Thos. Frognall Dibdin, D.D. *London: John Major.* MDCCCXXXVI.

3 *vols.*, 8*vo.*

Two volumes *extended* to THREE, by the *insertion* of upwards of Two HUNDRED fine and appropriate ILLUSTRATIONS consisting of ENGRAVED PORTRAITS, AUTOGRAPH LETTERS and PRINTED MATTER, all pertinent and incidental to the work. More than two-thirds of the PORTRAITS, One Hundred and Sixty-three in number; are INDIA PROOFS and PROOFS BEFORE LETTERS, a considerable number of which are impressions from PRIVATE PLATES; and all in the finest and most perfect condition. The Index, subsequently printed, and wanting in many copies, is bound up with the work. Among the PORTRAITS from PRIVATE PLATES are those of JOHN BRITTON.— THOMAS BAKER.— DAWSON TURNER.— CHARLES BUTLER.— FRANCIS LEWIS.— E. V. UTTERSON.— JAMES BINDLEY.— SIR M. M. SYKES.— WM. UPCOTT.— And others.

The Autographs being chiefly A.N.S., are therefore, well adapted to the size of the work, and embrace, among other well known names of the friends of the AUTHOR, and his associate members of the renowned *Roxburghe Club*, (to an account of which the second volume is exclusively devoted,) the following:

Thomas Amyot	Isaac D'Israeli	William Roscoe
The Author	Francis Douce	Earl Spencer
Marquis of Blandford	Henry Ellis	Sydney Smith
Philip Bliss	Hon. Thos. Grenville	Robert Southey
Charles Burney	Richard Heber	Francis Wrangham
Sir Francis Chantrey	Sir Thos. Lawrence	James Walsh

And numerous others.

There are also inserted the Broadside "*Address*," written and presented by DIBDIN to the DUKE of WELLINGTON, on the occasion of his visit to OXFORD, in 1834, with Autograph Notes over the Author's signature.— MS. "*Bill of Fare*" for the Roxburghe Club Dinner, June 17th, 1812.— "*The Ordre of the Tostes*," for "the Roxburghe Festival," printed in BLACK LETTER upon pink paper, and surmounted by the Arms of the Club.— "*List of Members*," of the Roxburghe Club, printed for the Club, on India paper.— "*Proceedings of a Meeting*" of the Club, at which it was resolved, that "each member shall subscribe Two Guineas towards a monument for CAXTON."— The celebrated large "Broadside" invitation to an extra *Roxburghe Club Dinner*, issued by DIBDIN and HAZLEWOOD, March 19th, 1825, signed JOHN FUST and WILLIAM CAXTON.— A Prospectus of the Decameron; on two leaves.— Original title pages to "JACK JUGGLER," and "THERSYTES," HAZLEWOOD's contributions to the Roxburghe Club in 1820; three leaves.— Invitation to "*The Decameronic Banquet.*" November 1st, 1817; two leaves.— And an outline drawing of the head of Roger Wilbraham, done in pencil after death, by Mr. Utterson, and obtained by the present owner from Mr. Utterson's copy of the Decameron. &c.

592 DIBDIN. A Bibliographical Antiquarian and Picturesque Tour in the Northern Counties of England and in Scotland. By the Reverend Thomas Frognall Dibdin, D.D.

London: Printed for the Author. MDCCCXXXVIII.

3 *vols.*, *imp.* 8*vo.*

One of A FEW COPIES ONLY in which nearly all the plates are on *India paper*; several of the plates in the text in *duplicate* upon *India paper* on separate leaves; and some of the full page plates in *duplicate* in two states.

Two volumes *extended* to THREE by the *insertion* of upwards of SEVENTY beautiful and appropriate ILLUSTRATIONS; all, with the exception of three, either *Proofs*, *India Proofs* or *India Proofs before letters* in the finest state, and comprising a number of impressions from PRIVATE PLATES of a high order of rarity; among which may be named those of JOHN TROTTER BROCKETT, engraved by Collard; DAWSON TURNER, engraved by Fox; DUKE OF BUCCLEUGH, drawn by Wilkie, and engraved by F. C. Lewis; and MARGARET, daughter of James I. of Scotland, engraved by Picart for MR. DIBDIN, an impression of which was recently priced by Mr. Quaritch at five guineas, and respecting which see the "Reminiscences." vol. III. p. 906. Note. The beautiful WATER COLOUR DRAWING of Exning Vicarage was executed by Mr.

Henry Farrar, expressly for this copy. The titles for the third volume have been produced in exact fac-simile specially for the set.

In this work the author concluded his tours. It is an essential companion to France and Germany; and, as it describes some collections that have ceased to exist, possesses an historical interest.

593 DIBDIN. Bibliomania; or Book-Madness; A Bibliographical Romance. Illustrated with Cuts. By Thomas Frognall Dibdin, D.D. New and Improved Edition ... including a Key to the assumed characters in the Drama. *London: H. G. Bohn.* MDCCCXLII.

3 *vols., Imp. 8vo.*

LARGE PAPER, of which *only fifty-five copies* were printed. One volume *extended* to THREE, with extra half titles and titles printed in exact fac-simile specially for this copy. The ILLUSTRATIONS, FOUR HUNDRED AND THIRTY in number, comprise an assemblage of PORTRAITS of the persons referred to in the work; nearly all of whom are represented. The engravings are uniformly of the *finest* character, and embrace *Two Hundred and Seventy-six* PROOFS, INDIA PROOFS, and PROOFS BEFORE LETTERS, many SCARCE; others RARE; and several impressions from PRIVATE PLATES, some of which are of *excessive rarity* and high cost; in fact, almost unprocurable at any price. At page vii., will be found an *autograph note* of the AUTHOR relating to the work; his PORTRAIT engraved by HODGETTS after PHILLIPS, of which only 75 impressions were struck off, graces the title page in the first volume.

Mr. John Allan's copy which contained 297 illustrations only, produced, at his sale, $720.

THREE SPLENDID VOLUMES.

This edition was undertaken by Mr. Walmsly. It contains a Key to the characters, etc., and a supplement, edited by Dr. Dibdin himself.

"You have contrived to strew flowers over a path which, in other hands, would have proved a very dull one; and all Bibliomanes must remember you long, as he who first united their antiquarian details with good-humored raillery and cheerfulness."— *Sir Walter Scott to Dr. Dibdin.*

594 DIBDIN. Bibliomania, or Book Madness. ... . *London:* 1842.

Roy. 8vo. BEST EDITION. *Now scarce.*

"The Bibliomania is written in dialogues or conversations, the characters introduced are well-known book collectors of the author's acquaintance. The great value of the work is in the notes, which abound with anecdotes of Books and Book Collectors, and an account of the rarer articles in their collections, and the prices at which they were sold, extracted from the sale catalogues. It will be always consulted as an authority."— *Lowndes.*

---

595 DICKENSON (J.) God's | Protecting Providence, | Man's | Surest Help and Defence, | in Times of greatest Difficulty, and | the most eminent Danger, evidenced in the | remarkable Deliverance of Robert | Barrow, with divers other Persons, | from the devouring Waves of the Sea, | amongst which they suffered Shipwreck; and also from the cruel devouring Jaws | of the inhuman Canibals of Florida. | Faithfully related by one of the Persons concern'd therein, Jonathan Dickenson. | The Fifth Edition. | *London: Printed and Sold by Mary Hinde, No. 2 in George-yard, Lombard-Street.* [*n. d.*]

8vo, 7 l., pp. 126, *Books, 2 l. Half calf.* Fine clean copy. RARE.

"A highly interesting volume."— *Rich,* I. p. 130.

596 [DICKINSON (John.)] Letters from a Farmer in Pennsylvania, to the Inhabitants of the British Colonies. *Boston: Edes & Gill.* 1768.

8vo, pp. 80. *Half crimson morocco.* EXCESSIVELY RARE.

See his "Political Writings." Vol. I. p. 135.

597 [DICKINSON.] Letters from a Farmer &c. [Another Edition.] *London: J. Almon.* 1768.

8vo, pp. iii., 118. *Half maroon morocco, gilt top,* UNCUT. A beautiful copy with a SCARCE PORTRAIT of the AUTHOR *inserted.*

"My Lord Hillsborough mentioned the Farmer's Letters to me, said he had read them, that they were well written, and he believed he could guess who was the author, looking in my face at the same time, as if he thought it was me. He censured the doctrines as extremely wild, &c."—*Franklin's Letter to his Son, Memoirs,* III. 306.

598 [DICKINSON.] An Essay on the Constitutional Power of Great-Britain over the Colonies in America; with the Resolves of the Committee for the Province of Pennsylvania, and their Instructions To their Representatives in Assembly. *Philadelphia: William and Thomas Bradford.* M,DCC,LXXIV.

8vo, pp. vii., 127, (1). *Half blue morocco, carmine edges.* Title page repaired where a name has been cut from the upper corner, otherwise a fine copy of a VERY RARE work, for which the author received the thanks of the Continental Congress.

599 DICKINSON. The Political Writings of John Dickinson, Esquire, Late President of the State of Delaware, and of the Commonwealth of Pennsylvania. ... *Wilmington: Bonsal and Niles.* 1801.

2 *vols., 8vo, pp. xvi.,* 416; 384, (14). *Half calf.* A fine copy. *Very scarce.* PORTRAIT of the AUTHOR *inserted.*

600 DIES IRÆ. [Translated by M. H. Bright.] *New-York: Privately Printed.* 1866.

8vo, half purple morocco, gilt top, UNCUT, *by* BRADSTREET. THIRTY COPIES only printed. This is one of the copies with the MS. correction on p. 9.

601 **Dies Irae.** [Translated by M. H. Bright.] *New York: Privately Printed.* 1866.

8vo, half red morocco, gilt top, UNCUT, *by* BRADSTREET. BLACK LETTER. 28 *copies only printed.*

A new version of the famous old monkish song.

602 DISOSWAY (G. P.) The Earliest Churches of New York and its Vicinity. By Gabriel P. Disosway, A.M. ... *New York: James G. Gregory.* M DCCC LXV.

8vo, pp. 416. *Woodcuts. Half green morocco, gilt top,* UNCUT.

603 [D'ISRAELI (Isaac.)] Quarrels of Authors; or some Memoirs for our Literary History including Specimens of Controversy to the Reign of Elizabeth. By the Author of "Calamities of Authors." *London: John Murray.* 1814.

3 *vols., sm. 8vo, half olive morocco, gilt top,* UNCUT.

604 D'ISRAELI. Amenities of Literature; consisting of Sketches and Characters of English Literature, illustrating the Literary, Political, and Religious Vicissitudes of the English People. By I. D'Israeli. ... Second Edition. *London: Edward Moxon.* 1842.

3 *vols.*, 8*vo*, *half crimson morocco*, *gilt top*, UNCUT. BEST EDITION.

605 DISRAELI. Amenities of Literature, consisting of Sketches and Characters of English Literature. By Isaac Disraeli. A New Edition, edited by his Son, the Right Hon. B. Disraeli. *Privately Printed Riverside Press*, *Cambridge.* 1864.

2 *vols.*, 8*vo*, *half green morocco*, *gilt top*, UNCUT. LARGE PAPER: 100 *copies printed.*

606 DISRAELI. Curiosities of Literature. By Isaac Disraeli. With a View of the Life and Writings of the Author by his Son. *Privately Printed Riverside Press*, *Cambridge.* 1864.

4 *vols.*, 8*vo*, *half green morocco*, *gilt top*, UNCUT. *Portrait.* LARGE PAPER: 100 *copies printed.*

"The nicknacks of literature collected in Mr. Disraeli's cabinet were selected from sources not generally accessible to ordinary readers. These volumes are not only admirably adapted to minister to the amusement of the lounger and refined trifler, but they have higher capacities, as curious and authentic pictures of the manners of ruder times, and records of the progress of letters from their rise in the dark middle ages, to almost the present era."

607 DIXON (W. H.) Personal History of Lord Bacon. From unpublished Papers. By William Hepworth Dixon of the Inner Temple. *Boston: Ticknor and Fields.* 1861.

8*vo*, *half blue morocco*, *gilt top*, UNCUT. Uniform with Bacon's Works. Fine PORTRAIT of BACON *inserted.* LARGE PAPER: 75 *copies only printed.*

See Bacon (F.) No. 102.

608 DOANE (G. W.) One World: One Washington. The Oration in the City Hall, Burlington, on Washington's Birthday, 1859; by request of the Lady Managers of the Mount Vernon Association, and Many Citizens of Burlington. By the Rt. Rev. George Washington Doane, D.D. ... *Burlington: N. J.* MDCCCLIX.

8*vo*, *pp.* 32. *Half green morocco*, *gilt top*, UNCUT. PROOF BEFORE LETTER PORTRAIT of WASHINGTON *inserted.*

609 DONCK (A. v. d.) Beschryvinge | Van | Nieuvv-Nederlant, | (Gelijck het tegenwoordigh in Staet is) | Begrijpende de Nature, Aert, gelegentheyt en vruchtbaerheyt | van het selve Landt; mitsgaders de proffijtelijcke ende gewenste toevallen, die | aldaer tot onderhoudt der Menschen, (soo uyt haer selven als van buyten inge- | bracht) gevonden worden. Als mede de maniere en ongemeyne Eygenschap- | pen vande Wilden ofte Naturellen vanden Lande. Ende een bysonder verhael | vanden wonderlijcken Aert ende het Weesen der Bevers. | Dær noch by-gevoeght is | Een Discours over de gelegentheyt van Nieuw-Nederlandt | tusschen een Nederlandts Patriot, ende een Nieuw

Nederlander. | Beschreven door | Adriaen van der Donck, | Beyder Rechten Doctoor, die tegenwoordigh | noch in Nieuw-Nederlandt is. | En hier achter by gevoeght | Het voordeeligh Reglement vande Ed : Hoog. Achtbare | Heeren de Heeren Burgermeesteren deser Stede, | betreffende de saken van Nieuw-Nederlandt. | Den tweeden Druck. | Met een pertinent Kærtje van t' zelve Landt verçiert, | en van veel druck-fouten gesuyvert. | *t'Aemsteldam*, | *By Evert Nieuwenhof*, *Boeck-verkooper*, *woonende op* | *'t Ruslandt*, *in't Schrijf-Boeck*, *Anno* 1656. | *Met Privilegie voor* 15 *Jaren.* |

4to, 4 *l.*, *pp.* 100, *Register*, (4), *Conditien*, 4 *l. Map. Crushed red levant morocco*, *paneled sides*, *corner ornaments*, *gilt top*, UNCUT, *by* F. BEDFORD. EXCESSIVELY RARE in *uncut* condition.

This second edition contains a map, which is not in the first. The map is entitled, "Nova Belgica, sive Nieuw Nederlandt," and is copied from the rare map of N. J. Vischer. *See* Asher's list of the "Maps and Charts of N. Netherland," p. 12.

"A large part of this very rare work is devoted to a description of the natives of the New Netherlands. Van der Donck arrived in New Amsterdam in 1642. He served as the sheriff of the colony of Rensselaerwyck, and purchased an estate on the Hudson, near the site of the village of Yonkers. Before this work was published, he had printed *An Exposition of the New Netherlands* (Hague, 1650,) in which the administrations of Kieft and Stuyvesant were vigorously assailed. A division of the work before us, found on page 52, is entitled, "Of the Manners and peculiar Customs of the Natives of the New-Netherlands." This is subdivided into twenty-two sections, each treating of some of the peculiarities of the savages of the state of New York. The whole covering pp. 52 to 81. The treatise possesses an interest beyond its rarity, in being the relation of an educated man, regarding the Indians of the island and neighborhood of New-York. The work was translated by Gen. J. Johnson, and printed in the sixth volume of the New York Historical Society."— *Field.*

610 DONCK. A Description of the New Netherlands, (as the same are at the Present Time ;) comprehending the Fruitfulness and Natural Advantages of the Country, and the Desirable Opportunities which it presents, within itself, and from Abroad for the Subsistance of Man ; which are not surpassed elsewhere. Together with Remarks on the Character and Peculiar Customs of the Savages, or Natives of the Land ; Also, a Particular Description of the Wonderful Nature and Habits of the Beaver. With a Dialogue between a Netherland Patriot and a New Netherlander, on the Advantages of the Country. Written by Adriaen Van der Donck, Doctor of both Laws, at present in the New Netherlands. To which are added, the Regulations of the Affairs of the Country, by the Council of the City of Amsterdam, etc. The second edition, with a map of the country. At Amsterdam, published by Evert Nieuwenhof, book-seller. Anno Domini, 1656. [*New York : Reprinted.* 1841.]

8vo, *half green morocco*, *gilt top*, *by* BRADSTREET. PORTRAIT of PETER STUYVESANT *inserted.*

Translated from the Original Work, by Gen. J. Johnson, for the "Collections of the New York Historical Society."

611 DONCK. Remonstrance of New Netherland, and the Occurrences there. Addressed to the High and Mighty Lords States General of the United Netherlands, on the 28th July 1649. With Secretary

Van Tienhoven's Answer. Translated from a copy of the original Dutch MS. By E. B. O'Callaghan, M.D.
Albany: Weed, Parsons & Company. 1856.

4to, pp. 65, (1). *Half green morocco.* Forms part of the "Documentary History of New York." A few copies only issued with a separate title *for presentation.*

"This is not a translation of that *Vertoogh* translated by Mr. Murphy for the New York Historical Society, and issued in a quarto volume by Mr. Lenox, but of the transcript of the Notarial copy of the Original MS. at the Hague."— *Introduction.*

612 [DORCHESTER.] Public Expression of Grief, for the Death of General George Washington, at Dorchester. [Followed by:] An Eulogy on General George Washington, who Died on the 14th of Dec. 1799. Pronounced at Dorcester Feb. 22, 1800. It being the Day recommended by Congress, for the National Lamentation of his Death. By Oliver Everett, Esq. A.M, ... *Charlestown:* M. DCCC.

8vo, pp. 6, 22.

613 [DORCHESTER.] The Fraternal Tribute of Respect Paid to the Masonic Character of Washington, in the Union Lodge in Dorchester, January 7th, A.L. 5800. *Charlestown:* M,DCCC.

8vo, pp. 14.

Published by the Town, and one copy delivered to each family. The collection is very rare. The Discourse was delivered by Thaddeus Mason Harris.

614 DOUCE (F.) Illustrations of Shakspeare, and of Ancient Manners; With Dissertations on the Clowns and Fools of Shakspeare; on the collection of Popular Tales entitled Gesta Romanorum; and on the English Morris Dance. By Francis Douce. The Illustrations on Wood by J. Berryman. *London: Longmans.* 1807.

2 *vols., 8vo, half green morocco, gilt top,* UNCUT. The short fore edge of the title in volume II., has been restored in this copy. PORTRAIT of MR. DOUCE *inserted.* BEST EDITION. VERY SCARCE. Clean and fine as when issued.

"Of this literary writer, notices are copiously strewed over the three volumes of the Bibliographical Decameron."— *Wrangham.*

615 DOUGLASS (F.) Narrative of the Life of Frederick Douglass, An American Slave. Written by Himself. *London:* 1847.

12mo. Portrait. Half green calf.

An edition not quoted in Sabin's Dictionary.

616 DOUGLASS (W.) A Summary, Historical and Political, of the First Planting, Progressive Improvements, and Present State of the British Settlements in North America. ... By William Douglass, M.D. ...
London: R. Baldwin. 1755.

2 *vols., 8vo, half calf antique.* A *fine copy.*

An exact reprint of the Boston edition of 1749, with the addition of a map.

617 DOWLING (J.) History of Romanism : from the Earliest corruptions of Christianity to the Present time. ... With Numerous Accurate and Highly Finished Engravings of its Ceremonies, Superstitions, Persecutions, and Historical Incidents. By Rev. John Dowling, A.M. *New-York : Edward Walker.* 1847.

8vo, green morocco, emblematically tooled and gilt sides, gilt edges, by WALKER. FINE COPY with 52 Illustrative Engravings.

618 [DOWSE (T.)] The Dowse Library. Proceedings of the Massachusetts Historical Society, relating to the Donations from Thomas Dowse ; with the Eulogy by Edward Everett. *Boston : Printed for Private Distribution.* 1859.

8vo, pp. v., 80, 3 *Plates. Cloth, gilt edges.* PRIVATELY PRINTED.

619 DRAKE (J. R.) The Culprit Fay, and other Poems. By John Rodman Drake. *New York : George Dearborn.* 1835.

8vo, half green morocco, gilt top, UNCUT. PORTRAIT of MR. HALLECK *inserted.*

620 DRAKE (S. G.) Biography and History of the Indians of North America ; comprising a General Account of them, and Details in the Lives of all the most distinguished Chiefs, and others, who have been noted, among the various Nations upon the Continent. Also a History of their Wars ; their Manners and Customs ; and the most celebrated Speeches of their Orators, from their first being known to Europeans to the Present Time. Likewise exhibiting an Analysis, of the most Distinguished, as well as Absurd Authors, who have written upon the great question of the first peopling of America. By Samuel G. Drake. Third Edition, with ... Additions ... Corrections and ... Engravings. *Boston : O. L. Perkins.* 1834.

8vo, pp. 518, 30. 8 *Plates. Half gray calf, gilt top,* UNCUT. SIXTEEN PORTRAITS *inserted.*

621 DRAKE. Indian Captivities ; being a Collection of the most remarkable Narratives of Persons taken Captive by the North American Indians ; or Relations of those who by Stratagem or desperate Valor, have effected the most surprising Escapes from their cruel hands. To which are added, Notes, Historical, Biographical, &c. By Samuel G. Drake. *Boston :* 1839.

12mo, pp. 360. *Half morocco.* A fine copy. *Very Scarce.* An interesting AUTOGRAPH LETTER of the AUTHOR relating to the composition of the work, and a PROOF BEFORE LETTER FRONTISPIECE *inserted.*

622 DRAKE. Biography and History of the Indians of North America, from its First Discovery. By Samuel G. Drake. ... Eleventh Edition. *Boston : Benjamin B. Mussey & Co.* 1851.

8vo, pp. 720. 39 *Plates. Half calf antique.* Of this edition FIFTY-SIX COPIES only were struck off on *superfine paper,* each of which had 39 steel and copper plates, with a printed list of the same.

The last and most complete edition, published under the eye of the author, of this very excellent and carefully compiled collection of the materials of Indian history. It is the result of a lifetime of labor, by one who spared no pains to be faithful to the completeness and truthfulness of history.

623 DRAKE. The History and Antiquities of Boston, the Capital of Massachusetts and Metropolis of New England, from its Settlement in 1630, to the Year 1770. Also, an Introductory History of the Discovery and Settlement of New England. With Notes, Critical and Illustrative. By Samuel G. Drake, A.M. ...
Boston: Published by the Author. 1856–7.

2 vols., imp. 4to, half red levant morocco, gilt top, UNCUT. LARGE PAPER; *100 copies only printed;* with the extra title page, and the scarce and fine PORTRAIT of the AUTHOR from a PRIVATE PLATE.

This SPLENDID SET contains ONE HUNDRED AND SIX ADDITIONAL ILLUSTRATIONS, many of which are SCARCE, and several PROOFS ON INDIA PAPER.

624 DRAKE. Result of Some Researches Among the British Archives for Information Relative to the Founders of New England: Made in the Years 1858, 1859 and 1860. Originally Collected for and Published in the New England Historical and Genealogical Register, and now Corrected and Enlarged. By Samuel G. Drake.
Boston: 1860.

4to, pp. 131. *Map and 2 Plates. Half blue morocco, gilt top,* UNCUT.

"The researches of Mr. Drake prove most satisfactorily that the Pilgrim Fathers did not belong to the higher circles of English society."

625 DRAKE. A Brief Memoir of Sir Walter Raleigh, prepared for and published in the New England Historical and Genealogical Register for April, 1862, and now Reprinted with Additions, by Samuel G. Drake. *Boston: Printed for the Author for private distribution.* 1862.

4to, pp. 55. *Portrait. Half green levant morocco, gilt top,* UNCUT. LARGE PAPER. *Only 25 copies printed.* An INDIA PROOF PORTRAIT of RALEIGH after ZUCHERRO *inserted.*

626 DRAKE. The Old Indian Chronicle; being a Collection of Exceeding Rare Tracts, written and published in the Time of King Philip's War, by Persons residing in the Country. To which are now added an Introduction and Notes, by Samuel G. Drake.
Boston: Samuel A. Drake. 1867.

4to, pp. ix., (3), 333. *Map. Half red morocco, gilt top,* UNCUT, *by* BRADSTREET.

627 DRAKE. A Particular History of the Five Years' French and Indian War in New England and Parts Adjacent, from its Declaration by the King of France, March 15, 1744, to the Treaty with the Eastern Indians, Oct. 16, 1749, sometimes called Governor Shirley's War. With a Memoir of Major-General Shirley, accompanied by his Portrait and other Engravings. By Samuel G. Drake.
Albany: Joel Munsell. 1870.

4to, pp. 312. *Portrait and Cuts. Half red morocco, gilt top,* UNCUT, *by* BRADSTREET.

"This very excellent and judicious collection of the principal incidents of the "Five Years War," contains, besides the Annals of that period, some personal narratives of much interest."—*Field.*

628 DRAYTON (J.) Letters written during a Tour through the Northern and Eastern States of America; by John Drayton.
Charleston, South-Carolina: Printed by Harrison and Bowen. M,DCC,XCIV.

8vo, pp. iv., (8), 3–138. 3 *Plates. Crimson morocco, gilt top,* UNCUT. An EXCEEDINGLY SCARCE PORTRAIT of the AUTHOR *inserted.* The work contains CURIOUS CONTEMPORARY VIEWS of New York city 80 years ago.

Mr. Drayton was a district judge, and subsequently Governor of South Carolina. This early production is but little known, and is EXTREMELY RARE.

629 DRAYTON. Memoirs of the American Revolution, from its Commencement to the year 1776, inclusive; as relating to the State of South Carolina; and occasionally referring to the States of North Carolina and Georgia. By John Drayton, L.L.D.
Charleston: A. E. Miller. 1821.

2 *vols., 8vo, pp. xxvii.,* 430; (2), 400. *Portrait. Half blue morocco, gilt top,* UNCUT. PORTRAIT *inserted.* A beautiful copy. SCARCE.

630 DRING (T.) Recollections of the Jersey Prison-Ship; taken, and prepared for Publication, from the Original Manuscript of the late Captain Thomas Dring, of Providence, R. I., One of the Prisoners. By Albert G. Greene. *Providence: H. H. Brown.* 1829.

12mo, pp. 167. *Plate. Half green morocco, gilt top.* FIRST EDITION. FINE COPY. EXCESSIVELY RARE.

Greene's copy sold for $21.00.

631 DRING. Recollections of the Jersey Prison-Ship; &c. [Another Edition.] *New York: P. M. Davis.* 1831.

12mo, pp. 167. *Plate. Half olive morocco, gilt top.* Folded Plan of "Wallabout Bay at the time of the Revolution." *inserted.* EXCESSIVELY SCARCE. Not recorded in Sabin's Dictionary.

This was the Davis copy, at whose sale it brought $30.

632 DRING. Recollections of the Jersey Prison-Ship; from the Original Manuscripts of Captain Thomas Dring, one of the Prisoners. Edited by Henry B. Dawson. *Morrisania: N. Y.* 1865.

Roy. 8vo, Portrait, Map and Plans. Half scarlet morocco, gilt top, UNCUT. *One hundred copies* only printed in this size.

633 DRUMMOND (W.) Poetical Works, of William Drummond of Hawthornden. Edited by William Turnbull.
London: John Russell Smith. 1856.

Sm. 8vo, half olive morocco, gilt top, UNCUT.

634 [DUANE (William.)] A Letter to George Washington, President of the United States; containing Strictures on his Address of the

Seventeenth of September, 1796, notifying his Relinquishment of the Presidential Office. By Jasper Dwight, of Vermont.
Printed at Philadelphia, for the Author, Dec. 1796.

8vo, pp. 48, 16. *Half green morocco, gilt top,* UNCUT. Contemporary PORTRAIT of WASHINGTON *inserted.* This copy contains "Washington's Farewell Address," pp. 16, following the letter, which was written under an assumed name.

635 DUCHÉ (J.) The Duty of Standing Fast in our Spiritual and Temporal Liberties, a Sermon Preached ... July 7th, 1775, Before the First Battalion of the City and Liberties of Philadelphia .... By the Reverend Jacob Duché, M.A.
Philadelphia: James Humphreys, Jun. 1775.

pp. iv., 25. DEDICATED TO GENERAL WASHINGTON.

[Also:] The American Vine, a Sermon preached ... before the Honourable Continental Congress, July 20th, 1775. Being the day recommended by them for a General Fast throughout the United English Colonies of America. By the Rev. Jacob Duché, M.A.
Philadelphia: James Humphreys, Jun. 1775.

8vo, pp. 34. *2 pieces in one vol. Half green morocco.* An interesting AUTOGRAPH LETTER and a fine ORIGINAL PORTRAIT of the AUTHOR *inserted.*

Two RARE Revolutionary Sermons. "Duché, like Galloway, a co-labourer in the early career of the Revolution, was supposed to be a firm supporter of the cause, and in consequence was appointed chaplain to the Continental Congress, but subsequently, from fear, or some other less laudable reason, after having put his hand to the plough, he looked back, and abandoned the cause."

636 [DUCHÉ.] Caspipina's Letters; containing Observations on a variety of subjects, Literary, Moral, and Religious. Written by a Gentleman who resided some time in Philadelphia. To which is added, The Life and Character of Wm. Penn, Esq.; Original Proprietor of Pennsylvania. ... *Bath: R. Cruttwell.* MDCCLXXVII.

2 vols., 16mo, bound in one. Half red morocco, gilt top, UNCUT. PORTRAIT of the AUTHOR *inserted.* An elegant copy, and RARE in *uncut* condition.

The life of William Penn, annexed to this edition of Duché, was written by Edmund Rack, of Bath, and the whole work was edited by him; it includes an entire reprint of "A brief account of the Province of Pennsylvania," published by Penn in 1681, in folio. Duché was "The Assistant Minister Of Christ's Church And St. Peter's In Philadelphia In North America," and his signature of "Tamoc Caspipina" forms the initial letters of those words.

637 DUCHÉ. Discourses on various Subjects, By Jacob Duché, M.A. Formerly Rector of Christ-Church and St. Peter's, in Philadelphia, and late Chaplain to the Asylum for Female Orphans in the Parish of Lambeth, Surry. The Third Edition. ... *London: T. Cadell.* 1790.

2 vols., 8vo, half olive morocco, gilt top, UNCUT. Frontispieces engraved by SHARP, from Drawings by BENJAMIN WEST.

Adams gives an interesting account of the scene when Duché made the first prayer in Congress, and in conclusion says, "Duché is one of the most ingenious men, and best characters, and greatest orators in the Episcopal order,—yet a zealous friend of liberty and of his country." "Duché's reputation, however, has a less amiable and honorable side; of him it has been written: 'He, whose sublime prayer as Chaplain of the Continental Congress, melted the hearts of his audience every time he bent to repeat it, fell away from his loyalty, and enjoys the sole infamy of having sought to corrupt Washington.' "—*Tuckerman's America*, p. 81.

638 DUER (W. A.) Letter, addressed to Cadwallader D. Colden, Esquire. In Answer to the Strictures, contained in his "Life of Robert Fulton." Upon the Report of the Select Committee to whom was referred a Memorial relative to Steam Navigation, presented to the Legislature of New York, at the Session of 1814. With an Appendix ... . By William Alexander Duer, Esquire. *Albany: E. and E. Hosford.* 1817.

8vo, pp. 127. *Half morocco.* TWO ILLUSTRATIONS *inserted.*
See Colden (C. D.) No. 433.

639 DUER. The Life of William Alexander, Earl of Stirling; Major General in the Army of the United States, during the Revolution: with Selections from his Correspondence. By his Grandson, William Alexander Duer, LL.D. *New York: Wiley & Putnam.* 1847.

8vo, pp. xii., 272. *Portrait and* 5 *Plans.* *Half calf, carmine edges.* Large and fine copy with TWENTY-FOUR ILLUSTRATIONS *inserted.*

640 DUER. Reminiscences of an Old Yorker. By the late William A. Duer, LL.D., President of Columbia College, etc. *New York: Printed for W. L. Andrews.* 1867.

4to, pp. 102. *Half crushed green levant morocco, gilt top,* UNCUT, *by* W MATTHEWS. *Privately Printed* for W. L. ANDREWS, ESQ., and only THIRTY-FIVE COPIES issued. An elegant and most desirable volume, with *Eighteen* ILLUSTRATIONS *inserted,* most of which are FINE INDIA PROOFS. An UNLETTERED PROOF of the RARE PORTRAIT of EGBERT BENSON from a PRIVATE PLATE is also inserted.

These articles on Old New York originally appeared in the "American Mail," 1847, and have become so scarce that but one copy could be obtained, from which to reprint this volume.

641 DUNHAM (J.) A Funeral Oration on George Washington, Late General of the Armies of the United States. Pronounced, at Oxford, Massachusetts, at the request of the Field Officers of the Brigade Stationed at that place, on the 15th Jan., 1800; ... By Josiah Dunham, A.M., Capt. 16th U. S. Regiment. *Boston:* [1800.]

8vo, pp. 20. UNCUT. *Scarce.*

642 [DUNLAP (William.)] André: a Tragedy in five acts: as now performing at the Theatre in New York. To which is added the Cow-Chase: a Satirical Poem. By Major André: With the proceedings of the Court Martial; and Authentic Documents concerning him. *London: printed for David Ogilvy and Son.* 1799.

8vo, pp. 110. *Half olive morocco, gilt top,* FINE and LARGE COPY. VERY SCARCE, and the ONLY COPY we are able to trace.

643 DUNLAP (W.) History of the American Theatre. By William Dunlap. ... *London: Bentley.* 1833.

4 *vols., 8vo.* *Purple morocco extra, gilt top,* UNCUT.

Two volumes *extended to* FOUR, with RUBRICATED TITLES printed expressly for the set; and ONE HUNDRED AND SIXTY-TWO ILLUSTRATIONS *inserted:* all fine impressions, and nearly one-fourth of which are PROOFS, and PRINTS on INDIA PAPER. The collection comprises numerous VERY RARE PORTRAITS, among which are fine ORIGINAL impressions of MR. AND MRS. HODGKINSON; JOHN HOWARD PAYNE; FENNELL; SIMPSON; MR. and MRS. JOHNSON; MRS. MERRY; JEFFERSON; MISS BRUNTON; MRS. DARLEY; HILSON; EDWIN; &c., and many others which are now almost unprocurable.

AN ELEGANT AND UNIQUE SET.

A SPLENDIDLY ILLUSTRATED COPY

OF

644 DUNLAP. History of the Rise and Progress of the Arts of Design in the United States. By William Dunlap. *New York:* 1834.

6 *vols.*, 8*vo*, *crushed green levant morocco*, *paneled sides*, *corner ornaments*, *gilt top*, UNCUT, in the best style of MR. MATTHEWS.

Two volumes *extended to* SIX, with RUBRICATED TITLES printed expressly for the set, and an INDIA PROOF VIGNETTE mounted in each. The *inserted* ILLUSTRATIONS exceed FIVE HUNDRED in number, ALL of which are UNEXCEPTIONALLY FINE and APPROPRIATE, and many of which could not, probably, now be duplicated.

This BEAUTIFULLY BOUND, and ELEGANTLY ILLUSTRATED work is one of the GEMS of this collection; and is, perhaps, at once, one of the MOST EXTENSIVELY as well as MOST TASTEFULLY ILLUSTRATED sets in existence. As intending purchasers will examine and decide for themselves, we refrain from attempting to describe the contents of this UNIQUE, ELEGANT, and HIGHLY INTERESTING BOOK, further than to quote what here follows from an intelligent correspondent of the New York Evening Mail. "Among the illustrations will be found portraits of almost all the prominent American artists named in the work, and engraved specimens, so far as they could be procured, of the style or manner of each individual painter or engraver. In illustrating this book its present owner has exhibited admirable judgment in the selection of specimens of the different styles of our artists. He has in all cases endeavoured to secure an impression from the very block or plate criticised or otherwise spoken of in the text. This is the true and only correct method of illustrating such works; here we have the engraving on one page and on the other a criticism of it — the artist and the critic communing as it were, together."

The following work which may be considered as a continuation of this, is uniform in size and style of binding, and should accompany it.

645 CUMMINGS (T. S.) Historic Annals of the National Academy of Design, New York Drawing Association, etc., with Occasional Dottings by the Way-side, from 1825 to the Present Time. By Thos. S. Cummings, N.A. ... *Philadelphia: George W. Childs.* 1865.

8*vo*, *pp.* 364. *Half green levant morocco*, *gilt top*, UNCUT, *by* W. MATTHEWS. A COLOURED *photographic* PORTRAIT of the AUTHOR, and THIRTY-FIVE ILLUSTRATIONS *inserted.* Uniform with the preceding No.

Published by subscription only, and now scarce. Contains the fullest account published of the controversies and difficulties attending the formation of the "National Academy of Design."

646 DUNLAP (W.) History of the Arts of Design. [Another Copy.] *New York:* 1834.

2 *vols.*, 8*vo*, *half crushed red levant morocco*, *gilt top*, UNCUT, *by* W. MATTHEWS. An UNLETTERED INDIA PROOF PORTRAIT of the AUTHOR, and one of MR. LESLIE, the artist, in same state, *inserted.*

A SPLENDID COPY.

647 DUNLAP. History of the New Netherlands, Province of New York, and State of New York, to the Adoption of the Federal Constitution. By William Dunlap.
New York: Printed for the Author. 1839-40.

2 vols., 8vo. Portrait of Peter Stuyvesant, and Maps. Half blue morocco, gilt top. A very large copy with an UNLETTERED ARTIST'S PROOF PORTRAIT of the AUTHOR, and other ILLUSTRATIONS *inserted.*

648 DUNTON (J.) The Life and Errors of John Dunton, ... with the Lives and Characters of more than a Thousand Contemporary Divines, and other persons of Literary Eminence. To which are added Dunton's Conversation in Ireland; Selections from his other Genuine Works; and a faithful Portrait of the Author. [Edited by John Nichols.] *London: J. Nichols, Son, and Bentley.* 1818.

2 vols., 8vo, pp. xxxii., 776. Portrait. Half green morocco, gilt top, UNCUT, *by* BRADSTREET. Very SCARCE in *uncut* condition.

Eighty-four pages are occupied with the account of his visit to New England, his opening a bookstore in Boston; intercourse with the Mathers, John Cotton, Eliot, Hubbard, Indian sachems, and several ladies of Boston, of some of whom he relates very curious particulars.

649 DUYCKINCK (E. A.) *and* (G. L.) Cyclopedia of American Literature; embracing Personal and Critical Notices of Authors, and Selections from their Writings, from the earliest period to the present day. ... By Evart A. and George L. Duyckinck.
New York: Charles Scribner. 1855-66.

3 vols., imp. 8vo. Half green levant morocco, gilt top, UNCUT. Griswold's pungent critique on the work pp. 32, now EXCESSIVELY RARE, and an article from the N. A. Review, pp. 30, both inlaid to the size of the work, are bound up with volume 1.

A FINE SET.

The work contains personal and critical notices of authors, and selections from their writings, with 225 woodcut portraits, 425 facsimile autographs, and 75 views of colleges, etc. The editions of a later date are on thinner paper. The Supplement, which forms the third volume in this set, contains sketches of the old Spanish writers on America by Buckingham Smith, and notices of early French writers by John Gilmary Shea.

650 DWIGHT (T.) The Conquest of Canaan; A Poem in Eleven Books. By Timothy Dwight.
Hartford: Elisha Babcock. M,DCC,LXXXV.

12mo, pp. (8), 304, (1). *Half calf.* Two PORTRAITS *inserted.* A fine copy of the First Epic Poem published in America.

DEDICATED TO GENERAL WASHINGTON.

651 DWIGHT. A Discourse delivered at New-Haven, Feb. 22, 1800; on the Character of George Washington, Esq., at the Request of the Citizens; By Timothy Dwight, D.D. ...
New Haven: 1800.

8vo, pp. 55. UNCUT.

652 DWIGHT. Travels in New-England and New-York. By Timothy Dwight, ... Illustrated with Maps, &c. *London: W. Bayne & Son.* 1823.

4 vols., 8vo, half calf, gilt top, UNCUT. BEST EDITION.

A most interesting and valuable work on the physics, geography, scenery, natural history, including geology, mineralogy, &c., vegetation, government, notices of eminent men and others, of the United States.

653 DWIGHT (T.) History of the Hartford Convention: with a Review of the Policy of the United States Government, which led to the War of 1812. By Theodore Dwight, Secretary of the Convention. *New York: N. and J. White.* 1833.

8vo, pp. 447. *Half calf, carmine edges.* LARGE and FINE COPY. SCARCE.

654 EATON (J. H.) The Life of Andrew Jackson, Major General in the Service of the United States: Comprising a History of the War in the South, from the Commencement of the Creek Campaign, to the Termination of Hostilities before New Orleans. ... By John Henry Eaton. *Philadelphia: Samuel F. Bradford.* 1824.

8vo, pp. 468. *Portrait. Half red morocco, gilt top,* UNCUT. An AUTOGRAPH LETTER of the AUTHOR, and PORTRAIT *inserted.*

655 ECCLESTON (T.) An | Epistle | by way of | Encouragement to Friends | to be frequent at | Week-Day Meetings. | By Theodore Eccleston. | *London Printed, and Reprinted by* | WILLIAM BRADFORD *in New York:* 1732.

12mo, pp. 8. *Polished calf, gilt top,* UNCUT, *by* F. BEDFORD. One of the RAREST EXAMPLES of BRADFORD'S PRESS.

656 ECHO. (THE) [*New York:*] *Printed at the Porcupine Press, by Pasquin Petronius.* [1807.]

8vo, pp. xv., 331, (10), 8 *Plates. Half green morocco, gilt top,* UNCUT.
The authors were Alsop, Dwight, Cogswell, Hopkins, and Trumbull.

657 EDDIS (W.) Letters from America, Historical and Descriptive; comprising Occurrences from 1769, to 1777, inclusive. By William Eddis, late Surveyor of the Customs, &c., at Annapolis, in Maryland.... *London: Printed for the Author.* M DCC XCII.

8vo, 25l., pp. 445. *Half purple levant morocco, gilt top,* UNCUT. FINE COPY, and SCARCE in *uncut* condition.

Valuable as indicating the state of public feeling anterior to the Revolution. "Mr. Eddis's letters are forty in number. The first contains an account of the country, the government, trade, manners and customs of the inhabitants, followed by others, giving an account of the progress of the war, till his departure from New York. The concluding letters narrate the difficulties and dangers which the author experienced, in consequence of his refusing to take the oath tendered him by the Americans."—*M. R. viii.* 124.

658 [EDDY (Thomas.)] An Account of the State Prison or Penitentiary House, in the City of New-York. By one of the Inspectors of the Prison. *New York: Isaac Collins and Son.* 1801.

8vo, half red morocco, gilt top, UNCUT, *by* BRADSTREET. Contains engraved Elevation and Ground Plan of the Old State Prison. VERY SCARCE.

659 EDINBURGH REVIEW. Selections from the Edinburgh Review; comprising the Best Articles in that Journal, from its Commencement to the present time. ... Edited by Maurice Cross.
London: Longman. 1833.

8vo, half crimson morocco, gilt top, UNCUT. An elegant set, and VERY SCARCE in *uncut* condition.

A judicious selection from the ablest journal of the day, comprising the brilliant essays of Lord Brougham, Lord Jeffrey, Sydney Smith, Lord Macaulay, and a host of other eminent writers.

660 EDWARDS (E.) Memoirs of Libraries; Including a Hand Book of Library Economy. By Edward Edwards.
London: Trübner & Co. 1859.

2 vols., roy. 8vo, half olive levant morocco, gilt top, UNCUT. LARGE PAPER; a *few copies only* printed.
Contains numerous *Engravings from early MSS., Facsimiles of Types, Bookbinding, etc.* This important work was in preparation thirteen years. Neither France nor Germany can boast of a work treating the subjects with a similar comprehensiveness, and in England the work has certainly had no predecessor.

661 EDWARDS. Libraries and Founders of Libraries. By Edward Edwards. *London: Trübner and Co.* 1865.

Roy. 8vo, half olive levant morocco, gilt top, UNCUT. LARGE PAPER; of which THIRTY COPIES ONLY were printed.

This valuable bibliographical work is in a large measure based upon documents hitherto unused, and upon personal examination of the principal collections which are described.

662 EDWARDS. Lives of the Founders of the British Museum: with Notices of its Chief Augmentors and other Benefactors. 1570–1870. By Edward Edwards. *London: Trübner and Co.* 1870.

2 vols., imp. 8vo, half crushed red levant morocco, gilt top, UNCUT, *by* W. MATTHEWS. LARGE PAPER; THIRTY COPIES ONLY printed. Two fine and rare PORTRAITS *inserted.* A SPLENDID COPY. UNIQUE, in TWO VOLUMES with RUBRICATED TITLES.

663 EDWARDS (J.) A Faithful Narrative of the Surprising Work of God in the Conversion of many Hundred Souls in Northampton, and the Neighbouring Towns and Villages of New-Hampshire, and New-England. In a Letter to the Reverend Dr. Benjamin Colman of Boston. By the Revd. Mr. Edwards, Minister of Northampton. And published with a large Preface, by Dr. Watts and Dr. Guyse. To which is added, True Grace, distinguished from the Experience of Devils; in a Sermon, preached before the Synod of New-York. A New American Edition.
Elizabeth-Town: Printed by Shepard Kolloch. M,DCC,XC.

12mo, pp. 125, 43. *Half calf.* FINE COPY of a RARE EDITION.

664 EGEDE (H.) A Description of Greenland. By Hans Egede, who was a Missionary in that Country for Twenty-five Years. A New Edition. With an Historical Introduction and a Life of the Author.

Illustrated with a Map of Greenland, and Numerous Engravings on Wood. *London: T. and J. Allman.* 1818.

8vo, pp. cxviii., 225. Map and Engravings. Half green morocco, gilt top, UNCUT, *by* BRADSTREET.

"Although the quaint relation of the Danish missionary Egede affords us little information regarding the natives of Greenland which has not often been printed, yet his narratives of incidents among them, and descriptions of their characteristics at that early day (1721), are valuable as historical records."— *Field.*

665 [ELIOT (John).] The | Holy Bible: | containing the | Old Testament | and the *New.* | Translated into the | Indian Language, | *and* | Ordered to be Printed by the *Commissioners* of *the Vnited Colonies* | in *New-England,* | At the Charge, and with the Consent of the | Corporation in *England* | *For the Propagation of the Gospel amongst the* Indians | *in* New-England. | Cambridge: Printed by *Samuel Green* and *Marmaduke Johnson.* | MDCLXIII. |

Small 4to.

Collation. Title, 1 l. Dedication to King Charles II., 2 l. List of Books 1 l. Text A to M *m m m m* in 4s. Title.— Wusku | Wuttestamentum, | Nul-Lordumun | Jesus Christ | Nuppoquohwussuaeneumun. | Cambridge: | Printed by *Samuel Green* and *Marmaduke Johnson.* | MDCLXI. | 1 l.; verso, blank; Text: Matthew to the end of Luke, sigs. A2 to verso of L4; John to Rev. Aa to verso of Xx3, all in 4s; 1 leaf blank. *VVame* | Ketoohomae uketoohomaongash | DAVID. | U to N in 4s; Noowomoo, 1 l. Size of printed page in full, $6\frac{5}{8}$ inches by $4\frac{5}{8}$ inches. OF THE LEAF, $7\frac{1}{2}$ BY $5\frac{7}{8}$ INCHES.

This is one of the copies having the DEDICATION TO KING CHARLES, of which, according to Thomas, (*Hist. of Printing.*) TWENTY COPIES ONLY *were printed.*

It has been newly bound by MR. FRANCIS BEDFORD, who pronounced it to be the FINEST COPY he had ever seen, and who thus describes his own work. "*Olive Levant gros grained morocco; Elegantly Ornamented back, and double paneled sides, Diamond Centre and Diamond Corners in rich Harleian style, joints inside richly hand tooled, and crimson silk linings against marble paper facings, double silk head bands, enclosed in a Solander Case of blue English morocco, full gilt and lettered back, lined with white velvet.*"

Mr. J. H. Trumbull's Translation of the Catechism at the end of the volume, of which *a few copies only* were printed for presentation to the owners of copies of the Bible, will accompany it. The Translation matches and ranges with the Solander case containing the Bible, and was also bound by MR. BEDFORD.

This copy was a duplicate from the Bodleian Library at Oxford, and reached the United States in 1862, seeking a purchaser at $1000. It was bought by Mr. Bruce, and again sold at the dispersion of his library in 1868, when the writer bought it for Mr. Rice, at a cost of $1150. It was then first discovered that the *leaf of contents* was wanting. Fortunately, however, an imperfect copy of the Bible happened to be accessible, from which the needed leaf was obtained, and Mr. Rice was made happy by the acquisition of what he imagined to be a perfect copy of Eliot's Indian Bible. At the sale of Mr. Rice's collection in 1870, it again changed hands, having been purchased by Mr. Bouton, from whom it was obtained by its present owner, who discovered that the leaf of contents inserted by Mr. Rice, was that belonging to the second edition, and replaced it with a GENUINE leaf from an imperfect copy of the FIRST EDITION then in his possession. The book is therefore now ABSOLUTELY PERFECT THROUGHOUT; a GENUINE FIRST EDITION from BEGINNING TO END, beyond cavil or question. It is without doubt, the FINEST COPY that has, for many years, been offered for sale, and is believed to be the BEST, in point of size, preservation, and internal condition (if we except the Bodleian Library stamp, on the reverse of the titles), of any on this side of the Atlantic. The Allan copy was slightly SHORTER. In this copy PROOF LEAVES are to be met with at every few pages, while in the Allan copy there were few or none. In short, it is a MATCHLESS COPY.

"Mr. Eliot, pastor of Roxbury, Mass., commenced, at the age of forty two, the study of the Natick Indian dialect, in which this work is printed. In 1649, having made some proficiency, he expressed a desire to translate a portion of the Scriptures into that language for the use of the Indians to whom he acted as a Missionary, and with the aid of an Indian, completed the translation of the entire Bible, including the Old and New Testament, in 1658, after a labor of eight years. This fact having been communicated to the Corporation established in London for the Propagation of the Gospel among the Indians of New-England, that body expressed themselves, in a letter dated 7th of May, 1659, on the subject of printing the work, in the following terms:

'As to the printing of the Bible in the Indian language; mensioned in Mr. Endicott's 'letter; which wee vnderstand is alreddy translated into the Indian tounge; wee conceuie 'will not onely be acceptable vnto God; but very proffitable to the poor heathen and will 'much tend to the promotion of the speritual part of this worke amongst them; and therfor 'wee offer it not only as our owne but as the judgment of others that the New Testament 'bee first printed in the Indian language.' The printing of that part was accordingly commenced by Samuel Green, of Cambridge, the same year. Writing in April, 1660, the Corporation add: 'We haue out of our desire to further a worke of soe great consernment 'hauing hopes that somethinge will bee collected in particulare with Relation to the printing 'of the ould Testament, agreed with an able Printer for three years.'"

Marmaduke Johnson accordingly arrived in this country to superintend the printing.

"It has been already stated that Mr. Eliot completed the immense labour of translating this Bible in 1658, but the printing of the Old Testament was not commenced until 1660. In September of that year, a sheet of Genesis was transmitted to England. '*The printers doubt not but to print a sheet every weeke, and compute the whole to amount to a hundred and fifty sheets.*' In September, 1661, the five books of Moses were printed; in September, 1662, the work was about half done, and completed in September, 1663. Three years were thus occupied in the completion of the Old Testament. The Corporation had already ordered, in April, 1663, 'that the Psalmes of David, in meter, shalbee printed in the Indian language.' On the 18th of Sept., following, twenty copies of the Bible were ordered to be sent to England, 'and as many of the Psalmes, if printed of before the shippes departure from hence.' The edition, including the Psalm books, consisted of upwards of 1000 copies. Three hundred and sixty-eight reams of paper were used in printing the Bible; the expense ranged from sixty to seventy shillings sterling a sheet. The cost of printing the Psalms was forty shillings a sheet, or £26, in the whole; of printing the 'Epistle dedicatory' to the Bible, £1, and of 'binding and clasping,' two shillings and sixpence per copy. JOHN RATCLIFF, the bookbinder, objected to this low price, and avowed in a petition to the Commissioners, 'that under 3s. 4d. or 3s. 6d. per book' he could not bind them and live comfortably, 'one Bible being as much as he could compleat in one day,' and find the materials."—O'CALLAGHAN.

Among the many points of interest which this book possesses, not the least is the fact, that it is the language of a nation no longer in existence, and is almost the only monument of the race; another, that it is the first edition of the Bible published in this country. The very sight of it caused the quaint Cotton Mather to exclaim: "*Behold, ye Americans, the greatest honour that ever you were partakers of! This ... is the only Bible that ever was printed in all America, from the very foundation of the World.*"

The names of the Books are retained as in the English versions, and such words as were unknown to the Indians are retained with an Indian termination, such as cherubim*lah*, &c. The longest word is, Mark, i, 40: Wutteppesittukqussunnoowehtunkquoh, signifying "kneeling down to him."

666 ELIOT. Communion of Churches: | or, | The Divine Management of Gospel Churches | by the Ordinance of | Councils, | Constituted in Order according to the | Scriptures. | As Also, | The Way of bringing all Christian | Parishes to be particular Reforming | Congregational Churches: | Humbly Proposed, | As a Way which hath so much Light from the | Scriptures of Truth, as that it may lawfully be | Submitted unto by all; and may, by the blessing | of the Lord, be a Means of Uniting those two | Holy and Eminent Parties, | The Presbyterians and Congregationals. | As Also | To Prepare for the hoped-for Resurrection of the | Churches; and to Propose a way to bring all | Christian Nations unto an Unity of the | Faith and Order of the

Gospel. | Written by John Eliot, Teacher of | Roxbury in N. E. | Psal. 1. 10. That ye may try the things that are excellent. | 1 John 4. 1. Try the Spirits. | *Cambridge: Printed by Marmaduke Johnson.* 1665.

16mo, title, pp. 38. *Crushed blue levant morooco, paneled sides, corner ornaments, filleted and gilt back, inside lined in highly polished blue levant morocco exquisitely tooled and gilt, gilt top,* UNCUT; A MOST BEAUTIFUL EXAMPLE of the BEST STYLE of F. BEDFORD.

ONE OF THE VERY EARLIEST NEW ENGLAND IMPRINTS.

The verso of the title reads: "Although a few Copies of this small Script are | Printed; yet it is not published, onely [*sic*] committed | privately to some Godly and Able hands, to be Viewed, | Corrected, Amended, or Rejected, as it shall be found to | hold weight in the Sanctuary Ballance [*sic*] or not. |...| The procuring of half so many copies written and | corrected, would be more difficult and chargeable, then [*sic*] | the Printing of these few | ... | John Eliot." | Beyond any doubt this is THE FIRST PRIVATELY PRINTED AMERICAN BOOK. Martin, in his "Catalogue of Books, Privately Printed," notices but seven titles during the entire century in which this interesting little volume was printed. This, the *only known copy* is uncut, and has manuscript alterations by a contemporary hand — probably by Eliot himself. It is, we believe, UNIQUE.

667 ELIOT *and* MAYHEW (Thomas.) Tears of Repentance: | Or, A further | Narrative of the Progress of the Gospel | Amongst the | Indians | in | New-England: | Setting forth, not only their present state | and condition, but sundry Confessions of sin | by diverse of the said Indians, wrought upon | by the saving Power of the Gospel; Together | with the manifestation of their Faith and Hope | in Jesus Christ, and the Work of Grace upon | their Hearts. | Related by Mr. Eliot and Mr. Mayhew, two Faithful Laborers | in that Work of the Lord. | Published by the Corporation for propagating the Gospel there, for the | Satisfaction and Comfort of such as wish well thereunto. | ... | *London: Printed by Peter Cole in Leaden-Hall, and are to be Sold at | his Shop, at the Sign of the Printing-Press in Cornhill, | near the Royal Exchange.* 1653.

Small 4to, pp. (36), 47. *Polished calf, gilt edges, by* W. PRATT. EXTREMELY RARE.
This copy brought $100 at the Rice Sale.

"The second tract on the subject, published by the corporation, by whom it is dedicated to the Lord General Cromwell: to whom there is also another dedication by Mr. Eliot. It contains also a letter from Richard Mather, dated in Dorchester, N. E." — *Rich.*

668 ELIOT (J.) A Biographical Dictionary, containing a Brief Account of the First Settlers, and other Eminent Characters among the Magistrates, Ministers, Literary and Worthy Men in New-England. By John Eliot, D.D. ... *Boston: Edward Oliver.* 1809.

8vo, pp. viii., 511, (1). *Half blue morocco, gilt top,* UNCUT. A fine copy, containing TWENTY-EIGHT *inserted* PORTRAITS of persons noticed in the work.

669 ELLET (Elizabeth Fries Lummis.) Domestic History of the American Revolution. By Mrs. Ellet. *New York: Charles Scribner.* 1854.

12mo, half green morocco, gilt top, UNCUT.

670 ELLET. The Women of the American Revolution. By Elizabeth F. Ellet. *New York: Charles Scribner.* 1854.

3 *vols.,* 12*mo, half green morocco, gilt top,* UNCUT.

671 ELLICOTT (A.) Journal of Andrew Ellicott, late Commissioner on behalf of the United States ... for Determining the Boundary Between the United States and the Possessions of his Catholic Majesty in America. Containing Occasional Remarks on the Situation, Soil, Rivers, Natural Productions, and Diseases of the different Countries on the Ohio, Mississippi, and Gulf of Mexico ... to which is added an Appendix ... *Philadelphia: Printed by William Fry.* 1814.

4to, pp. vii., 299, 151. 13 *Folded Maps and Plates. Half purple morocco, gilt top,* UNCUT. A beautiful copy, and VERY SCARCE in this condition.

One of the earliest books by an American author, which describes the vast regions traversed by the Commission, and indeed the pioneer account of regions then desert, and now teeming with life, activity and civilization.

672 ELLIOTT (C. W.) The New England History, from the Discovery of the Continent by the Northmen, A.D. 986, to the Period when the Colonies declared their Independence, A.D. 1776. By Charles W. Elliott ... . *New-York: Charles Scribner.* 1857.

2 *vols., 8vo, half blue morocco, gilt top,* UNCUT. *Sixty-six* ILLUSTRATIONS *inserted.* The inlaying in these volumes was *not* executed by MR. TRENT.

673 ELLIOTT (J. D.) Speech of Com. Jesse Duncan Elliott, U. S. N., delivered in Hagerstown, Md., On 14th November, 1843. ... *Philadelphia: G. B. Zieber & Co.* 1844.

8vo, half red imitation morocco.

A defence of his conduct at the battle of Lake Erie, and an extraordinary production.

674 ELLIS (G.) Specimens of the Early English Poets; to which is prefixed, an Historical Sketch of the Rise and Progress of the English Poetry and Language, with a Biography of each Poet. By George Ellis, Esq. The Fifth Edition Corrected. *London: Henry Washbourne.* 1845.

3 *vols., sm. 8vo, calf antique, by* RIVIERE. A FINE SET.

675 ELLIS (G. E.) An Oration delivered at Charlestown, Massachusetts, on the 17th of June, 1841, in Commemoration of the Battle of Bunker Hill. By George E. Ellis. *Boston: William Crosby & Co.* 1841.

8vo, pp. 72. *Half green morocco, gilt top,* UNCUT. *Twenty-eight* ILLUSTRATIONS *inserted.* An elegant copy.

676 ELLIS. "Commemoration of Washington." A Discourse (on the New Holiday,) Preached in Harvard Church, Charlestown on Sunday February 22nd, 1857. By George E. Ellis. *Charlestown: Abram E. Cutter.* 1857.

8vo, pp. 30. *Half green morocco, gilt top,* UNCUT.

677 ELLIS. I. The Aims and Purposes of the Founders of Massachusetts. II. Their Treatment of Intruders and Dissentients. Two

Lectures ... delivered before the Lowell Institute, on Jan. 8 and Jan. 12, 1869. By George E. Ellis.
Boston: Press of John Wilson and Son. 1869.

8vo, pp. 100. *Half blue morocco, gilt top,* UNCUT, *by* BRADSTREET. TWO PORTRAITS *inserted.*

678 ELLIS. Memoir of Jared Sparks, LL.D. By George E. Ellis. ...
Cambridge: Press of John Wilson & Son. 1869.

8vo, pp. 102. *Half crushed green levant morocco, gilt top,* UNCUT, *by* W. MATTHEWS. An elegant copy, ILLUSTRATED with FIFTEEN PORTRAITS, mostly PROOFS, INDIA PROOFS, and INDIA PROOFS BEFORE LETTERS; including an ARTIST'S TRIAL PROOF of an UNFINISHED PORTRAIT of WASHINGTON. FIFTY COPIES ONLY separately printed, from the "Proceedings of the Mass. Hist. Soc."

679 ELMER (J.) An Eulogium, On the Character of Gen. George Washington ... . Delivered At Bridge-Town, Cumberland County, New-Jersey, January 30th, 1800. By Jonathan Elmer, M.D. S.S.P.A.
Trenton: Printed by G. Craft. MDCCC.

8vo, pp. 25. *Half blue morocco, gilt top,* UNCUT. PORTRAIT of WASHINGTON *inserted.* EXCEEDINGLY RARE.

Not in Hough's Bibliographical List; and the *only copy* we have ever seen.

680 EMMET (T. A.) Catalogue of the Library belonging to Thomas Addis Emmet, M.D. *New York: Bradstreet Press.* 1868.

Roy. 8vo, pp. (1), 371. *Half red levant morocco, gilt top, uncut, by* W. MATTHEWS. *Sixty copies* printed for PRIVATE DISTRIBUTION. One of the finest issues of BRADSTREET'S PRESS.

681 EMMONS (N.) A Sermon on the Death of Gen. George Washington, preached February 22, 1800. By Nathaniel Emmons, D.D. Pastor of the Church in Franklin. *Wrentham: Mass.* 1800.

8vo, pp. 26. UNCUT, *and Very Scarce.*

682 EMMONS (R.) The Fredoniad: or, Independence Preserved. An Epick Poem on the Late War of 1812. By Richard Emmons, M.D.
Boston: William Emmons. 1827.

4 *vols., crown 8vo, half green morocco, gilt top,* UNCUT.

683 EMMONS. The Battle of Bunker Hill, or the Temple of Liberty; an Historic Poem in Four Cantos, Respectfully Dedicated to the Friends of Rational Liberty throughout the World. By the late Richard Emmons, M.D. Second Edition. *Boston:* 1841.

12mo, pp. 141. *Half red morocco.* TWO ILLUSTRATIONS *inserted.*

684 EMORY (W. H.) Report of the United States and Mexican Boundary Survey, made under the Direction of the Secretary of the Interior. By William H. Emory. *Washington:* 1857–59.

2 *vols., 4to, bound in* 3. *Half green morocco, gilt top.* Volume II. is comparatively *scarce.*

The title of this work, like many other of the government documents, conveys a very inadequate idea of its contents, which are partly as follows: Vol. I. Part I. General account, general description of the country, Lower Rio Bravo, &c. Astronomical and geodetic work, meteorology. Lithograph, 74 steel plates, 24 woodcuts, pp. xvi., 258. Part II. Geological reports, by Dr. C. C. Parry, Arthur Schott, Jas. Hall, and T. A. Conrad. 26 woodcuts, 21 steel plates, pp. xiii., 174. Vol. II. Part I. Botany of the boundary, by John Torrey, 61 plates, pp. 270. Cactaneæ of the boundary, by George Englemann, 75 plates, pp. 78. Part II. Zoology of the boundary — mammals of the boundary, by Spencer F. Baird, 27 plates, pp. 62. Birds of the boundary, by Spencer F. Baird, 25 colored plates, pp. 53. Reptiles, by S. F. Baird, 41 plates, pp. 35. Icthyology, by Charles Giraud 41 plates, pp. 85.

685 ENQUIRY (An) into the Causes of the Alienation of the Delaware and Shawanese Indians from the British Interest, ... Extracted from the Public Treaties, and other Authentic Papers relating to the Transactions of the Government of Pensilvania, and the said Indians, for near Forty Years; and explained by a Map of the Country. Together with the remarkable Journal of Christian Frederic Post, by whose Negotiations among the Indians on the Ohio, they were withdrawn from the Interest of the French, who thereupon abandoned the Fort and the Country. With Notes by the Editor explaining sundry Indian Customs, etc. Written in Pensylvania.
London: J. Wilkie. MDCCLIX.

8vo, pp. 184. *Map. Half crushed purple levant morocco, gilt top,* UNCUT, *by* F. BEDFORD. EXTREMELY RARE in this state.

CHARLES THOMSON, Secretary to Congress, was the author of this most interesting and valuable Enquiry.

"One of the principal causes of the hostility of the Pennsylvania Indians, was the wicked craft practiced upon them by Governor Thomas Penn, and other proprietors in 1737. Certain chiefs having been called together by the speculators, two persons were found to testify that they were present at a council fifty years before, at which as much land was ceded to William Penn, as a man could walk around in a day and a half. There was a chief living who could have proved this testimony false, but he was carefully kept in ignorance of the council, and by mean fraud, endless perjury, and tempting but specious gifts, the surreptitious deed was ratified. To locate as large a territory as possible, a trained pedestrian was employed, who was met at appointed stations by refreshments, and thus was enabled to traverse a route which cut off a million acres from the Indian territory. Less than one third that quantity of land was the amount which the Indians had been led to expect would be ceded. Endless conferences, and numerous councils, were followed by bloody massacres, that devastated the border settlements of Pennsylvania and Virginia, for twenty years. Mr. Thomson's work fully analyzes the cause of the *alienation*, which the heroic Quaker, Christian Post, hazarded his life to overcome."— *Field.*

See Post (C. F.) No. 1619.

686 EULOGIES and Orations on the Life and Death of General George Washington, First President of the United States of America. ...
Boston: W. P. & L. Blake. 1800.

8vo, pp. 304. *Half green morocco.* PORTRAIT of WASHINGTON, engraved by TANNER after SAVAGE, *inserted.* An elegant copy. RARE.

Contains a selection of 20 of the best pieces on the subject.

687 [EVANS (A.E.) *and* Sons.] The Print Collectors Manual. Catalogue of nearly Six Thousand Etchings and Engravings by Artists of every School and Period, comprising the Best Examples of every Eminent Engraver, from the Earliest Period to the Present Time,

with the Size and Price of each print. On sale by A. E. Evans & Sons, London. *London:* [1857.]

8vo, pp. 260, *iv.*, 50. *Half green morocco, gilt top,* UNCUT. VERY SCARCE.

688 [EVANS *and* Son.] Catalogue of Engraved British Portraits comprising Thirty Thousand Portraits of Persons connected with the History and Literature of Great Britain, the British Colonies, and the United States of America. Accompanied by concise Biographical Notices, the names of the Painter and Engraver, and the Size and Price of each Plate. *London: A. E. Evans & Son.* [*n. d.*]

2 *vols., 8vo, pp.* (2), 395; (1), 431. *Half green morocco, gilt top,* UNCUT. A fine set of Evans' catalogues, out of print, and SCARCE.

Indispensable to the intelligent illustrator.

689 EVANS (I.) A Discourse, delivered, on the 18th Day of December, 1777, the Day of Public Thanksgiving, appointed by the Honourable Continental Congress. By the Reverend Israel Evans, A.M. ... *Lancaster: Francis Bailey.* M,DCC,LXXVIII.

12mo, pp. 24. *Half green morocco,* UNCUT.

Published at the request of GEN. POOR, to be distributed among the soldiers of his brigade gratis.

690 EVANS (T.) Old Ballads, Historical and Narrative, with some of Modern Date; now first collected from rare Copies and MSS., none of which are inserted in Dr. Percy's Collection. With Notes. By Thomas Evans. [*London:*] *T. Evans.* 1784.

4 *vols., post 8vo, calf.* A fine copy.

One of the most desirable collections of old ballads ever published.

691 EVERETT (E.) The Mount Vernon Papers. By Edward Everett. *New York:* 1858–59.

Sm. 4to, half maroon morocco, gilt top, UNCUT.

The complete series of articles as *originally written* by Mr. Everett, and published in the New York Ledger; cut from that paper and mounted by TRENT upon 82 leaves of paper ruled in double columns and headed expressly for the purpose, with a COMPOSITE TITLE, and THREE ILLUSTRATIONS *inserted.*

692 EVERETT. Eulogy on Thomas Dowse, of Cambridgeport, Pronounced before the Massachusetts Historical Society, 9th December, 1858. By Edward Everett. With the Introductory Address by Robert C. Winthrop ... and an Appendix. *Boston: John Wilson and Son.* M.DCCC.LIX.

8vo, pp. 82. 2 *Portraits and View. Cloth extra, gilt edges. A few copies only* PRIVATELY PRINTED from the "Proceedings of the Mass. Hist. Soc."

693 EVERETT. The Life of George Washington. By Edward Everett. *New York: Sheldon and Company.* 1860.

8vo, pp. 348. *Half green morocco, gilt top,* UNCUT. LARGE PAPER; *One hundred copies only printed.* EIGHT ILLUSTRATIONS *inserted.*

694 [EVERETT.] Tribute of the Massachusetts Historical Society to the Memory of Edward Everett, January 30, 1865. *Boston:* 1865.

Impl. 8vo, pp. 90. *Portrait. Half green morocco, gilt top,* UNCUT. An AUTOGRAPH NOTE, and PORTRAIT of MR. EVERETT *inserted.*

695 [EVERETT.] Tribute to the Memory of ... Edward Everett, by the New-England Historic-Genealogical Society ... January 17 and February 1, 1865. *Boston:* MDCCCLXV.

4to, pp. 97. 2 *Portraits and* 2 *Plates. Half green morocco, gilt top,* UNCUT. LARGE PAPER; *only* 75 *copies printed.* AUTOGRAPH LETTER and PORTRAIT of MR. EVERETT *inserted.*

696 [EVERETT.] A Memorial of Edward Everett, from the City of Boston. *Boston: Printed by order of the City Council.* MDCCCLXV.

4to, pp. 315. 2 *Portraits. Half green morocco, gilt top,* UNCUT. LARGE PAPER; of which FIFTEEN COPIES only were left *uncut.* PORTRAIT of MR. EVERETT, and VIEW of his LIBRARY inserted.

697 EVERETT (O.) An Eulogy, on General George Washington. ... Pronounced at Dorchester, Feb. 22, 1800. It being the Day Recommended by Congress for the National Lamentation of his Death. By Oliver Everett, Esq. ... Published at the request of the Town. *Charlestown:* M,DCCC.

8vo, pp. 22. *Very Scarce.*

698 EXQUEMELIN (J.) Bucaniers | of | America: | Or, a true | Account | of the | Most remarkable Assaults | Committed of late years upon the Coasts of | The West Indies, | By the Bucaniers of Jamaica, and Tortuga, | Both English and French. | Wherein are contained more especially, | The Unparallel'd Exploits of Sir Henry Morgan, our English | Jamaican Hero, who sack'd Puerto Velo, burnt Panama, &c. | Written originally in Dutch, by John Esquemeling, one of the Bucaniers, | who was present at those Tragedies, and translated into Spanish by | Alonso de Bonne-maison, M.D. &c. | The Second Edition Corrected and Inlarged with two | Additional Relations, viz. the one of Captain Cook, and the other of | Captain Sharp. | Now faithfully rendered into English. | *London: Printed for William Crooke, at the Green Dra- | gon, without Temple-bar.* 1684.

2 *vols., 4to, bound in one. Gray calf, carmine edges.* A LARGE and FINE COPY of ALL FOUR PARTS, with the maps and plates complete. VERY SCARCE.

A copy was recently priced by Mr. Quaritch at £12.12.0.

699 [EXQUEMELIN.] The History of the Bucaniers of America. Containing, I. The Exploits and Adventures of Le Grand, Lolonois, Roche Brasiliano, Bat the Portuguese, Sir H. Morgan, &c. II. The dangerous Voyage and bold Attempts of Capt. Sharp, Watlin, Sawkins, Coxon, and others in the South Sea. III. A Journal of a Voyage into the South Sea by the Freebooters of America, from 1684 to 1689. IV. A Relation of a Voyage of the Sieur De Montauban, Captain of the Free-booters, in Guinea, in the Year 1695. Exhibit-

ing A particular Account and Description of Porto Bello, Chagre, and Panama, Cuba, Havanna, and most of the Spanish Possessions on the Coasts of the West-Indies, and also along the Coasts of the South Sea; with the Manner in which they have been invaded, attempted, or taken by these Adventurers. The Whole written in several Languages by Persons present at the Transactions. The Fifth Edition. *London: T. Evans and Richardson and Urquhart.* M.DCC.LXXI.

2 vols., 12*mo*, *pp.* (2), 318; 360, (12.) *Old calf.* FINE COPY of a SCARCE EDITION, unnoticed by Lowndes.

700 EXTRACTS From the Votes and Proceedings of the American Continental Congress, Held at Philadelphia on the 5th of September 1774. Containing the Bill of Rights, a List of Grievances, Occasional Resolves, the Association, an Address to the People of Great-Britain, and a Memorial to the Inhabitants of the British American Colonies. ... *Philadelphia: William and Thomas Bradford.* 1774.

8*vo*, *pp.* 36. *Half roan.*

701 FANNING (D.) The Narrative of Colonel David Fanning. (A Tory in the Revolutionary War with Great Britain): giving an Account of his Adventures in North Carolina, From 1775 to 1783, as Written by Himself. With an Introduction and Explanatory Notes.

Richmond, Va. Printed for private distribution only, 1861, *In the First Year of the Independence of the Confederate States of America.*

4*to*, *pp.* *xxv.*, 92. *Half calf, gilt top*, UNCUT. The ORIGINAL EDITION (on Piries paper) of this RARE TRACT, of which *only fifty copies* were printed.

The original manuscript belongs to Mr. Charles Deane, of Cambridge, Mass., who lent it to a friend, who re-lent it to a gentleman in the South, where it was copied, edited, and printed. The notes are by Governor Swain, of North Carolina, and Thomas H. Wynne, of Richmond.

702 FARIBAULT (G. B.) Catalogue d'ouvrages sur l'histoire de l'Amérique, et en particulier sur celle du Canada, de la Louisiane, de l'Acadie, et autres lieux, Ci-devant connus sous le nom de Nouvelle-France; avec des notes bibliographiques critiques, et littéraires. En Trois Partes. Rédigé par G. B. Faribault, Avocat.

Quebec: W. Cowan. 1837.

8*vo.* *pp.* 207. *Half purple levant morocco, gilt top*, UNCUT. A long and interesting AUTOGRAPH letter from the AUTHOR giving an account of the destruction of the Parliament Buildings and their precious literary contents, by fire, at Quebec, *inserted.* EXTREMELY SCARCE; we have never seen but ONE COPY sold.

Part I., contains the authors, arranged alphabetically. Part II., annonymous works arranged chronologically. Part III., a catalogue of maps, charts, and plans. The number of works described is 969, and to many of them are added descriptive notes.

703 FARNHAM (L.) A Glance at Private Libraries. By Luther Farnham. *Boston:* 1855.

8vo, pp. 79. *Half blue morocco, gilt top.* LARGE and FINE COPY. *Very Scarce.*

The principal collections noticed, are those of Webster, Ticknor, Livermore, Hosmer, Lawrence, Prescott, Everett, Chase, Crowninshield, Sparks, Parker, and Adams; seven of which are now dispersed.

704 FEDERALIST: (The) | A Collection | of | Essays, | written in Favour of the | New Constitution, | as agreed upon by the Federal Convention, | September 17, 1787. | *New York: J. and A. McLean.* M,DCC,LXXXVIII.

2 vols., 12mo, pp. vi., 227; *vi.,* 384. *Half olive morocco, gilt top,* UNCUT. An autograph inscription is on the upper corner of the title to the first volume. A FINE COPY of the FIRST EDITION. EXTREMELY RARE.

First edition in a collected form. Mr. Madison's papers were much changed in the subsequent editions. Nos. 2, 3, 4, 5, and 64, were written by Mr. Jay; Nos. 10, 14, 17, 18, 19, 21, 37 to 58, 62 and 63, were written by Mr. Madison; the remainder by Gen. Hamilton.

705 FELLOWS (J.) The Veil Removed; or Reflections on David Humphreys' Essay on the Life of Israel Putnam. Also, Notices of Oliver W. B. Peabody's Life of the same, S. Swett's Sketch of Bunker Hill Battle, Etc., Etc. By John Fellows. ... *New York: James D. Lockwood.* 1843.

12mo, pp. 231. *Half calf.*

706 FELT (J. B.) An Historical Account of Massachusetts Currency. By Joseph B. Felt. ... *Boston: Perkins & Marvin.* 1839.

8vo, pp. 259. *Half blue morocco, gilt top,* UNCUT. FOUR PIECES of Rhode Island CONTINENTAL CURRENCY *inserted.*

707 FELTMAN (W.) The Journal of Lieut. William Feltman of the First Pennsylvania Regiment, 1781–82. Including the March into Virginia, and the Siege of Yorktown. *Philadelphia: Henry Cary Baird.* 1853.

8vo, pp. 48. *Half calf, gilt top,* UNCUT.

708 FENN (J.) Paston Letters. Original Letters written during the Reigns of Henry VI., Edward IV., and Richard III., by various persons of rank or consequence; with Notes Historical and Explanatory, edited by John Fenn. A new edition by A. Ramsay. *London: Charles Knight & Co.* 1840.

2 vols., sq. 8vo, bound in one. Olive morocco, blank tooled sides, gauffered and gilt edges, by WRIGHT. An ELEGANT COPY.

A most singular and valuable work, containing many curious anecdotes relative to this turbulent and bloody, but hitherto dark, period of history, and elucidating not only public matters of state, but likewise the private manners of the age, &c.

709 FERGUSON (R.) The Works of Robert Ferguson. Edited, with Life of the Author and an Essay on his Genius and Writings, by A. B. G. *London: A. Fullarton and Co.* 1851.

12mo, half green morocco, gilt top, UNCUT.

710 FERRIAR (J.) The Bibliomania, An Epistle, to Richard Heber, Esq. By John Ferriar, M.D. *London: Cadell and Davies.* 1809.

PROOF PORTRAIT of DR. FERRIAR *inserted.* LARGE PAPER. EXCESSIVELY RARE.

[Also:] RATIONAL MADNESS: a Song, for the Lovers of Curious and Rare Books: adapted to the Popular Tune of "Liberty Hall," by J(ohn) M(ajor). *London:* [*n. d.*]

PRIVATELY PRINTED, and *fifty copies only.* VERY RARE.

4to, 2 pieces in one vol., half olive brown morocco, gilt top, UNCUT. Uniform with Dibdin's Works.

711 FERRIS (B.) A History of the Original Settlements on the Delaware, from its Discovery by Hudson to the Colonization under William Penn. To which is added an Account of the Ecclesiastical Affairs of the Swedish Settlers, and a History of Wilmington, from its First Settlement to the Present Time. Illustrated by Drawings. ... By Benjamin Ferris. *Wilmington: Wilson & Heald* 1846.

8vo, pp. 312. Map, 2 Plans, 4 Plates. Half calf.

712 [FESSENDEN (Thomas Green.)] Democracy Unveiled; or, Tyranny stripped of the Garb of Patriotism. By Christopher Caustic, L.L.D. &c. ... . Second Edition. *Boston: David Carlisle.* 1805.

12mo, pp. viii., 220. Half green morocco, gilt top, UNCUT. RARE PORTRAIT of PAINE, and PORTRAITS of GODWIN, and JEFFERSON, *inserted.*

713 [FESSENDEN.] Democracy Unveiled. Third Edition, with Large Additions. *New York: I.Riley and Co.* 1806.

2 vols., 12mo, half morocco, carmine edges.

714 FESSENDEN. Original Poems. By Thomas Green Fessenden, A.M. ... . *London: Hurst.* 1804.

Crown 8vo, half blue morocco, gilt top.

715 [FESSENDEN.] Terrible Tractoration!! A Poetical Petition against Galvanizing Trumpery, and the Perkinistic Institution. In Four Cantos. Most Respectfully addressed to the Royal College of Physicians, by Christopher Caustic, M.D., LL.D., A S S., ... First American, From the Second London Edition, Revised and Corrected by the Author, with Additional Notes. *New York: Samuel Stansbury.* 1804.

Crown 8vo, half blue morocco, gilt top. Uniform with the preceding No.

A defence of Perkins' metalic tractors in Hudibrastic verse.

716 FIELD (T. W.) Historic and Antiquarian Scenes in Brooklyn and its Vicinity, with Illustrations of some of its Antiquities. By T. W. Field. *Brooklyn:* 1868.

Imp. 8vo, pp. iv., 2 l., 96. 11 Plates and Map. Half red morocco, gilt top, UNCUT, by BRADSTREET. FIVE ILLUSTRATIONS *inserted.* ONE HUNDRED COPIES printed for PRIVATE DISTRIBUTION.

A collection of valuable and interesting papers relating to the Revolutionary, Colonial, and Indian History of Long Island.

717 FIELD. The Battle of Long Island, with connected Preceding Events, and the Subsequent American Retreat. Introductory Narrative. By Thomas W. Field. With Authentic Documents. *Brooklyn:* 1869.

Imp. 8vo, pp. xiii., ix., 549. 7 *Plates. Half morocco, gilt top,* UNCUT. LARGE PAPER: *only* 100 *copies printed.*

Two editions were issued at the same time, with the title as above; another forms Vol. II. of the "Memoirs of the Long Island Historical Society."

718 FIELD. An Essay toward an Indian Bibliography. Being a Catalogue of Books, relating to the History, Antiquities, Languages, Customs, Religion, Wars, Literature, and Origin of the American Indians, in the Library of Thomas W. Field. With Bibliographical and Historical Notes, and Synopses of the Contents of some of the Works least known. *New York: Scribner, Armstrong & Co.* 1873.

8vo, pp. iv., 430. *Half crushed red levant morocco, gilt top,* UNCUT, by W. MATTHEWS.

So far, the most extensive list of books on this subject. Mr. Field has devoted many years to the acquisition of the books, and his notes, which are numerous, convey much valuable information concerning not only the books, but the Indians themselves. We have made free use of his notes in the compilation of this catalogue.

"This bibliographical handbook, embracing a collection of about 1800 works, may be considered the chief, if not the only one of its kind. The author's notes are judicious and valuable, and have an interest beyond even the actual subject of the Essay. Collectors of Americana of every kind will derive pleasure and profit from a labour that evinces a wide range of study and experience."— *B. Quaritch.*

719 FILSON (J.) The Discovery, Settlement And present state of Kentucke: and An Essay towards the Topography, and Natural History of that important Country. To which is added, An Appendix, Containing, I. The Adventures of Col. Daniel Boon, one of the first Settlers, comprehending every important Occurrence in the political History of that Province. II. The Minutes of the Piankashaw Council, held at Post St. Vincents, April 15, 1784. III. An Account of the Indian Nations inhabiting within the Limits of the Thirteen United States, their Manners and Customs, and Reflections on their Origin. IV. The Stages and Distances between Philadelphia and the Falls of the Ohio, from Pittsburg to Pensacola, and several other Places.—The Whole illustrated by a new and accurate Map of Kentucke and the Country adjoining, drawn from actual Surveys. By John Filson. *Wilmington: Printed by James Adams.* 1784.

8vo, pp. 118. *Brown morocco, gilt edges.* A beautiful copy. VERY SCARCE. PORTRAIT of DANIEL BOONE *inserted.*

Although a map is announced in the title, it seems never to have been published; when found it is usually supplied from the French translation. The author, one of the first narrators of border warfare, was himself killed by the Indians of Ohio.

720 FILSON. Histoire de Kentucke, nouvelle colonie à l'ouest de la Virginie: contenant, 1°. La Découverte, l'Acquisition, l'Établisse-

ment, la Description topographique, l'Histoire Naturelle, &c. du Territoire : 2°. La Relation historique du Colonel Boon, un des premiers Colons, sur les guerres contre les Naturels : 3°. l'Assemblée des Piankashaws au Poste Saint Vincent : 4°. Un exposé succinct des Nations Indiennes qui habitent dans les limites des Treize États-Unis, de leurs mœurs & coûtumes, & des Réflexions sur leur Origine ; & autres Pièces : Avec une carte. Ouvrage pour servir de suite aux Lettres d'un Cultivateur Américain. Traduit de l'Anglois, de M. John Filson ; Par M. Farrand, de l'Académie des Arcades de Rome. *A Paris : Chez Buisson, Libraire.* M. DCC. LXXXV.

8vo, pp. xvi., 234. Map. Half brown morocco, gilt top. A LARGE and FINE COPY with the Map. RARE.

The translator has made some additions to the work.

721 FINDLEY (W.) History of the Insurrection, in the Four Western Counties of Pennsylvania : In the Year M.DCC.XCIV. With a Recital of the Circumstances specially connected therewith : and an Historical View of the Previous Situation of the Country. By William Findley. ... *Philadelphia : Printed by Samuel Harrison Smith.* M.DCC.XCVI.

8vo, pp. 328. Half maroon morocco, gilt top, UNCUT. Very fine copy. PORTRAIT *inserted.* RARE in *uncut* condition.

Known as the "History of the Whiskey Rebellion."

722 FISHER (C. F.) Catalogue of the Library of J. B. Fisher, Containing many Choice and Curious Books, ... Sold at Auction, 1866. Prepared by Charles F. Fisher. *Philadelphia :* 1866.

4to, half olive morocco, gilt top, UNCUT. *Ruled and priced.* LARGE PAPER. *Fifteen copies only printed.*

723 FISKE (T.) A Sermon, Delivered Dec. 29, 1799. At the Second Parish in Cambridge, Being the Lord's Day, Immediately following the Melancholy Intelligence of the Death of General George Washington. ... By Thadeus Fiske, A.M. ... *Boston :* 1800.

8vo, pp. 21. UNCUT.

724 FLINT (A.) A Discourse, Delivered at Hartford, Feb. 22, 1800, The Day set apart by Recommendation of Congress, to pay a Tribute of Respect to the memory of General George Washington. ... By Abel Flint. ... *Hartford :* 1800.

8vo, pp. (4), 22. UNCUT.

725 FLORIDA. The Discovery and Conquest of Terra Florida, by Don Ferdinando de Soto, and Six Hundred Spaniards, his Followers. Written by a Gentleman of Elvas, employed in all the Action, and translated out of Portuguese, by Richard Hakluyt. Reprinted from the Edition of 1611. Edited, with Notes and an Introduction, and

a Translation of a Narrative of the Expedition of Luis Hernandez de Biedma, Factor to the Same. By William B. Rye ... . *London: Printed for the Hakluyt Society.* M.DCCC.LI.

8vo, pp. lxvii., 200, v. Map. Half purple morocco, gilt top, UNCUT.

726 [FOLSOM (George.)] A Catalogue of Original Documents in the English Archives, relating to the Early History of the State of Maine. ... *New York: Privately Printed.* 1858.

Roy. 8vo., pp. iv., 137. Half red morocco, gilt top, UNCUT, by BRADSTREET. VERY SCARCE.

727 FONTANES (L.) Éloge Funébre de Washington. Prononcé dans le Temple de Mars, par Louis Fontanes, le 20 pluviôse an 8. [*Paris:* 1800.]

8vo, pp. 29.

728 FORBES (E.) An Eulogy moralized, on the Illustrious Character of the late General George Washington. ... Delivered at Gloucester, on the 22d of February, 1800. ... By Eli Forbes, A.M. ... To which is added, General Washington's Affectionate Address to the United States, declining their future suffrages for the Presidency. *Newburyport:* 1800.

8vo, pp. 40. UNCUT.

729 FORBES (R.) Jacobite Memoirs of the Rebellion of 1745. Edited from the Manuscripts of The Late Right Reverend Robert Forbes, A.M. ... By Robert Chambers. *Edinburgh: W. and R. Chambers.* 1834.

8vo, pp. xix., 511. Portrait. Half calf antique.

730 FORCE (P.) Tracts and other Papers, relating principally to the Origin, Settlement, and Progress of the Colonies in North America, from the Discovery of the Country to the Year 1776. Collected by Peter Force. *Washington: Peter Force.* 1836.

4 *vols., roy. 8vo, half olive morocco, gilt top,* UNCUT. A beautifully COLOURED PHOTOGRAPH of MR. FORCE, with his characteristic AUTOGRAPH SIGNATURE, *inserted.* The "Special Report," of the librarian of Congress giving an account of Mr. Force's library, (purchased by the United States) is laid in at the end of the first volume.

An interesting and valuable series of reprints of the rarest tracts relating to America. Now entirely out of print.

731 FORCE. American Archives; consisting of a Collection of Authentick Records, State Papers, and Letters and other notices of Public Affairs; the whole forming a Documentary History of the Origin and Progress of the North American Colonies; of the Causes and Accomplishment of the American Revolution, and of the Constitution of Government for the United States to the Final Ratification Thereof. *Washington:* 1837–53.

Fourth Series, 5 *vols., Fifth Series,* 4 *vols.; together.* 9 *vols., folio, half russia.* The other series have not been published.

This great storehouse of British Colonial and American history was printed by order of the United States Government. It was the intention to divide the work into six series, from 1493 to 1789. The nine volumes described are all that have appeared, and the further progress of the work is suspended. The manuscript of the unpublished portion is in the Library of Congress. *See N. Am. Rev.*, XLVI. 475. Also Sabin's *Dictionary*.

732 FORREST (E.) Catalogue of the Library of Edwin Forrest. Compiled by Joseph Sabin. *Philadelphia :* 1863.

8vo, half olive morocco, gilt top, UNCUT. PRIVATELY PRINTED, *and* 175 *copies only.* FINE PROOF PORTRAIT, and an interesting AUTOGRAPH LETTER of MR. FORREST *inserted.*

"My dear friend, it is not money that I play for now, but the excitement of the stage keeps me from rusting physically and mentally. It is wholesome to be employed in 'the labour we delight in.'"— *Extract.*

733 FOSTER (J.) A Discourse Delivered December 29, 1799; Occasioned by the Melancholy Death of George Washington. ... By John Foster, A.M. Pastor of the Third Church and Society in Cambridge. ... *Boston :* 1800.

8vo, pp. 22. UNCUT.

734 FOWLE (W. F.) Catalogue of the Choice Collection of Books belonging to William F. Fowle, Esq., of Boston, Mass. *Cambridge : Riverside Press.* 1865.

Imp. 8vo, pp. viii., 147. *Half red levant morocco, gilt top,* UNCUT, *by* W. MATTHEWS. LARGE PAPER: *only* 85 *copies printed.* Ruled and priced. VERY SCARCE.

This library, although it contained but 1,614 volumes, realized $17,522.19, an average of almost $11 per volume, the highest, probably, ever attained in this country up to its date.

735 FOX (C.) A Portrait of George Washington, from an Original Drawing, as he appeared while Reviewing the Continental Army on Boston Common, in 1776; A History of the Portrait, and Documentary Evidence in Proof of the Correctness of the Likeness. By Charles Fox. ... *Boston : Crocker & Brewster.* 1851.

8vo, pp. 37. *Portrait. Half green morocco, gilt top,* UNCUT. *Very Scarce.*

736 FOX (E.) The Revolutionary Adventures of Ebenezer Fox, of Roxbury, Massachusetts. *Boston : Munroe & Francis.* 1838.

8vo, pp. 238. *Portrait. Half calf.*

737 FOX (G.) *and* BURNYEAT (J.) A New-England | Fire-Brand Quenched, | being an Answer | unto a | Slanderous Book, Entituled; George Fox | Digged out of his Burrows, &c. Printed at Boston in the Year | 1676. by Roger Williams of Providence in New-England. | Which he dedicateth to the King, with Desires, That, if | the Most-High please, Old and New-England may Flourish, when | the Pope & Mahomet, Rome & Constantinople are in their Ashes. | Of a Dispute upon XIV. of his Proposals held and debated | betwixt him, the said Roger Williams, on the one Part, and | John Stubs, William Edmundson and John Burnyeat, on the other. | At Providence and Newport in Rhode-Island, in the Year 1672. | In which his Cavils

are Refuted & his Reflections Reproved. | In Two Parts. | As also, | an Answer to R. W.'s Appendix, &c. | With a | Post-Script Confuting his Blasphemous Assertions, | viz. Of the Blood of Christ, that was Shed, its being Corruptible | and Corrupted; and that Salvation was by a Man, that was Cor- | ruptible, &c. Where-unto is added, a | Catalogue of his Railery, Lies, Scorn & Blasphemies: And | his Temporizing Spirit made manifest. Also, The | Letters of W. Coddington of Rode-Island, and R. Scot of | Providence in New-England, Concerning R. W. And Lastly, Some | Testimonies of Antient & Modern Authors concer- | ning the Light, Scriptvres, Rvle & the Sovl of Man. | By George Fox and John Bvrnyeat. | *Printed in the Year* M DC LXXIX.

Two parts, 4to, 14*l., pp.* 233; 1*l.*, 255, (1). *Green wrinkled morocco, gilt edges.* BEAUTIFUL COPY. EXTREMELY SCARCE.

George Fox was the founder of the Society of Friends or Quakers. In the course of his public ministrations he visited America twice, where he spent two years. He was a voluminous writer. A list of his works fills no less than fifty-one pages in Smith's "Catalogue of Friends' Books." Charles Lamb speaks highly of Fox's writings. On one occasion Fox preached for five unbroken hours to an assemblage of patient Indians.

738 FOXE (L.) North-VVest Fox, | or, | Fox from the North-west passage. | Beginning | VVith King Arthvr, Malga, Octhvr, | the two Zeni's of Iseland, Estoitland, and Dorgia; | Following with briefe Abstracts of the Voyages of Cabot, | Frobisher, Davis, Waymouth, Knight, Hudson, Button, Gib- | bons, Bylot, Baffin, Hawkridge: Together with the | Courses, Distances, Latitudes, Longitudes, Variations, | Depths of Seas, Sets of Tydes, Currents, Races, | and over-Falls; vvith other Observations, Accidents and remarkable things, as our Miseries and | sufferings. | Mr. Iames Hall's three Voyages to Groynland, with a | Topographicall description of the Countries, the Salvages | lives and Treacheries, how our Men have been slayne | by them there, with the Commodities of all those | parts; whereby the Marchant may have Trade, and | the Mariner Imployment. | Demonstrated in a Polar Card, wherein are all the Maines, Seas, | and Islands, herein mentioned. | With the Author his owne Voyage, being the XVIth. | with the opinions and Collections of the most famous Ma- | thematicians, and Cosmographers; with a Probabilitie to | prove the same by Marine Remonstrations, compa- | red by the Ebbing and Flovving of the Sea, experimented | vvith places of our ovvn Coast. | By Captaine Lvke Foxe of Kingstone vpon Hull, Capt. | and Pylot for the Voyage, in his Majesties Pinnace | the Charles. | Printed by his Majesties Command. | *London,* | *Printed by B. Alsop and Tho. Favvcet, dwelling in Grubstreet.* | 1635.

4to, plate of a sphere 1 *l.*, 5 *l., pp.* 269, (3). *Map. Blue morocco, gilt edges.* EXCESSIVELY RARE in PERFECT CONDITION, as this copy is, and with a *fine impression* of the MAP from the ORIGINAL PLATE, with the Fox and Goose in one corner, which is not to be found in all copies.

After page 168 are two leaves paged 172, 170, 171, and blank, which are said to be cancelled leaves. There are several other errors in the pagination. After page 79 the next is page 100, and the *hiatus* is not supplied; the other errors are corrected by duplication; signature B b is incorrectly paged 225–232 instead of 205–212. This very rare collection of early voyages towards making a discovery of the North-West Passage, contains many important facts and judicious observations on the ice, tides, compass, northern lights, etc. Fox started on this expedition on the 28th April, 1631, and the result of his exploration is related in this *very rare volume*. The map is often deficient, or supplied by a facsimile.

We are UNABLE TO RECORD the PUBLIC SALE of a PERFECT COPY in the UNITED STATES.

739 A BEAUTIFULLY ILLUSTRATED WORK.

FRANCIS (J. W.) Old New York: or, Reminiscences of the Past Sixty Years. By John W. Francis, M.D., LL.D. With a Memoir of the Author, by Henry T. Tuckerman.
New York: W. J. Widdleton. MDCCCLXV.

4 *vols., imp. 8vo, pp. cxxxvi.,* 400. 2 *Portraits and Plate. Grass green crushed levant morocco, filleted and gilt back, paneled sides elegantly tooled and gilt, richly gilt broad inside borders, gilt top,* UNCUT, *by* W. MATTHEWS *in his* BEST STYLE.

A LARGE PAPER COPY, of which *only* 100 *were printed*. ONE volume extended to FOUR, with RUBRICATED TITLES printed expressly for the set, and upwards of FIVE HUNDRED FINE ILLUSTRATIONS, consisting of PORTRAITS and VIEWS, *inserted*; of which nearly Two HUNDRED are PROOFS, INDIA PROOFS, and INDIA PROOFS BEFORE LETTERS, embracing several PRIVATE PLATES, and FOUR WATER COLOUR DRAWINGS; all directly relating to the text, and uniformly in the FINEST and MOST UNEXCEPTIONABLE condition throughout. One of the finest examples of American bookbinding, and altogether a truly CHOICE, SUMPTUOUS, and UNIQUE set.

740 [FRANKLIN (B.)] Some Observations on the Proceedings against The Rev. Mr. Hemphill; with a Vindication of his Sermons. The Second Edition. *Philadelphia: Printed and Sold by* B. FRANKLIN. 1735.

12*mo, pp.* 32. *Polished calf, gilt edges, by* W. PRATT. EXTREMELY RARE.

One of the first, if not the VERY FIRST BOOK printed by Benjamin Franklin; to whom its authorship is positively ascribed.

741 [FRANKLIN. ?] Letters between Theophilus and Eugenio, on the Moral Pravity of Man, and the Means of his Restoration. Wrote in the East-Indies, And now First Published from the Original Manuscript.
Philadelphia: Printed and Sold by B. FRANKLIN. MDCCXLVII.

4*to, pp. iv.,* 64. *Half gray calf, gilt top,* UNCUT. EXTREMELY RARE. Probably written by Franklin, and an EARLY SPECIMEN of his press. FINE COPY.

742 [FRANKLIN. ?] Proposals relating to the Education of Youth in Pennsylvania. *Philadelphia:* M.DCC.XLIX.

8*vo, pp.* 32. *Half gray calf.* A beautiful copy, and a fine example of Franklin's press although without his imprint.

In the advertisement prefixed to this pamphlet, letters on the subject are requested to be addressed to B. Franklin, Printer, &c., from which it appears probable that he was the author.

743 [FRANKLIN.] Some Account of the Pennsylvania Hospital; From its first Rise, to the Beginning of the Fifth Month, called May, 1754.
Philadelphia: Printed by B. FRANKLIN and D. HALL. MDCCLIV.

4*to, pp.* 40. *Half gray calf.* Fine copy, with the AUTOGRAPH of PROUD the Historian; "E Libris Roberti Proudi 1761."

744 [FRANKLIN.] The Substance of a Council Held at Lancaster August the 28th, 1764. By a Committee of Presbyterian Ministers and Elders deputed from all Parts of Pennsylvania, in order to settle the ensuing Election of Members for the Assembly. Published At the Request of their respective Congregations.
Printed in the Year MDCCLXIV.

12mo, pp. 19. *Half gray calf, gilt top,* UNCUT. VERY SCARCE. Said to have been *written* and *printed* by Franklin.

Motto.

When Gospel Trumpeter surrounded
  With long-eared rout to Battle sounded,
And Pulpit Drum ecclesiastic,
  Was beat by Fist instead of a Stick
Such Priests deserve to have their A-se Kick'd.

745 [FRANKLIN.] Second | Protest, | with a | List of the Voters | against the | Bill | To Repeal the | American Stamp Act, | of | Last Session. | *A Paris,* | *Chez J. W. Imprimeur, Rue du Columbier Faux-* | *bourgh St. Germain, à l'Hotel de Saxe,* 1766. | *Prix, dit huit Sous,* | *Avec Approbation, & Privilege.*

8vo, pp. 15. *Claret morocco, gilt top,* UNCUT. UNIQUE.

DR. FRANKLIN'S COPY, WITH HIS MANUSCRIPT NOTES. This was purchased at the sale or Mr. Morrell's Library, from whose catalogue the following notice is reprinted: "Of this unique volume, possessing as it does the greatest historical interest, it is needless to say more than that I have always considered it one of the choicest, in point of rarity, in my collection. The following lines in Franklin's handwriting, on page 12, will serve as a specimen of the character of the notes (with which nearly every page is copiously filled): 'My Duty to the King & Justice to my Country, will, I hope, justify me if I likewise protest, which I do with all Humility, in behalf of myself and of Every American, and of our Posterity, against your Declaratory Bill, that the Parliament of Great Britain, hath not, never had, and of Right never can have, without our Consent given either before or after, Power to make Laws of sufficient Force to bind the Subjects in America in any Case whatever, and particularly in Taxation.'"

On the last leaf occurs the following, also in FRANKLIN'S HANDWRITING. "I have some little Property in America. I will freely spend nineteen Shillings in the Pound to defend my Right of giving or refusing the other Shilling, and after all, if I cannot defend that Right, I can retire chearfully with my little Family into the Boundless Woods of America which are sure to afford Freedom and Subsistance to any man who can bait a Hook or pull a Trigger."

746 [FRANKLIN.] The Examination of Doctor Benjamin Franklin, before an August Assembly, relating to the Repeal of the Stamp-Act, &c. [*n. p.* 1766.]

8vo, pp. 16. *Half green morocco,* UNCUT. RARE. *Contemporary* PORTRAIT *inserted.* Probably printed at Philadelphia. Issued without a title.

747 [FRANKLIN.] The Examination of Doctor Benjamin Franklin, Relative to the Repeal of the American Stamp Act, In MDCCLXVI.
[*n. p.*] MDCCLXVII.

8vo, pp. 50. *Half green morocco.* Fine copy. SCARCE.

748 [FRANKLIN.] Memoirs of the Late Dr. Benjamin Franklin; With a Review of his Pamphlet, entitled "Information to those who would wish to remove to America." *London: A. Grant.* 1790.

8vo, pp. 94. *Portrait. Half red morocco, gilt top,* UNCUT. *Scarce.*

An endeavor to depreciate the Doctor, and a flat contradiction of his representations as to emigration. *See M. Rev.*, IX. 83.

749 FRANKLIN. The Works of Benjamin Franklin; Containing Several Political and Historical Tracts not included in any Former Edition, and many Letters Official and Private not hitherto published; with Notes and a Life of the Author. By Jared Sparks.
Boston: Hilliard Gray & Co. 1836–40.

10 *vols., imp. 8vo, half crimson morocco, gilt top,* UNCUT. Uniform in size with the works of Washington, Adams, Webster, Bancroft, &c.

A UNIQUE and ELEGANT LARGE PAPER COPY of which *fifty sets only* were printed; containing upwards of ONE HUNDRED CHOICE ILLUSTRATIONS, including SIX FINE and RARE PORTRAITS of FRANKLIN, one of which is the renowned SNUFF BOX PORTRAIT, printed in tint, with the legend, "WHERE LIBERTY DWELLS THERE IS MY COUNTRY."

750 [FRANKLIN.] Letters to Benjamin Franklin, from his Family and Friends. 1751–1790. *New York: Charles B. Richardson.* 1859.

4to, half purple levant morocco, gilt top, UNCUT. LARGE PAPER. *Ten copies only* printed. TWENTY-FIVE CHOICE ILLUSTRATIONS *inserted,* two of which are photographs of figures which cannot be obtained in any other form, and FOURTEEN, PROOFS, INDIA PROOFS, and PROOFS BEFORE LETTERS; with a beautiful impression of the RARE PORTRAIT of ANDRÉ, painted by himself, and engraved by SHERWIN in 1781.

751 [FRANKLIN (B.) *and* SOWER (C.) A Collection of Seven Devotional Tracts; with Separate Titles and Imprints as described below, and a General Title to the whole. Printed by FRANKLIN and HALL: and CHRISTOPHER SOWER.]

Extract from a Treatise called the Spirit of Prayer. By William Law. *Philadelphia: Printed by* B. FRANKLIN and D. HALL. 1760.

A Discourse on Mistakes concerning Religion, Enthusiasm, &c. By Thomas Hartley. *Germantown:* CHRISTOPHER SOWER. 1759.

Christ's Spirit a Christian's Strength. By William Dell.
Germantown: CHRISTOPHER SOWER. 1760.

The Doctrine of Baptisms. By William Dell.
Philadelphia: Re-Printed by B. FRANKLIN *and* D. HALL. 1759.

The Trial of Spirits, both in Teachers and Hearers. By William Dell. *Philadelphia: Re-Printed by* B. FRANKLIN *and* D. HALL. 1760.

Liberty of the Spirit and of the Flesh Distinguished. By John Rutty. *Philadelphia: Re-Printed by* B. FRANKLIN *and* D. HALL. 1759.

Observations on the Inslaving, Importing, and Purchasing of Negroes. [By Anthony Benezet.]
Germantown: Printed by CHRISTOPHER SOWER. 1760.

8vo, polished calf, extra gilt, by F. BEDFORD. A FINE SET.

Books printed by Sower are EXTREMELY SCARCE. They were nearly all used to make cartridges at the battle of Germantown, where his printing office was then situated.

A UNIQUE COLLECTION.

752 FRELINGHUYSEN (F.) An Oration on the Death of Gen. George Washington: delivered in the Dutch Church, in New-Brunswick, on the 22d of February, 1800. By Major-General Frederick Frelinghuysen. ... *New-Brunswick, New Jersey:* 1800.

8vo, pp. 23.

753 FRENCH (B. F.) Historical Collections of Louisiana, embracing many Rare and Valuable Documents relating to the Natural, Civil and Political History of that State. Compiled with Historical and Biographical Notes, and an Introduction, By B. F. French. ... *New York: Wiley & Putnam.* 1846–53.

5 *vols., 8vo, half calf. A large and fine set.* VERY SCARCE.

This collection is almost wholly composed of memoirs and narratives, of the original explorers. Vol I. contains, with other historical material, La Salle's memoir of the discovery of the Mississippi, Joutel's journal, and Hennepin's account of the Mississippi. Vol. II. Marquette and Joliet's voyage to discover the Mississippi, De Soto's expedition, and Coxe's "Carolana." Vol. III. La Harpe's journal of the establishment of the French in Louisiana, Charlevoix's journal, etc. Vol. IV. Narratives of the voyages, missions, and travels among the Indians, by Marquette, Joliet, Dablon, Allouez, Le Clercq, La Salle, Hennepin, Membre, and Douay, with biographical and bibliographical notices of the missionaries and their works. By J. G. Shea. Vol. V. Dumont's memoir of transactions with the Indians of Louisiana, from 1712 to 1740, and Champégny's memoirs.

754 FRENCH. Historical Collections of Louisiana and Florida, including Translations of Original Manuscripts relating to their Discovery and Settlement, with Numerous Historical and Biographical Notes. By B. F. French. ... New Series. *New York: J. Sabin & Sons.* 1869.

8vo, half red morocco, gilt top, UNCUT, *by* BRADSTREET.

Contents: M. de Rémonville on the importance of establishing a colony in Louisiana; The expedition of P. Le Moyne d'Iberville to Louisiana; Annals of Louisiana, 1698–1722, by M. Penicaut; History of the first attempt of the Huguenots to colonize Florida, by René Laudonnière, translated by R. Hakluyt.

755 [FRENCH (James Clark.) *and* CAREY (Edward.)] The Trip of the Oceanus to Fort Sumter and Charleston, S.C. Comprising the Incidents of the Excursion, the Appearance at that time of the City, and the entire Programme of Exercises at the Re-raising of the Flag over the ruins of Fort Sumter, April 14th, 1865. *Brooklyn:* 1865.

8vo, pp. 172, (2). 6 *Plates. Half blue morocco, gilt top,* UNCUT.

756 FRENEAU (P.) The Poems of Philip Freneau. Written chiefly during the late War. *Philadelphia: Printed by Francis Bailey.* M DCC LXXXVI.

Sm. 8vo, pp. viii., 407. Half green morocco, carmine edges. FINE COPY, and the RAREST of all of the editions of Freneau's works.

757 [FRENEAU.] A Journey from Philadelphia to New-York, by way of Burlington and South-Amboy. [In Verse.] By Robert Slender, Stocking Weaver. Extracted from the Author's Journals.

Philadelphia : Francis Bailey. 1787.

8vo, pp. 28. *Half green morocco.* FINE COPY. EXTREMELY RARE.

758 FRENEAU. The Miscellaneous Works of Mr. Philip Freneau, containing his Essays and Additional Poems.

Philadelphia : Francis Bailey. MDCCLXXXVIII.

12mo, pp. xii., 429. *Half green morocco, carmine edges.* RARE. FINE COPY, with an AUTOGRAPH SIGNATURE of the AUTHOR *inserted.*

759 FRENEAU. Poems Written between the Years 1768 & 1794, by Philip Freneau of New Jersey: A New Edition, Revised and Corrected by the Author; Including a Considerable Number of Pieces never before Published. ...

Monmouth, (N. J.) : printed at the press of the Author, at Mount Pleasant, near Middletown-Point : M,DCC,XCV *and, of American Independence* XIX.

8vo, pp. (5), *x–xv.,* 455, (1). *Half green morocco.* LARGE and FINE copy. VERY SCARCE. *Inserted* is a Receipt for a subscription to the National Gazette, WRITTEN and SIGNED by FRENEAU. One of the RAREST of American autographs.

760 [FRENEAU.] Letters on Various Interesting and Important Subjects; many of which have appeared in the Aurora. Corrected and much Enlarged. By Robert Slender, O.S.M.

Philadelphia : Printed for the Author. 1799.

8vo, pp. 142, (1). *Half green morocco.* FINE COPY. RARE.

761 FRENEAU. Poems Written and Published during the American Revolutionary War, and now Republished from the Original Manuscripts, interspersed with Translations from the Ancients, and other pieces not heretofore in Print. By Philip Freneau. ... The Third Edition. ... *Philadelphia : Press of Lydia R. Bailey.* 1809.

2 *vols., 12mo, pp. iv.,* 280; 302, *xii.* 2 *Plates. Half green morocco.* FINE COPY, with the *engraved frontispieces,* wanting in many sets. VERY SCARCE.

762 FRENEAU. A Collection of Poems, on American Affairs, and a Variety of other Subjects, chiefly Moral and Political. Written between the Year 1797 and the Present time. By Philip Freneau. ...

New York : David Longworth. 1815.

2 *vols.,* 18*mo,* bound *in one. Half green morocco, gilt top,* UNCUT. FINE COPY, and VERY RARE in *uncut* condition.

Freneau enjoyed the friendship of Adams, Franklin, Jefferson, Madison, and Munroe, and the last three were his constant correspondents while they lived. His patriotic songs and ballads, which were superior to any metrical compositions then written in America, were everywhere sung with enthusiasm.

763 FRENEAU. Poems on Various Subjects, but chiefly Illustrative of the Events and Actors in the American War of Independence. By

Philip Freneau. Reprinted from the Rare Edition printed at Philadelphia in 1786. With a Preface. *London: J. R. Smith.* 1861.

Sm. 8vo, half red morocco, gilt top, UNCUT.

764 FRENEAU. Poems relating to the American Revolution. By Philip Freneau. With an Introductory Memoir and Notes, By Evert A. Duyckinck. *New York: W. J. Widdleton.* M.DCCC.LXV.

Imp. 8vo, half green morocco, gilt top, UNCUT. LARGE PAPER, *only* 100 *copies printed.*

This collection embraces all of Freneau's poems relating to the American revolution, gathered from the several volumes published by the author. No collection of this kind has been published in America since the edition, now exceedingly rare, published at Philadelphia in 1809. The Poems of the Revolution, by which the author's reputation was established, are now brought together in one volume for the first time.

765 FRISBIE (L.) An Eulogy on the Illustrious Character of the late General George Washington ... delivered at Ipswich, on the 7th day of January, 1800. By Levi Frisbie, A.M. ... To which is added, General Washington's Parential and Affectionate Address to his Country ... . *Newburyport:* 1800.

8vo, pp. 61. UNCUT.

766 FRIES (J.) The Two Trials of John Fries, on an Indictment for Treason; together with a Brief Report of the Trials of several other Persons, for Treason and Insurrection, in the Counties of Bucks, Northampton and Montgomery ... Begun at ... Philadelphia, April 11, 1799; continued at Norristown, October 11, 1799, and concluded at Philadelphia, April 11, 1800; before the Hon. Judges, Iredell, Peters, Washington and Chase. ... Taken in Short Hand by Thomas Carpenter. *Philadelphia: William W. Woodward.* 1800.

8vo, pp. 4, 226, 50. *Half green morocco.* VERY SCARCE. Title repaired where a name has been cut from the head margin.

Relates to the "Whiskey Insurrection."

767 FROISSART (*Sir* J.) Chronicles of England, France, and Spain, and the adjoining Countries. ... By Sir John Froissart. Translated from the French Edition. ... By Thomas Johnes, Esq. To which is prefixed a Life of the Author, An Essay on his Works, and a Criticism on his History. *London: W. Smith.* 1844.

2 *vols., royal 8vo, half crushed red levant morocco, gilt top,* UNCUT, *by* W. MATTHEWS.

The set of "ILLUMINATED ILLUSTRATIONS" which is *inserted* in this fine copy, contains beautiful impressions of the SEVENTY-TWO ILLUSTRATIONS IN GOLD AND COLOURS, of the FIRST ISSUE of 1844–45; published at twelve guineas. In consequence of the wear of the stones the subsequent issues are defaced and undesirable. The work itself is the FIRST EDITION of Smith's reprint. The numerous woodcuts are consequently *fine, strong,* and *brilliant* impressions.

TWO ELEGANT VOLUMES.

Sir Walter Scott, in his "Tales of my Landlord," thus speaks of the above: "Did you ever read Froissart?" "No," said Morton. "I have half a mind," said Claverhouse, "to contrive you should have six months' imprisonment in order to procure you that pleasure. His chapters inspire me with more enthusiasm than even poetry itself."

768 [FROISSART.] Illuminated Illustrations of Froissart. Selected from the MS. in the Bibliothèque Royale, Paris, and from other Sources. By H. N. Humphreys, Esq. *London: W. Smith.* 1844–45.

Roy. 8vo, 2 parts in 1 vol., half crushed red levant morocco, gilt top, UNCUT, *by* W. MATTHEWS. Uniform with the "Chronicles."

This is the text which accompanies and *describes* the "Illuminated Illustrations." It is a necessary pendant to the preceding No., and should accompany it.

"I rejoice you have met with Froissart; he is the Herodotus of a barbarous age; had he but had the luck of writing in as good a language he might have been immortal! His locomotive disposition (for then there was no other way of learning things), his simple curiosity, his religious credulity, were much like those of the old Grecian."— *Gray's Letters.*

769 FROTHINGHAM (R.) The Command in the Battle of Bunker Hill, with a Reply to "Remarks on Frothingham's History of the Battle, by S. Swett." ... By Richard Frothingham, Jr., ...
Boston: Charles C. Little and James Brown. 1850.

8vo, pp. 56, (1). *Half crimson morocco, gilt top,* UNCUT. PORTRAIT *inserted.*

770 FROTHINGHAM. History of the Siege of Boston, and of the Battles of Lexington, Concord, and Bunker Hill. Also, an Account of the Bunker Hill Monument. With Illustrative Documents. Second Edition. *Boston: Charles C. Little and James Brown.* 1851.

8vo, pp. ix., (1), 420. *Maps and plates. Half green morocco, gilt top,* UNCUT.

UNIQUE copy with *fifty-six* ILLUSTRATIONS *inserted:* together with Endicott's "Account of Leslie's Retreat." pp. 47; Hudson's "Doubts concerning the Battle of Bunkerhill." pp. 41; *inlaid* to the size of the volume by TRENT; and *ten leaves of mounted cuttings* bound in at the end. A MS. list of "Corrections and Additions" by the author, is also in the volume.

"In my judgment, Mr. Frothingham's work excels any that has appeared on insulated points of our history. It is the best of our historic monographs that I have seen. Its author has been patient in research, and very successful; has been most impartial; has brought to excellent materials a sound and healthy judgment, and after finishing all this, his work is pervaded with a modesty which lends a new charm to its merit."— *George Bancroft.*

771 FROTHINGHAM. Life and Times of Joseph Warren. By Richard Frothingham. Portrait and Fac-simile.
Boston: Little, Brown & Co. 1865.

8vo, half purple morocco, gilt top, UNCUT. Fine copy with TWENTY-ONE ILLUSTRATIONS *inserted.*

772 FULTON (R.) A Treatise on the Improvement of Canal Navigation; exhibiting the numerous Advantages to be derived from Small Canals, and Boats of Two to Five feet wide, containing from Two to Five Tons Burthen. ... Including Observations on the great Importance of Water Communications, with Thoughts on, and Designs for Aqueducts and Bridges of Iron and Wood. By R. Fulton, Civil Engineer. ... *London: I. and J. Taylor.* 1796.

4to, pp. xvi., 144. 17 *Plates. Half green morocco, gilt top,* UNCUT. Two PORTRAITS *inserted.* Beautiful copy. VERY RARE in *uncut* condition.

"But few of Fulton's admirers are aware that he wrote such a book, a few copies only, (of a small number printed) having reached this country." In the late Mr. Gowans' catalogue for 1866, a cut copy is priced at $25.

773 FULTON. A Treatise &c. [Another copy.]
London: I. and J. Taylor. 1796.

4to, half green morocco, gilt top, by BRADSTREET. PORTRAIT of the AUTHOR *inserted.*
LARGE PAPER.

Notwithstanding this copy has been trimmed, it is much larger than the uncut one; thus settling the question as to the work having been printed on large paper. It is the ONLY COPY KNOWN in such a form.

774 FURMAN (G.) Notes, Geographical and Historical, relating to the Town of Brooklyn, in Kings County, on Long Island. By Gabriel Furman. *Brooklyn: A. Spooner.* 1824.

Sm. 8vo, crushed crimson levant morocco, gilt top, UNCUT, *by* F. BEDFORD. A BEAUTIFUL COPY of this VERY RARE work, TOTALLY UNCUT, and as fine, in its present binding, as any copy in existence.

775 FURMAN. Notes, Geographical and Historical, &c. [Another Edition.] With Notes and a Memoir of the Author.
Brooklyn: Reprinted for the Faust Club. 1865.

Imp. 8vo, half purple morocco, gilt top, UNCUT. LARGE PAPER. 120 *Copies only printed.*

776 [FURMAN.] Catalogue of an Extensive and Valuable Private Library ... consisting of Rare Books, &c. [Collected by Gabriel Furman.] *New York:* 1846.

8vo, half olive morocco, gilt top, UNCUT. Ruled; with *names* and *prices.* Contains upwards of 300 titles of AMERICANA.

777 FURMAN (R.) Humble Submission to Divine Sovereignty the duty of a Bereaved Nation: A Sermon occasioned by the Death of His Excellency General George Washington ... Preached in ... Charleston, S. C., on the 22d of February, 1800, before the American Revolution Society, the State Society of the Cincinnati, and a numerous assemblage of Citizens. By Richard Furman, A.M. ...
Charleston: MDCCC.

8vo, pp. 28. VERY RARE.

778 **Fyssher (J.)** This treatyse concernynge the fruytful | saynges of Dauid the kynge and prophete in | the seuen penytencyall psalmes. Deuyded | in seuen sermons was made and compyled | by the ryght reuerente fader in god Johan | fyssher doctoure of dyuynyte & bysshop of | Rochester at the exortacyō and sterynge of | the moost excellēt princesse Margarete coū | -tesse of Rychemoūt and Derby & moder to | our souerayne lorde kynge Henry the VII. | [Colophon.] Here endeth the exposycyon of the VII. psalmes. En- | prynted at London in the Fletestrete at the sygne of the | sonne by Wynkyn de Worde prynter unto the moost ex | -cellent pryncesse my lady the kynges graūdame. In the | yere of our lorde god. M.CCCCC. and IX. the XII. daye | of the moneth of Juyn. |

Small 4to, **Black Letter,** 145 *unpaged leaves,* with the large device of WYNKYN DE WORDE on the last page. *Blue morocco, blind tooled back and sides, gilt edges.* A LARGE AND BEAUTIFUL COPY, AND IN THE MOST PERFECT CONDITION.

This elegant copy has been in the possession of Mr. Utterson, and the Rev. T. Corser, and is worthy of companionship with the choicest of books. It is of the GREATEST POSSIBLE RARITY in a fine and complete condition like this. There is a copy in the Lambeth Library, and one in the British Museum, and there was said to be a copy in the collection of Mr. Nuenburg, but it did not appear in the catalogue of his library. It is conspicuous by its absence from the Grenville collection, and from the library at Althorpe; nor did Mr. Heber succeed in obtaining it. Dibdin never saw a copy, but described it from Herbert's account. The present example is a very desirable one, as it rarely happens that an English book of so early a date, by one of the first printers, is found in such clean, sound state. Next after CAXTON, the name of his pupil, WYNKYN DE WORDE, is most famous in the annals of English typography. Although by birth a Lorrainer, he devoted himself to England, and did more than any other of the early English printers to spread knowledge by means of the press.

779 GAGE (T.) The English-American his Travail by Sea and Land; | or, | A New Svrvey | of the | VVest-India's, | containing | A Journall of Three thousand and Three hundred | Miles within the main Land of America. | Wherein is set forth his Voyage from Spain to St. John de Ulhua; | and from thence to Xalappa, to Tlaxcalla, the City of Angeles, and | forward to Mexico; With the description of that great City, | as it was in former times, and also at this present. | Likewise his Journey from Mexico through the provinces of Guaxaca, | Chiapa, Guatemala, Vera Paz, Truxillo, Comayagua; with his | abode Twelve years about Guatemala, and especially in the | Indian-towns of Mixco, Pinola, Petapa, Amatitlan. | As also his strange and wonderfull Conversion, and Calling from those | remote Parts to his Native Country. | ... | By the true and painfull endevours of Thomas Gage, now Preacher | of the Word of God at Acris in the County of Kent, Anno Dom. 1648. |
London: Printed by R. Cotes, etc. 1648.

Sm. folio, 5l., pp. 220, (12). *Half gray calf antique.* A beautiful copy.

This book is remarkable as the first and only extensive work by an English author upon the Spanish Indies as seen from within. It is most entertaining and instructive, notwithstanding the singularly superstitious tales that it narrates. Gage belonged to the Dominican order originally, but joined the English church before he wrote his travels. The 22d chapter relating to his journey to Rome, was suppressed in the subsequent editions.

780 GAGE (Thomas.) Letters of the Two Commanders-in-Chief, Generals Gage and Washington, and Major-Generals Burgoyne and Lee; with the Manifesto of General Washington to the Inhabitants of Canada. *New York: James Rivington.* 1775.

[Also:] Letters of Major General Lee, to the Right Hon. Earl Percy, and Major General John Burgoyne. With the Answers. *New York: James Rivington.* 1775.

[And:] Letters which lately passed between his Excellency Governor Tryon, and Whitehead Hicks, Esq., Mayor of the City of New York. *New York: James Rivington.* 1775.

In which Tryon demands protection for his person against an apprehended capture by the Provincial Congress; and sets forth the reasons for his ultimate flight to the Asia man-of-war.

8vo, 3 VERY RARE TRACTS, *in* 1 *vol.*, *pp.* 8 : 8, 4 : 8. *Half red morocco.*

781 GALLERY (The) of [British and Foreign] Portraits: with Memoirs. [By Distinguished Biographers.] *London: Charles Knight.* 1833–38.

7 *vols.*, *imp.* *8vo*, *half green levant morocco*, *gilt top*, UNCUT, *by* W. MATTHEWS. A SPLENDID COPY, with conspicuously BRILLIANT IMPRESSIONS of the 168 PORTRAITS. VERY SCARCE in this *spotless* and *uncut* state.

A very interesting series, engraved in the highest style of the Art, in the same manner as Lodge's Portraits, to which it forms an excellent companion, the portraits being different.

782 [GALLOWAY (Joseph.)] Letters to a Nobleman, on the Conduct of the War in the Middle Colonies. The Second Edition. *London: J Wilkie.* 1779.

8vo, *pp.* *viii.*, 101. *Map.* *Half blue morocco.* The LARGE FOLDED MAP is wanting in many copies.

This famous tract was written to demonstrate the shameful misconduct of the English generals in the American war.

783 [GALLOWAY.] A Letter to the Right Honourable Lord Viscount H—e, on His Naval Conduct in the American War. The Second Edition Corrected. *London: G. Wilkie.* 1779.

8vo., *pp.* (4), 50. *Half morocco*, UNCUT.

"The conduct of Admiral Howe is severely criticised. He is charged with the most palpable and criminal negligence and misconduct, in regard to the prosecution of the American war, leaving the reader to account for it, if he can, from connections with opposition at home, from secret favor to the American defection, from views of private interest, or from coöperation of all these unworthy principles." *See M. Rev.*, LXI. 467.

784 [GALLOWAY.] A Candid Examination of the Mutual Claims of Great-Britain, and the Colonies; with a Plan of Accomodation, on Constitutional Principles. By the Author of Letters to a Nobleman on the Conduct of the American War. [*London:*] *G. Wilkie.* MDCCLXXX.

8vo, *pp.* 116. *Half blue morocco*, *gilt top*, UNCUT.

A well-written Tory tract. "The effect of illiberal motives and unworthy passions. A principal object of this pamphlet is to reprobate the proceedings of the Congress; and for this purpose the author labors to maintain the unlimited supremacy of parliament over all the dominions of the crown, by arguments which have been often alleged, and sufficiently answered."— *M. Rev.*, LII. 537.

785 [GALLOWAY.] The Examination of Joseph Galloway, Esq., Late Speaker of the House of Assembly of Pennsylvania, before the House of Commons, in a Committee on the American Papers. With Explanatory Notes. The Second Edition. *London: J. Wilkie.* 1780.

8vo, *pp.* 85. *Half blue morocco*, *carmine edges.*

"Besides Mr. Galloway's very important evidence, this pamphlet contains many useful and interesting notes relative to the conduct of the war in America."— *M. Rev.*

786 [GALLOWAY.] A Letter from Cicero to the Right Hon. Lord Viscount H—e: occasioned by His late Speech in the H—e of C—ns. *London: J. Bew.* MDCCLXXXI.

8vo, pp. 43. *Half blue morocco, gilt top,* UNCUT.

Mr. Galloway here accuses Lord Howe, and his brother Sir William, of having most flagrantly, shamefully, and wickedly betrayed the trust reposed in them, in the command of the British naval and land forces in America."— *M. Rev.* "A thorough roasting and toasting of the two brothers, Lord, and Sir William Howe, commanding in America, for their blunders, selfishness, and misconduct, especially at Brooklyn on Long Island, at White Plains, the Brandywine, Germantown, Valley Forge, Princeton, New York, on the Raritan, the Delaware, etc."— *Stevens.*

787 [GALLOWAY.] A Reply to the Observations of Lieut. Gen. Sir William Howe, on a pamphlet, entitled Letters to a Nobleman: in which His Misrepresentations are Detected, and those Letters are Supported, by a Variety of New Matter and Argument. To which is added, An Appendix, Containing, I. Letter to Sir William Howe upon his Strictures on Mr. Galloway's Private Character. II. A Letter from Mr. Kirk to Sir William Howe, and his Answer. III. A Letter from a Committee to the President, of the Congress, on the State of the Rebel Army at Valley Forge, found among the Papers of Henry Laurens, Esq. By the Author of Letters to a Nobleman. The Second Edition, with Additions. *London: G. Wilkie.* MDCCLXXXI.

8vo, pp. (4), 157. *Half morocco, uncut.*

Mr. Galloway's defence of his own character and conduct against Sir William Howe.

788 [GALLOWAY.] Letter from Cicero to Cataline the Second. With Corrections and Explanatory Notes. *London: J. Bew.* MDCCLXXXI.

8vo, pp. vii., 104. *Half blue morocco, carmine edges.*

Under the assumed name of Cicero, Mr. Galloway attacks the Hon. Charles James Fox (whom he calls Cataline the Second), and the leaders of the opposition, with the view of exposing them to the indignation of the public.

789 [GALLOWAY.] Fabricius: Or, Letters to the People of Great Britain; on The Absurdity and Mischiefs of Defensive Operations only in the American War; and on The Causes of the Failure in the Southern Operations. *London: G. Wilkie.* MDCCLXXXII.

8vo, pp. 111. *Half blue morocco, gilt top,* UNCUT.

Galloway at first espoused American independency, but subsequently joined the home party and wrote against the Americans. Even at this late hour he scribbles for the recovery of the colonies and against their independence. Trumbull hits him hard, thus:—

"Did you not, in as vile and shallow way,
Fright our poor Philadelphian, Galloway,
Your Congress, when the loyal ribald
Belied, berated and bescribbled?
What ropes and halters did you send,
Terrific emblems of his end,
Till, lest he'd hang in more than effigy,
Fled in a fog the trembling refugee?"— *McFingal.*

790 [GALLOWAY.] The Claim of the American Loyalists Reviewed and Maintained upon Incontrovertible Principles of Law and Justice. *London: G. and T. Wilkie.* MDCCLXXXVIII.

8*vo, pp. viii.*, 138. *Half morocco.*

"Mr. Galloway was a member of Congress (and Speaker of the House of Assembly of Pennsylvania); he went over to the royal army in December, 1776, and continued with it till the evacuation of Philadelphia, in June, 1778, abandoning his estate and property to the value of above forty thousand pounds sterling."

791 GANO (S.) A Sermon on the Death of George Washington; delivered Lord's Day, January 5, 1800, before the Baptist Society in Providence. By Stephen Gano. ... *Providence:* 1800.

8*vo, pp.* 20. EXCEEDINGLY RARE.

792 GARDEN (A.) Anecdotes of the Revolutionary War in America, with Sketches of Character of Persons the most distinguished, in the Southern States, for Civil and Military Services. By Alexander Garden. ... *Charleston: Printed for the Author.* 1822.

8*vo, pp. xi.*, 459. *Half blue morocco, gilt top,* UNCUT. TWO PORTRAITS *inserted.* FINE COPY; entirely free from stains.

793 GARDEN. Anecdotes of the American Revolution, illustrative of the Talents and Virtues of the Heroes and Patriots, who Acted the Most Conspicuous Parts therein. By Alexander Garden. Second Series. *Charleston: A. E. Miller.* 1828.

12*mo, pp. ix.*, (3), 240. *Half blue morocco, gilt top,* UNCUT. FINE COPY.

794 GARDEN. Anecdotes of the American Revolution. Illustrative of the Talents and Virtues of the Heroes of the Revolution, who Acted the Most Conspicuous Parts therein. By Alexander Garden of Lee's Legion. *Reprinted: Brooklyn, N. Y.* 1865.

3 *vols.*, 4*to, half purple morocco, gilt top,* UNCUT. 150 *copies only printed.*

AN ILLUSTRATED COPY.

EIGHTY-EIGHT FINE PORTRAITS *inserted;* some PROOFS; some PROOFS BEFORE LETTERS; some RARE; all fine impressions. This edition contains additional anecdotes and notes by the editor, Thomas W. Field.

795 GARDINER (W.) Catalogue of Ancient and Modern Books, Selected with the Greatest Care, on sale by William Gardiner. *London:* 1810–14.

8*vo, half olive morocco, gilt top,* UNCUT. The SEVEN PARTS of Gardiner's Catalogue complete. VERY SCARCE.

Replete with original, uncommon, and characteristic bibliographical notes. Gardiner was the "Mustapha" of the "Bibliomania." *See* his memorable and incisive attack on Dibdin at the end of Catalogue Part I., for 1812. PORTRAIT of GARDINER, from a PRIVATE PLATE, and three leaves containing an account of the melancholy termination of his career *inserted.*

796 [GATFORD (Lionel.)] Publick | Good | Without Private | Interests: | Or, | A Compendious Remonstrance of the | present sad State

and Condition of the English | Colonie in Virginia. | With | A Modest Declaration of the severall Causes | (so far as by the Rules of Right, Reason and Religious Obser- | vation may be Collected) why it hath not prospered better hitherto | As also, | A Submissive suggestion of the most prudentiall probable wayes, and | meanes, both Divine and Civill (that the inexpert Remembrancer could | for the present recall to minde) for its happyer improvement | and advancement for the future. | Humbly presented to His Highness the Lord Protectour, | By a Person zealously devoted, | To the more effectual propagating of the Gospel in that Nation, | and to the inlargement of the Honour and Benefit, both of the said | Colonie, and this whole Nation, from whence they | have been transplanted. | *London*, | *Printed for Henry Marsh, and are to be sold at* | *the Crown in S. Paul's Church-yard.* 1657.

4to, 8 *l.*, *pp.* 26. *Half red morocco, gilt top*, UNCUT, *by* BRADSTREET. Reprinted in facsimile at Vienna for E. Tross, of Paris. SCARCE.

797 [GEARY (John W.)] IN MEMORIAM. *Philadelphia:* 1873.

4to, half green levant morocco, gilt top, UNCUT, *by* W. MATTHEWS. PRIVATELY PRINTED. One of the TWENTY-TWO "AUTOGRAPH COPIES," signed by the twenty surviving members of General Geary's Staff. Each signature, with the date, and the rank of the signer, occupies an entire page.

A beautiful tribute of respect for the memory of Gen. John W. Geary, late Governor of Pennsylvania.

798 GENERAL ADDRESS (The) (In Two Parts) Of the Outinian Lecturer to his Auditors. ... Descriptive of the Institution of the Outinian Society in the Hundredth year after the death of the benevolent William Penn, ... to secure the Advantages of Justice and Benevolence, with the aid of Ethical and Critical Lectures. ... *London: W. Nicoll.* 1822.

8vo, pp. (1), 56. 6 *Plates. Half red levant morocco, gilt top*, UNCUT, *by* W. MATTHEWS. Contains fine INDIA PROOF PORTRAITS of the PENN family.

799 GEORGIA. Observations upon the Effects of Certain Late Political Suggestions. By the Delegates of Georgia. Printed in the Year 1781. *Wormsloe:* 1847.

Folio, pp. 14. *Half maroon morocco, gilt top, uncut.* PRIVATELY REPRINTED for Mr. George Wymberly-Jones, and TWENTY-ONE COPIES only. VERY RARE.

800 GEORGIA. The Particular Case of the Georgia Loyalists; in addition to the General Case and Claim of the American Loyalists, which was lately published by order of their Agents. [*London*:] *February*. 1783.

8vo, pp. 16. *Half morocco.* VERY SCARCE.

801 GILBERT (B.) A Narrative of the Captivity and Sufferings of Benjamin Gilbert and his Family; who were Surprised by the Indians,

and taken from their Farms, on the Frontier of Pennsylvania. In the Spring, 1780. *London: James Phillips.* 1790.

12mo, pp. 123. *Half calf.* RARE.

Written by William Walton, to whom it was verbally narrated by Mr. Gilbert and his family after their return.

802 GILLISS (J. M.) The United States Naval Astronomical Expedition to the Southern Hemisphere during the years 1849–1852. ... By Lieut. J. M. Gilliss, assisted by Messrs. Macrae, Phelps, and Smith. *Washington:* 1855–56.

4to, 2 vols. bound in one, pp. xvi., 556; *xii.,* 300. 62 *Plates. Half olive morocco, gilt top.*

These volumes contain most interesting and useful information respecting the geography, natural history, industrial resources, etc. of the regions visited. The first volume has, besides maps, many COLOURED views; the second contains 14 beautifully COLOURED plates of birds, 3 COLOURED plates of Indian antiquities, 6 plates of reptiles, 5 of fishes and 4 of fossil mammalia. All the papers are by well-known American naturalists. The work has become scarce.

803 [GILPIN (Eliza.)] A Memorial of Henry D. Gilpin. *Philadelphia: Privately Printed.* 1860.

Roy. 8vo, pp. iii., (4), 211. *Portrait. Half morocco, gilt top,* UNCUT. PORTRAIT of MR. GILPIN *inserted.*

804 [GILPIN (Thomas.)] Exiles in Virginia: with Observations on the Conduct of the Society of Friends during the Revolutionary War, comprising the Official Papers of the Government relating to that period, 1777–1778. *Philadelphia: Publishea for the Subscribers.* 1848.

8vo, pp. 302. 3 *Facsimiles. Half olive morocco, gilt top,* UNCUT. Fine PORTRAIT of PENN *inserted.* SCARCE. Presentation copy from the Author.

805 GIRDLESTONE (T.) Facts Tending to Prove that General Lee, was never Absent from this Country, for any Length of Time, during the years 1767–1772, and that he was the Author of Junius. By Thomas Girdlestone, M.D. *London: P. Martin.* 1813.

8vo, pp. vii., 138. *Half calf, gilt top.* UNCUT. Contains the RARE and CURIOUS FULL LENGTH PORTRAIT of the GENERAL, with his dog; and two plates of facsimiles. PORTRAIT of HUGH BOYD *inserted.* VERY SCARCE.

806 GLASS (F.) A Life of George Washington in Latin Prose. By Francis Glass, A.M. ... Edited by J. N. Reynolds. Third Edition. *New York: Harper & Brothers.* 1836.

12mo, pp. 285, (30). *Portrait. Half green morocco, gilt top,* UNCUT. PORTRAIT of WASHINGTON *inserted.*

807 GLEASON (B.) An Oration Pronounced at ... Wrentham February 22, 1800, ... in Memory of Gen. George Washington. ... By Benjamin Gleason. *Wrentham: Mass.* 1800.

8vo, pp. 32. UNCUT.

808 [GLEIG (G. R.)] A Narrative of the Campaigns of the British Army at Washington, and New Orleans, ... in the years 1814 and

1815; with some Account of the Countries visited. By an Officer who served in the Expedition. *London: John Murray.* 1821.

8vo, calf. PORTRAIT of the AUTHOR *inserted.*

The Rev. gentleman was at the battle of New Orleans, and rather dislikes the Americans.

809 [GLOVER.] An Appeal to the Justice and Interests of the People of Great Britain, in the present Disputes with America. By an Old Member of Parliament. The Fourth Edition, Corrected. *London: J. Almon.* 1776.

[Also:] A Second Appeal to the Justice and Interests of the People, on the Measures respecting America. By the Author of the First. *London: J. Almon.* 1775.

[And:] A Speech intended to have been delivered in the House of Commons, in support of the Petition from the General Congress at Philadelphia. By the Author of An Appeal to the Justice and Interests of Great-Britain. *London: J. Almon.* 1775.

8vo, 3 Tracts in 1 vol., pp. 46; 90; 67. *Half olive morocco, carmine edges.*

"The author of these appeals is an able advocate for the colonists, and exposes the impolicy of raising a revenue in America against the will of the people."—*M. R.*

Attributed to Dr. Lee of Virginia; also to Lord Chatham, and with more probability to Mr. Glover.

810 [GOADBY (R.)] An Apology for the Life of Bampfylde-Moore Carew, commonly called the King of the Beggars. Being an Impartial Account of his Life ... wherein the great Number of Characters and Shapes he has appeared in through Great Britain, Ireland, and several other places of Europe, are related; with his Travels twice through great part of America. A particular Account of the Origin, Government, Language, Laws and Customs of the Gypsies; their method of electing their King, &c. ... The Ninth Edition. *London: R. Goadby.* 1775.

Sm. 8vo, pp. xxiv., iv., 347. *Portrait. Red morocco, super extra, gilt edges.* FINE COPY of the BEST EDITION, now VERY SCARCE. Contains a BRILLIANT IMPRESSION of the RARE 4to PORTRAIT, the largest and best of this singular character published, and seldom found with the book.

"Carew was born at Devon in 1693, was tried at Exeter about 1739 or 1740, and banished to Maryland, where he went at the cost of the public. He gives an amusing account of the country, and his adventures in Maryland, Virginia, New Jersey, New York, and Connecticut, till he embarked at New London for England. His accounts how he bamboozled and bled Whitefield, Thos. Penn, Gov. Thomas, and many others of good repute, are amusing, true or not."—*Stevens.*

811 GODDARD (D. A.) The Mathers Weighed in the Balances By Delano A. Goddard, M.A., and Found Not Wanting. *Boston: and London:* 1870.

16mo, pp. 32. *Cloth,* UNCUT. A FEW COPIES only PRIVATELY PRINTED on Whatman's handmade paper. VERY SCARCE.

812 [GODMAN (John D.)] Ode suggested by Rembrandt Peale's National Portrait of Washington.
Philadelphia: Printed by Jesper Harding. 1824.

8vo, half green morocco, gilt top, UNCUT. An INDIA PROOF impression of Peale's PORTRAIT of WASHINGTON *inserted.*

813 GOFFE (W.) Plan for seizing and carrying to New York Coll. Wm. Goffe the Regicide, As set forth in the affidavit of John London, Ap. 20, 1678. Published from the original in the office of the Secretary of State of New-York, by Franklin B. Hough, M.D. ...
Albany: Weed, Parsons & Co. M.D.CCC.LV.

Sm. 8vo, half red morocco, gilt top, UNCUT. *A few copies only printed.*

814 [GOMARA (F. Lopez. de)] The | Pleasant Historie of the | Conquest of the VVeast India, | now called new Spayne, | Atchieued by the vvorthy Prince | Hernando Cortes Marques of the valley of | Huaxacac, most delectable to Reade: | Translated out of the Spa- | nishe tongue, by T. N. | Anno. 1578. | *Imprinted at London by | Henry Bynneman.* | [1578.]

4to, **Black Letter.** *Title, pp.* (10), 405, (3). *Olive morocco, gilt edges, by* W. PRATT. LARGE and BEAUTIFUL COPY of the FIRST ENGLISH EDITION. EXCEEDINGLY RARE. The translator was Thomas Nicholas.

815 GORDON (W.) The History of the Rise, Progress, and Establishment of the Independence of the United States of America: Including an Account of the late War; and of the Thirteen Colonies, from their Origin to that Period. By William Gordon, D.D.
London: Printed for the Author. MDCCLXXXVIII.

4 *vols., 8vo, half green morocco, gilt top,* UNCUT. BEAUTIFUL COPY, with a RARE contemporary PORTRAIT opposite each title, and the VERY SCARCE PORTRAIT of the AUTHOR, *inserted.*

Dr. Gordon went to America in 1770, remained there until 1786, and wrote a considerable part of his work on the spot. Congress allowed him the inspection of such records as could with propriety be submitted to the perusal of a private person. Washington, Gates, Greene, Lincoln and Otho H. Williams, also allowed a liberal examination of their papers. "The accounts here given of American Affairs," says the author, "are so different in several respects from what have been the conceptions of many on each side of the Atlantic, that it was necessary to insert a variety of letters, papers, and anecdotes, to authenticate the narrative."

816 GORGES (F.) America | Painted to the Life. | The True | History | of | The Spaniards Proceedings in the Conquests of the | Indians, and of their Civil Wars among them- | selves, from Columbus his first Discovery, | to these later Times. | As Also, | Of the Original Undertakings of the Advancement of | Plantations into those parts; | ... | More especially, an absolute Narrative of the North | parts of America, and of the Discoveries and | Plantations of our English in | Virginia, New-England, and Berbadoes. | Publisht by Ferdinando Gorges, Esq; | ... | *London, Printed for Nath. Brook at the Angel in Cornhil.* 1659.

Title, 2 leaves, pp. 51. *Portrait and Map.*

Part II. A | briefe Narration | of the | Originall Undertakings | of the | Advancement | of | Plantations | Into the parts of | America. | Especially, | Shewing the beginning, progress | and continuance of that of | New-England. | Written by the right Worshipfull, Sir Ferdinando Gorges | Knight and Governour of the Fort and Island of | Plymouth in Devonshire. | *London: Printed by E. Brudenell, for Nath. Brook at the | Angell in Corn hill.* 1658.

Title, pp. 57.

Part III. America | Painted to the Life. | A | True History of the originall undertakings of the advancement | of Plantations into those parts, with a perfect relation of | our English Discoveries, shewing their beginning, progress, and | continuance, from the year, 1628. to 1658. declaring the forms of | their Government. ... | More | Especially an absolute Narrative of the North parts of America, and | of the discoveries and plantations of our English in | New-England. | Written by Sir Ferdinando Gorges Knight | and Governour of the Fort and Island of Plimouth in | Devonshire, one of the first and cheifest pro- | moters of those Plantations. | Publisht since his decease, by his Grand-child Ferdinando Gorges Esquire, | who hath much enlarged it, and added severall accurate Descripti- | ons of his owne. | ... | For the Reader's clearer understanding of the Country's they are lively described in a | compleat and exquisite Map. | Vivit post funera virtus. | *London; Printed by E. Brudenell, for Nathaniel Brook dwelling at | the Angel in Corn-hill.* 1658.

Title, 1*l., pp.* 236.

Part IV. America | Painted to the Life. | The | History | Of The | Spaniards Proceedings in America, their Con | quests of the Indians, and of their | Civil Wars among themselves. | From | Columbus his first Discovery, to these | later Times. | By | Ferdinando Gorges, Esq; | Ovid. Auri sacri fames quid non- | *London, Printed by T. F. for Nath. Brook at the Angel | in Cornhil.* 1659.

Title, 1 *leaf, pp.* 52, (17), *Books* 3.

4*to, crushed rich brown levant morocco, paneled sides elegantly tooled and gilt, edges gilt on carmine, by* W. MATTHEWS. A BEAUTIFUL COPY of this EXCESSIVELY RARE WORK. ALL FOUR PARTS with their respective TITLES, and the PORTRAIT and MAP COMPLETE.

This very rare book contains four distinct works, paged separately, the third of which is *Johnson's History of New England; or, Wonder Working Providence,* 1654, with a new title, &c. "It is altogether a very singular performance, containing a great deal of important information, relative to the early history of New England, and particularly of the District of Maine, which was originally granted to the author's grandfather, by whom the second work was written."—*Rich.*

817 GOSPEL ORDER | REVIVED, | Being an Answer to a Book lately set | forth by the Rev. Mr. Increase Mather, President | of Harvard Colledge etc. | Entituled | The Order of the Gospel, etc. | Dedicated to the Churches of Christ in New-England. | By sundry Ministers of the Gospel in New-England. | [*New York:*] *Printed* [*by William Bradford*] *in the year* 1700.

Sm. 4*to, pp.* (12), 40. *Polished calf, gilt edges, by* F. BEDFORD.

Opposite the title is the following curious and suggestive *Advertisement.*—"The *Reader* is desired to take Notice that the Press in *Boston* is so much under the aw of the Reverend Author, whom we answer and his friends, that we could not obtain of the Printer there to print the following sheets, which is the only true Reason why we have sent the Copy so far for its Impressions and where it was printed with some Difficulty."

A BEAUTIFUL COPY of this EXCESSIVELY RARE tract, respecting which Thomas, "Hist. of Printing," II. 90, says "This is the only book printed in New York, prior to 1700, that contained more than 20 pages." For an extended and interesting account of this most rare tract see Thomas. II. 458, *note.*

818 GRACE (H.) The History of the Life and Sufferings of Henry Grace of Basingstoke, in the County of Southampton, being a Narrative of the Hardships he underwent during several years Captivity among the Savages in North America, and of the Cruelties they

practice to their unhappy Prisoners. In which is introduced an Account of the several Customs and Manners of the different Nations of Indians; as well as a compendious Description of the Soil, Produce, and various Animals of those Parts. Written by Himself.
Reading: 1764.

12mo, pp. 56. *Half morocco.* Title in facsimile, otherwise a fine copy of one of the RAREST of Indian captivities. It is unnoticed by Mr. Field.

"The author's recital of the various hardships he underwent affords that painful entertainment we usually find in historical details of distress, especially when they have any thing of adventure in them, as is the case with the present artless but affecting narrative."—*M. R.*

819 GRAHAM (J. A.) A Descriptive Sketch of the Present State of Vermont, one of the United States of America. By J. A. Graham, LL.D. Late Lieutenant Colonel in the Service of the above State.
London: Printed for the Author. 1797.

8vo, pp. vii., 186, (1). *Portrait. Half crushed red levant morocco, gilt top, by* W. MATTHEWS. An elegant copy. Beautifully printed, and embellished with a fine PORTRAIT of the AUTHOR.

820 GRAHAM [(Samuel)]. Memoir of General Graham with Notices of the Campaigns in which he was engaged from 1779 to 1801. Edited by his Son Colonel James J. Graham.
Edinburgh: Privately Printed by R. & R. Clark. 1862.

Sm. 8vo, pp. xvii., (1), 318. *7 Plates. Half olive morocco, gilt top,* UNCUT.

Contains a graphic account of the romantic and tragic incidents connected with Captain Charles Asgill during the American Revolution. But few copies of this work were printed, and those only for private circulation among the friends and relatives of the family. *See Preface.*

821 GRAHAME (J.) The History of the United States of North America, from the Plantation of the British Colonies till their Revolt and Declaration of Independence. By James Grahame, Esq.
London: Smith, Elder and Co. 1836.

4 *vols., 8vo, half pale calf, gilt top,* UNCUT. An UNLETTERED INDIA PROOF PORTRAIT of the AUTHOR *inserted.*

"This historical work is the fruit of more than eleven years of intense meditation, eager research, industrious composition, and solicitous revisal."—*Author's Preface.*

"Mr. Grahame has published the best book that has anywhere appeared upon the History of the United States.—*N. A. Review.*

See Quincy (Josiah.) No. 1656.

822 [GRANT (*Mrs.* Anne.)] Memoirs of an American Lady: with Sketches of Manners and Scenery in America, as they existed previous to the Revolution. *London: Longman.* 1808.

2 *vols., 12mo, half blue morocco, gilt top,* UNCUT. Two PORTRAITS, one an ARTIST'S PROOF, of the AUTHOR *inserted.* ORIGINAL EDITION. RARE in *uncut* condition.

The "American Lady" means Mrs. Schuyler of Albany. Exceedingly instructive coneerning the manners and customs which prevailed in New York colony at the close of the eighteenth century.

823 GRAVES (W.) Two Letters from W. Graves Esq.: Respecting the Conduct of Rear-Admiral Thomas Graves in North America, during his accidental Command there for Four Months in 1781. [*London:* 1782.]

4to, pp. 48, 14, 9–19. *Plan. Half olive morocco.* A large and fine copy of the VERY SCARCE PRIVATELY PRINTED ORIGINAL EDITION. This copy contains manuscript notes and emendations evidently by its author, or compiler, and is much more voluminous in the body of the work, and in the appendices, than the following reprint.

824 GRAVES. Two Letters from W. Graves, Esq. [Another Edition.] *Morrisania:* 1865.

4to, pp. 4, 39. *Half blue morocco, gilt top,* UNCUT. *One Hundred Copies only printed.*

825 GRAVIER (G.) Découvertes et Établissements de Cavalier de la Salle de Rouen dans l'Amérique du Nord (Lacs Ontario, Érié, Huron, Michigan, vallées de l'Ohio et du Mississippi et Texas) Par Gabriel Gravier, ... *Paris:* 1870.

Roy. 8vo, pp. xii., 412. *Portrait, Plate, and Map. Half red morocco, gilt top,* UNCUT, *by* BRADSTREET.

The present work is the only narrative of the great discoveries achieved by "the Columbus of his age" in the great tract of country lying along and about the course of the Mississippi; and in fact over all the continent between Canada and the Gulf of Mexico. Hennepin's Travels are supplementary to those of Cavalier de la Salle.

See Joutel (Mons.) No. 1110.

826 GRAY (F. C.) Oration delivered before the Legislature of Massachusetts, At their Request, on the Hundredth Anniversary of the Birth of George Washington. By Francis C. Gray. *Boston: Dutton and Wentworth.* 1832.

8vo, pp. 80, *half blue morocco, gilt top,* UNCUT, *by* W. SMITH.

827 [GRAYDON (A.)] Memoirs of a Life, Chiefly Passed in Pennsylvania, within the last Sixty Years. With Occasional Remarks upon the General Occurrences, Character and Spirit of that Eventful Period. *Harrisburgh: Printed by John Wyeth.* 1811.

12mo, pp. 378, (1). *Half calf. Large* and *fine copy* of the SCARCE FIRST EDITION.

828 GRAYDON. Memoirs of his Own Time. With Reminiscences of the Men and Events of the Revolution. By Alexander Graydon. Edited by John Stockton Littell ... *Philadelphia: Lindsay & Blakiston.* 1846.

8vo, pp. xxiv., 13–504. *Half red morocco, gilt top, by* BRADSTREET. BEST EDITION. INDIA PROOF PORTRAIT of WASHINGTON *inserted.*

"The candour with respect to public occurrences which it displays — the views of manners in Pennsylvania prior to the memorable era of 1776, and the incidental sketches of historical characters, with which it is enriched, cannot fail to render this volume a valuable addition to the stock of general knowledge."—*Jno. Galt.*

829 GREELEY (H.) Letter of Horace Greeley to Messrs. George W. Blunt, John A. Kennedy, O. Stone, Stephen Hyatt, and 30 others, Members of the Union League Club.
[*New York* :] *Privately Printed.* 1867.

8*vo*, *boards*, UNCUT. A *few copies* printed for *private distribution* only.

"Understand, once for all, that I dare you and defy you, and that I propose to fight it out on the line that I have held from the day of Lee's surrender."— *Extract.*

830 GREEN (A.) A Discourse Delivered at Malden, January 8, 1800. A Day, Devoted by the Inhabitants, Publicly to Respect The Memory of the Illustrious George Washington, ... By Aaron Green, A.M. ...
Medford : [1800.]

8*vo*, *pp*. 23.

831 GREEN (A.) The Life of Ashbel Green, V.D.M. Begun to be written by Himself, in his Eighty-second year and continued to his Eighty-fourth. Prepared for the Press at the Author's Request, by Joseph H. Jones. ... *New York* : 1849.

8*vo*, *pp*. 628. *Portrait. Half calf.*

832 GREENE (B.) An Eulogy on George Washington, ... who died December 14th, 1799. Pronounced at Berwick, January 4th, 1800. By Benjamin Greene, A.M. *Portsmouth* : *New Hampshire.* 1800.

8*vo*, *pp*. 16. UNCUT. *Very Scarce.*

833 GREENE (G. W.) The Life of Nathaniel Greene, Major-General in the Army of the Revolution. By George Washington Greene.
New York : *G. P. Putnam and Son.* 1867–71.

3 *vols.*, *roy.* 8*vo*, *half green morocco*, *gilt top*, UNCUT, *by* BRADSTREET. PORTRAIT of GENERAL GREENE, and a MILITARY PROTECTION for MRS. GREENE during her journey on a visit to her husband, written and signed by GENERAL WASHINGTON, *inserted.*

834 GREENE STATUE. Proceedings in Congress attending the Reception of the Statue of Maj. Gen. Nathaniel Greene, of the Army of the Revolution, presented to the United States for the Capitol at Washington, by the State of Rhode Island. *Providence* : 1870.

4*to*, *pp*. 41. *Plate of Statue. Cloth*, UNCUT. VERY SCARCE. *Twenty copies only printed.* RARE INDIA PROOF PORTRAIT of GENERAL GREENE *inserted.*

835 **Gregorius (Magnus.)** INCIPIT LIBER REGULE PASTORAL GREGORII PAPE AD JOHĀNEM ARCHIEPISCOPUM RAUĒNENSEM PROLOGUS. *Moguntiæ* : *Per Joh. Fust et P. Schoffer.* [*circa* 1465.]

Sm. 4*to*, **Gothic Letter**, 152 *leaves*, 24 *lines to a page. Crushed green levant morocco, elegantly blank tooled after an antique design, gilt edges, by* THOMPSON *of* London. A BEAUTIFUL, CLEAN, and LARGE copy with ROUGH LEAVES.

A most interesting specimen of the press of FUST and SCHOIFFER, the INVENTORS of the art of Printing. It is beautifully printed in a fine bold Gothic type. The paper is as firm and crisp as the day it was printed. Described by Hain, vol. II. No. 7982.

"What was the world doing when this volume was printed, 1465? The Middle Ages were just expiring, and the era of Modern History about to dawn. America was undiscovered, the rich Mines of Mexico and Peru had not been travelled by their future conquerors, Columbus was in the world but a boy, an unrecognized atom in the vast aggregate of humanity, Henry the VIth was King of England, the struggle of the White and Red Roses had not commenced, the Glories of the Alhambra had not yet been revealed to the prying and intruding stranger, Venice was the grand emporium of Eastern Commerce, the Mistress of the Sea, etc. Such was part of the general aspect of the world when the first printing presses were set up."

836 GRENVILLE (*Lord.*) Bibliotheca Grenvilliana; or Bibliographical Notices of Rare and Curious Books, forming part of the Library of the Right Honourable Thomas Grenville: By John Thomas Payne and Henry Foss. *London:* 1842–72.

4 *vols., imp. 8vo, half crushed red levant morocco, gilt top,* UNCUT, *by* W. MATTHEWS. An UNLETTERED ARTIST'S PROOF PORTRAIT of LORD GRENVILLE *inserted.* A SPLENDID LARGE PAPER COPY of this valuable work of which SIXTEEN SETS ONLY were printed for sale. VERY RARE.

"The Trustees of the British Museum have just had printed Part III. of the 'Bibliotheca Grenvilliana,' completing the Catalogue of the library bequeathed to the British Museum, by the late Right Hon. Thomas Grenville, with a General Index. This third part has been drawn up with great care by Mr. Rye, the Keeper of the Printed Books. The general Index to the entire library is a most valuable feature in the present publication. Mr. Grenville, it may be mentioned, died on the 17th of December, 1846, and his magnificent library was received in the British Museum in January of the following year. The first part of the Catalogue of his library, drawn up by Messrs. Payne and Foss, was published in 1842, and the second part in 1848."—*Athenæum.*

837 GRESSWELL (Wm. P.) Annals of Parisian Typography, containing an Account of the Earliest Typographical Establishments of Paris; and notices and Illustrations of the most Remarkable Productions of the Parisian Gothic Press; compiled principally to shew its General Character; and its Particular Influence upon the Early English Press. By Rev. William Parr Gresswell. *London: Cadell and Davies.* 1818.

Roy. 8vo. LARGE PAPER. *Half olive morocco, gilt top,* UNCUT.

838 GRIFFITH (W.) An Oration, delivered To the Citizens of Burlington, on the 22d of February, 1800, In Commemoration of Gen. George Washington. ... By William Griffith, Esq. To which is added, A Prayer on the Same Occasion. By Charles H. Wharton, D.D. ... *Trenton:* M.DCCC.

8vo, pp. 25. UNCUT.

839 [GRIFFITHS (A. F.)] Bibliotheca Anglo-Poetica: or a Descriptive Catalogue of a Rare and Rich Collection of Early English Poetry: ... Illustrated by Occasional Extracts and Remarks, Critical and Biographical.

London: Printed for the Proprietors of the Collection. 1815.

Roy. 8vo, half olive morocco, gilt top, UNCUT. FINE COPY.

This extraordinary collection of old English poetry formed part of the extensive library of Thomas Hill (the Hull of Theodore Hook in his Gilbert Gurney), when he failed in business as a sugar baker. This portion of the library, its great value not being known to the creditors, was presented to him. He afterwards sold it to Messrs. Longman & Co., who employed Griffiths to make out this *catalogue raisonnée.* The initials at the beginning of each letter have very neat woodcuts of the poets from rare prints. It is now very scarce.

840 [GRISWOLD (R. W.)] Washington and the Generals of the American Revolution. With Sixteen Portraits on Steel, from Original Pictures. *Philadelphia:* 1847.

2 *vols.,* 12*mo, pp. xii.,* 324; 336. 16 *Portraits. Half green morocco.* Very scarce.

Written by R. W. Griswold. A controversy arose in consequence of the simultaneous issue of Headley's work (*See* No. 907), and it is said that *this* publication was suppressed.

841 GRISWOLD. The Republican Court or American Society in the Days of Washington. By Rufus Wilmot Griswold. With Twenty-one Portraits of Distinguished Women, engraved from Original Pictures by Woolaston, Copley, Gainsborough, Stuart, Trumbull, Pine, Malbone, and other contemporary Painters.
New York: D. Appleton and Company. M. DCCC. LV,

Roy. 8*vo, half olive morocco, gilt top,* UNCUT. A *selected copy* of the FIRST EDITION, with BRILLIANT IMPRESSIONS of the plates.

842 GRISWOLD (S). A Funeral Eulogium, pronounced at New-Milford, on the Twenty-second of February 1800; Being the day recommended by Congress for publicly testifying Respect to the Memory of George Washington. ... By Stanley Griswold. ...
Litchfield: [1800.]

8*vo, pp.* 24. *Very Scarce.*

843 G[ROOM] (S.) A | Glass | For the People of | New-England, | in which | They may see themselves and Spirits, and | if not too late, Repent and Turn from their | Abominable Ways and Cursed Contrivances: | That so the Lord God may turn away his Wrath, | which he will bring upon them (if they Repent not) for | their Blasphemies against himself, and for all the Mur- | ders and Cruelties done to his tender People, ever since | they usurped Authority to Banish, Hang, Whip, and | Cut Off Ears, and Spoil the Goods of Dissenters from | them in Religious Matters, while themselves disown | Infallibility in those things. By S. G. | ... | Printed in the Year, 1676.

4*to, pp.* 43. *Crushed red levant morocco, gilt edges, by* F. BEDFORD. FINE COPY.
One of the RAREST of early New-England Quaker Tracts.

844 GUILD (A.) The Librarian's Manual: a Treatise on Bibliography, comprising a Select and Descriptive List of Bibliographical Works; to which are added, Sketches of Publick Libraries. Illustrated with Engravings. By Reuben A. Guild, A.M. ...
New York: Charles B. Norton. MDCCCLVIII.

4*to, pp.* 10, 304. 16 *Engravings. Half green levant morocco, gilt top,* UNCUT. One of TEN COPIES ONLY printed on LARGE PAPER. Very RARE in this form.

The first part consists of a descriptive list of 495 separate works, comprising 1916 volumes of such Bibliographical books as are considered to be of the first importance for a library apparatus, including a copious American Bibliography. The second part contains historical sketches of fourteen of the largest public libraries in this country and Europe.

845 GUIREY (W.) A Funeral Sermon on the death of General George Washington. ... Delivered ... at Lynn, January 7, 1800. ... By the Rev. William Guirey. *Salem:* 1800.

8vo, pp. 22. *Scarce.*

846 GUIZOT (F. P. G.) Washington. By Monsieur Guizot. ... Translated by Henry Reeve, Esq. *London: John Murray.* 1840.

8vo, pp. xvi., 230. *Half green morocco, gilt top,* UNCUT. PORTRAIT of WASHINGTON *inserted.*

"The name of Mr. Sparks is strangely omitted from the title-page, a singular fact never accounted for."— G. ELLIS'S *Memoir of Jared Sparks.*

This translation has passed through many editions in many lands, under the name of "Guizot's Washington." In the Illustrated Catalogue of the Great Exhibition of 1851 (Vol. II. p. 693), there is "a casket in the Florentine style made to contain an autographical work by M. Guizot, entitled 'The Life of Washington.'"

847 GUTENBERG (J.) John Gutenberg, First Master Printer, His Acts, and most remarkable Discourses, and his Death. From the German, by C. W. *London: Trübner and Co.* 1860.

4to, pp. 141. *Half olive morocco, gilt top,* UNCUT. PRIVATELY PRINTED, and *only* 100 *copies.* View of GUTENBERG'S MONUMENT at Mentz *inserted.*

"Only a few copies allowed to be sold by the book-loving amateur who has produced this beautiful volume for presentation to his friends."

848 HACKE (W.) A Collection of Original Voyages: Containing I. Capt. Cowley's Voyage round the Globe. II. Captain Sharp's Journey over the Isthmus of Darien, and Expedition into the South Seas, Written by himself. III. Capt. Wood's Voyage thro' the Streights of Magellan. IV. Mr. Roberts' Adventures among the Corsairs of the Levant; his Account of their Way of Living; Description of the Archipelago Islands, Taking of Scio, &c. Illustrated with several Maps and Draughts. Published by Capt. William Hacke. *London: James Knapton.* 1699.

8vo, pp. (32), 45, 100, 53. *Books* 3. 4 *Maps and Plate. Mottled calf, carmine edges.* FINE LARGE COPY.

This Collection contains part of the original material for the History of the Buccaniers, Capt. Cowley's Voyage round the Globe, Capt. Sharp's Journey over the Isthmus of Darien and Expedition to the South Seas, Capt. Wood's Voyage to the Straits of Magellan, &c.

849 HAEGHOORT (G.) Keten Der Goddelyke Waarheden, Die Men geloven en betrachten moet Om Salig te worden, In haar natuurlyk verband kortlyk te same-geschakelt; Door Gerard Haeghoort, predikant te Second River. ...
Te Nieuw-York, Gedruckt by J. PETER ZENGER. 1738.

12mo, pp. iv., (1), 36. *Blue morocco,* UNCUT, *edges gilt on the rough.* FINE COPY. EXCEEDINGLY RARE.

850 **Haklupt (R.) The Principall Nabigations, Voiages and Discoueries of the English nation,** made by Sea or ouer Land, to the most remote and farthest distant Quarters of the earth at any time within the compasse of these 1500 yeeres: Deuided into three seuerall parts, according to the positions of the Regions whereunto they were directed. ... Including the English valiant attempts in searching almost all the corners of the vaste and new world of America, etc. By Richard Hakluyt. ... .

Imprinted at London by George Bishop and Ralph Newberie. 1589.

Folio, russia extra, gilt edges, by F. BEDFORD. LARGE and BEAUTIFUL COPY of the FIRST EDITION, with a folded MAP "Typus Cosmographicus Universalis," mounted on linen, opposite the title. This copy contains Baker's "Two Voyages to Guinee" in 1562, IN VERSE, and Sir John Mandeville's Travels, about 1360, occupying 28 leaves.

851 **Haklupt. The Principal Nabigations, Voiages, Traffiques, and Discoueries of the English Nation,** made by Sea or ouerland to the remote and farthest distant quarters of the Earth, etc. By Richard Hakluyt ... .

Imprinted at London, by George Bishop. 1599–1600.

3 *vols., folio, crushed blue levant morocco, gilt back, paneled sides, corner ornaments, gilt edges, by* F. BEDFORD.

A LARGE and SPLENDID COPY from the Library of Sir Francis Freeling, with the ORIGINAL VOYAGE TO CADIZ, continuously paged, at the end of the first volume. This is one of the copies with the date in the title 1599 instead of 1598. The voyage to Cadiz is rarely found in the work, but sometimes a very good facsimile is inserted. To discover the difference between the two see *Lowndes.*

A FINE COPY OF THE WHOLE OF THE VOYAGES. VERY RARE.

852 HAKLUYT'S Collection of the Early Voyages, Travels, and Discoveries of the English Nation. A New Edition, with Additions, and Supplemental Volume of Early Voyages. [Edited by R. H. Evans.] *London: R. H. Evans.* 1809–12.

5 *vols., roy. 4to, half crimson levant morocco, gilt top,* UNCUT. An ELEGANT and COMPLETE set. RARE in this state. 250 *copies only* printed.

The first three volumes and part of the 4th are exactly reprinted from the edition of 1599–1600. The remainder of the fourth and the whole of the 5th volume are occupied by reprints of various publications of Hakluyt and others of his time, which were also published in a separate volume in 1812. The Perkins copy, on large paper, sold for £32.

853 HAKLUYT. Divers Voyages touching the Discovery of America and the Islands adjacent, Collected and Published by Richard Hakluyt. ... Edited with Notes and an Introduction, by John Winter Jones, of the British Museum.

London: Printed for the Hakluyt Society. 1850.

8vo, 3 *p. l., pp. cxi.,* 171, 6. 2 *Maps, and Facsimile. Half purple morocco, gilt top,* UNCUT.

Hakluyt's first publication. It contains seven articles or voyages, the fifth of which is "The relation of Iohn Verazanus, a Florentine, of the lande by him discouered in the name of his Maiestie, written in Diepe, the eight of July, 1524," which is the earliest known account of Rhode Island.

854 HALE (J.) A Modest Enquiry | Into the Nature of | Witchcraft, | And | How Persons Guilty of that Crime | may be Convicted: And the means | used for their Discovery Discussed, | both Negatively and Affirmatively, | according to Scripture and | Experience. | By John Hale, | Pastor of the Church of Christ in Beverly. | Anno Domini, 1697. | ... | *Boston in N. E.* | *Printed by B. Green, and J. Allen, for* | *Benjamin Eliot under the Town House.* 1702.

Sm. 8vo, pp. 176. *Brown morocco, paneled sides, gilt edges.* EXCESSIVELY RARE, indeed the rarest of all of the works relating to the New England Witchcraft Delusion. We know of ONE OTHER COPY only.

855 HALKETT (J.) Historical Notes respecting the Indians of North America: with Remarks on the Attempts made to Convert and Civilise them. By John Halkett, Esq. *London:* 1825.

8vo, pp. viii., 408. *Half olive morocco, gilt top,* UNCUT. FRONTISPIECE *inserted.*

856 [HALL (*Major.*)] The History of the Civil War in America. Comprehending the Campaigns of 1775, 1776, and 1777. By an Officer of the Army.
London: T. Payne and Son, and J. Sewell. M.DCC,LXXX.

8vo, pp. (8), 413. *Map. Vol.* I., *all that was published. Polished calf, yellow edges, by* F. BEDFORD. *Scarce* PORTRAIT *of* WASHINGTON *inserted.*

857 HALL (H.) History of Vermont, from its Discovery to its Admission into the Union, in 1791. By Hiland Hall.
Albany: J Munsell. 1868.

8vo, pp. xii., 521. *Map. Half red levant morocco, gilt top,* UNCUT. *One of* 50 *copies only printed on* FINE PAPER.

858 HALLAM (A.) Introduction to the Literature of Europe, in the Fifteenth, Sixteenth, and Seventeenth Centuries. By Henry Hallam, F.R.A.S. *London: John Murray.* 1837–39.

4 *vols.,* 8*vo, half blue morocco, gilt top,* UNCUT. ORIGINAL and BEST EDITION.

859 [HALLECK (Fitz-Greene.)] FANNY.
New York: C. Wiley & Co. 1819.

8vo, pp. 49. *Portrait. Half green morocco, gilt top,* UNCUT.

The RARE FIRST EDITION, which contains some sharp stanzas suppressed in all other editions. This interesting copy has many MS. notes in the hand-writing of the late Mr. E. B. Corwin, and another, pointing out the numerous variations between this, and subsequent editions, and filling in the names left in blank by the Author.

860 HALLECK. FANNY: A Poem. By Fitz-Greene Halleck. [With Notes by the Author written expressly for this Edition.]
New York: 1866.

Imp. 8vo, half green morocco, gilt top, UNCUT. INDIA PROOF PORTRAIT of the AUTHOR engraved by BURT. 70 *Copies only* PRIVATELY PRINTED *for* W. L. ANDREWS, ESQ.

861 HALLECK. Lines to the Recorder. By Fitz-Greene Halleck. *New York:* 1866.

Imp. 8vo, half green morocco, gilt top, UNCUT. PRIVATELY PRINTED *for* W. L. ANDREWS, ESQ.; *and* 70 *copies only.* INDIA PROOF PORTRAIT of the AUTHOR, from a PRIVATE PLATE, *inserted.*

These beautiful reprints were edited by the Author, and will always be valuable as being, probably, the last publications containing Mr. Halleck's Annotations. The Portrait was engraved, from an original miniature by Rogers, especially for this edition.

862 HALLIWELL (J. O.) An Historical Sketch of the Provincial Dialects of England, Illustrated by Numerous Examples. By James Orchard Halliwell. *Albany: J. Munsell.* 1863.

Roy. 8vo, half blue morocco, gilt top, UNCUT. An original *Autograph Note* of MR. HALLIWELL, to Mr. Munsell, assenting to the republication of the work in the United States, (partially printed in the volume) *inserted.*

863 HALSEY (W.) An Oration delivered the Twenty-Second of February, MDCCC. Before the Brethren and a Select Audience in the Hall of St. John's Lodge No. 2, Newark, New-Jersey. By William Halsey, Esq. *Newark:* 1800.

8vo, pp. 23. UNCUT. An EXCEEDINGLY RARE Oration on the Death of George Washington.

864 HAMILTON (A.) Observations on Certain Documents contained in No. V. & VI. of "The History of the United States for the year 1796" in which the charge of Speculation against Alexander Hamilton late Secretary of the Treasury, is fully refuted. Written by Himself. *Philadelphia: John Fenno.* 1797.

8vo, pp. 37, *lviii. Half maroon morocco, gilt top,* UNCUT. SCARCE. ORIGINAL EDITION, and a fine copy, notwithstanding the upper margin of the title has been restored where a name has been cut from it.

Almost the whole of this edition was destroyed by the friends of General Hamilton.

865 HAMILTON. Observations on Certain Documents. [Another Edition.] *Philadelphia: Printed Pro Bono Publico.* 1800.

8vo, polished calf, gilt top, UNCUT, *by* F. BEDFORD. BEAUTIFUL COPY of this RARE EDITION, put forth by Hamilton's enemies.

"'Written by himself,' or this little book of 96 pages would most likely have been pronounced the greatest libel upon the greatest man New York ever produced. It has been claimed to the honor of his friends that they endeavored to suppress it. It was copyrighted, and never reprinted but once until recently, but scarce as it has become, it is now part of American literature. Hamilton was charged with 'a connection with one James Reynolds for purposes of improper pecuniary speculation.' 'My real crime,' confesses the late Secretary not without a blush, 'is an amorous connection with his [Reynolds] wife for a considerable time, with his privity and connivance.' That was how he came to be the private banker of the husband of Mrs. Reynolds, 'from whose conversation it was quickly apparent that other than pecuniary consolation would be acceptable,' p. 18. Truth never appeared so naked as in these confessions of Alexander Hamilton."—*Stevens.*

866 HAMILTON (J. C.) The Life of Alexander Hamilton. By his Son, John C. Hamilton. *New York: D. Appleton & Co.* 1840.

2 *vols., 8vo, half green levant morocco, gilt top,* UNCUT. Vol. II. is *very scarce.* FINE COPY, ILLUSTRATED with upwards of SEVENTY PORTRAITS and VIEWS many of which are RARE.

867 HAMILTON. The Works of Alexander Hamilton; comprising his Correspondence, and his Political and Official Writings, exclusive of the Federalist, Civil and Military. Published from the Original Manuscripts deposited in the Department of State, by order of the Joint Library Committee of Congress. Edited by John C. Hamilton, ...
New York: John F. Trow, ... M.DCCC.L.–LI.

7 vols., 8vo, half green morocco, gilt top. LARGE and FINE SET of this SCARCE and VALUABLE work, with an appropriate frontispiece *inserted* in each volume.

868 HAMILTON. History of the Republic of the United States of America, as traced in the Writings of Alexander Hamilton and of his Cotemporaries. By John C. Hamilton. ...
New York: andPhiladelphia: 1857–65.

7 vols., 8vo, half red morocco, gilt top. An appropriate frontispiece *inserted* in each volume.

869 HAMILTON (S.) The History of the National Flag of the United States of America. By Schuyler Hamilton, Capt. U. S. A.
Philadelphia: Lippincott, Grambo & Co. 1853.

12mo. Three plates of flags. Cloth.

870 HAMILTONIAD: or, the Effects of Discord. An Original Poem. In Two Books. With an Appendix; containing a number of Interesting Papers relative to the late Unfortunate Duel. By a Young Gentleman of Philadelphia. ...
Philadelphia: Printed for the Author. 1804.

8vo, pp. 55. Half green morocco, gilt top, UNCUT. VERY SCARCE. A fine impression of the RARE PORTRAIT of HAMILTON, engraved by LENEY; and one other *inserted*.

For another "Hamiltoniad" *see* [Williams (John.)] No. 2151.

871 HAMOR (R.) A Trve Discourse Of The | Present Estate Of Vir | ginia, and the successe of the Affaires | there till the 18 of Iune, 1614. | Together. | With A Relation Of the | seuerall English Townes and forts, the assu- | red hopes of that countrie, and the peace | concluded with the Indians. | The Christening of Powhatans daughter, | and her marriage with an English-man. | Written by Raphe Hamor the yon- | ger, late Secretarie in that Colony, | ... | *Printed at London, by Iohn Beale, for Wil- | liam Welby dwelling at the signe of the | Swanne, in Paul's Church-yard.* 1615.

Sm. 4to, pp. (8), 69. *Errata* 1 *p. Olive morocco, gilt back, paneled sides, centre and corner ornaments, edges gilt on carmine, by* REVIERE.

A BEAUTIFUL COPY of the EXCESSIVELY RARE ORIGINAL EDITION, of which we have seen but ONE OTHER COPY offered for sale in the United States viz: the Barney copy, which, although in very indifferent condition, sold for $150. This copy was purchased at the sale of the Bruce library for $170.00. It is in the VERY FINEST POSSIBLE CONDITION.

872 HAMOR. A Trve discovrse of the Present Estate of Virginia; and the Successe of the Affaires there till the 18 of Iune, 1614. ...

Written by Raphe Hamor the yonger, late Secretarie in that Colony. [*Albany: Reprinted.* 1860.]

Folio, half blue morocco, gilt top, UNCUT. 200 copies reprinted for Dr. C. G. Barney of Richmond, Va.

873 HANCOCK (J). An Oration; delivered March 5, 1774, at the Request of the Inhabitants of the Town of Boston: to Commemorate the Bloody Tragedy of the Fifth of March, 1770. By The Honourable John Hancock, Esq. ... *Boston: Printed by Edes and Gill.* M,DCC,LXXIV.

4to, pp. 20. *Half green morocco, gilt top,* UNCUT. RARE. A RARE and fine PORTRAIT of the AUTHOR; an AUTOGRAPH order WRITTEN and SIGNED by him, for "one best Beaver Hat," probably lost on an election bet; and a facsimile of Revere's engraving of "The Boston Massacre." *inserted.*

874 HANCOCK. An Oration; delivered March 5, 1774, at the Request of the Inhabitants of the Town of Boston: to Commemorate the Bloody Tragedy of the Fifth of March, 1770. By the Honorable John Hancock, Esq. ... *New Haven: Re-Printed by Thomas and Samuel Green.* M,DCC,LXXIV.

8vo, pp. 15. *Half calf, gilt edges.* RARE EDITION. SCARCE contemporary PORTRAIT of HANCOCK *inserted.*

Remarkable as being the only publication of this distinguished patriot.

875 HANCOCK. E. Pluribus Unum. British Cruelty Oppression and Murder. Two Orations. An Oration delivered by John Hancock Esq. at Boston, in Commemoration of the Evening of the 5th of March, 1770, when a number of Citizens were killed by a party of British Troops, quartered among them in a time of peace.

[Also:] An Oration delivered by Dr. Joseph Warren, at Boston, On The Same Subject. ... To which is added, An Account of the Captivity of Mrs. Jemimah Howe, taken by the Indians at Hinsdale, N. H. July 27, 1775. [*n. p.*] *P. M. Davis Publisher.* 1824.

Sm. 8vo, pp. 23. *Half red morocco, gilt top,* UNCUT. *Exceedingly scarce.* Contemporary PORTRAIT of HANCOCK *inserted.*

876 HANGER (G.) An Address to the Army; in Reply to Strictures, by Roderick McKenzie, (late Lieutenant in the 71st Regiment) on Tarleton's History of the Campaigns of 1780 and 1781. By the Hon. George Hanger. ... *London: James Ridgeway.* MDCCLXXXIX.

8vo, pp. xvi., 138, 8. *Half green morocco, gilt top,* UNCUT. VERY RARE. FINE COPY, uniform with "McKenzie's Strictures." No. 1306.

See Tarleton (B.) No. 1945.

877 HANGER. The Life, Adventures, and Opinions of Col. George Hanger. Written by Himself. With Advice to the Lovely Cyprians, and to the Fair Sex in general. Adventures in America, &c. *London: J. Debrett.* 1801.

2 vols., 8vo, half calf, carmine edges. FINE COPY.

Col. Hanger (afterward Lord Coleraine) served with distinction in the American War. See vol. II. page 427, for a curious prophecy relative to the late rebellion: "One of these days, the Northern and Southern powers will fight as vigorously against each other as they both have united to do against the British."

878 HANNA (J. S.) A History of the Life and Services of Captain Samuel Dewees, a native of Pennsylvania, and Soldier of the Revolutionary and Last Wars. Also, Reminiscences of the Revolutionary Struggle (Indian War, Western Expedition, Liberty Insurrection in Northampton County, Pa.) and Late War with Great Britain, in all of which he was Patriotically Engaged. ... By John Smith Hanna. *Baltimore: Printed by Robert Neilson.* 1844.

12*mo*, *pp.* 360. *Portrait, and Engravings. Half blue morocco, gilt top.* SCARCE.

879 HANSARD (T. C.) Typographia: an Historical Sketch of the Origin and Progress of the Art of Printing; with Practical Directions for conducting every Department in an Office: With a Description of Stereotype and Lithography. Illustrated by Engravings, Biographical Notices, and Portraits. By T. C. Hansard. *London:* 1825.

Roy. 8vo, half olive levant morocco, gilt top, UNCUT.

This is not a mere practical treatise, but a compendium of Ames, Herbert, Dibdin, and others, giving a complete history of the art, and much curious information respecting early printers, as well as practical information indispensable to authors and persons connected with literature. The perusal of this work will point out to authors the best method of arranging matter for press, besides saving them much time and trouble in correcting their proofs.

880 HANSARD. Treatises on Printing and Type-Founding. By T. C. Hansard. From the Seventh Edition of the Encyclopædia Britannica. *Edinburgh: Adam and Charles Black.* 1841.

8vo, half morocco, gilt top, UNCUT.

881 HANSON (E.) An Account of the Captivity of Elizabeth Hanson, Now or Late of Kachecky, in New-England: Who, with Four of her Children and Servant-Maid, was taken captive by the Indians, and carried into Canada. Setting forth the various remarkable Occurrences, sore Trials, and wonderful Deliverances which befell them after their Departure, to the Time of their Redemption. Taken in Substance from her own Mouth, by Samuel Bownas. The Second Edition. *London: Samuel Clark.* M.D.CCLX.

Sm. 8vo, pp. 28. *Half morocco, gilt edges.* VERY SCARCE.

882 HARBISON (M.) A Narrative of the Sufferings of Massy Harbison, from Indian Barbarity, giving an Account of her Captivity, the Murder of her Two Children, her Escape, with an Infant at her Breast; together with some Account of the cruelties of the Indians, on the Allegheny River &c., in the years 1790, '91, '92, '93, '94. Communicated by herself. *Pittsburgh: D. and M. Maclean.* 1828.

24*mo*, *pp.* 98. *Paneled calf, antique.* VERY SCARCE.

3 HARDIE (J.) An Account of the Malignant Fever lately prevalent in the city of New York. Containing a Narrative of its Rise, Progress and Decline, ... the Manner in which the Poor were Relieved ... a list of the Donations which have been presented for the Relief of the Sick ... a list of the Names of the Dead ... and a Comparative View of the Fever of the Year 1798 .... By James Hardie, A.M. .... *New York: Hurtin and M'Farlane.* 1799.

8vo, pp. 139, (9). *Half blue morocco.* SCARCE.

4 HARDIE. An Account of the Malignant Fever, which prevailed in the City of New-York, during the autumn of 1805. Containing, the Proceedings of the Board of Health, ... an Account of the Marine and Bellevue Hospitals, ... Record of Deaths, &c. ... By James Hardie, A.M. *New York: Southwick & Hardcastle.* 1805.

8vo, pp. 196. *Half blue morocco.* SCARCE.

5 HARDIE. An Account of the Yellow Fever which occurred in the City of New York, in the year 1822. To which is prefixed a brief sketch of the different Pestilential Diseases, with which this City was afflicted, in the years 1798, 1799, 1803 & 1805, with the opinion of several of our most Eminent Physicians, respecting the Origin of the Disease, its Prevention and Cure. To which is added a Correct List of all the Deaths by Yellow Fever during the late Season. ... By James Hardie, A.M. *New York: Samuel Marks.* 1822.

12mo, pp. iv., 120. *Half morocco.* VERY SCARCE.

6 HARIOT (T.) A briefe and true report | of the new found land of Virginia | of the commodities and of the nature and man | ners of the naturall inhabitants. Discouered by | the English Colony there seated by Sir Richard | Greinuile Knight In the yeere 1585. Which Rema | ined Vnder the gouernement of twelue monethes, | at the speciall charge and direction of the Honou- | rable Sir Walter Raleigh Knight, lord Warden | of the ſtanneries Who therein hath beene fauoured | and authoriſed by her Maiestie: | and her letters patents: | This fore book Is made in Engliſh | By Thomas Hariot ſeruant to the abouenamed | Sir Walter, a member of the Colony, and there | imployed in discouering. | Cum Gratia et Privilegio, Caes. Ma^{tis} Specia^{lis} | *Francoforti ad Moenvm* | *Typis Ioannis Wecheli, svmtibvs vero Theodori* | *De Bry anno* CIƆ IƆ XC. | *Venales reperivntvr in officina Sigismvndi Feirabendii* | [Colophon:] *At Franckfort,* | *inprinted by Ihon We* | *chel, at Theodore de Bry, own* | *coast and chardges.* | MDXC. | [*New York: reprinted for J. Sabin & Sons.* 1871.]

Folio, half morocco, UNCUT. *One hundred copies only printed.*

This first English edition is so rare, that only five or six copies are known. That which is described in the "Bibliotheca Grenvilliana," I. 185–186, had been bought by Lord Oxford, at Frankfort, about 1710, for £100. Another brought the same price at the Nassau sale, and Stevens's copy sold in Boston, in 1870, for $975.00.

This "reproduction" has been executed by the newly discovered process of Photo-Lithography. The imitation of the old style type is perfect, and the twenty-three quaint and curious Engravings by John White, the English painter who, at the command of Queen Elizabeth, accompanied Sir Walter Raleigh in his famous expedition, are reproduced with marvelous accuracy.

887 HARRIS (T. M.) A Discourse delivered at Dorchester, December 29, 1799, being the Lord's Day after hearing the distressing intelligence of the Death of General George Washington. ... By Thaddeus Mason Harris. *Charlestown:* MDCCC.

8vo, pp. 16.

888 HARRIS. The Journal of a Tour into the Territory Northwest of the Alleghany Mountains; made in the Spring of the Year 1803. With a Geographical and Historical Account of the State of Ohio. Illustrated with Original Maps and Views. By Thaddeus Mason Harris, A.M. ... *Boston: Manning & Loring.* 1805.

8vo, pp. 271. 2 *Maps and* 2 *Plates. Half calf,* UNCUT. FINE COPY. SCARCE.

889 HARRIS. Biographical Memorials of James Oglethorpe, Founder of the Colony of Georgia, in North America. By Thaddeus Mason Harris, D.D. ... *Boston: printed for the Author.* M DCCC XLI.

8vo, pp. xxii., 424. *Portrait, Plate, Map and Facsimile. Half red morocco, gilt top,* UNCUT. THREE PORTRAITS *inserted.*

The largest portion of this volume is occupied with a narrative of Oglethorpe's association with the settlement of Georgia, his wise treatment of the Indians, their fidelity and attachment to him, and sketches of their chiefs.

890 HARRIS (W. W.) The Battle of Groton Heights: a Collection of Narratives, Official Reports, Records, &c., of the Storming of Fort Griswold, and the Burning of New London by British Troops, under the Command of Brig.-Gen. Benedict Arnold, on the Sixth of September, 1781. With an Introduction and Notes. By William W. Harris. *New London:* 1870.

Roy. 8vo, pp. x., 123. *Half green morocco, gilt top,* UNCUT. 100 *copies only* PRIVATELY PRINTED.

891 [HARRISSE (Henry.)] Bibliotheca Americana Vetustissima. A Description of Works relating to America published between the Years 1492 and 1551. *New York: Geo. P. Philes.* MDCCCLXVI.

4to, half brown levant morocco, gilt top, UNCUT. LARGE PAPER; 99 *copies only printed.* AN ELEGANT COPY.

Elegantly printed on very superior paper. This is, in spite of a few typographical inaccuacies, the most complete and satisfactory work of its kind. The descriptions are exact, and a collation of each book is attached. Its arrangement is chronological, but an alphabetical index is added.

"It is the fashion to decry the works of this author, because of the few blunders that are met with in his text; but who can expect perfection in any book, especially one of bibliography? In spite of that portentous German voyager, 'Ander Schiffahrt,' Mr. Harrisse's Bibliotheca is the best and most useful bibliographical essay in existence upon the early literature relating to the New World." — *B. Quaritch.*

892 [HARRISSE.] Bibliotheca Americana Vetustissima. A Description of Works relating to America published between the Years 1492 and 1551. Additions. *Paris: Libraire Tross.* M.DCCC.LXXII.

Imp. 8vo, pp. xl., 199, (1). Engravings. *Half olive brown morocco, gilt top*, UNCUT, *by* W. MATTHEWS.

Contains one hundred and eighty-six articles, two thirds of which are new to collectors of books that relate to the New World.

893 [HARRISSE.] A Brief Disquisition Concerning the Early History of Printing in America. *New York: Privately Printed.* 1866.

Imp. 8vo, pp. 18. *Half red morocco, gilt top*, UNCUT, *by* BRADSTREET. EXTREMELY SCARCE. FIVE COPIES ONLY printed on HOLLAND PAPER. 25 *copies in all.*

894 [HARRISSE.] **Notes on Columbus.** *New York: Privately Printed.* MDCCCLXVI.

Folio, pp. vii., 227. 13 *Photographs. Crimson levant morocco, paneled and gilt sides, morocco joints, broad inside borders, gilt top*, UNCUT, *by* W. MATTHEWS.

A SPLENDID COPY of this MAGNIFICENT and almost UNATTAINABLE BOOK of which *ninety-nine copies only* were printed exclusively for PRIVATE DISTRIBUTION. The portrait of COLUMBUS photographed from DE BRY, has been transferred to page 162, and a brilliant impression of the ORIGINAL *inserted* in its stead.

A SUMPTUOUS VOLUME.

It is to the munificence of S. L. M. Barlow, Esq., of New York, that the possessors of this grand work are indebted for its production. It consists of a series of notes and extracts from rare books, relating to Columbus, with numerous valuable bibliographical and historical notes. It also contains an account of the poems, eulogies, essays, etc., in honour of Columbus, and is a treasury of fact and fancy, relative to the great navigator.

895 HARSHA (D. A.) The Life of the Rev. James Hervey. By D. A. Harsha, M.A. *Albany: J. Munsell.* 1865.

Imp. 8vo, half purple morocco, gilt top, UNCUT. FIFTY COPIES ONLY printed, THIRTY-FIVE of which were for presentation.

896 HARSHA. Life of the Rev. George Whitefield. By D. A. Harsha, M.A. *Albany: J. Munsell.* 1866.

Imp. 8vo, half purple morocco, gilt top, UNCUT. FIFTY COPIES ONLY printed, THIRTY-FIVE of which were for presentation.

897 HART (J. S.) An Essay on the Life and Writings of Edmund Spencer, with a Special Exposition of the Fairy Queen. By John S. Hart, A.M. *New York and London: Wiley and Putnam.* 1847.

8vo, green morocco, gilt edges. FINE COPY. SCARCE.

898 HART (L.) Religious Improvement of the Death of Great Men. A Discourse addressed to the Congregation in the North Society in Preston, ... Dec. 29, 1799, Occasioned by the Death of Gen. George Washington. ... By Levi Hart, A.M. ... *Norwich:* 1800.

8vo, pp. 26. VERY RARE.

899 HARTFORD CONVENTION. The Proceedings of a Convention of Delegates, from the States of Massachusetts, Connecticut, and Rhode

Island; the Counties of Cheshire and Grafton, in the State of New Hampshire; and the County of Windham, in the State of Vermont; Convened at Hartford in the State of Connecticut, December 15th, 1814. *Hartford: Printed by Charles Hosmer.* 1815.

8vo, pp. 39. *Half calf, gilt top,* UNCUT, *by* BRADSTREET.
The ORIGINAL ACCOUNT of the Hartford Convention. VERY SCARCE.

900 HARTLIB (Samuel.) The Reformed | Virginian | Silk-Worm, | or a Rare and New | Discovery | Of | A speedy way, and easie means, found out | by a young Lady in England she having made | full proof thereof in May, | Anno 1652. | For the feeding of Silk-worms in the woods, on the | Mulberry-Tree-leaves in Virginia: Who after fourty dayes | time, present their most rich golden-coloured silken | Fleece, to the instant Wonderful enriching of | all the Planters there, requiring from | them neither cost, labour, or hindrance | in any of their other emplo- | ments whatsoever. | And also to the good hopes, that the Indians, see- | ing and finding that there is neither art, skill, or pains | in the thing: they will readily set upon it, being | by the benefit thereof inabled to buy of the | English (in way of Truck for their | Silk-bottoms) all those things | that they most desire. | *London,* | *Printed by John Streater, for Giles Calvert at the* | *Black-Spread-Eagle at the West end* | *of Pauls,* 1655.

Sm. 4to, pp. (4), 40. *Crushed green levant morocco, gilt edges, by* DAVID of Paris.
A BEAUTIFUL COPY OF THIS VERY RARE WORK.

901 HARTSHORNE (C. H.) The Book Rarities in the University of Cambridge. Illustrated by Original Letters, and Notes, Biographical, Literary, and Antiquarian. By Rev. C. H. Hartshorne, M.A. *London: Longman.* 1829.

Imp. 8vo, pp. xiv., (1), 559. 22 *Engravings.* *Half olive levant morocco, gilt top,* UNCUT. LARGE VELLUM PAPER; TWENTY-FIVE COPIES only printed.

The original letters in this volume form a very interesting portion of its contents. Those of Ciofanos are filled with abuse of Aldus, Junior, whom he terms "*la Cornacchia Esopea,*" and of whose literary ability he speaks very slightingly. It also includes a reprint of "Capell's Shakesperiana."

902 [HARVEY (James B.)] Catalogue of the Library at Oakwood. *New York: Printed for the Owner.* 1870.

8vo, half red morocco, gilt top, UNCUT, *by* BRADSTREET. RULED and PRICED. One of TEN COPIES only printed on Whatman's drawing paper.

903 [HASSAL *Miss.*)] Secret History; or the Horrors of St. Domingo, in a Series of Letters, written by a Lady at Cape Francois, to Colonel Burr, late Vice-President of the United States, principally during the Command of Count Rochambeau. *Philadelphia: Bradford & Inskeep.* 1808.

12mo, pp. (4), 225. *Half green morocco, carmine edges.* SCARCE.

904 HAVEN (C. C.) Thirty Days in New Jersey Ninety Years ago: An Essay revealing New Facts in Connection with Washington and his Army in 1776 and 1777. By C. C. Haven. ... *Trenton:* 1867.

8vo, pp. 72. *Half green morocco, gilt top,* UNCUT, *by* BRADSTREET. FINE PORTRAIT of WASHINGTON *inserted.*

905 [HAWKS (Francis Lester.) A Criticism on Tucker's Life of Jefferson.] *New York:* 1837.

Forms *pp.* 1–58, of No. 1, of the New York Review, containing Dr. Hawks's memorable attack on the character of Thomas Jefferson.

[Also:] A Defence of the Character of Thomas Jefferson against a Writer in the New York Review. By a Virginian. [George Tucker.] *New York:* 1838.

8vo, 2 pieces in 1 vol., half green morocco, gilt top. VERY SCARCE.

906 HAYWOOD (J.). The Civil and Political History of the State of Tennessee, from its Earliest Settlement up to the year 1796; including the Boundaries of the State. By John Haywood. *Printed for the Author by Heiskel & Brown: Knoxville, Tenn.* 1823.

8vo, pp. (4), 504. *Mottled calf, yellow edges, by* F. BEDFORD. LARGE and BEAUTIFUL COPY of this EXCEEDINGLY RARE WORK.

"Contains a large portion of material relating to the border warfare with the Indians. The story of Indian conflicts and massacres is narrated with great detail and minuteness, filling much the larger portion of the work. The narrative of the formation of the State of Franklin, and the civil war which ensued, is a chapter of American history but little known, and scarcely exceeded in interest by any other."— *Field.*

907 HEADLEY (J. T.) Washington and his Generals. By J. T. Headley. ... *New York: Charles Scribner.* 1856.

2 vols., 12mo. Half green morocco, gilt top, UNCUT. SIXTEEN PORTRAITS of the GENERALS engraved on STEEL.

908 HEARD (F. F.) The Legal Acquirements of William Shakspere. By Franklin Fiske Heard. *Boston: John Kimball Wiggin.* 1865.

4to, half red morocco, gilt top, UNCUT. SIXTY COPIES ONLY printed. A SPLENDID PROOF IMPRESSION of the SHAKSPERE BUST engraved by WARD, from a painting by PHILIPS, *inserted.*

909 HEATH [(William.)] Memoirs of Major-General Heath. Containing Anecdotes, Details of Skirmishes, Battles, and other Military Events, during the American War. Written by Himself. *Printed at Boston, by I. Thomas, and E. T. Andrews. Aug.* 1798.

8vo, pp. 388. *Crushed red levant morocco, gilt top,* UNCUT, *by* F. BEDFORD. FINE ORIGINAL IMPRESSION of the RARE PORTRAIT of GEN. HEATH engraved by J. R. SMITH *inserted.*

Probably UNIQUE. We have never seen or heard of another copy which is ABSOLUTELY UNCUT. This identical copy brought $95 at the Rice Sale, without the portrait, and before it was bound by Bedford.

910 HEATH. Memoirs. [Another Copy.] *Boston:* 1798.

8vo, half calf, carmine edges. LARGE, and CLEAN COPY. An ORIGINAL IMPRESSION of the FXCESSIVELY RARE FULL LENGTH PORTRAIT of GEN. HEATH *inserted.*

911 HECKEWELDER (J.) An Account of the History, Manners, and Customs, of the Indian Nations, who once inhabited Pennsylvania and the neighbouring States. By the Rev. John Heckewelder, of Bethlehem. [Transactions of the Historical and Literary Committee of the Am. Phil. Soc. Vol. I.] *Philadelphia: Abraham Small.* 1819.

8vo, pp. l., iv., 3–465. *Half blue morocco, gilt top,* UNCUT. PORTRAIT of the AUTHOR *inserted.* SCARCE in any condition, *especially so* in such fine and *uncut* state.

Contents: Heckewelder's Account of the History, Manners, and Customs of the Indian Natives who once inhabited Pennsylvania, etc. pp. 350; Heckewelder and Duponceau on the Languages of the American Indians, pp. 100; Words, Phrases, and Short Dialogues in the Lenni Lenape Language, pp. 14.

912 HECKEWELDER. A Narrative of the Mission of the United Brethren among the Delaware and Mohegan Indians, from its Commencement, in the year 1740, to ... 1808. Comprising all the Remarkable Incidents which took place at their Missionary Stations during that period. Interspersed with Anecdotes, Historical Facts, Speeches of Indians, and other Interesting Matter. By John Heckewelder. ... *Philadelphia: McCarty & Davis.* 1820.

8vo, pp. xii., 17–429, (1). *Portrait. Half blue levant morocco, gilt top,* UNCUT.

"Heckewelder's narrative is a full and undoubtedly faithful record of all the details of the Mission, its wonderful success and its appalling destruction. He was able to give a thousand particulars from personal experience, and it is at once an interesting story, abounding in veritable incidents; and a valuable history, fortified by impregnable facts. Forty years of missionary life among the Delaware and Shawnese tribes, had amply fitted the author to record the facts which fell under his own knowledge."— *Field.*

913 HELPS (A.) The Life of Las Casas, "The Apostle of the Indies." By Arthur Helps. *Philadelphia: [i.e. London.]* 1868.

Post 8vo, pp. xix., 292. *Map. Half green morocco, gilt top,* UNCUT, *by* BRADSTREET.

914 HENLEY (D.) Proceedings of a Court Martial held at Cambridge, by order of Major General Heath, Commanding the American Troops ... for the Trial of Colonel David Henley, accused by General Burgoyne, of Ill Treatment of the British Soldiers, &c. ... The Second Edition. *London: J. Almon.* MDCCLXXVIII.

8vo, pp. 155. *Half blue morocco, gilt top, by* W. MATTHEWS. LARGE and FINE COPY. VERY SCARCE.

915 HENNEPIN (Louis.) A | New Discovery | of a | Vast Country in America, | Extending above Four Thousand Miles, | between | New France and New Mexico. | With a | Description of the Great Lakes, Cata- | racts, Rivers, Plants, and Animals: | Also, the Manners, Customs, and Languages, of the | several Native Indians; and the Advantage of | Commerce with those different Nations. | With a | Continuation: | giving an Account of the | Attempts of the Sieur De la Salle upon the | Mines of St. Barbe, &c. The taking of | Quebec by the English; With the Advantages | of a Shorter Cut to China and Japan. | Both Parts illustrated with Maps, and Figures, | and Dedicated to His Majesty K. William. | By L. Hennepin, now Resi-

dent in Holland. | To which is added, Several New Discoveries in North- | America, not publish'd in the French Edition. | *London : Printed for M. Bentley, J. Tonson, H. Bon- | wick, T. Goodwin and S. Manship.* 1698.

Part I. pp. (22), 299, (1) : *Part II. pp.* (32), 178, (2), 303–355. 2 *Maps*, 5 *Plates*. 8*vo*, *half calf, antique*. LARGE and FINE COPY of the first English edition ; differing in some respects from that of the following year.

" Hennepin was persecuted, and has been severely criticised, chiefly on account of his opposition to the Jesuits, and because he counselled William III. (in whose dominions he had sought for the freedom and safety which he could not find in France) to send out missionaries to the New World. His enemies considered such advice from a monk as heretical and detestable ; it simply proves the wiser, purer and more Catholic Christianity of Hennepin, who had no bigoted horror for other sects than his own."— *Stevens*.

916 HENNEPIN. A | New Discovery | of a | Vast Country in America, | Extending above Four Thousand Miles, | Between | New France & New Mexico ; | With A | Description of the Great Lakes, Cataracts, | Rivers, Plants, and Animals. | Also the Manners, Customs, and Languages of the several | Native Indians ; And the Advantage of Commerce with | those different Nations. | With a | Continuation | Giving an Account of the | Attempts of the Sieur de la Salle upon the | Mines of St. Barbe, &c. The Taking of Quebec | by the English ; With the Advantages of a | shorter Cut to China and Japan. | Both Illustrated with Maps and Figures ; and Dedicated | to His Majesty King William. | By L. Hennepin now Resident in Holland. | To which are added, Several New Discoveries in North | America, not Publish'd in the French Edition. | *London : Printed for Henry Bonwicke, at the Red Lion | in St. Paul's Church-Yard.* 1699.

Part I. pp. (20), 240. *Part II. pp.* (24), 216. 2 *Maps*, 7 *Plates*. 8*vo*, *calf, yellow edges*. The Maps are folded, and *laid in loose* for convenient reference.

A RARE EDITION which Dr. O'Callaghan says "*is not in any catalogue.*"— *Hist. Mag.*, II. 24.

Father Hennepin was commissioned by La Salle to explore the upper course of the Mississippi to its source, and ranks as the discoverer of the immense region watered by that river. One of the plates represents the first view ever taken of the Falls of Niagara.

917 HENRY (A.) Travels and Adventures in Canada and the Indian Territories, between the Years 1760 and 1776. In Two Parts. By Alexander Henry, Esq. *New York : I. Riley.* 1809.

8*vo*, *pp. viii.*, 330. *Half calf*, UNCUT. SCARCE.

" The author relates the incidents of his life as a fur-trader among the Indians on the shores of the upper great lakes ; of the surprise and massacre of the garrison of Fort Michilimackinac, of his own narrow escape from the slaughter, and his capture. His narrative of the details of his long captivity is very interesting, and has been deemed the most authentic we have, relating to the domestic habits of the northern Indians."— *Field*.

918 HENRY (J. J.) An Accurate and Interesting Account of the Hardships and Sufferings of that Band of Heroes, who Traversed the

Wilderness in the Campaign against Quebec in 1795. By John Joseph Henry, Esq. ... *Lancaster: Printed by William Greer.* 1812.

12mo, pp. 225. *Half calf.* Fine clean copy of the scarce FIRST EDITION.

919 HERBERT (C.) A Relic of the Revolution, containing a Full and Particular Account of the Sufferings and Privations of all the American Prisoners captured on the High Seas, and Carried into Plymouth, England, during the Revolution of 1776. ... Also, an Account of the Several Cruises of the Squadron under the Command of Commodore John Paul Jones, Prizes taken, etc, etc. By Charles Herbert, of Newburyport, Mass. ... *Boston: Charles H. Peirce.* 1847.

12mo, pp. 258. *Half green morocco, gilt top,* UNCUT. SCARCE.

920 HERRERA (A. de) The General History of the Vast Continent and Islands of America, commonly call'd the West-Indies, from the first Discovery thereof: with the best Accounts the People could give of their Antiquities. Collected from the original Relations sent to the Kings of Spain. By Antonio de Herrera. ... Translated into English by Capt. John Stevens. Illustrated with Cuts and Maps. *London: Printed for Jer. Batley.* M.DCC.XXV–XXVI.

6 *vols.,* 8*vo.* 2 *Maps and* 16 *Plates. Half calf antique. Fine clean set.*

"No one has ever disputed the fidelity of old Herrera, styled the Prince of Historians, to the sources of information then accessible, and no one has ever exceeded him in careful research, and interesting narration of aboriginal history. He sought and obtained many of the original documents, which the industry and spirit of the old missionaries and explorers made so numerous and voluminous. He copied, almost bodily, the MS. History of the Indies by Las Casas. Mr. Squier notices that he has transferred almost the entire MS. Relacion of Palacio, to chapters 8, 9, and 10 of the Eighth Book of his Fourth Decade. His work is a perfect treasure-house of the most valuable details, regarding the original state of the religion and manners of the Indians."—*Field.*

921 [HERVEY (N.)] The Memory of Washington; with Biographical Sketches of his Mother and Wife. Relations of Lafayette to Washington; with Incidents and Anecdotes in the Lives of the Two Patriots. *Boston: J. Munroe & Co.* 1852.

12mo, pp. 320. 2 *Plates. Half green morocco, gilt top.*

922 **Heures a l'Usaige de Rome,** tout a long sans rien requerir. Avec les figures de la destruction de Hierusalem et Calendrier [1518 à 1525]. PRINTED ON EIGHTY LEAVES OF PURE VELLUM WITHIN DECORATIVE BORDERS COLOURED ON GOLD GROUNDS, AND FILLETS, with FOURTEEN LARGE WOODCUTS of the usual Scriptural subjects, and NINETEEN of smaller size, finished as Ancient Missal Paintings. The capitals, of which there are many hundreds, are in COLOURS and GOLD. *Paris: Hardouyn.* [1518.]

Roy. 8*vo, elegantly bound in orange morocco extra, gilt edges, and in the* FINEST STATE OF PRESERVATION.

A BEAUTIFUL EXAMPLE of the press of HARDOUYN; FINELY ILLUMINATED IN GOLD AND COLOURS in imitation of the miniatures usually found in Manuscript Horæ, by GERMAIN HARDOUIN, who styled himself in "*Arte litterariæ picturæ peritissimus.*"

923 HEYLYN (P.) Cosmographie. ... Containing the Chorographie & History of the whole World. ... By Peter Heylyn.
London: Anne Seile. 1677.

Folio, half red morocco, gilt top, by BRADSTREET.

So much of the work as relates to AMERICA.

Collation. Engraved and printed titles, 2 l. To the Reader &c., 4 l. Introduction, pp. 24. Map, "Americæ Nova descriptio Impensis Annæ Seile 1663." Title, 1 l., Text, pp. 83–154. Appendix, pp. 155–162.

IN THE FINEST CONDITION.

924 HICKCOX (J. H.) An Historical Account of American Coinage. By John H. Hickcox. ... With Plates. *Albany: Joel Munsell.* 1858.

Imp. 8vo, pp. viii., 151. 5 Plates. Half blue morocco, gilt top, UNCUT. 200 copies PRIVATELY PRINTED.

925 **Hieronymi (St.) Expositio Symboli Apostolorum.**
[*Cologne: Ulric Zell. circa* 1460.]

Sm. 4to, 28 leaves, 27 lines to a page. Claret morocco, antique. Back and sides elegantly blind tooled, gilt edges, lettered on the side, by W MATTHEWS.

A VERY EARLY EDITION of this Father, having neither the name of the printer, his office, residence, nor date, but with the types of ULRIC ZELL (about) MCCCCLX. A FINE COPY, and a BEAUTIFUL SPECIMEN OF EARLY TYPOGRAPHY. ULRIC ZELL was the first printer at Cologne and a workman for Schoiffer, one of the first printers.

926 **Higden (Ranulph.) Polycronycon in whiche book ben comprised briefly many wonderful historyes by Ranulph monke of Chestre and afterward englisshed by one Trevisa vycarye of barkley and now at this tyme symply emprynted and sette in forme by me William Caxton and a lytel embelysshed fro tholde makyng and also have added suche storyes as I coulde fynde &c.**
Fynysshed per Caxton MCCCClxxxii.

Folio, thick gros grained brown levant morocco elegant, richly blind tooled entirely over the covers to an old English Caxton pattern, with Tudor Rose, Fleurs de Lis and Acorns, in exact facsimile of an early Caxton binding, gilt edges, by F. BEDFORD. EXTREMELY RARE.

This LARGE and ELEGANT copy of the POLYCHRONICON, than which "few of Caxton's books have excited more interest and research," is a SPLENDID EXAMPLE of typographical art from the hands of ENGLAND'S FIRST PRINTER nearly FOUR HUNDRED YEARS ago. It measures 7½ inches by 10½ inches on the leaf, and therefore, is fully up to the average size of all the copies referred to by Mr. Blades in his life of Caxton. Of the 29 copies enumerated by him all but five are imperfect, some being fragments merely, as in the case of one of those in the British Museum, which contains but six leaves only. A noticeable feature in Mr. Blades's list is that almost every incomplete copy is deficient in the earlier portions of the work, thus accounting for the fact that the two leaves of the Proheme alone, would probably command forty pounds in London.

This beautiful copy contains ALL the prefatory matter, except the Table of Contents, with which exception, and that of the "Liber Ultimus" written by Caxton himself in continuation of the history, it will be found to meet Mr. Blades's collation of the text in every particular. A few leaves have been repaired by Mr. Bedford in his neatest manner. In every other respect the volume is in a FINE STATE OF PRESERVATION.

The Charlemont copy, though imperfect, sold for £477.10.0.

927 HIGGINSON (Francis.) New-Englands | Plantation. | Or, | a Short and Trve | Description of the | Commodities and | Discommodities | of that Countrey. | Written by Mr. Higgeson, a Reuerend Diuine | now there resident. | Whereunto is added a Letter, sent by M[r]. Graues | an Enginere, out of New-England, | The third Edition, enlarged. | *London,* | *Printed by T. and R. Cotes. for Michael Sparke, dwelling* | *at the Signe of the Blue Bible in Greene-* | *Arbor.* 1630.

Sm. 4to, title, and 12 unpaged leaves. Crushed red levant morocco, gilt edges, by F. BEDFORD. LARGE and FINE COPY. EXTREMELY RARE.

Treating of the Indians, climate, soil, water, air and the animal and vegetable productions of New England.

"But whosoever desireth to know as much as yet can be discouered I aduise them to buy Captain John Smith's booke of the description of New-England in Folio; and there let the Reader expect to haue full content."—*Extract.*

928 HIGGINSON (J.) The | Cause of God | and His People in New-England, | as it was | Stated and Discussed | in | A Sermon Preached before the Honourable General | Covrt of the Massachvsets Colony, | on the 27 day of May, 1663. Being the Day | Of Election at Boston. | By John Higginson, Pastor of the Church | of Christ at Salem. ... | *Cambridg: Printed by Samuel Green.* 1663.

Sm. 4to, title, and pp. 24. Olive morocco, sides in compartments elegantly blank and gilt tooled, inside lined with polished crimson morocco paneled and gilt with centre and corner ornaments, morocco joints, gilt edges. A choice example of the best workmanship of PAWSON & NICHOLSON.

A VERY EARLY New England imprint. Printed in the same year with, and by one of the printers of ELIOT'S INDIAN BIBLE. RARE AUTOGRAPH SIGNATURE of the PRINTER *inserted.* The title page is mounted and each leaf on a guard, thereby insuring their preservation.

A FINE COPY, PRESQUE UNIQUE.

"This Reverend Person (John Higginson) has been always valued for his useful Preaching, and his holy Living, having formerly born his Testimony to, *the Cause of God, and his People in New-England,* in a Sermon so entituled, which he preached on the greatest Anniversary Solemnity, which occurr'd in the Land. "—*Magnalia.* Book III. p. 76.

929 [HIGGINSON (Stephen.)] Ten Chapters in the Life of John Hancock. The Writings of Laco, as published in the Massachusetts Centinel, in the months of February and March, 1789, with the addition of No. VII., which was omitted.

Printed at Boston. 1789. *Reprinted; New York.* 1857.

8vo, pp. 68. *Half green morocco, gilt top,* UNCUT. SCARCE. FOURTEEN ILLUSTRATIONS *inserted;* including FIVE PORTRAITS of HANCOCK, three of which are contemporary; and five leaves of mounted newspaper cuttings relating to the work. 150 *copies only printed;* 60 of which were destroyed by fire.

930 HINMAN (R. R.) A Historical Collection, from Official Records, Files, etc., of the Part sustained by Connecticut, during the War of the Revolution. With an Appendix, containing important Letters, Depositions, etc., written during the War. Compiled by Royal R. Hinman. ... *Hartford: E. Gleason.* 1842.

8vo, pp. 644. 2 *Portraits. Half green morocco, gilt top.*

931 HISTORICAL ANECDOTES, Civil and Military; in a Series of Letters, written From America, in the years 1777 and 1778, to different Persons in England; containing Observations on the General Management of the War, and on the Conduct of our Principal Commanders, in the Revolted Colonies, During that Period.

London: J. Bew. M.DCC.LXXIX.

8vo, pp. (6), 85. *Half red morocco, carmine edges.* FINE COPY. VERY SCARCE. We know only of *this*, and *the copy* in the Rice Library, which sold for $14.00. *See Rich.* I. 274.

"These letters seem to have been written by a zealous North British Loyalist; who chooses to demonstrate his aversion to the rebels and their cause, by bestowing, most liberally on both, the choicest flowers of scurrility."— *Monthly Review.*

932 HISTORICAL MAGAZINE, and Notes and Queries concerning the Antiquities, History, and Biography of America. [First Series, 1857 to 1866. 10 Vols. Second Series, 1867 to 1869. 6 Vols.]

Boston, & New York: 1857–69.

16 *vols.*, 4*to*, *half blue morocco, gilt top*, UNCUT.

933 HISTORY (The) of the British Empire, from the Year 1765, to the end of 1783. Containing An Impartial History of the Origin, Progress, and Termination of the American Revolution. By a Society of Gentlemen. *Philadelphia: R. Campbell & Co.* M.DCC.XCVIII.

2 *vols.*, 8*vo*, *pp.* 475; 452, 59. 2 *Portraits. Half maroon morocco. Curious portraits* of WASHINGTON and FRANKLIN.

These volumes are wholly occupied by a comprehensive history of the American Revolution.

934 HISTORY (The) of the Origin, Rise and Progress of the War in America between Great Britain and her Colonies, from its Commencement in the Year 1764, to the Time of General Gage's Arrival at Boston in 1774.

London, Printed. Boston, in the State of Massachusetts: Reprinted by Thomas and John Fleet ... M,DCC,LXXX.

[Continued as:] THE HISTORY of the Rise and Progress of the War in North-America, from the Time of General Gage's Arrival at Boston, in May, 1774.

London, Printed. Boston, in the State of Massachusetts: Reprinted by Thomas and John Fleet ... M,DCC,LXXX.

"End of the first volume" are the last words in the book; whereas the previous volume of 90 pp. is in fact the first. The next title is a continuation.

THE HISTORY of the War in America between Great Britain and her Colonies. Vol. II.

London, Printed. Boston [as before]. M.DCC.LXXX.

This concludes the series and is in fact Vol. III.

3 *vols.*, 8*vo*, *pp.* 90; 381, 34; 84, 4. *Crushed blue levant morocco, gilt top*, UNCUT, *by* F. BEDFORD. A COMPLETE SET of one of the SCARCEST WORKS in this collection. We know of NO OTHER COMPLETE SET in any of our public or private Libraries.

935 HISTORY (The) of the War in America, Between Great Britain and Her Colonies, from its Commencement to the Conclusion in 1783. In which its Origin, Progress, and Operations are faithfully related, together with Anecdotes and Characters of the different Commanders, ... To which is added, A Collection of Interesting and Authentic Papers tending to elucidate the History.
Dublin: Printed for the Company of Booksellers. 1779–85.

3 vols., 8vo, half russia.

Seldom found complete, the third volume, which is supplementary, having been published six years subsequent to the two first. This copy contains the *large folded sheet* giving the names and rank of the killed, wounded and missing of the British forces at the battles of Concord, and Bunkerhill, which is frequently wanting.

936 HITCHCOCK (E.) A Discourse on the Dignity and Excellence of the Human Character; Illustrated in the Life of General George Washington, ... delivered February 22, 1800, ... at Providence. By Enos Hitchcock, D.D. ... *Providence:* 1800.

8vo, pp. 35. UNCUT. SCARCE.

937 HOAR (L.) The Sting of Death | and | Death Unstung | Delivered in two | Sermons | In which is shewed | the Misery of the Death of those that Dye in their Sins, & out | of Christ, and the Blessedness of theirs that Dye in the Lord. | Preached on the occasion of the Death of the truly noble and virtuous | The Lady Mildmay. | By Leonard Hoar, M.D. | Sometime Preacher of God's Word in Wanstead. | ... | *Boston: Printed by John Foster.* 1680.

Sm. 4to, pp. (8), 24. *Crimson morocco, gilt edges.* A RARE and VERY EARLY Boston imprint. The Epistle Dedicatory, pp. 6, is signed by Josiah Flint of Dorchester.

938 HOFFMAN (M.) A Treatiſe upon the Eſtate and Rights of the Corporation of the City of New York, ... as Proprietors. By Murray Hoffman, Eſq. *New York: McSpedon & Baker.* 1853.

8vo, half calf, UNCUT.

939 HOGG (J.) The Jacobite Relics of Scotland: being the Songs, Airs, and Legends, of the Adherents to the House of Stuart. Collected and Illustrated by James Hogg.
Edinburgh: William Blackwood. 1819–21.

2 vols., 8vo, polished calf, yellow edges. FINE COPY.
Recently priced in an English sale catalogue at £5. 15. 6.

940 HOGG. The Jacobite Relics &c. [Another copy.]
Edinburgh: William Blackwood. 1819–21.

2 vols., 8vo, half crushed green levant morocco, gilt top, UNCUT, *by* W. MATTHEWS. EXCEEDINGLY SCARCE in this fine *uncut* state.

"The Songs of a nation, more than any other influence, preserve its annals in their lights and shades of feeling. The days when the Stuarts claimed the throne of Scotland formed a stirring period in the national history, and around them have been thrown by the poet's art, interest, and romance that can never die; the famous Ettrick Shepherd revelled in the Songs and Legends of the Jacobite times, he was unwearied in his search after these Scotch Airs and Songs, sparing neither time nor toil in order to obtain the best versions."

941 [HOGG.] A Queer Book. By The Ettrick Shepherd. [James Hogg.] *Edinburgh: William Blackwood.* 1832.

12mo, pp. ii., 379. Half calf. An Autograph Note WRITTEN and SIGNED by the AUTHOR *inserted.*

942 HOLBROOK (J. E.) North American Herpetology; or, a Description of the Reptiles inhabiting the United States. By John Edwards Holbrooke, M.D. ... *Philadelphia: J. Dobson.* 1842.

5 *vols., 4to, half crushed red levant morocco, gilt top,* UNCUT, *by* W. MATTHEWS. A SPLENDID COPY of an uncommon set of books.

The first systematic work, on the Reptiles of the United States, ever attempted. The PLATES, 157 in number, are beautifully COLOURED; and it appears to be in every way worthy of a place in the library of the Naturalist by the side of Wilson's great work on our Birds. Complete sets, like the present, are VERY SCARCE, the fourth and fifth volumes, of which a small edition only was printed, being rarely found with the other three.

943 HOLCOMBE (H.) A Sermon, Occasioned By the Death of Lieutenant-General George Washington ... . Delivered in ... Savannah, Georgia, January 19th, 1800. ... By Henry Holcombe, Minister of the Word of God in Savannah. [*Savannah:* 1800.]

4to, pp. 16, (2). UNCUT. *Very Scarce.*

944 [HOLDEN (Oliver.)] Sacred Dirges, Hymns, and Anthems, Commemorative of the Death of General George Washington, the Guardian of his Country, and the Friend of Man. An Original Composition. By a Citizen of Massachusetts.
Printed at Boston: by I. Thomas and E. T. Andrews. [1800.]

Oblong 4to, pp. 24. Boards, UNCUT. VERY RARE.

945 [HOLLANDI (Henri.)] Herωologia Anglica; clarissimorum et doctissimorum aliquot Anglorum, qui floruerunt ab A.B. 1500 usque ad 1620, vivæ effigies, vitæ et elogia, authore H. H. Anglo-Britanno.
Impensis Crispini Passæi Chalcogr. et Jansonii Bibliop. Arnhem. *s. a.* [1620.]

Sm. folio, old russia; from the ALLAN Collection, containing 64 PORTRAITS, and 2 MONUMENTS. BRILLIANT IMPRESSIONS. A GENUINE, EARLY, and TALL COPY issued before those with the post praefatio. The engraved title is mounted, and the fore-margin of several leaves a little wormed, notwithstanding which it is a desirable copy of this beautiful series of English Portraits, the first ever issued.

As few copies are perfect we add the COLLATION:— Title; Text: Augustissimo, 1 leaf; Praefatio, 2 leaves; Ejusdem, a leaf; Encomium, a leaf; iret, a leaf; non jam, *leaf with portrait;* pp. 1–240, with a PORTRAIT on nearly every leaf. SEPARATE PLATES, Monument of Queen Elizabeth at p. 40; Frobisher's portrait, at p. 96; J. Balaeus, at p. 164.

This book (says Walpole) was the first regular collection of English Heads, and though it had probably a wide circulation upon its appearance, it is at this time in a complete state, very rare. What greatly enhances its merits is, that all the portraits, also the two monuments are drawn from original pictures.

946 [HOLLIS (Thomas.)] The Trve Sentiments of America: contained in a Collection of Letters sent from the Hovse of Representatives of the Province of Massachvsetts Bay to several persons of high rank in this Kingdom: Together with certain papers relating to a svpposed Libel on the Governor of that Province, and a Dissertation [by John Adams] on the Canon and Fevdal Law. *London: J. Almon.* 1768.

8vo, pp. 158. *Half green morocco. Large and fine copy.*

"The collecting and publication of these important papers in England is due to Thomas Hollis, an ardent friend of the Colonies in London. They include the celebrated letter written by Samuel Adams to Dennis De Berdt, Agent for the House of Representatives in England, dated January 12, 1768, adopted by the Colonial Legislature and signed by the Speaker. Until recently there were doubts as to the authorship of this document, but all uncertainty is now removed, Mr. Bancroft having in his possession the original draft in the handwriting of Mr. Adams. In speaking of this Mr. Bancroft says, "On the sixth day of January, and for the evening and morning of many succeeding days, the paper was under severe examination. Seven times it was revised; every word was weighed, every sentence considered; and each seemingly harsh expression tempered and refined. At last, on the twelfth of January, the letter was adopted, to be sent to the Agent, communicated to the British Ministry, and published to the world, as expressing the unchangeable opinions of Massachusetts."— *History of the United States*, Vol. VI. p. 120–125.

947 HOLLISTER (G. H.) The History of Connecticut, from the First Settlement of the Colony, to the Adoption of the Present Constitution. By G. H. Hollister. ... Second Edition, Enlarged and Improved. *Hartford: Case, Tiffany & Co.* 1857.

2 *vols., 8vo, pp.* 613; 758; 17 *Portraits. Half purple morocco, gilt top,* UNCUT.

948 HOLMES (A.) A Sermon Preached at Cambridge, ... December 29, 1799, Occasioned by the Death of George Washington. ... By Abiel Holmes. ... [And Hymn.] *Boston:* 1800.

8vo, pp. 22, (1). *Half blue morocco, gilt top,* UNCUT, *by* BRADSTREET.

949 HOLMES. The Counsel of Washington, Recommended in a Discourse, Delivered at Cambridge, February 22, 1800. By Abiel Holmes. ... *Boston*: 1800.

8vo, pp. 23, *half blue morocco, gilt top,* UNCUT *by* BRADSTREET. EXCEEDINGLY RARE.

950 HOLMES. The Annals of America, from the Discovery by Columbus in the year 1492 to the year 1826. By Abiel Holmes, D.D. ... Second Edition. *Cambridge: Hilliard and Brown.* 1829.

2 *vols., 8vo, pp. xvi.,* 584; (1), 599. *Half maroon levant morocco, gilt top,* UNCUT. FINE COPY of the BEST EDITION. SCARCE.

"One of the best works of the kind ever published. Everything of importance in the history of America is related in a concise manner, with copious and interesting notes and references to the original authorities.— It is out of print and SCARCE."— *Rich.*

951 HOLMES (J.) Historical Sketches of the Missions of the United Brethren for Propagating the Gospel among the Heathen, from their

Commencement to the year 1817. By the Rev. John Holmes. ... Second Improved Edition. *London: Printed for The Author.* 1827.

8vo, pp. viii., 470. *Half blue levant morocco, gilt top,* UNCUT.

The author was Minister of the Brethren's Congregation in Dublin, and gives an account of their Missionary labors from their commencement to 1818. The Missions chiefly described are in Greenland, Labrador, among the Delaware and Iroquois Indians, the West Indies, South America, etc.

952 HOMANS (J. S.) A Cyclopædia of Commerce and Commercial Navigation: edited by J. Smith Homans ... and by J. Smith Homans Jr. ... *New-York: Harper & Brother.* 1859.

2 *vols., roy. 8vo, pp.* 2007. *Half blue morocco, gilt top,* UNCUT.

953 HOME (J.) Douglas, a Tragedy. By John Home, Esq. *Edinburgh:* 1798.

8vo, half morocco, LARGE PAPER; PORTRAIT *of the* AUTHOR *and one of* MR. WOOD *in the character of Glenalvon, the only one of him known, and other plates.*

A very curious and scarce subscription edition. The present is the ONLY COPY we ever met with.

954 HOMES of American Authors; comprising Anecdotical, Personal, and Descriptive Sketches, by Various Writers. Illustrated with Views of their Residences from original drawings, and a Facsimile of the MS. of each Author. *New York: G. P. Putnam & Co.* 1853.

Sq. 8vo, pp. viii., 366. 19 *Plates,* 15 *Wood Engravings,* 16 *Facsimiles. Half blue morocco, gilt top,* UNCUT.

955 HOMES of American Statesman: with Anecdotical, Personal, and Descriptive Sketches, by Various Writers. Illustrated with Engravings on Wood, from Drawings by Döpler, and Daguereotypes: and Facsimiles of Autograph Letters. *New York: G. P. Putnam and Co.* 1854.

Sq. 8vo, pp. viii., 469. 45 *Views,* 17 *Facsimiles. Half blue morocco, gilt top,* UNCUT. TWENTY-THREE PORTRAITS *inserted;* embracing those of *all* the Statesmen noticed in the work, that of Henry Wheaton excepted.

956 HONEYWOOD (ST. J.) Poems by St. John Honeywood, A.M. With Some Pieces in Prose. *New York: T. & J. Swords.* 1801.

12mo, *pp. viii.,* 159. *Calf, yellow edges.*

957 HOOKE (W.) New | Englands | Teares, | for old | Englands | Feares, | Preached in a Sermon on July 23, | 1640. being a day of Publike Humiliation, | appointed by the Churches in behalfe of our | Native Countrey in time of | feared dangers. | By William Hooke, Minister of God's | Word; Sometime of Axmouth in Devonshire, | now of Taunton in New England, | Sent over to a worthy Member of the honourable | House of Commons, who desires it may be for | publike

good. | *London :* | *Printed by E. G. for Iohn Rothwell and Henry Overton, and* | *are to be sould at the Sunne in Paul's Church-* | *yard, and in Pope's-head Alley.* 1641.

4to, pp. (4), 23. *Green morocco, gilt edges, by* F. BEDFORD. LARGE and FINE COPY, with *many rough leaves.* RARE.

" A Sermon preached to some in New-England for Old England's sake." There appears to have been two editions printed in the same year.

958 [HOOKER (Thomas.)] The | Vnbelievers | Preparing for | Christ. | By T. H. *London : Printed by Tho. Cotes for Andrew Crooke, and are to be* | *sold at the Blacke Beare in Saint Pauls Church-* | *yard.* 1638.

4to, 204, (4), 119, 4. *Blue morocco antique, blank tooled sides, gilt edges, by* HAYDAY. BEAUTIFUL COPY.

959 [HOOKER.] The | Sovles | Preparation | for Christ. | Or, | A Treatise | of Contrition. | Wherein is discovered | Hovv God breakes the heart, | and wounds the Soule in the con- | version of a Sinner to Himselfe. | The fourth Edition. | *London,* | *Printed by the Assignees of T. P. for T. Nickoles, and* | *are to bee sold at the signe of the Bible, in* | *Popes-head Ally.* 1638.

4to, pp. (6). 242. *Blue morocco ; uniform with the preceding No.*

960 [HOOKER.] The | Sovles | Hvmiliation. | The second Edition. | *London,* | *Printed by I. L. for Andrew Crooke, at the* | *Signe of the Beare in Paul's Church-yard.* | 1638.

4to, pp. 223, (8). *Blue morocco ; uniform with the preceding No.*

961 [HOOKER.] The Soules | Implantation. | A Treatise | Containing, | The broken Heart, | ... | The Preparation of the Heart, | ... | The Soules ingraffing into Christ, | ... |Spirituall Love and Joy, | ... | *London,* | *Printed by R. Young, and are sold by Fulke Clifton* | *on New Fish-street-hill.* | 1637.

4to, pp. (2), 266. *Blue morocco, uniform with the preceding No.*

The author was the first minister of Cambridge, Mass., and one of the founders of the colony of Connecticut. He appeared with such majesty in the pulpit, that it was pleasantly said of him " he could put a king into his pocket." He has been called the Luther of New England.

962 HOOKER. The Danger | of | Desertion : | or | a Farvvell (sic) Sermon | of Mr. Thomas Hooker, | Sometime Minister of God's Word at Chains- | ford in Essex ; but now of New England. | Preached immediately before his departure | out of old England. | Together | with Ten Particvlar | rules to be practiced every day by | Converted Christians. | *London,* | *Printed by G. M. for George Edwards in the* | *Old Baily in Green-Arbour, at the signe* | *of the Angell.* 1641.

4to, pp. (4), 29. *Polished calf, gilt edges, by* W. PRATT. A FINE COPY of this SCARCE historical sermon.

" Hooker was a son of thunder."— MATHER's *Magnalia.*

963 HOPKINSON (F.) The Miscellaneous Essays and Occasional Writings of Francis Hopkinson, Esq. *Philadelphia: T. Dobson.* M,DCC,XCII.

3 vols., 8vo, half green morocco, gilt top, UNCUT. Fine clean copy. Rarely found *uncut.* PORTRAIT of the AUTHOR, an Autograph Letter WRITTEN, and a United States Draft SIGNED by him *inserted.*

964 HOPKINSON. The Old Farm and the New Farm: a Political Allegory. By Francis Hopkinson ... with an Introduction and Historical Notes by Benson J. Lossing, M.A.

New York: Dana and Co. 1857.

12mo, pp. 76. *Half morocco, gilt top,* UNCUT. PORTRAIT of the AUTHOR *inserted.*

965 **Hore Beate Marie Virginis,** secundum Usum Romanum, cum Calendario. PRINTED ON 114 LEAVES OF PURE VELLUM, with 19 large ILLUMINATED PAINTINGS THE SIZE of THE PAGE, and 34 smaller Miniatures likewise in GOLD AND COLOURS; all the capitals are RUBRICATED AND GILT. *Paris: Kerver.* MCCCCC.

Sm. 4to, blue morocco, inlaid and richly tooled back, gold filleted sides, gilt edges. In the finest state of preservation.

A MOST BEAUTIFUL EXAMPLE of the RARE FIRST EDITION, "*Secundum Usum Romanum,*" PRINTED BY KERVER, with a date, and a fine specimen of his early and celebrated Press; the ornamental illuminations are of equal merit, and interesting specimens of French Art; the Costumes being of a rich and varied character.

"Thielmann Kerver, who commenced to publish his 'Hours' in 1497, at first used the press of Jean Philippe; but he soon printed for himself, for we remark that from the end of this same year, 1497, he printed for Jean Richard of Rouen, and for Pierre Regnault of Caen, who, in 1492 had employed Pigouchet. He lived then on Pont St. Michel. Three years after, he sold his shop to Gillett Remacle, bookseller, for whom he printed 'Hours' in 1500, 1501, 1502 and 1503, in the Rue St. Jacques, where he died in 1522. His widow succeeded him at the end of this year. She continued until 1556 to publish books of liturgy in all forms. One remarkable thing is, that though the editions are very numerous, the '*Hours*' of Kerver are rarer than those of *Vostre* or of the two *Hardouins.* This comes probably from the fact that few were printed upon vellum, and that the copies on paper have been destroyed. Besides, among those which appeared before 1520, only the first, with borders round the pages, are worthy of being collected; and these borders are desirable for the arabesque, a style in which he excelled. It is supposed that Kerver rarely used painting to decorate his books, for but few have come down to us thus ornamented." — *Brunet.*

966 **Hore Intemerate Virginis Dei Genetricis Marie** secundum usum ecclie Romane: ... Parisiis novit impssis p. Egidiū Hardouyn. **Black Letter.** PRINTED ON 124 LEAVES OF PURE VELLUM, with 16 large and VERY FINE EARLY WOODCUTS, some on WHOLE PAGES, some on half, and 17 smaller woodcuts, BRILLIANT IMPRESSIONS, also many hundred capitals ILLUMINATED in GOLD and COLOURS. *Paris: Hardouyn. s. a.* (1508.)

Sm. 8vo, crushed brown levant morocco, sides elegantly blank and gilt tooled in the Grolier style, vellum linings, edges gilt on the round. In a blue morocco pull-off Case, by F. BEDFORD.

A RARE and BEAUTIFUL EXAMPLE of early French Typography.

967 HORNE (R. H.) Orion, an Epic Poem. In Three Books. By R. H. Horne. (Price One Farthing.) *London: J. Miller.* 1843.

Crown 8vo, pp. (4), 137. *Half orange morocco, gilt top,* UNCUT. Beautifully printed on INDIA PAPER.

The RARE FIRST EDITION, and one of the copies published and sold for ONE FARTHING. There were three editions published at that price, and a limited number printed. One copy only was sold to each applicant. They were out of print in a few hours, the price was then risen to 5s. and some thousands were sold in a short space of time.

968 HORNE (T. H.) An Introduction to the Study of Bibliography. To which is prefixed a Memoir on the Public Libraries of the Antients. By Thomas Hartwell Horne. Illustrated with Engravings. *London: T. Cadell & W. Davies.* 1814.

2 vols., roy. 8vo, half maroon levant morocco, gilt top, UNCUT. LARGE PAPER; TWENTY COPIES ONLY printed. An Autograph Note *written* and *signed* by the AUTHOR *inserted.* EXCEEDINGLY SCARCE.

969 HOROLOGIŪ DEUOTIONIS. [2d leaf] Incipit in horologiū deuotionis plogus circa vitam Christi iesu. [Colophon] Explicit Horologium deuotionis. [*Mayence: Circa.* 1480.]

Sm. 8vo, brown morocco antique, blank and gilt tooled sides, corner ornaments, edges gilt on carmine, vellum linings, by F. BEDFORD.

A BEAUTIFUL and MOST DESIRABLE specimen of EARLY TYPOGRAPHY, and of the art of ENGRAVING on WOOD and on METAL in its infancy. It consists of 122 leaves with 37 engravings of the size of the page engraved on wood and on metal "*en manierè criblee.*" It is an *undescribed edition* and remarkable on account of the *curious* Engravings. The verso of the 5th leaf is blank.

970 HORRY (P.) *and* Weems (M. L.) The Life of General Francis Marion, a Celebrated Partisan Officer in the Revolutionary War, against the British and Tories in South Carolina and Georgia. By Brig. Gen. P. Horry, of Marion's Brigade: and M. L. Weems. *Philadelphia: Joseph Allen.* 1833.

12mo, sheep. ILLUSTRATIONS *on wood, by* DR. ANDERSON.

971 [HORSMANDEN (Daniel.)] A | Journal | of the | Proceedings | in | The Detection of the Conspiracy | formed by | Some White People, in Conjunction with Negro and other Slaves, | for | Burning the City of New-York in America, | And Murdering the Inhabitants. | Which Conspiracy was partly put in Execution, by Burning His Majesty's House in | Fort George, within the said City, on Wednesday the Eighteenth of March, 1741, and | setting Fire to several Dwellings and other Houses there, within a few Days succeeding. | And by another Attempt made in Prosecution of the same infernal scheme, by putting | Fire between two other Dwelling Houses within the said City, on the Fifteenth Day of | February, 1742; which was accidentally and timely discovered and extinguished. | Containing. |

I. A Narrative of the Trials, Condemnations, Executions, and Behaviour of the | several Criminals, at the Gallows and Stake, with their Speeches and Confessions; with | Notes, Observations and Reflections occasionally interspersed throughout the whole. |

II. An Appendix, wherein is set forth some additional Evidence concerning the said | Conspiracy and Conspirators, which has come to Light since their Trials and | Executions. |

III. Lists of the several Persons (Whites and Blacks) committed on Account of the | Conspiracy; and of the several Criminals executed; and of those transported, with | the Places whereto. | By the Recorder of the City of New-York. | ... | *New York:* | *Printed by James Parker, at the New Printing-Office.* 1744.

4to, title, pp. vi., 206, 1 *blank leaf,* 16. *Crushed blue levant morocco, paneled sides, corner ornaments, edges gilt on carmine, by* F. BEDFORD. LARGE and SUPERB COPY of this EXCESSIVELY RARE WORK.

The only copy that has been sold in New York during many years was in the Bruce sale. It was bought for Mr. Rice and resold with his Collection when it brought $140.00, and was a copy much inferior to this. Mr. Quaritch, in a recent catalogue, offers a copy for £45, and remarks "I know of no other copy sold in the London market." The work had become so scarce even in 1810, that the editor of the edition of that year intimates that he experienced the greatest difficulty in finding a copy. Parker (the printer of this volume) was an apprentice to Bradford, and succeeded to the business in 1742.

Nos. 972, and 973, are Reprints.

972 [HORSMANDEN.] A Journal of the Proceedings in the Detection of the Conspiracy Formed by some White People, in conjunction with Negro and other Slaves, for burning the City of New York in America and murdering the Inhabitants. ... By the Recorder of the City of New-York. ...
Printed at New-York: London, Reprinted and Sold by John Clarke. 1747.

8vo, pp. viii., 425, (7). *Half crushed red levant morocco, gilt top,* UNCUT, by W. MATTHEWS. AN ELEGANT COPY. Equally RARE, though not perhaps so valuable as the preceding No. *We have never seen another copy.*

973 HORSMANDEN. The New York Conspiracy, or a History of the Negro Plot, with the Journal of the Proceedings against the Conspirators at New-York in the years 1741–2. Together with several interesting Tables, ... By Daniel Horsmanden, Esq.
New York: Southwick & Pelsue. 1810.

8vo, pp. 385, (7). *Half crushed blue levant morocco, gilt top,* UNCUT, *by* W. MATTHEWS. BEAUTIFUL COPY. VERY RARE in *uncut* condition.

For an Account of this alleged Conspiracy and the Trial, see Chandler's *American Criminal Trials, Vol.* I. p. 211.

974 HOSACK (D.) Memoir of DeWitt Clinton: with an Appendix, containing numerous Documents, Illustrative of the Principal Events of his Life. By David Hosack, M.D. F.R.S.
New York: J. Seymour. 1829.

2 *vols, 4to, half green morocco, gilt top,* UNCUT.

A SUPERBLY ILLUSTRATED COPY, and an elegant tribute to the memory of New York's GREATEST STATESMAN. One volume EXTENDED to TWO, with RUBRICATED TITLES printed expressly for the set, and upwards of ONE HUNDRED PORTRAITS and VIEWS *inserted:* TWENTY of which are FINE INDIA PROOFS, and many SCARCE and RARE. Included are SEVEN fine and different PORTRAITS of CLINTON, an Autograph Note SIGNED, and an Official Document wholly in his HANDWRITING, with his SIGNATURE and a fine impression of the Seal of the State of New York attached.

TWO BEAUTIFUL VOLUMES.

975 HOSMER (Z.) Catalogue of the Valuable and Choice Library of Zelotes Hosmer, Esq. of Cambridge, Mass. *Boston:* 1861.

Roy. 8vo, half olive morocco, gilt top, UNCUT. With *prices* and *names.* Particularly rich in early English literature, bibliography, and rare editions of the Greek and Latin classics.

976 HOUDIN (M. G.) A Funeral Oration on the Death of George Washington: Delivered in ... Albany, ... on the Twenty-second of February, 1800. By Michael Gabriel Houdin, Major in the late Revolutionary Army of the United States. *Albany:* [1800.]

Sm. 4to, pp. 11. *Portrait.* UNCUT, and SCARCE.

977 HOUGH (F. B.) A History of St. Lawrence and Franklin Counties, New York, from the Earliest Period to the Present Time. By Franklin B. Hough, A.M., M.D. *Albany: Little & Co.* 1853.

Roy. 8vo, pp. 719, (1). *Portraits, Maps, and Plans. Half green levant morocco, gilt top,* UNCUT. One of TWENTY-FIVE COPIES printed on FINE PAPER, with ADDITIONAL ILLUSTRATIONS.

978 HOUGH. A History of Jefferson County in the State of New York, from the Earliest Period to the Present Time. By F. B. Hough, A.M. M.D. *Albany: J. Munsell.* 1854.

8vo, pp. 601. *Portraits and Plates. Half green levant morocco, gilt top,* UNCUT. PORTRAIT of the AUTHOR *inserted.*

979 HOUGH. Papers Relating to the Island of Nantucket, with Documents relating to the Original Settlement of that Island, Martha's Vineyard, and other Islands adjacent, known as Duke's County, while under the Colony of New York. Compiled from Official Records .... By Franklin B. Hough, ... *Albany:* [*J. Munsell.*] 1856.

Sm. 4to, pp. xviii., 162, (1). *Half morocco.* PRIVATELY PRINTED: *and only* 150 *copies. Very scarce.* This copy wants the Map.

980 HOUGH. History of Lewis County, in the State of New York, from the Beginning of its Settlement to the Present Time. By Franklin B. Hough. ... *Albany: Munsell & Rowland.* 1860.

Roy. 8vo, pp. iv., 319. 22 *Portraits. Half green levant morocco, gilt top,* UNCUT. One of TWENTY-FIVE COPIES printed on FINE PAPER, and NOT FOR SALE. PROOF PORTRAIT of the AUTHOR *inserted.*

981 HOUGH. Bibliographical List of Books and Pamphlets containing Eulogies, Orations, Poems, or other Papers, relating to the Death of General Washington, or to the Honors Paid to His Memory. By Franklin B. Hough. *Albany: Privately Printed.* 1865.

Imp. 8vo, pp. 59. *Half green morocco, gilt top,* UNCUT. TWENTY-FOUR COPIES only PRIVATELY PRINTED, on tinted paper, with RUBRICATED TITLE.

982 HOUSE (The) of Wisdom in a Bustle; a Poem, Descriptive of the Noted Battle Lately Fought in C–ng–ss. By Geoffry Touchstone. *Philadelphia: Printed for the Author.* 1798.

8vo, pp. 27. *Half red morocco.* VERY SCARCE. *Rare caricature engraving* of the incidents referred to in the text *inserted.*

983 HOWE (H.) Historical Collections of Virginia; containing a Collection of the most interesting Facts, Traditions, Biographical Sketches, Anecdotes, &c., relating to its History and Antiquities, together with Geographical and Statistical Descriptions. To which is appended, an Historical and Descriptive Sketch of the District of Columbia. Illustrated by over 100 Engravings ... . By Henry Howe. *Charleston: S. C. Babcock & Co.* 1845.

8vo, pp. 544. *Map. Half calf. Carmine edges.*

984 [HOWE (Robert.)] A Candid and Impartial Narrative of the Transactions of the Fleet, under the Command of Lord Howe, from the Arrival of the Toulon Squadron, on the Coast of America, to the Time of his Lordship's Departure for England. With Observations. By an Officer then serving in the Fleet. The Second Edition, Revised and Corrected, with a Plan of the Situation of the Fleet, within Sandy-Hook. *London: J. Almon.* [1779.]

8vo, pp. 58. *Plan. Half maroon morocco.* SCARCE. The large folded PLAN of "The Fleet within Sandy Hook" is wanting in many copies.

Praises Lord Howe, and abuses the Ministry, particularly Lord Sandwich.

985 [HOWE (W.)] Two Letters from Agricola to Sir William Howe; to which are annexed, by the same author, Political Observations. *London: J. Millidge.* 1779.

8vo, pp. 63. *Half maroon morocco.* SCARCE.

"The author is very severe on Sir William Howe, whom he charges with the most shameful indolence and languor, in the conduct of the American war, which he accuses him of protracting, to the utter distress and ignominy of his country, while possessed of every superiority and advantage for putting a speedy and glorious end to the contest."—*Monthly Review.*

986 HOWE (W.) The Narrative of Lieut. Gen. Sir William Howe, in a Committee of the House of Commons, on the 29th of April, 1779, Relative to his Conduct, during his Late Command of the King's Troops in North America: To which are added, some Observations upon a Pamphlet, entitled, Letters to a Nobleman. The Third Edition. *London: H. Baldwin.* MDCCLXXXI.

4to, pp. 110. *Half calf.* LARGE CLEAN COPY. SCARCE.

An able vindication of the noble commander, in reply to various authors who had joined in the cry against him.

987 HOWELL (J.) EPISTOLÆ HO-ELIANÆ: Familiar Letters Domestic and Foreign, divided into Four Books; Partly Historical, Political, Philosophical: upon Emergent Occasions. By James Howell, Esq. ... The Ninth Edition, very much Corrected. *London: J. Darby.* 1726.

8vo, gray calf, carmine edges, by NUTT.

Thefe letters, relating to one of the moft interefting periods of Englifh Hiftory, the reigns of James I. and Charles I. difcover a variety of literature, and abound with much entertaining and ufeful information. They were written, Ant. Wood informs us, by the Author when confined in the Fleet prison for debt.

988 HOWGILL (F.) The | Deceiver | of the | Nations | Discovered : | and his | Cruelty | Made Manifest. | And | How he hath deceived the Nations, and wrought his | Works of Darkness, more hiddenly under the Mask of Higher | Power and Holy Church; and so persecutes the Righteous | Seed, and makes them suffer under the Name of evil Doers, | in these latter daies. | More especially his cruel Works of Darkness laid open and re- | proved in Maryland in Virginia, And the sad Sufferings of | the Servants of the Lord there, by his cruel Instruments. | ... | By a Lover of Mercy and Truth, | Fra. Howgill. |
London : Printed for Thomas Simmons, ... 1600.

4to, pp. 27. *Half morocco.* Head line of one leaf slightly injured.
A VERY RARE TRACT relating to Maryland.

989 HUBBARD (J. N.) Sketches of Border Adventures, in the Life and Times of Major Moses Van Campen, a Surviving Soldier of the Revolution. By his grandson John N. Hubbard A.B.
Bath, N. Y. : R. L. Underhill & Co. 1842.

8vo, pp. 310. *Half olive morocco, gilt top.* FOUR ILLUSTRATIONS *inserted.* FINE COPY. VERY SCARCE.

990 HUBBARD (William.) A | Narrative | of the Troubles with the | Indians | In New-England, from the first planting thereof in the | year 1607, to this present year 1677. But chiefly of the late | Troubles in the two last years, 1675. and 1676. | To which is added a Discourse about the Warre with the | Pequods | In the year 1637, | By W. Hubbard, Minister of Ipswich. | *Published by Authority.* | *Boston :* | *Printed by John Foster, in the year* 1677.

pp. (14), 132, (8), 7–12. *Narrative* 88. *Map.*

[Also :] The Happiness of a People | In the Wisdome of their Rulers | Directing | And in the Obedience of their Brethren | Attending | Unto what Israel ougho to do : | Recommended in a | Sermon | Before the Honourable Governour and Council, and | the Respected Deputies of the Mattachusets Colony | in New-England. | Preached at Boston, May. 3d. 1676. being the day of | Election there. | By William Hvbbard Minister of Ipswich. | *Boston, Printed by John Foster.* 1676. |

pp. (8), 63.

Sm. 4to, crushed blue levant morocco, gilt edges, by F. BEDFORD. FINE COPY.

The rare and curious MAP often wanting is in the finest condition, and is described as follows on the map itself: "*A map of New England, being the first that ever was here cut, and done by the best pattern that could be had, which being in some places defective, it made the other less exact; yet doth it sufficiently show the situation of the country, and conveniently well the distance of places, &c.*"

This book has been frequently reprinted, and will always remain an authority upon the subjects of which it treats. The Sermon which follows the Narrative is, bibliographically speaking, a necessary part of the work. We have never seen a copy in the original binding which did not contain it. It possesses in itself high bibliographical interest, for, according to Thomas's *History of Printing*, it is probably THE FIRST BOOK PRINTED IN BOSTON, all the printing in the British Colonies, previous to 1676, being done at Cambridge, and in that year the FIRST PRESS was set up at Boston. The entire work was reprinted at London in the following year, a copy of which is offered in a recent catalogue of Mr. Quaritch at £25. Concerning this London edition see Field's "Bibliography."

991 HUBBARD. Narrative | of the | Indian Wars | in | New-England, | From the first Planting thereof in the Year 1607, to | the Year 1677. | Containing | A Relation of the Occasion, Rise and Progress | of the War with the Indians, in the Southern, Wes- | tern, Eastern and Northern Parts of said Country. | By William Hubbard, A.M. | Minister of Ipswich. | ... |
Boston: Printed and sold by John Boyle. . . . 1775.

12*mo, pp. viii.,* 288. *Crushed red levant morocco, gilt edges, by* F. BEDFORD. The second American edition. VERY SCARCE.

"The whole country was the seat of war, and every man procured his bread in jeopardy of his life." — *Preface.*

992 HUBBARD. A General History of New England, from the Discovery to MDCLXXX. By the Rev. William Hubbard, Minister of Ipswich, Mass. Second Edition, Collated with the Original MS.
Boston: Little and Brown. 1848.

8*vo, pp.* 676. *Half crimson morocco, gilt top,* UNCUT. TWENTY-FOUR ILLUSTRATIONS *inserted.*

993 HUBBELL (H.) Arnold, or the Treason of West Point: a Tragedy, in Five Acts. By Horatio Hubbell. *Philadelphia:* 1847.

12*mo, pp.* 76. *Half red morocco.*

994 HUBLEY (B.) The History of the American Revolution, including the most Important Events and Resolutions of the Honourable Continental Congress during that period and also, the most interesting Letters and Orders of His Excellency General George Washington, Commander-in-Chief of the American Forces. By Benrard Hubley. Vol. I. [All published.]
Northumberland, Pennsylvania: Printed for the Author, by Andrew Kennedy. 1805.

8*vo, pp.* (4), 606, (1). *Half red levant morocco, gilt top,* UNCUT. SCARCE PROOF PORTRAIT *of* WASHINGTON *inserted.* A BEAUTIFUL COPY of one of the RAREST and most important Histories of the American Revolution.

995 HUDSON (C.) Doubts Concerning the Battle of Bunker's Hill. Addressed to the Christian Public. By Charles Hudson.
Boston: MDCCCLVII.

12*mo, half crimson morocco, gilt top.*

996 HUDSON (D.) History of Jemima Wilkinson, a Preacheress of the Eighteenth Century; containing an Authentic Narrative of her

Life and Character, and of the Rise, Progress, and Conclusion of her Ministry. By David Hudson. *Geneva: (N. Y.) S. P. Hull.* 1821.

12mo, pp. 208, *xx.* *Half gray calf,* UNCUT. Fine copy. VERY SCARCE.

Relates chiefly to the proceedings of Friends in Rhode Island. She insisted on the Shaker doctrine of celibacy, and the exercises of their religious meetings resembled those of that sect.

997 HUGGINS (J. R. D.) Hugginiana; or Huggins's Fantasy, being a Collection of the most esteemed Modern Literary Productions. Exposing the Art of making a Noise in the World, without beating a Drum or Crying Oysters; and showing how, like Whittington of old, who rose from nothing to be Lord Mayor of London, a mere Barber may become an Emperor, if he has but spirit enough to assume, and talents enough to support the title. By John Richard Desborus Huggins. *New York: Printed by H. C. Southwick, Wall street. Most Excellent Printer to his most Barberous Majesty.* 1808.

12mo, pp. 288. 7 *Plates.* *Half red morocco, gilt top,* UNCUT. VERY SCARCE.

998 HULL (W.) Defence of Brigadier General W. Hull. Delivered before the General Court Martial, of which Major General Dearborn was President, at Albany, March, 1814. With an Address to the Citizens of the United States. Written by Himself. Copied from the Original Manuscript, and published by his authority. To which are prefixed, The Charges against Brigadier General Hull, as Specified by the Government. *Boston: Wells and Lilly.* 1814.

12mo, pp. xlvi., 215. *Half calf,* UNCUT. *Scarce.*

999 HULL. Memoirs of the Campaign of the North Western Army of the United States A.D. 1812. In a Series of letters addressed to the Citizens of the United States. With an Appendix Containing a brief Sketch of the Revolutionary Services of the Author. By William Hull, late Governour of the Territory of Michigan, and Brigadier General in the Service of the United States. *Boston: True & Greene.* 1824.

8vo, pp. 229, *x.* *Half blue morocco, gilt top,* UNCUT, *by* W. MATTHEWS. Author's Autograph Signature at the end of the text.

1000 HULL. Revolutionary Services and Civil Life of General William Hull; Prepared from his Manuscripts, by his Daughter, Mrs. Maria Campbell: together with the History of the Campaign of 1812, and Surrender of the Post of Detroit, by his Grandson, James Freeman Clarke. *New-York: D. Appleton & Co.* M DCCC XLVIII.

8vo, pp. xx., 17–482. *Half blue morocco, gilt top,* UNCUT, *by* W. MATTHEWS. Uniform with the preceding No.

1001 HUMBLE (The) | Petition | and | Address | Of the General Court Sitting at | Boston in New-England, | unto | The High and Mighty |

Prince | Charles | The Second. | And presented unto His Most-Gracious | Majesty Feb. 11, 1660. | [*London:*] *Printed in the Year.* 1660.

Sm. 4to, brown calf, gilt edges, by F. BEDFORD. Fine Copy.

A MOST RARE BOOK relating to the early history of New England. Signed "John Endecot Govr. In the Name, and with the Consent of the General Court." Printed in the Hutchinson "Collection of Papers." p. 325.

1002 HUMBLE ADDRESS | (The) | of the | Publicans | of | New England, | To which King you please. | With Some | Remarks | Upon it. | *A Publican is a Creature that lives upon the* | *Commonwealth.* | [*London:*] *Printed in the Year*, 1691.

Sm. 4to, pp. 35. *Polished calf, carmine edges, by* F. BEDFORD. FINE COPY of a book of EXTREME RARITY.

1003 HUMBOLDT (A. de) Researches, concerning the Institutions & Monuments of the Ancient Inhabitants of America, with Descriptions & Views of some of the most Striking Scenes in the Cordilleras. Written in French by Alex. de Humboldt, and Translated into English by Helen Maria Williams. *London: Longman.* 1814.

2 *vols., 8vo, pp. iv.,* 411; 324. 19 *Plates. Half red levant morocco, gilt top,* UNCUT, *by* W. SMITH.

This translation of the text of Humboldt's celebrated *Vues de Cordilleras*, is a valuable adjunct to the great folio of plates, for all students not familiar with the language of the original.

1004 HUME (A.) The Learned Societies and Printing Clubs of the United Kingdom: being an Account of their respective Origin, History, Objects, and Constitution. With full details respecting their published Works and Transactions. ... By Rev. A. Hume. ... *London: G. Willis.* 1853.

Sm. 8vo, half olive morocco, gilt top, UNCUT.

Contains lists of the books issued by the Camden, Shakspeare, Maitland, Bannatyne, Roxburghe, and all the other Societies.

1005 HUMPHREY (H. B.) Catalogue of the Valuable Library of Henry B. Humphrey, Esq., ... Sold May 9th, 1871. *Cambridge: Riverside Press.* 1871.

8vo, pp. vii., 444. *Paper,* UNCUT.

1006 HUMPHREYS (D.) An Historical Account of the Incorporated Society for the Propagation of the Gospel in Foreign Parts. Containing their Foundation, Proceedings, and the Success of their Missionaries in the British Colonies to the year 1728. By David Humphreys, D.D. Secretary to the Honourable Society. *London: J. Downing.* M.DCC.XXX.

8vo, pp. xxxi., 356. 2 *Maps. Polished calf, yellow edges, by* F. BEDFORD.

This society was incorporated in 1701. The whole of this volume relates to the proceedings of the missionaries in different parts of North America, together with the state of religion there: and is illustrated with two maps, one of Carolina, the other of New England, &c., by Herman Moll.

1007 HUMPHREYS (D.) The Miscellaneous Works of David Humphreys, Late Minister Plenipotentiary from the United States of America to the Court of Madrid. *New York: T. & J. Swords.* 1804.

8vo, pp. xv., 394, (14). *Portrait, and Plate. Half green morocco, gilt top,* UNCUT, *by* BRADSTREET. EIGHT ILLUSTRATIONS *inserted.* FINE COPY. SCARCE in *uncut* condition.

1008 HUMPHREYS. Miscellaneous Works. [Another copy.] *New York:* 1804.

8vo, half calf. NINETEEN ILLUSTRATIONS *inserted.* A presentation copy from the AUTHOR to DR. JENNER.

1009 HUMPHREYS. An Essay on the Life of the Honourable Major General Israel Putnam. Addressed to the State Society of the Cincinnati in Connecticut, and first published by their Order. By Col. David Humphreys. With Notes and Additions. With an Appendix, containing an Historical and Topographical Sketch of Bunker Hill Battle. By S. Swett. *Boston: Samuel Avery.* 1818.

12mo, pp. 276. *Portrait* (inlaid). *Half morocco, gilt top,* UNCUT, *by* BRADSTREET.

1010 HUMPHREYS. The Conduct of General Washington, respecting the Confinement of Capt. Asgill, placed in its True Point of Light. By David Humphreys. With a preface and appendix. *New York: Printed for the Holland Club.* 1859.

8vo, pp. 35. *Half green levant morocco, gilt top,* UNCUT, *by* W. MATTHEWS. No. 19 of A FEW COPIES only printed.

1011 HUMPHREYS (H. N.) A History of the Art of Printing, from its Invention to its wide-spread Developement in the Middle of the 16th Century. Preceded by a Short Account of the Origin of the Alphabet, and of the successive Methods of Recording Events and Multiplying MS. Books before the Invention of Printing. By H. Noel Humphreys. ... With One Hundred Illustrations. ... *London: Bernard Quaritch.* 1867.

Imp. 4to, illuminated cloth, UNCUT. No. 126 of the FIRST ISSUE of 300 copies only, with the publisher's certificate to that effect *inserted.*

"The illustrations of this work, which, unlike fac-similes produced by hand, must *necessarily* be absolute reproductions of their originals, exceed one hundred in number, and frequently consist of representations of entire pages from many of the most interesting books produced by the early printers. Among them may be mentioned an entire folio page from the first printed Bible, the magnificent work of Gutenberg, richly adorned with ornamental borderings by a contemporary German illuminator. An entire page from the celebrated Psalter of Schœffer, in which the large capitals are PRINTED IN COLOURS, in rivalry with the illuminators of the time. Pages from the first books printed in ITALY, FRANCE, SPAIN, FLANDERS, and HOLLAND, accompany the accounts of the introduction of the printing press to those countries; and several such entire pages in fac-simile illustrate the description of the works of WILLIAM CAXTON, the founder of the printing press in England. In addition to these and many illustrations of other kinds, will be found a very interesting and an abundant series of examples from the most richly decorated of the French "HORÆ," and from the profusely illustrated German books produced in the first half of the sixteenth century."

1012 HUMPHREYS. Master Pieces of the Early Printers & Engravers. A Series of Facsimiles from Rare and Curious Books, remarkable for Illustrative Devices, Beautiful Borders, Decorative Initials, Printers Marks, Elaborate Title-pages, &c. By H. Noel Humphreys. ... *London: H. Sotheran & Co.* 1870.

Imp. 4to, illuminated cloth, gilt edges. SUBSCRIPTION COPY, with fine early impressions of the SEVENTY CURIOUS PLATES.

"The great beauty of many of the books produced by the Early Printers, both as regards the remarkable and various character of their Types, and the exquisitely designed Initials and Borderings with which their pages are enriched, is scarcely known and appreciated beyond the narrow circle of enthusiastic bibliographers who have made the first works that issued from the printing press a subject of special study; and it is to make them more widely known that the present work has been projected. The greater part of the examples are now published for the first time, and have never appeared in any other bibliographical work. They comprise designs by WOHLGEMUTH, DURER, BURGEMAIR, CRANACH, and others equally celebrated."

1013 HUNT (C. H.) Life of Edward Livingston. By Charles Haven Hunt. With an Introduction by George Bancroft. *New York: D. Appleton and Co.* 1864.

Roy. 8vo, pp. xxiv., 448. 2 Portraits. Half green morocco, gilt top, UNCUT. LARGE PAPER; 75 copies only printed. THIRTY FINE ILLUSTRATIONS, some of which are RARE, and an AUTOGRAPH LETTER of MR. LIVINGSTON *inserted.*

1014 [HUNT (Freeman.)] American Anecdotes. Original and Select. By an American. *Boston: Putnam & Hunt.* 1830.

2 vols., 12mo, pp. 300; 300. Half calf, gilt top, UNCUT. RARE *in any condition*; especially so *uncut.*

Contains four hundred and eighty-seven anecdotes, mostly relating to the American Revolution, with an index.

1015 HUNT (G. J.) The Historical Reader: Containing the late War, between the United States and Great Britain, from June, 1812, to February, 1815. Written in the Ancient Historical Style. ... By Gilbert J. Hunt. Third Edition. ... *New York: David Longworth.* 1819.

12mo, pp. 233. Half calf, UNCUT. *Scarce* and *curious.*

1016 HUNTER (J. D.) Memoirs of a Captivity among the Indians of North America, from Childhood to the Age of Nineteen; with Anecdotes Descriptive of their Manners and Customs. ... By John D. Hunter. The Third Edition, with Additions. *London: Longman & Co.* 1824.

8vo, pp. xi., 468. Portrait. Half red morocco, gilt top, UNCUT.

1017 HUNTINGTON (A.) A Sermon delivered at Topsfield, January 5, 1800. Occasioned by the Death of George Washington. ... By Asahel Huntington, A.M. ... *Salem:* 1800.

8vo, pp. 32. EXCEEDINGLY RARE. The ONLY COPY seen by Dr. Hough. Contains "An Historical Sketch" of General Washington.

1018 HUNTINGTON (E.) An Oration delivered at Middletown, in the State of Connecticut, February 22, A.D. 1800. [On the Death of General Washington.] By Enoch Huntington, A.M. ... *Middletown:* 1800.

8vo, pp. 9.

1019 HUNTINGTON (J.) [Funeral Eulogy by General J. Huntington, and Oration by Lyman Law, delivered at New-London January 11th, 1800. On the Death of General Washington. *New London: Jan.* 20, 1800.]

8vo, pp. 17. VERY SCARCE. *Published without a title page.*

1020 HUTCHINS (T.) A Topographical Description of Virginia, Maryland, Pennsylvania, and North Carolina, comprehending the Rivers Ohio, Kenhawa, Siota, Cherokee, Wabash, Illinois, Mississippi, &c. The Climate, Soil and Produce, whether Animal, Vegetable, or Mineral; ... By Thomas Hutchins, Captain in the 60th Regiment of Foot. With a Plan of the Rapids of the Ohio, a Plan of the several Villages in the Illinois Country, ... and an Appendix containing Mr. Patrick Kennedy's Journal up the Illinois River. ... *Boston: John Norman.* MDCCLXXXVII.

Sm. 8vo, pp. 32. 2 *Engraved Plans, and Table of Distances. Half red morocco, gilt top,* UNCUT, *by* W. MATTHEWS. VERY SCARCE.

"The greater part," says Hutchins, "done from my own Surveys preceding and during the last war, and since in many reconnoitering tours between 1764, and 1775."

1021 HUTCHINSON (F.) An Historical Essay concerning Witchcraft. ... By Francis Hutchinson, D.D. ... The Second Edition, with Considerable Additions. *London: R. Knaplock.* MDCCXX.

8vo, pp. (32), 336. *Half olive morocco, gilt top,* UNCUT. A FINE COPY of the BEST EDITION, and VERY SCARCE in *uncut* condition.

Contains much interesting matter, and develops many celebrated impostures; it gives an account of the Suffolk Witches, the hanging of threescore in the years 1645–6, in Suffolk; the tryal of two women before Lord Chief Baron Hale, and their execution at Bury St. Edmonds, 1664. It also gives an account of the Witchcraft troubles at Salem, Boston, and Andover, in New England.

1022 HUTCHINSON (Thomas.) The History of the Colony of Massachusetts-Bay, from the First Settlement thereof in 1628, until its Incorporation with the Colony of Plimouth, Province of Main, &c., by the Charter of King William and Queen Mary, in 1691. ... By Mr. Hutchinson Lieutenant-Governor of the Massachusetts Province. The Second Edition. *London: M. Richardson.* M DCC LX. From 1691, until the Year 1750. Volume II. The Second Edition. *London: G. Kearsley.* M DCC LXVIII.

pp. (4), *iv.*, 566; (2), *iv.*, 539. PORTRAIT of the AUTHOR *inserted.*

[Also:] The History of the Province of Massachusetts Bay, from 1749 to 1774, comprising a Detailed Narrative of the Origin and

Early Stages of the American Revolution. By Thomas Hutchinson, Esq., formerly Governor of the Province. Edited from the Author's MS. by his grandson, the Rev. John Hutchinson, M.A.
London: John Murray. M DCCC XXVIII.

pp. xx., 551. PORTRAIT *inserted.*

3 *vols.*, 8*vo*, *half green morocco*, *gilt top*, UNCUT. This copy of the third volume contains the DEDICATION and PREFACE, 16 pages, which were omitted in one-half of the edition. COMPLETE SETS in such FINE, PERFECT, and *uncut* condition as the present, are EXCEEDINGLY SCARCE.

1023 [HUTCHINSON.] A Collection of Original Papers Relative to the History of the Colony of Massachusetts-Bay.
Boston: New England. Printed by Thomas and John Fleet. 1769.

8*vo*, *pp. ii.*, 576. *Half green morocco*, *gilt top*, UNCUT. A BEAUTIFUL COPY, uniform with the preceding No., and EXCESSIVELY RARE in *uncut* condition.

"This collection of papers was published by Lieut.-Gov. Hutchinson, 'to support and elucidate the principal facts related in the first part of the History of Massachusetts Bay, and may serve as an appendix to it.' 'The author of that History was possessed of many other ancient and very curious original papers, which are irrecoverably lost by an unfortunate event sufficiently known.' (This alludes to the destruction of his papers by a mob, at the time of the Riots in Boston on account of the Stamp Act, in 1765.)"—*Rich.*

For an interesting account of the various editions of Hutchinson's History, *see* Deane's *Hutchinson Bibliography*, No. 538, *Supra.*

1024 [HUTCHINSON.] The Speeches of His Excellency Governor Hutchinson, to the General Assembly of the Massachusetts Bay. At a Session begun and held on the Sixth of January, 1773. With the Answers of His Majesty's Council and the House of Representatives respectively. [Published by order of the House.]
Boston: Edes & Gill. 1773.

8*vo*, *pp.* 126. *Half green morocco.* SCARCE.

1025 [HUTCHINSON.] The Letters of Governor Hutchinson, and Lieut. Governor Oliver, &c. Printed at Boston. And Remarks thereon. With the Assembly's Address, and the Proceedings of the Lord's Committee of Council. Together with the Substance of Mr. Wedderburn's Speech relating to those Letters. And the Report of the Lord's Committee to his Majesty in Council. The Second Edition.
London: J. Wilkie. 1774.

8*vo*, *pp.* (4), 142.

"These are the celebrated letters written in 1767, '68 '69, which mysteriously found their way back to Boston, it is supposed through Dr. Franklin, and brought matters to a crisis there. Nothing except the "Tea Party" ever created a greater political sensation in Boston, or more speedy results than the publication by authority of the General Court of these letters."

[Also :] A Faithful Account of the Whole of the Transactions relating to a late Affair of Honour between J. Temple, and W. Whately, Esqrs., containing a particular History of that unhappy Quarrel. Likewise the whole of their Letters that passed on the Occasion, with those signed Antenor, An Enemy to Villains of Every Denomination, &c. &c. *London: R. Snagg.* 1774.

8*vo*, *pp.* 38.

Mr. Temple was accused of having surreptitiously obtained the letters of Governor Hutchinson and Lieutenant-Governor Oliver, from Mr. Whately, which produced the duel to which this pamphlet relates. The letters in question were procured by Dr. Franklin. *See* Sparks's *Franklin, Vol. iv., pp.* 405–455.

8vo, 2 vols. bound in 1. Half blue morocco. VERY SCARCE.

1026 [HUTCHINSON. Documents of the Senate and House of Representatives of the Commonwealth of Massachusetts; containing the correspondence and proceedings, relative to the controversy between that Commonwealth and the Massachusetts Historical Society respecting the ownership and possession of the "Hutchinson Papers" so called. *Boston:* 1868–71.]

2 vols., thin 8vo, half green morocco, gilt top. Uniform with the History and the Papers to which they form an important addition.

1027 HYMNS AND ODES, Composed on the Death of Gen. George Washington: adapted to the 22d day of February, and dedicated to those who please to sing them! *Portsmouth: (N. H.) January,* 1800.

[*Reprinted at New York, in* 1868, *for the Washington Club.*] *Imp. 8vo, half green morocco, gilt top,* UNCUT, *by* BRADSTREET. TWELVE COPIES only printed on WHATMAN'S DRAWING PAPER. INDIA PROOF PORTRAIT of WASHINGTON from a PRIVATE PLATE *inserted.*

1028 IMLAY (G.) A Topographical Description of the Western Territory of North America: ... Containing the Discovery, Settlement, and Present State of Kentucky; ... by J. Filson. ... An Account of the Indian Nations inhabiting within the Limits of the XIII States. ... The Culture of Indian Corn, Hemp, Flax, Hops, Tobacco, &c. ... Observations on the ancient Works, the native Inhabitants of the Western Country, &c.; by Major Jonathan Heart. A Historical Narrative and Topographical Description of Louisiana and West Florida, ... by Mr. Thomas Hutchins. Account of the Soil, growing Timber, and other Productions of several Lands, particularly the Genesee Tract. ... Remarks for the Information of those who wish to become Settlers in America, by Dr. Franklin. Topographical Description of Virginia, Pennsylvania, Maryland, and North Carolina, by Mr. Tho. Hutchins. Mr. Patrick Kennedy's Journal up the Illinois River, &c. Description of the State of Tenasee, and of the South-Western Territory, ... By Gilbert Imlay. ... The Third Edition, with great Additions. *London: J. Debrett.* 1797.

8vo, pp. xii., 598, (28). 3 *Maps and Plate. Half blue morocco, gilt top,* UNCUT. Beautiful copy. PORTRAIT of DANIEL BOONE *inserted.*

"AN invaluable work to all Western Historians, and indeed indispensable; containing *thirteen* of the earliest treatises."— *S. G. Drake.*

1029 IMPARTIAL (An) History of the War in America, between Great Britain and her Colonies, from Its Commencement to the end of the Year 1779. ... . Illustrated with a Variety of beautiful Copper Plates, representing real and animated Likenesses of those celebrated Generals who have distinguished themselves in the important Contest.
London: R. Faulder. 1780.

8vo, pp. xi., 608, 44. *Half maroon morocco, gilt top,* UNCUT. MAP, and 13 *full length* PORTRAITS of American and British Generals, being those of Generals Washington, Gates, Arnold, Wooster, Putnam, Charles Lee, Com. Hopkins, Samuel Adams, Hancock, Franklin, Gen. Howe, Admiral Howe, and American Rifleman. A VERY FINE COPY, quite free from the plate *set offs* which disfigure all other copies we have ever seen.

1030 INDENTURE OF AGREEMENT, 4th July, 1760, between Lord Baltimore and Thomas and Richard Penn, Esquires, Settling the Limits and Boundaries of Maryland, Pennsylvania, and the Three Lower Counties of Newcastle, Kent and Sussex, in Delaware.
Philadelphia: Kite & Walton. 1851.

Sm. folio, pp. 31. *Half calf, gilt top,* UNCUT.

Originally printed by B. Franklin. This edition was *privately reprinted,* on writing paper, for E. D. Ingraham, of Philadelphia.

1031 INDIANS. A Treaty held at the Town of Lancaster, in Pennsylvania, by the Honourable the Lieutenant-Governor of the Province, and the Honourable the Commissioners for the Province of Virginia and Maryland, with the Indians of the Six Nations, in June, 1744. *Philadelphia: Printed and sold by* B. FRANKLIN, *at the New Printing Office, near the Market.* MDCCXLIV.

Folio, pp. 39. *Paneled calf, gilt top,* UNCUT. FINE COPY. EXTREMELY RARE. TWO COPIES ONLY, including the present, are known to have been offered for sale in this city.

1032 INDIANS. An Account of Conferences held, and Treaties made, between Major-general Sir William Johnson Bart. and the chief Sachems and Warriours of the Mohawks, Oneidas, Onondagas, Cayugas, Senekas, Tuscaroras [and other] Indian Nations in North America, at their Meetings on different Occasions, at Fort Johnson in the County of Albany, in the Colony of New York, in the Years 1755 and 1756. With a Letter from the Rev. Mr. Hawley to Sir William Johnson, written at the Desire of the Delaware Indians. And a Preface giving a short Account of the Six Nations, some Anecdotes of the Life of Sir William, and Notes illustrating the whole; Also an Appendix Containing an Account of Conferences between several Quakers in Philadelphia, and some of the Heads of the Six Nations in April 1756. *London: A. Millar.* MDCCLVI.

8vo, pp. xii., 3–77. *Half claret morocco.* RARE contemporary PORTRAIT of SIR WILLIAM JOHNSON *inserted.* VERY SCARCE. Not in Field's *Bibliography.*

1033 INGERSOLL (C. J.) Historical Sketch of the Second War between the United States of America, and Great Britain, declared by Act of Congress, the 18th of June, 1812, and concluded by peace, the 15th of February, 1815. By Charles J. Ingersoll. Vol. I. Embracing the Events of 1812–13. Vol. II. Embracing the Events of 1814.— Vols. III. and IV. Embracing the Events of 1814–15. *Philadelphia:* 1845–52.

4 *vols.*, 8*vo*, *half green morocco*, UNCUT. An *Autograph Note Signed* of the AUTHOR *inserted. Complete sets*, as this is, are EXCEEDINGLY SCARCE.

1034 INGLEBY (C. M.) A Complete View of the Shakspere Controversy, concerning the Authority and Genuineness of Manuscript Matter affecting the Works and Biography of Shakspere, published by J. Payne Collier, as the Fruits of his Researches. By C. M. Ingleby, LL.D. *London: Nattali and Bond.* 1861.

8*vo.*, *half red morocco*, *gilt top*, UNCUT.

1035 [INGRAHAM (Edward D.)] A Sketch of the Events which preceded the Capture of Washington, by the British, on the twenty-fourth of August, 1814. *Philadelphia: Carey & Hart.* 1849.

8*vo*, *pp. iv.*, 66. *Plan. Half morocco*, *gilt top*, UNCUT. PORTRAIT and *Autograph Note Signed* of the AUTHOR *inserted.*

With a valuable map showing the Potomac River, a Sketch of the march of the British Army under Gen. Ross, 19th to the 29th of August, 1814, and a plan of the Battle of Bladensburg.

1036 [IRVING (Washington.)] History of New York, from the Beginning of the World to the End of the Dutch Dynasty. ... By Diedrich Knickerbocker. *Glasgow: John Wylie & Co.* 1821.

8*vo*, *half purple morocco*, *gilt top*, UNCUT. RARE. SIX COPIES were printed on this paper, of which, this is the ONLY ONE in the United States. SCARCE PORTRAIT of the AUTHOR *inserted.*

1037 [IRVING.] The Sketch Book of Geoffrey Crayon, Gent[n]. Author's Revised Edition. With Original Designs by F. O. C. Darley. Engraved by Childs, Herrick, etc. *New York: G. P. Putnam.* 1848.

Sq. 8*vo*, *rich claret morocco*, *blank filleted sides*, *gilt edges*, *by* W. MATTHEWS. LARGE TINTED PAPER; 50 *copies only printed.* A BEAUTIFUL and VERY RARE edition containing FINE INDIA PROOF ILLUSTRATIONS by DARLEY.

1038 [IRVING.] Tales of a Traveller. By Geoffrey Crayon Gent[n]. With Illustrations by F. O. C. Darley. Engraved by Eminent Artists. *New York: G. P. Putnam.* 1850.

Sq. 8*vo. Uniform in size and binding with the preceding No.* The SEVENTEEN ILLUSTRATIONS by DARLEY are FINE INDIA PROOFS. LARGE TINTED PAPER; 50 *copies only printed.*

1039 [IRVING.] A History of New York, from the Beginning of the World to the End of the Dutch Dynasty. ... By Diedrich Knickerbocker. With Illustrations by F. O. C. Darley. Engraved by Eminent Artists. *New York: G. P. Putnam.* 1850.

Sq. 8*vo. Uniform with the preceding No.* FINE INDIA PROOF impressions of DARLEY'S beautiful ILLUSTRATIONS. LARGE TINTED PAPER. 50 *copies only printed.*

1040 IRVING. Bracebridge Hall. By Washington Irving. Illustrated With Fourteen Original Designs by Schmolze. *New York: G. P. Putnam.* 1858.

Sq. 8*vo. Uniform in size and binding with the preceding No.* The ILLUSTRATIONS by SCHMOLZE are BRILLIANT PROOFS on INDIA PAPER. Two additional ILLUSTRATIONS *inserted.* LARGE TINTED PAPER; 50 *copies only printed.*

This, together with the three preceding works, forms a fine and VERY SCARCE LARGE PAPER SET of the most admired of Irving's writings.

A MAGNIFICENT COPY

OF

IRVING'S LIFE OF GEORGE WASHINGTON

SPLENDIDLY ILLUSTRATED AND SUMPTUOUSLY BOUND.

1041 IRVING. The Life of George Washington. By Washington Irving. [5 vols.] *New York: George P. Putnam.* 1855–59.

[Also:] BATTLE OF GUILFORD COURT-HOUSE, Comprising Chapter XX. of Volume IV. of Irving's Life of George Washington, in the Manuscript of the Author. *Written at Sunnyside:* 1857.

[And:] TUCKERMAN (H. T.) The Character and Portraits of Washington. By Henry T. Tuckerman. *New York: G. P. Putnam.* 1859.

Together 7 vols., roy. 4to, extended to 12 vols. LARGE PAPER, *of which* ONE HUNDRED AND TEN copies of the "LIFE," and ONE HUNDRED AND FIFTY-SIX copies of the "CHARACTER" were respectively printed. Superbly bound in *polished green levant morocco of a uniform shade throughout; paneled sides elegantly tooled and gilt, and corner ornaments with Washington's monogram in centre, the whole after an original design prepared expressly for the work; back in unison; broad inside borders beautifully inlaid, tooled and gilt on polished green morocco; rich watered silk linings; morocco joints; gilt top,* UNCUT; *each volume in a* SLIP-CASE *lined with velvet finished chamois leather; by* W. MATTHEWS: a MASTERPIECE of ARTISTIC BOOKBINDING, described by *himself* in a letter, which accompanies the set, and from which the following is an extract.

"I have never felt so great a responsibility in binding a set of books before. The material, consisting of so large a number of engravings and letters, of every size and shape, requiring strength and flexibility alike, and their correct arrangement, was of itself sufficient, but to forward true, and handsomely finish twelve volumes, so that either one may be taken as a sample of the rest, is an effort not easily accomplished in the art of bookbinding. In all these particulars I think I have never been more successful. In the minute correctness of the finishing I will challenge the world to produce so many volumes so exact and so perfect in their ornamentation. Mr. Gibson has been steadily employed on them since July 10th, to December 1st, and is unequalled as an exact finisher and designer. The exact amount of wages paid this workman was $502.97.— I may add that no workman ever worked more faithfully, and the exactness of so large a piece of work is a marvel of modern patience, no finisher or expert could detect which volume was done first or last. Aside from the binding you have the most exquisitely illustrated set of books that ever went through my hands, the book is worthy of the binding, and I shall feel happy to hear you say the binding is worthy of the book."

Independent of the one hundred and two India proof plates which form a part of the original work, many of which are *genuine unlettered first proofs* obtained directly from MR. PUTNAM in advance of their issue, this TRULY MATCHLESS COPY of the LIFE OF WASHINGTON contains ONE THOUSAND SEVEN HUNDRED *inserted* ILLUSTRATIONS, of the most choice description; comprising TWO HUNDRED and TWENTY-TWO PORTRAITS of WASHINGTON; EIGHT HUNDRED and SIXTY-ONE PORTRAITS of his COMPEERS and ASSOCIATES; TWO HUNDRED and EIGHTY-TWO VIEWS; ONE HUNDRED and FIFTY-NINE SUBJECTS; NINETY-EIGHT AUTOGRAPH LETTERS, NOTES, &c., including TEN of GEN. WASHINGTON; SEVENTEEN MAPS; FIFTEEN FACSIMILES; and EIGHTEEN SHEETS of Snowden's "Coins and Medals of Washington" &c.; of which nearly FOUR HUNDRED and FIFTY are PROOFS, INDIA PROOFS, and PROOFS BEFORE LETTERS in the finest condition; SEVENTY-ONE are beautifully COLOURED photographs, and

SIXTY-TWO are WATER COLOUR DRAWINGS. EXTRA RUBRICATED TITLES, with an ENGRAVED VIGNETTE mounted in each, were printed by MR. MUNSELL expressly for this set.

The illustrations are distributed throughout the volumes in the following manner.

Vol. I. Contains Seventy-seven Portraits, Seventeen Subjects, Forty-one Views, and Four Autograph Letters, comprising, GOV. ROBERT DINWIDDIE. L. S.— GEN. BRADDOCK. L.S.— SIR WM. JOHNSON. A.L.S.— SIR JEFFREY AMHERST. L.S.

Vol. II. Contains One Hundred and Seven Portraits, Twenty-three Subjects, Twenty-nine Views &c., and Six Autograph Letters &c., comprising, GEORGE WASHINGTON. Two A.L.S.— PHILIP SCHUYLER. A.L.S.— ARCHIBALD ROBERTSON. A.L.S.— JOHN HANCOCK. *Superscription and Sig.*— ETHAN ALLEN. A.N.S.

Vol. III. Contains One Hundred and Six Portraits, Three Subjects, Fifty Views, and Three Autograph Letters, comprising, GEN. CHARLES LEE. A.L.S.— GEN. SCHUYLER. A.L.S.— COL. MARINUS WILLETT. A.L.S.

Vol. IV. Contains Eighty-nine Portraits, Fifty-four Subjects, Twelve Views, and Three Autograph Letters, comprising, HENRY LAURENS. Pres. of Congress. A.L.S.— GEN. GREEN. A.L.S.— GEN. BENEDICT ARNOLD. A.L.S.

Vol. V. Contains One Hundred and One Portraits, Ten Subjects, Thirty-two Views, and Nine Autograph Letters, &c., comprising, MRS. MARTHA WASHINGTON. A.L.S. — COL. PETER GANSEVOORT. A.L.S. — GEN. HEATH. *Military Order Signed.*— GEN. LORD STIRLING. A.L.S.— GEN. JAMES CLINTON. A.L.S.— GOV. JOHN TRUMBULL. *Sup. and Sig.* GEN. BURGOYNE.— *Note in third person.*— REV. MR. BRUDENELL. A.L.— GEN. BURGOYNE. A.N.S.

Vol. VI. Contains One Hundred and Nineteen Portraits, Twelve Subjects, Twenty-eight Views &c., and Twenty-five Autograph Letters &c., among which are the following: BARON DE KALB. A.L.S.— GEN. GATES. A.L.S.— GEN. SMALLWOOD. A.L.S.— GEN. MIFFLIN. *Aut. Sig.*— ELIAS BONDINOT. *Aut. Sig.*— BARON STEUBEN. A.O.S.— GEN. CONWAY. A O.S.— CHIEF-JUSTICE MARSHALL. *Sup. and Sig.*— GEN. STIRLING. A.L.S.— GEN. WASHINGTON. L.S. In the handwriting of COL. TILGHMAN.— BENJAMIN FRANKLIN, ARTHUR LEE, and JOHN ADAMS. *Signatures* to a diplomatic note, *written* by MR. ADAMS.— GEN. WASHINGTON. L.S. In the handwriting of COL. JOHN LAURENS.— GEN. ROBERT HOWE. A.L.S.— GEN. LINCOLN. A.L.S.— BENJAMIN FRANKLIN. Two L.S.— GEN. GEO. CLINTON. A.L.S.— GEN. LAMB. A.D.S.— GEN. WAYNE. A.L.S.— GEN. DU PORTAIL. A.L.S.— COUNT DE ESTAING. A.L.S.— &c.

Vol. VII. Contains Ninety-four Portraits, Nineteen Subjects, Twenty-four Views &c., and Fourteen Autograph Letters &c., comprising, GEN. WASHINGTON. L.S. In the handwriting of COL. VARICK.— GEN. ST. CLAIR. A.L.S.— GEN. LINCOLN. A.L.S.— GEN. O. H. WILLIAMS. A.D.S.— COL. TIMOTHY PICKERING, A.L.S.— MARQUIS CORNWALLIS. A.L.S.— GEN. WASHINGTON. L.S. In handwriting of COL. ALEX. HAMILTON.— GEN. MORGAN LEWIS. A.L.S.— GEN. MARION. A.L.S.— TERMS of the CAPITULATION of FORT MOULTRIE, the ORIGINAL DOCUMENT signed by CHARLES HUDSON, and WILLIAM SCOTT.— GEN. GATES. A.L.S.— GEN. SCHUYLER. A.L.S.— COL. AARON OGDEN. *Sup. and Sig.*— WASHINGTON IRVING. Page of the Volume in his *handwriting*.

Vol. VIII. Contains One Hundred and Seven Portraits, Fourteen Subjects, Twenty-nine Views &c., and Fourteen Autograph Letters &c., among which are the following: COUNT DE GRASSE. N.S.— COL. WM. JACKSON. A.D.S.— CHANCELLOR LIVINGSTON. A.L.S.— THADDEUS KOSCIUSZKO. A.L.S.— GEN. KNOX. L.S.— GEN. LAFAYETTE. A.L.S.— COL. DAVID HUMPHREYS. A.L.S.— GEN. WEEDEN. A.L.S.— GEORGE WASHINGTON. A.N. *in third person.*— GEORGE WASHINGTON. *Pen and Ink Survey of one his farms, executed by himself.*— BUSHROD WASHINGTON. A.O.S.— JOHN ADAMS, and THOMAS JEFFERSON. *Signatures* to a diplomatic note *written* by Mr. ADAMS.— &c.

Vol. IX. Contains One Hundred and Thirty-seven Portraits, Five Subjects, Twenty-four Views, etc., and Eleven Autograph Letters, etc., comprising, WASHINGTON IRVING. *Sup. and Sig.*— GEORGE WASHINGTON, and THOMAS JEFFERSON. *Signatures* to a State Document, with a fine impression of the seal of the U. S., affixed.— THOMAS JOHNSON, DAVID STEWART, and DANIEL CARROLL. *Signatures* to a Washington City Improvement Bond.— ROBERT MORRIS. A.L.S.— ALEX. HAMILTON. L.S.— GEN. KNOX. L.S.— JAMES MADISON. A.L. *in third person.*— COL. JOSEPH HABERSHAM. A.L.S.— ALEX HAMILTON. A.L. *In third person.*— GEN. JON. WILLIAMS. *Sup. and Sig.*

Vol. X. Contains One Hundred and Twenty-seven Portraits, Two Subjects, Thirteen Views, and Seven Autograph Letters, etc., comprising, TIMOTHY PICKERING. A.L.S.—

GEORGE WASHINGTON. A.L.S.—RUFUS KING. *Sup. and Sig.*—OLIVER WOLCOTT. L.S.—JOHN ADAMS. A.L.S.—REMBRANDT PEELE, A.L.S.— WASHINGTON'S EXECUTORS. A.L.S.

The "MS. CHAPTER." Contains an INDIA PROOF PORTRAIT of the AUTHOR engraved by HALPIN from the picture by MARTIN, and a RUBRICATED TITLE PAGE printed by MR. MUNSELL expressly for the volume.

The "CHARACTER AND PORTRAITS," which has been treated as an independent work and entirely irrespective of the LIFE, etc., contains (in addition to the Twelve Illustrations published with the volume, all of which are selected India proofs, and India proofs before letters,) FORTY-FOUR *inserted* ILLUSTRATIONS, of which FORTY-ONE are PORTRAITS of WASHINGTON, many of them VERY RARE, and embracing FIVE UNLETTERED INDIA PROOF impressions and ONE PROOF impression from PRIVATE PLATES, besides FIFTEEN other UNLETTERED INDIA PROOF impressions of the FIRST CLASS.

The numerous portraits which constitute so large an element in the illustration of this unrivalled set are uniformly brilliant impressions, selected with the most fastidious care, and of the finest description throughout. Many of them were imported from England, France, and Germany, during the preparation of the work, especially for its embellishment, as they could not *then*, nor could they *now*, be obtained in this Country, and many large and expensive engravings were reduced in order to obtain a single good head of some notable personage prominent in the text. They represent nearly every eminent character referred to in the work, and are thought to comprise every thing that is rare, curious, or fine in that connection, including TWENTY BEAUTIFUL PORTRAITS of FRANKLIN, and the pair of Washington and Franklin, painted and etched by CHARLES WILSON PEELE, which are SO RARE that fifty dollars have been paid for an impression of the Franklin head alone. The portraits of Washington were *selected* from an assemblage of upwards of four hundred, the result of many years of discriminative collecting by the present owner of the work. They are ALL in fine condition, ALL essentially different, comprehend every known rare or curious portrait of that illustrious character, and their duplication, under almost any circumstances, may well be questioned.

The coloured photographs mostly represent persons whose portraits have not been publicly engraved. They were executed in the best and most careful manner by an accomplished artist, irrespective of cost, *exclusively* for these volumes. The Water Colour Drawings, which chiefly represent the various Head-Quarters of Washington, and other notable localities, were mostly taken on the spot expressly for this copy of the work.

The Autograph letters, notes, and documents are of the highest interest, and of much historical value, nearly all relating and pertinent to the period, circumstance, or event referred to in the narrative. Many of them possess no inconsiderable value as autographs merely, such, for instance, as those of MRS. WASHINGTON, BENEDICT ARNOLD, ETHAN ALLEN, COL. PETER GANSEVOORT, GEN. ROBERT HOWE, BARON DE KALB, KOSCIUSZKO, DE ESTAING, LAFAYETTE and others.

The Inlaying of many hundreds of the engravings was intrusted *carte blanche* to MR. GEORGE TRENT, who executed the work in the most artistic and satisfactory manner.

An ardent admirer of the character of Gen. Washington, the owner of these volumes spent the leisure of ten years, and no small amount of money, in their *con amore* preparation. They are in the FINEST STATE OF PRESERVATION, PERFECT IN EVERY DETAIL, the TEXT and PLATES, without any exception, PURE and SPOTLESS from beginning to end throughout, and we do not hesitate to assert, that, take them all in all, they constitute THE FINEST, MOST COMPLETE, AND MOST DESIRABLE ILLUSTRATED LIFE OF WASHINGTON EVER PRODUCED.

1042 IRVING. The Works of Washington Irving. New Edition. Revised. *New York: G. P. Putnam.* 1860–63.

16 *vols., sq. 8vo, half olive morocco, gilt top,* UNCUT; the ELEGANT LARGE PAPER EDITION, printed on *slightly tinted paper*, of which only *one hundred copies were issued.*

ONE HUNDRED AND FORTY-FOUR ILLUSTRATIONS *inserted;* comprising a COMPLETE SET of LESLIE'S celebrated illustrations for "Knickerbocker," and the "Sketch Book," several of which are INDIA PROOFS, and a full page of "Knickerbocker" in the MANUSCRIPT of the AUTHOR. The illustrations by DARLEY, in the "Sketch Book," are upon INDIA PAPER; and the fifteen engravings which illustrate "Bracebridge Hall," are BRILLIANT INDIA PROOFS. Complete sets of LESLIE'S ILLUSTRATIONS are VERY RARE, and difficult to obtain at almost any price.

1043 IRVING (P. M.) The Life and Letters of Washington Irving. By his Nephew; Pierre M. Irving.
New York: G. P. Putnam. 1862–64.

4 *vols., sq. 8vo. Uniform in size and binding with the* Works. LARGE PAPER; 110 *copies only printed.*

AN ELEGANT AND BEAUTIFULLY ILLUSTRATED COPY.

Containing ONE HUNDRED and FORTY *inserted* illustrations, besides those that belong in the work, the inferior portion of which has been thrown out, and replaced with FINER IMPRESSIONS. Many of the additional illustrations are PROOFS, and PROOFS ON INDIA PAPER. A facsimile of the curious letter addressed by MR. IRVING to the publisher is inserted at p. 120. Vol. IV., and contains the passage relating to the "Mousing Philadelphia Publishers," which was suppressed in the printed copy.

1044 [IRVING.] Sketch Book of Geoffrey Crayon Gent. Artist's Edition. Illustrated with One hundred and Twenty Engravings on Wood, from Original Designs. *New York: G. P. Putnam.* M.DCCC.LXIV.

Sq. roy. 8vo, half olive morocco, gilt top, UNCUT. LARGE PAPER; *only* 100 *copies printed.* FOUR ILLUSTRATIONS *inserted,* including two beautiful PROOF PORTRAITS of the AUTHOR; and impressions of the CANCELLED HALF TITLE and TITLE drawn by W. HART, engraved by RICHARDSON, and probably *not* in any other copy.

1045 IRVING (W.) PAULDING (J. K.) *and* IRVING (W.) Salmagundi; or the Whim-Whams and Opinions of Launcelot Langstaff, Esq., and Others. By William Irving, James Kirke Paulding, and Washington Irving. Printed from the Original Edition, with a Preface and Notes by Evert A. Duyckinck. *New York: G. P. Putnam.* 1860.

Sq. 8vo, Uniform in size and binding with Irving's Works. THREE ILLUSTRATIONS *inserted.*

1046 IRVING MEMORIAL. Washington Irving. Mr. Bryant's Address on his Life and Genius. Addresses by Everett, Bancroft, Longfellow, Felton, Aspinwall, King, Francis, Greene. Mr. Allibone's Sketch of his Life and Works. With Eight Photographs.
New York: 1860.

Sq. 8vo. pp. 113, 63. *Uniform in size and binding with the works.* TWENTY-TWO ILLUSTRATIONS *inserted;* several of which are fine INDIA PROOFS.

1047 IRVINGIANA. A Memorial of Washington Irving.
New York: Charles B. Richardson. 1860.

4to, pp. lxxiv. Portrait and Facsimile, boards, UNCUT; LARGE PAPER. 110 *copies only printed.* VERY SCARCE.

1048 IZARD (George.) Official Correspondence with the Department of War, relative to the Military Operations of the American Army under the Command of Major General Izard on the Northern Frontier of the United States, in the Years 1814 and 1815.
Philadelphia: Thomas Dobson. 1816.

8vo, pp. vii., 152. *Half crimson morocco, gilt top,* UNCUT.

1049 JACKSON (J.) Memoir of the Last Sickness of General Washington, and its Treatment by the attendant Physicians. By James Jackson, M.D. *Boston: Privately Printed.* 1860.

12mo, pp. 31. *Green morocco, gilt top, by* W. SMITH. An *unpublished* PORTRAIT of WASHINGTON *inserted.*

1050 JACKSON (J.) A Treatise on Wood Engraving, Historical and Practical. With upwards of Three Hundred Illustrations Engraved on Wood, by John Jackson. *London: Charles Knight and Co.* 1839.

Imp. 8vo, half purple morocco, gilt top, UNCUT. ORIGINAL and BEST EDITION.

This fine copy contains the "MAP OF JERUSALEM," and the view of "THE PARSONAGE AT OVINGHAM," both in tint, and not in all copies. SEVENTEEN ILLUSTRATIONS *inserted*, including some fine PROOF, and INDIA PROOF PORTRAITS, among which are those of THOMAS and JOHN BEWICK, HOLLAR, HOLBEIN, RUBENS, and others; a splendid etching of RUBENS by Hess, and a beautifully engraved portrait of ALBERT DURER by Steinla; also an impression of the large full length figure of "St. BERNARDIN," dated 1454, copied from the original in the Royal Library at Paris, and one of the figure of the "VIRGIN AND CHILD." being a facsimile of the *earliest known woodcut with the name of the artist attached, circa* 1454. Of these two last mentioned, FORTY COPIES only were taken and the stones then destroyed. The following is a necessary pendant to this work.

1051 CHATTO (W. A.) A Third Preface to "A Treatise on Wood Engraving, Historical and Practical;" Exposing the Fallacies contained in the First, Restoring the Passages Suppressed in the Second, and containing an Account of Mr. John Jackson's Actual Share in the Composition and Illustration of that Work. In a Letter to Stephen Oliver. By Wm. A. Chatto, Author of the First Seven Chapters of the Work, and the Writer of the Whole as Originally Printed. *London: Printed for the Author.* 1839.

Imp. 8vo, pp. 36. *Uniform with the Treatise in size and binding.* PRIVATELY PRINTED, and VERY RARE. *Autograph Note* of the AUTHOR *inserted.*

The rare, pungent, and incisive Third Preface, without which the "Treatise on Wood Engraving," cannot be considered complete.

1052 JACKSON (W.) Eulogium, on the Character of General Washington, ... Pronounced before the Pennsylvania Society of the Cincinnati, on the Twenty-second day of February, Eighteen Hundred ... at Philadelphia. By Major William Jackson, Aid-de-camp to the late President of the United States ... . *Philadelphia:* 1800.

8vo, pp. 44.

1053 [JACOB (John J.)] A Biographical Sketch of the Life of the late Capt. Michael Cresap. *Cumberland Md.: printed for the Author.* 1826.

12mo, pp. 124. *Polished calf, gilt edges, by* F. BEDFORD. A FINE COPY of this RARE BOOK. Fisher's copy, much inferior to this, sold for $31.00.

"The strange fate which led this border warrior from the silent forests, to die in the crowded city, and lie within a few feet of the ceaseless sounding of the million feet which tread Broadway, is not less remarkable than the fortune which befell his memory when dead. Made the object of the hatred and detestation of the civilized world, by Jefferson's publication of Logan's speech, Captain Cresap, worn down with anxiety and ill health, did not hesitate to collect a company of his formidable riflemen, and march to aid his countrymen at the siege of Boston. He however was only able to reach New York, where he died in October, 1775, and was buried in Trinity church-yard."— *Field.*

1054 JACOB. A Biographical Sketch of the Life of the Late Captain Michael Cresap. By John J. Jacob.
Cincinnati: William Dodge. 1866.

Small 4to, pp. 158. *Half maroon morocco, gilt top,* UNCUT. PORTRAIT *inserted.*
A reprint of the preceding No., with Notes, and an Appendix.

1055 JAMES I. The Works of James I, King of Scotland. Containing the King's Quair, Christis Kirk on the Grene, and Peblis to the Play.
Perth: 1786.

12mo, brown morocco, gilt top, UNCUT. *Portrait.* VERY SCARCE.
For an admirable sketch of James I, and his poems, *see* "A Royal Poet." in Irving's *Sketch Book. See* also *Allibone.*

1056 JAMES (E.) A Narrative of the Captivity and Adventures of John Tanner, (U. S. Interpreter of the Saut de Saint Marie,) during Thirty Years residence among the Indians in the Interior of North America. Prepared for the Press By Edwin James, M.D. ...
New York: G. & C. & H. Carvill. 1830.

8vo, pp. 426. *Portrait. Half red morocco, gilt top,* UNCUT, *by* BRADSTREET. *Duplicate* INDIA PROOF PORTRAIT *inserted.*
The narrative was related *viva voce* by Tanner to Dr. James, Mr. Field remarks that "His relation of his life among the Northern Indians, is probably the most minute, if not authentic detail of their habits, modes of living, and social customs, ever printed."

1057 JAMES (W.) An Inquiry into the Merits of the Principal Naval Actions between Great Britain and the United States; comprising an Account of all British and American ships of War, reciprocally Captured and Destroyed, since the 18th of June, 1812. By William James. *Halifax, N. S.: Printed for the Author.* 1816.

8vo, pp. vi., 102. *Half russia. Fine copy.* VERY SCARCE.
This author considered that little credit for naval or other exploits was due to the Statesmen; and evinced great disgust at the American idea that "they are an intelligent, active and enlightened people, beyond all former example."

1058 JAMES. A Full and Correct Account of the Chief Naval Occurrences of the late War between Great Britain and the United States of America; preceded by a cursory examination of the American Accounts of their Naval Actions fought previous to that period: to which is added an Appendix; with Plates. By William James. ...
London: T. Egerton. 1817.

8vo, pp. xv., (1), 528, *ccxvi.,* (16). *Plate. Half russia, gilt top,* UNCUT.

1059 JAMES. A Full and Correct Account of the Military Occurrences of the late War between Great Britain and the United States of America. With an Appendix and Plates. By William James.
London: Printed for the Author. 1818.

2 vols., 8vo, pp. xxxii., 476; 582, (16). 4 Maps. Half russia, gilt top, UNCUT.

"A work of which it is not too high praise to assert that it approaches as nearly to perfection, in its own line, as any historical work perhaps ever did."— *Edinburgh Review.*

1060 JAMES. Warden Refuted; being a Defence of the British Navy against the Mis-representations of a Work recently published at Edinburgh, entitled "A Statistical, Political, and Historical Account of the United States ... by D. B. Warden ... ." In a Letter to the Author of that Work; by William James; ...
London: J. M. Richardson. 1819.

8vo, pp. 48. Half russia, gilt top, uncut.

See Warden (D. B.) No. 2040.

1061 JAMES (W. D.) A Sketch of the Life of Brig. Gen. Francis Marion, and A History of his Brigade, from its Rise in June, 1780, until Disbanded in December, 1782; with Descriptions of Characters and Scenes, not heretofore published. Containing also, an Appendix, with Copies of Letters which passed between Several of the Leading Characters of that day; principally from Gen. Greene to Gen. Marion. By William Dobein James, A.M., during that period one of Marion's Militia. At present one of the Associate Judges in Equity, South-Carolina. *Charleston, S. C.: Printed by Gould and Riley.* 1821.

8vo, pp. 182, 39. Crushed green levant morocco, gilt top, UNCUT, *by* F. BEDFORD. Two scarce and fine PORTRAITS *inserted.* SPLENDID COPY of one of the RAREST of all Revolutionary Biographies, and seldom found *uncut.*

1062 [JARVIS (Russell.)] A Biographical Notice of Com. Jesse D. Elliot; Containing a Review of the Controversy between him and the late Commodore Perry; and a History of the Figure Head of the U. S. Frigate Constitution. ... By a Citizen of New York.
Philadelphia: Printed for the Author. 1835.

12mo, pp. 480. Half calf.

1063 JAY (John.) New Plottings in Aid of the Rebel Doctrine of State Sovereignty. Mr. Jay's Second Letter on Dawson's Introduction to the Federalist. Exposing its Falsification of the History of the Constitution; its Libels on Duane, Livingston, Jay and Hamilton; and its relation to recent efforts by Traitors at home, and Foes abroad, to maintain the Rebel doctrine of State Sovereignty, for the Subversion of the Unity of the Republic and the Supreme Sovereignty of the American People. *New York: American News Co.* 1864.

8vo, pp. 54, viii. Half red morocco, gilt top, by BRADSTREET. SUPPRESSED, and VERY SCARCE.

1064 JAY. New Plottings to Aid the Rebellion. [Third Edition.] *New York: James G. Gregory.* 1864.

8vo, pp. 50. *Half red morocco, gilt top, by* BRADSTREET. Also suppressed, and very scarce.

1065 JAY (W.) The Life of John Jay; with Selections from his Correspondence and Miscellaneous Papers. By his Son William Jay. *New York: J. & J. Harper.* 1833.

2 *vols.*, *8vo, pp. viii.*, 520; (4), 502. *Portrait. Half calf, gilt top,* UNCUT. An *Autograph Letter,* and THREE different PORTRAITS of MR. JAY *inserted.*

1066 [JEFFERSON (Thomas.)] A Summary View of the Rights of British America. Set forth in some Resolutions intended for the Inspection of the present Delegates of the People of Virginia, now in Convention. By a Native, and Member of the House of Burgesses. The Second Edition. [Dedication to the King signed Tribunus.] *Williamsburg, printed. London: Reprinted for G. Kearsley.* 1774.

8vo, pp. xvi., 5–44. *Half morocco. Very Scarce.*

"This summary was intended to convey to the late convention of the delegates of Virginia the sentiments of one of their members, who was prevented from attending."

1067 [JEFFERSON.] Notes on the State of Virginia; written in the Year 1781, somewhat corrected and enlarged in the winter of 1782, for the use of a Foreigner of distinction, in answer to certain queries proposed by him respecting 1. Its Boundaries. 2. Rivers. 3. Sea ports. 4. Mountains, &c. [*Paris.*] MDCCLXXXII.

8vo, pp. (2), 391. *Crushed green levant morocco, edges gilt on carmine, by* W. MATTHEWS. BEAUTIFUL COPY of the ORIGINAL EDITION, PRIVATELY PRINTED, and EXTREMELY RARE.

"This edition of Mr. Jefferson's celebrated Notes was evidently printed in Paris; but as Mr. Jefferson did not reach France until the year 1784, the date on the title probably is not that of the year in which it was printed, but of the year in which the manuscript was completed. A copy presented to M. Malesherbe had the following note, in Mr. Jefferson's handwriting. 'Mr. Jefferson having had a few copies of these notes printed to present to some of his friends, and to some estimable characters beyond that line, takes the liberty of presenting a copy to M. de Malesherbe, as a testimony of his respect to his character. Unwilling to expose them to the public eye, he begs the favour of M. de M. to put them into the hands of no person on whose care and fidelity he cannot rely, to guard them against publication.' "—*Rich.*

It is not known of how many copies the privately printed edition consisted; but they were unquestionably very few, rendering it one of the SCARCEST BOOKS in the whole American collection.

1068 JEFFERSON. Notes on the State of Virginia. Written by Thomas Jefferson. Illustrated with A Map, including the States of Virginia, Maryland, Delaware, and Pennsylvania. *London: John Stockdale.* M. DCC. LXXXVII.

8vo, pp. (4), 382. *Map. Half calf, gilt top,* UNCUT. Scarce contemporary PORTRAIT of JEFFERSON *inserted.* FINE COPY. SCARCE.

1069 JEFFERSON. Notes on the State of Virginia. By Thomas Jefferson: illustrated with a Map, including the States of Virginia, Mary-

land, Delaware and Pennsylvania. A New Edition, prepared by the Author, containing Notes and Plates never before published.
Richmond: J. W. Randolph. 1853.

8vo, pp. iv., (4), 275. *Map, 2 Plates, and Folded Sheet. Half green morocco, gilt top,* UNCUT. PORTRAIT *inserted.*

Printed from President Jefferson's own copy of Stockdale's edition, containing many additions and corrections, and a map and plates. Also: Letters from Gen. Dearborn and Judge Gibson relating to the Murder of Logan; a Topographical Analysis of Virginia for 1790; and Translations of all Jefferson's Notes in Foreign Languages by Prof. Schele de Vere.

1070 JEFFERSON. Memoirs, Correspondence, and Private Papers of Thomas Jefferson, late President of the United States. ... Edited by Thomas Jefferson Randolph.
London: Henry Colburn and Richard Bentley. 1829.

4 *vols.*, *8vo, half green morocco, gilt top,* UNCUT.

The contents of these volumes are not embraced in the Congressional Publications.

1071 JENINGS (E.) The Candor of Henry Laurens, Esq.; Manifested by his Behaviour to Mr. Edmund Jenings. [*London:*] *July*, 1783.

4to, pp. 38. *Half blue morocco, gilt top,* UNCUT. PRIVATELY PRINTED. VERY SCARCE.

1072 JENINGS. A Full Manifestation of what Mr. Henry Laurens falsely denominates Candor in himself, and Tricks in Mr. Edmund Jenings. *London: Printed in the year* 1783.

4to, pp. (4), 80. *Half blue morocco, gilt top,* UNCUT. PRIVATELY PRINTED. VERY SCARCE.

An answer to the pamphlet entitled "State of the Case by which his Candour to Mr. Edmund Jennings is manifested and the Tricks of Mr. Jennings detected," by Henry Laurens.

This, together with the preceding No. and Laurens' "State of the Case," comprise a complete series of the publications relating to the "*Pitiful Quarrel*" between Messrs. Jenings and Laurens. The *three* books are *very rarely* found together.

See Laurens (Henry.) No. 1193.

1073 JENNINGS (D.) An Abridgment of the Life of the late Reverend and Learned Dr. Cotton Mather, of Boston in New England. Taken from the Account of him published by his Son, the Rev. Mr. Samuel Mather. Proposed as a Pattern to all Christians, who desire to excel in Holiness and Usefulness, and especially to younger Ministers. By David Jennings. *London: J. Oswald.* 1744.

12mo, pp. xii., (4), 143. *Polished calf, gilt edges, by* F. BEDFORD. SCARCE.

1074 JESSE (J. H.) Memoirs of the Court of England during the Reign of the Stuarts, including the Protectorate. By John Heneage Jesse. Plates. *London: Bentley.* 1840.

4 *vols.*, *8vo, half green morocco, gilt top,* UNCUT. FORTY-SEVEN PORTRAITS, chiefly FINE IMPRESSIONS from LODGE, *inserted.*

1075 JESSE. Memoirs of the Court of England from the Revolution in 1688 to the Death of George the Second. By John Heneage Jesse. Plates. *London: Bentley.* 1846.

3 *vols.*, 8*vo*, *half green morocco*, *gilt top*, UNCUT. THIRTEEN FINE PORTRAITS *inserted*, several of which are INDIA PROOFS. Uniform with the preceding No.

1076 JESSE. The Pretenders and their Adherents. Memoirs of the Chevalier, Prince Charles Edward, and their Adherents. By John Heneage Jesse. *London : Bentley.* 1846.

2 *vols.*, 8*vo*, *half green morocco*, *gilt top*, UNCUT. Two PORTRAITS *inserted.* Uniform with the preceding No.

The above works by MR. JESSE have become VERY SCARCE. "We know of no series of books, that of Horace Walpole perhaps excepted, in which so much information is conveyed in so agreeable a manner as in this series of historical anecdotical works."

1077 JÉSUITES. Relations des Jésuites Contenant ce qui s'est passé de plus remarquable dans les Missions des Pères de la Campagnie de Jésus dans la Nouvelle-France. *Quebec : Augustine Coté.* 1858.

3 *vols.*, *roy.* 8*vo*, *half green morocco*, *gilt top*, UNCUT. VERY SCARCE.
The EMPEROR MAXIMILLIAN'S COPY, with his book-plate.

"The most extraordinary and valuable collection ever made of the narratives of a class of men who, two centuries before what we term civilization, had prostrated the forests, explored the vast territories covered by them, recorded the peculiarities of the natives, and in many instances bestowed upon them the blessings of Christianity. These relations, for many years looked upon through the haze of sectarian distrust, were lightly esteemed by the students of American history, but the more their character and statements were investigated, the more important and valuable they appeared. They have become the sources from which we must draw almost all the historic material of New York and Canada, during the first century and a half of their exploration by Europeans. It was to perpetuate these monuments of the early history of Canada, that Parliament ordered their publication in this form."— *Field.*

1078 JEWETT (C. C.) On the Construction of Catalogues of Libraries, and their Publication by means of Separate, Stereotyped Titles. With Rules and Examples. By Charles C. Jewett. ... Second Edition. *Washington :* 1853.

Roy. 8*vo*, *pp. xii.*, 96. *Half green morocco*, *gilt top*, UNCUT.

A well written summary of all that has been done towards solving this difficult subject. Librarians and Private collectors will find in it many valuable and practical hints.

1079 JOGUES (I.) Novum Belgium : An Account of New Netherland in 1643–4. By Rev. Father Isaac Jogues .... With a Facsimile of his Original Manuscript, his Portrait, a Map, and Notes. By J. G. Shea. *New York : Privately Printed.* 1862.

4*to*, *pp.* 55. 4 *leaves of Facsimile*, 2 *Portraits*, *Map and View*. *Half blue morocco*, *gilt top*, UNCUT. *Small Edition.*

Edited, for the first time, from the Jesuit MS. Narrative dated 1646.

1080 JOHNSON (C.) A General History of the Pyrates, from their first Rise and Settlement in the Island of Providence, to the present Time. With the remarkable Actions and Adventures of the two Female Pyrates Mary Read and Anne Bonney ; Contained in the following chapters. Introduction. I. Of Capt. Avery. II. Of Capt. Martel. III. Of Capt. Teach. IV. Of Capt. Bonnet. V. Of Capt. England. VI. Of Capt. Vane. VII. Of Capt. Rackam. VIII. Of Capt. Davis. IX. Of Capt. Roberts. X. Of Capt. Anstis. XI. Of Capt. Worley. XII. Of Capt. Lowther. XIII. Of Capt. Low. XIV. Of Capt. Evans. XV. Of Capt. Phillips. XVI. Of Capt. Spriggs. And their several Crews. To which is added a short Abstract on the Statute and Civil Law in Relation to Pyracy. The Second Edition, with considerable Additions. By Captain Charles Johnson. *London: T. Warner.* 1724.

8vo, pp. (20), 17–427. 3 *Plates. Half calf antique. Fine copy.* VERY SCARCE.

This RARE WORK embodies a great quantity of matter relating to the Colonial History of British America, nowhere else extant, as, the Adventures of Blackbeard, and his Capture by Lieut. Maynard in the James River, Va. The Life and Career of Capt. Kyd, &c.

1081 JOHNSON (J.) Typographia, or the Printers' Instructor: including an Account of the Origin of Printing, with Biographical Notices of the Printers of England, from Caxton to the close of the Sixteenth Century: A Series of Ancient and Modern Alphabets and Domesday Characters; ... By J. Johnson, Printer. *London: Longman.* 1824.

2 *vols., 8vo, half olive morocco, gilt top,* UNCUT. Beautiful copy of the ROXBURGHE EDITION. LARGEST PAPER; of which a FEW COPIES ONLY were printed. Frontispiece *inserted* in each volume.

This invaluable work is too often regarded merely as a book for printers, whereas it contains more information respecting early printed books than is to be found in any other and more costly volumes. In its compilation Johnson was assisted by Dibdin, Wilkins, Baber, and other well known Bibliographers.

1082 JOHNSON (J. B.) Eulogy on General George Washington. A Sermon, delivered February 22d, 1800, in ... Albany, before the Legislature of the State of New York. By Rev. John B. Johnson. ... *Albany:* 1800.

8vo, pp. 22.

1083 JOHNSON (J.) Traditions and Reminiscences chiefly of the American Revolution in the South: including Biographical Sketches, Incidents and Anecdotes, few of which have been published, Particularly of Residents in the Upper Country. By Joseph Johnson, M.D., of Charleston, S. C. *Charleston, S. C.: Walker & James.* 1851.

8vo, pp. viii., 592. *Map and Plans. Half blue morocco, gilt top.* An elegant copy with an *Autograph Letter* of the AUTHOR relating to the work, and THIRTY-SEVEN ILLUSTRATIONS *inserted,* some of which are INDIA PROOFS, and some VERY RARE.

We know of no book of such recent date, which is so difficult to procure in *any* condition.

1084 JOHNSON (Mrs.) A Narrative of the Captivity of Mrs. Johnson. Containing an Account of her Sufferings, during Four Years, with the Indians and French. Together with an Appendix; containing the Sermons preached at her Funeral, ... with sundry other interesting Articles. Third Edition Corrected, and Considerably Enlarged. *Windsor, Vt.:* 1814.

12mo, pp. 178. *Half morocco.* VERY SCARCE.

One of the most interesting of all the Indian Captivities. She was captured at Charlestown, New Hampshire, in 1754, carried through what is now Vermont to Canada where she resided several years, and returned to New Hampshire by the way of England and New York.

1085 [JOHNSON (Samuel.)] Ethica: or the First Principles of Moral Philosophy; and especially that Part which is called Ethics. In a Chain of necessary Consequences from certain Facts. The Second Edition. *Philadelphia: printed by* B. FRANKLIN *and* D. HALL, *at the New Printing-Office, near the Market.* 1752.

8vo, pp. viii., 103. *Half gray calf.* FINE COPY. RARE.

1086 [JOHNSON.] Noetica: or the First Principles of Human Knowledge. Being a Logick, Including both Metaphysics and Dialectic, Or the Art of Reasoning. With a brief Pathology, and an Account of the gradual Progress of the Human Mind, from the first Dawnings of Sense to the highest Perfection, both Intellectual and Moral, of which it is capable. To which is prefixed, A Short Introduction to the Study of the Sciences. *Philadelphia: Printed by* B. FRANKLIN *and* D. HALL, *at the New Printing-Office near the Market.* 1752.

8vo, pp. xxiv., 103. *Half gray calf.* FINE COPY. RARE.

1087 [JOHNSON.] Taxation no Tyranny; an Answer to the Resolutions and Address of the American Congress. *London: T. Cadell.* MDCCLXXV.

8vo, pp. 91. *Half red morocco.*

The six works next following, form a series of Answers &c. to "Taxation no Tyranny." They are uniformly bound, and each numbered at the bottom of the back, in the order of their publication.

"This tract claims its importance from the celebrity of its author. It was written in the sixty-sixth year of his age, when he was at the meridian of his fame. Mr. Bancroft in his seventh volume describes it at length as an exemplification of the tone of public sentiment then prevailing in England. It called forth several replies, each of which is aimed at pointing out the fallacy that lurks in its title as well as in all its reasonings." — *J. R. Bartlett.*

1088 [JOHNSON.] Taxation, Tyranny. Addressed to Samuel Johnson, LL.D. *London: J. Bew.* 1775.

8vo, pp. 80.

The style and argument of this performance deserve commendation, but in some cases the author appears not to be well acquainted with facts in regard to the dispute.

1089 [JOHNSON.] Resistance No Rebellion: in Answer to Dr. Johnson's "Taxation no Tyranny." *London: J. Bell.* MDCCLXXV.

8vo, pp. (4), 35.

This reply, "by way of parody," appears to be in general well conducted, and capable of affording much entertainment, with some information.

1090 [JOHNSON.] A Defence of the Resolutions and Address of the American Congress, in Reply to "Taxation No Tyranny." By the Author of Regulus. ... *London: J. Williams.* [1775.]

8vo, pp. 96.

"This pamphlet contains many very harsh, and some very just strictures on the doctrines and tenets advanced by Dr. Johnson, whose pamphlet has been honoured with unmerited notice."— *M. Review.*

1091 [JOHNSON.] An Answer to a Pamphlet entitled "Taxation no Tyranny." Addressed to the Author and to Persons in Power. *London: J. Almon.* MDCCLXXV.

8vo, pp. 63. *Gilt top,* UNCUT.

The "Monthly Review" styles this one of the best of the answers to Dr. Johnson's Pamphlet.

1092 [JOHNSON.] The Pamphlet, entitled, "Taxation no Tyranny," Candidly Considered, and its Arguments, and Pernicious Doctrines, Exposed and Refuted. *London: W. Davis.* [1775.]

8vo, pp. 131. *Gilt top,* UNCUT.

1093 [JOHNSON.] The Right of the British Legislature to Tax the American Colonies Vindicated, and the Means of Asserting that Right proposed. The Second Edition, with Additions. *London: T. Beckett.* MDCCLXXV.

8vo, pp. 88.

"Perhaps no two pamphlets did more good to the American cause than Dr. Johnson's '*Taxation no Tyranny*,' and Mr. Wesley's '*Calm Address*,' both intended to have quite a contrary effect from that which was produced by them. This arose from the numerous and able answers which were immediately circulated by lovers of truth, and enemies to oppression, in which the specious arguments of the ministerial hirelings were at once confuted and shown in their true light."— *Rich.*

1094 [JOHNSON.] Hypocrisy Unmasked; Or, A Short Inquiry into the Religious Complaints of our American Colonies. To which is added, A Word on the Laws against Popery in Great Britain and Ireland. *London: W. Nicoll.* MDCCLXXVI.

12mo, pp. 24. *Half morocco, gilt top,* UNCUT. *Very Scarce.*

The object of the author seems to be to defend the "*Quebec Bill*," which protects the Canadians in the exercise of the Roman Catholic religion. The American Colonies classed this Bill among their grievances. The author of the tract in question shows that many of the colonies extended the same rights to Roman Catholics that the Quebec Bill did to the Canadians.

1095 JOHNSON (W.) Sketches of the Life and Correspondence of Nathanael Greene, Major General of the Armies of the United States, In the War of the Revolution. Compiled chiefly from Original Materials. By William Johnson, of Charleston, South-Carolina. *Charleston: Printed for the Author, by A. E. Miller,* ... 1822.

2 *vols., 4to, pp. xi.,* 515, (1); 477, 11. *Portrait,* 7 *Engraved Plans, and Map. Half green morocco, gilt top,* UNCUT. AN ELEGANT COPY, almost free from stains; containing the APPENDIX 11 pp. *subsequently printed,* and *not* in all copies. PORTRAIT *inserted.*

1096 JOHNSTON (C.) A Narrative of the Incidents attending the Capture, Detention, and Ransom of Charles Johnston, of Botetourt County, Virginia, who was made Prisoner by the Indians, on the River Ohio, in the year 1790. Together with an interesting Account of the Fate of his Companions ... one of whom suffered at the Stake. To which are added Sketches of Indian Character and Manners, with illustrative Anecdotes.

New York: J. & J. Harper. 1827.

12*mo, pp.* 264. *Half red morocco, gilt top,* UNCUT. SCARCE.

1097 JOHNSTONE (*Chevalier.* de) Memoirs of the Rebellion in 1745 and 1746. By the Chevalier de Johnstone .... Containing a Narrative of the Progress of the Rebellion, from its Commencement to the Battle of Culloden: the Characters of the Principal Persons engaged in it, and Anecdotes respecting them; ... with an Account of the Sufferings and Privations of the Author ... before he effected his Escape to the Continent, &c. &c. Translated from a French MS. originally deposited in the Scots College at Paris ..., Third Edition. *London: Longman.* 1822.

8*vo, pp. lxxii.,* 456. 2 *Portraits, and Plan. Half green morocco, gilt top,* UNCUT. An *Autograph Letter* of the famous MAJOR LOCKHART *inserted.*

"A very interesting work, written under the influence of disappointment and ill humour. Some of the stories are altogether fictitious."— *Lowndes.*

Includes the Author's Adventures in Cape Breton, Canada, &c.

1098 JOHONNOT (J.) The Remarkable Adventures of Jackson Johonnot, of Massachusetts, who served as a Soldier in the Western Army, in the Expedition under Gen. Harmar, and Gen. St. Clair. Containing an account of his Captivity, Sufferings, and Escape from the Kickappo Indians. Written by Himself. ... *Greenfield: Mass.* 1816.

8*vo, half morocco, gilt top,* UNCUT, *by* BRADSTREET. VERY SCARCE. Brought $16.00 at HUGHES's Sale in Cincinnati, 1871.

1099 JONES (C. C. Jr.) Historical Sketch of Tomo-chi-chi, Mico of the Yamacraes. By Charles C. Jones, Jun:

Albany: J. Munsell. 1868.

8*vo, pp.* 133. *Half red levant morocco, gilt top,* UNCUT.

"The large-minded and heroic Indian chief, who welcomed Oglethorpe to the lands of his nation, and fed and protected the infant colony during those early years, when disease and the Spaniards threatened its existence, well deserved a biography. No hero of the colonies of North America, even the boasting Captain John Smith, the zealous Roger Williams, or the noble Oglethorpe himself, better deserved an enduring monument than Tomo-Chi-Chi."— *Field.*

1100 JONES (H.) The | Present State | of | Virginia. | Giving | A particular and short Account of the In- | dian, English, and Negroe Inhabitants of that | Colony. | Shewing their Religion, Manners, Government, | Trade, Way of Living, &c. with a Description of | the Country. | From whence is inferred a short View of | Maryland and North Carolina. | To which are added, | Schemes and Propositions for the better promotion of | Learning, Religion, Inventions, Manufacturers, and Trade in | Virginia, and the other Plantations. | For the Information of the Curious, and for the Service of such | as are engaged in the Propagation of the Gospel and Advancement | of Learning, and for the Use of all Persons concerned in the | Virginia Trade and Plantation. | [Motto.] By Hvgh Jones, A.M. Chaplain to | the Honourable Assembly, and lately Minister of | James-Town, &c. in Virginia. | *London: Printed for J. Clarke, at the Bible, under the Royal-* | *Exchange.* M DCC XXIV.

8vo, 2 l., pp. viii., 151, (1). *Crushed red levant morocco, gilt edges, by* F. BEDFORD. EXCEEDINGLY SCARCE.

"One of the scarcest works relating to Virginia published in this century. The author thinks that the settlement of America by the Europeans is a fulfilment of the scriptural text on his title-page, *Japhet* being the English, *Shem* the Indians, and *Canaan* the Negroes."—*Rich.*

1101 [JONES (Ignatius.)] Random Recollections of Albany, from 1800 to 1808: with some Additional Matter. Second Edition. [Also: Recollections of Hudson, by the same Author.]
Albany: Charles Van Benthuysen. 1850.

8vo, pp. 90, 78. *Half green morocco, gilt top.* FINE COPY. *Very Scarce.*

1102 JONES (John P.) Memoirs of Rear-Admiral Paul Jones. ... Now First Compiled from his Original Journals and Correspondence: including an Account of his Services under Prince Potemkin. Prepared for Publication by Himself.
Edinburgh: Oliver & Boyd. MDCCCXXX.

2 vols., 12mo, half calf.

1103 JONES (J. S.) A Defence of the Revolutionary History of the State of North Carolina from the Aspersions of Mr. Jefferson. By Jo. Seawell Jones, of Shocco, North Carolina.
Boston: Charles Bowen. 1834.

12mo, pp. xii., 343. *Half olive morocco, gilt top,* UNCUT. PORTRAIT *inserted.*

1104 JOSSELYN (J.) New-Englands | Rarities | Discovered: | in | Birds, Beasts, Fishes, Serpents, | and Plants of that Country. | Together with | The Physical and Chyrurgical Remedies | wherewith the Natives constantly use to | Cure their Distempers, Wounds, | and Sores. | Also | A Perfect Description of an Indian Sqva, | in all her Bravery; with a Poem not | improperly conferr'd upon her. | Lastly | A Chronological Table | of the most remarkable Passages in that | Country amongst the English. | Illustrated with Cvts. | By John Josselyn, Gent. | *London, Printed for G. Widdowes at the* | *Green Dragon in St. Pauls Church yard,* 1672.

Sm. 8vo, pp. (4), 114, (2). *Winged Dragon, and Plate. Red levant morocco, paneled and gilt sides, gilt edges, by* F. BEDFORD. BEAUTIFUL COPY. VERY RARE. This copy has the *folded* and *unpaged plate* at page 54, which is sometimes wanting.

"The earliest work on the Natural History of New England."—*Rich.*

The description of the "Indian Squaw in all her *bravery*," together with the "poem not improperly conferred upon her," occupy pp. 99 to 102. The description of Indian medicaments, and the use made of various herbs by the natives, occupy much of the remainder of the work.

1105 JOSSELYN. An | Account | Of Two | Voyages | To | New-England. | Wherein you have the setting out of a Ship, | with the charges; The prices of all necessaries for | furnishing a Planter and his Family at his first com- | ing; A Description of the Countrey, Natives and | Creatures, with their Merchantil and Physical use; | The Government of the Countrey as it is now pos- | sessed by the English, &c. A large Chronological Ta- | ble of the most remarkable passages, from the first dis- | covering of the Continent of America, to the year | 1673. By John Josselyn Gent. | *London, Printed for Giles Widdows, at the Green-Dragon | in St. Paul's-Church-Yard*, 1674.

12mo, pp. (8), 279, (3). *Maroon morocco, gilt edges.* AN UNUSUALLY LARGE COPY of a PARTICULARLY RARE and interesting work.

"The relation is curious and faithful — when the author makes his own remarks they are in the oddest, most uncouth expressions imaginable." — *Locke.*

1106 JOSSELYN. An Account of Two Voyages to New England, Made during the years 1638, 1663. By John Josselyn Gent. [Also :] New-England's Rarities Discovered in Birds, Beasts, Fishes, Serpents, and Plants of that Country. By John Josselyn, Gent. With an Introduction and Notes By Edward Tuckerman, M.A.
Boston: William Veazie. MDCCCLXV.

2 *vols., roy.* 4*to, half crushed blue levant morocco, gilt top,* UNCUT, *by* BRADSTREET. LARGE PAPER, 25 *copies only printed.*

Not merely reprints. The copious, interesting, and valuable annotations lend a new value to the works.

1107 JOURNAL of the Principal Occurrences during the Siege of Quebec by the American Revolutionists under Generals Montgomery and Arnold in 1775–6: containing Many Anecdotes of Moment never yet published, collected from some Old Manuscripts Originally Written by an Officer, during the Period of the Gallant Defence made by Sir Guy Carleton. ... To which are added a Preface and illustrative Notes by W. J. P. Shortt. *London: Simpkin and Co.* 1824.

8*vo. pp. xv.,* III. *Polished calf.* VERY SCARCE.

1108 JOURNAL of the Proceedings of the Congress held at Philadelphia, September 5, 1774. *Philadelphia: Printed by William and Thomas Bradford; at the London Coffee House.* M,DCC,LXXIV.

The original edition, with the first device of the Confederate States; twelve hands grasping a column based on Magna Charta, and surmounted by the cap of liberty and the motto, "*Hanc tuemur.*"

[Also :] JOURNAL of the Proceedings of the Congress, held at Philadelphia; May 10, 1775.
Philadelphia: Printed by William and Thomas Bradford. MDCCLXXV.

8*vo,* 2 *vols. bound in one. pp.* 144; *iv.,* 239. *Half blue morocco, gilt top,* UNCUT. RARE in such FINE *uncut* condition.

"DR. FRANKLIN, it is believed, caused the *first part* of this volume to be issued in London, in January, 1775. Its effect was startling, for it proclaimed to the discriminating British

Public (if there was at that time such a body) that the English language had acquired new vigor and clearness in being transplanted to the Western shores. The pith, point, and force of these Public Papers, astonished the politicians and statesmen of Westminster, and delighted the friends of the Colonies."— *Stevens.*

1109 JOURNALS (The) of the Proceedings of Congress. Held at Philadelphia, from January to May, 1776.
Philadelphia: Printed by R. Aitken. MDCCLXXVI.

8vo, pp. 93. 237. *Half blue morocco, gilt top,* UNCUT. Uniform with the preceding No. and EQUALLY RARE.

1110 JOUTEL (*Mons.*) A | Journal | of the Last | Voyage | perform'd by | Monsr. de la Sale, | to the | Gulph of Mexico, | To find out the | Mouth of the Missisipi River; | Containing, | An Account of the Settlements he endeavour'd to | make on the Coast of the aforesaid Bay, his | unfortunate Death, and the Travels of his | Companions for the Space of Eight Hundred | Leagues across that Inland Country of America, | now call'd Louisiana, (and given by the King of | France to M. Crozat,) till they came into Canada. | Written in French by Monsieur Joutel, | A Commander in that Expedition; | And Translated, from the Edition just publish'd at Paris. | With an exact Map of that vast Country, and a Copy of the | Letters Patents granted by the K. of France to M. Crozat. | *London: Printed for A. Bell.* 1714.

8vo, title, pp. xxi., (9), 205, (5). *Map. Half calf antique.* FINE COPY. VERY SCARCE.

Mr. Parkman, in speaking of the journey of Joutel in which he accompanied La Salle, says, "Of the three narratives of this journey, those of Joutel, Cavalier and Douay, the first is by far the best. That of Cavalier seems the work of a man of confused brain and indifferent memory. Joutel's account is of a very different character, and seems to be the work of an honest and intelligent man. Douay's account is brief, but it agrees with that of Joutel in most essential points."— *France and England in North America.* Part Third. p. 356.

1111 JUAN *and* ULLOA. A Voyage to South America: Describing at large the Spanish Cities, Towns, Provinces, &c. on that extensive Continent: ... by Don George Juan, and Don Antonio de Ulloa. ... Translated from the Original Spanish; with Notes and Observations; and an Account of the Brazils. By John Adams, Esq., of Waltham Abbey. The Fifth Edition. Illustrated with Plates.
London: John Stockdale. 1807.

2 *vols., 8vo, pp. xxvii.,* 479; *iv.,* 419, 14. *Map and 7 Folded Plates. Half gray calf, carmine edges.* LARGE and CLEAN copy of the BEST EDITION.

1112 JUMEL (E. B.) Obituary of Madame Eliza B. Jumel. In the New York Times of July 18th, 1865. *New York:* 1865.

4to, half blue morocco, gilt top, UNCUT. *Thirty copies only* PRIVATELY PRINTED. PORTRAIT of MADAM JUMEL, VIEW of her RESIDENCE, and PORTRAIT of AARON BURR *inserted.*

1113 JUNIUS. Including Letters by the Same Writer, under other Signatures, (Now first collected) to which are added, his Confidential Correspondence with Mr. Wilkes, and his Private Letters addressed to Mr. H. S. Woodfall. With a Preliminary Essay, Notes, Facsimiles, &c. Second Edition. *London: Printed by G. Woodfall.* 1814.

2 *vols.*, 8*vo*, *half orange morocco, gilt top*, UNCUT. BEST EDITION. One of BOCQUET's fine PORTRAITS *inserted* in front of each volume.

1114 JUSTICE (The) and Necessity of Taxing the American Colonies, Demonstrated. Together with a Vindication of the Authority of Parliament. *London: J. Almon.* 1766.

8*vo*, *pp.* 36. *Half red morocco.*

"This is, in truth, a most fiery politician, and his pamphlet a mere firebrand. In reply to the objections of the colonists to a standing army, he says that they have need of the *gentlemen of the blade*, to polish and refine their manners, to rub off the rust of puritanism, etc."—*Monthly Review.*

1115 KALM (P.) Travels into North America; containing its Natural History, and A circumstantial Account of its Plantations and Agriculture in general, with the Civil, Ecclesiastical and Commercial State of the Country. The Manners of the Inhabitants, and several curious and Important Remarks on various Subjects. By Peter Kalm. ... Translated into English By John Reinhold Forster, F.A.S. Enriched with a Map, several Cuts for the Illustration of Natural History, and Some additional Notes. *Warrington: and London.* MDCCLXX-LXXI.

3 *vols.*, 8*vo*, *pp.* *xvi.*, 400, (1); 352; *viii.*, 310, (14). *Map and* 6 *Plates.* *Half calf.* LARGE and FINE copy of the BEST EDITION. VERY SCARCE.

1116 KALM. Travels into North America. The Second Edition. *London: T. Lowndes.* 1772.

2 *vols.*, 8*vo*, *pp.* *xii.*, 414; *iv.*, 423, (8). *Map and* 6 *Plates.* *Half blue morocco, gilt top*, UNCUT, *by* BRADSTREET. BEAUTIFUL COPY.

"A valuable work as regards the Natural History, Geography and State of the Country at the time of the author's visit."

1117 KANE (E. K.) The U. S. Grinnell Expedition in Search of Sir John Franklin. A Personal Narrative. By Elisha Kent Kane, M.D. U.S.N. *New York: Harper & Brothers.* 1854.

8*vo*, *pp.* 552. 2 *Maps and* 12 *Plates.* *Many Wood-cuts.* *Half maroon morocco, gilt top*, UNCUT. An unlettered India proof PORTRAIT of the AUTHOR *inserted.*

1118 KANE. Arctic Explorations: the Second Grinnell Expedition in Search of Sir John Franklin, 1853, '54, '55. By Elisha Kent Kane, M.D. U.S N. Illustrated by upwards of Three Hundred Engravings, from Sketches by the Author. ... *Philadelphia: Childs & Peterson.* 1856.

2 *vols.*, 8*vo*, *pp.* 464; 467. *Half blue morocco, gilt top*, UNCUT.

1119 KAPP (F.) The Life of Frederick William Von Steuben. Major-General in the Revolutionary Army. By Frederick Kapp. With an Introduction by George Bancroft.
New York: Mason Brothers. 1859.

2 vols., 8vo, half green morocco, gilt top, UNCUT. AN ILLUSTRATED COPY. One volume extended to TWO, with RUBRICATED TITLES printed expressly for the work, and SIXTY-TWO ILLUSTRATIONS *inserted.*

1120 KAY (J.) A Series of Original Portraits and Caricature Etchings, by the late John Kay, Miniature Painter, Edinburgh. With Biographical Sketches and Illustrative Anecdotes.
Edinburgh: Hugh Paton. 1837–38.

2 vols., 4to, half calf. LARGE PAPER, with the list of Subscribers. BRILLIANT IMPRESSIONS of the THREE HUNDRED and FIFTY-SIX curious and expressive PLATES. VERY SCARCE in any form.

"The Works of John Kay illustrate an interesting epoch in the history of the Scottish Capital. Throughout the greater part of half a century this Artist devoted himself with enthusiasm to his novel undertaking; and while he contributed in no common degree to gratify and amuse the public of his own day, his graphic productions form a record which cannot fail to prove acceptable in after times, indeed this curious and valuable work forms a complete record of the public characters of every grade and kind, including many distinguished strangers, who made a figure in Edinburgh for nearly half a century."

1121 [KAY. A Series of Coloured Portraits of Remarkable Persons. By John Kay. *Edinburgh:* 1836.]

Sm. 4to, half calf. Ten coloured etchings. Published without a title page. VERY RARE. The *only copy* we have ever seen.

1122 KEITH (G.) The | Presbyterian and Independent | Visible Churches | in | New-England | And else-where, | Brought to the Test, and examined accor- | ding to the Doctrine of the holy Scriptures, | in their Doctrine, Ministry, Worship, Consti- | tution, Government, Sacraments and Sabbath | Day, and found to be No True Church of | Christ. | More particularly directed to these in New Eng- | land, and more generally to those in Old- | England, Scotland, Ireland, &c. | With | A Call and Warning from the Lord to the People | of Boston and New-England, to Repent, &c. And two | Letters to the Preachers in Boston; and an Answer to the | Gross Abuses, Lyes and Slanders of Increase Mather and | Samuel Norton, &c. | By George Keith. | *Philadelphia, Printed and Sold by* WILL. BRADFORD, | *Anno* 1689.

Sm. 8vo, pp. (12), 232. Blue morocco, gilt edges. EXCEEDINGLY RARE. One of the EARLIEST ISSUES of BRADFORD'S PRESS.

1123 KEITH. The Pretended | Antidote | Proved | Poyson: | Or, The true Principles of the Christian | & Protestant Religion Defended, | And the Four Counterfit Defenders | thereof Detected and Discovered; the | names of which are James Allen, Joshua | Moodey, Samuel Willard, and Cotten Mather, | who call themselves Ministers of the Gospel | in Boston, in their pretended Answer to my | Book called,

The Presbyterian & Independent | Visible Churches in New-England, and else- | where brought to the Test, &c. And G. K. | cleared not to be guilty of any Calumnies | against these so called Teachers of New-Eng- | land, &c. | By George Keith. | With an Appendix by John Delavall, by | way of Animadversion on some Passages in a | Discourse of Cotton Mathers before the ge- | neral Court of Massachusets, the 28th of the | Third Moneth 1690. | *Philadelphia, Printed by* WILL. BRADFORD, 1690.

Sm. 8vo, pp. (2), 224. *Crushed blue levant morocco, paneled sides, gilt edges, by* F. BEDFORD. BEAUTIFUL COPY of this MOST RARE VOLUME.

1124 KEITH. A | Serious Appeal | to all the more Sober, Impartial & Judicious People | in | Nevv-England | to whose Hands this may come, | Whether Cotton Mather in his late Address, &c. hath not | extreamly failed in proving the People call'd Quakers guilty | of manifold Heresies, Blasphemies and strong Delusions, | and whether he hath not much rather proved himself ex- | treamly Ignorant and greatly possessed with a Spirit of | Perversion, Error, Prejudice and envious Zeal against them | in general, and G. K. in particular, in his most uncharit- | able and rash Judgment against him, | Together with a Vindication of our | Christian Faith | In those Things Sincerely Believed by us, especially respect- | ing the Fundamental Doctrines and Principles of | Christian Religion. | By George Keith. | *Printed and Sold by* WILLIAM BRADFORD *at Philadelphia in Pennsyl- | vania, in the year* 1692.

Sm. 4to, pp. (4), 67. *Half calf.*
An EXTREMELY RARE piece in answer to Cotton Mather.

1125 KEITH. Truth and Innocency, Defended against Calumny and Defamation, in a late Report spread abroad Concerning the Revolution of Humane Souls, With a further Clearing of the Truth, by a plain Explication of my Sence, &c. By George Keith.
[*Philadelphia: William Bradford.* 1692.]

Sm. 4to, pp. 20. *Half blue morocco, gilt edges.*

For place, printer's name and date, see "*Books lately Printed, and to be Sold by William Bradford in Philadelphia,* 1692." at the end of "Some of the Fundamental Truths, &c." No. 1132.

1126 KEITH. A Testimony against That False and Absurd Opinion Which some hold, viz.: That all True Believers and Saints immediately after the Bodily Death attain to all the Resurrection they expect, and enter into the fullest Enjoyment of Happiness. And also That the Wicked, immediately after Death, are raised up to receive all the Punishment they are to expect. By George Keith.
[*Philadelphia: William Bradford.* 1692.]

Sm. 4to, pp. 12. *Half blue morocco.*
For place, printer and date, *see* as in the preceding No.

1127 [KEITH (George.) *and* BUDD (Thomas.)] An Appeal from the Twenty-eight Judges To The Spirit of Truth & true Judgment In all Faithful Friends, called Quakers, that meet at this Yearly Meeting at Burlington, the 7 month, 1692.

[*Philadelphia: William Bradford.* 1692.]

Sm. 4*to*, *half blue morocco*, EXTREMELY RARE. Signed by George Keith; Thomas Budd; and four others.

For place, printer, and date of publication see "*Books to be sold by William Bradford in Philadelphia*, 1692." at the end of "A True Copy of Three Judgements." No. 1133.

This book was printed at Philadelphia, in 1692, by *William Bradford*, for which he was imprisoned, upon the charge of "uttering and spreading a malicious and seditious paper." His tools and type were taken away from him, and this was the beginning of the persecution which afterwards drove him, with his printing, from Philadelphia to New York, in 1693. For an account of his arrest and committal to prison, evidently written by himself, see the POSTSCRIPT at the end of this tract.

1128 [KEITH *and* BUDD.] The Plea of The Innocent Against the False Judgment of the Guilty. Being a Vindication of George Keith and his Friends, who are joyned with him in this present Testimony, from the False Judgment, Calumnies, False Informations and Defamations of Samuell Jenings, John Simcock, Thomas Lloyd, and others joyned with them, being in Number Twenty-Eight. Directed by way of Epistle to faithful Friends of Truth in Pennsilvania, East and West-Jarsey, and else-where, as Occasion requireth.

[*Philadelphia: William Bradford.* 1692.]

Sm. 4*to*, *pp.* 24. *Half blue morocco.* Signed by George Keith, and Thomas Budd.

For imprint, see list of "*Books, etc.*," at the end of "Some of the Fundamental Truths, &c.," above referred to.

1129 [KEITH.] The | Christian Faith | of the People of God, called in Scorn, | Quakers | in Rhode-Island (who are in Unity with all faithfull Brethren | of the same Profession in all parts of the World) | Vindicated | From the Calumnies of Christian Lodewick, that formerly | was of that Profession, but is lately fallen therefrom. | As also from the base Forgeries, and wicked Slanders of | Cotton Mather, called a Minister at Boston, who hath greatly | commended the said Christian Lodewick, and approved his false | Charges against us, and hath added thereunto many gross, | impudent and vile Calumnies against us and our Brethren, in his | late Address, so called, to some in New-England, the which in | due time may receive a more full answer, to discover his Igno- | rance, Prejudice and Perversion against our Friends in gene- | ral and G. K. in particular, whom he hath most unworthily | abused. | To which is added some Testimonies of our Antient | Friends to the | true Christ of God; | &c. ... | *Printed and Sold by* WILLIAM BRADFORD at *Philadelphia in Pennsyl-* | *vania, in the Year* 1692.

Sm. 4*to*, *pp.* 16. *Calf, gilt edges.* EXTREMELY RARE. Signed by George Keith, and twelve others.

The "Testimonies," which fill eight pages, are signed by Will. Bradford. Unnoticed in Smith's *Quaker Bibliography*.

1130 [KEITH *and* BUDD.] False Judgements Reprehended: And A Just Reproof to Tho. Everndon, And his Associates and Fellow-Travellers, For the false and rash Judgement T. E. gave against G. K. and his faithful Friends and Brethren, at the public Meeting at Philadelphia the 27. of 10. Mon. 1692. .... [Signed, George Keith, Thomas Budd.]

[Also:] A brief Answer to two Papers procured from Friends in Maryland, the one concerning Thomas Budd's favouring John Lyman &c. the other concerning his owning George Keith's Principles and Doctrines. [Signed by Thomas Budd.]

Printed [by William Bradford at Philadelphia.] in the Year 1692.

Sm. 4*to*, *pp.* 8, 4. *Half blue morocco.* The imprint is at the end of the tract.
Not in Smith's *Bibliography.*

1131 [KEITH.] Some Reasons and Causes of the Late Seperation that hath come to pass at Philadelphia betwixt us, called by some the Seperate Meeting, and Others that meet apart from us. More particularly opened to Vindicate and Clear us and our Testimony in that respect, viz: That the Seperation lyeth at their Door, and They (and not We) are justly chargeable with it. With An Account of our Sincere Christian Faith. [*Philadelphia: William Bradford.* 1692.]

Sm. 4*to*, *pp.* 36. *Half blue morocco.*

For imprint see list of "*Books, etc.,*" at the end of "Some of the Fundamental Truths, &c.," referred to above.

1132 KEITH. Some of the Fundamental Truths of Christianity. Briefly hinted at, by Way of Question and Answer. With a Postscript by the Author G. K. The Third Edition.

[*Philadelphia: William Bradford.* 1692.]

Sm. 4*to*, *pp.* 15, (1). *Half blue morocco.*

At the end of this VERY RARE tract is a list of "*Books lately Printed and to be Sold by William Bradford in Philadelphia,* 1692."
Not in Smith's *Bibliography.*

1133 [KEITH.] A True Copy of three Judgements given forth by a Party of Men, called Quakers at Philadelphia, against George Keith and his Friends. With two Answers to the said Judgements. [Also:] An Expostulation with Samuell Jenings, Thomas Lloyd and the rest of the twenty-eight Unjust Judges &c. ... [Signed by Thomas Budd, William Bradford, and five others.]

[*Philadelphia: William Bradford.* 1692.]

Sm. 4*to*, *pp.* 9, 7, (1). *Half blue morocco.* VERY RARE.

At the end of this tract, which is unnoticed in Smith's *Bibliography*, occurs "*Books to be Sold by William Bradford in Philadelphia.* 1692." in which, and in the list referred to in the preceding number, nearly all the untitled and undated books printed by Bradford, and in this catalogue, will be found. In addition to the interesting Book-list with its prices ranging from 4 *d.* to 9 *d.* per volume, there is the following curious note concluding the final page.

"And whereas it is reported, That the Printer being a favourer of G. K. he will not print for any other, which is the reason that the other Party appear not in print as well as G. K. These are to signifie, that the Printer hath not yet refused to print any thing for either Party, and also signifies that he doth not refuse, but is willing and ready to print anything for the future that G. K's Opposers shall bring to him."

1134 [KEITH.] The | Heresie and Hatred | Which was falsely Charged upon the | Innocent | Justly returned upon the | Guilty. | Giving some brief and impartial Account of the most ma- | terial Passages of a late Dispute in Writing, that hath | passed at Philadelphia betwixt | John Delavall and George Keith, | With some intermixt Remarks and Observations on | the whole. | *Printed and Sold by* WILLIAM BRADFORD *at Philadelphia, Anno Dom.* 1693.

Sm. 4to, pp. 22, (1). *Calf, gilt edges, by* F. BEDFORD. A BEAUTIFUL COPY nearly UNCUT. Signed George Keith at end. MOST RARE.

On the last page occurs the following curious and suggestive notice.

"THE PRINTERS ADVERTISEMENT. That notwithstanding the various Reports spread concerning my refusing to Print for those that are George Keith's Opposers, These are to Signifie. That I have never refused, but often proffered to Print anything for them, and do now again signifie, that if John Delavall or any other of his Brethern have any thing to print, I am most willing to do it for them; not that I want to beg their Work, I need it not, but to leave them without Excuse, that if they be any way wronged or falsely charged by what is published in Print to the World, they may have equal priviledge to Vindicate themselves as Publickly; though I have little cause to make this offer to them, considering their many Abuses to me."—W. B.

1135 [KEITH.] New-England's Spirit of Persecution | Transmitted To | Pennsilvania, And the Pretended Quaker found Persecuting the True | Christian-Quaker, | In the | Tryal | Of | Peter Boss, George Keith, Thomas Budd, | and William Bradford, | At the Sessions held at Philadelphia the Nineth, Tenth and | Twelfth Days of December, 1692. Giving an Account | of the most Arbitrary Proceedure of that Court. | *Printed [by William Bradford] in the Year* 1693.

Sm. 4to. Title. pp. 38. *Calf, gilt top,* UNCUT. A BEAUTIFUL COPY, and of EXTREME RARITY.

In a note to the *only copy* of this book which has ever been sold in New York (in 1845) it is claimed that this is the FIRST BOOK PRINTED IN NEW YORK. In the following note, its present owner has, we think, settled the question in favour of Philadelphia.

Doubts have been entertained whether this volume was really printed at Philadelphia, on the ground that the printer having suffered imprisonment for printing and publishing "An Appeal" would not likely have ventured to issue a work of this character there and thereby subject himself to a probable recurrence of farther difficulty with the Authorities. It has been surmised that the tract might have been printed at New York, but in that case Bradford could have had no possible reason for withholding his name from the title page. On the other hand, our printer, having been discharged from arrest and had his press restored to him by Gov. Fletcher on the sole ground of his having been imprisoned for "a religious difference," could not have had any misgivings whatever respecting the publication of a bare recital of the trial and its attendant circumstances, with its present imprint. Nor was one of his resolute character, smarting under what he conceived to be an outrage and a wrong, likely to suspend its publication during the five months which elapsed between the termination of his trial, and his settlement at New York.

It is a tract of the greatest possible rarity; of much historical interest in connexion with the earliest efforts to establish the press in the middle colonies; and gives a very curious and

30

interesting insight into the social economy and manners of the early Quaker settlers in Pennsylvania; as well as some account of Printers and Printing at the time.

The following is a reprint.

1136 [KEITH.] The | Tryals | of | Peter Boss, George Keith, | Thomas Budd, and William Bradford, | Quakers, | For several Great Misdemeanours | (As was pretended by their Adversaries) | before | A Court of Quakers: | At the Sessions held at *Philadelphia, in* | *Pensylvania*, the Ninth Tenth and | Twelfth Days of December, 1692. | Giving also an Account of the most Arbitrary Pro- | ceedure of that Court. | *Printed first Beyond-Sea, and now Reprinted in London for* | *Richard Baldwin.* 1693.

Sm. 4*to*, *pp.* 34. *Calf, gilt edges.* FINE COPY. EXCEEDINGLY RARE.

1137 KEITH. A Refutation of a dangerous and hurtful Opinion maintained by Mr. Samuell Willard, an Independent Minister at Boston, and President at the Commencement in Cambridge in New England, July 1, 1702. ... Sent to him in Latin soon after the Commencement, and since Translated into English. By George Keith, M.A. [*New York: William Bradford.* 1702.]

Sm. 4*to*, *pp.* 7. *Half blue morocco.* FINE COPY. VERY RARE.

"Writ at Boston in N. England the 2d day of July, 1702. and after some time sent in Latine to Mr. Willard, by G. K."— *Work.* p. 7.

See on same page, an announcement of the two following tracts as being in the press. This tract was evidently not seen by Mr. Smith, who gives a fragment only of the title.

1138 KEITH. A | Reply to Mr. Increase Mather's | Printed Remarks | on a | Sermon | Preached by G. K. at Her Majesty's Chappel | in Boston, the 14th of June, 1702. In Vindication of the Six good Rules in | Divinity there delivered. | Which he hath attempted (though very Feebly and Unsuc- | cessfully) to Refute. | By George Keith, M.A. | *Printed and Sold by* WILLIAM BRADFORD *at the Bible in* | *New-York*, 1703.

Sm. 4*to*, *pp.* 35. *Calf, gilt edges, by* HAYDAY. A BEAUTIFUL COPY, and of GREAT RARITY.

Apparently not seen by Mr. Smith who gives five words only of the title.

1139 KEITH. The | Spirit | of | Railing Shimei | and of | Baal's Four Hundred Lying Prophets | Entered into | Caleb Pusey | and his | Quaker-Brethren in Pennsilvania, | who Approve him. Containing an Answer to his and their Book, falsly | called, Proteus Ecclesiasticus, Detecting many of their gross | Falshoods, Lyes, Calumnies, Perversions and Abuses, as well | as his and their gross Ignorance and Infidelity contained in | their said Book. | By George Keith, A.M. | *Printed and Sold by* WILLIAM BRADFORD *at the Sign of the Bible* | *in New York:* 1703.

Sm. 4*to*, *pp.* (6) 61. *Calf, gilt edges.* FINE COPY. VERY RARE.

Dedicated to His Excellency Coll. Francis Nicholson, Her Majesties Lieut. and Governour General of the Dominion of Virginia.

1140 [KEITH *and* EVANS (Evan.)] Some of the many false, scandalous, blasphemous, & self-contradictory Assertions of William Davis, faithfully collected out of his Book, printed Anno 1700. entituled, Jesus the Crucified Man, the Eternal Son of God, &c. in exact quotations word for word, without adding or diminishing. [*New York: William Bradford.* 1703.]

Sm. 4to, pp. 12. *Half blue morocco.* Dated at Philadelphia, the 26th of March, 1703. Signed by George Keith, and Evan Evans.

This rare tract is wholly occupied by Keith's account of his public recantation from, and denouncement of Quakerism, under the patronage, and protection of the Rev. Evan Evans, the then Minister of Christ Church, and Rector of Philadelphia. The proceedings became so turbulent, that Keith and his newly acquired friends, were turned out of the Meeting-house in which they assembled, into the street; while the Quaker mayor, William Shippen, fearing a breach of the peace, sent "the constable" also a quaker, "with his constables staff" to disperse them, which he did; an act that caused much animadversion at the time.

1141 KEITH. The | Power | of the | Gospel in the | Conversion of Sinners | in a | Sermon | Preach'd at | Annapolis In Maryland. | By George Keith M.A. | July the 4th | *Printed and are to be Sold by Thomas Reading,* | *at the Sign of tho (Sic) George Anno Domini.* MDCCIII.

Sm. 4to, pp. (1), 19. *Half morocco.* VERY RARE.

There was no press at Annapolis until 1726. Before that time the colony printing was done at Philadelphia and New York by W. Bradford. *See* Thomas, *Hist. of Printing.* II. 127.

1142 KEITH. The Notes of the | True Church | With the Application of them to the | Church of England, | And the great Sin of Separation from Her. | Delivered in A | Sermon | Preached at | Trinity Church in New-York, | Before the Administration of the holy Sacrament | of the Lord's Supper. | The 7th of November, 1703. | By George Keith, M.A. | *Printed and Sold by* WILLIAM BRADFORD *at the Sign of the Bible* | *in New-York,* 1704.

Sm. 4to, pp. (8), 20. *Calf, gilt edges, by* HAYDAY. FINE COPY. EXCEEDINGLY RARE.

1143 KEITH. The great Necessity & Use | of the | Holy Sacraments | of | Baptism & the Lord's Supper, | delivered in a | Sermon | preached at | Trinity-Church in New-York, | the 28th of November, 1703 | by George Keith, M.A. | *Printed and Sold by* WILLIAM BRADFORD *at the Sign of the Bible* | *New York,* 1704.

Sm. 4to, pp. 24. *Calf, gilt edges, by* HAYDAY. FINE COPY, and of GREAT RARITY.

1144 KEITH. An | Answer | to Mr. Samuell Willard | (One of the Ministers at Boston in New-England) | his | Reply | To my Printed Sheet, called, A Dangerous and | hurtful Opinion maintained by him, viz. | That the Fall of Adam, and all the Sins of Men necessarily | come to pass by virtue of Gods Decree, and his Determin- | ing both of the Will of Adam, and of all other Men to | sin. | By George Keith, M.A. | *Printed and Sold by* WILLIAM BRADFORD *at the Sign of the Bible* | *in New-York,* 1704.

Sm. 4to, 2 l., pp. 41. Polished calf, gilt edges, by HAYDAY. *Fine copy.* VERY RARE.

Dedicated to His Excellency Edward Viscount Cornbury Captain General and Governour in Chief in and over Her Majesties Provinces of New-York, and New-Jersey, &c.

1145 [KEITH.] Some brief Remarks upon a late Book entituled "George Keith once more brought to the Test, &c.," having the name of Caleb Pusey at the end of the Preface and C. P. at the end of the Book. [*New York: William Bradford.* 1704.]

Sm. 4to, pp. 20. Half blue morocco. MOST RARE.

Dated March 2, 1704, and signed George Keith.

At the end of the tract is a certificate signed by William Bradford respecting the manner of his discharge from arrest by Gov. Fletcher. A great part of the volume is occupied with that subject.

1146 KEITH. A | Journal | of | Travels | from | New-Hampshire | to Caratuck, | on the Continent of | North-America. By George Keith, A.M. | Late Missionary from the Society for the Pro- | pagation of the Gospel in Foreign Parts; and | now Rector of Edburton, in Sussex. | *London: | Printed by Joseph Downing, for Brab. Aylmer, at the Three-Pigeons | over-against the Royal-Exchange in Cornhill,* 1706.

Sm. 4to, pp. (4), 92. *Red morocco, gilt edges, by* F. BEDFORD. LARGE and ELEGANT COPY. SCARCE.

Page 89 contains an "Account of the several Treatises" written and published "in print, in North America," by George Keith, "within the time of his abode there, in the years 1702 and 1703 to 1704." The list mentions nine printed sermons and controversial tracts, principally anti-Quaker. Mather, Willard, Pusey and others wrote in reply. A complete set of these ten, bound in one volume, was presented to the Society for the Propagation of the Gospel. Keith had to get his answer to Mather printed in New York, "the Boston printer not daring to offend the independent preachers there."

1147 KEITH (I. S.) National Affliction, and National Consolation! A Sermon, on the Death of General George Washington, ... delivered on the Twelfth of January, One Thousand Eight Hundred, ... in Charleston, South Carolina. By Isaac Stockton Keith, D.D. ... *Charleston:* 1800.

8vo, pp. 30. RARE.

1148 KEITH (*Sir* W.) The | History | of the | British Plantations in America, | With | A Chronological Account of the most remarkable | Things, which happen'd to the first Adventurers | in their several Discoveries of that New World. | Part I. | Containing the History of Virginia; with Remarks on the | Trade and Commerce of that Colony. | By Sir William Keith, Bart. | *London:* M.DCC.XXXVIII.

4to, pp. (8), 187. 2 *Maps. Green morocco, gilt edges.* A SPLENDID SPOTLESS, and LARGE COPY. *Very Scarce.*

"The first of an intended series of Colonial Histories, which was not continued. Sir William Keith was Governor of Pennsylvania from 1717 to 1726. The work was printed at the expence of the Society for the Encouragement of Learning."

1149 KELLY (J.) A Complete Collection of Scotish Proverbs Explained and made Intelligible to the English Reader. By James Kelly, M. A. *London: William and John Innys.* 1721.

8vo, pp. (14), 400, (18). *Half morocco. Fine copy.* RARE *and Curious.*

1150 KEMP. (J.) A Sermon Delivered in Christ Church, Cambridge, in Maryland, on the Twenty-second of February, 1800, ... on the Death of General George Washington. ... By James Kemp, A.M. ... *Easton:* [1800.]

8vo, pp. 15. UNCUT. *Very Scarce.*

1151 KENDALL (J.) A Discourse Delivered at Plymouth, February 22d, 1800, at the request of the Inhabitants, ... as a Testimony of Grief for the Death of George Washington, ... who Died Dec. 14, 1799. By James Kendall, A.M. ... *Boston:* 1800.

8vo, pp. 24. UNCUT.

1152 KENNEDY (P.) An Answer to Paine's Letter to General Washington: Including Some Pages of Gratuitous Counsel to Mr. Erskine. By P. Kennedy, Esq.
Philadelphia: Republished by William Cobbett. Jan. 1798.

8vo, pp. 42. *Half green morocco, gilt top.* Rare and curious contemporary engraved FRONTISPIECE *inserted.* VERY SCARCE.

See Paine (Thomas.) No. 1541.

1153 [KENNETT (White.)] Bibliotheca Americanæ Primordia. An Attempt towards laying the Foundation of an American Library, in several Books, Papers, and Writings, humbly given to the Society for Propagation of the Gospel in Foreign Parts, for the perpetual Use and Benefit of their Members, their Missionaries, Friends, Correspondents and Others concern'd in the Good Design of Planting and promoting Christianity within her Majesty's Colonies and Plantations in the West-Indies. By a Member of the said Society.
London: Printed for J. Churchill. 1713.

4to, pp. (2), *xvi., iii.*, 275, (224). *Half purple levant morocco.* LARGE PAPER; measuring 9¼ inches by 8⅛ inches on the leaf. Scarce PORTRAIT of the AUTHOR *inserted.* RARE. The ONLY COPY we have ever seen on large paper.

"In this catalogue will be found about twenty original tracts relating to Newfoundland; above fifty concerning Virginia; one hundred, or more, of New England: and so on in proportion to the other colonies." — *Preface.*

"This, as far as it goes, is the best Catalogue of Books relating to America extant, the titles being copied at full length with the greatest exactness, together with name of the printer, and the number of pages in each volume. It unfortunately contains only the books given to the society by White Kennett, Bishop of Peterborough. It is rich in English tracts relating to New England."— *Rich.*

The collection which it refers to has disappeared — some scattered and neglected remains of it, were found a few years since among the archives of the Society at Lambeth.

1154 KETTELL (S.) Specimens of American Poetry, with Critical and Biographical Notices. By Samuel Kettell.
Boston: S. G. Goodrich. MDCCCXXIX.

3 *vols.*, 12*mo, half blue morocco.*

This collection embraces specimens of the poetry of 188 American Poets, beginning with Cotton Mather, and ending with J. G. Whittier. The third volume contains a bibliographical and chronological list of American poets.

1155 [KIDD (William.)] A Full Account of the Proceedings In Relation to Capt. Kidd. In two Letters. Written by a Person of Quality to a Kinsman of the Earl of Bellomont in Ireland.
London: Printed and Sold by the Booksellers of London and Westminster. MDCCI.

Sm. 4to, pp, (8), 51. *Half calf.* Fine copy. VERY SCARCE.

"No unimportant man has caused more fear, speculation, and gold-digging, than Captain Kidd. Along the shores of New England and Long Island, from his day to this, men have dug in the dead of night, directed, as they thought, by the witch hazel or the divining-rod, to find his buried gold, and none have found it. 'The Pirate Kidd' was long a bugbear to frighten children, and a name to arouse the cupidity of men."— *C. W. Elliott's New-England History.*

1156 [KIDD.] The Arraignment, Tryal and Condemnation of Captain William Kidd, for Murther and Piracy upon six several indictments, at the Admiralty-Sessions, at the Old-Bailey. On Thursday the 8th, and Friday the 9th, of May, 1701.
London: Jonathan Robinson. 1703.

Sm. 8vo, (pp. 27). Half morocco. VERY SCARCE.

Extracted from "An Exact Abridgement of all the Tryals ... relating to High Treasons, Piracies, &c." published at London as above.

Captain Kidd was employed by the Earl of Bellomont, to act against the pirates who infested the North American coast in 1696, but turned pirate himself. He was afterwards taken at Boston, sent to England, tried, and hung with several others.

1157 KIDDER (F.) Military Operations in Eastern Maine and Nova Scotia during the Revolution, chiefly compiled from the Journals and Letters of Colonel John Allan, with Notes and a Memoir of Col. John Allan. By Frederic Kidder. *Albany: Joel Munsell.* 1867.

Roy. 8vo, pp. x., 336. Map. Half green morocco, gilt top, UNCUT, *by* BRADSTREET.

"This narrative of the sufferings and devotion of a Revolutionary hero, hitherto but little known to the people whose cause he espoused, is entirely devoted to the minutiæ of seven years' residence among the Micmacs, Maracheets, Passammaquody, and Penobscot Indians, during which he acted as their chief or superintendent, and influenced their neutrality during the conflict."— *Field.*

1158 KIDDER. History of the First New Hampshire Regiment in the War of the Revolution. By Frederic Kidder.
Albany: J. Munsell. 1868.

8vo, half red morocco, gilt top, UNCUT, *by* W. SMITH. PORTRAIT *inserted.*

The first history of a Revolutionary Regiment that has been written.

1159 KING (C.) A Memoir of the Construction, Cost, and Capacity of the Croton Aqueduct, compiled from official documents: together with an account of the Civic Celebration on the Fourteenth of October, 1842, on occasion of the Completion of the Great Work; preceded by a Preliminary Essay on Ancient and Modern Aqueducts. By Charles King. *New York:* 1843.

4to, half calf. Printed for private distribution. SCARCE.

1160 KING (J.) Thoughts on the Difficulties and Distresses in which the Peace of 1783, has involved the People of England; on the Present Disposition of the English, Scots and Irish, to Emigrate to America; and on the Hazard they run (without certain Precautions) of rendering their Condition more Deplorable. ... By John King. With an Appendix. The Sixth Edition. *London: T. Davies.* 1783.

8vo, pp. 71. *Half morocco.*

The appendix contains an account of Col. Edmund Fanning the notorious Long Island Tory.

1161 KING (W.) A Discourse Delivered in Chelsea, in the City of Norwich, Jan. 5, 1800, as a Token of Humiliation before God, on account of the Death of Gen. George Washington. ... By Walter King. ... *Norwich:* 1800.

8vo, pp. 22. UNCUT. VERY RARE.

1162 KINKER (J.) Treurzang, bij het plechtig vieren der Nagedachtenis van Washington, en de maatschappij van verdiensten felix meritis, Den 21 Maart 1800. Uitgesproken doo Mr. Johannes Kinker, ... *Te Amsterdam, bij. J. ten Bruck.* 1800.

8vo, 18 *leaves.* Engraved Frontispiece. One of the RAREST of its class.

1163 KINLOCH (F.) Eulogy on George Washington. By Francis Kinloch Of Georgetown, S. C. *New York: Privately Printed.* 1867.

Roy. 8vo, pp. 19. *Half green morocco, gilt top,* UNCUT. Sixty copies only privately reprinted. INDIA PROOF PORTRAIT *inserted.*

A reprint of a supposed unique original printed at Georgetown, S. C. in 1800.

1164 KIP (W. I.) The Early Jesuit Missions in North America: Compiled and Translated from the Letters of the French Jesuits, with Notes. By the Rev. William Ingraham Kip, M.A. *New York: Wiley and Putnam.* 1846.

12mo, pp. xiv., (4), 321. *Half red morocco, gilt top.*

1165 [KIP (W. I.)] The Olden Time in New York. By a Member of the New York Genealogical and Biographical Society. I. New York Society in Olden Time. II. Traces of American Lineage in England. *New York: G. P. Putnam & Sons,* 1872.

4to, pp. 64. *Half polished green levant morocco, gilt top,* UNCUT, *by* W. MATTHEWS. A few copies only printed. TWENTY-ONE FINE ILLUSTRATIONS *inserted,* embracing NINE INDIA PROOFS, some BEFORE LETTERS; and several PRIVATE PLATES.

A CHOICE and BEAUTIFUL VOLUME, by the BISHOP of CALIFORNIA.

1166 KIRKLAND (J. T.) A Discourse occasioned by the Death of General George Washington. Delivered Dec. 29, 1799. By John Thornton Kirkland. ... To which is added the Valedictory Address of the late President, to the People of the United States. *Boston:* 1800.

8vo, pp. 22, 22. UNCUT.

1167 KLOSE (C. L.) Memoirs of Prince Charles Stuart, (Count of Albany,) Commonly called the Young Pretender; with Notices of the Rebellion in 1745. By Charles Louis Klose. ... Second Edition. *London: Henry Colburn.* 1846.

2 vols., 8vo, half green morocco, gilt top, UNCUT. Uniform with Jesse's Works, *supra.*

1168 KNAPP (S. L.) The Life of Thomas Eddy; Comprising an extensive Correspondence with many of the most Distinguished Philosophers and Philanthropists of this and other Countries. By Samuel L. Knapp. ... *New York: Conner & Cooke.* 1834.

8vo, half calf, UNCUT. PORTRAIT *inserted.* SCARCE.

1169 KNAPP. The Life of Aaron Burr. By Samuel L. Knapp. *New York: Wiley & Long.* 1835.

12mo, pp. 290. *Half green morocco.* TWO PORTRAITS *inserted.*

1170 KNIGHT (C.) William Caxton, the First English Printer. A Biography. By Charles Knight. *London: Charles Knight and Co.* 1844.

12mo, half olive morocco, gilt top, UNCUT.

1171 KNIGHT. The Old Printer and the Modern Press. By Charles Knight. *London: John Murray.* 1854.

Sm. 8vo, half olive morocco, gilt top, UNCUT.

"The Father of Printing could not have found a more suitable or a more enthusiastic biographer."—*Patriot.*

1172 KNIGHT. The English Cyclopædia. Conducted by Charles Knight. BIOGRAPHY. [Volumes I. to VI. Complete.] *London: Bradbury and Evans.* 1856.

4to, 6 vols. bound in 3, half blue morocco, gilt top, UNCUT.

1173 KNIGHT (Sarah Kemble.) The Journals of Madam Knight, and Rev. Mr. Buckingham. From the Original Manuscripts written in 1704 and 1710. *New York: Wilder & Campbell.* 1825.

Sm. 8vo, pp. 129. *Half red morocco, gilt top,* UNCUT. A fine copy of the FIRST EDITION, now VERY SCARCE.

Mad. Knight's Journal consists of an account of a journey from Boston to New York in the year 1704. That of the Rev. Mr. Buckingham of the Expedition against Canada in 1710 and 1711.

1174 KNIGHT. Journal of Madam Knight. *Philadelphia.* [*n. d.*]

4to, half red morocco, gilt top, UNCUT. Cut from "Littell's Living Age;" and mounted on ruled paper with a composite title page, in MR. TRENT's neatest manner. Contains nine columns of introductory matter not in the original work.

1175 KNOX (J.) An Historical Journal of the Campaigns in North-America, for The Years 1757, 1758, 1759 and 1760: containing The Most Remarkable Occurrences of that Period; particularly The Two Sieges of Quebec, &c. &c. ... By Captain John Knox. *London: Printed for the Author.* MDCCLXIX.

2 vols., 4to, pp. (16), 405, (1); (1), 465, (1). *Map and 2 Portraits. Half green levant morocco, gilt top,* UNCUT, *by* BRADSTREET. BEAUTIFUL COPY. VERY SCARCE in *uncut* condition.

"A very valuable collection of materials towards a History of our Late War, and Conquests in America, as well as for a Description and Natural History of the Country, in which this attentive and industrious author personally served; and the best original authority for the death of Wolfe and the Conquest of Canada."— *M. Review.*

1176 KOHL (J. G.) A Popular History of the Discovery of America, from Columbus to Franklin. By J. G. Kohl. Translated from the German by Major R. R. Noel. *London: Chapman and Hall.* 1862.

2 vols., sm. 8vo, half red morocco, gilt top, UNCUT, *by* BRADSTREET. PORTRAITS of JACQUES CARTIER and VESPUCIUS *inserted.*

1177 [KOOP (M.)] Historical Account of the Substances which have been used to describe Events, and to convey Ideas, from the earliest date to the Invention of Paper. Printed on the First Useful Paper manufactured solely from Straw. *London:* 1800.

Roy. 8vo, half calf. Fine large copy. Eighty-two pages printed on STRAW PAPER, with an appendix printed on paper made from WOOD, the first example of paper so made.

1178 LAHONTAN (*Baron.*) New Voyages to North-America. Containing An Account of the several Nations of that vast Continent; their Customs, Commerce, and Way of Navigation upon the Lakes and Rivers; the several Attempts of the English and French to dispossess one another; with the Reasons of the Miscarriage of the former; ... A Geographical Description of Canada, and a Natural History of the Country, with Remarks upon their Government, and the Interest of the English and French in their Commerce. Also a Dialogue between the Author and a General of the Savages, giving a full View of the Religion and strange Opinions of those People: ... To which is added, A Dictionary of the Algonkine Language, which is generally spoke in North-America. Illustrated with Twenty-three Maps and Cuts. Written in French by the Baron Lahontan, ... Done into English. The Second Edition. A great Part of which never Printed in the Original. *London: John Brindley.* 1735.

2 vols., 8vo, pp. (24), 280; 304. 23 *Plates. Half gray calf antique.* FINE CLEAN COPY.

"Becoming intimate with the Indians, La Hontan formed the plan of an Expedition to the eastern regions beyond the Mississippi, *and was the first person* to make known, by communication from the Indians, the existence of the Rocky Mountains, the Columbia River, and the Ocean, or 'Great Salt Lake.'"— *Murray.*

1179 LAFAYETTE (*Marquis.* de) Epistle from the Marquis de Lafayette to General Washington. *Edinburgh: Mundell & Son.* 1800.

8vo, pp. (2), 32. UNCUT. EXCEEDINGLY RARE. The ONLY COPY seen by Dr. Hough.

This rare Poetical Piece was written during the lifetime of General Washington, but was not printed until after his death.

1180 [LAING (William *and* David.)] Select Remains of the Ancient Popular Poetry of Scotland. [Edited by William and David Laing. With Notes, Dissertations and an Appendix.]
Printed at Edinburgh: MDCCCXXII.

4to, green morocco super extra, gilt edges, by CLARKE *and* BEDFORD. AN ELEGANT COPY. VERY RARE. 108 copies only PRIVATELY PRINTED, all but 27 of which were destroyed by Fire.

Most of the pieces in this volume are in no other collection.

1181 LALLEMANT (H.) Lettres Envoiées de la Novvelle France au R. P. Iacqves Renavlt Prouincial de la Compagnie de Iesvs en la Prouince de la France, par le R. P. Hier. Lallemant Superieur des Missions de la dite Compagnie en ce nouueau Monde.
A Paris, Chez Sebastien Cramoisy, M.DC.LX.

Sm. 8vo, pp. 49, (3). *Brown morocco, paneled sides, gilt edges.* A FEW COPIES ONLY reprinted for Mr. James Lenox, all for presents. PRESENTATION COPY to the Baron Sobolewski.

1182 LAMB (R.) An Original and Authentic Journal of Occurrences during the late American War, from its Commencement to the year 1783. By R. Lamb, late Sergeant in the Royal Welsh Fuzileers.
Dublin: 1809.

8vo, pp. xxiv., 438. *Half calf, gilt top,* UNCUT. VERY SCARCE in this condition. This FINE COPY has the PLAN at page 158 which is often wanting.

1183 LAMB. Memoir of His Own Life, by R. Lamb, formerly a Sergeant in the Royal Welsh Fuzileers. *Dublin:* 1811.

8vo, pp. 296. *Half calf, gilt top,* UNCUT. FINE COPY and VERY SCARCE in *uncut* condition. Uniform with the preceding No.

1184 LANDAIS (P.) The Second Part of the Memorial to Justify Peter Landais' Conduct, during the Late War.
New York: Samuel Loudon. [1787?]

4to, pp. 52. *Half red morocco, gilt top,* UNCUT. COLOURED PHOTOGRAPH of LANDAIS *inserted.*

A Tract of EXTREME RARITY. The author, a native of France, was appointed by Congress captain of the frigate Alliance, the finest vessel then in its service. He was with Paul Jones in the memorable action between the Serapis and the Bon Homme Richard, was dismissed from the service for questionable conduct in that affair, and wrote this in answer to "Charges and Proofs respecting the conduct of Peter Landais." For nearly forty years he continued to press his claim for restoration to rank, during which time he resided in this city and was well known to most of its inhabitants.

1185 LANGDON (C.) An Oration on the Virtues and Death of Gen. Geo. Washington, ... delivered at Castleton, February 22d, 1800, By Chauncy Langdon. ... *Rutland:* [1800.]

8vo, pp. 24. UNCUT and RARE.

1186 [LANGWORTHY (Edward.)] Memoirs of the Life of the late Charles Lee, Esq., ... Second in Command in the Service of the United States of America during the Revolution: to which are

added his Political and Military Essays, also, Letters to, and from many Distinguished Characters, both in Europe and America.
London: J. S. Jordan. 1792.

8vo, pp. xii., 439. *Half calf*, UNCUT. PORTRAIT *inserted.* SCARCE.

1187 [LANGWORTHY.] Anecdotes of the late Charles Lee Esq. ... Second Edition. With an Appendix of Additional Papers and Letters.
London: J. S. Jordan. 1797.

8vo, pp. xii., 446. *Half calf.* LARGE and FINE COPY. SCARCE.

Contains many curious particulars relating to the War between Great Britain and her Colonies.

1188 LANMAN (J. H.) History of Michigan, Civil and Topographical, in a Compendious Form; with a View of the Surrounding Lakes. By James H. Lanman. With a Map.
New York: E. French. 1839.

8vo, pp. xvi., 398. *Map. Calf, red edges.* LARGE and FINE COPY.

1189 LA ROCHE-HÉRON (C. de) Les Servantes de Dieu en Canada. Essai sur l'Histoire des Communautes Religieuses de Femmes de la Province. Edition Revue, Corrigée, Augmentée et Spécialmente Préparée pour le Canada. Par C. De Laroche-Héron.
Montreal: 1855.

8vo, pp. 158, (1). *Half green morocco, gilt top.* VERY SCARCE.

1190 LATHROP (J.) INNOCENT BLOOD CRYING TO GOD FROM THE STREETS OF BOSTON. A Sermon occasioned by the Horrid Murder of Messieurs Samuel Gray, Samuel Maverick, James Caldwell, and Crispus Attucks, with Patrick Carr, since dead, and Christopher Monk, judged irrecoverable, and several others badly wounded, by a Party of Troops under the Command of Captain Preston: on the Fifth of March, 1770, and preached on the Lord's-Day following: By John Lathrop, A.M. *London: E. and C. Dilly.* MDCCLXX.

4to, pp. 22. *Half red morocco, gilt top*, UNCUT. A FINE CLEAN COPY of one of the RAREST VOLUMES relating to the BOSTON MASSACRE.

1191 LATOUR (*Major* A. L.) Historical Memoir of the War in West Florida and Louisiana in 1814–15. With an Atlas. By Major A. Lacarriere Latour. ... Written originally in French, and Translated for the Author, by H. P. Nugent, Esq.
Philadelphia: John Conrad and Co. 1816.

2 *vols., 8vo, pp. xx.*, 264, *cxc. Portrait and* 8 *Maps. Half crushed green levant morocco, gilt top*, UNCUT, *by* W. MATTHEWS. An ELEGANT COPY of this VERY SCARCE work. Two PORTRAITS *inserted.* The second volume contains the 8 maps alone.

"Major Latour's narrative of the military events is minute and interesting, and the appendix contains an invaluable collection of state papers."— *N. A. Review.*

1192 LATROBE (J. H. B.) The History of Mason and Dixon's Line; contained in an Address, delivered by John H. B. Latrobe, of Maryland, before the Historical Society of Pennsylvania, November 8, 1854. *Philadelphia:* 1855.

8vo, pp. 52. *Half red morocco, gilt top.* Fine PORTRAITS of WILLIAM PENN, and LORD CALVERT *inserted.*

1193 LAURENS (Henry.) Mr. Laurens' True State of the Case. By which his Candor to Mr. Edmund Jenings is manifested, and the Tricks of Mr. Jenings are detected. [*Privately Printed, London.*] 1783.

4to, pp. 77. *Half green morocco, gilt top,* UNCUT. PORTRAIT of MR. LAURENS *inserted.* VERY SCARCE.

See Jenings (E.) Nos. 1071, and 1072.

1194 **Laus Patriae Celestis.** Translation of an Ancient Latin Hymn. By O. A. M. [Truly translated from an elaborate and elegant Production of the Middle Ages, written by an Abbot of Clugni, who flourished in the 12th century.] *Albany: J. Munsell.* 1867.

12*mo, half blue morocco, gilt top,* UNCUT. TWENTY-FIVE COPIES only printed for PRIVATE DISTRIBUTION.

1195 LAUZUN (*Duke.* de) Memoirs of the Duke de Lauzun. Written by Himself. Second Edition. *London:* 1822.

12*mo, pp. ix.,* 211. *Half calf.* Fine copy. VERY SCARCE.

The Duc de Lauzun accompanied Count Rochambeau in the French Expedition to America. His Memoirs comprise many curious particulars of the conduct of the War, General Washington, &c.

1196 LAWSON (D.) Christ's Fidelity | the only | Shield | Against | Satan's Malignity. | Asserted in a | Sermon | Deliver'd at Salem-Village, the | 24th of March, 1692. Being Lecture- | day there, and a time of Publick | Examination, of some Suspected | for Witchcraft. | By Deodat Lawson, Minister | of the Gospel. | The Second Edition. | *Printed at Boston, in New-England, and Reprinted | in London, by R. Tockey, for the Author;* | 1704.

12*mo, pp.* (12), 120. *Purple levant morocco, gilt edges, by* W. PRATT. BEAUTIFUL COPY of this VERY RARE work.

Relating to the Salem Witchcraft Delusion. The appendix contains "some remarkable things relating to the afflicted and accused."

1197 [LAWSON (James.)] Poems: Gleanings from Spare Hours of a Business Life. *New York:* 1857.

8vo, pp. 156. *Extra cloth, gilt edges.* A FEW COPIES only PRIVATELY PRINTED; all for presentation.

1198 [LAWSON.] Liddesdale: or the Border Chief. A Tragedy. [*New York:* 1861.]

Roy. 8vo, pp. 114, *Green morocco extra, gilt edges.* PRIVATELY PRINTED, and 100 copies only.

1199 [LAWSON.] Giordano. A Tragedy.
Printed, not Published. Yonkers. 1867.

Imp. 8vo, pp. 98. *Crushed red levant morocco, beveled boards, broad inside richly gilt borders, morocco joints, silk linings, gilt edges, by* W. SMITH. PRIVATELY PRINTED and FORTY COPIES only.

1200 LAWSON (J.) The | History | of | Carolina ; | containing the | Exact Description and Natural History | of that | Country : | Together with the Present State thereof. | And | A Journal | Of a Thousand Miles, Travel'd thro' several | Nations of Indians. | Giving a particular Account of their Customs, | Manners, &c. | By John Lawson, Gent. Surveyor-General | of North-Carolina. | *London : | Printed for W. Taylor at the Ship, and J. Baker at the Black- | Boy, in Pater-noster-Row.* 1714.

4to, pp. (6), 258, (1). *Map, and Plate. Wrinkled red morocco, corner ornaments, gilt edges, by* F. BEDFORD. An unusually LARGE and FINE COPY of this VERY SCARCE work, with the MAP, and the RARE PLATE, wanting in many copies.

1201 LEAKE (I. Q.) Memoir of the Life and Times of General John Lamb, an Officer of the Revolution, who Commanded the Post at West Point at the time of Arnold's Defection, and his Correspondence with Washington, Clinton, Patrick Henry, and other Distinguished Men of his Time. By Isaac Q. Leake. *Albany : J. Munsell.* 1857.

8vo, pp. x., 431. *Portrait and Plans. Half calf, gilt top,* UNCUT. FINE PAPER COPY with THIRTEEN ILLUSTRATIONS *inserted.*

1202 LECHFORD (T.) Plain Dealing. | Or, | Nevves | from | New-England. | A short view of New-England's | present Government, both Ecclesiasticall and Civil, | compared with the anciently-received and esta- | blished Government of England, in some materiall points ; fit for the gravest | consideration in these times. | By Thomas Lechford of Clements Inne, | in the County of Middlesex, Gent. | *London : | Printed by W. E. and I. G. for Nath : Butter, at the Signe | of the pyde Bull neere S. Austins gate.* 1642.

4to, pp. (8), 80. *Polished calf, gilt edges, by* W. PRATT. A FINE COPY of the ORIGINAL and EXTREMELY RARE edition.

For an account of this highly esteemed work, and of its author, *see* Hutchinson's *Hist. of Mass. Bay.* I. 451.

1203 LEE (A.) Observations on Certain Commercial Transactions in France, laid before Congress. By Arthur Lee, Esquire.
Philadelphia : Printed by E. Bailey. 1780.

4to, pp. 51. *Half olive morocco, carmine edges.* VERY RARE.

An exposition of the extravagant and wasteful expenditure of the public money by Franklin, and his nephew Jonathan Williams, during their official residence at Paris. Crisp and pungent. Williams charged Mr. Lee with "the delight of glutting his soul with the carnage of his (Williams') character, &c."

1204 LEE. Extracts from a Letter written to the President of Congress, by the Honorable Arthur Lee, Esquire. In Answer to a Libel pub-

lished in the Pennsylvania Gazette, of the Fifth of December, 1778, by Silas Deane, Esquire. In which every Charge or Insinuation against him in that Libel, is fully and clearly refuted.
Philadelphia: F. Bailey. M.DCC.LXXX.

Sm. 4to, pp. 74. *Half calf.* VERY RARE.

A tract not only of great rarity but of much historical interest; which, together with the preceding No., "Deane's Address," and the "Paris Papers," (both in this collection), may some time afford material for an instructive and interesting episode in the history of the Revolution, in which Franklin, Williams, Paul Jones, and Deane, may, possibly, be brought to occupy the same niche.

See Deane (Silas.) Nos. 543, 544, and 545.

1205 LEE (C.) Proceedings | of a | General Court Martial, | Held at Brunswick, | in the State of New-Jersey, | by Order of | His Excellency | General Washington, | Commander in Chief | Of the Army of | The United States of America, | For the Trial of | Major General Lee. | July 4th, 1778. | Major General Lord Stirling, President. | *Philadelphia: | Printed by John Dunlap, in Market | Street.* MDCCLXXVIII.

Folio, pp. 62. *Purple levant morocco, rich inside borders, gilt edges, by* W. MATTHEWS. FINE COPY. ORIGINAL EDITION. EXCESSIVELY RARE. A few copies only printed. RARE contemporary mezzotint PORTRAIT of GEN. LEE *inserted.*

1206 LEE. Proceedings of a General Court-Martial, ... for the Trial of Major General Lee. July 4th, 1778. *Cooperstown: N. Y.* 1823.

Roy. 8vo, pp. 134. *Half calf,* UNCUT. FINE COPY of the VERY RARE REPRINT of the trial of General Lee, of which a few copies only were PRIVATELY PRINTED.

1207 LEE. Proceedings of a General Court-Martial, ... for the Trial of Major-General Lee. July 4th, 1778.
New York: Privately Reprinted. 1864.

Roy. 8vo, pp. 239. *Half blue morocco, gilt top,* UNCUT. One hundred copies only PRIVATELY REPRINTED. AN UNLETTERED INDIA PROOF PORTRAIT of GEN. LEE *inserted.*

1208 LEE (H.) [A Funeral Oration, delivered at the German Lutheran Church, Philadelphia, on Thursday the 26th December, 1799, in Honor of the Memory of George Washington. ... By Major-General Henry Lee. *Philadelphia:* 1800.]

8vo, pp. 17. UNCUT. Government Edition. Issued without a title page.

1209 LEE. Funeral Oration on the Death of General Washington, Delivered at the Request of Congress, by Major-General Henry Lee, Member of Congress from Virginia.
Boston: Joseph Nancrede. [1800.]

8vo, pp. 15. UNCUT. SCARCE EDITION.

1210 LEE. A Funeral Oration In Honour of the Memory of George Washington. Prepared and Delivered at the Request of Congress, at the German Lutheran Church, Philadelphia, on Thursday, the

26th of December. By Major-Gen. Henry Lee, One of the Representatives from Virginia. *Brooklyn: Printed by Thomas Kirk.* 1800.

8vo, pp. 16.

Probably the FIRST BOOK printed in BROOKLYN, L.I., where the press was first introduced by THOMAS KIRK, in June, 1799.

1211 LEE. Oration. [Same Title.] Second Edition. *Brooklyn: Thomas Kirk.* 1800.

8vo, pp. 16. UNCUT.

1212 LEE. A Funeral Oration On the Death of George Washington, ... Delivered at the Request of Congress. ... To which is subjoined, An Eulogy: by Judge Minot. *London: Button.* 1800.

8vo, pp. 28. UNCUT.

Of the three hundred and fifty (more or less) orations on the death of Washington, this is considered to be the most meritorious, as the number of editions through which it passed sufficiently indicates.

1213 LEE. Memoirs of the War in the Southern Department of the United States. By Henry Lee, Lieutenant Colonel Commandant of the Partisan Legion during the American War. *Philadelphia: Bradford and Inskeep.* 1812.

2 *vols.*, *8vo, pp.* (4), 423; (4), 486. 2 *Portraits.* *Half crimson morocco, gilt top*, UNCUT. PORTRAIT of the AUTHOR *inserted.* FINE COPY.

1214 LEE. Memoirs of the War. A New Edition, with Corrections left by the Author, and with Notes and Additions by H. Lee, the Author of the Campaign of '81. *Washington: Peter Force.* 1827.

8vo, pp. 466. *Half red morocco, gilt top*, UNCUT, *by* BRADSTREET. FINE COPY, and unusually free from the stains found in all copies. Two PORTRAITS of the AUTHOR, one an ARTIST'S UNLETTERED PROOF *inserted.*

1215 LEE (H.) The Campaign of 1781 in the Carolinas; with Remarks Historical and Critical on Johnson's Life of Greene. To which is added an Appendix of Original Documents, relating to the History of the Revolution. By H. Lee. *Philadelphia: E. Littell.* 1824.

8vo, pp. 511, *xlvii.* *Half blue morocco, gilt top*, UNCUT. PORTRAIT of GEN. GREENE *inserted.* FINE COPY. Very Scarce.

1216 LEE. Observations on the Writings of Thomas Jefferson, with Particular Reference to the Attack they contain on the Memory of the Late Gen. Henry Lee. In a Series of Letters, By H. Lee. Second Edition, with an Introduction and Notes, by Charles Carter Lee. *Philadelphia: J. Dobson.* 1839.

8vo, pp. xix., 262. *Half blue morocco, gilt top*, UNCUT. PORTRAIT *inserted.*

The first edition has become very rare, mainly on account of its having been rigidly suppressed, and as far as possible destroyed throughout Virginia. The worshippers of the memory of Jefferson could not bear such an expose and therefore it was doomed to destruction.

1217 LEE (R. H.) Memoir of the Life of Richard Henry Lee, and his Correspondence with the most Distinguished men in America and

Europe, Illustrative of their Characters, and of the Events of the American Revolution. By his Grandson, Richard H. Lee, of Leesburg, Virginia. *Philadelphia:* 1825.

2 vols., 8vo, pp. 299; 238. *Half maroon morocco, gilt top,* UNCUT. TWENTY-ONE PORTRAITS *inserted.*

1218 LEE. Life of Arthur Lee, LL.D., Joint Commissioner of the United States to the Court of France, and Sole Commissioner to the Courts of Spain and Prussia, during the Revolutionary War. With his Political and Literary Correspondence and his Papers on Diplomatic and Political Subjects ... By Richard Henry Lee. ... *Boston: Wells and Lilly.* 1829.

2 vols., roy. 8vo, pp. 431; 399. *Half crimson morocco, gilt top,* UNCUT. THREE PORTRAITS *inserted.*

THE FIRST BOOK PRINTED SOUTH OF MASSACHUSETTS.

1219 L[EEDS] (D[aniel.]) The | Temple of Wisdom | For the | Little World, | In Two Parts. | The First Philosophically Divine, treating of | The Being of all Beeings, | And whence everything hath its original, as | Heaven, Hell, Angels, Men and Devils, Earth, | Stars and Elements. | And particularly of all Mysteries concerning the *Soul;* and | of *Adam* before and after the Fall. | Also, a Treatise of the four Complexions, with | the Causes of spiritual Sadness &c. | *To which is added*, A Postscript to all Students in | Arts and Sciences. | The Second Part, Morally divine, Contains | *First.* Abuses Stript and Whipt, by *Geo. Wither*, with his | discription of Fair Virtue. | *Secondly.* A Collection of Divine Poems from *Fr. Quarles.* | *Lastly.* Essayes and Religious Meditations of Sir *Francis* | *Bacon* Knight. | Collected, Published and intended for a general Good, | By D. L. | *Printed and Sold* by WILLIAM BRADFORD *in Philadelphia*, | *Anno.* 1688.

Title 1 *leaf. Preface* 3 *pages. To the Doctors,* 3 *pages. pp.* 1 *to* 125. 1 *unnumbered page.* 1 *blank leaf. Second Title, with full imprint* 1688. 1 *page. To the Reader* 1 *page. pp.* 3 *to* 48. *Third Title, "Printed in the Year* 1688." 1 *page. pp.* 50 *to* 86. 1 *page Errata.*

12mo. Blue levant morocco extra, gilt edges, by F. BEDFORD.

Concerning this probably UNIQUE VOLUME, see Bacon's Works, Montague's Edition, Vol. XVI., note No. 31, in which Mr. Montague observes "it is a fact not unworthy of notice, that the first book published in Philadelphia, consists partly of Lord Bacon's Essays. It is entitled 'The Temple of Wisdom,' printed by William Bradford, Philadelphia, 1688." It is one of the RAREST among rare American books, for NO OTHER COPY IS KNOWN TO EXIST. The volume is in a fine state of preservation, clean, fresh, and crisp, as when first published.

1220 LEEDS (D.) The Rebuker | Rebuked | in a Brief | Answer | To Caleb Pusey his | Scurrilous Pamphet (sic), | Entituled, | A Rebuke to Daniel Leeds, &c. | Wherein William Penn his Sandy Foundation is fairly | quoted, showing that he calls Christ, The Finite | Impotent

Creature. | By Daniel Leeds. | *Printed and Sold by* WILLIAM BRADFORD *at the Bible in* | *New York*, 1703.

Small 4to, pp. 11. *Calf, gilt edges, by* HAYDAY. FINE COPY. VERY RARE.

1221 LEEDS. The Great Mistery of Fox-Craft Discovered. And the Quaker Plainness & Sincerity Demonstrated, ... Introduced with two Letter (sic) written by G. Fox to Coll. Lewis Morris, deceased, exactly Spell'd and Printed as in the Originals, which are now to be seen in the Library at Burlington in New Jersey, and will be proved (by the likeness of the Hand, &c.) to be the Hand-Writing of the Quaker's Learned Fox, if denyed. To which is Added, A Postscript, with some Remarks on the Quaker-Almanack for this year 1705. [*New York: William Bradford.* 1705.]

Small 4to, pp. 16. *Calf, gilt edges, by* HAYDAY.

Contains curious illustrations of the illiteracy of the great Quaker leader George Fox, and is so RARE that it has escaped the notice of Mr. Smith, whose "Catalogue of Friends' Books" is a monument of untiring industry and research.

1222 LEEDS (T.) The American Almanack for the Year of Christian Account 1731. Being the third after Bissextile or Leap Year. By Titan Leeds, Philomat. *Printed and sold by* WILLIAM BRADFORD *in New York, and* ANDREW BRADFORD *in Philadelphia.* [1731.]

8 *vols.*, 12*mo, polished calf, gilt edges, by* F. BEDFORD. After 1733, the imprint reads "*Printed and Sold by* WILLIAM BRADFORD *in New York.*"

This is a series of EIGHT of these EXCEEDINGLY RARE productions of BRADFORD'S PRESS, embracing the years 1731. '32. '33. '37. '38. '39. '42. and 1743., uniform in size and binding, and in the finest condition. A remarkable instance of the well known thrifty habit of the printer occurs in that for the year 1738; a portion thereof being printed upon paper one side of which having previously been used, the printed sides were pasted face to face, and the sheets of the Almanack printed on the blanks. These have been carefully separated by Mr. Bedford, and exhibit a curious example of printing-house economy. In that for 1739, in May, is found the often quoted entry, "the printer born the 20th, 1663." which, notwithstanding the inscription (1660) upon his tomb-stone, is now generally admitted to have been the date of his birth. It would be very difficult, if indeed it were possible, to obtain a MORE DESIRABLE, FINER, or MORE INTERESTING SPECIMEN of BRADFORD'S PRESS than these HANDSOME LITTLE VOLUMES present.

1223 **Legendæ Catholicæ.** A Lytle Boke of Seyntlie Gestes. *Imprinted at Edinburgh in the Year of the Incarnation.* MDCCCXL.

Sq. 12*mo, pp. xvi.*, (2), 257. *Half green morocco, gilt top*, UNCUT. FORTY COPIES only printed. EXTREMELY RARE.

"This very curious collection of poetical hagiologies is selected from the well-known Auchinleck MS. supposed to have been written in some North of England Monastery about the latter end of the XIIIth or commencement of the XIVth century. It contains the following legends:—Pope Gregory; St. Margaret; St. Katherine; Mary Magdalen; Joachim and Anne; and Our Lady's Mother. Only 40 copies were printed, under the editorial care of W. Turnbull, Esq.

This is the book the extraordinary preface to which has been so often quoted in reference to the case of Mr. Turnbull, both in the House of Lords and Commons. The dedication is To the 'memory of Peter Ribadeneira of the Society of Jesus.' In his remarks on the state of the MS. the editor says, 'It has been sadly mutilated by some sacrilegious hand for the sake of the illuminations. Would to God that for his pains the Vandal had been served after a similar fashion, and been qualified to chant shrill treble within the choir of the Sistine chapel.'"

1224 [LEGGETT (William.)] Liesure Hours at Sea: being a few Miscellaneous Poems. By a Midshipman of the United States Navy. *New York:* 1825.

12mo, half green levant morocco, gilt top, UNCUT, *by* F. BEDFORD. INDIA PROOF PORTRAIT of the AUTHOR *inserted.* FINE COPY. VERY SCARCE.

1225 LE GRAND (M.) Fabliaux or Tales, abridged from French Manuscripts of the XIIth and XIIIth Centuries by M. Le Grand, Selected and Translated into English Verse, by the late G. L. Way, Esq. With a Preface, Notes, and Appendix, by the late G. Ellis, Esq. A New Edition Corrected. *London: J. Rodwell.* 1815.

3 *vols., 8vo, half green morocco, gilt top,* UNCUT. FINE COPY. SCARCE in *uncut* condition.

"The Fabliaux are as frequently revolting for their naked grossness, as they are interesting for the lively pictures which they present of Life and Manners. Yet these were the chosen literary pastimes of the fair and gay during the times of Chivalry."—*Sir W. Scott.*

1226 LENDRUM (J.) A Concise and Impartial History of the American Revolution. To which is prefixed, a General History of North and South America, ... and a View of the Progress, Character, and Political State of the Colonies previous to the Revolution. From the Best Authorities. By John Lendrum. *Trenton: James Oram.* 1811.

2 *vols., 12mo, pp.* 415; *viii.,* 228. 2 *Maps. Half calf.* PORTRAIT *inserted.*

1227 [LEONARD (Daniel.)] Massachusettensis; or a Series of Letters, containing a Faithful State of many important and striking Facts, which laid the Foundation of the Present Troubles in the Province of the Massachusetts-Bay. ... . Originally addressed to the People of that Province. ... By a Person of Honor upon the Spot.
Boston: Printed. London: Re-printed for J. Mathews. MDCCLXXVI.

8vo, pp. viii., 118. *Half olive morocco.* SCARCE.

"On my return from Congress," says John Adams, "in November, 1774, I found the Massachusetts Gazette teeming with political speculations, and Massachusettensis shining like to the moon among the lesser stars. I instantly knew him to be my friend Sewell, and was told he excited great exultation among the Tories, and many gloomy apprehensions among the Whigs."

Notwithstanding this positive statement it is now ascertained that these letters were written by Daniel Leonard of Taunton.

See *John Adams's Works,* II. 405. Also *Boston Transcript,* April 18, 1851.

1228 LEONARD (D. A.) An Oration occasioned by the Death of Gen. George Washington. Pronounced ... in the City of New York, on February, 22, 1800. ... By David A. Leonard, A.B. *New York:* 1800.

8vo, pp. 22. EXCEEDINGLY RARE.

1229 LE PAGE DU PRATZ (M.) The History of Louisiana, or of the Western Parts of Virginia and Carolina: Containing a Description of the Countries that lie on Both Sides of the River Mississippi: With an Account of the Settlements, Inhabitants, Soil, Climate, and Products. Translated from the French of M. Le Page Du Pratz;

With some Notes and Observations relating to our Colonies. A New Edition. *London: T. Becket.* M.DCC.LXXIV.

8vo, pp. (8), *xxxvi.*, 387. 2 *Maps. Half crushed red levant morocco, gilt top,* UNCUT, by W. MATTHEWS. ELEGANT COPY. VERY SCARCE in *uncut* condition.

1230 [LESLIE (Charles.)] A Short and Easie Method with the Deists. Wherein the Certainty of the Christian Religion is demonstrated, by infallible Proof from Four Rules, which are Incompatible to any Imposture that ever yet has been, or that can possibly be. In a Letter to a Friend. The Eighth Edition. *London: Printed by J. Applebee and Sold by John Checkley, at the Sign of the Crown and Blue-Gate, over against the West-End of the Town-House in Boston,* 1723. [Followed by] The Speech of Mr. John Checkley upon his Tryal at Boston in New England, for publishing "A Short and Easie Method with the Deists, &c." to which is added, The Jury's Verdict, His Plea in Arrest of Judgment, and the Sentence of the Court. Second Edition. [And] A Specimen of a True Dissenting Catechism upon Right True-Blue Dissenting Principles, &c. *London: J. Applebee.* 1738.

8vo, 3 *pieces in* 1 *vol., half crushed blue levant morocco, gilt edges, by* W. MATTHEWS. BEAUTIFUL COPY of this RARE work.

It is of the highest interest in connection with the liberty of the press in New England. Checkley was prosecuted at the Inferior Court in Boston, in 1724, for publishing and selling this book, which was called, "a false and scandalous libel, tending to draw into dispute his present Majesty's title to the Crown, scandalizing the ministers of the gospel, established by law in this Province; falsifying the Holy Scriptures, representing the Church of Rome as the present Mother Church; and tending to raise divisions, jealousies and animosities among his Majesty's loving subjects of this Province." He was convicted but appealed to the Superior Court, where, after a long speech in his own defence, the jury brought in a verdict against him. The Court sentenced him to pay a fine of £50 to the King, and to give two sureties in the sum of £100 for his good behavior for six months.

See Thomas' *History of Printing.* II. 427. Also: Stevens' *Nuggets.* No. 535.

1231 LESTER (C. E.) The Artists of America: a Series of Biographical Sketches of American Artists; with Portraits and Designs on Steel. By Charles Edwards Lester. *New York: Baker & Scribner.* 1846.

8vo, pp. vi., 257. *Half green morocco, gilt top,* UNCUT. FIVE PORTRAITS, and five pages of additional matter, "An Hour with Rembrandt Peale," *inserted.*

1232 LESTER *and* FOSTER (A.) The Life and Voyages of Americus Vespucius; With Illustrations concerning the Navigator, and the Discovery of the New World. By C. Edwards Lester, and Andrew Foster. *New York: Baker & Scribner.* 1846.

8vo, pp. 431. *Half calf.* LARGE and FINE COPY.

Contains also: an account of the discoveries of Vasco de Gama, beyond the Cape of Good Hope. Letters of Paolo Toscanelli to Columbus; Marco Polo and his travels, &c.

1233 L[ETCHWORTH] (T[homas.]) A | Morning and Evening's | Meditation, | or, a | Descant | on the | Times. | A | Poem. | *London: Printed.* | *Philadelphia: Re-printed and Sold by* B. | FRANKLIN *and* D. HALL. 1766.

Sm. 8vo, pp. 58. *Half gray calf.* VERY RARE. We have never seen but ONE OTHER COPY.

1234 LETTER (A) from a Veteran, to the Officers of the Army Encamped at Boston. *America: Printed in the Year* 1774.

8vo, pp. 19. *Half morocco.* EXTREMELY SCARCE.

Remarkably well written, and attributed to the British General Prescott..— Tudor's *Otis.* p. 466.

1235 LETTER (A) from a Virginian to the Members of the Congress to be held at Philadelphia on the 1st of September, 1774. *Boston:* 1774.

8vo, pp. 55. *Half morocco,* UNCUT.

The author appears to have made an unsuccessful effort to dissuade the members of the congress from adopting the non-importation and non-exportation agreements.

1236 LETTER (A) to the Inhabitants of the Province of Quebec. Extract from the Minutes of the Congress.
Philadelphia: William and Thomas Bradford. 1774.

8vo, pp. 37–50. *Half green morocco,* UNCUT.

An official letter from the Colonial Congress, inciting the Canadians to join the thirteen United Colonies in their opposition to Great Britain.

1237 LETTER (A) from the Nobility, Barons, and Commons of Scotland in the year 1370, ... directed to Pope John: wherein they declare their firm Resolutions to adhere to their King Robert the Bruce, as the restorer of the safety and Liberties of the People, ... but withall, they notwithstanding declare, that if the King should offer to subvert their civil Liberties, they will disown him as an Enemy, and choose another to be King, for their own defence. Translated from the original, in Latine ... by Sir George MacKenzie of Rosehaugh. ...
Edinburgh: Reprinted in the year 1689. *New York: Privately Printed.* 1861.

Sm. 4to, half red morocco, gilt top, UNCUT. THIRTY COPIES only PRIVATELY PRINTED. The engraved cuts of the arms of Douglass, and Lockhart, were executed by Dr. Anderson in his 86th year; his charge for the work was three dollars! An autograph letter of the late MR. BALMANNO giving an account of the printing of the volume is *inserted.*

1238 LETTERS (The) of Valens, (which originally appeared in the London Evening Post) with Corrections, Explanatory Notes, and a Preface by the Author. *London: J. Almon.* MDCCLXXVII.

8vo, pp. ii., xv., 160. *Blue morocco, gilt top,* UNCUT. VERY SCARCE.

Presentation copy from JOHN ALMON, the publisher of the work, "To HIS EXCELLENCY GENERAL WASHINGTON," with Washington's BOOK PLATE on the inside lining of the original cover. It was presented by GEN. WASHINGTON to COLONEL RICHARD VARICK on the day previous to breaking up Head Quarters at Newburgh, and remained in his possession until his death, after which it was obtained by its present owner at the sale of Col. Varick's effects.

"In these well-written, spirited, and anti-ministerial letters, the author takes a view of the policy of the American War, its objects, its conduct, and the motives of Government for engaging in it."— *Rich.*

1239 LETTERS Written in London by an American Spy. From the year 1764 to the year 1785. *London: J. Bew,* MDCCLXXXVI.

8vo, pp. xxi., 167. *Half calf.* FINE *copy.* RARE.

"These letters are said to be the correspondences of a Quaker with his friends in Philadelphia; and, while they display the honest bluntness of a sect, are animated by a warm philanthropy, true religion, and sound sense."— *Critical Review.*

1240 LETTERS and Papers relating Chiefly to the Provincial History of Pennsylvania, with some Notices of the Writers. Privately Printed. *Philadelphia:* 1855.

12mo, pp. cxxxviii., 312. *Half brown morocco, gilt top,* UNCUT. PORTRAIT of WILLIAM SHIPPEN *inserted.* EXTREMELY SCARCE.

Edited by Thomas Balch, and known as *The Shippen Papers.*

1241 LEVASSEUR (A.) La Fayette in America in 1824 and 1825; or, Journal of a Voyage to the United States: by A. Levasseur, Secretary to Gen. La Fayette during his journey. Translated by John D. Godman, M.D. *Philadelphia: Carey and Lea.* 1829.

2 *vols.,* 12*mo, half olive morocco, gilt top,* UNCUT. *Contemporary* PORTRAIT *of* LAFAYETTE *inserted. Original edition.* VERY SCARCE.

1242 LEWIS (E.) An Eulogy, on the Life and Character of His Excellency George Washington, Esqr. ... Delivered at Lenox, February 22, 1800. By Eldad Lewis Esquire. ... *Pittsfield: (Mass.) March,* 1800.

12*mo, pp.* 20. A VERY RARE Poetical Eulogy.

1243 LEWIS (J.) The Life of Mayster **Wyllyam Caxton,** of the Weald of Kent; the First Printer in England. In which is given an Account of the Rise and Progress of the Art of **Pryntyng** in England, during his Time, till 1493. Collected by John Lewis, Minister of Mergate in Kent. *London: Printed in the Year.* M.DCC.XXXVII.

Roy. 8vo, pp. xxii., 156, (4). *Portrait and* 2 *Plates. Red morocco, edges gilt on carmine.* LARGE THICK PAPER. 150 *Copies only printed.* VERY SCARCE.

This copy possesses an additional leaf, paged 158, printed on much thinner paper, containing the Character of Caxton by Bp. Bale and a note respecting Sir Walter Manny from Froissart.

1244 LEWIS (M.) Celebration of the Centennial Anniversary of the Birth of George Washington, New-York, February 22, 1832. With An Oration delivered ... before the Common Council and Citizens ... By Maj. Gen. Morgan Lewis. ... *New-York: G. F. Hopkins & Son.* 1832.

8*vo, pp.* 11, 32. *Half morocco.* PORTRAIT of GENERAL LEWIS *inserted.* VERY SCARCE.

1245 LIBERTY A Poem. By Rusticus. *Philadelphia: John Dunlap.* MDCCLXVIII.

4*to, pp.* 27. *Half calf.* A fine specimen of colonial book-making.

The author attributed the Stamp Act to Mr. Grenville.

1246 LIBRARY OF NEW ENGLAND HISTORY. *Boston:* MDCCCLXV-LXVII.

5 *vols.,* 4*to, half blue levant morocco extra, gilt top,* UNCUT, *by* BRADSTREET. LARGE PAPER. THIRTY-FIVE COPIES ONLY PRINTED.

These volumes, the most elegant of their class, merit a passing notice. They are not mere reprints of the rare and valuable works whose titles they bear, as each work has a copious introduction, and is profusely annotated by an eminent New England scholar. The series is complete so far as published; one volume of an intended Virginia series is included, that being the only one issued when the work was stopped.

Their Titles are briefly as follows:

I. Mourt's Relation or Journal of the Plantation at Plymouth. With an Introduction and Notes by Henry Martyn Dexter. *Boston: John Kimball Wiggin.* M DCCC LXV.

II. & III. The History of King Philip's War. By Benjamin Church. With an Introduction and Notes by Henry Martyn Dexter.
Boston: J. K. Wiggin and Wm. Parsons Lunt. MDCCCLXVII.

IV. Plain Dealing. Or News from New England. By Thomas Lechford. With an Introduction and Notes by J. Hammond Trumbull.
Boston: J. K. Wiggin and Wm. Parsons Lunt. MDCCCLXVII.

Virginia Series I. A True Relation of Virginia. By Captain John Smith. With an Introduction and Notes by Charles Deane. Map in Fac-simile.
Boston: Wiggin and Lunt. MDCCCLXVI.

AN ELEGANT SET.

1247 LIBRI (G.) Monuments Inédits ou peu Connus, faisant partie du Cabinet de Guillaume Libri, et qui se rapportent à l'Histoire de l'Ornementation chez différents Peuples. Seconde Édition, augmentée de plusieurs Planches. *Londres:* 1864.

Folio, in a port-folio.

Of this SPLENDID and UNIQUE work only 150 copies were executed. It contains 65 large Plates, exhibiting numerous specimens of richly ornamented Early Bookbindings, Illuminated Manuscripts, Drawings by Raffaelle, Michael Angelo, Da Vinci, Rubens, Guercino, splendid Works of Art in Gold, Ivory, &c. Early Engraved Maps, Antiquities in Gold by the Aborigines of America, &c., all beautifully executed in facsimile of the originals, in GOLD, SILVER, and COLOURS; with Descriptions in English and French.

1248 LINCOLN (A.) Tribute of Respect of the Citizens of Troy to the Memory of Abraham Lincoln. *Albany: J. Munsell.* 1865.

4to, half green morocco, gilt top, UNCUT. INDIA PROOF PORTRAIT, and PROOF VIEW of "Lincoln's Early Home" *inserted.*

1249 [LIND (John.)] An Answer to the Declaration of the American Congress. *London: T. Cadell.* 1776.

8vo, pp. 132. *Half crimson morocco, gilt top,* UNCUT, *by* BRADSTREET.

Each article of the Declaration of Independence is carefully examined and every assertion disputed. In a short "review" at the end of the volume, the author thus expresses himself. "The opinions of the modern Americans on Government, like those of their good ancestors on witchcraft, would be too ridiculous to deserve any notice, if like them, too contemptible and extravagant as they be, they had not led to the most serious consequences."

1250 L[INGARD](R.) A | Letter of Advice | To A Young | **Gentleman** | Leaving the | UNIVERSITY | Concerning his Behaviour | and Conversation in the | WORLD. | By R. L. | *Printed and Sold by VV. Bradford,* | *Printer to his Majesty, King* | *William, at the Bible in* | *New York.* 1696.

16mo. Title 1l. Advertisement 2l. pp. 45. *Crushed purple levant morocco, broad inside borders, gilt edges.* AUTOGRAPH SIGNATURE of the PRINTER *inserted.* In the FINEST STATE OF PRESERVATION.

The EARLIEST BOOK known to have been printed in the COLONY OF NEW YORK; the Laws of the Colony excepted, which were printed in chapters, from time to time as passed, and collected into a volume at the end of each session.

THIS IS THE ONLY COPY KNOWN TO EXIST.

It was purchased at the sale of E. B. Corwin's Library, and although it cannot claim to be the earliest example of printing in the Colony of New York, it is certainly

THE FIRST BOOK PRINTED IN NEW YORK

that has come under our notice, or of which we have any account. It is a reprint of an English work, a copy of which was described in one of Mr. Thorpe's catalogues some years ago.

1251 LINN (J. B.) The Death of Washington. A Poem in imitation of the manner of Ossian. By Rev. John Blair Linn, A.M. ... *Philadelphia:* 1800.

8vo, pp. 26. *Very scarce.*

1252 LINN (W.) A Funeral Eulogy, occasioned by the Death of General Washington. Delivered February 22d, 1800, before the New York State Society of the Cincinnati. By William Linn, D.D. *New York:* 1800.

8vo, pp. 44.

1253 LINN. The Blessings of America. A Sermon preached in the Middle Dutch Church, on the Fourth July 1791, being the Anniversary of the Independence of America: at the request of the Tammany Society, or Columbian Order. By William Linn, D.D. *New-York:* M, DCC, XCI.

8vo, pp. 39. *Half crimson morocco.* VERY SCARCE.

1254 LINSCHOTEN (J. H. Van) Semper Eadem. | John | Hvighen Van | Linschoten. | his Discours of Voyages | into y[e] Easte & West | Indies. | Deuided into Foure Bookes | *Printed at London by* | *John Wolfe* | *Printer to y[e] Honorable Cittie of* | *London* | *I. W.* | [1598.]

Collation. Five prel. leaves; text, pp. 197. 'The Second Booke, etc. 1598.' Title, and pp. 197–295. 'The Thirde Booke, etc. 1598.' Title, and pp. 307–447. 'The Fovrth Booke, etc. 1598.' Title, and pp. 451–462. With 12 copper-plate maps.

Folio, **Black Letter**, *with the frontispiece and the whole of the* 12 GENUINE ENGLISH MAPS *engraved by* ROGERS, ELSTRACKE *and* BECKIT; *remarkably* FINE COPY *in russia extra, gilt edges, by* F. BEDFORD. VERY RARE.

1255 LINSCHOTEN. Voyages. [Another Copy.] *London:* [1598.]

Folio. **Black Letter.** *Crushed blue levant morocco, gilt edges, by* F. BEDFORD. BEAUTIFUL COPY, with a SPLENDID IMPRESSION of the engraved title, all the TWELVE MAPS; and a SELECTION of TWENTY-SEVEN of the BEST ENGRAVINGS from the Dutch edition *inserted.*

"This inestimable book, a treasure of all the learning respecting the East and West-Indies and the navigation thither, at the end of the sixteenth century, has been in the highest esteem for nearly a century, and was given to each ship sailing to India, as a log-book. Hence the many editions (6 in Dutch, 3 in French, and 1 in Latin), which is also the cause why *fine* copies, especially with *all* the plates and maps, are so *very rare.* A large part of the book is occupied by translations of original Spanish and Portuguese documents on geography, ethnography, statistics, navigation, etc., and in these respects it is of the highest importance and authority. The description of America occupies pages 17 to 82 of the third part."— *F. Muller.*

1256 LIPPARD (G.) Washington and his Generals; or Legends of the Revolution. By George Lippard. With a Biographical Sketch of the Author, by Rev. C. Chauncey Burr.
Philadelphia: G. B. Zieber & Co. 1847.

8vo, half green morocco. PORTRAIT *inserted.*

1257 LISLE (H. M.) An Oration delivered at Hingham, ... on Saturday the 22d of February, 1800, the Anniversary of the Birth, and the day appointed by the Government of the United States for Public National Mourning for the Death of ... General George Washington. By Henry Maurice Lisle. ... *Boston:* 1800.

8vo, pp. 22. UNCUT, *and* RARE.

1258 [LIVERMORE (George.)] Remarks on Public Libraries. From the North American Review, for July, 1850. For Private Distribution only. *Cambridge:* 1850.

8vo, half morocco, gilt edges. VERY SCARCE.

1259 LIVERMORE. An Historical Research respecting the Opinions of the Founders of the Republic on Negroes as Slaves, as Citizens, and as Soldiers. ... By George Livermore. Fifth Edition. *Boston:* 1863.

4to, cloth, gilt top, UNCUT. LARGE PAPER. 50 copies PRIVATELY PRINTED *for presentation only.*

1260 LIVERMORE. An Historical Research. [Another Copy.]
Boston: 1863.

Roy. 8vo, half blue morocco, gilt top, UNCUT. TWO PORTRAITS *inserted.* FINE PAPER. 50 *copies only* PRIVATELY PRINTED.

1261 [LIVINGSTON (William.)] A | Review | of the | Military Operatons | in | North America; | from | The Commencement of the French Hostilities | on the Frontiers of Virginia in 1753, to the Surrender | of Oswego, on the 14th of August, 1756. | Interspersed | With Various Observations, Characters, and Anecdotes; necessary to | give Light into the Conduct of American Transactions in general; | and more especially into the political Management of Affairs in | New-York. | In a Letter to a Nobleman.
London: Printed for R. and J. Dodsley. MDCCLVII.

4to, pp. (4), 144. *Half green morocco, gilt top, by* BRADSTREET. LARGE and FINE COPY. VERY SCARCE.

1262 LIVINGSTON. [Same Title as the preceding No.] To which are added, Colonel Washington's Journal of his Expedition to the Ohio, in 1754, and several Letters and other Papers of Consequence, found in the Cabinet of Major General Braddock, after his Defeat near Fort Du Quesne; and since published by the French Court. None of these Papers are contained in the English Edition.
Dublin: Printed for P. Wilson and J. Exshaw, in Dane-Street. M.DCC.LVII.

12mo, pp. 276. Crushed red levant morocco, paneled sides, rich inside borders, gilt edges, by W. MATTHEWS. AN ELEGANT COPY. RARE.

"Washington's Journal commences at page 191, and with Braddock's Papers occupies the remainder of the volume. This portion of the work is a translation of the *Memoire contenant le Precis des Faits,* printed by the French Court, charging Washington with the assassination of Jumonville, and reprinted by Hugh Gaine in 1757, under the title of "Memorial containing a Summary View of Facts, etc."—*Field.*

The *Precis des Faits* and the "Memorial," are both in this Collection. *See* Nos. 1380, and 1381.

1263 LODGE (E.) Portraits of Illustrious Personages of Great Britain. ... With Biographical and Historical Memoirs of their Lives and Actions. By Edmund Lodge, Esq., F.S.A.
London: Harding and Lepard. 1835.

Roy. 8vo, 12 vols., bound in 6. Green levant morocco, broad outside and inside gilt borders, gilt edges, by "MACKENZIE BOOK-BINDER TO THE KING." A BEAUTIFUL SET with MOST BRILLIANT IMPRESSIONS of the TWO HUNDRED AND FORTY PORTRAITS.

This is one of the copies published by Harding, in which the impressions are uniformly fresh and fine. Such sets are becoming QUITE SCARCE, in consequence of the attraction they present to the illustrator.

1264 LONG (J.) Voyages and Travels of an Indian Interpreter and Trader, describing the Manners and Customs of the North American Indians; with an Account of the Posts situated on the River St. Lawrence, Lake Ontario, &c. To which is added a Vocabulary of the Chippeway Language. ... By J. Long.
London: Printed for the Author. MDCCXCI.

4to, pp. xi., 295. Map. Half blue levant morocco, gilt top, UNCUT, *by* W. MATTHEWS. INDIA PROOF PORTRAIT *inserted.* AN ELEGANT COPY; clean as when issued.

"The author engaged in the service of the Hudson's Bay Company in 1768, and journeyed as a fur trader among the Indians of Canada for nineteen years. His knowledge of the character, customs, and domestic life of the Indians was therefore the most thorough and intimate. His relations are characterized by candour and intelligence, tinged a little with the disappointments, which most of the servants of the Company who have written accounts of their experiences, seem to have suffered."—*Field.*

1265 LORD (W. W.) André; a Tragedy. In Five Acts. By W. W. Lord. *New York: Charles Scribner.* 1856.

Sm. 8vo, pp. 138. Half green morocco, gilt top, UNCUT. PORTRAIT of ANDRÉ *inserted.*

1266 LOSKIEL (G. H.) History of the Mission of the United Brethren among the Indians of North America. In Three Parts. By George Henry Loskiel. Translated from the German by Christian Ignatius Latrobe. *London: Printed for the Brethren's Society.* 1794.

8vo, pp. xii., 159, 234, 233, (22). Map. Half blue morocco, gilt top, UNCUT. *Map mounted on fine linen.* BEAUTIFUL COPY.

1267 LOSSING (B. J.) The Pictorial Field-Book of the Revolution; or, Illustrations, by Pen and Pencil, of the History, Biography, Scenery, Relics, and Traditions of the War for Independence. By Benson

J. Lossing. With Several Hundred Engravings on Wood, by Lossing and Barritt, chiefly from Original Sketches by the Author.
New York: Harper & Brothers. 1851–52.

2 *vols., roy. 8vo, half green morocco, gilt top,* UNCUT.

Bound from carefully *selected* numbers of the now exceedingly scarce FIRST EDITION, with BRILLIANT and PERFECT IMPRESSIONS of the nearly ELEVEN HUNDRED highly finished woodcuts. A pungent review of the work, (20 pp.) is *inserted* at the end of the first volume..

1268 LOSSING. Mount Vernon and its Associations, Historical, Biographical, and Pictorial. By Benson J. Lossing. Illustrated by Numerous Engravings, chiefly from Original Drawings by the Author, Engraved by Lossing and Barritt.
New York: W. A. Townsend and Co. 1859.

Sq. 8vo, pp. 376. 139 *Engravings. Half green morocco, gilt top,* UNCUT. Fine copy. THIRTY-THREE ILLUSTRATIONS *inserted.*

1269 LOSSING. The Life and Times of Philip Schuyler. By Benson J. Lossing [Vol. 1. only.] *New York:* 1860.

8vo, pp. 504. *Half red morocco, gilt top,* UNCUT. PORTRAIT and BOOK-PLATE of GEN. SCHUYLER *inserted.* No more of this edition was published.

1270 LOSSING. Life of Washington; a Biography; Personal, Military, and Political. By Benson J. Lossing.
New York: Virtue and Company. [1860.]

3 *vols., imp. 8vo, half green levant morocco, gilt top,* UNCUT. Bound from *selected original parts,* with FINE IMPRESSIONS of the EIGHTY ENGRAVINGS, many of which are INDIA PROOFS.

1271 LOSSING. The Home of Washington and its Associations, Historical, Biographical, and Pictorial. New Edition, Revised, with Additions. By Benson J. Lossing. Illustrated by Numerous Engravings. ... *New York: W. A. Townsend.* 1865.

Sq. imp. 8vo, pp. 376. 140 *Engravings. Half green morocco, gilt top,* UNCUT. LARGE PAPER. 100 *copies only printed.*

Inserted are THIRTY-FIVE beautiful illustrations, upwards of TWENTY of which are INDIA PROOFS, and INDIA PROOFS BEFORE LETTERS. A *selected copy* with FINE and PERFECT impressions of the ONE HUNDRED AND FORTY ENGRAVINGS contained in the work.

1272 LOSSING. The Hudson, from the Wilderness to the Sea. By Benson J. Lossing. Illustrated by Three Hundred and Six Engravings on Wood, from Drawings by the Author, and a Frontispiece on Steel. *New York: Virtue and Yorston.* 1866.

Sm. 4to, pp. vii., 464. *Half green morocco, gilt top,* UNCUT. One of TWELVE COPIES ONLY of the FIRST EDITION which were left uncut. EXCELLENT IMPRESSIONS of the numerous Wood Engravings.

1273 LOSSING. Vassar College and its Founder. By B. J. Lossing.
New York: 1867.

Roy. 8vo, pp. 175. PORTRAIT, and EIGHTY-SIX beautiful and highly finished Engravings on Wood. *Cloth extra, gilt edges.* Printed for PRIVATE DISTRIBUTION only.

1274 LOSSING. The Pictorial Field-Book of the War of 1812; or, Illustrations, by Pen and Pencil, of the History, Biography, Scenery, Relics, and Traditions of the Last War for American Independence. By Benson J. Lossing. With Several Hundred Engravings on Wood, by Lossing and Barritt, Chiefly from Original Sketches by the Author. *New York: Harper & Brothers.* 1868.

Roy. 8vo, pp. 1084. *Half crushed green levant morocco, gilt top,* UNCUT, by BRADSTREET. SPLENDID COPY, *bound from selected parts,* with remarkably FINE IMPRESSIONS of the EIGHT HUNDRED AND EIGHTY-TWO ENGRAVINGS.

1275 LOSSING. A Memorial of Alexander Anderson, M.D., the First Engraver on Wood in America. ... By Benson J. Lossing. *New York: Printed for the Subscribers.* 1873.

Imp. 8vo, pp. (6), 107. 38 *Engravings. Half green levant morocco, gilt top,* UNCUT, *by* W. MATTHEWS. LIMITED EDITION.

THIRTY-TWO ILLUSTRATIONS *inserted;* including SEVENTEEN INDIA PROOFS, some BEFORE LETTERS; several PRIVATE PLATES, and a SPLENDID IMPRESSION of the VERY RARE large engraving by ANDERSON after REDINGER.

AN ELEGANT VOLUME.

1276 LOVE (C.) A Poem on the Death of General Washington, Late President of the United States. In Two Books. By Charles Love. *Alexandria: Virginia.* A.D., M,DCCC.

12mo, pp. 60. UNCUT. EXCEEDINGLY RARE. The *only copy* referred to in Dr. Hough's List.

1277 LOVELL (J.) Oration delivered April 2d, 1771, at the Request of the Inhabitants of the Town of Boston; to Commemorate the Bloody Tragedy of the Fifth of March, 1770. By James Lovell, A.M. *Boston: Printed by Edes and Gill by Order of the Town of Boston.* 1771.

4to, pp. 19. *Half green morocco, gilt top,* UNCUT. VERY RARE. *Beautiful Copy.*

1278 [LOVETT (John.)] A Tribute to Washington, for February 22d, 1800. *Troy:* 1800.

4to, pp. 15. UNCUT. *Dedicated to* JOHN JAY.

Concerning the Author of this RARE poetical piece of 280 lines, see Woodworth's *Troy.*

1279 LOWNDES (W. T.) The Bibliographer's Manual of English Literature containing an Account of Rare, Curious, and Useful Books. ... With Bibliographical and Critical Notices, Collations, ... and Prices. ... By William Thomas Lowndes. *London: W. Pickering.* 1834.

4 *vols., 8vo, half purple levant morocco, gilt top,* UNCUT. FINE COPY.

Invaluable to the Collector or Librarian, as it gives an account of the rare, curious and useful books, published in or relating to Great Britain and Ireland, from the invention of printing; with Bibliographical and Critical Notices, collations of the rarer articles, and the prices at which they have been sold in the present century. The type of this is larger than, and much superior to that of the following edition.

1280 LOWNDES. The Bibliographer's Manual of English Literature. ... By William Thomas Lowndes. New Edition Revised, Corrected and Enlarged ... By Henry G. Bohn. *London: Bell & Daldy.* 1869.

6 *vols., crown 8vo, half red morocco, gilt top,* UNCUT, *by* BRADSTREET. ELEGANT COPY. LARGE PAPER. *Only* 250 *sets printed.*

There is no substitute for "The Bibliographer's Manual." Undertaken originally to supply an obvious desideratum felt by all readers and book-buyers, it forms at once a key to the riches of English literature for the student, and a guide in the formation of a library for the collector. In its present enlarged form it comprises notices of upwards of *one hundred thousand distinct books* published in Great Britain and Ireland, from the invention of printing to the date of its publication.

1281 LOWNDES. The British Librarian, or Book Collector's Guide to the formation of a Library, in all Branches of Literature, ... With Prices, Critical Notes, References, and an Index of Authors and Subjects. ... By William T. Lowndes.

London: Whittaker and Co. 1839-40.

Thick 8vo, half purple morocco, gilt top, UNCUT.

Eleven parts; comprising "Religion and its History.," all that were published; this, the most valuable Bibliography of Theological Literature ever attempted having been interrupted by the death of the Author.

Uniform with No. 1279.

1282 LOWVILLE ACADEMY. Semi-Centennial Anniversary, Celebrated at Lowville, N. Y. July 21st and 22nd, 1858. [Edited by F. B. Hough.] *Lowville: Published by the Home Committee.* 1859.

Roy. 8vo, pp. 133. 12 *Portraits and View. Half morocco, gilt top,* UNCUT. LARGE PAPER: 23 *copies only printed,* and containing some Engravings not in the *small paper* copies.

1283 LUCAS (E.) Journal and Letters of Eliza Lucas. Now first printed. *Wormsloe:* 1850.

Roy. 4to, pp. 30. *Half brown morocco, gilt top,* UNCUT. NINETEEN COPIES PRIVATELY PRINTED for Mr. George Wymberly-Jones. This copy is one of FIVE ONLY printed on T H paper. The *Inscription* and the *Colophon* are each printed on a leaf of *vellum.* EXTREMELY RARE.

The writer of this journal was the wife of Chief Justice Pinckney of South Carolina, and the mother of General Charles Cotesworth Pinckney, and General Thomas Pinckney.

1284 [LUCOMBE (Philip.)] A Concise History of the Origin and Progress of the Art of Printing; ... Compiled from those who have wrote on this Curious Art. *London: W. Adlard and J. Browne.* 1770.

8vo, pp. (12), 494, 12. *Portrait. Half calf, carmine edges. Fine Copy.* VERY SCARCE. Author's own copy with his book-plate. Two PORTRAITS of the AUTHOR, *inserted.*

1285 LUDEWIG (H. E.) The Literature of American Local History; a Bibliographical Essay. By Hermann E. Ludewig.

New York: Printed for the Author. M.DCCC.XLVI.

8vo, pp. xx., 180. *Half crushed red levant morocco, gilt top, by* W. MATTHEWS. PRIVATELY PRINTED, and VERY SCARCE.

This beautiful copy contains the SUPPLEMENT, subsequently printed, mounted and inlaid on ten leaves by TRENT; also two AUTOGRAPH LETTERS of the AUTHOR, and one of MR. MUNSELL, all relating to this copy, and of a *very interesting* character.

1286 LYNDSAY (*Sir* D.) The Poetical Works of Sir David Lyndsay of the Mount, Lion King at Arms, under James V. A New Edition, Corrected and Enlarged: with a Life of the Author; Prefatory Dissertations; and an appropriate Glossary. By George Chalmers, F.R.S. *London: Longman.* 1806.

3 *vols., sm. 8vo, half green morocco, gilt top,* UNCUT. FINE COPY of the BEST EDITION. EXCEEDINGLY SCARCE.

It is a mistake to suppose that this excellent book is superseded by that recently published in two small volumes, as the latter *omits several passages in the text,* and contains merely a *selection* from Chalmers's *most valuable* and *interesting* notes. The author was Lion King-at-Arms under James V. The estimate in which he is held at the present day, after the lapse of nearly three centuries have fallen on his unknown grave, may be given in the following lines of Scott:—

"Still is thy name of high account,
And still thy verse has charms —
Sir David Lindsay of the Mount,
Lord Lyon King-at-Arms."

1287 [LYON (L.) *and* HAWS (S.)] Military Journals of Two Private Soldiers 1758–1775, with numerous Illustrative Notes to which is added, a Supplement, containing Official Papers on the Skirmishes at Lexington and Concord. *Poughkeepsie:* 1855.

8vo, pp. 128. *Half purple morocco, gilt top. Scarce.*

The journal of Lemuel Lyon, contains some incidents of the fatal expedition during the French and Indian war of 1758, against Fort Ticonderoga. The work was edited by Abraham Tomlinson, with notes by B. J. Lossing.

1288 MABLY (Abbé. de) Remarks concerning the Government and the Laws of the United States of America; in Four Letters, addressed to Mr. Adams. ... From the French of the Abbé de Mably; with Notes, by the Translator. *London: J. Debrett.* 1784.

8vo, pp. 280. *Half gray calf, carmine edges. Large* and *fine copy.*

It was the questions in this book which caused Mr. Adams to write his Defence of the Constitution of the United States.

1289 [M'AFEE (Robert B.)] History of the Late War in the Western Country, comprising a Full Account of all the Transactions in that Quarter, from the Commencement of Hostilities at Tippecanoe, to the Termination of the Contest at New Orleans on the Return of Peace. *Lexington: Worsley & Smith.* 1816.

8vo, pp. viii., 534, (2). *Half blue levant morocco, gilt top,* UNCUT, *by* W. MATTHEWS. SEVEN PORTRAITS *inserted.* A Beautiful copy, with the PREFACE, frequently wanting. EXCESSIVELY RARE in *uncut* condition.

"The author of this now scarce work, sought and obtained a large amount of information, regarding the Indian wars of the western frontier, from the actors engaged in them. His narrative, therefore, contains much material, which later histories either do not possess, or only copy from his pages."— *Field.*

1290 M'CALL (H.) The History of Georgia, containing Brief Sketches of the most Remarkable Events, up to the Present Day. By Capt. Hugh M'Call. *Savannah: Seymour & Williams.* 1811–16.

2 *vols.*, 8*vo*, *pp. viii.*, 376; *vii.*, 424. *Crushed blue levant morocco, gilt top*, UNCUT, *by* F. BEDFORD. A SPLENDID COPY of one of the RAREST of State Histories. TWO PORTRAITS *inserted.*

"Although the title indicates the intention to bring the history down to the date of publication, the narrative is suspended with the declaration of peace in 1783. Both volumes are largely devoted to the history of the border warfare with the Creeks and Cherokees. Numerous incidents relating to the savages of these nations, and their sanguinary attacks upon the frontiers, with sketches of their chiefs, and of the loyalist refugees who led them, are narrated. These were derived in many instances directly from the lips of some of the survivors of these bloody scenes, from manuscripts, or from printed documents, no longer accessible to the student of history."— *Field.*

1291 MACAULAY (T. B.) Lays of Ancient Rome. By Thomas Babington Macaulay. Seventh Edition. *London: Longmans.* 1846.

8*vo*, *half green morocco, gilt top*, UNCUT.

"A Riverside Recollection from Bishop Doane to Rev. Dr. Ogilby, Christmas, 1848."

1292 MACAULAY. The History of England from the Accession of James the Second. By Thomas B. Macaulay. Eleventh Edition. *London: Longmans.* 1856–61.

5 *vols.*, 8*vo*, *half olive morocco, gilt top*, UNCUT. BEST EDITION. An INDIA PROOF PORTRAIT *inserted* in front of each volume.

1293 MACCLINTOCK (S.) An Oration Commemorative of the late Illustrious General Washington; Pronounced at Greenland, February 22d, 1800. ... By Samuel MacClintock, D.D. *Portsmouth:* 1800.

8*vo*, *pp.* 16. RARE.

1294 M'CLUNG (J. A.) Sketches of Western Adventure: containing an Account of the most interesting Incidents connected with the Settlement of the West, from 1755 to 1794. Together with an Appendix. By John A. M'Clung. *Philadelphia: Grigg & Elliot.* 1832.

12*mo*, *pp.* 360. *Half olive morocco, gilt top*, UNCUT. FOUR PORTRAITS *inserted.* ORIGINAL EDITION. RARE in *uncut* state.

Although bearing the imprint of Philadelphia, the work was really published at Maysville, Ky.

1295 M'CLURE (D.) A Discourse; Commemorative of the Death of General George Washington, ... Delivered at East Windsor, Connecticut, February 22, 1800. By David M'Clure, A.M. *East Windsor:* 1800.

8*vo*, *pp.* 23. UNCUT.

1296 M'CRIE (T.) The Life of John Knox: containing Illustrations of the History of the Reformation in Scotland; with Biographical Notices of the Principal Reformers, and Sketches of the Progress of Literature in Scotland, during a great part of the Sixteenth Century. ...

By Thomas M'Crie, D.D. ... The Second Edition. Corrected and Enlarged. *Edinburgh:* 1813.

2 vols., 8vo, half red morocco, gilt top, UNCUT. A FINE COPY with THIRTY-FIVE ILLUSTRATIONS *inserted.*

1297 [M'CULLOCH (James H.)] Researches on America; Being an Attempt to settle Some Points relative to the Aborigines of America, &c. ... By an Officer of the United States Army. *Baltimore: Coale and Maxwell.* 1816.

8vo, pp. (8), 130, (1). *Half gray calf,* UNCUT. VERY SCARCE.
The original sketch of a work afterwards much amplified.

1298 M'GREGOR (J.) British America. By John M'Gregor, Esq. The Second Edition. *Edinburgh: William Blackwood.* 1833.

2 vols., 8vo, pp. xxiv., 561; *xiv.,* (1), 606. 15 *Maps. Half calf.*

1299 M'GUIRE (E. C.) The Religious Opinions and Character of Washington. By E. C. M'Guire. *New York: Harper & Brothers.* MDCCCXXXVI.

12mo, pp. 414. *Half green morocco.* PORTRAIT *inserted.*

1300 McIAN (R. R.) The Clans of the Scottish Highlands, illustrated by appropriate Figures, displaying their Dress, Tartans, Arms, Armorial Insignia, and Social Occupations, from Original Sketches, by R. R. McIan, Esq. With accompanying description ... by James Logan, Esq. *London: Ackerman and Co.* 1845.

2 vols., folio, crushed green levant morocco, paneled and gilt sides, broad emblematically gilt inside borders, morocco joints, gilt edges. An ORIGINAL SUBSCRIBER'S COPY bound from numbers. The SEVENTY-TWO BEAUTIFULLY COLOURED FULL LENGTH FIGURES in this copy are INCOMPARABLY SUPERIOR to those of subsequent issues from the worn stones.

TWO SPLENDID VOLUMES.

"One of the most valuable and interesting works of modern times. The portraits are painted by a veritable Highlandman — an artist of the true stamp, who is familiar with his subject."— *Art Union.*

"The tartans given by Messrs. McIan and Logan we know have always been received as the veritable patterns."— *Morning Post.*

1301 MACKENZIE (A. S.) Life of Paul Jones. By Alexander Slidell Mackenzie, U.S.N. *Boston: Hilliard, Gray, and Company.* 1841.

2 vols., sm. 8vo, pp. xiii., 260; *ix.,* 308. *Half calf.*

1302 MACKENZIE. Life of Stephen Decatur, A Commodore in the Navy of the United States. By Alexander Slidell Mackenzie, U.S.N. *Boston: Little and Brown.* 1846.

Roy. 8vo, pp. xi., 443. *Facsimile. Half crimson morocco, gilt top,* UNCUT. LARGE PAPER; a *few copies only* printed.

1303 MACKENZIE (W. L.) Sketches of Canada and the United States. By William L. Mackenzie. *London: Effingham Wilson.* 1833.

Sm. 8vo, pp. xxiv., 504. *Half calf, gilt top,* UNCUT. Fine copy. VERY SCARCE.

1304 MACKENZIE. The Lives and Opinions of Benjamin F. Butler, ... and Jesse Hoyt. ... By W. L. Mackenzie. *Boston: Cook & Co.* 1845.

8vo, pp. 152. *Half green morocco, gilt top.* PORTRAIT *inserted.*

1305 MACKENZIE. The Life and Times of Martin Van Buren: the Correspondence of his Friends, Family, and Pupils: together with Brief Notices, Sketches, and Anecdotes, illustrative of the Public Career of many other Prominent Characters. By William L. Mackenzie. *Boston: Cooke & Co.* 1846.

8vo, pp. xii., 308. *Half green morocco, gilt top,* UNCUT. PORTRAIT *inserted.* Uniform with the preceding No.

"These volumes gave so much offence to the parties concerned, that their sale was prohibited by injunction. They made some uncomfortable revelations touching the actions and conduct of many of the leading democratic politicians who figured largely during Gen. Jackson's time."— *W. Gowans.*

1306 MACKENZIE (R.) Strictures on Lt. Col. Tarleton's "History of the Campaigns of 1780 and 1781, in the Southern Provinces of North America," wherein Military Characters and Corps are vindicated from Injurious Aspersions, and several Important Transactions placed in their proper point of view. In a series of Letters to a Friend. By Roderick Mackenzie late Lieutenant in the 71st Regiment. To which is added a Detail of the Siege of Ninety-Six, and the Re-capture of the Island of New Providence.

London: Printed for the Author. M.DCC.LXXXVII.

8vo, pp. vi., 186. *Half green morocco, gilt top,* UNCUT. FINE COPY. VERY SCARCE. Uniform with "Hanger's Reply." No. 876.

See Tarleton (B.) No. 1945.

The author defends Lord Cornwallis, and is very severe on Lieut. Col. Tarleton's "*History*," in which, he says, "some facts have been withheld, and some mutilated, while others are raised to a pitch of importance, to which, if historical justice had been the author's object, they are by no means entitled."

1307 M'KINNEY (T. L.) History of the Indian Tribes of North America, with Biographical Sketches and Anecdotes of the principal Chiefs. Embellished with One Hundred and Twenty Portraits from the Indian Gallery in the Department of War, at Washington. By Thomas L. M'Kinney, late of the Indian Department, Washington, and James Hall, Esq., of Cincinnati. *Philadelphia:* 1838–44.

3 *vols., folio, half red levant morocco extra, full gilt backs, morocco joints, gilt top,* UNCUT, *by* W. MATTHEWS. A SPLENDID SET of the ORIGINAL ISSUE.

As early as 1824, the practice was begun of taking portraits of the principal Indians who came to Washington, and depositing them in the War Department. Under the management of Col. M'Kinney, Superintendent of Indian Affairs, the number rapidly increased, till a very interesting gallery was formed. They were chiefly painted by Mr. King, an artist of high repute, who has been remarkably successful in transferring to his canvas the strong lineaments of the Indian countenance. Col. M'Kinney conceived the plan of making this rare and curious collection more valuable to the world by publishing a series of engraved portraits exactly copied and colored from these paintings. With each portrait is connected a biographical sketch of the individual whom it is intended to represent, interspersed with anecdotes and narrations. The work contains also a historical account of the various Indian tribes within the borders of the United States.

1308 M'KINNON (J. D.) Descriptive Poems. By John D. M'Kinnon, containing Picturesque Views of the State of New York.
New York: T. and J. Swords. 1802.

12mo, pp. (4), 79. *Half calf, gilt top,* UNCUT. *Very scarce.*

1309 MACLEANE (L.) An Essay on the Expediency of Innoculation and the Seasons most proper for it. Humbly Inscribed to the Inhabitants of Philadelphia, by Laughlin Macleane, M.D.
Philadelphia: Printed by William Bradford. 1756.

8vo, pp. 39, (1). *Half maroon morocco, gilt top,* UNCUT. *Very Scarce.*
One of the earliest American works on the subject.

1310 MACWHORTER (A.) A Funeral Sermon preached in Newark, December 27, 1799, a day of Public Mourning, observed by the Town for the universally Lamented General Washington. ... To which is Subjoined his last Address to his Beloved Countrymen. By Alexander Macwhorter, D.D. *Newark:* MDCCC.

8vo, pp. 22. RARE. A small portion of the upper margin of the title is cut off. The Address is wanting.

1311 MADISON (J.) A Discourse on the Death of General Washington ... delivered on the 22d of February, 1800, in the Church in Williamsburg. By James Madison, D.D., Bishop of the Protestant Episcopal Church in Virginia, and President of William and Mary's College. The Second Edition Corrected. *New York:* 1800.

8vo, pp. 42. UNCUT.

1312 MADISON. A Discourse. The Third Edition. *New York: Printed. London: Reprinted for John Hatchard.* 1800.

8vo, UNCUT, and EXCEEDINGLY SCARCE.

1313 MADISON Agonistes; or the Agonies of Mother Goose. Fragment of a Political Burletta as acting or to be acted, on the American Stage. To which are added, Sundry other Monologues, Dialogues, Songs, &c., as Spoken or Sung on the Boards of the Great Political Theatre of Europe. *London: Printed by D. Deans.* 1814.

8vo, pp. 103. *Half calf.* SCARCE.

Among the Dramatis Personæ are Randolpho and Adamo, Members of Congress, Mother Jeff, Miss Paterson, King of Westphalia, &c.

1314 MADISON (J.) The Papers of James Madison. ... Being his Correspondence and Reports of Debates during the Congress of the Confederation and his Reports of Debates in the Federal Convention; now published from the Original Manuscripts, ... under the Superintendence of Henry D. Gilpin.
Washington: Langtree & O'Sullivan. 1840.

3 *vols., 8vo, pp. lx.,* 580, *xxii.; xxii.,* 581–1242; *xiv.,* 1243–1624, *ccxlvi., and* 16*l. of Facsimiles. Half red morocco, gilt top.* LARGE and FINE COPY. SCARCE. FOUR PORTRAITS *inserted.*

1315 MADISON. Selections from the Private Correspondence of James Madison, From 1813 to 1836. Published by J. C. McGuire, Exclusively for Private Distribution. *Washington :* MDCCCLIX.

4to, pp. vi., 9–419. Dark olive morocco, embossed sides, gilt edges. BEAUTIFUL COPY. EXCEEDINGLY SCARCE.

1316 MADISON. Letters and other Writings of James Madison, Fourth President of the United States. Published by Order of Congress. *Philadelphia : J. B. Lippincott & Co.* 1865.

4 *vols., 8vo, pp. li.,* 658; *xxxvii.,* 617; *lx.,* 670; *lvii.,* 694. *Half crimson morocco, gilt top,* UNCUT. TWO PORTRAITS *inserted.* SCARCE.

1317 MAGAW (S.) An Oration commemorative of the Virtues and Greatness of General Washington; Pronounced in ... Philadelphia, Before the Grand Lodge of Pennsylvania, on the Twenty-second day of February, Eighteen Hundred. By Samuel Magaw, D.D. *Newfield:* 1800.

8vo, pp. 23. VERY RARE.

1318 MAINE. Collections of the Maine Historical Society. [Vols. I.–III. only.] *Portland:* 1831–53.

3 *vols., 8vo, half calf.* Vol. I. is of the *Original Edition,* printed by Day Fraser & Co., and of rare occurrence, nearly the whole impression having been destroyed by fire.

1319 MAINE. Collections of the Maine Historical Society. *Portland:* 1831–69.

7 *vols., 8vo, cloth. Complete to date.* SCARCE.

"The First Series embraces a large collection of particular and local histories of towns, biographical sketches of remarkable men, topographical descriptions, etc., the natural history of the State, accounts of the former and present modes of cultivation and improvements that have been made in husbandry. It describes the vegetable productions, and minerals, gives observations on the weather and climate, an account of epidemic diseases, accurate bills of mortality, much information relating to the primitive inhabitants of the State, and a vast amount of other information both local and concerning New England generally. The New Series consists of documentary history relating to the discovery of Maine."

1320 MAITLAND (S. R.) The Dark Ages: A Series of Essays, intended to illustrate the State of Religion and Literature in the Ninth, Tenth, Eleventh, and Twelfth Centuries. ... By the Rev. S. R. Maitland, F.R.S. ... *London : Rivingtons.* 1844.

8vo, pp. xxiii., 498. *Half purple morocco, gilt top,* UNCUT. VERY SCARCE.

1321 MAJOR (R. H.) The Life of Prince Henry of Portugal, surnamed the Navigator; and its Results: Comprising the Discovery, within one Century, of Half the World. With New Facts in the Discovery of the Atlantic Islands; a Refutation of French Claims to Priority in Discovery; Portuguese Knowledge (subsequently lost) of the Nile Lakes; and the History of the Naming of America. From Authentic Cotemporary Documents. By Richard Henry Major. ... Illustrated with Portraits, Maps, Etc. *London : A. Asher & Co.* 1868.

Roy. 8vo, pp. lii., 487. 4 Portraits, 7 Maps, 2 Engravings. Half green morocco, gilt top, UNCUT, *by* BRADSTREET.

"The author has illustrated his book with curious maps, which throw a striking light on ancient geography, and on the early discovery of the Portuguese; and his examination of some of the old voyages, deserves attention."—*Edinburgh Review.*

"'The Life of Prince Henry' is a piece of good work, full of new matter, and of high mark in European letters." —*Athenæum.*

1322 MANTE (T.) The | History | of the | Late War | in | North-America, | and the | Islands of the West-Indies, | including | the Campaigns of MDCCLXIII, and MDCCLXIV | against his Majesty's Indian Enemies. | By Thomas Mante, | Assistant Engineer during the Siege of the Havanna, | and Major of a Brigade in the Campaign of 1764. | *London : | Printed for W. Strahan, and T. Cadell in the Strand.* MDCCLXXII.

4to, pp. (4), *viii.*, 542, (1). 18 *Maps. Half morocco, gilt top,* UNCUT. A BEAUTIFUL COPY, FINE and CLEAN as when published; with ALL the LARGE FOLDED MAPS. Seldom found complete, and of the GREATEST RARITY in UNCUT condition.

It is probable that but few copies were printed, though the large and beautiful plans and military maps, (which give it so great a value) must have made its production a work of much expense. The introduction contains an account of Washington's escape from assassination, by an Indian, in December, 1753.

1323 **Manuscript. Hore Beate Marie Virginis,** a French MS. of the XVth Century, finely written on one hundred and fifteen leaves of PURE VELLUM, and PROFUSELY DECORATED THROUGHOUT; the embellishments are executed with great skill, and consist of broad arabesque borders to every page, very numerous CAPITAL LETTERS, seventeen MINIATURES, and sixteen LARGE ILLUMINATIONS OF SINGULAR BRILLIANCY AND FRESHNESS OF COLOUR, surrounded by borders of superior design, the WHOLE OF THE ILLUSTRATIONS RICHLY FINISHED IN BURNISHED AND IN DULL GOLD. A BEAUTIFUL EXAMPLE OF MEDIÆVAL ART, IN THE BEST PRESERVATION. *Sæc. XV.*

8vo, brown levant morocco, richly tooled and gilt sides after a Grolier pattern, vellum fly-leaves, gilt edges. In a pull-off case covered in blue morocco, lined inside with white velvet, by F. BEDFORD. Size of leaf 7 inches by 4¾ inches.

1324 MARQUETTE (J.) Recit des Voyages et des Decouvertes du R. Père Jacques Marquette de la Compagnie de Jesus, en l'année 1673 et aux suivantes; la Continuation de ses Voyages par le R. P. Claude Alloüez, et le Journal Autographe du P. Marquette en 1674 & 1675. Avec la Carte de son Voyage tracée de sa main.

[Also:] Dreuillette (G.) Narré du Voyage faict pour la Mission des Abnaquiois et des Connaissances tiréz de la Nouvelle Angleterre et des dispositions des Magistrats de cette Republique pour le secours contre les Iroquois, ès années 1648 & 1649. Par le R. Père Gabriel Dreuillette de la Compagnie de Jesus.
[*Albany: Weed, Parsons & Co.* 1855.]

8vo, 2 vols., bound in 1, pp. (9), 169, (1), *Map and Facsimile : and pp.* (4), 33. *Green morocco,* UNCUT. EXTREMELY RARE. A FEW COPIES ONLY PRIVATELY PRINTED from the Original MSS. for Mr. James Lenox, exclusively for presentation. This was Baron Sobolewski's copy.

1325 MARRANT (J.) A Narrative of the Life of John Marrant, of New York, in North America; giving an Account of his Conversion when only fourteen years of age, his leaving his Mother's House from religious motives, wandering several Days in the Desert without Food, and being at last taken by an Indian Hunter among the Cherokees, where he was condemned to die. With an account of his Conversion of the King of the Cherokees, and his Daughter, &c. The whole authenticated by the Rev. W. Aldridge. *Leeds:* 1810.

8vo, pp. 24. *Half olive morocco,* UNCUT. RARE.

1326 MARSH (E. G.) An Oration, delivered at Wethersfield, February 22, 1800; on the Death of General George Washington. ... By Ebenezer Grant Marsh. *Hartford:* 1800.

8vo, pp. 16. UNCUT.

1327 MARSHALL (C.) Passages from the Diary of Christopher Marshall, kept in Philadelphia and Lancaster during the American Revolution. Edited by William Duane, — 1774–1777.
Philadelphia: Hazard & Mitchell. 1839.

12mo, pp. 174, *xix. Errata. Half calf.*

1328 MARSHALL (J.) The Life of George Washington, Commander in Chief of the American Forces, during the War which established the Independence of his Country, and First President of the United States. Compiled under the inspection of the Honorable Bushrod Washington, from Original Papers bequeathed to him by his deceased Relative. To which is prefixed, an Introduction, containing a Compendious View of the Colonies planted by the English on the Continent of North America. By John Marshall. ...
London: Richard Phillips. 1804–7.

3 *vols., 4to. Half green levant morocco, gilt top,* UNCUT, *by* W. MATTHEWS.

A SPLENDID COPY, CLEAN and FINE as when issued. Inserted are SIX RARE PORTRAITS of WASHINGTON, a RARE INDIA PROOF PORTRAIT of CABOT, and one of the AUTHOR. This edition contains all the ORIGINAL MAPS and PLATES, some of which were omitted in the American edition.

Incomparably the BEST Life of Washington.

1329 MARTIN (J.) A Bibliographical Catalogue of Books Privately Printed: including those of the Bannatyne, Maitland and Roxburghe Clubs, and of the Private Presses at Darlington, Auchinleck, Lee Priory, Newcastle, Middle Hill, and Strawberry Hill. By John Martin. *London: J. and A. Arch.* 1834.

2 *vols., imp. 8vo, half crushed red levant morocco, gilt top,* UNCUT, *by* W. MATTHEWS. LARGE PAPER. 50 copies only printed. DUPLICATE PLATE IN COLOURS. ELEGANT COPY.

The Accounts of the various Clubs, and Private Presses, are not included in the more recent edition.

1330 MARTIN (L.) The Genuine Information, delivered to the Legislature of the State of Maryland, Relative to the Proceedings of the General Convention, lately held at Philadelphia; by Luther Martin, Esquire, Attorney General of Maryland, and one of the Delegates in the said Convention. Together with A Letter to the Hon. Thomas C. Deye, Speaker of the House of Delegates, an Address to the Citizens of the United States, and some Remarks relative to a Standing Army and a Bill of Rights.

Philadelphia: Printed by Eleazer Oswald. M.DCC.LXXXVIII.

8vo, pp. viii., 93. *Half gray calf, gilt top,* UNCUT, *by* BRADSTREET. VERY SCARCE. FINE COPY with an AUTOGRAPH LETTER of the AUTHOR *inserted.*

1331 [MARTYN (Benjamin.)] An Impartial Enquiry into the State and Utility of the Province of Georgia.

London: W. Meadows. MDCCXLI.

8vo, pp. 104. *Half blue morocco, gilt top,* LARGE and FINE COPY. SCARCE.

"A very well written Tract, defending the Colony from the malignant reports that had been industriously circulated."— *Rich.*

1332 [MARTYR (Peter.)] The | History of Trauayle | in the | VVest and East Indies, and other | countreys lying eyther way, | towardes the frutefull and rych | Moluccaes. | As | in Mascouia, Persia, Arabia, Syria, Ægypte, | Ethiopia, Guinea, China in Cathaye and | Giapan: VVith a discourse of | the Northwest pas- | sage. | ... | Gathered in parte, and done into Englyshe by | Richarde Eden. | Newly set in order, augmented, and finished | by Richard VVilles. | *Imprinted at London | by Richarde Iugge.* | 1577. | *Cum Priuilegio.*

4to, 10 *p. l.,* 466 *l. Errata and Table* 6 *l. Russia extra, gilt leaves, by* JENKINS & CECIL. VERY RARE.

"The great historical importance of this book is not yet fully appreciated. Besides the first three Decades of Peter Martyr it contains a translation of that Author's paper on the recently discovered Islands, first printed in 1521 to supply the loss of Cortes's First Relation. It also contains the Bull of Pope Alexander (in Latin and English) dividing the world between Spain and Portugal; as well as translations of the most important parts pertaining to maritime discovery and the new world, of Ziegler, Paulus Jovius, Vespucci, Maximilianus Transylvanus, Oviedo, Gomara, Andreas de Corsali, Cadamosto, Butrigarius, the Classic Authors, etc." — *Stevens.*

For an extended notice of this edition see *Rich,* No. 15.

1333 [MARTYR.] The | Historie Of | The West Indies, | Containing the Actes and Aduentures | of the Spaniards, which haue conquered | and peopled those Countries, inriched with vari- | etie of pleasant relation of the Manners, | Ceremonies, Lawes, Gouernments, | and Warres of the | Indians. | Published in Latin by Mr. Hakluyt, | and translated into English by M. Lok. Gent. | ... | *London, | printed for Andrew Hebb, and are to be sold at the Signe | of the Bell in Paul's Church-yard.* [1597.]

4to, 3*l. Text* 318 *l.* With the "Epistola Dedicatoria," 2*l,* (evidently inserted from another edition.) *Blue morocco, gilt edges.* A remarkably LARGE and FINE COPY of the RAREST of the English versions of Peter Martyr.

Its date is uncertain. White Kennett, a good authority, places it at 1597. Rich gives the date as 1612; but in either case it is doubtless the same work.

1334 [MARTYR.] The | Famovs | Historie of | the Indies: | Declaring the aduentures of | the Spaniards, which haue conque- | red these Countries, with Varietie of Relations | of the Religions, Lawes, Gouernments, Manners, | Ceremonies, Customs, Rites, Warres, | and Funerals of that People. | Comprised into sundry Decads. | Set forth first by Mr. Hackluyt, and now pub- | lished by L. M. Gent. | The second Edition. | *London:* | *Printed for Michael Sparke dwelling at the signe* | *of the blue Bible in Green-Arbor*, 1628.

4to, 3 l., Text 318 l. Brown levant morocco, paneled and gilt sides, corner ornaments, gilt edges, by F. BEDFORD. CONTEMPORARY PORTRAIT of MARTYR *inserted.*

A BEAUTIFUL COPY of a work of MUCH RARITY.

"Martyr possessed eminent ability and learning, and is believed to be the first writer who noticed in his works the discovery of America by his countryman Columbus; as he is the first who published a treatise descriptive of the peculiarities of the natives of the New World, the first decade having been printed in 1504, and the first three decades in 1516. It was not until 1530, that the complete work in eight decades was printed. Eden translated the first edition of three decades, and printed it with some matters copied from Oviedo and other authors, in 1555. Willes followed his example, and produced the three decades with part of the fourth, and some additional material drawn from several historians. The first complete English edition was printed in 1597."—*Field.*

1335 MARY-LAND. A Relation of The successefull beginnings of the Lord Baltemore's Plantation in Mary-Land; Being an extract of certaine Letters written from thence, by some of the Aduenturers to their friends in England. Anno Domini 1634.
[*Albany: J. Munsell.* 1865.]

4to, pp. 23. Map. Half red morocco, gilt top, UNCUT; 150 *copies printed* from a transcript of the original work in the British Museum.

1336 [MASERES (Francis.)] Considerations on the Expediency of Admitting Representatives from the American Colonies into the British House of Commons. *London: B. White.* 1770.

8vo, pp. 41. Half blue morocco.

1337 [MASERES.] The Canadian Freeholder: in Three Dialogues, between an Englishman and a Frenchman, settled in Canada. Shewing the Sentiments of the Bulk of the Freeholders of Canada concerning the late Quebec-Act; with some Remarks on the Boston-Charter Act, and an Attempt to shew the great Expediency of Immediately Repealing both those Acts of Parliament, and of making some other Useful Regulations and Concessions to his Majesty's American Subjects, as a Ground for Reconciliation with the United Colonies in America. *London:* 1776–79.

3 vols., 8vo, pp. 483; xxii., 404; xlii., 399–810. Calf. FINE COPY. SCARCE.

The dialogues are between a sensible and substantial Canadian freeholder of the Roman Catholick religion and an English Protestant gentleman, and are intended to convey a true representation of the sentiments of the French, or Canadian, inhabitants of that province, &c.

1338 MASON (J.) A | Brief History | of the | Pequot War: | Especially | Of the Memorable Taking of their Fort at | Mistick in Connecticut | In | 1637. | Written by | Major John Mason, | A principal Actor therein, as then Chief Captain and Com- | mander of Connecticut Forces. | With an Introduction and some Explanatory Notes, | By the Reverend | Mr. Thomas Prince. | *Boston, Printed & Sold by S. Kneeland & T. Green | in Queen-Street,* 1736.

12mo, pp. (1), *vi., x.,* 22. *Crushed red levant morocco, gilt edges, by* W. PRATT. EXCESSIVELY RARE. A small portion of the head-lines, cut off in binding, has been supplied in fac-simile, and so admirably done as almost to escape detection. The margins otherwise are good, and it is believed, despite the above unimportant defect, that this is as fine a copy of this rare book as can be procured.

Major Mason was one of the first settlers of Dorchester, in 1630. From that place he removed about the year 1635 and assisted in laying the foundation of a new colony. After the Pequot War, in which he took a prominent part, he was appointed by the Governor of Connecticut, Major-General of all their forces, which office he continued to hold till his death. He was elected Deputy-Governor of the Colony in 1660, which place he held for ten years. He died at Norwich in 1672 or 1673, at the age of 72.

An uncut copy was recently sold at private sale, for $160.

1339 MASON. Brief History of the Pequot War. *New York: Reprinted by J. Sabin & Sons.* 1869.

8vo, half red morocco, gilt top, UNCUT, *by* BRADSTREET. PORTRAIT of THOMAS PRINCE *inserted.* An elegant facsimile reprint of the preceding No.

1340 MASON (J. M.) A Funeral Oration, delivered in ... the City of New York, on the 22d day of February, 1800, being the day rccommended by Congress to the Citizens of the United States, publicly to testify their Grief for the Death of Gen. Washington. ... By John M. Mason, A.M. ... *New-York:* 1800.

8vo, pp. 23. UNCUT.

1341 MASON. A Funeral Oration on Gen. Washington, Delivered Feb. 22, 1800. By Appointment of a Number of the Clergy of New-York. By John M. Mason, A.M. The Second Edition. *New-York:* 1800.

8vo, pp. 32. UNCUT.

1342 MASSACHUSETTS. A | Word of Comfort | To a | Melancholy Country. | Or the | Bank of Credit | Erected in the | Massachusetts-Bay, | Fairly Defended by a Discovery of the | Great Benefit Accruing by it to the | Whole Province; With a Re- | medy for Recovering a Civil State | when Sinking under Desperation by a | Defeat on their Bank of Credit. | By Amicus Patriæ. | ... | *Boston: Printed in the Year,* 1721.

12mo, pp. (4), 58. *Polished calf, gilt edges, by* W. PRATT. EXTREMELY RARE.

Of special interest in connection with the Currency Question. "The Want of Money (or a Sufficient Medium of Trade) is the greatest of all Interruptions in a Common Wealth; and puts by, or Obstructs the carrying on of a Business in a Flourishing Manner."—*Extract from Title.*

1343 MASSACHUSETTS. Collections of the Massachusetts Historical Society. [Complete to 1871.] *Boston:* 1792–1871.

41 *vols., 8vo, half red morocco, gilt top,* UNCUT, with the exception of Vol. IV. of the third series, none of which were left uncut. AN ELEGANT SET. *Seldom found complete.* A FRONTISPIECE *inserted* in nearly every volume.

A most important collection, containing the only reprints of many of the earliest and most rare books relating to the history of this country.

1344 MASSACHUSETTS. Proceedings of the Massachusetts Historical Society. [Complete to 1873.] *Boston:* 1859–73.

10 *vols., 8vo, half olive morocco, gilt top,* UNCUT. Many Portraits and Facsimiles. Several PORTRAITS *inserted.*

1345 MASSACHUSETTS. Speeches of the Governors of Massachusetts, from 1765 to 1775; and the Answers of the House of Representatives, to the same; with their Resolutions and Addresses for that period. And other Public Papers, relating to the Dispute between this Country and Great Britain, which led to the Independence of the United States. *Boston: Russell and Gardner.* 1818.

8*vo, pp.* 424. *Half green morocco, gilt top,* UNCUT. VERY SCARCE.

Known as the "Massachusetts State Papers." Collected and Edited by Alden Bradford.

1346 MASSACHUSETTS. The Journals of each Provincial Congress of Massachusetts in 1774 and 1775, and of the Committee of Safety, with an Appendix, containing the proceedings of the County Conventions. Narratives of the Events of the nineteenth of April, 1775. Papers relating to Ticonderoga and Crown Point, and other Documents, illustrative of the early History of the American Revolution. Published agreeably to a Resolve passed March 10, 1837, under the Supervision of William Lincoln.
Boston: Dutton & Wentworth, Printers to the State. 1838.

8*vo, pp. lix.,* 778. *Half blue morocco, carmine edges.* FINE COPY. SCARCE.

1347 MASSACHUSETTS. Records of the Governor and Company of the Massachusetts Bay in New England. [1628–1686.] Printed by Order of the Legislature. Edited by Nathaniel B. Shurtleff, M.D.
Boston: From the Press of William White. 1853–4.

6 *vols., 4to, cloth, gilt top,* UNCUT.

Highly important for the History of Massachusetts. *A few copies only printed* at the public expense, and now EXCEEDINGLY SCARCE.

1348 MASSACHUSETTS. Report of a Committee appointed by the Massachusetts Historical Society on Exchanges of Prisoners during the American Revolutionary War. [Also:] Mr. Bancroft's Letter [to the New York Historical Society] on the Exchange of Prisoners during the American War of Independence. [And:] Mr. Bancroft and his Boston Critics. *Boston: and New York:* 1861–62

8*vo,* 3 *pieces in* 1 *vol., half green morocco, gilt top,* UNCUT.

1349 MASSACHUSETTS. Proceedings of a Convention of Delegates from several of the New-England States, held at Boston, August 3–9, 1780, to advise on affairs necessary to promote the most Vigorous Prosecution of the War, and to provide for a Generous Reception of our French Allies. ... With an Introduction and Notes, by Franklin B. Hough. *Albany: J. Munsell.* 1867.

Sm. 4to, pp. 80. *Half green morocco, gilt top,* UNCUT, *by* BRADSTREET. 100 *copies only printed.*

1350 MATHER (C.) Late | Memorable Providences | Relating to | Witchcrafts and Possessions, | Clearly Manifesting, | Not only that there are Witches, but | that Good Men (as well as others) | may possibly have their Lives shortned | by such evil instruments of Satan. | Written by Cotton Mather Minister of the | Gospel at Boston in New-England. | The Second Impression. | Recommended by the Reverend Mr Richard | Baxter in London, and by the Ministers of | Boston and Charlestown in New-England. | *London,* | *Printed for Tho. Parkhurst at the Bible and* | *Three Crowns in Cheapside near Mercers-* | *Chapel.* 1691.

12*mo, pp.* (22), 144. *Polished calf, gilt edges, by* F. BEDFORD. FINE COPY of one of the EARLIEST and RAREST American works referring to the subject.

"The latest witchcraft frenzy was in New England in 1692, when the execution of witches became a calamity more dreadful than the sword or the pestilence." — *Robinson's Theol. Dict.*

1351 MATHER. The Wonders of the Invisible World: | Being an Account of the | Tryals | of | Several Witches, | Lately Executed in | New-England: | And of several Remarkable Curiosities | therein Occurring. | By Cotton Mather. | Published by the Special Command of his Excellency the | Governour of the Province of the Massachusetts-Bay in New- | England. | The Second Edition | *Printed first, at Boston in New-England, and Reprinted at London, for* | *John Dunton, at the Raven in the Poultrey.* 1693.

4*to, pp.* 62. *Blue morocco, gilt top,* UNCUT, *by* F. BEDFORD. A BEAUTIFUL COPY, and of the GREATEST RARITY in *uncut* condition.

1352 [MATHER.] The Bostonian Ebenezer. | Some | Historical Remarks, | On the State of | Boston, | The Chief Town of New-England, | and of the English America. | With Some, | Agreeable Methods, | For | Preserving and Promoting, the Good | State of That, as well as any | other Town, in the like Circumstances. | Humbly Offer'd, By a Native of Boston. | *Boston, Printed by B. Green & J. Allen, for* | *Samuel Phillips, at the Brick Shop,* 1698.

12*mo, pp.* 82. *Polished red morocco, inside lined with polished green calf, rich inside gilt borders, centre ornaments, gilt edges, by* PAWSON *and* NICHOLSON. EXCESSIVELY RARE.

The RAREST of any of the numerous productions of Cotton Mather. *See* his Life by his Son, Samuel Mather, p. 164. Also the "Magnalia."

1353 MATHER. Magnalia Christi Americana: or, the Ecclesiastical History of New England, From Its First Planting in the Year 1620, unto the Year of our Lord, 1698. In Seven Books. ... By the Reverend and Learned Cotton Mather, M.A. And Pastor of the North Church in Boston, New-England.

London: Thomas Parkhurst. MDCCII.

Folio, LARGE PAPER; *purple levant morocco, blank and gilt tooled back and sides, inside lined with polished russia elegantly tooled and gilt in the Grolier manner, russia fly leaves, morocco joints, gilt edges.* The large PORTRAIT, reduced to an oval, and a CHARACTERISTIC AUTOGRAPH LETTER of the AUTHOR, both inlaid by MR. TRENT, precede the title.

This GRAND LARGE PAPER COPY, measuring 14½ inches by 9¼ inches on the leaf, is ABSOLUTELY PERFECT in every particular, including the two leaves of Books &c. at the end, and is considered to stand UNSURPASSED in beauty of CONDITION, and probably in point of SIZE. It is a truly MAGNIFICENT COPY, and of the HIGHEST DEGREE OF RARITY upon LARGE PAPER.

"To those who are interested in the early history of our country, it may be well to remark, that for accuracy in historical occurrences they will do well to rely upon other authorities; but if they wish to obtain a general view of the state of society and manners, they will probably nowhere find so many materials for this purpose, as in the work of this pedantic and garrulous writer."

1354 [MATHER.] Psalterium Americanum. | The Book of | Psalms, | In a Translation Exactly conformed | unto the Original; | but all in | Blank Verse, | Fitted unto the Tunes commonly used | in our Churches. Which Pure | Offering is accompanied with | Illustrations, digging for Hidden | Treasures in it; And Rules to | Employ it upon the Glorious and | Various Intentions of it, | Whereto are added, | Some other Portions of the Sacred | Scripture, to Enrich the | Cantional. | *Boston: in N. E.* | *Printed by S. Kneeland, for B. Eliot,* | *S. Gerrish, D. Henchman, and* | *J. Edwards, and Sold at their Shops,* 1718.

12mo, Title, xxxv., (1), 426. *Blue morocco, paneled sides, gilt edges.* RARE, and CURIOUS.

"In this singular publication, which is a close translation of the Hebrew, Dr. Mather has not only disregarded the modern practice of breaking the lines, whether rhymed or not, but he has run out (to use a printer's phrase) the whole matter; so that while each psalm looks exactly like prose, and may be read as such, it is, in fact, modulated so that it may be sung as lyric verse.

The learned Doctor says that in the 'twice seven versions' which he has seen, the authors 'put in as large an Heap of poor Things, which, are intirely their own, — meerly for the sake of preserving the *Clink* of the *Rhime*; Which after all is of small consequence unto a Generous Poem; and of none at all unto the Melody of Singing."

The following extract from the xxiii. Psalm is a specimen of the translation and arrangement. By omitting the words in BLACK LETTER the verse is adapted to short metre. 'The Director of the Psalmody, need only say. Sing with the **Black Letter**, or sing without the **Black Letter**, and the tune will be sufficiently directed.

1. My Shepherd is th' ETERNAL God: || I shall not be in [**any**] want: ||

2 In pastures of tender grass || He [**ever**] makes me lie down: || To waters of tranquillities || He gently carries me, [**along.**] ||

3. My *feeble and my wandring* Soul || He [**kindly**] does fetch back again; || In the plain paths of righteousness || He does lead [**and guide**] me along, || because of the regard He has [**ever**] unto His *Glorious* Name. ||'" — *J. R. Bartlett.*

1355 MATHER. India Christiana. | A Discourse, | Delivered unto the | Commissioners, | for the | Propagation of the Gospel among | the American Indians | which is | Accompanied with several Instru- | ments relating to the Glorious | Design of Propagating our Holy | Religion, in the Eastern | as well as the Western, Indies. | An Entertainment which they that are | Waiting for the Kingdom of God | will receive as Good News | from a far Country. | By Cotton Mather, D.D. | and F.R.S. | *Boston in New-England:* | *Printed by B. Green.* 1721.

Sm. 8vo, Title, ii., 94, (1). Polished blue levant morocco, richly ornamented sides, broad inside borders, edges gilt on carmine, by F. BEDFORD. A BEAUTIFUL COPY of this MOST RARE work. It contains the slip at the end, "Corrigenda," usually wanting.

1356 MATHER. The | Christian Philospher: | A | Collection | of the | Best Discoveries in Nature, | with | Religious Improvements. | By Cotton Mather, D.D. | And Fellow of the Royal Society. | *London:* | *Printed for Eman. Matthews at the Bible in* | *Pater-noster-Row.* M.DCC.XXI.

Sm. 8vo, pp. viii., (1), 304. Polished calf, edges gilt in the round, by F. BEDFORD. ELEGANT COPY. VERY SCARCE.

"Hereby hangs a funny tale. About the year 1714, Cotton Mather in Boston was dubbed with F.R.S., a trinity of capitals which flattering his vanity he adopted and wore, though somewhat against his previous teachings in regard to worldly distinctions. The first of his 383 books that came out after the receipt of this polished handle bore F.R.S. after his name, much to the astonishment of his rivals, and amusement of his fellow citizens. He immediately wrote to the Secretary of the Royal Society thanking him, and continued through life to be an active correspondent, all but the first letter being still preserved by the Society. The letter of thanks, however, for some reason never got among the records, but eventually fell among autograph-mongers, and found its way to New York. Some, in the Doctor's lifetime, said he had been hoaxed, and never was really elected, while others, and among them his son, manfully contended that he was really one of the Philosophers. This book was written during the controversy to show that he was both competent and willing to be an F.R.S. To this day the question is not settled — Was Cotton Mather an F.R.S.? There is nothing in the Society's records to show it, though the names of a dozen other Americans are recorded." — *Stevens.*

1357 [MATHER.] Parentator. | Memoirs | of | Remarkables | in the | Life | and the | Death | of the | Ever-Memorable | Dr. Increase Mather. | Who Expired August 23, 1723. | *Boston: Printed by B. Green, for* | *Nathaniel Belknap, at the Corner of* | *Scarlets-Wharff.* 1724.

Sm. 8vo, Title, pp. x., xv., 239, (6). Portrait. Polished green levant morocco, paneled and gilt sides, edges gilt on carmine, by F. BEDFORD. AN ELEGANT COPY of this VERY RARE BOOK, with a fine impression of the PORTRAIT engraved by STURT.

Rewritten and issued with the following title.

1358 [MATHER.] Memoirs | of the | Life | of the late Reverend | Increase Mather, D.D. | Who died August 23, 1723. | With a Preface by the Reverend Edmund | Calamy, D.D. | *London:* | *Printed for John Clark and Richard* | *Hett at the Bible and Crown in the Poultry,* | *near Cheapside.* MDCCXXV.

8vo, pp. (8), 88. Red morocco, gilt top, UNCUT, *by* F. BEDFORD. Fine impression of the SCARCE PORTRAIT of INCREASE MATHER engraved by R. WHITE *inserted.* AN ELEGANT COPY. RARE in *uncut* condition.

1359 MATHER (I.) A Brief | History | of the | War | with the | Indians | in | New-England. | From June 24. 1675. (when the first

Englishman was Murder- | ed by the Indians) to August 12. 1676. when Philip, | alias Metacomet, the principal Author and | Beginner of the War, was slain. | Wherein the Grounds, Beginning, and Progress of the War, is summarily | expressed. Together with a serious Exhortation to the | Inhabitants of that Land. | By Increase Mather, Teacher of a Church of | Christ, in Boston in New-England. | .... | *London, Printed for Richard Chiswell, at the Rose and Crown in St. Paul's | Church-Yard, according to the Original Copy Printed | in New-England.* 1676.

4to, *pp.* (6), 51, 8. *Polished blue levant morocco, paneled sides, corner ornaments, rich inside borders, edges gilt on carmine, by* F. BEDFORD. LARGE and BEAUTIFUL copy. EXCEEDINGLY RARE.

Lowndes quotes this book as having only occurred for sale at Puttick's in 1859. The New England edition is not mentioned by him, nor elsewhere, so far as we have been able to ascertain. Perhaps no copy of it exists. The preface mentions the labours of Eliot, "this now aged servant of the Lord," and his famous Natic Bible.

1360 MATHER. Κομήτογραφια | Or A | Discourse Concerning | Comets ; | wherein the Nature of Blazing Stars | is Enquired into : | With an Historical Account of all the Comets which have appeared, from the Beginning of the | World unto this present year, M.DC.LXXXIII. | Expressing | The Place in the Heavens, where they were seen, | Their Motion, Forms, Duration ; and the Re- | markable Events which have followed | in the World, so far as they have been | by Learned Men Observed. | As also two Sermons | Occasioned by the late Blazing Stars. | By Increase Mather, Teacher of a Church, | at Boston in New England. | *Boston, in New England.* | *Printed by S. G. for S. S. and Sold by J. Browning.* | *At the corner of the Prison Lane next to the Town-* | *House.* 1683.

Sm. 8vo, *pp.* (12), 143 ; (1), (8), 38 ; (2), 32. *Polished calf, gilt edges by* W. PRATT. A FINE COPY of this RARE WORK, with the Two SERMONS and their respective *title pages*, one or the other of which is frequently wanting.

An Address "To the Reader," pp. 4, is signed "John Sherman." The "two Sermons" are, "Heaven's Alarm. Second Impression 1682," which has a separate title-page, and "The Latter Sign," which has continuous signatures with "Heaven's Alarm."

1361 MATHER. An | Essay | For the Recording of | Illustrious | Providences, | Wherein an Account is given of | many Remarkable and very Me- | morable Events, which have hap- | pened in this last Age : | Especially in | New-England. | By Increase Mather, | Teacher of a Church at Boston in | New-England. | ... | *Boston in New-England* | *Printed by Samuel Green for Joseph Browning,* | *And are to be sold at his Shop at the corner of* | *the Prison Lane.* 1684.

Sm. 8vo, *pp.* (22), 372, (8). *Red morocco, gilt edges, by* F. BEDFORD. A FINE COPY of the FIRST EDITION of this MOST RARE WORK.

A very singular collection of remarkable Sea Deliverances, Accidents, Remarkable Phenomena, Witchcrafts, Apparations, connected with the Inhabitants of New England. *See* a long notice of the volume in the *New Retrospective Review*, No. 1, Nov. 1852.

1362 MATHER. A Further | Account | of the | Tryals | of the | New-England Witches. | With the | Observations | of a Person who was upon the Place several | Days when the suspected Witches were | first taken into Examination. | To which is added, | Cases of Conscience | Concerning Witchcrafts and Evil Spirits Per- | sonating Men.| Written at the Request of the Ministers of New-England. | By Increase Mather, President of Harvard Colledge. | *London: Printed for J. Dunton, at the Raven in the Poultrey.* | 1693.

4to, pp. 10, (4), 39, (5). *Books 2l. Crushed blue levant morocco, gilt top,* UNCUT, *by* W. MATTHEWS. A SPLENDID COPY, with the SECOND TITLE often wanting, and an impression of the SCARCE PORTRAIT of the AUTHOR engraved by WHITE *inserted.* Of EXTREME RARITY in such FINE and *uncut* state.

1363 MATHER. De | Successu Evangelii | Apud | Indos | Occidentales. | In Novâ-Angliâ; | Epistola. | Ad Cl. Virum | D. Johannem Leusdenum | Linguæ Sanctæ in Ultrajectinâ Acade | miâ Professorem, Scripta, | A Crescentio Mathero | Apud Bostonienses V.D.M. nec non Collegii | Harvardini quod est Cantabrigia Nov-An- | glorum, Rectore. | Londoni, Typis J. G. 1688 | Jam recusua, & successu Evangelii apud In- | dos Orientales aucta. | *Ultrajecti,* | *Apud Wilhelmum Broedeleth,* | *Anno* 1699.

12mo, pp. 16. *Polished calf, gilt edges, by* F. BEDFORD. LARGE and FINE COPY. RARE. ["Of the Success of the Gospel among the American Indians, in New England.] This is the third edition, having been printed in London in 1688, and at the same place as this, in 1697. Copies of either edition are not easy to procure."— *Field.*

1364 MATHER. Early History of New England; being a Relation of Hostile Passages between the Indians and European Voyagers and First Settlers; and a full Narrative of Hostilities, to the Close of the War with the Pequots, in the year 1637; also a detailed Account of the Origin of the War with King Philip. By Increase Mather. With an Introduction and Notes, By Samuel G. Drake.
Boston: Printed for the Editor. 1864.

4to, pp. 319. *Portrait. Half crimson morocco, gilt top,* UNCUT.

1365 MATHER (I.) *and* (C.) The History of King Philip's War. By the Rev. Increase Mather, D.D. Also, a History of the Same War, by the Rev. Cotton Mather, D.D. To which are added An Introduction and Notes By Samuel G. Drake. ... *Albany: J. Munsell.* 1862.

4to, pp. 281. 3 *Portraits. Half crimson morocco, gilt top,* UNCUT. SCARCE PORTRAIT *of* COTTON MATHER, engraved by HOPWOOD *inserted.*

1366 [MATHER (Richard.)] Church-Government | and | Church-Covenant | Discussed, | In an Answer of the Elders of the seve- | rall Churches in | New-England | To two and thirty Questions, sent over | to them by divers Ministers in England, to de- | clare their judgements therein. | Together with an Apologie of the said Elders in | New-England for Church-Covenant, sent over | in Answer to Master Bernard in the | Yeare 1639. | As also in an Answer to nine Positions about Church- | Government. | And now published for the satisfaction of all who desire | resolution in those points. | *London*, | *Printed by R. O. and G. D. for Benjamin Allen*, | *Anno Dom.* 1643.

4to, pp. (4), 84; (2), 78. *Calf, gilt edges, by* LEIGHTON. VERY SCARCE.

The "Apologie" has a separate title-page and paging; the "Answer unto nine Positions" has a separate title-page, but is paged continuously with the "Apologie," omitting pp. 47, 48. As the address "To the Reader" is signed "H. Peter," the work has sometimes wrongly been ascribed to him.

1367 MATHER (R.) *and* TOMPSON (W.) A | Modest & Brotherly | Ansvver | To Mr. Charles Herle his Book, | against the Independency of Churches. | Wherein his four Arguments for the Govern- | ment of Synods over particular Congregati- | ons, are friendly Examined, and | clearly Answered. | Together, with Christian and Loving Ani- | madversions upon sundry other observable passa- | ges in said Booke. | All tending to declare the true use of Synods, and the | power of Congregational Churches in the points of | electing and ordaining their owne Officers, | and censuring their Offendors. | By Richard Mather Teacher of the | Church at Dorchester; and William | Tompson Pastor of the Church at | Braintree in New-England. | ... | *London, Printed for Henry Overton in Popes-head alley.* 1644.

4to, pp. (4), 58. *Green morocco, gilt edges, by* W. MATTHEWS. FINE COPY. VERY SCARCE.

1368 MATHER (S.) The | Life | of the | Very Reverend and Learned | Cotton Mather, | D.D. & F.R.S. | Late Pastor of the North Church in Boston. | Who Died, February 13, 1727, 8. | By Samuel Mather, M.A. | *Boston, New-England:* | *Printed for Samuel Gerrish, in Cornhill.* | MDCCXXIX.

8vo, 12 l., pp. 186. *Mottled calf, gilt edges, by* W. PRATT. LARGE and BEAUTIFUL COPY. VERY SCARCE.

At the end is a list of no less than 383 works written by Cotton Mather.

1369 [MATHER (Samuel.)] An | Attempt to Shew, | That America must be Known to the | Ancients; | made at the Request, and to gratify the Curiosity, | of an Inquisitive Gentleman: | To which is added | an Appendix, | Concerning the American Colonies, | and some | Modern Managements against | them. | By an American Englishman. | Pastor of a Church in Boston, New-England. | *Boston New-England:* | *Printed by J. Kneeland.* | MDCCLXXIII.

8vo, pp. 35. *Half purple morocco.* LARGE and FINE COPY. RARE.

"A work of equal Learning and Patriotism." "It maintains that the posterity of Japhet, by Magog, were the primary inhabitants of America; a warlike people, well qualified to make those Ancient Encampments which have been discovered at the West." — *Is. Thomas.*

It is so rare that *Rich* had never seen a copy, but refers to the Catalogue of Harvard College Library.

1370 MAUDUIT (I.) A Short View of the History of the New England Colonies, with respect to their Charters and Constitution. By Israel Mauduit. The Fourth edition. To which is now added, An

Account of a Conference between the late Mr. Grenville and the several Colony Agents, in the year 1764, previous to the passing the Stamp Act. Also the original Charter granted in the 4th of Charles I. and never before printed in England.
London: J. Wilkie. MDCCLXXVI.

8vo, pp. 100. *Half red morocco.* SCARCE.

1371 [MAUDUIT.] Remarks upon Gen. Howe's Account of his Proceedings on Long Island, in the Extraordinary Gazette of October 10, 1776. The Second Edition. *London: Fielding & Walker.* 1778.

8vo, pp. 54. *Half blue morocco. Very Scarce.*

1372 [MAUDUIT.] Observations upon the conduct of Sir W——m H——e at the White Plains; as related in the Gazette of December 30, 1776. *London: J. Bew.* 1779.

8vo, pp. 44. *Half red morocco. Very Scarce.*

1373 [MAUDUIT.] Strictures on the Philadelphia Mischianza or Triumph upon leaving America Unconquered. With Extracts containing the Principal Part of a Letter, published in the "American Crisis." In order to shew how far the King's Enemies think his General deserving of Public Honours. N.B. A flattering Account of this Mischianza was published in the "Philadelphia Gazette," and copied into the "Morning Post," the 13th of July last; and a Larger one by a still more flattering Panegyrist, may be found in the "Gentleman's Magazine" for August last. *London: J. Bew.* 1779.

8vo, pp. 42. *Half red morocco.* PORTRAIT *of the* AUTHOR *inserted. Very Scarce.*
For an extended note respecting this tract, see *Rich.* I. 277.

1374 [MAUDUIT.] Three Letters to Lord Viscount Howe. With Remarks on the Attack at Bunker's Hill. The Second Edition. To which is added a Comparative View of the Conduct of Lord Cornwallis and General Howe. *London: G. Wilkie.* 1781.

8vo, pp. 48. *Half green morocco. Very Scarce.*

1375 MAYER (B.) Memoir of Jared Sparks, LL.D. By Brantz Mayer.
Baltimore: Printed for the Author. 1867.

4to, pp. 36. *Half green morocco, gilt top,* UNCUT, *by* BRADSTREET. LARGE PAPER, of which *fifty copies only* were PRIVATELY PRINTED. THREE PORTRAITS *inserted.*

1376 MAYHEW (J.) The Snare broken. A Thanksgiving-Discourse, Preached at the Desire of the West Church in Boston, N. E. Friday May 23, 1766. Occasioned by the Repeal of the Stamp-Act. By Jonathan Mayhew, D.D. Pastor of said Church.
Boston: R. & S. Draper. 1766.

8vo, pp. viii., 44. *Half purple morocco.* VERY SCARCE.
Dedicated to the Right Honorable William Pitt, Esq.

1377 MAYHEW (M.) The | Conquests and Triumphs | of | Grace: | Being | A Brief Narrative of the Success which the | Gospel hath had among the Indians of | Martha's Vineyard (and the Places adjacent) | in New-England. | With | Some Remarkable Curiosities, concerning the | Numbers, the Customs, and the present Cir- | cumstances of the Indians on that Island. | Further Explaining and Confirming the Account | given of those Matters, by Mr. Cotton Mather, | in the Life of the Renowned Mr. John Eliot. | By Matthew Mayhew. | Attested by the Reverend Mr. Nath. Mather, and others. | Whereunto is Added | An Account concerning the Present State of Christianity | among the Indians, in other Parts of New-England: | Expressed in the Letters of several Worthy Persons. | best acquainted therewithal. | *London, Printed for Nath. Hiller, at the Princes Arms | in Leadenhall-street, over against St. Mary Axe*, 1695.

Sm. 8vo, pp. 68, (1). *Blue levant morocco, paneled and gilt sides, corner ornaments, inside lined with highly polished morocco, elegantly gilt borders, morocco joints, gilt top,* UNCUT, *by* F. BEDFORD. A SPLENDID COPY, and of the HIGHEST DEGREE OF RARITY.

We cannot record the public sale of ANY COPY in the United States. It is unnoticed by Kennett, Ternaux, Rich, Stevens, Field, and other bibliographers.

1378 MEAD (S.) A Sermon delivered December 29th, 1799; Occasioned by the Death of General George Washington. ... By Samuel Mead, A.M., Pastor of a Church in Danvers. ... *Salem:* 1800.

8vo, pp. 24. UNCUT and RARE.

1379 [MEIN (John.)] Sagittarius's Letters | and | Political Speculations. | Extracted | From the Public Ledger. | Humbly Inscribed | To the Very Loyal and Truly Pious Dr. Samuel | Cooper, Pastor of the Congregational Church in Brattle | Street. | *Boston: | Printed by Order of the Select Men and Sold at Dona- | tion Hall, for the benefit of the distressed Patriots.* | MDCCLXXV.

8vo, pp. 127. *Polished calf, gilt edges, by* W. PRATT. FINE COPY, with many rough leaves. VERY SCARCE.

"A strong Tory, anti-Puritanical publication, full of hits against the Pilgrim Fathers and their descendants, with a great deal of personal gossip, and, on the whole, a book of considerable historic interest. To the New York, Philadelphia, and Southern antiquarian explorers after scraps against the early New Englanders, this little volume will prove a mine, and afford salt and spice enough for many Fourth of July orations."—*Stevens.*

1380 MÉMOIRE | contenant le | Précis Des Faits, | avec leurs | Piéces Justificatives, | Pour server de Résponse aux Observations | envoyées par les Ministres d' Angleterre, | dans le Cours de l' Europe. | *A Paris, | De L' Imprimerie Royale.* | M.DCCLVI.

12mo, pp. viii., 275. *Crimson morocco, richly ornamented sides, edges gilt on carmine, by* W. MATTHEWS. LARGE and ELEGANT COPY. EXTREMELY RARE.

"The very curious history of this memoir deserves attention from all students of American history. At the surrender of Fort Necessity by Washington, his Journal of the Expedition, together with the letters of Braddock to the British Ministry, and his instructions to Washington, were seized by the French victors. They were immediately transmitted to France, and by order of the French king, printed and sent to every court of Europe, as indicating the aggressive character of the British. From evidence drawn from these documents, they charge Washington with the murder of Jumonville. This was the second publication of any of Washington's writings, and the first notice the public had of his Journal. It was translated and printed in New York, in 1757, under the title of *A Memorial*, etc., and the same year in Dublin under the title of *Review of Military Operations in N. A., and Journal of Major Washington.* It is very clear from the French relation that Jumonville was approaching Washington on an embassy of peace, but that Washington, unwilling to trust him, had ordered his advance to be fired upon."—*Field.*

See Livingston (William.) Nos. 1261, and 1262.

The following is a Translation.

1381 MEMORIAL (A) Containing a Summary View of Facts, with their Authorities. In Answer to the Observations sent by the English Ministry to the Courts of Europe. Translated from the French. *New York: J. Parker.* 1757.

8vo, pp. iv., 190. Crushed red levant morocco, rich inside borders, gilt edges, by W. MATTHEWS. LARGE and BEAUTIFUL COPY with many rough leaves. EXTREMELY RARE.

See Livingston (W.) No. 1262.

1382 MERLE D'AUBIGNÉ (J. H.) History of the Great Reformation of the Sixteenth Century in Germany, Switzerland, &c. By J. H. Merle D'Aubigné. ... *London: D. Walther.* 1841–53.

5 vols., 8vo, half olive morocco, gilt top, UNCUT.

1383 MERRICK (P.) An Eulogy on the Character of the late Gen. George Washington: The Pride of America, the Glory of the World. Pronounced ... at Brookfield ... the 22d of February, 1800. By Pliny Merrick, Esq. ... *Brookfield: Mass.* 1800.

8vo, pp. 14. UNCUT.

1384 MERRYWEATHER (F. S.) Bibliomania in The Middle Ages. Or Sketches of Bookworms, Collectors, Bible Students, Scribes, and Illuminators, from the Anglo Saxon and Norman Periods, to the Introduction of Printing into England; with Anecdotes, illustrating the History of the Monastic Libraries of Great Britain, in the Olden Time. By F. Somner Merryweather. *London: Merryweather.* M.DCCC.XLIX.

Sm. 8vo, pp. iv., 218. Half olive morocco, gilt top. SCARCE.

1385 MESSINGER (R.) An Oration, delivered at Old York, on the Death of George Washington. ... By the Rev. Rosewell Messinger, Pastor ... in Old York, Maine. *Charlestown:* 1800.

8vo, pp. 16. UNCUT.

1386 METCALF (S. L.) A Collection of some of the most interesting Narratives of Indian Warfare in the West, containing an Account of the Adventures of Colonel Daniel Boone, one of the first Settlers of Kentucky, comprehending the most important occurrences relative to its early history. Also, an account of the Manners, and Customs of the Indians, their Traditions and Religious Sentiments, their Police or Civil Government, their Discipline and method of War; to which is added, an Account of the Expeditions of Genl's Harmer, Scott, Wilkinson, St. Clair, & Wayne. The whole compiled from the best authorities, By Samuel L. Metcalf.

Lexington : Ky. Printed by William G. Hunt. 1821.

8vo, pp. 270. *Errata* 5 *lines. Half gray calf, gilt top,* UNCUT. PORTRAIT of DANIEL BOONE *inserted.* A BEAUTIFUL COPY, and EXTREMELY RARE in *uncut* condition.

"A compilation, principally from available sources, of the narratives which in their original form had, even at the date of its publication, become scarce. It includes Colonel Boone's *Narrative*, first printed in Filson's *Kentucky*, at Wilmington, 1784; Dr. Knight's and Slover's *Narratives of Captivity*, originally published (s. l. s. d.); and Colonel James Smith's *Narrative of Captivity*, printed in 1799."—*Field.*

1387 MICHAUX (F. A.) *and* NUTTALL (T.) The North American Sylva; or, a Description of the Forest Trees of the United States, Canada, and Nova Scotia. ... Translated from the French of F. A. Michaux. With Notes by J. J. Smith. ... *Philadelphia.* 1853. [Also:] The North American Sylva; or, a Description of the Forest Trees of the United States, Canada, and Nova Scotia, not described in the work of F. A. Michaux, ... by Thomas Nuttall, ...

Philadelphia: 1852–53.

6 *vols., imp. 8vo, half green levant morocco, gilt top,* UNCUT. PORTRAIT of MICHAUX *inserted.* AN ELEGANT COPY of one of the FINEST WORKS ever published in America, containing nearly 300 BEAUTIFULLY COLOURED ENGRAVINGS of American forest trees.

"A production of unrivalled interest and beauty, giving descriptions and illustrations of all the Forest Trees of North America, from the Arctic limits of arborescent vegetation to the confines of the tropical circle; and the most complete work of the kind. It is handsomely printed on fine paper and ranges in size and appearance with the beautiful works of AUDUBON."

This edition should not be confounded with those of a later date with impressions from the now much worn stones.

1388 MILLER (A.) A Sermon Occasioned by the Death of General Washington. Delivered at Greenbush, on the 22d Day of February, 1800. By Alexander Miller, A.M. *Albany:* 1800.

8vo, pp. 15.

1389 [MILLER (John.)] Fly Leaves; or, Scraps and Sketches, Literary, Bibliographical and Miscellaneous, consisting of Notes on Antiquarian and Historical Subjects, Collections towards neglected Biography, ... Choice Specimens of Ancient Poetry, chiefly from unpublished MSS. ... With numerous Bibliographical Notices Etc.

London: John Miller. 1854–55.

12mo, 2vols. bound in 1, *pp. x.,* 189; *xii.,* 180. *Half olive morocco, gilt top.* VERY SCARCE. First and Second Series, all ever published.

1390 MILLER (J.) A Description of the Province and City of New York; with Plans of the City and Several Forts as they existed in the Year, 1695. By the Rev. John Miller. Now first printed from the Original Manuscript. To which is added, a Catalogue of an extensive Collection of Books relating to America, on sale by the Publisher. *London: Thomas Rodd.* MDCCCXLIII.

8vo, pp. 43. 6 *Folded Plans. Rodd's Cat. pp.* (4), 21–116. *Half red morocco, gilt top,* UNCUT, *by* BRADSTREET. VERY SCARCE in *uncut* condition.

"As it contains some curious particulars respecting the state of society in the province at that time, and is moreover of particular local interest, as giving plans of the town and the several forts, the Publisher thought he would be rendering an acceptable service to those persons who take an interest in tracing the rise and growth of the great commercial emporium of the western world, by causing a few copies to be printed, and thus preserving it from the chance of being lost or destroyed."— *Preface.*

1391 MILLER. A Description of the Province and City of New York; with Plans of the City and Several Forts as they existed in the year 1695. By John Miller. A New Edition, with an Introduction and copious Historical Notes. By John Gilmary Shea, LL.D. *New York: William Gowans.* 1862.

4to, pp. 127. *Gowans' Cat. pp.* 24. *Half calf, gilt top,* UNCUT. LARGE PAPER; 50 *copies only printed.* TWO FINE INDIA PROOF ILLUSTRATIONS *inserted.*

Forms No. 3 of Gowans' "Bibliotheca Americana."

1392 MILLER (S.) A Sermon Delivered December 29, 1799; occasioned by the Death of General George Washington, late President of the United States. ... By Samuel Miller, A.M. ... *New York:* 1800.

8vo, pp. 39. *Half morocco,* UNCUT.

1393 MILTON (J.) The Works of John Milton in Verse and Prose Printed from the Original Editions with a Life of the Author By the Rev. John Mitford *London William Pickering* 1851

8 *vols., 8vo, half purple levant morocco, gilt top,* UNCUT. Only 500 copies of this valuable and beautiful edition were printed. It is now VERY SCARCE.

The most beautiful reproduction of an old author ever published. The types used were cast expressly for this edition, in exact imitation of the original copies. Printed on ancient wire-wove paper.

1394 MINER (C.) History of Wyoming, in a Series of Letters from Charles Miner, to his Son William Penn Miner, Esq. *Philadelphia: J. Crissy.* 1845.

8vo, pp. 488, (2), 104. 2 *Maps. Cuts. Half maroon morocco, gilt top,* UNCUT. An interesting AUTOGRAPH LETTER of the AUTHOR, solely relating to the work; and SIXTEEN ILLUSTRATIONS *inserted.*

The ONLY UNCUT COPY we have ever met with.

"This is the most nearly complete of all the histories of the valley, which has been the scene of such tragic events, as have elicited the interest of some in every civilized land. The work is much the largest of these narratives, and includes a 'Copy of Lt. Col. Adam Hubley's Journal on the Western Expedition, against the Indians under the Command of Major General Sullivan, 1779. By Simon Stevens, Lancaster, Pa. Aug. 9, 1845.'"— *Field.*

1395 MINOT (G. R.) An Eulogy on George Washington, ... who Died December 14, 1799. Delivered before the Inhabitants of the Town of Boston, ... By George Richards Minot, A.M. *Boston:* [1800.]

8vo, pp. 24. UNCUT.

1396 MINOT. An Eulogy on George Washington. Second Edition. *Boston :* [1800.]

8vo, pp. 24. UNCUT.

1397 MINOT. Continuation of the History of the Province of Massachusetts Bay, from the year 1748. With An Introductory Sketch of Events from its Original Settlement. By George Richards Minot. ... *Boston : Manning & Loring.* 1798–1803.

8vo, 2 vols. bound in 1, *pp.* 304; 222. *Half green morocco, gilt top,* UNCUT. Uniform with Hutchinson's History. Two PORTRAITS *inserted.*

"The second volume was published in 1803, after the death of the author. It brings the history down to the year 1765, and was apparently intended as a continuation of Hutchinson."—*Rich.*

1398 MINOT. The History of the Insurrections in Massachusetts, in the year Seventeen Hundred and Eighty-six, and the Rebellion Consequent thereon. By George Richards Minot, A.M. Second Edition. *Boston : James W. Burdett & Co.* 1810.

8vo, pp. 192. *Half green morocco, gilt top,* UNCUT, *by* BRADSTREET. FINE COPY. PORTRAIT of the AUTHOR *inserted.* SCARCE.

Rich says, "This insurrection is more generally known as *Shay's Rebellion,* from the name of the person who took the lead in it, and relating to whom there is a ballad extant in Massachusetts commencing —

My name is Shays; in former days
In Pelham I did dwell, sirs, &c."

1399 MINUTES of Conferences, Held at Lancaster, In August 1762, With the Sachems and Warriors of Several Tribes of Northern and Western Indians.
Philadelphia : Printed and Sold by B. FRANKLIN & D. HALL, *at the New-Printing-Office, near the Market.* MDCCLXIII.

Folio, pp. 36. *Calf antique, paneled sides, gilt top,* UNCUT. FINE COPY. VERY SCARCE. Almost UNIQUE in *uncut* condition.

1400 MINUTES | of the | Trial and Examination | of | Certain Persons, | in the | Province of New York, | Charged with being Engaged in a | Conspiracy against the Authority | of the Congress, | and | The Liberties of America. | *London : Printed for J. Bew.* M DCC LXXXVI.

8vo, pp. iv., 45. *Half red morocco.* FINE COPY. EXTREMELY RARE.

In the preface to those "Minutes," it is stated that they were "discovered (on the late capture of New York by the British troops) among the papers of a person who appears to have been Secretary to the Committee." They relate to a conspiracy against Congress, and particularly against Washington, whom the conspirators proposed to carry off.

"A Mr. Matthews," says the *Monthly Review,* "who was prominent in the conspiracy, was condemned to suffer death, but Congress resolved to postpone the execution of the sentence, and ordered him to be carried into Connecticut, there to be imprisoned till further orders."

The work contains some curious scandal about Washington, and *Mary Gibbons,* "a girl from New Jersey, of whom General Washington was very fond, and whom he maintained genteelly at a house near Mr. Skinner's."

1401 MISSALE ROMANUM. A MANUSCRIPT OF THE FOURTEENTH CENTURY; beautifully written upon ONE HUNDRED AND FORTY LEAVES OF PURE VELLUM, and ornamented with THIRTEEN MINIATURES within rich borders THE FULL SIZE OF THE PAGE, and hundreds of Capitals; the whole MOST BEAUTIFULLY ILLUMINATED in Colours and Gold. The Miniatures in this most CHOICE and DESIRABLE example of Mediæval Art are of much artistic merit and of GREATLY SUPERIOR EXECUTION to those generally met with.

Small octavo, crushed red levant morocco, richly paneled and gilt back and sides, broad inside borders, gilt edges, by W. MATTHEWS. IN THE FINEST STATE OF PRESERVATION.

"It was written in 1380, and is a small octavo of superior execution. It contains thirteen miniatures of grouped figures, one of which represents a lady, with a gaily attired knight, while Death, in the form of a skeleton, steals up behind, and transfixes her with his dart: designed, doubtless, to represent the uncertainty of life. The costume is of the time of Charles V. of France, and seems as *outré* to us as our fashions would have appeared then. The large letters are in gold, and the whole profusely ornamented."— *Rev. Dr. W. Bacon Stevens.*

1402 MITCHEL (J.) Nehemiah | on the | Wall | in | Troublesom Times; | or, | A Serious and Seasonable Improvement of that great | Example of Magistratical Piety and Prudence, Self-denial | and Tenderness, Fearlesness and Fidelity, unto In- | struction and Encouragement of present and | succeeding Rulers in our Israel. | As it was delivered in a Sermon Preached at | Boston in N. E. May 15, 1667. being the | Day of Election | there. | By that faithful Servant of Christ | Mr. Jonathan Mitchel, late Pastor of | the Church of Christ at Cambridge. | *Cambridge: | Printed by S. G. and M. J.* 1671.

Sm. 4to, pp. (4), 34. *Polished calf, yellow edges by* W. PRATT. FINE COPY. EXCEEDINGLY RARE.

One of the *earliest* Massachusetts Election Sermons. S. G. and M. J. are the initials of Samuel Green and Marmaduke Johnson, the printers of ELIOT'S INDIAN BIBLE.

1403 MITCHELL (S. L.) The Life, Exploits, and Precepts of Tammany; the Famous Indian Chief. Being the Anniversary Oration pronounced before the Tammany Society, or Columbian Order, ... May 12, 1795. By Samuel Latham Mitchell, M.D. ... *New York: J. Buell.* M.DCC.XCV.

8vo, pp. 36. *Half green morocco.* TWO PORTRAITS of the AUTHOR *inserted,* and THREE other ILLUSTRATIONS laid in the volume. FINE COPY. VERY SCARCE.

1404 MOCQUET (J.) Travels and Voyages into Africa, Asia, and America, the East and West-Indies; ... Performed by Mr. John Mocquet. ... Enriched with Sculptures. Translated from the French, by N. Pullen, Gent. *London: W. Newton.* 1696.

Small 8vo, pp. (32), 352. *Cuts. Half calf.* VERY SCARCE.

1405 MOHAWK. The Book of | Common Prayer, | and Administration of the | Sacraments, | and other | Rites and Ceremonies | of the | Church, | according to the use of the | Church of England: | together with | A Collection of Occasional Prayers, and | divers Sentences of | Holy Scripture, | Necessary for Knowledge and Practice. | Formerly collected, and translated into the Mohawk Language | under the direction of the Missionaries of the Society for the | Propagation of the Gospel in Foreign Parts, to the Mohawk | Indians. | A New Edition : | to which is added | The Gospel according to St. Mark, | Translated into the Mohawk Language, | By Captn Joseph Brant, | An Indian of the Mohawk Nation. | *London :* | *Printed by C. Buckton, Great Putney Street,* | *Golden Square,* 1787.

8vo, English and Indian Titles, pp. iii., 505, (1). Frontispiece and 18 Copperplates by PEACHEY. *Crushed blue levant morocco, paneled and gilt sides, gilt edges, by* F. BEDFORD. FINE COPY. VERY SCARCE.

The Frontispiece represents the reception of the Mohawk delegation by George III. For an interesting account of this and other editions of the Mohawk Prayer Book see Field's "*Essay*" No. 273.

1406 MONARDES. Ioyfvll Newes | Out of the New-found | VVorlde. | Wherein are declared, the rare and | singuler vertues of diuers Herbs, Trees, | Plantes, Oyles & Stones, with their ap- | plications, as well to the vse of Phisicke, as of | Chirurgery : which being well applyed, bring | such present remedie for all diseases, as may | seeme altogether incredible : notwith- | standing by practice found out | to be true. | Also the portrature of the said Hearbs, | verie aptly described : | Englished by John Frampton Marchant. | Newly corrected as by conference with | the olde copies may appeare. Wher- | vnto are added three other bookes | treating of the Bezaar stone, the herb | Escuerconera, the properties of Iron | and Steele in Medicine, and the be- | nefit of Snow. | *London,* | *Printed by E. Allde, by the assigne of* | *Bonham Norton.* | 1596.

Sm. 4to. Title, pp. 4, 374. Brown morocco, gilt edges. A remarkably LARGE and FINE COPY of this RARE WORK, fresh and crisp as when published. The first three leaves have been re-margined by TRENT in his neatest manner.

This edition contains three additional books, not in the former. It commences with a notice cf Columbus's discovery, and among other curious matter contains a long article on tobacco.

Consequent on the erroneous pagination of all copies of this edition, it is generally collated as above. The actual number of *leaves* however in a perfect copy, as this is, is 183 in all.

1407 MONRO (R.) A Description of the Genesee Country, in the State of New York: in which the Situation, Dimensions, Civil Divisions, Soil, Minerals, Produce, Lakes and Rivers, Curiosities, Climate, Navigation, Trade and Manufactures, Population, and other interesting matters relative to that country, are impartially described. ... By Robert Monro. *New York : Printed for the Author.* 1804.

8vo, pp. 16. Map. Half green morocco, gilt top, UNCUT. FINE COPY. VERY SCARCE.

1408 MONTAIGNE (M. de) Works of Michael de Montaigne comprising his Essays, Journey into Italy, and Letters, with Notes from all the Commentators, Biographical and Bibliographical Notices &c.

By W. Hazlitt. A New and Carefully Revised Edition edited by O. W. Wight. *Cambridge: Riverside Press.* 1864.

4 vols., roy. 8vo, half olive morocco, gilt top, UNCUT. LARGE PAPER. *Only* 75 *copies printed.* SCARCE.

"Montaigne and Howell's Letters are my bed-side books. I like to hear them tell their old stories over and over again. I am informed that both of them tell coarse stories. I don't heed them, it was the custom of their time as it is of Highlanders and Hottentots to dispense with a part of dress which we all wear in cities."— *W. M. Thackeray.*

1409 [MONTANUS (Arnoldus.)] Die Unbekante | Neue Welt, | oder | Beschreibung | des Welt-teils | Amerika, | und des | Sud-Landes: | Darinnen vom Vhrsprunge der Ameriker und Sudlän- | der, und von den gedenckwürdigen Reysen der Europer darnach zu. | Wie auch | Von derselben Festen Ländern, Inseln, Städten, Festungen, Dörfern, | vornähmsten Gebeuen, Bergen, Brunnen, Flüssen, und Ahrten der Tiere, | Beume, Stauden, und anderer fremden Gewächse; Als auch von den | Gottes-und Götzen-diensten, Sitten, Sprachen, Kleider-trachten, | wunderlichen Begabnissen, und so wohl alten als neuen | Kriegen, ausführlich gehandelt wird; | Durch und durch mit vielen nach dem Leben in Ameriken selbst | entworfenen Abbildungen gezieret. | Durch Dr. O. D. | *Zu Amsterdam,* | *Bey Jacob von Meurs, auf der Keysersgraft, in der Stadt Meurs,* | 1673.

Folio. Engraved and Printed Titles, pp. (4), 658, (22). 6 *Portraits,* 32 *Folded Views,* 16 *Maps, and* 70 *Large Plates in the Text. Half green levant morocco, carmine edges.* LARGE and CLEAN COPY, with BRILLIANT IMPRESSIONS of the PLATES.

Contains Fine Portraits of Columbus, Vespucius, Magellan, Montezuma, Pizarro &c. and the EARLIEST VIEWS of New Amsterdam, i. e. New York, in 1670. The half-page plates printed in the text represent the games, festivals, occupations, battles, religious rites, cannibalism, habitations, manners and customs of the Indians.

"This German edition is much scarcer than the Dutch original. Asher says that he had met with only one copy in the Netherlands, viz. that in the Royal Library of the Hague."— *F. Muller.*

1410 [MONTCALM (*Marquis.* de)] Letters from the Marquis de Montcalm, Governor General of Canada; to Messrs. De Bereyer & De la Molé in the years 1757, 1758 and 1759. With an English translation. *London: J. Almon.* 1777.

8vo, pp. 28. *French and English on opposite pages. White vellum, by* W. PRATT.

These letters, purporting to have been written by so distinguished a man as the Governor General of Canada, the last of them but a few days before the fall of Quebec and the death of both Generals Montcalm and Wolfe, have attracted great interest, while their genuineness has been suspected. But "it has been reserved," says Mr. Henry Stevens in an extended note on the subject, "for Mr. Francis Parkman, the historian, in 1869, to settle almost to a demonstration that the Montcalm letters are forgeries."

See Mr. Stevens's long and exceedingly interesting note on this SCARCE WORK, extracted from his "Bibliotheca Historica," and *inserted* before the title page in this copy.

1411 MONTCALM. Eloge Historique de Monsieur le Marquis De Montcalm. (Extrait du "Mercure de France." de 1760.) [Also, Three other Tracts, relating to the Early History of Canada.] *Quebec:* 1855.

8vo, half green morocco, gilt top, UNCUT. VERY SCARCE. AUTOGRAPH NOTE of MR. FARIBAULT, author of "Catalogue d'Ouvrages &c." *inserted.*

1412 MOODY (J.) Lieut. James Moody's Narrative of his Exertions and Sufferings in the Cause of the Government, since the year 1776; Authenticated by Proper Certificates. The Second Edition.
London: Richardson & Urquhart. MDCCLXXXIII.

8vo, pp. (2), 57, (7). *Half calf.* FINE COPY. VERY SCARCE. Second and BEST EDITION, containing matter not embraced in the first.

"Moody, a New Jersey farmer, was so much harassed by mobs, associations and committees, that, driven into the British lines, he became an active, and in some instances successful partizan against his countrymen." From 1776 to 1782 he was a Spy, a Ranger and Scout in the service of the British. A portion of the time he was attached to General Skinner's New Jersey Tory Brigade.

1413 [MOORE (Clement C.)] Observations upon certain Passages in Mr. Jefferson's Notes on Virginia, which appear to have a Tendency to Subvert Religion and Establish a False Philosophy.
New York: 1804.

8vo, pp. 32. *Half calf, gilt top,* UNCUT. *Very Scarce.*

1414 MOORE. Poems. By Clement C. Moore, LL.D.
New York: Bartlett & Welford. 1844.

12mo, pp. 216. *Half crimson morocco, gilt top,* UNCUT. THICK PAPER. A few copies only printed for PRIVATE DISTRIBUTION.

1415 MOORE (F.) A Voyage to Georgia. Begun in the Year 1735. Containing, An Account of the Settling the Town of Frederica, in the Southern Part of the Province; and a Description of the Soil, Air, Birds, Beasts, Trees, Rivers, Islands, &c. With the Rules and Orders made by the Honourable the Trustees for that Settlement; including the Allowances of Provisions, Cloathing, and other Necessaries to the Families and Servants which went thither. Also A Description of the Town and County of Savannah, in the Northern Part of the Province; the Manner of dividing and granting the Lands, and the Improvements there: With an Account of the Air, Soil, Rivers, and Islands in that Part. By Francis Moore. ...
London: Jacob Robinson. 1744.

Sm. 8vo, pp. 108, (1). *Half purple morocco.* LARGE and FINE COPY. EXTREMELY SCARCE.

"The numbers of the Indian tribes, the location of their territories, and the dealings of the wise and pacific Oglethorpe with them, form the subject of much of the volume. Many incidents in the life of the good chief Tomo-chi-chi, are given."— *Field.*

1416 MOORE (F.) Songs and Ballads of the American Revolution. With Notes and Illustrations, by Frank Moore.
New York: D. Appleton & Company. MDCCCLVI.

12mo, pp. xii., 394. *Half green morocco, gilt top,* UNCUT.

1417 MOORE. Materials for History. Printed from Original Manuscripts. With Notes and Illustrations. By Frank Moore. First Series. [All published.] *New York: Printed for the Zenger Club.* 1861.

4to, pp. 240. *Half red morocco, gilt top,* UNCUT. PORTRAIT. 250 *Copies only printed.* PORTRAIT *inserted.* Contains the Laurens Correspondence, rarely found complete.

1418 MOORE. Rebellion Record : (The) A Diary of American Events, with Documents, Narratives, Illustrative Incidents, Poetry, Etc. Edited by Frank Moore, ... With an Introductory Address, on the Causes of the Struggle, and the Great Issues before the Country By Edward Everett. *New York: G. P. Putnam.* 1861–1868.

12 vols., imp. 8vo, half crushed red levant morocco, gilt top, UNCUT, *by* W. MATTHEWS.

A SPLENDID SET, bound from SELECTED NUMBERS with PICKED IMPRESSIONS of the numerous engravings. ONE HUNDRED and THIRTY PORTRAITS *inserted,* many of which are PROOFS, and UNLETTERED PROOFS on INDIA PAPER. An impression of the red, white, and blue cover, discontinued after the first number, is also *inserted.* This set is ABSOLUTELY PERFECT THROUGHOUT, a condition to which very many copies cannot lay claim.

The work is an impartial embodiment of all that is valuable on the subject, and is for the Rebellion what Almon's Remembrancer is for the Revolution.

1419 MOORE. Diary of the American Revolution. From Newspapers and Original Documents. By Frank Moore. *New York: Privately Printed.* 1865.

2 vols., imp. 8vo, half maroon morocco, gilt top, UNCUT. LARGE PAPER; 100 *copies printed,* with the NUMEROUS FINE PORTRAITS and VIEWS on INDIA PAPER.

1420 MOORE (G. H.) "Mr. Lee's Plan, March 29, 1777." The Treason of Charles Lee Major General Second in Command in the American Army of the Revolution. By George H. Moore. ... *New York: Charles Scribner.* 1860.

8vo, pp. xii., 115. *2 Portraits and 2 Facsimiles. Half red morocco, gilt top,* UNCUT.

A manuscript, accidentally discovered, has at length settled this vexed question, to the shame of the treacherous officer. Mr. Moore has presented the subject, with notes and facsimiles, in the most careful manner.

1421 MOORE. Historical Notes on the Employment of Negroes in the American Army of the Revolution. By George H. Moore. *New York: Charles T. Evans.* 1862.

8vo, pp. 24. Half crimson morocco, gilt top, UNCUT. PORTRAIT *inserted.*

1422 MOORE. Notes on The History of Slavery in Massachusetts. By George H. Moore. ... *New York: D. Appleton & Co.* M DCCC LXVI.

8vo, pp. iv., 256. Half purple morocco, gilt top, UNCUT.

1423 MOORE. [Correspondence concerning Moore's Notes on the History of] Slavery in Massachusetts. Two Letters from the Historical Magazine, September and October, 1866. I. From George Davis, Esq. II. From George H. Moore, Esq. *New York:* 1866.

8vo, pp. 12. Half red morocco, gilt top, UNCUT, *by* BRADSTREET. *Privately Printed.* SCARCE.

1424 MOORE (H.) A Dictionary of Quotations from Various Authors in Ancient and Modern Languages, with English Translations. ... By Hugh Moore, Esq. *London: Whittaker Treacher & Co.* 1831.

8vo, calf, marbled edges.

1425 MOORE (H.) Memoir of Col. Ethan Allen; containing the most Interesting Incidents connected with his Private and Public Career. By Hugh Moore. *Plattsburgh: O. R. Cook.* 1834.

12mo, pp. 252. *Half green morocco.* VERY SCARCE.

1426 MOORE (M.) The Memoirs and Adventures of Mark Moore, late an Officer in the British Navy. Interspersed with a Variety of original Anecdotes, selected from his Journals, when in the Tuscan, Portuguese, Swedish, Imperial, American, and British Service, in each of whieh he bore a Commission. Written by Himself. ... *London: Printed for the Author.* 1795.

8vo, pp. xi., 267. *Half calf. Rare* and *Curious.*

Moore was by birth an American, and an officer in the British Navy, afterwards an "itinerant play-house adventurer, etc." The work is dedicated to the Right Honourable Richard Earl Howe.

1427 MORGAN (A.) Anti-Paedo-Rantism; | or | Mr. Samuel Finley's | Charitable Plea for the Speechless | Examined and Refuted: | The Baptism of Believers | Maintain'd; | And The Mode of it, by Immersion, | Vindicated. | By Abel Morgan, at Middletown, | in East-Jersey. | *Philadelphia:* | *Printed by* B. FRANKLIN, *in Market-Street.* | M,DCC,XLVII.

12mo, pp. 174. *Half gray calf.* FINE COPY. VERY RARE. This copy has the scarce Appendix, (six leaves), with separate title and imprint, and continuously paged, which is frequently wanting.

"Written by Abel Morgan, pastor of a Baptist church at Middletown, in New Jersey. It is said to have been the first book written in America relating to the baptismal controversy, notwithstanding which, it is but rarely mentioned in bibliographical works."

1428 MORISON (W.) An Oration Delivered at the Request of the Officers of the Assembled Cavalry and Infantry, and Other Militia Officers, on the 22d of February, 1800, in the West Parish of Londonderry, in Commemoration of the Death of General George Washington. By William Morison. *Newburyport:* [1800.]

8vo. Title, pp. 21–32. VERY RARE.

1429 MORISON. A Sermon delivered at the request of the Elders, ... of the Presbyterian Society in the West Parish of Londonderry, January 1st, 1800, on the Death of General George Washington. By William Morison. *Newburyport:* [1800.]

8vo, pp. 18. UNCUT. EXCEEDINGLY RARE. The *only copy* noticed in Dr. Hough's List.

1430 MORRELL (T.) A Sermon on the Death of General George Washington. By Thomas H. Morrell. ... Delivered on the 22d of February, 1800, in the City of Baltimore. *Baltimore:* [1800.]

12mo, pp. 29. *Very scarce.*

1431 MORRELL (T. H.) Bibliotheca Americana. Catalogue of the entire Private Library of Mr. T. H. Morrell; comprising ... Books on the History and Antiquities of America. ... Sold ... November, 1866. *New York:* 1866.

4to, half crimson morocco, gilt top, UNCUT. LARGE PAPER; 12 copies only printed. RULED and PRICED.

1432 MORRELL. Bibliotheca Americana: Catalogue of the Choice Collection of Books, belonging to T. H. Morrell. [Sold January, 1869.] *New York:* 1869.

4to, half red morocco, gilt top, UNCUT, *by* BRADSTREET. LARGE PAPER. Six copies only printed. PRICED.

1433 [MORRIS (Gouverneur.)] Observations on the American Revolution. Published according to a Resolution of Congress, by their Committee. For the Consideration of those who are desirous of comparing the Conduct of the opposed Parties, and the several Consequences which have flowed from it.

Philadelphia: Styner & Cist. MDCCLXXIX.

8vo, pp. 122. *Half green morocco.* Reprinted the same year, in the "Remembrancer."

1434 MORRIS. An Oration, upon the Death of General Washington, By Gouverneur Morris. Delivered ... at New-York on the 31st Day of December, 1799. ... *New York:* 1800.

8vo, pp. 24. UNCUT.

1435 MORRIS (J.) An Oration, delivered in South-Farms, in Litchfield, February 22, 1800, Commemorative of the Death of General George Washington, who died December 14th, 1799, ... By James Morris, Esq. *Litchfield:* [1800.]

8vo, pp. 29. EXCEEDINGLY RARE.

1436 MORSE (J.) A Prayer and Sermon, delivered at Charleston, December 31, 1799, on the Death of George Washington. ... With an additional Sketch of his Life. By Jedediah Morse, D.D. ... To which is Prefixed the Proceedings of the Town in Respectful Testimony of the Distinguished Talents & Pre-eminent Virtues of the Deceased. Written by Josiah Bartlett, Esq.

London: Printed by J. Bateson. 1800.

8vo, pp. 44, 36. UNCUT. EXCEEDINGLY SCARCE.

1437 MORSE. Annals of the American Revolution; or a Record of the Causes and Events which produced, and terminated in the Establishment and Independence of the American Republic. Interspersed with numerous appropriate Documents and Anecdotes. To which is prefixed a summary Account of ... some of the principal Indian Wars ... and a Biography of the principal Military Officers, who were instrumental in achieving our Independence. ... By Jedediah Morse, D.D. *Hartford:* 1824.

8vo, pp. (4), 400, 50. 5 *Plates. Half gray calf, red edges.* FINE COPY. SCARCE.

1438 MORTON (N.) New-England's | Memorial ; | or, | A brief Relation of the most Memorable and | Remarkable Passages of the Providence of | God, manifested to the | Planters | of | New-England in America | With special Reference to the first Colony | thereof, Called | New-Plimouth | ... | Published for the Use and Benefit of | present and future Generations. | By Nathaniel Morton, ... | *Boston, Reprinted for Daniel Henchman, at the Corner | Shop over-against the Brick-Meeting-House.* 1721.

Sm. 8vo, pp. (10), 248. *Crushed red levant morocco, paneled sides, gilt edges, by* W. PRATT. FINE COPY. VERY SCARCE.

The first edition of this work was printed in small 4to, at Cambridge, N. E., in 1669. Of this second edition, as above, there would seem to have been another issue, with a different title, in the same year.

"Morton's Memorial is a work of high authority and is confined chiefly to Plymouth Colony. It was compiled principally from manuscripts of his uncle William Bradford, and comprises the period between 1620 and 1646. The journals of Edward Winslow also furnished materials for the work."—*J. R. Bartlett.*

1439 MORTON. New-England's Memorial: or, A brief Relation of the most Memorable and Remarkable Passages of the Providence of God, manifested to the Planters of New-England, in America: With special Reference to the first Colony thereof, Called New Plymouth. ... Published for the Use and Benefit of present and future Generations. By Nathaniel Morton. ...
Newport: Reprinted and Sold by S. Southwick. M,DCC,LXXII.

Sm. 8vo, pp. viii., 208, (8). *Polished calf, red edges.* FINE COPY. Contains 16 columns of subscribers names.

The third edition of one of the rarest and most important books relating to New England history.

1440 MORTON (T.) New English Canaan | or | New Canaan. | Containing an Abstract of New England, | Composed in three Bookes. | The first Booke setting forth the originall of the Natives, their | Manners and Customes, together with their tractable Nature and | Love towards the English. | The second Booke setting forth the naturall Indowments of the | Country, and what staple Commodities it | yealdeth. | The third Booke setting forth, what people are planted there, | their prosperity, what remarkable accidents have happened since the first | planting of it, together with their Tenents and practise | of their Church. | Written by Thomas Morton, of Clifford's Inne gent, upon tenne | yeares Knowledge and experiment of the | Country. | *Printed at Amsterdam, | By Jacob Frederick Stam. | In the yeare* 1637.

4to, pp. 188, (3). *Crushed green levant morocco, paneled and gilt sides, corner ornaments, gilt edges, by* F. BEDFORD. BEAUTIFUL COPY.

A book of such EXTREME RARITY that Mr. Frederik Muller the eminent bookseller of Amsterdam remarks "Although this book is printed in my native place, Amsterdam, *I have never seen nor heard of it here.*" We know of ONLY ONE OTHER COPY in the United States. It is interspersed with Poems by various authors, including one by Ben Jonson not included in his works.

Its author, who appears to have possessed a jovial, and somewhat roystering temperament, found himself ill associated with the puritanical founders of New England. Allen says of him that, "he fell into great licentiousness, and became the lord of misrule;" he supplied the Indians with arms, that they might hunt for him, and was by this means, perhaps, an instrument in endangering the safety of the colonists. On the occasion of giving to Pasonagessit the name of Maremont, under his auspices, a pine-tree eighty feet in height, with buck's horns at the top, was planted in the ground, around which the company danced with such hilarity, as the good cheer they had not failed to provide inspired; much to the dissatisfaction of the stricter colonists, by whom he was for this offence sent out of the colony as a prisoner. Mr. Duyckinck remarks, that although the book professes to have been printed at Amsterdam, it was probably executed in London. Morton returned to the colonies after its appearance, and was imprisoned in Boston for a year, ostensibly on account of the libel it promulgated against the colonies.

1441 MOSELY (J. O.) An Oration, [Occasioned by the Death of Gen. Washington.] delivered at East-Haddam, ... at the request of the Inhabitants of the First Society in that Town, on the 22d of Feb. A.D. 1800. By Jonathan Ogden Mosely. *Hartford:* 1800.

8vo, pp. 18.

1442 MOTHERWELL (W.) Minstrelsey: Ancient and Modern, with an Historical Introduction and Notes. By William Motherwell. *Glasgow: John Wylie.* 1827.

Sm. 4to, half green morocco, gilt top, UNCUT. ORIGINAL and BEST EDITION. VERY SCARCE.

One of the most interesting and best selected collections of the kind ever printed, and very highly praised by Sir Walter Scott. The work consists of cv. pages of Introduction and 414 pages of the Ballads and Poetical Legends and Tales, to each of which is prefixed an introductory notice: and is further illustrated with a frontispiece and 2 plates, also 33 of the old airs engraved on 9 plates. It is now quite out of print, and very scarce.

1443 MOULTON (J. W.) View of the City of New-Orange, (now New-York,) as it was in the Year 1673. With Explanatory Notes. By Joseph W. Moulton, Esq. *New York: C. S. Vanwinkle.* 1825.

8vo, pp. 40. *Plate of New York in* 1673. *Half maroon morocco, gilt top,* UNCUT. FINE COPY. RARE in this condition.

1444 MOULTON. New York 170 years ago: with a View and Explanatory Notes. By Joseph W. Moulton. *New York: Wm. G. Boggs.* 1843.

8vo, pp. 24. *Plate. Half maroon morocco, gilt top,* UNCUT. Two ILLUSTRATIONS *inserted.* FINE COPY. RARE in *uncut* state. Uniform with the preceding No.

See Yates (J. V. N.) *and* Moulton (J. W.) No. 2198.

1445 MOULTRIE (W.) Memoirs of the American Revolution, so far as it related to the States of North and South Carolina, and Georgia. Compiled from the most Authentic Materials, the Author's Personal Knowledge of the various events, and including an Epistolary Correspondence on Public Affairs, with Civil and Military Officers at that period. By William Moultrie, late Governor of the State of South Carolina. ... *New York: Printed for the Author.* 1802.

2 *vols., 8vo, pp.* 506; 446. *Portrait. Half calf antique.* LARGE and CLEAN COPY. PORTRAIT of the AUTHOR *inserted.*

1446 MOUNTGOMERY (R.) A | Discourse | Concerning the design'd | Establishment | of a New | Colony | to the | South of Carolina, | in the | Most delightful Country of the | Universe. | By Sir Robert Mountgomery, Baronet. | *London:* | *Printed in the Year.* 1717.

8*vo. Title, pp.* 30. *Folded Engraved Plan,* "representing the Form of Setling (*sic*) the Districts, or County Divisions in the Margravate of Azilia." *Red morocco, gilt edges, by* F. BEDFORD. BEAUTIFUL COPY. VERY RARE.

"A very curious tract. Sir Rob. Montgomery having obtained a grant of all the land between the rivers Alatamaha and Savanna, now part of Georgia, which he called *Azilia*, issued these proposals for settling the colony."— *Rich.*

1447 [MOURT (G.)] A Relation or | Iournall of the beginning and proceedings | of the English Plantation setled at Plimoth in New | England, by certaine English Aduenturers both | Merchants and others. With their difficult passage, their safe arriuall, their | ioyfull building of, and comfortable planting them- | selves in the now well defended Towne | of New Plimoth. | As also a Relation of Fovre | seuerall discoueries since made by some of the | same English Planters there resident. | I. In a iourney to Pvckanokick the habitation of the Indians great- | est King Massasoyt: as also their message, the answer and entertainment | they had of him. | II. In a voyage made by ten of them to the Kingdome of Nawset, to seeke | a boy that had lost himselfe in the woods: with such accidents as befell them | in that voyage. | III. In their iourney to the Kingdome of Namaschet, in defence of their | greatest King Massasoyt, against the Narrohiggonsets, and to reuenge the | supposed death of their Interpreter Tisquantum. | IIII. Their voyage to the Massachusets, and their entertainment there. | With an answer to all such obiections as are any way made | against the lawfulnesse of English plantations | in those parts. | *London,* | *Printed for Iohn Bellamie, and are to be sold at his shop at the two* | *Greyhounds in Cornhill neere the Royall Exchange.* 1622.

4*to. Title, pp.* (10), 72. *Polished red levant morocco, paneled sides, rich inside borders, gilt edges, by* F. BEDFORD.

BEAUTIFUL COPY OF THE EXCESSIVELY RARE ORIGINAL EDITION.

The head lines having been cut into by a former binder, were restored by Harris of London, in so skilful a manner as almost to escape observation.

"MOURT'S RELATION" is the CHIEF CORNER STONE, of a New England Library.

1448 MUHLENBERG (H. A.) The Life of Major-General Peter Muhlenberg of the Revolutionary Army. By Henry A. Muhlenberg. *Philadelphia: Carey and Hart.* 1849.

12*mo, pp.* 456. *Half maroon morocco, gilt top,* UNCUT. An AUTOGRAPH LETTER of GEN. MUHLENBERG *inserted.* FINE COPY. SCARCE.

1449 MULLER (F.) Catalogue of Books, Maps, Plates on America, and of a Remarkable Collection of Early Voyages, offered for sale by Frederik Muller, at Amsterdam. ... With Bibliographical and Historical Notes and presenting an Essay towards a Dutch-American Bibliography. ... *Amsterdam: Frederik Muller.* 1872.

8vo, pp. viii., 288. 3 *Facsimiles. Half red morocco, gilt top,* UNCUT, *by* BRADSTREET.

"This is much more than a catalogue, it is a tolerably complete Bibliography of Dutch Books relating to America, contains translations of the titles, with critical and other notes concerning the books, and is a most desirable addition to a bibliographical collection."—Sabin's *Bibliopolist.*

1450 MUNSELL (C.) A Collection of Songs of the American Press, and other Poems relating to the Art of Printing. Compiled by C. Munsell. *Albany: N. Y.* 1868.

Sm. 8vo, pp. viii., 206, (1). *Half olive morocco, gilt top,* UNCUT, *by* WM. SMITH. A few copies only printed.

"This little volume has been put in type by a juvenile Typographer, as an exercise in his professional studies, for gratuitous circulation among his friends."—*Note.*

1451 MUNSELL (J.) The Typographical Miscellany. By Joel Munsell. *Albany: J. Munsell.* 1850.

8vo, pp. (6), 268. *Cuts. Half blue morocco.*

1452 MUNSELL. Annals of Albany. By Joel Munsell. *Albany: J. Munsell.* 1850–59.

10 *vols.,* 12*mo, half green morocco, gilt top,* UNCUT. VERY SCARCE in this COMPLETE and *uncut* condition.

1453 MUNSELL. A Chronology of Paper and Paper Making. By Joel Munsell. *Albany: J. Munsell.* 1857.

8vo, pp. vii., 110. *Half maroon morocco, gilt top,* UNCUT. 200 copies only printed. Contains specimens of Japanese paper, and paper made from straw.

In this interesting work no less than 110 substances are named from which paper can be made, including *Espartero,* or Spanish grass, and cane from the Southern states.

1454 [MUNSELL'S HISTORICAL SERIES.] *Albany: J. Munsell.* 1857–61.

10 *vols., roy. 4to, half crushed purple levant morocco, gilt top,* UNCUT. LARGE PAPER; of which SIX COMPLETE SETS ONLY were printed, as attested by MR. MUNSELL on the fly-leaf in Vol. I. TWENTY FINE ILLUSTRATIONS *inserted,* mostly INDIA PROOFS, and INDIA PROOFS BEFORE LETTERS.

AN ELEGANT SET.

The series consists of the following works:

I. Commissary Wilson's Orderly Book. Expedition of the Britiſh and Provincial Army, under Major-General Jeffrey Amherſt, againſt Ticonderoga and Crown Point, 1759. Map. [Annotated by Dr. E. B. O'Callaghan.] 1857.

II. A Narrative of the Cauſes which led to Philip's Indian War, of 1675 and 1676, by John Eaſton, of Rhode Iſland; with other Documents concerning this Event in the Office of the Secretary of State of New York. Map. With an Introduction and Notes. By Dr. F. B. Hough. 1858.

III. Orderly Book of the Northern Army, at Ticonderoga and Mt. Independence, from Oct. 17, 1776, to Jan. 8, 1777, with Biographical and Explanatory Notes. Portrait. [Annotated by the Publiſher.] 1859.

IV. Diary of the Siege of Detroit in the War with Pontiac. Alſo, a Narrative of the Principal Events of the Siege by Maj. Robert Rogers; a Plan for conducting Indian Affairs by Col. Bradſtreet; and other Authentick Documents never before printed. Edited with Notes by Franklin B. Hough. 1860.

V. Obſtructions to the Navigation of Hudſon's River; embracing the Minutes of the Secret Committee appointed by the Provincial Convention of New York, July 16, 1776, and other Original Documents relating to the Subject. Together with papers relating to the Beacons. Map. By E. M. Ruttenber. [Annotated by the Publiſher.] 1860.

VI. The Loyal Verſes of Joſeph Stanſbury and Dr. Jonathan Odell; relating to the American Revolution. Now First Edited by Winthrop Sargent. 1860.

VII. Orderly Book of Lieut. Gen. John Burgoyne, from his Entry into the State of New York until his Surrender at Saratoga, 16th Oct., 1777. From the Original Manuscript deposited at Washington's Head Quarters, Newburgh, N. Y. Map, Portraits, and Fac-ſimile. Edited by E. B. O'Callaghan. 1860.

VIII. Early Voyages up and down the Miſſiſſippi, by Cavelier, St. Coſmé, Le Sueur, Gravier and Guignas. With an Introduction, Notes, and an Index, by J. G. Shea. 1861.

IX & X. Proceedings of the Commiſſioners of Indian Affairs, appointed by Law for the Extinguiſhment of Indian Titles in the State of New York. ... With an Introduction and Notes, by Dr. F. B. Hough. Three Maps. 1861.

1455 MUNSELL. The Every Day Book of History and Chronology: embracing the Anniversaries of Memorable Persons and Events, in every Period and State of the World, from the Creation to the Present Time. By Joel Munsell. *New York: D. Appleton & Co.* 1858.

Roy. 8vo, pp. 537. *Half blue morocco, gilt top,* UNCUT.

An immense collection of memorable events, arranged under every day of the year, as they occurred; consisting of deaths of eminent men, battles, and occurrences of every kind, with full indexes.

1456 [MUNSELL'S SERIES OF AMERICAN LOCAL HISTORY.] *Albany: J. Munsell.* 1863–68.

9 *vols., roy. 8vo, half blue morocco, gilt top,* UNCUT. One of TWENTY-EIGHT SETS only printed on LARGE PAPER, as *attested* in MR. MUNSELL'S AUTOGRAPH NOTE in Vol. I.

The series consists of the following works:

I. Pioneer History of the Champlain Valley: being an Account of the Settlement of the town of Willsborough, by William Gilliland, together with his Journal and other Papers, and a Memoir, and Historical and Illustrative Notes, by Winslow C. Watson, Esq. 1863.

pp. 231.

II. Sir Charles Henry Frankland, Baronet; or, Boston in Colonial Times. By Elias Nason, M.A. 1865.

pp. 129.

III. Random Recollections of Albany, 1800 to 1808, by Gorham A. Worth; with Notes [by the publisher,] and numerous portraits and plates. 1866.

pp. 114.

IV. History of Lake Champlain, from its First Exploration by the French in 1609, to the close of the year 1814. By Peter S. Palmer. 1866.

pp. iv., 276. INDIA PROOF PORTRAIT *inserted.*

V. The Sexagenary, or Recollections of the Revolutionary War, [by S. De Witt Bloodgood, Esq.] Portraits of Schuyler, Burgoyne and Lady Harriet Ackland. 1866.

pp. 234.

VI. Letters and Journals relating to the War of the American Revolution, and the capture of the German Troops at Saratoga. By Mrs. General Riedesel; Translated ... by William L. Stone. 1867.

pp. 235. INDIA PROOF PORTRAIT *inserted.*

VII. Tah-Gah-Jute; or, Logan and Cresap, an Historical Essay, by Brantz Mayer. (A vindication of Capt. Cresap against the charge of murdering the family of Logan, etc.) 1867.

pp. 204. INDIA PROOF PORTRAIT *inserted.*

VIII. and IX. Memoirs and Letters and Journal of Major-General Riedesel, during his Residence in America. Translated from the Original German of Max von Eelking. By William L. Stone. 1868.

2 vols., pp. viii., 306; 284, (1). PORTRAIT and PLATES.
INDIA PROOF PORTRAIT *inserted.*

1457 MUNSELL. Collections on the History of Albany, from its Discovery to the Present Time. With Notices of its Public Institutions, and Biographical Sketches of Citizens Deceased, by J. Munsell. *Albany: J. Munsell.* 1865–71.

4 *vols., imp. 8vo, half maroon morocco, gilt top,* UNCUT. LARGE PAPER. FIFTY COPIES only printed.

These are a continuation of the "Annals of Albany," containing new matter and upwards of eighty portraits, views, maps, &c. The 4th vol. contains, besides the usual variety, the Baptisms and Marriages recorded in the Dutch church, arranged alphabetically by families, and embrace nearly every family from 1630 to 1800, also a Street Directory, showing the location of first settlers and transfers of lots from about 1650, onward: compiled by Prof. J. Pearson; a work of great labor and research.

1458 MURAT (A.) A Moral and Political Sketch of the United States of North America, by Achille Murat, ci-devant Prince Royal of the two Sicilies, and Citizen of the United States; with a Note on Negro Slavery, by Junius Redivivus. *London: E. Wilson.* 1833.

Post 8vo, half calf. Map.

"In this purple book the 'nephew of my uncle' defends and upholds negro slavery *in America*, though perhaps, were it brought nearer home to his own business and bosom, like many other philosophers, he would have sung a different tune. Lest these sentiments, so repugnant to British feeling, might give to the book a baleful influence, a neutralizing appendage by another hand is added, combating the Prince's facts, inferences and opinions."—*Stevens.*

1459 [MURPHY (Henry C.)] A Catalogue of an American Library, Chronologically Arranged. 1480–1800.. [*Brooklyn:* 1850?]

8vo, pp. 57, (1), *half red morocco, gilt top,* UNCUT. A FEW COPIES ONLY printed for presentation. MR. LUDEWIG'S copy with PORTRAIT and AUTOGRAPH of MR. MURPHY *inserted.*

Prepared for his own amusement, by its respected owner, a quarter of a century ago, this EXCEEDINGLY RARE Catalogue falls far short of even an approximate description of his now rich and probably unrivalled collection of books relating to the History, Geography, Ethnology and Philology of America.

1460 [MURPHY.] A Catalogue of an American Library. [Another Copy.] [*Brooklyn*: 1850?]

Roy. 8vo, pp. 57, (1). *Wrinkled claret morocco, gilt top,* UNCUT, *by* W. MATTHEWS. LARGE PAPER; TWENTY-FIVE COPIES ONLY printed for PRIVATE DISTRIBUTION. TWO FINE PORTRAITS representing MR. MURPHY at different periods of his life, and an AUTOGRAPH LETTER written by him, descriptive of the volume, *inserted.*

1461 [MURPHY.] Jacob Steendam, Noch Vaster. A Memoir of the First Poet in New Netherland with his Poems Descriptive of the Colony. *The Hague: The Brothers Giunta D'Albani.* 1861.

8vo, pp. 59. *Portrait. Half green morocco, gilt top,* UNCUT. Printed for PRIVATE DISTRIBUTION, and EXTREMELY SCARCE.

Reprinted with many additions in Mr. Murphy's "Anthology of New Netherland." 1865.

1462 [MURPHY.] Poetry of Nieuw-Neder-Landt: comprising Translations of Early Dutch Poems Relating to New York, &c. With Memoirs of the Authors, by the Translator. *Williamstadt:* MDCCCLXVI.

8vo. Title, pp. 9–206. *Portrait and Plate. Half orange morocco, gilt top,* UNCUT. *One copy only printed* on this paper. PORTRAIT of the TRANSLATOR *inserted.*

1463 MURRAY (J.) An Impartial History of the Present War in America; Containing An Account of its Rise and Progress, The Political Springs thereof, with its various Successes and Disappointments, on Both Sides. By the Rev. James Murray, of Newcastle. *Newcastle upon Tyne: ... T. Robson. ...* [*n. d.*]

3 *vols., 8vo, pp.* 573; 576; 332. 31 *Portraits and Maps. Half calf antique.* A LARGE, CLEAN, and UNEXCEPTIONABLE COPY, in which EVERY PORTRAIT and MAP is a carefully SELECTED and FINE impression.

The title of Vol. III., after "The Political Springs," reads: "Of the War now carrying on between Great Britain And the United Powers of France, Spain, and America." The volume ends abruptly at page 332, and is of EXTREME SCARCITY.

Mr. Rice's copy sold for $64.50.

1464 MYCALL (J.) A Funeral Address, on the Death of the late General George Washington; Interspersed with Sketches of, and Observations on, his Life and Character. Delivered in ... Harvard, February 22, 1800. By John Mycall. ... *Boston:* [1800.]

8vo, pp. 27. UNCUT, and RARE.

1465 MYSTERY REVEAL'D; (The) or Truth brought to Light. Being a Discovery of some Facts, in Relation to the Conduct of the M——y, which however extraordinary they may appear, are yet supported by such Testimonies of Authentic Papers and Memoirs; as neither Confidence, can out-brave; nor Cunning invalidate. By a Patriot. Monstrum Horrendum! *London: W. Cater.* 1759.

8vo. Title, pp. 319. *Red morocco, gilt edges, by* F. BEDFORD. FINE COPY. VERY SCARCE.

"The above title conveys no adequate idea of the contents of this very interesting book. The first part is a statement of affairs, and an analysis of them, from the Peace of Utrecht, till some months after Braddock's Defeat. The second part contains the Original Documents or Vouchers for the Narratives. These comprise the memorials and letters that passed between the English and French officers in Canada and Nova Scotia, and other English colonies, especially on the Ohio, from 1751 to 1755, including the chief papers that fell into the hands of the French after the surrender of Fort Necessity, and Braddock's Defeat, such as Washington's Journal and Letters, Stobo's Letter to Washington, Braddock's Letters, etc., etc., some of which papers are re-translations from the French."—*Stevens.*

1466 NANTUCKET. Papers relating to the Island of Nantucket, with Documents relating to the Original Settlement of that Island, Martha's Vineyard, and other Islands adjacent, known as Duke's County, while under the Colony of New York. Compiled from Official Records in the Office of the Secretary of State at Albany, New York. By Franklin B. Hough. *Albany: [J. Munsell.]* 1856.

4*to, pp. xviii.*, 163. *Map. Half green levant morocco, gilt top,* UNCUT, *by* W. SMITH. EXTREMELY RARE in *uncut* condition, nearly every copy of the 100 *only printed,* having been cut and bound for presentation.

1467 NARRAGANSETT CLUB. Publications of the Narragansett Club. First Series, Vols. I. to VI. [All published.] *Providence:* 1866–74.

6 *vols.,* 4*to, folded sheets,* UNCUT, *in cases.* LARGE PAPER. 25 COPIES ONLY PRINTED, excepting as respects Vol. VI., of which 150 copies were struck off.

The series embraces the following works:

I. Bibliographical Introduction to the Writings of Roger Williams. By Reuben Aldridge Guild, A.M. A Key into the Language of America. Edited by James Hammond Trumbull, A.M. Letter of John Cotton. Mr. Cotton's Letter Examined and Answered. Edited by Reuben Aldridge Guild, A.M. MDCCCLXVI.

II. John Cotton's Answer to Roger Williams. Edited by Rev. J. Lewis Diman. [Also:] Queries of Highest Consideration. Edited by Reuben Aldridge Guild, A.M. MDCCCLXVII.

III. The Bloody Tenent of Persecution. Edited by Samuel L. Caldwell. MDCCCLXVII.

IV. The Bloody Tenent yet more Bloody. Edited by Samuel L. Caldwell. MDCCCLXX.

V. George Fox Digg'd out of his Burrowes. Edited by Rev. J. Lewis Diman. MDCCCLXXII.

VI. Letters of Roger Williams, 1632 to 1682. Now first collected. Edited by John Russell Bartlett. MDCCCLXXIV.

1468 NARRATIVE of a Voyage to the Spanish Main, in the ship, "Two Friends"; the occupation of Amelia Island, by M'Gregor, &c. Sketches of the Province of East Florida; and Anecdotes illustrative of the Habits and Manners of the Seminole Indians: with an Appendix, containing a detail of the Seminole War, and the execution of Arbuthnot and Ambrister. *London: J. Miller.* 1819.

8*vo, pp. ix.*, (9), 328. *Half calf.*

"The narrator gives the results of his observations regarding the people and government of Florida, during the last days of its occupation by the Spaniards. The details of the seizure of Arbuthnot and Ambrister two Indian traders, on the soil of a friendly power, themselves citizens of another friendly government, engaged in a lawful commerce, their trial and execution by General Jackson, for selling arms to the Seminoles, whom they believed, and whom history records, to have been justly fighting against aggression, are also related at length."— *Field.*

1469 NARRATIVE (A) of the Miseries of New-England, by Reason of an Arbitrary Government Erected there. *London:* 1689.

Sm. 4to, polished calf, gilt edges, by F. BEDFORD. FINE COPY. VERY SCARCE.

Forms Part X. of "A Sixth Collection of Papers &c." the whole of which is in the volume, with title, and imprint.

1470 NATIONAL PORTRAIT GALLERY of Distinguished Americans. Conducted by James B. Longacre and James Herring. *Philadelphia:* 1836–40.

5 vols., 4to, half green morocco, gilt top, UNCUT. A FINE and GENUINE LARGE PAPER COPY with ORIGINAL and MOST BRILLIANT IMPRESSIONS of the one hundred and forty-four PORTRAITS, one alone excepted, which is a later impression. Several of those engraved by DURAND are PROOFS from his own collection.

Few such copies are now extant, and up to this date nothing has come from the hands of American engravers at all equal to the delicacy of handling, and beauty of finish of these fine portraits.

1471 NATIVE AMERICAN. (The) A Gift for the People. *Philadelphia: Hector Orr.* 1845.

Roy. 8vo, half red levant morocco, gilt edges. FINE COPY. VERY SCARCE.

This volume is appropriately printed with *red* ink, in *blue* borders, on *white* paper and contains numerous portraits of eminent Americans, including two rare half-lengths of Washington, one of them engraved by Longacre from the MINIATURE by TROTT. The work was edited by the Printer, Hector Orr, and contains Washington's Farewell Address, Declaration of Independence, Constitution of the U. S., Address of the Native American Conventions, and Address of the State [Penna.] Convention, 1845.

1472 NEAL (D.) The History of New England containing an Impartial Account of the Civil and Ecclesiastical Affairs of the Country to the Year of our Lord, 1700. To which is added, The Present State of New England. With a New and Accurate Map of the Country. And an Appendix containing their Present Charter, their Ecclesiastical Discipline, and their Municipal Laws. By Daniel Neal. ... *London: J. Clark.* MDCCXX.

2 vols., 8vo. Title, pp. vi., x., (2), 330. Title, (2), 331–712. Index, xv. Map. Half calf antique. FINE COPY, with the SCARCE PORTRAIT of the AUTHOR *inserted.*

Thomas Prince thus speaks of this work: "In 1720 came out Mr. Neal's *History of New England*, which I was glad to see, and pleased with both his spirit, style and method. And though he has fallen into many mistakes which are commonly known to us, some of which he seems to derive from Mr. Oldmixon's New England; ... yet considering the materials this worthy writer was confined to, and that he was never here; it seems to me scarce possible, that any under his disadvantages should form a better. In comparing him with the authors from whence he draws, I am surprised to see the pains he has taken to put the materials in such a regular order: And to me it seems as if many parts of his work cannot be mended."— *Chronology of New England. Pref.* p. *iii.*

1473 NEILSON (C.) An Original, Compiled and Corrected Account of Burgoyne's Campaign, and the Memorable Battles of Bemis's Heights, Sept. 19, and Oct. 7, 1777, from the most Authentic Sources of Information; including many Interesting Incidents connected with the same; and a Map of the Battle Ground. By Charles Neilson, Esq. *Albany: Printed by J. Munsell.* 1844.

12*mo*, *pp.* 291, (1). *Map. Half calf.* TWO PORTRAITS *inserted.* SCARCE.

1474 NELL (W. C.) The Coloured Patriots of the American Revolution, with Sketches of several distinguished Coloured Persons: to which is added, a brief Survey of the Condition and Prospects of Coloured Americans. By William C. Nell. With an Introduction, by Harriet Beecher Stowe. *Boston: Robert F. Wallcut.* 1855.

12*mo*, *pp.* 396. *Facsimile. Cuts. Half calf.* THREE PORTRAITS, and AUTOGRAPH SIGNATURE of FREDERICK DOUGLASS *inserted.* SCARCE.

1475 NEW-ENGLAND. New | Englands | First Fruits; | in Respect, | First of the | Conversion of some, | Conviction of divers, | Preparation of sundry | of the Indians. | 2. Of the progress of Learning, in the Colledge at | Cambridge in Massachusetts Bay. | With | Divers other speciall Matters concerning that Countrey. | Published by the instant request of sundry Friends, who desire | to be satisfied in these points by many New-England Men | who are here present, and were eye or eare- | witnesses of the same. | ... | *London,* | *Printed by R. O. and G. D. for Henry Overton, and are to be* | *sold at his Shop in Popes-head-Alley.* 1643.

4*to*, *pp.* (2), 26. *Crushed red levant morocco, richly gilt borders, inside lined with polished blue morocco beautifully tooled and gilt after an elegant original design, morocco joints, gilt edges, by* W. MATTHEWS. A SUPERB EXAMPLE of American binding.

THE FIRST and one of the RAREST of the series of reports sent from New England relative to the conversion of the Aborigines.

1476 NEW ENGLAND. A Brief | Relation | of the | State | of | New England. | From the Beginning of that | Plantation | To this Present Year, 1689. | In a Letter to a Person of Quality. | Licensed, July 30th, 1689. | *London,* | *Printed for Richard Baldwine, near the Black Bull in the* | *Old-Baily,* 1689.

Sm. 4*to*, *pp.* 18. *Polished calf, gilt edges, by* W. PRATT. LARGE and FINE COPY of this EXTREMELY SCARCE, and interesting EARLY ACCOUNT of NEW-ENGLAND.

1477 NEW ENGLAND. The | Revolution | in | New England | Justified, | and the People there Vindicated | from the Aspersions cast upon them | by Mr. John Palmer, | in his Pretended Answer to the | Declaration, | Published by the Inhabitants of Boston, and the | Country adjacent, on the day when they se- | cured their late Oppressors, who acted by an | Illegal and Arbitrary Commission from the | Late King James. | *Printed for Joseph Brunning at Boston* | *in New England.* 1691.

4to, pp. (6), 48. *Crushed red levant morocco, gilt top,* UNCUT. FINE, LARGE *and* CLEAN COPY. EXCESSIVELY RARE.

"To the Reader." is signed by E. R. and S. S., which, Palfrey, *Hist. of New England.* III. 514, says undoubtedly represent Edward Rawson, and Samuel Sewall.

See Byfield (N.) No. 313.

1478 NEW-ENGLAND. News from New-England, Being A True and last Account of the present Bloody Wars carried on betwixt the Infidels, Natives, and the English-Christians, and Converted Indians of New-England, declaring the many Dreadful Battles Fought betwixt them: As also the many Towns and Villages burnt by the merciless Heathens. And also the true Number of all the Christians slain since the beginning of that War, as it was sent over by a Factor of New-England to a Merchant in London.

London: Printed. 1676. *Boston: N. E., Reprinted for Samuel G. Drake.* 1850.

Sm. 4to, half morocco.

The original tract is of exceeding rarity, so much so that, not long since, but one copy was known to be in this country.

1479 NEW ENGLAND. New England's Trials. Declaring the Successe of 80 Ships employed thither within these eight yeares; and the Benefit of that Countrey by Sea and Land. With the present estate of that happie Plantation, begun but by 60 weake men in the yeare 1620. And how to build a Fleete of good Shippes to make a little Nauie Royall. Written by Captaine Iohn Smith, sometimes Gouernour of Virginia, and Admirall of New England. The Second Edition. *London, printed by William Iones,* 1622.

[*Reprinted, Providence.* 1867.]

Imp. 8vo, pp. (1), (32). *Half blue morocco, gilt top,* UNCUT. LARGE PAPER. SIXTY COPIES ONLY printed; all for presentation.

This elegant reprint was put forth by Mr. J. C. Brown, of Providence, strictly for private circulation. By way of satirizing the large paper mania, which had run to a ridiculous extreme, there were *sixty* copies of the work printed on large paper and *ten* on small.

1480 NEW-NETHERLAND. Beschryvinge | Van | Nieuvv-Nederlant, | (Gelijck het tegenwoordigh in Staet is) | Begrijpende de Nature, Aert, gelegentheyt en vruchtbaerheyt | van het selve Landt; mitsgaders de proffijtelijcke ende gewenste toevallen, die | aldaer tot onderhoudt der Menschen, (soo uyt haer selven als van buyten inge- | bracht) gevonden worden. Als mede de maniere en ongemeyne Eygenschap- | pen vande Wilden ofte Naturellen vanden Lande. Ende een bysonder verhael | vanden wonderlijcken Aert ende het Weesen der Bevers. | Daer noch by-gevoeght is | Een Discours over de gelegentheyt van Nieuw-Nederlandt | tusschen een Nederlandts Patriot, ende een Nieuw Nederlander. | Beschreven door | Adriaen van der Donck, | Beyder Rechten Doctoor, die tegenwoordigh | noch in Nieuw-Nederlandt is. | En hier achter by gevoeght | Het voordeeligh

Reglement vande Ed : Hoog. Achtbare | Heeren de Heeren Burgermeesteren deser Stede, | betreffende de saken van Nieuw-Nederlandt. | Den tweeden Druck. | Met een pertinent Kaertje van t' zelve Landt verçiert, | en van veel druck-fouten gesuyvert. | *t'Aemsteldam*, | *By Evert Nieuwenhof*, *Boeck-verkooper*, *woonende op* | *'t Ruslandt*, *in't Schrijf-boeck*, *Anno* 1656. | *Met Privilegie voor* 15 *Jaren*.

Sm. 4*to*, *pp.* 4 *l.*, 100, (4), 4 *l.* *Map.* *Crushed green levant morooco*, *paneled and gilt sides*, *gilt edges*, *by* F. BEDFORD. A LARGE and ELEGANT COPY of this RARE WORK, pronounced by Mr. Bedford to be one of the SOUNDEST and BEST copies that ever passed through his hands.

This second edition contains a map, which is not in the first. The map is entitled, "Nova Belgica, sive Nieuw Nederlandt," and is copied from the rare map of N. J. Vischer. *See* Asher's list of the "Maps and Charts of N. Netherland," p. 12. It is usually followed by "Conditien, Die door de Heeren Burgermeesteren der Stadt Amsterdam, volgens't gemaecte accoort met de West-Indische Compagnie, ende de Approbatie van hare Hog. Mog. de Heeren Staten Generael der Vereenighde Nederlanden daer op gevolght, gepresenteert werden aen alle de gene, die als Coloniers na Nieuw-Nederlandt Willen vertrecken ... *t'Amsterdam Met Consent* ... etc. *By Evert Nieuwenhoff* ... 1656." 4to, 4 l. In Puttick and Simpson's catalogue, No. 2202, 1860, a copy is described as the second and best impression of the second edition, containing some variations in the preliminary leaves, which we think is an error. For a translation, *see* "N. Y. Hist. Soc. Coll.," Second Series, Vol. 1. After page sixteen, both editions are alike.

1481 NEW NETHERLAND. Vertoogh van Nieu Nederland, and Breeden Raedt aende Vereenichde Nederlandsche Provintien. Two Rare Tracts printed in 1649–50. Relating to the Administration of Affairs in New Netherland. Translated from the Dutch by Henry C. Murphy. *New York* : 1854.

4*to*, *pp.* *viii.*, 190. *Map.* *Half green morocco*, *gilt top*, UNCUT. ONE HUNDRED AND TWENTY-FIVE COPIES ONLY PRINTED for Mr. James Lenox; all for presentation. EXTREMELY SCARCE.

A companion volume to "Vries' Voyages," No. 2024.

1482 NEW TESTAMENT (The) of Our Lord and Saviour Jesus Christ. With Engravings on Wood from Designs by Fra Angelica, Pietro Perugino, Francesca Francia, Lorenza di Credi, Fra Bartolommeo, Titian, Raphael, Gaudenzio Ferrari, Daniel di Volterra, and others. *London* : *Longman*. 1865.

4*to*, *crushed blue levant morocco*, *paneled sides*, *gilt top*, UNCUT, *by* W. MATTHEWS. AN ELEGANT COPY. Illustrated with BORDERS, ORNAMENTS, and INITIAL LETTERS, copied from the finest Italian MSS. of the 15th and 16th centuries, and by numerous other ENGRAVINGS ON WOOD, from the old masters; numerous MEDALLIONS are introduced in the margins.

The *finest book* of WOOD ENGRAVINGS ever produced in any country. The work was produced under the general superintendence of Mr. Henry Shaw, F.S.A.

1483 NEW-YORK. The | Laws | Of His Majesties | Colony of New-York, | As they were Enacted by the Governour, Council | and General Assembly (for the time being), in divers | Sessions, the first of which began April 9th, 1691. | *Printed by* WILLIAM BRADFORD,

Printer to the Kings most Excellent | Majesty for the Colony of New-York. 1719.

Folio, pp. (12); 1–88; 155–194; 239–290; 207–253; 246–324; "*An Ordinance for Regulating Fees.*" 20 *pp. Gray calf, sprinkled edges.* LARGE, CLEAN, *and* PERFECT COPY. EXCEEDINGLY SCARCE.

1484 NEW-YORK. An Account of the Interment of the Remains of 11,500 American Seamen, Soldiers and Citizens, who fell Victims to the Cruelties of the British, on Board their Prison Ships at the Wallabout, During the American Revolution. With a Particular Description of the Grand & Solemn Funeral Procession, which took place on the 26 May, 1808. And an Oration, Delivered at the Tomb of the Patriots, by Benjamin De Witt, M.D. ... Compiled by the Wallabout Committee.
New York: Printed by Frank White and Co. 1808.

12*mo, pp.* 96. *Half green morocco, gilt top,* UNCUT. VERY RARE. View of the TOMB OF THE MARTYRS *inserted.*

1485 NEW-YORK. An Account of the Procession, together with Copious Extracts from the Oration, delivered at the Walla-Bout; (L. I.), April 6, 1808. Upon laying the Corner-stone of the Vault, which is to contain the Relics of that Portion of American Seamen, Soldiers, and Citizens, who perished in the Cause of Liberty and their Country, on board the Prison Ships of the British, at the Wallabout during the Revolutionary War. Also, the Letter addressed to Thomas Jefferson, President of the United States, by the Tammany Society, and his Answer. [*New York:* 1808.]

12*mo, half morocco, gilt top,* UNCUT. Title page repaired. A little tract of MUCH RARITY. *See* Romaine (B.) No. 1721. Also; [Taylor (George.)] No. 1946.

1486 NEW-YORK. Collections of the New-York Historical Society.
New York: 1811–59.

9 *vols.,* 8*vo, half calf, sprinkled edges.* FINE, COMPLETE and LARGE set in nearly UNCUT state.

"There are many papers of great merit in these volumes, among which will be found De Witt Clinton's "Discourse on the Geographical, Political, and Historical View of the Red Men of New York."— La Salle's "Account of his last Expedition and Discoveries."— Dr. Jarvis' "Discourse on the Religion of the Indian Tribes of N. A."— Verrazano's "Voyages."— "Indian Tradition of first Settlement of New York."— Lambretchten's "History of New Netherlands."— Vander Donk's "Description of New Netherlands."— "Extract from De Vries' Voyages."— Juet's "Journal of Hudson's Voyages."— "Dermer's Letter, giving an Account of the Indians of N. E."— Mr. H. C. Murphy's "Complete Translation of De Vries' Voyages."— "Narrative of Captivity, and Martyrdom of Father Jogues, by the Mohawks."— "Short Sketch of the Mohawks," by J. Megapolensis.— "Memoir on Dutch and Indian," by Benson.— "Narrative of Marquis De Nouville's Expedition against the Senecas.— &c."— *Field.*

1487 NEW-YORK. Proceedings, of the New-York Historical Society.
New York: 1844–49.

7 *vols.*, 8*vo*, uniform in size and binding with the "Collections," combined with which, this forms a COMPLETE SET of the Society's SCARCE and VALUABLE publications.

"Among the numerous papers read before the Society, and published in these volumes, are many of more than ordinary interest, among which may be mentioned Mr. Bartlett's "Progress of Ethnology."— Schoolcraft's "Aboriginal Names of New York."— Thompson's "Indian Names of L. I."— Schoolcraft's "Siege and Defence of Fort Stanwix."— "Employment of the Indians by the English in the Revolutionary War."— Van Rensselaer's "Memoir on the French and Indian Expedition against N. Y. and the burning of Schenectady, 1689."— Schoolcraft's "Notices of Tumuli in Florida, and burial places of Indian Tribes."— Gilman's "Defeat of Gen. St. Clair."— Morgan's "Territorial Limits of the Iroquois."— Peter Wilson's "Address on the Iroquois."— O'Callaghan's "Jesuit Relations, with a Bibliographical Sketch of each."— "Champlain in the Onondaga Valley."— Long's "Ancient Architecture in America.— &c."— *Field.*

1488 NEW-YORK. Collections of the New-York Historical Society. Publication Fund Series. *New York:* 1868–72.

5 *vols.* 8*vo.* *Cloth* UNCUT. *All yet published.*
Printed for the Subscribers to the Fund, and not for Sale.

1489 NEW-YORK. Catalogue of the Museum and Gallery of Art of the New-York Historical Society. *New York:* 1862.

8*vo*, *half red morocco*, *gilt top*, UNCUT.

1490 NEW-YORK. Journal of the Votes and Proceedings of the General Assembly of the Colony of New-York, from 1766 to 1776, inclusive. Reprinted in pursuance of a joint resolution of the Legislature of the State of New-York, passed 30th April, 1820. *Albany: Printed by J. Buell.* 1820.

Folio. *Gray calf*, *carmine edges.* BEAUTIFUL COPY. VERY SCARCE.

Contains the SIX LEAVES subsequently printed, without which no copy is complete. The leaves referred to come in, in the following order. Following page 118, 13th Geo. III., *one leaf.*— Following page 104, 14th Geo. III., *one leaf.*— Following page 10, 15th Geo. III., *two leaves.*— Following page 90, 15th Geo. III., *two leaves.*

"In March 1820, on finding that only one copy of the original Journals from 1766 to 1776 was known to exist, the General Assembly of New York voted to reprint a small edition of fifty copies only. The volume has now become EXCESSIVELY RARE."— *Stevens.*

1491 NEW-YORK. Journals of the Provincial Congress, Provincial Convention, Committee of Safety and Council of Safety of the State of New York. 1775–1776–1777. *Albany: Printed for Thurlow Weed.* 1842.

2 *vols.*, *folio*, *calf.*

1492 NEW-YORK. Journal of the Legislative Council of the Colony of New-York. 1691–1775. Published by Order of the Senate of the State of New-York. *Albany:* 1861.

2 *vols.*, *folio*, *half calf.* *A few copies only reprinted.*

This book is by no means so common as is generally supposed, the greater part of the edition having been destroyed in Weed, Parsons & Co.'s fire.

1493 NEW-YORK. Natural History of New-York. *Albany:* 1842–67.

4*to*, 22 *parts bound in* 19 *volumes.* *Half crimson morocco*, *gilt top*, *by* PAWSON *and* NICHOLSON, *the last issued volume excepted which is in cloth.* With the large GEOLOGICAL MAP on rollers, and an assignment of an original subscriber's right to the remainder of the work when published.

This LARGE, CLEAN, and PERFECT SET, complete so far as published, is one of the FULL COLOURED COPIES which are now EXTREMELY SCARCE. It contains upwards of THIRTEEN HUNDRED FULL PAGE PLATES, comprising over TWO THOUSAND BEAUTIFULLY COLOURED FIGURES of Animals, Birds, Fishes, Reptiles, Insects, Plants, Flowers, Fruits, &c., coloured to the special order of the present owner, in a manner superior to that of the ordinary copies of the work. The compiler knows of no other set equal to this in point of completeness and condition.

The work is arranged under the following divisions.

I. ZOOLOGY. Mammalia, 33 Plates. Ornithology, 141 Plates. Reptiles and Amphibia, 79 Plates. Mollusca, 53 Plates. By James E. de Kay. 6 Parts, bound in 4 Volumes. 1842–44.

II. BOTANY. Flora, 161 Plates. By John Torrey, M.D. ... 2 Volumes. 1843.

III. MINERALOGY. Upwards of 500 Figures, and 10 Plates. By Lewis C. Beck. 1842.

IV. GEOLOGY. Comprising the Geology of the First Geological District. 46 Plates. By W. W. Mather. Second Geological District. 15 Plates. By Ebenezer Emmons, M.D. Third Geological District. Numerous Woodcuts. By Lardner Vanuxem. Fourth Geographical District. Nearly 200 Illustrations, Maps, Views, and Sections. By James Hall. 4 Parts, bound in 3 Volumes. 1842–43.

V. AGRICULTURE. Nearly 200 Plates, Maps, and Views. By Ebenezer Emmons. 5 Parts, bound in 4 Volumes. 1846–49.

VI. PALÆONTOLOGY. 355 Plates. By James Hall. 5 Volumes. 1849–67.

"The preparation of this splendid work by the ablest scientific men of the country has cost the State (of New York) more than 200,000 dollars, and is a brilliant example of enlightened legislative liberality. As a work embracing every department of Natural History, it must find a place in the library of all scientific men, as well as of all persons of taste and refinement."

1494 NEW-YORK. The Documentary History of the State of New-York. Arranged under direction of the Hon. Christopher Morgan, Secretary of State. By E. B. O'Callaghan, M.D. *Albany: Weed, Parsons & Co., Public Printers.* 1850–51.

4 *vols.*, 4*to*, *half blue morocco, gilt top.* FINE SET.

"A most valuable collection, consisting of Documents connected with the early history of the colony, the Indian Aborigines, and its affairs down to the year 1800; reprints of historical manuscripts, rare memoirs, accounts of early settlers; Indian biography, history, difficulties; biographical and genealogical accounts of families; early tours into various parts of the country; statistical accounts; land titles; the Leisler papers; Sir William Johnson's papers; the Rumsey and Fitch steam-boat controversy; churches, wars, disputes, &c., all taken from the manuscript archives of the State. The maps, seals and coins are particularly worthy of attention."

1495 NEW-YORK. Documents Relative to the Colonial History of the State of New-York; Procured in Holland, England and France, by John Romeyn Brodhead, Esq., Agent. ... Edited by E. B. O'Callaghan, M.D. [With Index Complete.] With a General Introduction by the Agent. *Albany: Weed, Parsons and Company.* 1856–1861.

11 *vols.*, 4*to*, *half blue morocco, gilt top.* Uniform with the "Documentary History."

"The Public Records of the State of New York are, chiefly, in the office of the Secretary of State at Albany. They are as various in their character, as they are voluminous in their extent. Most of them relate to, and illustrate the History of the State; and without them no accurate or detailed knowledge of that history can be gained." These volumes contain translations of all the Early Dutch Records, besides a mass of Documents bringing the History of the State down to its political existence as a member of an independent federation.

1496 NEW-YORK. Catalogue of the New-York State Library. Books, Maps, Manuscripts, Medals &c.
Albany: Charles Van Benthuysen. 1855–58.

4 *vols., roy. 8vo, half green morocco.* A COMPLETE SET of the LATEST ISSUE, now VERY SCARCE.

1497 NEW-YORK. Reminiscences of New-York and its Vicinity. [By Henry B. Dawson, and William J. Davis.] *New York:* 1855.

12*mo, pp.* 350. *Half orange morocco, gilt top,* UNCUT. FIFTY COPIES ONLY printed, all for presentation. EXCESSIVELY SCARCE. TWENTY ILLUSTRATIONS *inserted.* Pages 58–64 are by William J. Davis.

1498 NEW YORK CITY During the American Revolution. Being a Collection of Original Papers (now first published) from the Manuscripts in the possession of the Mercantile Library Association of New York City. *New York: Privately Printed for the Association.* 1861.

4*to, pp.* 194, (1). 2 *Maps. Half red morocco, gilt top,* UNCUT. NINE ILLUSTRATIONS *inserted,* mostly INDIA PROOFS BEFORE and AFTER LETTERS.

1499 NEW YORK. An Address delivered at the Celebration by the New York Historical Society, May 20, 1863, of the Two Hundredth Birth Day of Mr. William Bradford, who Introduced the Art of Printing into the Middle Colonies of British America. By John William Wallace of Philadelphia. Published with an Introductory Note, in Pursuance of a Resolution of the New York Historical Society. Parts omitted in the Delivery being now Inserted.
Albany: N. Y. J. Munsell. 1863.

8*vo, pp.* (4), 114. *Cloth, gilt top,* UNCUT. With the THREE FOLDED FACSIMILES, and the "Order of the Services," which are not in all copies.

1500 NEW YORK. Procès Verbal or the Ceremony of Installation of President of the New York Historical Society, as it will be Performed February 8, 1820. *New York: Printed for the use of the Members.* 1820.
[*Reprinted.* 1864.]

Roy. 8vo, pp. 14. *Half green morocco, gilt top,* UNCUT. THIRTY-FIVE COPIES ONLY privately reprinted. PORTRAIT *inserted.*

A satirical piece upon the installation of Dr. Hosack as President of the New York Historical Society.

1501 NEW YORK. Addresses of the City of New York to George Washington, with his Replies. *New York:* 1867.

4*to, pp. viii.,* 14. *Facsimile. Half green morocco, gilt top,* UNCUT. LARGE PAPER. NO. 1. of FIVE COPIES ONLY privately printed on WHATMAN'S DRAWING PAPER. FIVE PORTRAITS of WASHINGTON *inserted,* all, with one exception, beautiful UNLETTERED INDIA PROOFS, together with TWO other PORTRAITS in similar state.

1502 NICHOLS (J.) Literary Anecdotes of the Eighteenth Century. ... 9 vols. [Also:] Illustrations of the Literary History of the Eighteenth Century. Consisting of Authentic Memoirs and Original Letters of Eminent Persons. ... By John Nichols, F.S.A. Numerous illustrations. 8 vols. *London:* 1812–58.

17 vols., 8vo, half maroon morocco, gilt top, UNCUT. FIFTY-NINE PORTRAITS *inserted.* FINE and VERY CLEAN set. RARE in *uncut* condition.

"It is impossible, in a small space, to give anything like an adequate idea of the vast amount of curious information which these volumes contain. The hundreds of literary celebrities which are brought forward, not merely by passing anecdotes, but by highly valuable memoirs and sketches, and the extensive bibliographical and literary matter which they contain, render them one of the most permanently interesting collections ever published."

"Having perused, with inexpressible delight, sixteen volumes of this work, (the 17th not yet in America) we claim a right to expatiate with enthusiasm on its abounding merits."—*Allibone.*

1503 NICHOLLS (J. F.) The Remarkable Life, Adventures and Discoveries of Sebastian Cabot, of Bristol, the Founder of Great Britain's Maritime Power, Discoverer of America, and its first Colonizer. By J. F. Nicholls. ... *London: Sampson Low & Co.* 1869.

Sq. 8vo, pp. xv., 190. Portrait and Map. Half red morocco, gilt top, UNCUT, *by* BRADSTREET.

For a long, and appreciative note, see an extract from Stevens' "Bibliotheca Historica," inserted before the title, in this copy.

See Stevens (H.) No. 1910.

1504 NICHOLSON (J. B.) A Manual of the Art of Bookbinding: ... designed for the Practical Workman, the Amateur, and the Book-Collector. By James B. Nicholson.

Philadelphia: Henry Carey Baird. 1856.

Large 12mo, pp. 318. Cuts, Plates, and Specimens of Paper. Blue levant morocco, gilt edges, by PAWSON & NICHOLSON. Now out of print and VERY SCARCE.

1505 NILES (H.) Principles and Acts of the Revolution in America: or, an Attempt to Collect and Preserve some of the Speeches, Orations, and Proceedings, with Sketches and Remarks on Men and Things, and other Fugitive or Neglected Pieces, belonging to the Revolutionary Period in the United States. ... By H. Niles.

Baltimore: 1822.

Roy. 8vo, pp. viii., 495. Half red levant morocco, gilt top, UNCUT. *Clean* as when issued. VERY SCARCE in *uncut* state.

1506 NILES (S.) The Vanity of Man, Considered in a Sermon Delivered February 22d, 1800, Commemorating the Death of George Washington. ... By Samuel Niles, Pastor of the Church in Abingdon. *Boston:* 1800.

8vo, pp. 23. Errata.

1507 NOAH'S DOVE. A Little | Olive Leaf | Put in the Mouth of that | (So Called) | Noah's Dove, | and sent Home again to let her Master

Know | That the Waters are abated from off the face | of the Ground, | And that for the Sake of | Jesus Christ, | Whose Servant to the End of my Life I shall | Endeavour To Be. | *Printed and Sold by* WILLIAM BRADFORD *at the Sign of the Bible* | *in New-York.* 1704.

Sm. 4*to*, *pp.* (4), 31. *Polished calf, gilt edges, by* F. BEDFORD. One of the RAREST issues of BRADFORD's press. We have never either seen or heard of *another copy*. It is probably UNIQUE.

1508 NORTH AMERICAN REVIEW (The) and Miscellaneous Journal. From its Commencement in 1815, to and including the year 1856. With the General Index from 1815 to the End of the 25th Vol. *Boston:* 1815–56.

84 *vols.*, 8*vo*, *half green morocco.* A fine set.

After vol. XIII. the words "and Miscellaneous Journal," on the title are omitted.

1509 NORTHMORE (T.) Washington, or Liberty Restored: A Poem, in Ten Books. By Thomas Northmore, Esq. *Baltimore: John Vance & Co.* 1809.

12*mo*, *pp.* *viii.*, 253. *Half green morocco, gilt top,* UNCUT. PORTRAIT of WASHINGTON *inserted.*

1510 NORTON (J.) Abel being Dead yet speaketh; | or, The | Life & Death | of that deservedly Famous Man of God, | Mr. John Cotton, | Late Teacher of the Church of | Christ, at Boston in | New-England. | By John Norton, Teacher | of the same Church. | *London,* | *Printed by Tho. Newcomb for Lodwick Lloyd, and* | *are to be sold at his Shop next the Castle-* | *Tavern in Cornhill.* 1658.

Sm. 4*to*, *pp.* 51. *Books* (5). *Polished calf, gilt edges, by* F. BEDFORD. FINE COPY. EXTREMELY SCARCE.

1511 NORTON. Three Choice and Profitable | Sermons | Upon Several Texts of Scripture; | viz. | Jer. 30. 17. John 14. 3. Heb. 8. 5. | By that Reverend Servant of Christ, | Mr. John Norton | Late Teacher of the Church of Christ at Boston in N. E. | The First of them being the Last Sermon which | he Preached at the Court of Election at Boston. | The Second was the Last which he Preached on the Lord's-day. | The Third was the Last which he Preached on his Weekly-Lecture-Day. | Wherein | (Beside many other excellent and seasonable Truths) is shewed, | the Lords Sovereignty over, and Care for his Church and People, | in order to both their Militant and Triumphant condition; | and their Fidelity and good affection towards himself. | *Cambridge:* | *Printed by S. G. and M. I. for Hezekiah Usher of Boston.* 1664.

[Also:] A Copy | of the | Letter | Returned by the | Ministers of New-England | to | Mr. John Dury | about his | Pacification. | Faithfully Translated out of the Original Manuscript written in | Latine, by the Reverend Author of the Three | former Sermons | ... | By a Lover of Truth and Peace. | *Published in the Year* 1664.

Sm. 4to, pp. (6), 38; (6), 12. *Crimson morocco, gilt edges.* A FINE COPY of this EXCESSIVELY RARE TRACT.

One of the EARLIEST Cambridge, N. E. imprints, by the printers of, and contemporaneous with Eliot's Indian Bible. There was no press at Boston until several years after this date.

1512 NOTES AND QUERIES, a Medium of Intercommunication for Literary men, Artists, Antiquaries, Genealogists, etc. [From the beginning in 1849, to December 1867; being Series I. 12 vols. and Index; Series II. 12 vols. and Index; Series III. 12 vols. and Index.] *London:* 1849–67.

39 *vols., 4to, half green morocco, gilt top,* UNCUT. Covers and advertisements bound in at the end of each volume. AN ELEGANT SET of the FIRST THREE SERIES with INDEXES complete. VERY SCARCE in this fine condition.

A work of constantly increasing value and importance and one that no library should be without. Sets are now difficult to procure complete, and are daily enhancing in value; the earlier series and several of the Indexes have been for some time out of print.

1513 NOVA BRITANNIA. Offering Most Excellent fruites by Planting in Virginia. Exciting all such as be well affected to further the same. *London: Printed for Samuel Macham.* 1609.
Reprinted at the Chiswick Press for J. Sabin, New York. 1867.

Sm. 4to, Black Letter, 20 leaves. Crushed red levant morocco, gilt top, UNCUT, *by* F. BEDFORD. 250 *copies only printed.*

The most elegant of any of the modern reprints.

Dr. FRANCIS L. HAWKS, the editor of this edition, states, that "within his knowledge there are but *two* tracts, earlier than this, concerning what was called "Virginia." One was published in 1605 and the other in 1608. In Heber's catalogue, mention is made of a still earlier work — Brereton's "Briefe and true relation of the Discovery of the North part of Virginia, 1602," to which list we add Thomas Hariot's "*Virginia*," 1588.

1514 NUTS for Future Historians to Crack. Collected by Horace W. Smith. Containing the Cadwallader Pamphlet, Valley Forge Letters, etc. *Philadelphia: Horace W. Smith.* 1856.

8vo, pp. 90. *Half blue morocco, gilt top,* UNCUT.

AN ILLUSTRATED AND UNIQUE VOLUME.

With FIFTY engraved PORTRAITS, VIEWS, &c.; three photographs; an autograph letter cf the editor respecting the work; sixteen pages of cuttings, mounted by TRENT, all relating to the volume; WILLIAM B. REED's Reply, pp. 22, privately printed and EXCESSIVELY SCARCE; and THREE additional and UNPUBLISHED TITLE PAGES *inserted.* The first title has a woodcut of GEN. SAM. SMITH mounted in the blank space, without the oval. The second has the full length figure of JUSTICE, within the oval, with heads of REED and ARNOLD suspended in the evenly poised scales, the heads beautifully drawn in pencil by EHNINGER. The third is as published with the volume. The fourth has the figure of JUSTICE, within the oval, with fine photographic heads of REED and ARNOLD suspended in the scales. The VERY RARE PRIVATE PLATE of MARGARET MORRIS, and the rare and curious B.B.E. MIS-NAMED PORTRAIT of JOHN DICKINSON will be found in the volume.

1515 O'CALLAGHAN (E. B.) History of New Netherland; or, New York under the Dutch. By E. B. O'Callaghan, M.D. Second Edition.
New York: D. Appleton & Company. 1855.

2 vols., 8vo, pp. 493; 608. *Portrait,* 3 *Maps, and* 2 *Sheets of Facsimiles. Half calf.* FINE LARGE COPY. TWO PORTRAITS *inserted.*

1516 O'CALLAGHAN. A List of Editions of the Holy Scriptures, and Parts thereof, printed in America previous to 1860. With Introduction and Bibliographical Notes. By E. B. O'Callaghan.
Albany: Munsell & Rowland. 1861.

Imp. 8vo, half blue levant morocco, gilt top, UNCUT. 150 copies only printed. Contains FACSIMILES of the Title Pages to Eliot's Indian Bible.

1517 OGDEN (U.) Two Discourses, Occasioned by the Death of General George Washington. ... By the Rev. Uzal Ogden, D.D., Rector of Trinity Church, Newark, in the State of New-Jersey, Delivered in that Church, and in the Church in Union with it, at Belleville, December 29th, 1799, and January 5th, 1800. ...
Newark: Matthias Day. MDCCC.

8vo, pp. 46. UNCUT. Contains the RARE PORTRAIT of WASHINGTON, engraved by TIEBOUT, and wanting in many copies.

1518 [OGLETHORPE (James.)] A | New and Accurate Account | of the | Provinces | of | South-Carolina | and | Georgia: | With many curious and useful Observati- | ons on the Trade, Navigation and Planta- | tions of Great-Britain, compared with her | most powerful maritime Neighbours in an- | tient and modern Times. | *London:* | ... *J. Worrall* ... 1732.

8vo. Title, pp. 76. *Half maroon morocco:* LARGE *and* CLEAN COPY. EXCEEDINGLY SCARCE. Some copies have the date of 1733. This appears to be the tract referred to by Nichols, (*Lit. Anecd.* II. p. 19.) as written by Gov. Oglethorpe. *See* RICH. *Bib. Am. I.* 45.

1519 OLD ENGLAND FOR EVER, or, Spanish Cruelty display'd; Wherein the Spaniards' Right to America is impartially Examined and found Defective, their Pretensions founded in Blood, supported by Cruelty, and continued by Oppression. ... With an Account of their Intolerable Oppression and Barbarous Treatment of the poor Indians, and the Shocking and Tragical Methods used to deprive them of their Countrey, and obtain Possession of their rich Mines &c. ...
London: 1740.

Sm. 8vo, pp. 320. *Half calf antique.* VERY SCARCE.

1520 ONDERDONK (H. Jr.) Documents and Letters intended to illustrate the Revolutionary Incidents of Queens County; with Con-

necting Narratives, Explanatory Notes, and Additions. [Also:] Revolutionary Incidents of Suffolk and Kings Counties, with an Account of the Battle of Long Island, and the British Prisons and Prison-Ships at New York. By Henry Onderdonk, Jr.
New-York: Leavitt & Company. 1846–1849.

2 vols., 12mo, pp. 264; 268. *2 Maps. Half calf, carmine edges.*

1521 ORATION, (An) in Memory of Gen. George Washington. Delivered at Lovett's Hotel on the evening of the 22d February, 1800, before a Literary Society; and published by their Order. By a Member. *New York:* 1800.

12mo, pp. 23. *Half blue morocco, gilt top,* UNCUT, *by* BRADSTREET. VERY RARE.

1522 ORATIONS, delivered at the Request of the Inhabitants of the Town of Boston, to Commemorate the Evening of the Fifth of March, 1770; when a number of Citizens were killed by a party of British Troops, quartered among them, in a Time of Peace. Second Edition. *Boston: W. T. Clap.* 1807.

Sm. 8vo, pp. 198, (1). *Half green levant morocco, gilt top,* UNCUT, *by* F. BEDFORD. ELEGANT COPY. VERY SCARCE.

The orations are by James Lovell, A.M.; Dr. Benj. Church; Dr. Joseph Warren, (of Bunker Hill fame); Benj. Hichborn; William Tudor; Jonathan Mason, Jr.; Thos. Dawes, Jr.; and John Hancock, (the last of which is remarkable as being the only publication of this distinguished patriot). Also, an oration by Perez Morton, on the reinterment of the remains of Joseph Warren, April 8th, 1776.

1523 ORDERLY BOOK (The) of that portion of the American Army stationed at or near Williamsburg, Va., under the Command of Gen. Andrew Lewis, from March 18th, 1776, to August 28th, 1776. Printed from the Original Manuscript, with Notes and Introduction. By Charles Campbell, Esq. *Richmond: Va. Privately printed.* 1860.

4to, pp. (4), *xi.,* 100. *Half blue morocco, gilt top,* UNCUT. *One hundred copies only printed.* VERY SCARCE.

Forms No. 1. of "Historical Documents from the Old Dominion." All that was published.

1524 [O'REILLY (Henry.)] Notices of Sullivan's Campaign, in the Revolutionary Warfare in Western New York: embodied in the Addresses and Documents connected with the Funeral Honors rendered to those who fell with the gallant Boyd in the Genesee Valley, including the Remarks of Gov. Seward at Mount Hope.
Rochester: William Alling. 1842.

12mo, pp. 192. *Plate. Half green morocco.* VERY SCARCE.

This rare little volume was "published pursuant to a resolution adopted by the people assembled in Livingston County, to preserve a record of the honors paid to the soldiers whose blood first consecrated to freedom the soil of the Genesee Valley." The plate represents the "Hill of the Revolutionary Patriots at Mt. Hope, Rochester."

1525 [OSBORN (Langdon.)] The Vision of Rubeta, an Epic Story of the Island of Manhattan. With Illustrations done on *Stone*. *Boston: Weeks, Jordan and Company*. MDCCCXXXVIII.

8vo, pp. xviii., (2), 424. 4 *Plates. Half green morocco, gilt top*, UNCUT.

The work is mainly an attack on W. L. Stone, Chas. King, and the "Commercial Advertiser." E. A. Poe is said to have asserted that it was the only American satire ever written.

1526 [OSBORN.] A Critical Examination of the Poem entitled "The Vision of Rubeta." With an Inquiry concerning its Author. [*New York*:] *April*, 1839.

8vo, pp. vii., 42. *Half green morocco, gilt top*, UNCUT, *by* BRADSTREET. PORTRAIT of WILLIAM L. STONE *inserted*. VERY SCARCE.

1527 OSGOOD (D.) A Discourse, Delivered December 29, 1799, the Lord's-Day immediately following the Melancholy Tidings of the Loss sustained by the Nation in the Death of its most Eminent Citizen George Washington. ... By David Osgood, D.D. Pastor of the Church in Medford. *Boston*: 1800.

8vo, pp. 19. UNCUT.

1528 OTHER SIDE OF THE QUESTION; (The) or, A Defence of the Liberties of North-America. In Answer to a late Friendly Address to All Reasonable Americans, on The Subject of our Political Confusions. By a Citizen. *New-York: Printed by James Rivington, Hanover-Square*. M.DCC.LXXIV.

8vo, pp. 30. *Half green morocco*. VERY SCARCE.

1529 OTIS (J.) The Rights of the British Colonies Asserted and Proved. By James Otis, Esq. *London: J. Almon*. [1765.]

8vo, pp. 120. *Half green morocco*. VERY SCARCE.

The writer, a native of Boston, was one of the first and most influential of the controversialists on the popular side. This piece was read in MS. to the Mass. House of Representatives, and was published with their knowledge though not by their orders. The Instructions of May, 1764, in the Appendix, were drawn by Samuel Adams. *See* Kennedy's Wirt. II. 49.

1530 OTTLEY (W. Y.) An Inquiry concerning the Invention of Printing; in which the systems of Meerman, Heinecken, Santander, and Koning are Reviewed; including also Notices of the early use of Wood-Engraving in Europe, the Block Books, etc. By the late William Young Ottley, Esq. With an Introduction by J. Ph. Berjeau. Illustrated with Thirty-seven Plates, and numerous Wood-Engravings. *London: Joseph Lilly*. MDCCCLXII.

4to, pp. xlii., 377. *Half purple levant morocco, gilt top*, UNCUT. 200 copies only printed. FIVE ILLUSTRATIONS *inserted*.

One of the most important books ever produced on the vexed question of the Invention of Printing. The author reviews the systems of Meerman, Heinecken, Santander, and Koning, and has the courage to assert the claims of Holland to that honor.

1531 P (G.) Lex Parliamentaria : | or, a | Treatise | of the | Law and Custom | of the | Parliaments | of | England. | By G. P. Esq : | *London Printed, and Reprinted in New-York* | *and Sold by* WILLIAM and ANDREW BRADFORD | *in New York and Philadelphia.* 1716.

12*mo*, *pp.* (6), 184. *Crushed red levant morocco, paneled and gilt sides, edges gilt on carmine, by* F. BEDFORD. BEAUTIFUL COPY. VERY RARE.

We are unable to trace the sale of *any copy* of this most rare book. There is a copy in the library of the Massachusetts Historical Society, and it appeared in the Catalogue of H. A. Brady's sale, but being one of the books which did not belong to him it was not sold.

1532 PACKARD (A. S.) History of the Bunkerhill Monument. By Professor [Alpheus S.] Packard, of Bowdoin College. *Portland :* 1853.

8*vo*, *pp.* 33. *Plate. Half crimson morocco, gilt top.*

1533 PACKWOOD (G.) Packwood's Whim ; Packwoodiana ; or, the Goldfinch's Nest ; or The Way to get Money and be Happy. Giving ... Information how to lay out One Halfpenny, and how it will produce Thirty-five Thousand Guineas. ... And further, to make this Publication worth your money, that there may be no Grumbling, an Half Crown is placed within the leaves. By George Packwood. A New Edition, with Double Additions. *London :* [1808 ?]

8*vo pp.* 94. *Half red morocco, gilt top,* UNCUT. PORTRAIT.

1534 PAINE (T.) An Eulogy on the life of General George Washington. ... Written At the request of the citizens of Newburyport, and delivered at the first Presbyterian Meeting-House in that town, January 2d, 1800. By Thomas Paine, M.A. *Newburyport :* 1800.

8*vo*, *pp.* 22. UNCUT.

The author afterwards had his name changed to ROBERT TREAT PAINE, in order that he might not be confounded with Thomas Paine, Author of "Common Sense," &c.

1535 PAINE (R. T.) The Works, in Verse and Prose, of the Late Robert Treat Paine, Jr., Esq., with Notes. To which are prefixed Sketches of his Life, Character and Writings. [By Charles Prentiss.] *Boston : J. Belcher.* 1812.

8*vo*, *pp. lxxxviii.*, (2), 464, (1). *Portrait. Half green morocco, gilt top,* UNCUT.

1536 [PAINE (Thomas.)] Common Sense ; addressed to the Inhabitants of America. ... A New Edition with several Additions in the Body of the Work. To which is added an Appendix ; together with an Address to the People called Quakers. ... [Also :] Additions to Common Sense ; addressed to the Inhabitants of America. [And :] Plain Truth : Addressed to the Inhabitants of America. Containing

Remarks on a late Pamphlet, entitled Common Sense: Wherein are shewn, that the Scheme of Independence is Ruinous, Delusive, and Impracticable: That were the Author's Asseverations, respecting the Power of America, as Real as Nugatory, Reconciliation on liberal Principles with Great Britain, would be exalted Policy; and that, circumstanced as we are, Permanent Liberty, and True Happiness, can only be obtained by Reconciliation with that Kingdom. Written by Candidus. ... Second Edition. *London: John Almon.* 1776.

8vo, 3 pieces in 1 vol., pp. (6), 54; 47; (4), 47. *Half blue morocco.*

Plain Truth "is written with such outrageous zeal, and contains so many scurrilous reflections against the author of 'Common Sense' and the supposed favorers of independency, that we may safely conclude, from its having been printed in Philadelphia, that the congress either do not aim at a separation from this country, or that their government is not of the tyrannical nature which some have chosen to represent it."—M. R. LIV. 502. Dr. Parr says that this tract produced a wonderful effect throughout America and England.

1537 [PAINE.] Public Good, being an Examination Into the Claim of Virginia to the Vacant Western Territory, and of the Right of the United States to the Same. To which is added, Proposals for laying off a new State, to be applied as a Fund for Carrying on the War, or Redeeming the National Debt. By the Author of Common Sense. *Philadelphia: Printed by John Dunlap.* M,DCC,LXXX.

8vo, pp. 38. *Half gray calf, gilt top,* UNCUT. *Very scarce.*

1538 PAINE. Letter addressed to the Abbe Raynal on the Affairs of North America. In which the Mistakes in the Abbe's Account of the Revolution of America are corrected and cleared up. By Thomas Paine, M.A. ... *Philadelphia: Robert Aitken.* 1782.

8vo, pp. 77. *Half gray calf, gilt top,* UNCUT. PORTRAITS of PAINE and RAYNAL *inserted.*
This famous piece passed through several editions.
See Raynal (Abbé,) No. 1673.

1539 PAINE. The Writings of Thomas Paine, Secretary for Foreign Affairs to the Congress of the United States of America, in the Late War. *Albany: State of New York, Charles R. & George Webster.* [1792.]

8vo, half gray calf, carmine edges. VERY SCARCE. The list of subscribers contains nearly six hundred names, thirty of which are those of Members of Congress.
DEDICATED TO GEORGE WASHINGTON.

1540 PAINE. A Letter to George Washington, President of the United States of America. On Affairs Public and Private. By Thomas Paine. ... *Philadelphia: Benj. Franklin Bache.* 1796.

8vo, pp. 76. *Half green morocco, gilt top,* UNCUT. PORTRAIT of PAINE *inserted.*

1541 PAINE. Letter from Thomas Paine to George Washington, dated Paris, July, 1796. To which is added, Thomas Paine's Letter, dated Federal City, Nov., 1802. Also, his Speech in the National Convention on the Trial of Louis XVI.

Baltimore: Printed by G. Douglas. 1802.

8vo, pp. 44. *Half green morocco, gilt top,* UNCUT. *Very scarce.*

Mr. Paine was no admirer of Washington and thus addresses him: "Elevated to the chair of the Presidency, you assumed the merit of everything to yourself; and the natural ingratitude of your constitution began to appear. You commenced your presidential career by encouraging and swallowing the grossest adulation; and you travelled America from one end to the other to put yourself in the way of receiving it. You have as many addresses in your chest as James the Second. As to what were your views, for you are not great enough to have ambition, though you are little enough to have vanity, they cannot be inferred from expressions of your own; but the partizans of your politics have divulged the secret." He also attacks the military skill of Washington.

See Kennedy (P.) No 1152. Also, [Cobbett (W.)] No. 409.

1542 PAINE. Tom Paine's Jests; being an entirely New and Select Collection of Patriotic Bon Mots, Repartees, Anecdotes, Epigrams, Observations, etc., on Political subjects. By Thomas Paine, and other Supporters of the Rights of Man. To which is added, A Tribute to the Swinish Multitude, Being a choice collection of Patriotic Songs. *Philadelphia: Printed for Matthew Carey.* MDCCXCVI.

12mo, pp. 72. *Half maroon morocco.* VERY SCARCE.

It is questionable whether Paine had anything to do with this scarce little tract. It is however one of the earliest American Jest Books.

1543 [PAINE.] The Life of Thomas Pain, with a Review of his Writings; particularly of Rights of Man, Part First and Second. By Francis Oldys, A.M., of the University of Philadelphia. The Fifth Edition, corrected and enlarged. *London: John Stockdale.* 1792.

[Also:] A Narrative of Facts, relating to a Prosecution for High Treason; including the Address to the Jury, which the Court refused to hear; with Letters to the Attorney General ... and the Defence the Author had prepared, if he had been brought to Trial. The Second Edition. By Thomas Holcroft.

London: H. D. Symonds. 1795.

[Followed by:] A Narrative of the Sufferings of T. F. Palmer and W. Skirving, during a voyage to New South Wales, 1794, on board the Surprise Transport. By Thomas Fyshe Palmer, B.A. ... The Second Edition. *Cambridge: Printed by Benjamin Flower.* 1797.

8vo, 3 works in 1 vol., pp. viii., 166; 215; 79. *Half calf.* From the Ingraham Collection.

Oldys's "Life of Pain," is usually attributed to George Chalmers, who, however, denied the charge. Oldys is a *pseudonym.*

1544 [PAINE.] The Life of Thomas Paine, Author of Common Sense, &c. By James Cheetham. [pp. 347.] *New York:* 1809.

[Also:]

The Speeches of the Hon. Thomas Erskine, in the Court of King's Bench, June 28, 1797, ... on the Trial The King versus Thomas

Williams, for publishing the Age of Reason, written by Thomas Paine ... . [pp. 23.] *London: J. Debrett.* 1797.

The Trial of Daniel Isaac Eaton, ... in the Court of King's Bench, ... July the Tenth, 1793; for selling a supposed Libel, A Letter Addressed to the Addressers by Thomas Paine. [pp. 65.] *London: Daniel Isaac Eaton.* [1793.]

Observations on Certain Documents contained in No. V & VI of "The History of the United States for the Year 1796," in which the Charge of Speculation against Alexander Hamilton, late Secretary of the Treasury, is fully Refuted. Written by Himself. [pp. 37, lviii.] *Philadelphia: John Fenno.* 1797.

8vo, 4 works in 1 vol., gray calf. Fine copies. VERY SCARCE.

Inserted in this volume are, William B. Reed's Review of John Alberger's Oration on the 106th Birthday of Thomas Paine. pp. 58. Extracted from the N. A. R. for July, 1843.— Remarks on the Pretensions of Thomas Paine, author of "Common Sense," to the Character of a Poet. pp. 10. Extracted from the Portfolio.— And in the hand-writing of Mr. E. D. Ingraham; Copy of a Letter from Paine, to John Fellows, July 31st, 1805. 8 pp.— Copy of a Letter from Paine to B. F. Bache, January 20th, 1797. 4 pp.— And, Paine's Reflections on the Death of Lord Clive. 13 pp. An interesting volume from the INGRAHAM Collection.

1545 PAINE. The Political and Miscellaneous Works of Thomas Paine. *London: R. Carlile.* 1819.

2 vols., 8vo, half calf.

1546 [PAINE.] The Life of Thomas Paine, by Thomas Clio Rickman. *London: T. C. Rickman.* 1819.

[Also:] The Theological Works of Thomas Paine. *London: R. Carlile.* 1819.

8vo, 2 works in 1 vol., half calf. Uniform with the preceding No.

"The engraving of Mr. Paine by Sharp, prefixt to this work is the only true likeness of him; it is from his portrait by Romney, and is perhaps the greatest likeness ever taken by any painter; to that eminent artist I introduced him in 1792, and it was by my earnest persuasion that he sat to him."— *Preface to the Life.* p. xiv.

1547 [PAINE.] A Dialogue between the Ghost of General Montgomery just arrived from the Elysian Fields; and an American Delegate in a Wood near Philadelphia. [*Philadelphia:*] 1796. [*New York: Reprinted.* 1865.]

8vo, pp. 16, half blue morocco, gilt top, UNCUT. One of 80 *copies only* PRIVATELY PRINTED.

1548 [PAINE. PAINEIANA. An Extensive Collection of Pamphlets Relating to that Celebrated Character. *v.p. v.d.*]

5 vols., 8vo, half gray calf. Uniform in size.

These volumes contain nearly forty contemporaneous publications, issued between the years 1788 and 1820, and directly relating to Thomas Paine, his conduct, character and writings. Many of them are rare, all are curious and interesting, and they throw much light upon the status and habits of that extraordinary man, and the degree of estimation in which he was held by his contemporaries. It would be difficult, even if it were possible, to make a similar assemblage now, at almost any cost. The pamphlets are severally in the finest condition, many of them uncut, and as a memorial of the man, whose pen, during the troublous times of the American revolution, was "mightier than the sword," they are of much interest and value.

1549 PALFREY (J. G.) History of New England during the Stuart Dynasty. By John Gorham Palfrey. *Boston: Little, Brown & Co.* 1865.

3 *vols., imp. 8vo, pp.* xxxi., (2), 636; *xx.*, 640; *xxii.*, 659. 4 *Maps. Half purple morocco, gilt top,* UNCUT. LARGE PAPER. *One hundred copies only printed.*

1550 PAPERS Relating to America. [Respecting the Encounter between his Majesty's Ship Leopard, and the American Frigate Chesapeake.] Presented to the House of Commons, 1809. *London: A. Strahan.* 1810.

8vo, pp. viii., 178, (4). *Half calf. Fine copy.* VERY SCARCE.

1551 PAPERS Relating to Pemaquid and parts adjacent in the present State of Maine, known as Cornwall County, when under the Colony of New York. Compiled from Official Records in the office of the Secretary of State at Albany, N. Y. By Franklin B. Hough. *Albany: Weed, Parsons & Companie.* 1856.

Roy. 8vo, pp. vii., 136. *Half blue levant morocco, gilt top,* UNCUT. PORTRAIT *of the* EDITOR *inserted. One of* 50 *copies only printed on* FINE PAPER.

1552 PAPERS Relating to the Island of Nantucket, With Documents relating to the Original Settlement of that Island, Martha's Vineyard, and other Islands adjacent, known as Duke's County, While under the Colony of New York. Compiled from Official Records in the Office of the Secretary of State at Albany, New York. By Franklin B. Hough. *Albany: [J. Munsell.]* 1856.

4to, pp. xviii., 163. *Map. Half morocco.* 150 *copies only* PRIVATELY PRINTED.

I was reluctant to go back to old style printing, but the patron of this work, Hon. J. V. L. Pruyn, at whose expense it was issued, induced me to import the types from Caslon of London, the American founders being then deficient of an assortment, and workmen being unacquainted with the peculiarities of the style of work, I set up all the types with my own hands. It was the forerunner of what I termed my "Historical Series."—*Munsell.*

1553 PARISH (E.) An Oration, delivered at Byfield, February 22d, 1800, ... on the Death of General George Washington. By the Rev. Elijah Parish, A.M. *Newburyport:* [1800.]

8vo, pp. 32. UNCUT. VERY SCARCE.

1554 PARKER (I.) An Oration on the Sublime Virtues of General George Washington ... . Pronounced before the Inhabitants of Portland, February 22d, 1800. ... By Isaac Parker. *Portland:* [1800.]

8vo, pp. 24. SCARCE.

1555 PARKINSON (R.) A Tour in America, in 1798, 1799, and 1800, exhibiting Sketches of Society and Manners, and a particular Account of the American System of Agriculture, with its Recent Improvements. By Richard Parkinson, late of Orange Hill near Baltimore. *London: J. Harding.* 1805.

2 vols., 8vo, pp. (8), 319; (8), 320–735. *Half calf.*

Parkinson was an English agriculturist, who came to this country, recommended by Sir John Sinclair, to superintend the farms of General Washington, respecting whom the book abounds in curious details, that seem to have been generally overlooked by his biographers.

1556 PARKMAN (F. Jr.) History of the Conspiracy of Pontiac, and the War of the North American Tribes against the English Colonies after the Conquest of Canada. By Francis Parkman, Jr. *Boston: Little, Brown & Co.* 1866.

Roy. 8vo, pp. xxiv., 632. *Maps. Half crimson morocco, gilt top,* UNCUT. PORTRAIT *inserted.* LARGE PAPER; *seventy-five copies only printed.*

1557 PARKMAN. France and England in North America. A Series of Historical Narratives. By Francis Parkman. Part First. Pioneers of France in the New World. *Boston: Little, Brown & Company.* 1866.

Roy. 8vo, pp. xxii., 420. *Portrait. Half crimson morocco, gilt top,* UNCUT. LARGE PAPER; *seventy-five copies only printed.* Uniform with the preceding No.

1558 PARKMAN. France and England in North America. ... By Francis Parkman. Part Second. The Jesuits in North America in the Seventeenth Century. *Boston: Little, Brown and Company.* 1867.

Roy. 8vo, pp. lxxxix., 463. *Map. Half crimson morocco, gilt top,* UNCUT. LARGE PAPER; *seventy-five copies only printed.* Uniform with the preceding No.

1559 PARKMAN. France and England in North America. ... By Francis Parkman. Part Third. The Discovery of the Great West. *Boston: Little, Brown and Company.* 1870.

Roy. 8vo, pp. xxi., 425. *Map. Half crimson morocco, gilt top,* UNCUT. LARGE PAPER; *seventy-five copies only printed.* Uniform with the preceding No.

"The charm which Mr. Parkman's books assert on the attention of every reader, is not wholly derived from the pleasing style of his writing. His perfect knowledge of Indian life and manners, acquired by personal experience, and his exhaustion of the literature of his subject, as it is found in printed works, unedited manuscripts, and authenticated tradition, give new interest to the subjects of which he treats."—*Field.*

1560 PARSONS (U.) The Life of Sir William Pepperell, Bart., the only Native of New England who was created a Baronet during our connection with the Mother Country. By Usher Parsons. Third Edition. *Boston: Little, Brown and Company.* 1856.

Sm. 8vo, pp. xvi., 356. *Portrait, Map, and Plate. Half blue morocco, gilt top,* UNCUT.

1561 PARTON (J.) The Life and Times of Aaron Burr, Lieutenant Colonel in the Army of the Revolution, United States Senator, Vice President of the United States, &c. By J. Parton. *New York: Mason Brothers.* 1858.

8vo, pp. 706. *Half green morocco, gilt top,* UNCUT. A UNIQUE COPY, with an A.L.S. of the AUTHOR, an A L.S. of AARON BURR, a LOCK OF HAIR cut from his head after death, accompanied by evidences of its authenticity, and TWENTY-FIVE ILLUSTRATIONS *inserted.*

1562 PARTON. Life of Andrew Jackson. By James Parton. *New York: Mason Brothers.* 1860.

2 vols., roy. 8vo, half green morocco, gilt top, UNCUT.

AN ILLUSTRATED COPY.

Containing FOUR AUTOGRAPH LETTERS of the AUTHOR relating to the work, and nearly NINETY ILLUSTRATIONS *inserted.*

1563 PARTON. Life and Times of Benjamin Franklin. By James Parton. *New York: Mason Brothers.* 1865.

2 vols., imp. 8vo, half purple levant morocco, gilt top, UNCUT. LARGE PAPER; 100 *copies only printed.*

1564 PATRIOTIC ADDRESSES. A Selection of the Patriotic Addresses, to the President [John Adams] of the United States. Together with the President's Answers. Presented in the Year One Thousand Seven Hundred and Ninety-eight. ... *Boston: John W. Folsom.* 1798.

12mo, pp. 360. *Half blue morocco, carmine edges.* SCARCE.

1565 PATRIOTS (The) of North America: A Sketch. With Explanatory Notes. *New York: Printed in the Year,* M,DCC,LXXV.

8vo, pp. iv., 47. *Half red morocco.*

In this RARE and CURIOUS revolutionary poem the States are characterized as School Boys, and notwithstanding "a tory here reviles the whigs in verse," it is a clever performance with curious notes.

1566 PATTEN (W.) A Discourse, delivered in the 2d Congregational Church, Newport, December 29, 1799: occasioned by the Death of General George Washington. ... By William Patten, A.M. *Newport:* 1800.

8vo, pp. 19. RARE.

1567 PATTIE (J. O.) The Personal Narrative of James O. Pattie, of Kentucky, during an Expedition from St. Louis, through the Vast Regions between that place and the Pacific Ocean, and thence back through the City of Mexico to Vera Cruz, during Journeyings of Six Years; in which he and his Father, who accompanied him, suffered unheard of Hardships and Dangers, had various Conflicts with the Indians, and were made Captives, in which Captivity his Father died: together with a Description of the Country, and the various Nations through which they passed. Edited by Timothy Flint. *Cincinnati: E. H. Flint.* 1833.

8vo, pp. 300. 5 *Plates. Half gray calf.* FINE COPY. VERY SCARCE.

"The narrative of Pattie's expedition and captivity has more than the ordinary interest and value, which attaches to the stories of adventurers. He crossed the continent of America on a route which his party were the first to pursue. He encountered tribes of Indians who then saw a white man for the first time, and his narrative has the merit of being given in a candid, unexaggerated style, which impresses us with its veracity. The story of the perilous expedition, the frightful extremities to which his party were reduced, the fights with the savages, and his final capture, are all narrated with spirit and candor."— *Field.*

1568 PAULDING (J. K.) The Backwoodsman. A Poem. By James K. Paulding. *Philadelphia: M. Thomas.* 1818.

8vo, pp. 198. *Half red morocco, gilt top,* UNCUT, *by* BRADSTREET. An *unlettered proof* PORTRAIT of the AUTHOR *inserted.* VERY SCARCE.

1569 PAULDING. A Life of Washington. By James K. Paulding. *New York: Harper & Brothers.* 1840.

2 *vols.,* 16*mo, half green morocco, gilt top.*

1570 PAULDING (J.) Affairs and Men of New Amsterdam, in the time of Governor Peter Stuyvesant. Compiled from Dutch Manuscript Records of the period. By John Paulding. *New York: Casper C. Childs.* 1843.

12*mo, pp.* 161, (2). *Half red morocco. Scarce.*

1571 [PAULDING (W. K.)] History of the City of New York. By David T. Valentine. *New York: G. P. Putnam & Company.* 1853.

8vo, half calf. THIRTY-THREE ILLUSTRATIONS, and an additional appendix *inserted.*

This work was compiled by William K. Paulding, although published over the name of Mr. Valentine.

1572 PAYSON (P.) A Sermon delivered at Chelsea, January 14, 1800. ... on the Sorrowful Event of the Death of General Washington. By the Rev. Phillips Payson, A.M. *Charlestown:* 1800.

8vo, pp. 15. UNCUT.

1573 PEALE (Rembrandt.) Original Autograph Letters Written by the Friends and Relatives of Washington, on the Portrait painted by Rembrandt Peale. [1854.]

Imp. 4to, red levant morocco, richly tooled and gilt back and sides, gilt edges, with clasp. BEAUTIFULLY EXECUTED MANUSCRIPT TITLE-PAGE by Mr. George Becker, of Philadelphia.

This EXTRAORDINARY, HIGHLY INTERESTING, and ABSOLUTELY UNIQUE ASSEMBLAGE of WASHINGTONIAN MEMENTOES, is one of the DESIDERATA of this Collection. Its contents consist of eight pages relating to GENERAL WASHINGTON, partly original, and partly selected, in the handwriting of MR. PEALE, with a fine original signature of WASHINGTON mounted at the bottom of the last leaf, together with TWENTY-SIX ORIGINAL MANUSCRIPT LETTERS from his FRIENDS and RELATIVES, as follows:

SAMUEL BRECK.	A.L.S.	EDWARD LIVINGSTON.	A.L.S.
JOHN MARSHALL.	"	CHARLES CARROLL OF CARROLLTON.	"
BUSHROD WASHINGTON.	"	JOHN EAGER HOWARD.	"
RICHARD PETERS.	"	WILLIAM WHITE.	"
WILLIAM TILGHMAN.	"	CHARLES WILSON PEALE.	"
WILLIAM JACKSON.	"	GEORGE W. P. CUSTIS.	"
WILLIAM RUSH.	"	ROBERT GOODLOE HARPER.	L.S.
OLIVER WOLCOT.	L.S.	RUFUS KING.	A.L.S.
ANDREW JACKSON.	A.L.S.	SAMUEL SMITH.	"
WILLIAM CRANCH.	"	ALLAN MCLANE.	L.S.

ROBERT WHARTON.	A.L.S.	JAMES THACHER.	A.L.S.
BENJAMIN TALLMADGE.	"	TIMOTHY PICKERING	"
DANIEL UDREE.	"	A FOREIGN OFFICER.	"

Followed by GEN. WASHINGTON to CHARLES WILSON PEALE. A.L.S.— BENJAMIN FRANKLIN to the same. A.L.S.— THOMAS JEFFERSON to the same, A.L.S.— A Special Passport for REMBRANDT PEALE wholly written and signed by MR. JEFFERSON, as then, President of the United States.—And an A.L.S. of WASHINGTON IRVING to Rembrandt Peale. All in the finest state of preservation, mounted on tinted leaves, and ruled. A fragment of WASHINGTON'S COFFIN, from the old vault at Mount Vernon, duly authenticated, is attached to the inside of the under cover.

This very interesting collection, relating, as it does, entirely to a single important historical object, and forming a galaxy of the autographs of the most illustrious of the great and good men of the period of the Revolution, possesses a value far beyond that of a mere collection of autograph letters, inasmuch as many of the writers minutely describe the countenance, features, person and character of Washington; the circumstances under which they met him; some in the field; others under the hospitable roof of Mount Vernon; and relate interesting reminiscences of the events which brought them into his presence. The volume was arranged by the eminent artist himself, and accompanied him during his lecturing tours throughout the United States. It consequently exhibits some exterior evidence of use, although in most excellent preservation.

A UNIQUE WASHINGTONIAN MEMORIAL.

1574 [PEALE. Twenty-seven Fine Portraits, One View, a Pamphlet issued by Mr. Peale, and an Autograph Letter written and signed by him, all relating to, and designed to illustrate the Album. The Portraits embrace those of almost every Individual whose Autograph occurs in that volume.]

Folio, 4to, and 8vo, in a port-folio.

1575 PECK (G.) Wyoming; its History, Stirring Incidents, and Romantic Adventures. By George Peck. With Illustrations.

New York: Harper & Brothers. 1858.

12mo, pp. 432. *Woodcuts. Half maroon morocco, gilt top,* UNCUT. TWO PORTRAITS *inserted.*

1576 PENHALLOW (S.) The History of the Wars of New-England with the Eastern Indians, or a Narrative of their continued Perfidy and Cruelty, from the 10th of August, 1703, to the Peace renewed 13th of July, 1713. And from the 25th of July, 1722, to their Submission 15th December, 1725, which was ratified August 5th, 1726. By Samuel Penhallow.

Cincinnati: Reprinted for Wm. Dodge. 1859.

4to, pp. 138, 36. *Half maroon morocco, gilt top,* UNCUT. 150 copies only printed. *Portrait* of BENJAMIN COLMAN *inserted.*

Contains also "Lovewell's Fight." Gardener's Account of the "Pequot Warres," and "The Gospel in New-England."

1577 PENN (W.) A | Letter | from | William Penn | Popprietary (*sic*) and Governour of | Pennsylvania | In America, | To the | Committee | of the | Free Society of Traders | of that Province, residing in London. | Containing | A General Description of the Said Province, its Soil, Air, Water, Seasons and Produce, | both Natural and Artificial, and the good Encrease thereof. | ... To which is added, an Account of the City of | Philadelphia | Newly laid out. | Its Scituation between two Navigable Rivers, Delaware and Skulkill, | with a | Portraiture or Plat-form thereof, | ... | *Printed and Sold by Andrew Sowle, ... London.* 1683.

Folio, pp. 10. *Half blue morocco, gilt top, by* BRADSTREET. The Plat-form alluded to in the title is wanting.

One of the first printed accounts of Pennsylvania by the founder of the colony. It is so RARE that we are unable to trace the sale of *any other copy* in this country. The title at length will be found in RICH. p. 108.

1578 [PENN (William.)] Information and Direction | To | Such Persons as are inclined | to | America, | More | Especially Those related to the Province | of | Pennsylvania. | [*London:* 1684 ?]

Folio, pp. 4. *Half maroon morocco, gilt top, by* BRADSTREET.

This tract, written by William Penn, is unknown to Rich, and is not described by any bibliographer. It is of the *greatest rarity*, and of interest as exhibiting the terms upon which Penn disposed of his lands.

1579 PENNSYLVANIA. The Charters of the Province of Pennsylvania and City of Philadelphia. [Also :] A Collection of all the Laws of the Province of Pennsylvania, Now in Force. Published by Order of Assembly.
Philadelphia: Printed and Sold by B. FRANKLIN. MDCCXLII.

Folio, pp. 30; 562, *Appendix iv.*, 24; *Table xi.* *Half gray calf.* LARGE and CLEAN COPY, with *three imprints* of BENJAMIN FRANKLIN.

1580 PENNSYLVANIA. A Brief | State | of the | Province | of | Pennsylvania, | in which | the Conduct of their Assemblies for several | Years past is impartially examined, and the | true Cause of the continual Encroachments of | the French displayed, more especially the secret | Design of their late unwarrantable Invasion | and Settlement upon the River Ohio. | To which is annexed, | An easy Plan for restoring Quiet in the public Mea- | sures of that Province, and defeating the ambitious | Views of the French in time to come. | In a Letter from a Gentleman who | has resided many Years in Pennsylvania | to his Friend in London. | The Second Edition. | *London: Printed for R. Griffiths* .... 1755.

8vo, pp. 45. *Half green morocco, gilt top,* UNCUT, *by* F. BEDFORD. VERY RARE in *uncut* condition.

" From the answer to this pamphlet (see following No.) it would appear that its author was probably the Rev. William Smith, author of 'Discourses,' etc., 1759, assisted, according to a MS. note in a copy of the same work, by Dr. Franklin."— *Rich.*

1581 PENNSYLVANIA. An | Answer | To an invidious Pamphlet, intituled, | A Brief State of the Province of | Pensylvania. | Wherein are exposed | The many false Assertions of the Author or | Authors, of the said Pamphlet, with a | View to render the Quakers of Pensylvania | and their Government obnoxious to the | British Parliament and Ministry ; | and the | Several Transactions, most grosly misrepre- | sented therein, set in their true light. | *London :* | ... *S. Bladon* ... | MDCCLV.

8vo, pp. 80. *Half green morocco, gilt top,* UNCUT, *by* F. BEDFORD. EXCESSIVELY RARE in this *fine* and *uncut* state.

"This answer is said to be the production of one Cross, formerly an attorney's clerk, who was convicted of forgery, sentenced to be hanged, but after some time obtained the favour of transportation; and did us the honour to take up his residence in this province."—*Smith's* "Brief View." p. 13.

1582 PENNSYLVANIA. A | Brief View | of the Conduct of | Pennsylvania, | for the year 1755 ; | So far as it affected the General Service of the | British Colonies, particularly the Expedition | under the late General Braddock. | With an Account of the Shocking Inhumanities | committed by Incursions of the Indians upon the | Province in October and November ; which occasioned | a Body of the Inhabitants to come down, while the | Assembly were sitting, and to insist upon an imme- | diate Suspension of all Disputes, and the Passing of | a Law for the Defence of the Country. Interspers'd with several interesting Anecdotes and original | Papers relating to the Politics and Principles of | the People called Quakers : Being a Sequel to | a late well-known Pamphlet, | entitled, | A Brief State of Pennsylvania. | In a Second Letter to a Friend in London. | ... | *London : R. Griffiths.* 1756.

8vo, pp. 88. *Green morocco, gilt top,* UNCUT, *by* F. BEDFORD. EXCESSIVELY RARE in *uncut* condition. An AUTOGRAPH LETTER written and signed by BENJAMIN FRANKLIN relating to the subject matter of the volume *inserted.*

This work, written anonymously by Dr. Wm. Smith, is in continuation of his "Brief State, &c." An elaborate notice of the work will be found in the Monthly Review. XII. 192. XIV. 208.

1583 PENNSYLVANIA. A | True and Impartial State | of the Province of | Pennsylvania. | Containing, | An exact Account of the Nature of its Government; the Power | of the Proprietaries, and their Governors ; ... | The Rights and Privileges of the Assembly, and People, ... | With a True Narrative of the Dispute between the Governors and Assemblies ... | The whole being a full Answer to the Pamphlets intitled A | Brief State, and a Brief View, &c. of the Conduct of Pennsylvania. | ... | *Philadelphia* : | *Printed by W. Dunlap.* ... | M,DCC,LIX.

8vo, pp. v., 3–173, 34, (1). *Half green morocco, yellow edges, by* F. BEDFORD. VERY RARE.

This rare book has never been reprinted. It completes a series relating to one of the most stirring periods in the provincial history of Pennsylvania. We have never before met with the entire series embodied in any sale catalogue.

1584 PENNSYLVANIA. An Enquiry into the Causes of the Alienation of the Delaware and Shawanese Indians from the British Interest, and into the Measures taken for recovering their Friendship. Extracted from the Public Treaties, and other Authentic Papers relating to the Transactions of the Government of Pensilvania and the said Indians, for near Forty Years; and explained by a Map of the Country. Together with the Remarkable Journal of Christian Frederic Post, by whose Negotiations, among the Indians on the Ohio, they were withdrawn from the Interest of the French, who thereupon abandoned the Fort and Country. With Notes by the Editor [Charles Thomson] explaining sundry Indian Customs, &c. Written in Pensylvania. *London: J. Wilkie.* 1759.

8vo, pp. 184. *Map. Half blue levant morocco, gilt top,* UNCUT, *by* F. BEDFORD. FINE COPY. EXCESSIVELY RARE in *uncut* condition.

See Post (C. F.) No. 1619.

1585 PENNSYLVANIA. Memoirs of the Historical Society of Pennsylvania. [4 Vols.] *Philadelphia:* 1826–40.

[Also:] The Bulletin of the Historical Society of Pennsylvania. Vol. 1. 1845–47. [All ever published.] *Philadelphia:* 1848.

[And:] Collections of the Historical Society of Pennsylvania. Vol. 1. [No more published.] *Philadelphia:* 1853.

6 *vols., 8vo, half olive morocco,* UNCUT. A FINE and COMPLETE set.

This valuable series having been published from time to time in separate parts, during a period of nearly thirty years, complete sets, like the present, are VERY SCARCE.

1586 PENNSYLVANIA. Memoirs of the Historical Society of Pennsylvania. [The Publication Fund Series, Complete to date.] *Philadelphia:* 1864–74.

8 *vols., roy. 8vo, half morocco, gilt top,* UNCUT, except the three volumes last issued, which are in *cloth uncut.* FOURTEEN PORTRAITS *inserted* in the bound volumes. Published only for Subscribers to the Publication Fund, and *not for sale.*

The series contains The History of Braddock's Defeat.—History of the Insurrection in Pennsylvania, in 1794.—The Case of Major André.—Military Journal of Major Denny, 1781–95.—The Penn and Logan Correspondence, 1700–1750.—Acrelius' History of New Sweden.—&c.

1587 [PENNY HISTORIES. A Collection of Twenty one Curious and Uncommon Scotch and English Chap-Books. *v.p. v.d.*]

12*mo, calf. From the* INGRAHAM *Collection.*

1588 [PERCY (Thomas.)] Reliques of Ancient English Poetry: Consisting of old Heroic Ballads, Songs, and other Pieces of our Earlier Poets. Together with some few of Later Date. A New Edition. *London: L. A. Lewis.* 1841.

3 *vols., post 8vo, half red morocco, gilt top,* UNCUT.

1589 PERKINS (H.) Catalogue of the very Valuable and Important Library formed by the late Henry Perkins, Esq. Comprising many Splendid Illuminated Manuscripts, Ancient Bibles, Examples of

Printing on Vellum, Choice Specimens of Early Typography, the Four First Folio Editions of Shakespeare, &c. *London:* 1873.

Imp. 8vo, half red morocco, gilt top, UNCUT, *by* BRADSTREET. Contains 10 engraved *fac-similes* from the rarest volumes. Tastefully *underlined* in red and purple inks, and *ruled,* with *prices.* An ELEGANT COPY of this already VERY SCARCE catalogue.

1590 [PETERS (Samuel A.)] A | General History | of | Connecticut, | from its | First Settlement under George Fenwick, Esq. | To its | Latest Period of Amity with Great Britain; | including | a Description of the Country, | And many curious and interesting Anecdotes. | To which is added, | An Appendix, wherein new and true Sources of the present | Rebellion in America are pointed out; together with the particu- | lar Part taken by the People of Connecticut in its Promotion. | By a Gentleman of the Province. | *London:* | *Printed for the Author.* | MDCCLXXXI.

8vo, pp. x., 436. Crushed green levant morocco, back and sides elegantly tooled and gilt, broad inside borders, gilt top, UNCUT *by* W. MATTHEWS.

A SUMPTUOUS COPY. VERY RARE.

We have never sold another uncut copy. Contains a wonderful account of the Upper Cohoes Falls, "where water is consolidated without frost, by pressure, by swiftness, between the pinching, sturdy rocks, to such a degree of induration that no iron crow can be forced into it." Also a curious account of the ancient custom of courtship by "bundling."

1591 PERRY (M. C.) Narrative of the Expedition of an American Squadron to the China Seas and Japan, performed in the years 1852, 1853, and 1854, under the command of Commodore M. C. Perry, United States Navy, by order of the Government of the United States. ... *Washington:* 1856.

3 vols., 4to, half brown morocco, gilt top.

"In this valuable scientific work the first successful attempt at producing a coloured lithograph, in imitation of a drawing, is introduced. Vol. I. Contains the narrative of the expedition, illustrated by 89 fine lithographic plates, 78 wood-cuts, and 4 maps. Vol. II. A collection of reports, by various naval officers on the agriculture, botany, natural history, meteorology, topography, ethnography and geology of the places visited by the expedition, illustrated as follows. Agriculture, 4 plates; natural history — mammals, 2 plates; birds 6 plates, colored; fishes, 10 plates, colored; conchology, 5 plates, (2 colored); meteorology, 16 plates; maps 16 (14 large folding ones), and fac-similes of the treaty in Japanese characters. Vol. III. Observations on the zodiacal light from April 2, 1853, to April 22, 1855, with conclusions from the data thus obtained, by the Rev. George Jones, with 352 charts."

1592 [PERRY (O. H.)] Inauguration of the Perry Statue, At Cleveland, on the Tenth of September, 1860; Including the Addresses and other Proceedings, with a Sketch of William Walcutt, the Sculptor. *Cleveland: O.* 1861.

4to, pp. 128. Half blue morocco, gilt top, UNCUT. LARGE PAPER. *Eleven copies only* printed on this size. Two ILLUSTRATIONS *inserted,* one an *unlettered India proof* PORTRAIT of COMMODORE PERRY.

1593 PHELPS (R. H.) A History of Newgate of Connecticut, at Simsbury, now East Granby; its Insurrections and Massacres; the Imprisonment of the Tories in the Revolution, and the Working of its Mines. Also some account of the State Prison at Wethersfield. By Richard H. Phelps. *Albany : J. Munsell.* 1860.

4to, pp. 151. *Portrait. Half morocco, gilt top,* UNCUT. *Author's edition.* LARGE FINE PAPER. *Ten Copies only printed.*

1594 PHILADELPHIA. The Charter, Laws, and Catalogue of Books, of the Library Company of Philadelphia.
Philadelphia : printed by B. FRANKLIN *and* D. HALL. MDCCLXIV.

Sm. 8vo, pp. 150. *Half gray calf.* FINE COPY. *Very Scarce.*

1595 PHILAGATHOS. [*pseudonym*] A Poem, Commemorative of Goffe, Whalley, and Dixwell, Three of the Judges of Charles I. who, at the Restoration, took Refuge and Died in America. To which is prefixed, an Abstract of their History. By Philagathos.
Boston : Samuel Hall. 1793.

8vo, pp. 28. *Half red morocco, gilt top,* UNCUT. VERY RARE. A fine *original impression* of the facsimile of the "Death Warrant of Charles I." *inserted.*

1596 PHILOBIBLION. (The) A Monthly Bibliographical Journal. Containing Critical Notices of, and Extracts from, Rare, Curious, and Valuable Old Books. *New York : Geo. P. Philes & Co.* 1862–63.

2 *vols., 4to, half maroon morocco, gilt top,* UNCUT. Printed on India paper. SCARCE. Nearly all the surplus copies were accidentally destroyed by water.

1597 PICKELL (J.) A New Chapter in the Early Life of Washington, in Connection with the Narrative History of the Potomac Company. By John Pickell. *New York : D. Appleton & Co.* 1856.

8vo, pp. 178. *Half green morocco.* TEN ILLUSTRATIONS *inserted.*

1598 PICKERING (J.) A Vocabulary, or Collection of Words and Phrases which have been supposed to be peculiar to the United States of America, to which is prefixed an Essay on the present state of the English Language in the United States. ... By John Pickering.
Boston : Cummings and Hilliard. 1816.

8vo, pp. 206. *Half calf, gilt top,* UNCUT. SCARCE *in such fine condition.*
See Webster (Noah.) No. 2099.

1599 PICKETT (A. J.). History of Alabama, and incidentally of Georgia and Mississippi, from the earliest period. By Albert James Pickett. Second Edition. *Charleston : Walker and James.* 1851.

2 *vols., sq. 12mo, pp. xix.,* 377; *viii.,* 445. *Map and Woodcuts. Half blue morocco, gilt top, by* BRADSTREET. *A remarkably* LARGE *and* FINE COPY.

1600 PIERCE (J.) A Eulogy on George Washington the Great and the Good, Delivered, on the Anniversary of his Birth, At Brookline, and published at the Request of its inhabitants. By John Pierce. ...
Boston : 1800.

8vo, pp. 24. UNCUT. *Scarce.*

1601 PIERCE (W. L.) The Year: A Poem, in three Cantoes (*sic*). By William Leigh Pierce, Esq. *New York: David Longworth.* 1813.

12*mo*, *half calf*, *gilt top*, UNCUT. A long AUTOGRAPH LETTER from the AUTHOR, to the publisher, solely relating to the work, *inserted.*

A poetical review of the principal political occurrences of the year 1812; now VERY SCARCE.

1602 PIERPONT (J.) The Portrait. A Poem delivered before the Washington Benevolent Society, of Newburyport, on the evening of October 27, 1812. By John Pierpont.

Boston: Bradford and Read. 1812.

8*vo*, *pp.* 36. *Half green morocco, gilt top*, UNCUT. PORTRAIT of WASHINGTON *inserted.*

1603 PIETAS | ET | GRATULATIO | Collegii Cantabrigiensis | Apud Novanglos. | *Bostoni-Massachusettensium* | *Typis J. Green & J. Russell.* MDCCLXI.

4*to*, *pp. xiv.*, (2), 106. *Half blue morocco, gilt edges.* LARGE and FINE COPY. VERY RARE.

This very rare volume, consisting of gratulatory poems upon the accession of George III. to the throne, contains the first specimen of Greek printing executed in America. It is preceded by a fulsome address, wherein the youthful monarch, then in his 23d year, is told that he may lay claim to a higher title even, than "Father of his people," and may "justly be said to be the Patron of Mankind." Mr. Duyckinck devotes five columns of his "*Cyclopaedia*" to a description of this curious work.

1604 [PITT (William.)] The Celebrated Speech of a Celebrated Commoner. A New Edition Corrected.

London: Stephen Austin. MDCCLXVI.

8*vo*, *pp.* 17. *Half blue morocco.*

Composed of extracts from one of Mr. PITT's Speeches, relative to the Stamp Act.

1605 PLAIN QUESTION (The) upon the Present Dispute with our American Colonies. The Third Edition.

London: J. Wilkie. M.DCC.LXXVI.

12*mo*, *pp.* 24. *Half morocco, gilt top*, UNCUT.

"One great purpose of this little ministerial handbill, is to prove that there is nothing new or unprecedented in the exercise of Parliamentary authority over the colonies. The writer, however, appears to have been very ignorant of the subject, and very badly instructed by his employers."—*Monthly Review.* LIV. 330.

1606 PLYMOUTH. The First Plymouth Patent: Granted June 1, 1621. Now first printed from the Original Manuscript. Edited by Charles Deane. *Cambridge: Privately Printed.* MDCCCLIV.

4*to*, *pp.* 16. *Crushed olive brown levant morocco, paneled and gilt sides, broad inside gilt borders, morocco joints, gilt edges, by* W. MATTHEWS. From the Crowninshield Collection.

ONE OF FOUR COPIES PRINTED ON VELLUM.

On a fly-leaf, in the hand writing of the editor, is the following note; "Four copies on vellum, in the Libraries of E. A. Crowinshield, Esq. George Livermore, Esq. James Lenox, Esq. Charles Deane. January 1st, 1855." This volume was consequently printed upwards of three years previous to the printing of the first sheet of Professor Allen's Vellum

Philidor, which is claimed to have been the first attempt at Vellum Printing in America. Philadelphia must therefore relinquish its claim to that honour in favour of Cambridge, and this volume be regarded as one of an edition of four copies only of the FIRST WORK PRINTED ON VELLUM IN THE UNITED STATES.

See Allen (G.) No. 32.

1607 POEM (A) on Reading the Presidents Address; with a Sketch of the Character of a Candidate for the Presidency. *Philadelphia: Ormrod and Conrad.* 1796.

8vo, pp. 7. *Half green morocco, gilt top,* UNCUT. *Very Scarce.* An impression of the scarce PORTRAIT of WASHINGTON engraved by Tanner *inserted.*

1608 POETIC REMAINS of Some of the Scottish Kings. Now first collected. By George Chalmers, Esq. *London: John Murray.* 1824.

8vo, pp. vii., 208. *Portrait and Facsimile. Half morocco. A few copies only printed.* Contains the scarce full length PORTRAIT of JAMES I. and the FACSIMILE of his Charter.

The above most interesting volume contains the life of King James I.; the King's Quair; Poem of Peblis to the Play, said to be written by King James I., and first published from the Maitland MSS. in the Pepysian Collection, at Cambridge; Lives of James the IVth and Vth of Scotland; Christ's Kirk on the Green; The Gaberlunzie Man; The Lament of Mary Queen of Scots; Darnley's Ballad; Short Account of James VI., and his Sonnet and Psalm; Majesty in Misery, or Imploration to the King of Kings, written by King Charles I., in his durance at Carisbrooke Castle. It is a valuable volume to the Scottish Collector, and contains numerous and copious notes, explaining the meaning of the Scottish words.

1609 POETICAL VAGARIES (The) of a Knight of the Folding-Stick of Paste-Castle. To which is annexed, the History of the Garret &c. &c. Translated from the Hieroglyphics of the Society. By a Member of the Order of the Blue String. *Gotham: The Author.* 1815.

16mo, pp. 143. *Plate and Cuts. Half morocco, gilt top,* UNCUT. *Very scarce.*

1610 [POETRY OF THE REVOLUTION. A Collection of Popular Poems, written During, and Relating to the American Revolution.]

8vo, 4 pieces in 1 vol., half green morocco, carmine edges.

The titles of these Curious, Facetious, and Rare brochures are as follows:

I. The Poor Man's Advice to his Poor Neighbours: A Ballad, to the tune of Chevy-Chase. [*pp.* 19.] *New-York: Printed in the Year* M.DCC.LXXIV.

II. The Association, &c. of the Delegates of the Colonies, at the Grand Congress, held at Philadelphia, Sept. 1, 1774, Versified, and adapted to Music, Calculated for Grave and Gay Dispositions; with a short Introduction. By Job Jingle, Esq. Poet Lauerate to the Congress [*pp.* 22.] *Printed in the Year* M,DCC,LXXIV.

III. A Dialogue, between a Southern Delegate, and his Spouse, on his Return from the Grand Continental Congress. A Fragment, inscribed to the Married Ladies of America, by Mary V.V. [*pp.* 14.] *Printed in the Year.* M,DCC,LXXIV. Attributed to Mr. Jefferson.

IV. The Patriots of North America: A Sketch. With Explanatory Notes. [*pp. iv.,* 47.] *New-York: Printed in the Year.* M,DCC,LXXV. Imperfect; wanting sig. E.

1611 POLITICAL DEBATES. "Upon the whole, I will beg leave to tell the House what is really my opinion. It is, that the Stamp Act be repealed absolutely, totally, and immediately." The Great Commoner. *Paris: J. W., Imprimeur*, MDCCLXVI.

8vo, pp. 18. *Half morocco.*

Although this bears the imprint of Paris, it was, doubtless, printed in London.

WASHINGTON'S AUTOGRAPH.

1612 POLITICAL MAGAZINE (The) and Parliamentary, Naval, Military, and Literary Journal. No. XLIV. For March 1783. [*London:* 1783.]

8vo, blue morocco, uncut. With the original blue wrapper as published.

A genuine waif from WASHINGTON'S LIBRARY, with his name WRITTEN BY HIMSELF in two places. An impression from the ORIGINAL COPPER of his Book-plate; and an interesting letter from Mr. Robert Bell, Jr. who assisted in packing Washington's library previous to its removal from Mount Vernon, in 1860, and to whom, then, and there, this most interesting volume was presented by Mr. John A. Washington, *inserted.*

AN INTERESTING RELIC OF WASHINGTON, IN THE FINEST CONDITION.

1613 POOLE (W. F.) An Index to Periodical Literature. By Wm. Fred. Poole, A.M. ... *New York: Charles B. Norton.* 1853.

8vo, pp. x., (2), 533. *Half calf. A fine copy.* VERY SCARCE.

This useful work is the index to 12 British and 63 American Reviews and Magazines.

1614 [POOLE *and* OTHERS.] The Popham Colony. A Discussion of its Historical claims; with a Bibliography of the Subject. *Boston: J. K. Wiggin & Lunt.* 1866.

8vo, pp. 72. *Half brown morocco, gilt top,* UNCUT, *by* BRADSTREET. 300 *copies printed.*

1615 [POOLE (William F.)] The Mather Papers. Cotton Mather and Salem Witchcraft. [Reprinted from the "Boston Daily Advertiser," of October 28, 1868.] *Boston:* 1868.

Sm. 8vo, pp. 23. *Half blue morocco, gilt top,* UNCUT. *One hundred copies only printed.*

1616 POOLE (W. F.) Cotton Mather and Salem Witchcraft. By William Frederick Poole. [Reprinted from the "North American Review," for April, 1869.] *Boston:* 1869.

Roy. 8vo, pp. 63. *Half blue morocco, gilt top,* UNCUT, *by* BRADSTREET. *One hundred copies only printed.* INDIA PROOF PORTRAIT *of* COTTON MATHER *inserted.*

See Upham (C. W.) No. 2007.

1617 PORTER (D.) Two Discourses: The First Occasioned by the Death of General Washington, delivered at Spencertown, January 19, 1800. The Second, delivered on a Thanksgiving Occasion, at the same place, December 13, 1799. By David Porter. ... *Hudson:* M.DCCC.

12mo, pp. 33. VERY RARE.

1618 PORTER (E.) An Eulogy on George Washington, late Commander of the Armies, ... of the United States of America. ... Delivered Jan. 14, 1800, before the Inhabitants of the Town of Roxbury. ... By Eliphalet Porter. ... *Boston:* [1800.]

8vo, pp. 22. *With the* "Farewell Address," *in* 22 *additional pages.*

1619 POST (C. F.) The Second Journal of Christian Frederick Post, On a Message from the Governor of Pensilvania to the Indians on the Ohio. *London: J. Wilkie.* MDCCLIX.

8vo, pp. 67. *Polished calf, yellow edges, by* F. BEDFORD. *Beautiful copy.* VERY RARE.

"This journal is the sequel to that printed by Charles Thompson, Secretary to the Continental Congress, in his *Enquiry into the Causes of the Alienation of the Delaware and Shawanese Tribe of Indians.* It exhibits in a still stronger light the intrepidity and self-devotion of this noble Quaker. Since the days of Regulus no more perilous mission has been undertaken by a single man. Braddock had been defeated, and eight hundred white soldiers slain. Forbes was preparing for his invasion of the Indian territory. Pitiless massacre reigned on both sides. Rewards that would have tempted all the fierce borderers a year before, were offered in vain, until Christian Post, rejecting all offers of compensation, and solely for peace and mercy's sake, set out upon his mission. Every step through the wilderness, the most appalling dangers thickened around him. A hundred times were savage arms raised to destroy him, and a hundred times by little less than miracles, the blows were averted."—*Field.*

See Pennsylvania. No. 1584. Also, [Thomson (Charles.)] No. 1964.

1620 POTTER (I. R.) Life and Remarkable Adventures of Israel R. Potter, (a Native of Cranston, Rhode-Island,) who was a Soldier in the American Revolution, and took a Distinguished part in the Battle of Bunker Hill (in which he received three wounds,) after which he was taken Prisoner by the British, conveyed to England, where for 30 years he obtained a livelihood for himself and family, by crying "Old Chairs to Mend," through the Streets of London. ... *Providence: Printed by Henry Trumbull.* 1824.

12mo, pp. 108. *Plate,* "*Old Chairs to Mend.*" *Half morocco. Fine copy.*

This eventful and interesting narrative of poor Potter, has gone through several editions, notwithstanding which it is QUITE SCARCE. This copy is of the FIRST EDITION.

1621 POUCHOT (M.) Memoir upon the Late War in North America, between the French and English, 1755–60. Followed by Observations upon the Theatre of Actual War, and by New Details concerning the Manners and Customs of the Indians; with Topographical Maps. By M.— Pouchot, ... Translated and Edited by F. B. Hough. With additional Notes and Illustrations. *Printed for W. E. Woodward: Roxbury.* 1866.

2 *vols., imp. 8vo, pp. iv.,* 268; 283. 8 *Plans,* 6 *Views,* 6 *Maps and Portrait. Half blue morocco, gilt top,* UNCUT. Two ILLUSTRATIONS *inserted. One copy only printed on this paper.*

The original work is scarcely known in our public libraries, although a valuable statement of the events of the period from a French view of them, no where else given.

1622 POWER (J.) A Handy Book about Books, for Book-Lovers, Book-Buyers, and Book-Sellers. Attempted by John Power.
London: John Wilson. 1870.

8vo, pp. xiv., (2), 217, (1). 8 *Plates. Original ornamented boards, gilt top,* UNCUT.

No owner of a library can afford to dispense with it. It contains a large amount of information on Bibliography and Typography, together with a Chronological Table, a Bookseller's Directory, a Collection of Useful Receipts, a Dictionary of Terms, and other useful information of a miscellaneous character, interesting to book-collectors.

1623 POWNALL (T.) The Administration of the British Colonies. The Fifth Edition. Wherein their Rights and Constitution are discussed and stated. By Thomas Pownall. ...
London: J. Walter. MDCCLXXIV.

2 *vols., 8vo, pp.* (2), *xv.,* 288; *xi.,* 308. *Half calf.* BEST EDITION.

The various editions of this excellent work are a good index of the progress of knowledge in England of the affairs of the Colonies. Gov. Pownall's experience in America, and his position after his return, enabled him to speak with authority.

1624 POWNALL. A Topographical Description of such parts of North America as are contained in the (annexed) Map of the Middle British Colonies, &c. in North America. By T. Pownall. M.P. ...
London: J. Almon. MDCCLXXVI.

Folio, pp. vi., 46, 16. *Map. Half red levant morocco, gilt top, by* W. MATTHEWS. VERY SCARCE in such fine condition. A presentation copy from Mr. Pownall to Dr. Ingenhausen. Enriched with numerous valuable manuscript notes, additions, and corrections, in the handwriting of the author.

A republication of Evans's map and analysis of 1755, with improvements and additions. Governor Pownall says that "a pirated copy of Evans's map, was in a most audacious manner, published by Jeffreys, and falsely sold as Evans's map improved, by which that very laborious and ingenious, but poor man, was deprived of the benefit of his work. Owing to the ignorance of the engraver it can scarcely be called a copy, and, as respects the face of the country, might as well be a map of the moon."

1625 [POWNALL.] A Memorial Most Humbly Addressed to the Sovereigns of Europe, on the Present State of Affairs, between the Old and New World. *London: J. Almon.* 1780.

[Also:] A Memorial Addressed to the Sovereigns of America, by T. Pownall, late Governor, Captain-General, Vice-Admiral, &c. of the Provinces, now States, Massachusetts-Bay and South-Carolina; and Lieutenant-Governor of New-Jersey.
London: J. Debrett. MDCCLXXXIII.

8vo, 2 *pieces in* 1 *vol., pp.* (2), *viii.,* 127; (4), 139. *Half gray calf.* FINE COPIES.

A presentation set to Baron Albenslabor, the manuscript inscription to whom, occupies nearly an entire page. The "Memorial to the Sovereigns of Europe," which was published anonymously, in this copy has Mr. Pownall's autograph signature at the end of the text.

The Memorial to the Sovereigns of Europe which presupposes the independence of America, the editor says "was written by a gentleman lately deceased, who, from some misfortune in his personal relations, left England and took up his residence in the Azores." "It is written," says the Monthly Review, "with so much clearness of information and strength of argument, that it is probably the work of some eminent master, who chooses to conceal himself behind a peculiar style and a fictitious tale."

1626 PRAED (W. M.) The Poetical Works of Winthrop Mackworth Praed. New and Enlarged Edition.
New York: Redfield. 1860.

2 vols., sq. 8vo, half red morocco, gilt top, UNCUT. EDITOR'S EDITION. *Fifty copies only printed.*

1627 [PRENTISS (Charles.)] The Life of the Late Gen. William Eaton; Several Years an Officer in the United States Army, Consul at the Regency of Tunis on the Coast of Barbary and Commander of the Christian and other forces that marched from Egypt through the desert of Barca, in 1805, and Conquered the City of Derne, which led to the Treaty of Peace between the United States and the Regency of Tripoli; Principally compiled from his Correspondence and other Manuscripts.
Brookfield: Printed by E. Merriman & Co. 1813.

8vo, pp. 448. *Half red morocco, gilt top,* UNCUT. THIRTY ILLUSTRATIONS *inserted.*

1628 PRESCOTT (W. H.) History of the Reign of Ferdinand and Isabella, the Catholic, of Spain. By William H. Prescott. A New Edition, Revised, with Additions. *London: R. Bentley.* 1839.

3 vols., 8vo, half blue morocco, gilt top, UNCUT.

1629 PRESCOTT. History of the Conquest of Mexico; with a Preliminary View of the Ancient Mexican Civilization, and the Life of the Conqueror, Hernando Cortés. By William H. Prescott. ...
London: R. Bentley. 1843.

3 vols., 8vo, half blue morocco, gilt top. UNCUT.

1630 PRESCOTT. History of the Conquest of Peru, with a Preliminary View of the Civilization of the Incas. By William H. Prescott. ... Second Edition. *London: R. Bentley.* 1847.

2 vols., 8vo, half blue morocco, gilt top, UNCUT.

The above uniform set of Prescott's Historical Writings is upon much finer paper, and printed in a much better manner than the American editions.

1631 PRICE (R.) Two Tracts on Civil Liberty, [and] the War with America, ... [Comprising:] Observations on the Nature of Civil Liberty, the Principles of Government, and the Justice and Policy of the War with America. By Richard Price, D.D. The Eighth Edition, with Corrections and Additions. *London: T. Cadell.* 1778.

[Also:] Observations on the Importance of the American Revolution, and the Means of making it a Benefit to the World. ... By Richard Price. LL.D. *Dublin: L. White.* 1785.

[And:] A Review of Dr. Price's Writings, on the Subject of the Finances of this Kingdom. ... By William Morgan. F.R.S.
London: T. Cadell. 1792.

8vo, 3 Pieces in 1 vol., half blue morocco.

"The author of these observations must be ranked among the most respectable writers on the affairs of America. In him we see the warm pleader united with the sound reasoner, the intelligent politician, and (above all) the independent man."

1632 PRIEST (J.) American Antiquities, and Discoveries in the West: being an exhibition of the Evidence that an ancient population of partly civilized Nations, differing entirely from those of the present Indians, peopled America, many centuries before its Discovery by Columbus. And Inquiries into their Origin, with a copious description of many of their Stupendous Works now in ruins. With conjectures concerning what may have become of them. ... By Josiah Priest. Third Edition Revised. *Albany: Hoffman and White.* 1833.

8vo, pp. 400. 3 *Engravings. Cuts. Half red levant morocco, gilt top, by* F. BEDFORD.
"Notwithstanding 22,000 copies of this work were published in thirty months, in four editions, for subscribers, it is now *quite scarce* in perfect condition."— *Munsell.*

1633 PRINCE (J.) Part of a Discourse delivered on the 29th of December, upon the close of the Year 1799, recommending the Improvement of Time. By John Prince, LL.D. *Salem:* [1800.]

8vo, pp. 24. UNCUT.

Preached on the Sabbath after receiving the melancholy news of the Death of General Washington.

1634 PRINCE (S.) Catalogue of the Very Valuable Library of the late Rev. Samuel Prince, M.A. Sold December, 1865. *London:* 1865.

8vo, cloth uncut. Ruled, with names and *prices.* Rich in AMERICANA, SHAKSPEREIANA, &c.

1635 PRINCE (T.) A | Chronological History | of | New-England | In the Form of | Annals: | Being | A summary and exact Account of the most | material Transactions and Occurrences relating to this | Country, in the Order of Time wherein they hap | pened, from the Discovery by Captain Gosnold in 1602, | to the Arrival of Governor Belcher, in 1730. | With an Introduction, | ... | By Thomas Prince, M.A. | Vol. I. | *Boston: N. E.* | *Printed by Kneeland & Green for S. Gerrish,* | MDCCXXXVI.

Sm. 8vo, crushed crimson levant morocco, gilt edges, by W. MATTHEWS. *An excellent copy.* VERY SCARCE.

Morrell's copy sold for $25. Roche's for $23.

1636 PRINCE. Same Title. A New Edition. [Edited by Nathan Hale.] [*Boston:*] *Cummings, Hilliard, & Company.* 1826.

8vo, pp. 439. *Half calf, gilt top,* UNCUT. *Very scarce,* in this condition, no more than FIFTEEN COPIES having been left *uncut.*

1637 PRINCE. Same Title. Third Edition. To which is added, a Memoir of the Author, an attempt towards a perfect Catalogue of his Writings, a Genealogy of his Family, and the names of the

Subscribers to the original edition. By Samuel G. Drake. [Portraits and Plates.] *Boston:* 1852.

8vo, calf. FINE COPY. THIRTY COPIES *only printed.* EXCEEDINGLY SCARCE.

1638 PRINCE. A Sermon Deliver'd at the South-Church in Boston, New-England, August 14, 1746. Being the Day of General Thanksgiving for the Great Deliverance of the British Nations, by the Glorious and Happy Victory near Culloden ... By Thomas Prince, M.A. ... *Boston: Printed. London: Reprinted and sold by John Lewis.* 1747.

8vo, pp. 39. *Half morocco.* RARE.

1639 PRINCE. Catalogue of the American Portion of the Library of the Rev. Thomas Prince. With a Memoir, and List of his Publications, by Wm. H. Whitmore. *Boston: Wiggin & Lunt.* 1868.

12mo, pp. xxv., 166. *Half green levant morocco, gilt top,* UNCUT, *by* W. SMITH. PORTRAIT of MR. PRINCE *inserted.*

1640 PRINCE SOCIETY. Publications of the Prince Society. *Boston:* [*v.d.*]

This Society, named in honor of the Rev. Thomas Prince, the eminent Antiquary and Annalist of America, consists of 100 members, and prints 150 copies of each book on small, and ten on large paper.

The series consists of the following works:

I. & II. The Hutchinson Papers. A New Edition. Collated with and Corrected from the Original Manuscript, and Edited, with Illustrative Notes. *Albany, N. Y.: Printed by Joel Munsell.* 1865.

2 vols., pp. xv., ii., 324; *vii.,* 354. *Three fine* PORTRAITS *laid in.*

III. New England's Prospect. A true, lively, and experimentall description of that part of America, commonly called New-England: ... By William Wood. [Edited by Charles Deane.] *Boston: Printed by John Wilson & Son.* 1865.

pp. xxxi., (8), 131. MAP.

IV. Dunton's Letters; Written from New England, A.D. 1686. By John Dunton. In which are described his Voyages by Sea, his Travels on Land, and the Characters of his Friends and Acquaintances. Now first published from the Original Manuscript, in the Bodleian Library Oxford. With Notes and an Appendix, by W. H. Whitmore. *Boston: Printed by T. R. Marvin & Son.* 1867.

pp. xxiv., 340. *Cuts. An* INDIA PROOF PORTRAIT of INCREASE MATHER *laid in.*

V. & VI. The Andros Tracts: being a Collection of Pamphlets and Official Papers issued during the Period between the Overthrow of the Andros Government and the Establishment of the Second Charter of Massachusetts. Reprinted from the Original Editions and MSS. With Notes and a Memoir of Sir Edmund Andros, by W. H. Whitmore *Boston: Printed by T. R. Marvin & Son.* 1868–69.

2 vols. PORTRAITS.

VII. Sir William Alexander and American Colonization. Including Three Royal Charters; a Tract on Colonization; a Patent of the County of Canada and of Long Island; and the Roll of the Knights Baronets of New Scotland; with Annotations and a Memoir by the Rev. Edmund F. Slafter, A.M. *Boston: Printed by John Wilson and Son.* 1873.

pp. vii., (1), 283. PORTRAIT.

7 vols., roy. 4to, UNCUT. LARGE PAPER. *Only* TEN COMPLETE SETS *printed.*

1641 PRINTING. [A Series of Essays on Printing, comprising,] I. A Memoir on the Origin of Printing. In a Letter addressed to John Topham, Esq. II. An Historical Essay on the Origin of Printing. Translated from the French of M. De La Serna Santander. III. Biographical Memoirs of William Ged: including a particular Account of his Progress in the Art of Block Printing.
Newcastle: 1819–20.

8vo, 3 pieces bound in one vol., pp. iv., 72; xiv., 93; vi., 48. Polished calf, gilt edges, by F. BEDFORD. *Small Editions.* VERY SCARCE. *An elegant volume.*

1642 PROCEEDINGS (The) of the Executive of the United States, Respecting the Insurgents. 1794. *Philadelphia: John Fenno.* M,DCC,XCV.

8vo, pp. 130. *Half morocco. Fine copy.* VERY SCARCE.

Relating to the "WHISKEY INSURRECTION." 500 copies printed by order of the Senate of the United States, to be delivered with the Message of the President of 19th November, 1794.

1643 PROCEEDINGS of the General Society of the Cincinnati, with the Original Institution of the Order. To which are annexed, the Act of Incorporation, by the State of Pennsylvania; The By-Laws of the Pennsylvania Society, and the Testimonial to the Memory of General Washington, as Adopted and Communicated by the last meeting of the General Society. ... *Philadelphia: J. Ormrod.* 1801.

8vo, pp. 82. Half green morocco, gilt top, UNCUT. *One hundred copies only printed.* PORTRAIT of WASHINGTON *inserted.*

1644 PROCLAMATIONS for Thanksgiving, issued by the Continental Congress, Pres't Washington, by the National and State Governments on the Peace of 1815, and by the Governors of New York since the Introduction of the Custom. ... [Edited by F. B. Hough, M.D.] *Albany: Munsell and Rowland.* 1858.

Imp. 8vo, pp. xvii., 183. Half green morocco, gilt top, UNCUT. 150 *copies only printed.* THIRTY-NINE PORTRAITS of the GOVERNORS *inserted.*

1645 PROUD (R.) The History of Pennsylvania, in North America, from the Original Institution and Settlement of that Province, under the first Proprietor and Governor William Penn, in 1681, till after the year 1742. With an Introduction, Appendix, etc. etc. .... By Robert Proud. *Philadelphia: Zachariah Poulson, Junior.* 1797.

2 vols., 8vo, pp. 508; 373, 146. Portrait and Map. Half crushed red levant morocco, gilt top, UNCUT; *by* W. MATTHEWS. AN ELEGANT COPY with a FINE *and* GENUINE AUTOGRAPH LETTER WRITTEN *and* SIGNED *by* WILLIAM PENN, referring to events alluded to in the text *inserted.*

1646 PSALMS. The | Whole | Booke of Psalmes | Faithfully | Translated into English | Metre. | Whereunto is prefixed a discourse de- | claring not only the Lawfullnes, but also | the necessity of the heavenly Ordinance | of singing Scripture Psalmes in | the Churches of | God. | Imprinted | 1640. | *Cambridge:* 1862.

8vo, blue morocco, gilt back, paneled and gilt sides, broad inside gilt borders, gilt top, UNCUT. A BEAUTIFUL COPY of this elegant reprint of the FIRST BOOK printed in the British American Colonies.

ONE OF TWELVE COPIES ONLY PRINTED ON THICK PAPER.

"In the reproduction of this quaint volume every *word*, every *letter*, and indeed every *point* has been sedulously collated with a perfect impression of the original work struck at Cambridge in the year 1640. Indeed, so exact and faithful has the compositor been in following the original copy, that the bad spacing, omission of spaces, irregular justification, bad divisions, broken type, letters inverted, mixed lower-case letters with italics, and typographical errors are strictly reproductions of the printer's errors of the olden time."— *Preface.*

The copy of the *original* edition in the Crowninshield library was sold by its purchaser, Henry Stevens of London, to the British Museum for *one hundred and fifty guineas.*

1647 PSALMS. A New Version of the Psalms of David Fitted to the Tunes used in Churches. By N. Brady, D.D. Chaplain in Ordinary, and N. Tate, Esq.; Poet Laureat to His Majesty. [With an Appendix containing a number of Hymns taken Chiefly from Dr. Watts's Scriptural Collection.] *Boston: N. E. Printed by J. Kneeland, and S. Adams, For Thomas Leverett.* MDCCLXV.

12mo, pp. 276, 84. *Music, pp.* 17. *Blue morocco, gilt edges.* VERY SCARCE.

1648 PULTENEY (W.) Thoughts on the Present State of Affairs with America, and the Means of Conciliation. By William Pulteney, Esq. The Fifth Edition. *London: J. Dodsley.* MDCCLXXVIII.

[Also:] Considerations on the Present State of Public Affairs, and the Means of Raising the Necessary Supplies. By William Pulteney, Esq. *London: J. Dodsley.* MDCCLXXIX.

8vo, 2 pieces in 1 vol., pp. (4), 111; (4), 52. *Half morocco.* FINE COPIES.

Concerning the "Thoughts," Mr. Stevens remarks, "this is a well written and fair statement of the case as to whether or not the Americans were aiming at Independence from 1754, and how the difficulty may now be settled without a separation. Dr. Franklin's celebrated letters to Gov. Shirley, afterwards in 1766 printed in London, are given in the Appendix. The prophesying letters of General Montcalm, published the year before, are criticised and pronounced *fictitious* at page 41."

1649 PURCHAS (S.) Hakluytus Posthumus, or Purchas, his Pilgrimes, containing Peregrinations and Discoveries in the remotest North and East parts of Asia, called Tartaria and Asia, by Englishmen and others, and Voyages and Discoveries of the North parts of the World, by Land and Sea, Polar Regions and North-West of America, also English Northern Navigation, and Discoveries of Greenland, the North-West Passage, and other Arctic Regions; Voyages and Travels to and in the New World, called America, and of the Seas and Islands adjacent. By Samuel Purchas, D.D. *London:* 1625–26.

5 vols., folio, olive morocco, paneled and gilt sides, broad inside borders, gilt edges, by CLARKE & BEDFORD. An ELEGANT, EXTREMELY LARGE, and full margined copy, from the famous SOBOLEWSKI COLLECTION, with brilliant impressions of the Original Frontispiece, and the

Original Map of Virginia, and measuring 12⅞ inches by 8½ inches on the leaf; collating with Lowndes, and perfect and complete, except, that the map of Nova Scotia is wanting. It is by far the most desirable copy we have ever met with, being absolutely free from any taint whatever of the mildew which disfigures and endangers very many copies, and is perfectly CLEAN, FRESH, and CRISP throughout. A copy was lately priced in an English catalogue at £100.

Purchas says in his Preface that he has incorporated the substance of more than *twelve hundred* writers of Voyages and Travels. "His work," says Granger, in his Biogr. Hist. "is not only valuable for the various instruction and amusement contained in it, but is also very estimable on a national, and I may add, a religious account."

"We owe to the zeal and vast erudition of this laborious man, one of the most celebrated collections of Voyages which has ever appeared, valuable alike for the abundance of its materials and its importance in the history of Early Discoveries, especially those of the English."— *Biographie Universelle.*

1650 PURPLE (E. R.) Genealogical Notes of the Colden Family in America. By Edwin R. Purple.
New York: Privately Printed. 1873.

4to, pp. 24. *Green cloth extra, gilt top,* UNCUT. FIFTY COPIES *only printed.*

1651 PURPLE (S. S.) Bradford Family. Genealogical Memorials of William Bradford, the Printer. By Samuel S. Purple, M.D.
New York: Privately Printed. 1873.

4to, pp. 8. *Plate. Green cloth extra, gilt top,* UNCUT. FIFTY COPIES *only printed.*

1652 QUARITCH (B.) Bibliotheca Xylographica, Typographica et Palæographica. Catalogue of Block Books, and of Early Productions of the Printing Press in All Countries, and a Supplement of Manuscripts. For Sale by Bernard Quaritch. *London:* 1873.

8vo, half red morocco, gilt top, by BRADSTREET.

The most extraordinary, rare and valuable collection, ever offered for sale by any bookseller. The catalogue, which abounds in interesting and valuable bibliographical notes, contains upwards of 170 pages, and a table of contents chronologically arranged.

1653 QUINCY (J. Jr.) Observations on the Act of Parliament commonly called the Boston Port-Bill; With Thoughts on Civil Society and Standing Armies. By Josiah Quincy, Jr.
Boston: N. E. Edes and Gill. 1774.

[Also:] The American Vine, a Sermon, preached in Christ-Church, Philadelphia, before the Honourable Continental Congress, July 20th, 1775. ... By the Rev. Jacob Duché, M.A. *Philadelphia:* MDCCLXXV.

8vo, 2 tracts in 1 vol., pp. 82; 34. *Half blue calf. Very scarce.*

"One peculiarly unlucky circumstance attending our American disputes may be added to the rest, namely, that our fellow-subjects there are as well read in the nature and grounds of civil and religious liberty as ourselves; and this shrewd commentary on the *Boston Port Bill* will incline us to entertain a respectable opinion of their law pleaders."— *Monthly Review.*

1654 QUINCY (J.) An Oration Delivered before the Washington Benevolent Society of Massachusetts, on the Thirtieth day of April, 1813, being the Anniversary of the First Inauguration of President Washington. By Josiah Quincy. *Boston:* 1813.

8vo, pp. 29, (3). *Half green morocco, gilt top,* UNCUT. *Portrait of* WASHINGTON *inserted.*

1655 QUINCY. Memoir of the Life of Josiah Quincy, Jr., of Massachusetts. By his son, Josiah Quincy. *Boston: Cummings, Hilliard, & Company.* 1825.

8vo, pp. viii., 498. *Half green morocco, gilt top,* UNCUT. *Two* PORTRAITS *inserted,* one a COLOURED photograph of J. QUINCY, JR.

1656 QUINCY. The Memory of the late James Grahame, the Historian of the United States, Vindicated from the Charges of "Detraction" and "Calumny" preferred against him by Mr. George Bancroft, and the Conduct of Mr. Bancroft towards that Historian stated and exposed. By Josiah Quincy. *Boston: Crosby and Nichols.* 1846.

8vo, pp. 59. *Half calf, gilt top,* UNCUT. PROOF PORTRAIT of MR. GRAHAM *inserted.* VERY SCARCE.

See Mr. Bancroft's explanatory rejoinder to this pamphlet, in the "Memorandum" forming pages 27 and 28 of the ninth volume of his History of the United States.

1657 QUINCY. Memoir of the Life of John Quincy Adams. By Josiah Quincy, LL.D. *Boston: Phillips, Sampson and Company.* 1858.

8vo, pp. x., 429. *Portrait. Half green morocco, gilt top,* UNCUT. Presentation copy from the AUTHOR to LORD LYNDHURST, with the Author's Inscription, and an Autograph Note addressed to his Lordship, whose book plate remains in the volume. PORTRAIT *inserted.*

1658 RALEIGH (W.) The Discovery of the Large, Rich, and Beautiful Empire of Guiana, with a Relation of the Great and Golden City of Manoa (which the Spaniards called El Dorado), etc. Performed in the year 1595. By Sir W. Ralegh, Kt. ... Reprinted from the Edition of 1596, With some Unpublished Documents relative to that Country. Edited with copious Explanatory Notes and a Biographical Memoir, by Sir Robert H. Schomburgk. Ph. D. ... *London: Printed for the Hakluyt Society.* M.DCCC.XLVIII.

8vo, pp. lxxv., xv., 240. *Map. Half purple morocco, gilt top,* UNCUT.

1659 RAMSAY (A.) The Poems of Allan Ramsay. A New Edition, corrected and enlarged; with a Glossary. ... A Life of the Author, ... and Remarks on his Poems. ... *London: Cadell and Davies.* 1800.

2 vols., 8vo, pp. clxxviii., 380; viii., 608. Portrait and Facsimile. Half calf, antique. BEST EDITION. SCARCE.

Edited by G. Chalmers and Lord Woodhouselee.

1660 RAMSAY. The Gentle Shepherd, a Pastoral Comedy, by Allan Ramsay. To which is prefixed a ... Memoir of the Author, and a Critique on his Writings. With a Head, and Twelve Beautiful Characteristic Engravings, ... and a Full and Correct Glossary. *Edinburgh: Printed by James Ballantyne and Company.* 1808.

4to, pp. (2), *xxx.*, (2), 121. *Portrait and* 13 *Plates. Half green morocco.* LARGE and FINE COPY with all the beautiful characteristic COLOURED PLATES, from designs by DAVID ALLAN. *Fifty copies only printed.* VERY SCARCE.

1661 RAMSAY. The Gentle Shepherd, a Pastoral Comedy; with Illustrations of the Scenery: An Appendix, containing Memoirs of David Allan, the Scots Hogarth; ... and a Comprehensive Glossary. To which are prefixed an Authentic Life of Allan Ramsay. ... *Edinburgh:* 1808.

2 vols., roy. 8vo. Half calf antique. Large copy. Contains PORTRAIT of RAMSAY and 14 FINE ENGRAVINGS of the scenes referred to in the text. BEST EDITION. VERY SCARCE.

1662 RAMSAY. The Ever Green, being a Collection of Scots Poems, wrote by the Ingenious before 1600. Published by Allan Ramsay. *Glasgow: J. Cameron.* 1824.

2 vols., 12mo, half green morocco, gilt top, UNCUT. PORTRAIT of RAMSAY *inserted.*

1663 RAMSAY (D.) The History of the Revolution of South-Carolina, from a British Province to an Independent State. By David Ramsay, M.D. Member of the American Congress. *Trenton: Printed by Isaac Collins.* M.DCC.LXXXV.

2 vols., 8vo, pp. xx., 453; *xx.,* 574. 5 *Maps. Half crimson morocco, gilt top,* UNCUT. FOUR PORTRAITS *inserted.* Beautiful copy. VERY SCARCE in this condition.

Ramsay "possessed in an eminent degree the power of compression. His book is complete. We once heard good old General Lafayette say of his History of the Revolution, 'he has put every thing into it; he abbreviates like Florus.'"— *G. W. Greene.*

1664 RAMSAY. The History of South Carolina, from its First Settlement in 1670 to the year 1808. By David Ramsay, M.D. *Charleston: David Longworth.* 1809.

2 vols., 8vo, pp. xii., 478; *iv.,* 602. *Map and Plan. Half green morocco, gilt top,* UNCUT. FOUR PORTRAITS *inserted.* Elegant copy. VERY SCARCE in *uncut* condition.

1665 RAMSAY. The History of the American Revolution. By David Ramsay, M.D. of South-Carolina. A New Edition. *London: John Stockdale.* 1793.

2 vols., 8vo, pp. xii., 357; (4), 360. *Half blue morocco, gilt top,* UNCUT. THREE PORTRAITS *inserted.* VERY FINE COPY.

"The author gives a candid and intelligent account of the revolution he witnessed. He had access to all the official papers of the United States. It is impossible for the English student to judge of these transactions without reading this work."— *Prof. Smyth's Lectures.*

1666 RAMSAY. An Oration on the Death of Lieutenant-General George Washington, ... who Died Dec. 14, 1799. Delivered in St. Michael's Church, January 15, 1800. At the Request of the Inhabitants of Charleston, South Carolina, ... By David Ramsay, M.D. *Charleston:* MDCCC.

8vo, pp. (4), 30. *Half blue morocco, gilt top,* UNCUT.

1667 RAMSAY. Life of George Washington, Commander in Chief of the Armies of the United States in the War which established their Independence; and First President of the United States. By David Ramsay, M.D. ... *London: T. Cadell and W. Davies.* 1807.

8vo, pp. viii., 464. *Portrait. Half green morocco, gilt top,* UNCUT.

This copy contains BOTH PORTRAITS, one published with the English, the other with the American edition. It also contains the DEDICATION published with each of the above editions.

1668 RAMSAY. Memoirs of the Life of Martha Laurens Ramsay, who Died in Charleston, S. C., on the 10th of June, 1811, ... with an Appendix, containing Extracts from her Diary, Letters, and other private papers; and also, from Letters written to her by her Father, Henry Laurens, 1771–1776. By David Ramsay, M.D. *Glasgow:* 1818.

12mo, pp. 234. *Half calf, carmine edges.*

1669 RAND (G. C.) *and* AVERY. Specimen Book of Printing. [With a Description of their Printing House Illustrated by numerous Engravings on Wood.] *Boston:* [1865.]

Roy. 8vo, green cloth extra.

See Thomas (I.) No. 1960. Also, Trow (J. F.) No. 1989.

1670 RANDALL (H. S.) The Life of Thomas Jefferson. By Henry S. Randall, LL.D. *New York: Derby and Jackson.* 1858.

3 *vols., 8vo, half green morocco, gilt top,* UNCUT. FINE COPY. NINETY ILLUSTRATIONS *inserted.*

1671 RAYMOND (H. J.) The Life and Public Services of Abraham Lincoln. ... Together with His State Papers, including his Speeches, Addresses, Messages, Letters, and Proclamations, and the closing Scenes connected with his Life and Death. By Henry J. Raymond. To which are added Anecdotes and Personal Reminiscences of President Lincoln, by Frank B. Carpenter. ... *New York: Derby and Miller.* 1865.

2 *vols., 8vo, half crushed green levant morocco, gilt top,* UNCUT, *by* W. MATTHEWS. One volume extended to two by the *insertion* of nearly ONE HUNDRED FINE ILLUSTRATIONS; forty of which are INDIA PROOFS and INDIA PROOFS BEFORE LETTERS.

TWO BEAUTIFUL VOLUMES.

1672 RAYNAL (Abbé.) A Philosophical and Political History of the British Settlements and Trade in North America. From the French of Abbé Raynal. *Edinburgh:* M.DCC.LXXVI.

2 vols., 12mo, pp. 240; 231. *Half blue calf. Fine copy.* VERY SCARCE.

"These celebrated volumes of Abbé Raynal treat of every thing that can be sought for connected with the East and West Indies."—*Professor Smyth.*

1673 RAYNAL. The Revolution of America. By the Abbé Raynal. ... *London: Lockyer Davis.* MDCCLXXXI.

"The translator procured a copy of the original unpublished manuscript from the Abbé Raynal, and without his knowledge or consent, published it in French, at the same time with this translation."—*Rich.*

[Also:] Letter addressed to the Abbé Raynal on the Affairs of North-America. In which the Mistakes in the Abbé's Account of the Revolution of America are corrected and cleared up. By Thomas Paine, M.A. ... *London: John Stockdale.* MDCCLXXXII.

Sm. 8vo, 2 vols. bound in one, pp. xvi., 181; (2), 83. *Half brown morocco.*

1674 READ (J. M. Jr.) A Historical Inquiry concerning Henry Hudson, his Friends, Relatives and Early Life, his connection with the Muscovy Company and Discovery of Delaware Bay. By John Meredith Read, Jr. *Albany: J. Munsell.* MDCCCLXVI.

4to, pp. vi., 209. *Plate. Half maroon morocco, gilt top,* UNCUT. INDIA PROOF PORTRAIT *inserted.* LARGE PAPER. *Forty Copies only printed.*

1675 [REED (J.)] Remarks | on a | Late Publication | in the | Independent Gazetteer; | with a | Short Address | to the | People of Pennsylvania, | on the many | Libels and Slanders | which have | lately appeared against the Author. | *Philadelphia:* | *Printed by Francis Bailey, in Market-Street.* | M,DCC,LXXXIII.

Contemporary PORTRAIT of GEN. REED *inserted.* FINE COPY.

[Also:] A | Reply | to | General Joseph Reed's | Remarks, | on a | Late Publication | in the | Independent Gazetteer, | With some Observations on his | Address | to the | People of Pennsylvania. | [By John Cadwallader.] *Philadelphia:* | *Printed and Sold by T. Bradford, in Front-Street, the Fourth* | *Door below the Coffee-House,* MDCCLXXXIII.

Photographic PORTRAIT *of* GEN. CADWALLADER, also a private etching of the same by H. B. Hall, *inserted.* One corner of the title of this otherwise FINE COPY has been repaired, but without injury to the lettering.

2 vols., sm. 8vo, pp. 72; 54. *Gray calf, uniform.*

These ORIGINAL EDITIONS are two of the rarest pieces in Pennsylvania literature. The occasion of the dispute was the assertion, by Gen. Cadwallader, that in Dec., 1776, before the battle of Trenton, Gen. Reed was so much depressed by the sad state of American affairs as to meditate withdrawing from the service. This assertion Gen. Reed denies, and Gen. Cadwallader defends, in very heated and bitter language. The dispute was revived on the publication of the ninth volume of Mr. Bancroft's history.

See Reed (W. B.) in "Bancroftiana." No. 114. Also: Mrs. Warren's "American Revolution." Chap. XII.

1676 [REED.] A Reply to Gen. Joseph Reed's Remarks .... By Gen. John Cadwallader. With the Letters of Gen. George Washington, Gen. Alexander Hamilton, Major David Lenox, Dr. Benjamin Rush, Gen. P. Dickinson, Gen. Henry Laurens and others. [*Trenton: Reprinted.* 1846.]

12mo, pp. 36. *Half green morocco. Fine copy.* VERY SCARCE.

1677 [REED.] A Reprint of the Reed and Cadwallader Pamphlets. With an Appendix. [*Philadelphia:*] MDCCCLXIII.

Roy. 8vo, pp. iv., 82, 44, 12. *Half purple morocco, gilt top,* UNCUT. TWO PORTRAITS *inserted.* 199 *copies printed,* all for subscribers.

Includes the *privately printed* "Correspondence between Willlam B. Reed and John Penington and Son" in relation to this reprint, *not* in all copies.

1678 REED (W. B.) Life and Correspondence of Joseph Reed, Military Secretary of Washington, at Cambridge; Adjutant-General of the Continental Army; Member of the Congress of the United States; and President of the Executive Council of the State of Pennsylvania. By his Grandson, William B. Reed.
Philadelphia: Lindsay and Blakiston. 1847.

2 *vols., 8vo, pp.* 437; 507. *Portrait. Half blue levant morocco, gilt top,* UNCUT, *by* W. MATTHEWS. PORTRAIT *inserted.* VERY SCARCE in *uncut* condition. Beautiful copy.

1679 [REED.] The Life of Esther de Berdt, afterwards Esther Reed, of Pennsylvania. Privately Printed.
Philadelphia: C. Sherman, Printer. 1853.

12mo, pp. 336. *Half red morocco.* PORTRAIT of ESTHER DE BERDT *inserted. Printed for* PRIVATE CIRCULATION *only.* VERY SCARCE.

1680 [REICHEL (W. C.)] A Memorial of the Dedication of Monuments erected by the Moravian Historical Society, to mark the Sites of Ancient Missionary Stations in New York and Connecticut.
New York: C. B. Richardson. 1860.

8vo, pp. viii., 5–184, (1). 5 *Engravings. Half blue morocco.*

1681 RELATION de ce qui s'est passé de plvs remarqvable avx Missions des Pères de la Compagnie de Iésvs, en la Novvelle France, ès années 1676 et 1677. Imprimée pour la première fois, selon la Copie du MS. Original restant à l'Université-Laval Quebec. [*Albany:* 1854.]

12mo. Title, pp. 165. *Brown morocco, gilt edges. A few copies only printed for* Mr. James Lenox. This was Baron Sobolewski's copy, with Mr. Lenox's inscription on the fly-leaf. EXCEEDINGLY SCARCE.

1682 REMINISCENCES of the French War; Containing Rogers' Expeditions with the New-England Rangers under his command, as published in London in 1765; with Notes and Illustrations. To which is added an Account of the Life and Military Services of Maj. Gen.

John Stark; with Notices and Anecdotes of other Officers, distinguished in the French and Revolutionary Wars.
Concord: N. H. T. H. Roby. 1831.

12mo, pp. 275. *Portrait. Half blue morocco, gilt top,* UNCUT. SCARCE.

1683 REPORT of a Committee of the Linnæan Society of New England, relative to a Large Marine Animal, supposed to be a Serpent, seen near Cape Ann, Mass., in August, 1817.
Boston: Cummings and Hilliard. 1817.

8vo, pp. 52. 2 *Plates. Half morocco,* UNCUT. Long folded plate of the Sea-Serpent. VERY RARE.

1684 REPORT of a French Protestant Refugee, in Boston, 1687: Translated from the French by E. T. Fisher. *Brooklyn: N. Y.* 1868.

4to, pp. 42. *Half blue morocco, gilt top,* UNCUT, *by* BRADSTREET. 125 copies PRIVATELY PRINTED for Mr. J. Carson Brevoort.

1685 RETROSPECT (A) of the Boston Tea-Party. With a Memoir of George R. T. Hewes, a Survivor of the little Band of Patriots who drowned the Tea in Boston Harbour, in 1773. By a Citizen of New York. [J. Hawkes?] *New York:* 1834.

Sm. 8vo, pp. 209, (1). *Portrait. Half red morocco, gilt top,* UNCUT, *by* F. BEDFORD. BEAUTIFUL COPY. SCARCE in such fine *uncut* condition.

1686 RETROSPECTIVE REVIEW. (The)
London: C. and H. Baldwyn. 1820.

[Also:] The Retrospective Review and Historical and Antiquarian Magazine. Edited by Henry Southern, Esq., ... and N. H. Nicolas. Second Series. *London: Baldwin.* ... 1827.

[Followed by:] The Retrospective Review. Consisting of Criticisms upon, Analyses of, and Extracts from Curious, Valuable, and Scarce old Books. *London: John Russell Smith.* MDCCCLIII.

18 *vols., 8vo, half red morocco, gilt top,* UNCUT. Clean as when issued. A SPLENDID SET, and RARE in this COMPLETE and *uncut* state.

The three series complete, forming "An excellent review of early English literature. The criticisms in the first series were written by George Robinson, Esq., W. Gray, Esq., Mr. Sergeant Talfourd, Joseph Parkes, Esq., etc., the whole being under the superintendence of H. Southern, Esq. The second series was edited by Henry Southern and Nicholas Harris Nicolas. The papers in the third series were chiefly written by Thomas Wright, Esq., J. O. Halliwell, Esq., and M. A. Lower, Esq."—*Lowndes.*

Somerby's copy sold, in June, 1869, for $117.00.

1687 REVOLUTIONARY RELICS, or Clinton Correspondence; comprising the Celebrated Papers found in Andre's boots; Private and Confidential Letters from Washington, Hamilton, Lafayette, and other distinguished Officers and Statesmen of the American Revolution; illustrating in vivid colours, the Characters, Domestic Relations,

Private Feelings, Thoughts, and Movements of the Principal Actors in that thrilling drama. Published originally in the New York Herald. *New York: Herald Office.* 1842.

Imp. 8vo, half green morocco, gilt top, UNCUT. PORTRAITS of ANDRÉ and ARNOLD *inserted.* VERY SCARCE.

1688 RHODES (J.) The Surprising Adventures and Sufferings of John Rhodes, a seaman of Workington. Containing An Account of his Captivity and Cruel Treatment during eight Years with the Indians, and five Years in different Prisons amongst the Spaniards in South-America. By a Gentleman perfectly acquainted with the Unfortunate Sufferer. *Newark:* 1799.

12mo, pp. 268. *Half morocco.*

" A reprint of the New York edition, in larger type. There is nothing in this narrative to attest its truth, and the internal evidence is not sufficient to settle the question of its veracity. It contains some curious details of the customs of the Indians of Central America." — *Field.*

1689 RICE (J. A.) Catalogue of Mr. John A. Rice's Library. Sold 1870. *New York: J. Sabin & Sons.* 1870.

Roy. 8vo, pp. xvi., 566. *Half red morocco, gilt top,* UNCUT, *by* BRADSTREET. With printed prices at the end of the volume. One of TWENTY-FIVE COPIES printed on English laid paper for presents only.

This grand collection of books was, up to the issuing of the present catalogue, the finest that had ever been offered for sale in the United States. The total amount realized was over $42.000.

1690 RICH (O.) [A Complete Collection of the Bibliographical Works of Obadiah Rich; as described below.]

I. A Catalogue of Books, Relating principally to America, Arranged under the Years in which they were Printed. *London: O. Rich.* 1832.

pp. 129. *Advertisement* 1*l.* *Books relating to America.* 1493–1700. *pp.* 16. *Books Relating to America.* 1493–1700. *Supplement. pp.* 8. *Catalogue of the Duplicates of Mr. Rich's American Collection. pp.* 48.

II. Bibliotheca Americana Nova; or, A Catalogue of Books in Various Languages, Relating to America, Printed since the Year 1700. Compiled principally from the Works themselves. By O. Rich. ... [Vol. I. 1700–1800.] *London: O. Rich. New York: Harper and Brothers.* 1835.

Notice 1*l.* *Title* 1846, 1*l.* *Title* 1835, 1*l.*, *on the obverse of which is* " 250 copies printed in all: For sale in England, 100. To Send to America 150." *Dedication* 1*l.*, *pp.* 424. *Supplement of Additions and Corrections, Title* 1*l.*, *pp.* 425–517. *Rich's Catalogue of Books Relating to America, pp.* 40.

III. Bibliotheca Americana Nova. A Catalogue of Books Relating to America, in various Languages, including Voyages to the Pacific and round the World, and Collections of Voyages and Travels printed since the Year 1700. Compiled principally from the works themselves by O. Rich. ... Vol. II. 1801–1844. *London: Rich & Sons.* 1846.

pp. 4, 412. *Catalogue of Books relating to America on sale by Mr. Rich, pp.* 24.

3 *vols., 8vo, half green levant morocco, gilt top*, UNCUT. A FINE and COMPLETE SET in unexceptionable condition, and VERY SCARCE.

" All of Rich's Catalogues are important, and eagerly sought for by book Collectors, especially the earlier ones, which have come to be exceedingly scarce. " — *Guild's Librarian's Manual.*

1691 RICHARDSON (C.) A New Dictionary of the English Language. By Charles Richardson. *London: W. Pickering.* 1839.

2 *vols.*, 4*to*, *russia. A fine copy.*

Richardson's Dictionary appeared in 1833–9: since then there have been numerous issues with fresh titles and later dates. The book being stereotyped, there is no difference in the copies.

1692 RIDDLE (J. E.) A Copious and Critical Latin-English Lexicon; Founded on the German Latin Dictionaries of Dr. William Freund. By the Rev. Joseph Esmond Riddle, M.A. Second Edition. *London: Longman.* 1851.

4*to*, *pp. viii.*, 1400. *Cloth*, UNCUT.

1693 RIEDESEL (*Madame.* de) Letters and Memoirs Relating to the War of American Independence, and the Capture of the German Troops at Saratoga. By Madame de Riedesel. Translated from the original German. [By M. de Wallenstein.] *New-York: G. & C. Carvill.* 1827.

12*mo*, *pp.* 323. *Half purple morocco, gilt top*, UNCUT. VERY SCARCE.

FOURTEEN ILLUSTRATIONS, and eight leaves of cuttings, mounted by TRENT, *inserted*; embracing an AUTOGRAPH LETTER of the TRANSLATOR; an AUTOGRAPH LETTER of GEN. DE RIEDESEL to Gen. Gates requesting a passport for his Aid de Camp, with the reply of John Armstrong, A.D.C.; a fine impression of the ORIGINAL PORTRAIT of LADY ACKLAND; and the EXCESSIVELY RARE engraving of "HANCOCK'S WAREHOUSE FOR TARRING AND FEATHERING."

"They trace national events, and delineate the state of society in this country at one of its momentous epochs."— *Translator.*

1694 RIKER (J. Jr.) The Annals of Newtown, in Queens County, New-York: Containing its History from its First Settlement, together with many Interesting Facts concerning the adjacent Towns; also, a particular account of numerous Long Island Families now spread over this and various other States of the Union. By James Riker, Jr. *New York: D. Fanshaw.* 1852.

8*vo*, *pp.* (2), 437. 2 *Maps. Half olive morocco, gilt top*, UNCUT.

1695 RIPLEY (E.) A History of the Fight at Concord, on the 19th of April, 1775. With a Particular Account of the Military Operations and Interesting Events of that ever Memorable Day; showing that then and there the First Regular and Forcible Resistance was made to the British Soldiery, and the First British Blood was Shed by Armed Americans, and the Revolutionary War thus commenced. By the Rev. Ezra Ripley, D.D., with other Citizens of Concord. Second Edition. *Concord: Herman Atwill.* 1832.

Roy. 8*vo*, *pp.* 40. *Half crimson morocco, gilt top*, UNCUT. *Scarce* PORTRAIT of HANCOCK *inserted.*

1696 RISE, (The) Progress, and Present State, of the Dispute between the People of America, and the Administration.

London: W. Bailey. 1775.

Sm. 8vo, pp. 56. *Half morocco, gilt top,* UNCUT. RARE. *Curious Etched Frontispiece.*

Contains an authenticated account of the "Concord Fight." It is not included in any Bibliography, nor have we ever met with *another copy.*

1697 RITNER (J.) Vindication of General Washington from the Stigma of Adherence to Secret Societies. By Joseph Ritner, Governor of the Commonwealth of Pennsylvania, communicated by request of the House of Representatives, to that body, on the 8th of March, 1837, with the Proceedings which took place on its reception. Together with a Letter to Daniel Webster, and his Reply.

Boston: Printed by Ezra Lincoln. 1841.

8vo, pp. 48. *Half green morocco, gilt top,* UNCUT. TWELVE ILLUSTRATIONS *inserted,* including the scarce MASONIC PORTRAIT, also an impression of the very rare BILLINGS PORTRAIT of WASHINGTON.

1698 RITSON (J.) The Caledonian Muse: a Chronological Selection of Scottish Poetry from the Earliest Times. Edited by the late Joseph Ritson, Esq. With Vignettes engraved by Heath, after the designs of Stothard. *London: Printed* 1785. *R. Triphook.* 1821.

8vo, pp. iv., 232. *Half green morocco.* FINE COPY. VERY SCARCE. Some copies have a portrait of the editor which is wanting in this.

This volume, the second poetical work edited by Ritson, was nearly ready for publication in 1785, when a fire in the printer's warehouse destroyed the introduction, and its completion was abandoned.

1699 RITSON. The Life of King Arthur: from Ancient Historians and Authentic Documents. By Joseph Ritson, Esq.

London: Payne and Foss. 1825.

Crown 8vo, pp. (6), *xliii.,* 172. *Half crimson morocco, gilt top,* UNCUT.

1700 RITSON. Memoirs of the Celts or Gauls. By Joseph Ritson, Esq.

London: Payne and Foss. 1827.

Crown 8vo, pp. xiv., 369. *Half crimson morocco, gilt top,* UNCUT.

1701 RITSON. Annals of the Caledonians, Picts, and Scots; and of Strathclyde, Cumberland, Galloway, and Murray. By Joseph Ritson, Esq. *London: Payne and Foss.* 1828.

2 *vols., crown 8vo, pp.* (6), 262; (4), 341. *Half crimson morocco, gilt top,* UNCUT.

"As bitter as gall and as sharp as a razor,
And feeding on herbs like a Nebuchadnezzar;
His diet too acrid, his temper too sour,
Little Ritson came out with his two volumes more."—*Scott.*

1702 RITSON. Ancient Songs and Ballads, from the Reign of King Henry the Second to the Revolution. Collected by Joseph Ritson, Esq. *London: Payne and Foss.* 1829.

2 *vols., crown 8vo, pp.* (8), *ciii.*, 169; (6), 326. *Half crimson morocco, gilt top,* UNCUT.

"This edition is reprinted from a copy of the former one (Ancient Songs from the Time of King Henry the Third to the Revolution), corrected, enlarged, and much improved by the author."—*Lowndes.*

1703 RITSON. Fairy Tales, now first collected: to which are prefixed Two Dissertations: I. On Pygmies. II. On Fairies. By Joseph Ritson, Esq. *London: W. Pickering.* 1831.

Crown 8vo, pp. vi., 207. *Half crimson morocco, gilt top,* UNCUT.

1704 RITSON. Robin Hood: a Collection of All the Ancient Poems, Songs, and Ballads, now extant relative to that Celebrated English Outlaw. To which are prefixed Historical Anecdotes of his Life. By Joseph Ritson, Esq. Second Edition. *London: W. Pickering.* 1832.

2 *vols., crown 8vo, pp. viii., cxxxv.*, 148; *vi.*, 261. *Half crimson morocco, gilt top,* UNCUT. WOODCUTS by BEWICK. Out of print and VERY SCARCE; there was not a single copy in Mr. Pickering's sale catalogue.

"This edition contains several additions made by Ritson in his own copy, and the Editor (his Nephew) has added in the Appendix the Tale of Robin Hood and the Monk, which Ritson did not know was in existence. The woodcuts are better struck off and clearer."—*Lowndes.*

1705 RITSON. Pieces of Ancient Popular Poetry: from Authentic Manuscripts and Old Printed Copies. By Joseph Ritson, Esq. Second Edition. Adorned with Cuts. *London: W. Pickering.* 1833.

Crown 8vo, pp. xvi., 172. *Half crimson morocco, gilt top,* UNCUT.

1706 RITSON. The Letters of Joseph Ritson, Esq. Edited chiefly from Originals in the Possession of his Nephew. To which is prefixed a Memoir of the Author by Sir Harris Nicolas, K.C.M.G. *London: W. Pickering.* 1833.

2 *vols., crown 8vo, pp.* (4), *lxxxi.*, 224; 248. *Half crimson morocco, gilt top,* UNCUT.

Contains a collection of Ritson's letters from an early part of his life, comprising a period of nearly thirty years.

The preceding twelve volumes form the *entire series* of the various productions of Ritson, as published by Payne and Foss, and William Pickering; and are uniformly bound by MATTHEWS & RIDER. Complete sets, in such fine condition, are VERY SCARCE, as several of the volumes have long been out of print.

1707 ROBIN (*Abbé.*) New Travels | through | North-America: | In a Series of Letters; | Exhibiting, the History of the Victorious Campaign of the | Allied Armies, under His Excellency Gen. Washington, | and the Count de Rochambeau, in the Year 1781. | ... Also, | Narrations of the capture of General Burgoyne, | and Lord Cornwallis, with their Armies ; | ... | Translated from the Original of the Abbé Robin ; | one of the Chaplains to the French Army in America. | *Philadelphia :* | *Printed and Sold by Robert Bell, in Third-Street.* | M,DCC,LXXXIII.— *Price Two Thirds of a Dollar.*

8vo, pp. 112. *Polished calf, gilt top,* UNCUT, *by* F. BEDFORD. PORTRAIT *inserted.* AN ELEGANT COPY of the EXCESSIVELY RARE FIRST EDITION.

From Mr. Morrell's Collection.

1708 ROBINS (C.) A History of the Second Church, or Old North, in Boston. To which is added, A History of the New Brick Church. With Engravings. By Chandler Robbins, Minister of the Second Church. *Boston : Printed by John Wilson & Son.* 1852.

8vo, pp. viii., (2), 320. 5 *Plates. Half crimson morocco, gilt top,* UNCUT.

Contains FINE PORTRAITS of INCREASE MATHER, COTTON MATHER, JOHN LATHROP, HENRY WARE, and the AUTHOR.

1709 ROBBINS (T.) An Oration, Occasioned by the Death of General George Washington, delivered at Danbury, on a day appointed to Commemorate that Melancholy Event. January ii, MDCCC. To which is added a Sketch of his Life. By Thomas Robbins, A.M. *Danbury :* [1800.]

8vo, pp. 16. EXCEEDINGLY RARE. The *only copy* noticed by Dr. Hough.

1710 [ROBINSON (Matthew.)] Considerations on the Measures carrying on with respect to the British Colonies in North America. The Second Edition. With Additions and an Appendix relative to the present State of Affairs on that Continent. ... *London : R. Baldwin.* [1774.]

8vo, pp. (4), 176, 45. *Half olive morocco. A fine copy.*

"The author is one of the most candid and best informed of any of the late writers on the interests of Great Britain and her Colonies."— *Monthly Review.*

1711 [ROBINSON.] Considerations &c. [Another Edition.] *New York : John Holt.* 1774.

8vo, pp. 73. *Half morocco,* UNCUT.

"There is neither King or Sovereign Lord on Earth, who has, beyond his own Domain, Power to lay one Farthing on his Subjects, without the Grant and Consent of those who pay it; unless he does it by Tyranny and Violence — Philippe de Commines, Chap. 108."— *Motto on Title.*

1712 ROCHAMBEAU (*Count.* de) Memoirs of the Marshal Count de Rochambeau, relative to the War of Independence of the United States. Extracted and Translated from the French by M. W. E. Wright, Esq. *Paris :* 1838.

8vo, pp. (6), 114. *Half green morocco, gilt top,* UNCUT. TWO PORTRAITS of GEN. ROCHAMBEAU *inserted. Privately Printed.* VERY SCARCE.

1713 ROCHE (R. W.) Catalogue of the Private Library of Mr. Richard W. Roche. [Rich in Americana. Sold 1867.] *New York:* 1867.

8vo, pp. 251. *Half olive morocco, gilt top,* UNCUT. One of a *few copies* printed on thick laid paper. RULED and PRICED.

1714 ROGERS (G.) George Washington, crowned by "Equality, Fraternity, and Liberty." A Democratic Poem, dedicated unto Youth. By George Rogers. *New York: Leavitt Trow & Co.* 1849.

12mo, pp. 168. *Half green morocco, gilt top,* UNCUT. PORTRAIT of WASHINGTON *inserted.*

1715 [ROGERS (*Major* Robert.) THE ORIGINAL MANUSCRIPT DIARY OF THE SEIGE OF DETROIT, IN THE WAR WITH PONTIAC. Also, a Narrative of the Principal Events of the Siege. 1763–65.]

Sm. 4to, 213 *pages. Original binding, in a morocco pull-off case, lettered.* IN FINE CONDITION, and PERFECT PRESERVATION.

From this Precious Historical Manuscript written by the hand of the redoubtable Major himself, the Fourth Volume of "MUNSELL'S HISTORICAL SERIES" was prepared under the editorial care of Dr. Hough, who thus describes it. "The Diary printed in the following Pages, we believe to be now for the first time published, and although its Author is unknown, we have Reason to infer from several Allusions to himself, and References to other Records kept along with it, that he was the Secretary of the Commandant, and that he was fully in his Confidence. The Manuscript is all in one Hand-writing, and is written upon about half a dozen Sizes of Paper, which were evidently in loose Sheets at the Time, and have since been bound in one Volume. It was purchased from a Book-seller in London, and its former Owner had begun to print it; but finding, after getting through thirty-two pages, that the Sheets had not been bound in Chronological order, the Enterprize was abandoned, until it came into the Hands of the Publisher of the present Series. It bears conclusive Evidence of Authenticity, and is believed to offer new and valuable Contributions to our Knowledge of the Events to which it relates." The thirty-two pages alluded to as having been printed by a former owner accompany the Manuscript.

The Journals of Major Rogers published in 1765, terminate with February, 1761, and contain no allusion to the events recorded in this manuscript. There is, therefore, but little doubt that it was designed, that this diary should form a portion, if not the whole, of the Continuation to which Major Rogers alludes in the Advertisement at the end of his Journals above referred to.

1716 ROGERS. Journals of Major Robert Rogers: Containing An Account of the several Excursions he made under the Generals who commanded upon the Continent of North America, during the Late War. From which may by (*sic*) collected The most material Circumstances of every Campaign upon that Continent, from the Commencement to the Conclusion of the War.

London: Printed for the Author. MDCCLXV.

8vo, pp. viii., 236. *Green morocco, gilt edges, by* W. SMITH. ELEGANT COPY. VERY SCARCE.

"The journals of this celebrated partisan chief afford us many interesting details of border warfare, in the French and Indian War, which ended seventeen years before the Revolution. It was while associated with Rogers that General Putnam is said to have experienced those wonderful adventures, with the relation of which our youthful nerves have so often thrilled. It is however remarkable, that Major Rogers does not even mention the name of Putnam. The last page (237), is unnumbered and entitled, 'Advertisement.' It announces a continuation, or second part of the journal, which never appeared, as the subscriptions of a guinea a copy were probably not sufficiently numerous."— *Field.*

1717 ROGERS. A Concise Account of North America: Containing A Description of the several British Colonies, ... Also of the interior, or Westerly Parts of the Country, upon the Rivers St. Lawrence, the Mississippi, Christino, and the Great Lakes. To which is subjoined, an Account of the several Nations and Tribes of Indians residing in those Parts... . By Major Robert Rogers.
London: Printed for the Author. MDCCLXV.

8vo, pp. viii., 264. Green morocco, gilt edges, by W. SMITH. BEAUTIFUL COPY. VERY SCARCE. Uniform with the preceding No.

"This historical essay by the famous partisan officer and Indian fighter, although by no means equal to his Journal in interest, is not without merit. In the 'Concise Account' of the several colonies, he mingles many particulars of the Indian nations, but its especial interest is to be found in the section of this volume devoted to the 'Customs, Manners, and Government of the Indians,' pp. 205 to 264. These relations are the result of his own personal experience among the savages."—*Field.*

1718 [ROGERS.] Ponteach: or the Savages of America. A Tragedy.
London: Printed for the Author. MDCCLXVI.

8vo, pp. 110. Crushed blue levant morocco, gilt edges, broad inside borders, by F. BEDFORD. *Thick Paper Copy.* VERY RARE.

"I am not aware of the existence of any copy besides my own and that in the Library of the British Museum."—*Parkman's History of Pontiac.*

"Pontiac was assassinated in 1779, during a war between the Ioways and Ottawas. He was a great man."—Stone's *Life of Brant.* I. 25.

1719 ROGERS (T. J.) A New American Biographical Dictionary; or Remembrancer of the Departed Heroes, Sages, and Statesmen, of America; confined exclusively to those who have signalized themselves in either capacity, in the Revolutionary War which obtained the independence of their country. Third Edition: with Important Alterations and Additions. Compiled by Thomas J. Rogers.
Easton: Penn. Thomas J. Rogers. 1824.

8vo, pp. 504. Half green morocco, gilt top, UNCUT, *by* BRADSTREET. *Fine copy.* VERY SCARCE.

1720 ROGERS (W.) The Prayer, delivered on Saturday the 22d of February, 1800, in the German Reformed Church, Philadelphia; Before the Pennsylvania Society of the Cincinnati. By William Rogers, D.D. ... *Philadelphia:* 1800.

8vo, pp. 12. VERY SCARCE.

Delivered on the occasion of the Death of Gen. Washington.

1721 ROMAINE (B.) Review [of] the Tomb of the Martyrs, adjoining the United States Navy Yard, Brooklyn City, in Jackson Street, who died in the Dungeons and Pestilential Prison-ships, in and about the City of New-York, during the Seven Years of our Revolutionary War. By Benjamin Romaine. ... *New York: 4th July,* 1839.

Imp. 8vo, half green morocco, gilt top, UNCUT. View of the "JERSEY PRISON-SHIP" *inserted. Scarce.*

See [Taylor (George.)] No. 1946.

1722 ROMANS (B.) A Concise | Natural History | of | East and West Florida; | Containing | An Account of the natural Produce of all the Southern | Part of British America, in the three | Kingdoms of Nature, particularly the Animal and | Vegetable. | Likewise, | The artificial Produce now raised, or possible to be raised, | and manufactured there, with some commercial and po- | litical Observations in that part of the World; and a cho- | rographical Account of the same. | To which is added, by Way of Appendix, | Plain and easy Directions to Navigators over the Bank of | Bahama, the Coast of the two Floridas, the North of | Cuba, and the dangerous Gulph Passage. Noting also, | the hitherto unknown watering Places in that part of | America, intended principally for the Use of such Ves- | sels as may be so unfortunate as to be distressed by | Weather in that difficult Part of the World. | By Captain Bernard Romans. | Illustrated with twelve Copper Plates, | and Two whole Sheet Maps. | Vol. I. | *New-York*: | *Printed for the Author*, M,DCC,LXXV.

8vo, pp. 4, *viii.*, 342, (2), *lxxxix.*, (3). 1 *folded sheet, and* 10 *engravings; including the frontispiece, the dedication to John Ellis, and* 3 *full page maps. Crushed blue levant morocco, edges gilt on carmine, by* F. BEDFORD. A LARGE, FINE *and* PERFECT COPY *of this* EXCESSIVELY RARE BOOK, *with many rough leaves.*

This extremely rare work is so seldom found in any other than a fragmentary condition, that we are unable to refer to the full collation of any complete copy. No copy has ever been found with either of the whole sheet Maps, and all are more or less deficient in the number of Plates referred to in the title page. From the arrangement and tenor of the title, as well as from the sense of the "advertisement," at the end of the volume, we are clearly of opinion, that it was the author's design to distribute the "twelve copper plates, And Two whole Sheet Maps" throughout the two volumes into which he intended to divide the work; hence we do not hesitate to pronounce the present a *perfect* copy as well as the *finest one* within our knowledge.

The work was issued in the following year with an abridged title, less preliminary matter, and without the Appendix, but the text in the body of the work is the same in both editions. In the "Advertisement," above referred to, the author announces his intention to issue a second volume, to be accompanied by maps, adding, that "it is now in the press." It does not appear, however, that it ever was published. The plates are curious specimens of early Continental engraving; they were drawn and etched by Romans himself, who throughout the book uses a small i for the personal pronoun.

"This rare book contains an engraved dedication to Ellis the Naturalist, and six other plates etched by the author. Another copy with the date 1775, and called Volume I., has an appendix of 89 pages and 3 Maps."—*Rich.* I. 467.

1723 RONDTHALER (E.) The Life of John Heckwelder. By the Rev. Edward Rondthaler, of Nazareth, Pa. Edited by B. H. Coates, M.D. *Philadelphia: Townsend Ward.* 1847.

8vo, pp. 149. *Portrait. Half olive morocco, gilt top,* UNCUT.

1724 ROXBURGHE GARLAND. (A) *London: Printed by Bensley and Son.* 1817.

16mo, pp. 20. *Half green morocco, gilt top,* UNCUT. VERY SCARCE.

Printed for presents to the members of the Roxburghe Club only, at the expense of James Boswell, Esq. The contents are: "A Pleasant Pinte of Poetical Sherry," from Pasquil's Palinodia, 1630. "The Coronation of Canary," from Jordan's Fancy's Festivals, a Masque, 1697, and a humourous poem on the Roxburghe Club, by the Editor himself.

1725 ROXBURGHE REVELS. (The) The Roxburghe Club Finished by the Athenæum, and Joseph Haslewood, Esq. Finished by Himself. *London:* 1834.

4to, half olive morocco, gilt top, UNCUT, *by* W. MATTHEWS. Uniform with the Dibdin Collection.

A BEAUTIFUL and UNIQUE volume containing Twenty-eight double column pages cut from the Athenæum, *inlaid* back to back and *ruled* in red and black in the most artistic manner by TRENT; with RUBRICATED TITLE PAGE printed by MR. MATTHEWS expressly for the volume, and THIRTEEN FINE ILLUSTRATIONS *inserted*, embracing several PORTRAITS from PRIVATE PLATES, INDIA PROOFS, AND INDIA PROOFS BEFORE LETTERS.

1726 ROXBURGHE REVELS, and other Relative Papers; including Answers to the Attack on the Memory of the late Joseph Haslewood, Esq. F.S.A. With Specimens of his Literary Productions. *Edinburgh: Printed for Private Circulation.* M.DCCC.XXXVII.

4to, pp. ix., 144. *Half olive morocco, gilt top,* UNCUT, *by* W. MATTHEWS. Uniform with the Dibdin Collection. *Only a few copies printed.* VERY RARE.

THREE BEAUTIFUL PROOF PORTRAITS *inserted;* together with the "Catalogue," "List of Members," and "Rules and Regulations" of the ROXBURGHE CLUB, printed on the Club paper, bound in at the end of the volume. The Defence of Mr. Haslewood was written by Dr. Dibdin.

1727 RUSH (R.) Washington in Domestic Life. From Original Letters and Manuscripts. By Richard Rush. *Philadelphia: J. B. Lippincott and Co.* 1858.

8vo, pp. 85. *Half green morocco, gilt top.* EIGHT ILLUSTRATIONS *inserted.*

1728 RUSHTON (E.) Expostulatory Letter to George Washington, of Mount Vernon, in Virginia, on his continuing to be a Proprietor of Slaves. By Edward Rushton. *Liverpool: Printed.* 1797.

12mo, pp. 24. *Half green morocco, gilt top,* UNCUT. VERY RARE.

Apparently privately printed. "In July last the following letter was transmitted to the person to whom it is addressed, and a few weeks ago it was returned under cover, without a syllable in reply. As children that are crammed with confectionary, have no relish for plain and wholesome food; so men in power, who are seldom addressed but in the sweet tones of adulation, are apt to be disgusted with the plain and salutary language of truth. To offend was not the intention of the writer; yet the president has evidently been irritated; this however is not a bad symptom, for irritation causelessly excited, will frequently subside into shame, and to use the language of the moralist 'where there is yet shame, there may in time be virtue.' Liverpool, February 20th, 1797."— *Extract.*

It was also issued as a broadside.

1729 RUSKIN (J.) The Seven Lamps of Architecture. By John Ruskin. With [Fourteen] Illustrations Drawn and Etched by the Author. *London: Smith, Elder, and Co.* 1849.

Imp. 8vo, half scarlet morocco, gilt top, UNCUT. VERY SCARCE.

FIRST EDITION, with MR. RUSKIN'S OWN ETCHINGS, which, in the later editions were copied by engravers.

1730 RUSKIN. The Stones of Venice. I. The Foundations. II. The Sea-Stories. III. The Fall. By John Ruskin. With [Fifty-three] Illustrations Drawn by the Author.
London: Smith, Elder, and Co. 1851–53.

3 *vols., imp. 8vo, half scarlet morocco, gilt top,* UNCUT. FIRST EDITIONS, with BEAUTIFUL IMPRESSIONS of the plates.

"No one who has visited Venice can read this book without having a richer glow thrown over his remembrances of that city; and for those who have not, Mr. Ruskin paints it with a firmness of outline and vividness of colouring that will bring it before the imagination with the force of reality. His descriptions are the perfection of word-painting, and there is this additional charm in them, that the intellect and heart are sure to be gratified by profound thoughts and noble sentiments."—*Literary Gazette.*

"These volumes are full of fine things, and of true things."—*Athenæum.*

1731 RUSKIN. Modern Painters. By John Ruskin. [Illustrated with Eighty-seven Engravings on Steel.]
London: Smith, Elder, and Co. 1851–60.

5 *vols., imp. 8vo, half scarlet morocco, gilt top,* UNCUT. UNLETTERED INDIA PROOF PORTRAIT of J. M. W. TURNER *inserted.* FIRST EDITIONS, excepting Vol. I. which is of the *fifth*, and Vol. II. which is of the *third* edition.

Complete sets of the *earliest editions*, of the Great Art Works of John Ruskin have become almost unattainable, as several of the volumes have long been out of print. The present one is uniformly bound, spotlessly clean, quite perfect, and with unsurpassed impressions of the numerous beautiful illustrations.

"To Mr. Ruskin art has a deep moral and religious significance, both in its uses and in its connection with the character and condition of the artist. Every touch is, for him, the thought of a human intellect and the voice of a human heart. He seems to kiss the very footsteps of that art of which he is the great expositor."—*London Times.*

1732 RUSSELL (J. M.) A Funeral Oration, on General George Washington. By John Miller Russell, Esq. *Boston:* 1800.

8vo, pp. 22. UNCUT. VERY RARE.

1733 RUTGERS *vs.* WADDINGTON. Arguments and Judgement of the Mayor's Court of the City of New York, in a Cause between Elizabeth Rutgers and Joshua Waddington.
New York: Printed by S. Loudon. M,DCC,LXXXIV.

8vo, pp. 47. *Half morocco.* EXCESSIVELY RARE.

The editor of the following *reprint* has stated that he paid fifty dollars for his copy of this tract under the impression that no other one existed. A copious and interesting account of this celebrated case, will be found in Hamilton's "Life of Hamilton," II. 245, in which the biographer states, that the commencement of Hamilton's professional career, and the first exertion of his talent as an advocate, were made in "this mighty cause."

1734 [RUTGERS *vs.* WADDINGTON.] An Address from the Committee appointed at Mrs. Vandewater's on the 13th Day of September, 1784. To the People of the State of New York.
New York: Printed by Shepard Kollock. M.DCC.LXXXIV.

8vo, pp. 16. *Half red morocco, gilt top,* UNCUT.

The defendant's side of the case in this famous trial, which caused the greatest popular excitement at the time of its occurrence. EXTREMELY RARE, and evidently unknown to the editor of the following reprint of the trial. This and the preceding No. embrace two of the RAREST TRACTS KNOWN relative to the Revolutionary History of the City of New York.

1735 RUTGERS *vs.* WADDINGTON. The Case of Elizabeth Rutgers versus Joshua Waddington, Determined in the Mayor's Court, in the City of New York, August 7, 1786. With an Historical Introduction by Henry B. Dawson. *Morrisania: N. Y.* 1866.

Roy. 8vo, pp. xlvi., 47. *Half red morocco, gilt top,* UNCUT. 100 *copies only printed.*

1736 RUTTY (J.) The | Liberty | of the | Spirit | and of the | Flesh | Distinguished: | in an Address to those Captives in Spirit | among the People called Quakers, who are | commonly called Libertines. | By John Rutty, | An unworthy Member of that Community. | *Dublin: Printed. Philadelphia: Re-printed by* B. FRANKLIN *and* D. HALL. 1759.

8vo, pp. 64. *Half gray calf.* LARGE and FINE COPY.

1737 SABIN (J.) A Dictionary of Books Relating to America, From its Discovery to the Present Time. By Joseph Sabin. *New York: Joseph Sabin.* 1867–75.

7 *vols., imp. 8vo;* 5 *vols., cloth,* UNCUT, *and* 2 *vols., in parts.* All yet published. LARGE PAPER. *One hundred copies printed.*

The purchaser of this set will be required to assume the subscription undertaken by the present owner. It is the most thorough work of the kind ever attempted, and indispensable to the collector of an American library.

1738 SABIN (J.) & SONS. THE AMERICAN BIBLIOPOLIST. A Literary Register and Monthly Catalogue of Old and New Books, and Repository of Notes and Queries. [Vols. I.–V.] *New York:* 1869–73.

5 *vols., 8vo, in parts,* UNCUT.

1739 SABINE (L.) Biographical Sketches of Loyalists of the American Revolution with an Historical Essay. By Lorenzo Sabine. *Boston: Little, Brown and Company.* 1864.

2 *vols., 8vo, pp. xii.*, 608; 600. *Half red morocco, gilt top,* UNCUT. BEST EDITION.

1740 SAFFORD (W. H.) The Blennerhassett Papers, Embodying the Private Journal of Harman Blennerhassett, and the hitherto unpublished Correspondence of Burr, Alston, Comfort Tyler, Devereaux, Dayton, Adair, Miro, Emmett, Theodosia Burr Alston, Mrs. Blennerhassett, and others, their contemporaries; developing the purposes and aims of those engaged in the attempted Wilkinson and Burr Revolution; embracing also the first account of the "Spanish

Association of Kentucky," and A Memoir of Blennerhassett, by William H. Safford. *Cincinnati: Moore, Wilstach, & Baldwin.* 1864.

8vo, pp. 665. 3 *Portraits. Half green morocco, gilt top,* UNCUT. SIXTEEN PORTRAITS *inserted,* including an UNLETTERED INDIA PROOF of MRS. ALSTON, and a fine impression of the scarce PORTRAIT of MIRANDA.

1741 ST. CLAIR (Arthur.) Proceedings | of a | General Court Martial, | Held at White Plains, | in the State of | New York, | By Order of his Excellency | General Washington, | Commander in Chief | Of the Army of | The United States of America, | For the Trial of | Major General St. Clair, | August 25, 1778. | Major General Lincoln, President. | *Philadelphia:* | *Printed by Hall and Sellers, in Market Street.* | MDCCLXXVIII.

Folio, pp. 52. *Blue levant morocco, gilt edges, by* W. MATTHEWS. PORTRAIT of ST. CLAIR *inserted.* A fine copy of one of the RAREST of the series of Revolutionary military trials, with the RARE FOLDED PLAN.

We are unable to trace the public sale of more than *one copy.*

1742 ST. CLAIR. A Narrative of the Manner in which the Campaign against the Indians, in the Year One thousand seven hundred and ninety-one, was conducted, under the command of Major General St. Clair, together with his Observations on the Statements of the Secretary of War and the Quartermaster General, relative thereto, and the Reports of the Committees appointed to inquire into the causes of the failure thereof. Taken from the Files of the House of Representatives in Congress.

Philadelphia: Printed by Jane Aiken. 1812.

8vo, pp. xix., (24), 273. *Half blue morocco, gilt top,* UNCUT. *Two* PORTRAITS, one an *unlettered India proof,* of ST. CLAIR *inserted.* FINE COPY. VERY SCARCE.

"A narrative, of the terrible defeat and slaughter, of eight hundred soldiers by the Ohio Indians. St. Clair's voluminous defense is rendered nugatory and futile by the passionate ejaculations of Washington, when Major Denny called him from a dinner-party, to announce the defeat. Overcome with surprise and indignation, Washington cursed the beaten general with exceeding fervor, adding, 'Did not my last words warn him against a surprise.'"—*Field.*

1743 ST. JOHN (J. A.) The History of the Manners and Customs of Ancient Greece. By J. A. St. John. *London: Richard Bentley.* 1842.

3 *vols., 8vo, calf, marbled edges.* FINE COPY.

"A masterly picture of the Hellenic family, not in their political relations only, but in the still more attractive aspect of their social history and domestic life."—*Athenæum.*

1744 ST.-MEMIN (M. de) The St.-Memin Collection of Portraits; consisting of Seven hundred and Sixty Medallion Portraits, principally of distinguished Americans, photographed by J. Gurney & Son, from proof impressions of the original copperplates, engraved by M. de St.-Memin, from Drawings taken from life by himself, during his exile in the United States from 1793 to 1814. To which are prefixed a

Memoir of M. de St.-Memin, and Biographical Notices of the Persons whose Portraits constitute the Collection, compiled from Authentic and original sources by the publisher.
New York: Elias Dexter. 1862.

Folio, pp. viii., 104. *Embossed green cloth extra,* UNCUT. Made up from SELECTED COPIES of the photographs, lined and inlaid by MR. TRENT, and the CHOICEST of SIX COPIES ONLY so prepared.

"As the engraved copper-plates were delivered by M. de St.-Memin to the parties whose portraits had been taken, there would have been no collection of them in existence had he not reserved for his own use a few impressions of each of the plates which he had engraved. These he retained until his death in 1852, when they were purchased by a gentleman of Dijon, who retained possession of them until 1859; they then passed into the hands of the late James B. Robertson, who sent them to this country."— *Preface.*

1745 SALEM WITCHCRAFT; or the Adventures of Parson Handy, from Punkapog Pond. Second Edition, with Corrections.
New York: Elam Bliss. 1827.

12mo, pp. 70, (1). *Half red morocco.* VERY SCARCE.

1746 SALEM WITCHCRAFT: Comprising More Wonders of the Invisible World, Collected by Robert Calef; and Wonders of the Invisible World, by Cotton Mather. Together with Notes and Explanations by Samuel P. Fowler. *Boston: Wm. Veazie.* MDCCCLXV.

4to, pp. 450. *Portrait. Half olive levant morocco, gilt top,* UNCUT. LARGE PAPER; 100 *copies only printed.*

For a severe critique on this reproduction, *see* Deane's "Spurious Reprints &c." No. 539.

1747 SALT-PETRE. Several Methods of Making Salt-Petre; recommended to the Inhabitants of the United Colonies, by their Representatives in Congress. *Philadelphia: W. and T. Bradford.* 1775.

8vo, pp. 12. *Half morocco, gilt top,* UNCUT. EXCESSIVELY RARE.

Published by order of the Congress, with the *autograph signature* "Richard Varick Secy.," at the end of the text.

1748 [SAMPSON (Deborah.)] The Female Review: | or, | Memoirs | of an | American Young Lady; | whose Life and Character are Peculiarly | Distinguished — being a Continental Soldier, | for nearly Three Years in the late Ameri- | can War. | During which Time, | she performed the Duties of every Depart- | ment, into which she was called with punc- | tual Exactness, Fidelity and Honor, and pre- | served her Chastity inviolate by the most | artful concealment of her sex. | With an | Appendix, | containing | characteristic Traits, by different Hands: | her taste for Economy, principles of Domes- | tic Education, &c. | By a Citizen of Massachusetts. | *Dedham: Printed by | Nathaniel and Benjamin Heaton, | For the Author.* | M,DCC,XCVII.

12mo, pp. 258, (6). *Portrait. Green morocco, carmine edges.* FINE and PERFECT copy of the EXCESSIVELY RARE ORIGINAL EDITION; with the PORTRAIT, and LIST OF SUBSCRIBERS complete.

This remarkable woman was twice severely wounded in action, was pensioned by Congress, and received a compensation from the State of Massachusetts, in consideration of her military services.

Reprinted with the following title.

1749 [SAMPSON.] The Female Review. Life of Deborah Sampson the Female Soldier in the War of the Revolution. With an Introduction and Notes by John Adams Vinton.
Boston : J. K. Wiggin. ... MDCCCLXVI.

Sm. 4to, pp. 267. *Portrait. Half green morocco, gilt top,* UNCUT. Two hundred and fifty copies printed.

1750 [SANDERS (Daniel Clark.)] A | History | of the | Indian Wars | with the | First Settlers of the Uni- | ted States, | particularly | in New England. | Written in Vermont. | *Montpelier : Vt. Wright and Sibley.* | 1812.

16*mo, pp.* 319. *Brown morocco, gilt edges.* EXTREMELY RARE.

Mr. Field remarks : "the mystery which surrounded the authorship, history, and origin of this very rare volume, has been slowly dispelled by successive fragments of information. So few copies have survived the holocaust to which it was devoted, that its very existence was unknown to the most zealous collectors of Indian and Vermont history. Published anonymously, without preface, it was known to but few that the author was the Rev. Daniel Clark Sanders, President of the University of Vermont Immediately after its appearance, some person, evidently a personal enemy of the author, published an acrimonious critique upon the book, in the *Liberal and Philosophical Repository.* The animus of the critic was evidenced, not only by the bitterness of his language, but by his ignorance of the subject of Indian wars, being more profound than that of the author of the book he scored. Such was the effect of the article upon either Mr. Sanders, or the publishers, that the work was suppressed. But very few copies could have escaped the hands that were now as zealous to destroy, as they had lately been to create. In fact, so nearly complete was the destruction of the book, that it was forgotten by those who professed to know most of its author, his biographers. Neither Thompson, Williams, nor Hemmenway, who published memoirs of Sanders mention his authorship of the Indian wars."

1751 SANDERSON (J.) Biography of the Signers to the Declaration of Independence. By John Sanderson. [And Others.]
Philadelphia : 1820–27.

9 *vols., imp. 8vo, half russia, gilt top,* UNCUT. BEAUTIFUL COPY. LARGE PAPER. EXCESSIVELY RARE. We know of but ONE OTHER COPY on large paper. This was the Wight copy, and is probably the FINEST ONE ever sold.

Vols. I. and II. were edited by John Sanderson; III., IV., V., and VI., by Robert Waln. In vols. VII.–IX., the editor is not named.

1752 SANDERSON. Biography of the Signers &c. [Another Copy.]
Philadelphia : 1820–27.

9 *vols., 8vo, half green morocco, gilt top,* UNCUT.

A LARGE, CLEAN and FINE COPY with NINETY-NINE ILLUSTRATIONS *inserted,* embracing, among others, a COMPLETE SET of those in Brotherhead's edition, all FIRST PROOFS ON INDIA PAPER, and mounted in MR. TRENT's best manner.

A MOST DESIRABLE SET.

1753 SANDERSON. Sanderson's Biography of the Signers to the Declaration of Independence. Revised and Edited by Robert T. Conrad.
Philadelphia : 1852.

Imp. 8vo, pp. 834. *Green morocco, gold filleted sides, gilt edges.*

AN ELEGANT VOLUME with SIXTY-FOUR ILLUSTRATIONS *inserted*, including an INDIA PROOF SET of Brotherhead's RESIDENCES of the Signers.

1754 SANTAREM (*Viscount.*) Researches respecting Americus Vespucius and his Voyages. By the Viscount Santarem. ... Translated by E. V. Childe. *Boston: Little and Brown.* 1850.

16*mo*, *pp.* 221. *Half green morocco, gilt top,* UNCUT.

An interesting work, which throws much light on obscure portions of history, of value to our own historiographers.

1755 SARGENT (*Col.* W.) Diary of Col. Winthrop Sargent, Adjutant-General of the United States Army during the Campaign of MDCCXCI. [Under Major General St. Clair, against the Western Indians.] Now first printed. *Wormsloe: [Phila.]* MDCCCLI.

4*to*, *pp.* 58. 2 *Plates. Half purple morocco, gilt top,* UNCUT. 46 *Copies only* PRIVATELY PRINTED for Mr. George Wymberley-Jones. EXCESSIVELY RARE.

In addition to the Diary of the progress of, and daily occurrences in the force under Gen. St. Clair, this work also contains Col. Sargent's NARRATIVE of the terrible and disastrous defeat which closed the Campaign.

1756 SARGENT. A Journal of the General Meeting of the Cincinnati, in 1784. By Major Winthrop Sargent. ... Edited by Winthrop Sargent. Thirty-nine Copies Reprinted. *Philadelphia:* 1859.

8*vo*, *pp.* 59. *Half blue morocco, gilt top,* UNCUT. PRIVATELY PRINTED. RARE. TWO PORTRAITS, and two lines of manuscript in the *handwriting* of GEN. WASHINGTON *inserted.*

1757 [SARGENT (Winthrop.)] The Loyalist Poetry of the Revolution. [Edited by Winthrop Sargent.] *Philadelphia:* MDCCCLVII.

Sm. 4*to*, *pp. xi.*, 218. *Half green levant morocco, gilt top,* UNCUT. *Ninety-nine copies printed,* all for subscribers. VERY RARE. The SUPPRESSED LEAF is inserted at page 126.

Fisher's copy sold for $85.

1758 SARGENT. The Loyal Verses of Joseph Stansbury and Doctor Jonathan Odell; relating to the American Revolution. Now first edited by Winthrop Sargent. *Albany: J. Munsell.* 1860.

4*to*, *pp. xxi.*, 199. *Half green morocco, gilt top,* UNCUT. One of a *few copies only* printed for the editor upon paper designed to match that of the "Loyalist Poetry." VERY SCARCE.

"It is well known that, during our Revolutionary War, a very large part, if not an actual majority, of the American people remained more or less attached to the cause of the Crown. And considering how much of the education and intelligence of the community was included in their ranks, it will not be surprising to find that the Loyalists of that day were far from remiss in their efforts to vindicate their own conduct, or to attack that of their opponents. But as from the outset, with very rare exceptions, the press over all the continent was in the hands of the Whigs, they were thus shut out for the time from the popular ear; and since the close of the struggle, their literary productions have sunk into oblivion. Nevertheless, much of the Loyalist poetry of that season possesses a degree of vigor and of real merit worthy of a better cause and a better fate; and Mr. Sargent has rendered an acceptable service in rescuing it from neglect."

1759 SARGENT. The Life and Career of Major John André, Adjutant-General of the British Army in America. By Winthrop Sargent. *Boston:* MDCCCLXI.

8*vo*, *pp. xiv.*, 471. *Half red morocco, gilt top,* UNCUT. LARGE PAPER. Seventy-five copies printed.

A UNIQUE COPY; containing FIFTY-SIX *inserted* ILLUSTRATIONS, upwards of THIRTY of which are PROOFS, INDIA PROOFS, and INDIA PROOFS BEFORE LETTERS; including the rare and fine PORTRAIT of MISS SNEYD, engraved by Hopwood, a PROOF ON INDIA PAPER. The scarce PORTRAIT of the same, IN TINT, engraved by Bartolozzi, a PROOF BEFORE LETTERS. A fine impression of the very rare PORTRAIT of TARLETON engraved by Blackberd. A beautiful UNLETTERED PROOF, IN TINT, of LAFAYETTE engraved by Le Clair. An ORIGINAL SEPIA DRAWING of GEN. AMHERST, and a FINE SEPIA DRAWING of Washington's HEAD QUARTERS at Newburgh. The whole forming a MOST BEAUTIFUL COPY of a work of great interest and merit, now VERY SCARCE.

1760 SAVAGE (E.) An Eulogy on Gen. George Washington, who died Dec. 14, 1799; delivered at St. Peter's Church, in Salem, the 22d of February, 1800; ... the day assigned by Government for a General Mourning throughout the United States. By Ezekiel Savage, A.M. *Salem:* 1800.

8vo, pp. 23. *Half blue morocco, gilt top,* UNCUT, *by* BRADSTREET. VERY RARE.

1761 SAVANNAH. The Siege of Savannah, by the Combined American and French Forces, under the Command of Gen. Lincoln, and the Count D'Estaing, in the Autumn of 1779. *Albany: J. Munsell.* 1866.

4to, pp, 187. *Half red morocco, gilt top,* UNCUT. 100 *copies printed.* Edited by Franklin B. Hough.

1762 SAVANNAH. The siege of Savannah, in 1779, as Described in Two Contemporaneous Journals of French Officers in the Fleet of Count D'Estaing. [Edited by Charles C. Jones.] *Albany: J. Munsell.* 1874.

4to, pp. 77. *Plan. Cloth,* UNCUT.

Printed from a Manuscript in the possession of Mr. J. Carson Brevoort. The large folded plan of the siege was photo-lithographed from the original formerly in the possession of Lord Rawdon; now in the collection of Mr. Brevoort.

1763 SCHOHARIE COUNTY. History of Schoharie County, and Border Wars of New York; containing also a Sketch of the Causes which led to the American Revolution; and interesting Memoranda of the Mohawk Valley; together with much other Historical and Miscellaneous matter never before published. Illustrated with more than Thirty Engravings. By Jeptha R. Simms. *Albany: Munsell & Tanner, Printers.* 1845.

8vo, pp. 672. *Half red morocco. Fine Copy.* NINE PORTRAITS *inserted.* VERY SCARCE. Out of print twenty years ago.

1764 SCHOOLCRAFT (R. H.) Notes on the Iroquois; or Contributions to American History, Antiquities and General Ethnology. By Henry R. Schoolcraft. *Albany: Erastus H. Pease & Co.* 1847.

8vo, pp. xiv., (1), 498. 35 *Illustrations. Half blue morocco, gilt top,* UNCUT.

1765 SCHOOLCRAFT. Historical and Statistical Information respecting the History, Condition, and Prospects of the Indian Tribes of the

United States: Collected and Prepared under the Direction of the Bureau of Indian Affairs, per Act of Congress of March 3d, 1847. By Henry R. Schoolcraft, LL.D. Illustrated by S. Eastman, Capt. U.S.A. Published by authority of Congress.
Philadelphia: Lippincott, Grambo, & Co. 1851–57.

6 vols., roy. 4to, Part I. pp. 568, *and* 76 *Plates.— Part II. pp.* 608, *and* 80 *Plates.— Part III. pp.* 636, *and* 45 *Plates.— Part IV. pp.* 668, *and* 41 *Plates.— Part V. pp.* 712, 36 *Plates, and* 9 *Cuts.— Part VI. pp.* 756, 58 *Plates, and* 6 *Cuts. Half maroon morocco, gilt top,* UNCUT. The LARGE PAPER Government Edition, and a MAGNIFICENT COPY.

"This great work is a complete *Thesaurus* — an overflowing treasury of knowledge, respecting the Aborigines of America. It embraces their history, ethnography, antiquities, and languages; their ancient and modern geography; their manners and customs, religion and superstitions; their agriculture, commerce, and trade; their ornamental arts, and their physical and intellectual peculiarities. All these subjects are treated, not in a general and summary manner, but in detail, each topic being patiently and thoroughly discussed and exhausted; the work, although mainly executed by the author's own hand, having received the contributions of many *savans* thoroughly conversant with particular subjects embraced in its pages. The result is such a work as could have been produced in no other way. It is the most complete and thorough collection of treatises relating to the Indians, and comprises also the only general history of the aboriginal race, which has ever been published. It is a Library of Indian history and ethnography, and embraces within itself the substance of all that is known concerning the tribes as tribes, and the race as a race. To the scholar, the historian, the statesman, and the philologist, such a work is indispensable. No public or well appointed private library can be considered complete without it; and the general reader who wishes for satisfactory and reliable information about the Indians ,as they are at the present time, or as they have been at any previous period since America was discovered, must have recourse to these volumes. The illustrations of the Archives are executed in the most complete and finished style, literally 'without regard to expense;' and, as a whole, they comprise one of the proudest monuments of American art."

1766 SCHROEDER (J. F.) Maxims of Washington; Political, Social, Moral, and Religious. Collected and Arranged by John Frederick Schroeder, D.D. *New York: D. Appleton and Company.* 1855.

12mo, pp. xxiv., 13–423. *Half green morocco.* PORTRAIT of WASHINGTON *inserted.*

1767 SCHROEDER. Life and Times of Washington: Containing a Particular Account of National Principles and Events, and of the Illustrious Men of the Revolution. By John Frederick Schroeder, D.D. Illustrated with Highly Finished Steel Engravings, from Original Designs of Historical Scenes, and Full Length Portraits. By Alonzo Chappel. *New York: Johnson, Fry, and Company.* [1857–59.]

4 vols., 4to, half green morocco, gilt top, UNCUT. An ELEGANT and BEAUTIFULLY ILLUSTRATED COPY; consisting of Two Volumes extended to FOUR, with RUBRICATED TITLE PAGES printed expressly for the set, and containing nearly TWO HUNDRED ILLUSTRATIONS, in addition to fifty published with the work. The insertions are uniformly FINE and CLEAN impressions throughout, and embrace many VERY RARE VIEWS and PORTRAITS, now almost unattainable, among which are several of GEN. WASHINGTON. A large proportion of the whole are PROOFS, INDIA PROOFS, and PROOFS BEFORE LETTERS. The work was bound from parts carefully selected at the time of publication, is in the finest condition, and would form a desirable acquisition to *any* library.

1768 SCOTLAND DELINEATED. A Series of Views of the Principal

Cities and Towns, particularly of Edinburgh and its Environs; of the Cathedrals, Abbeys and other Monastic Remains; the Castles and Baronial Mansions; the Mountains and Rivers, the Sea-Coast, and other Grand and Picturesque Scenery. From drawings made by the most eminent English Artists. Accompanied by copious Letter Press, comprising Histories of the City and Castle of Edinburgh, and Palace of Holyrood; with Historical and Antiquarian Notices, and Curious and Original Anecdotes of the Principal Scenes and Events illustrated throughout the work. By John Parker Lawson, M.A. *London: Day and Son.* [*n. d.*]

Roy. 4to, pp. 285. 72 Plates. Green morocco super extra; richly gilt and inlaid back; paneled, beveled and gilt sides with the cross of St. Andrew inlaid in white, studded with parti-coloured morocco, and surrounded with an inlaid and gilt red morocco border; elegantly inlaid and gilt broad inside borders; morocco joints; gilt and gauffered edges, by GREGORY, *of Bath, England.*

A SPLENDID VOLUME.

1769 SCOTLAND ILLUSTRATED. A Series of One Hundred and Twenty Fine Steel Engravings after Drawings by Bartlett, Allom, &c. With Letter Press Descriptions by William Beattie, M.D. *London:* 1838.

2 vols., 4to, half blue morocco, gilt edges. FIRST EDITION, with fine impressions of the plates.

1770 SCOTT (J. M.) Blue Lights, or the Convention. A Poem, in four cantos. By Jonathan M. Scott, Esq.
New York: Charles N. Baldwin. 1817.

Relating to the Hartford Convention.

[Also:] The Sorceress, or Salem Delivered. A Poem, in four cantos. By Jonathan M. Scott, Esq.
New York: Charles N. Baldwin. 1817.

18mo, 2 vols. bound in 1. pp. xi., 150; xii., 120. Half gray calf, gilt top, UNCUT. Both of these poetical pieces are VERY RARE.

The "Sorceress" relates to the imputing to divers parties in New England the crime of Witchcraft, and for which many of both sexes were executed.

1771 SCOTT (*Sir* Walter.) Minstrelsy of the Scottish Border: consisting of Historical and Romantic Ballads, collected in the Southern Counties of Scotland; with a few of modern date, founded on Local Tradition. Third Edition.
Edinburgh: James Ballantyne and Co. 1806.

3 vols., 8vo, pp. clxvi., 282; (8), 434; (8), 471. Half green morocco, gilt top, UNCUT. PORTRAIT of the AUTHOR *inserted.* Beautiful copy. VERY SCARCE.

1772 SCOTT. The History of Scotland. By Sir Walter Scott, Bart.
London: 1829.

2 vols., 12mo, pp. xii., 352; xii., 438. Half green morocco, gilt top, UNCUT. Sixteen lines of the manuscript of the work in the HAND-WRITING of the AUTHOR *inserted.*

1773 SCOTT. Catalogue of the Library at Abbotsford.
Edinburgh: M.DCCC.XXXVIII.

4to, pp. vi., (2), 464. *Half blue levant morocco, gilt top,* UNCUT. INDIA PROOF PORTRAIT of SIR WALTER SCOTT *inserted.* Major Scott's contribution to the Bannatyne Club. VERY SCARCE.

This very valuable catalogue was compiled by the late Mr. Cochrane, of the London Library, St. James's Square. It contains very numerous references to the works of Sir Walter Scott, where he refers to, or quotes, the various books in the library.

"The nature and extent of the collection throw light in a remarkable manner on the history of its founder. The reader has before him a faithful inventory of the materials with which the National Poet and Novelist had stored his mind before he began his public career, and of the zeal with which he watched the progress of literary enterprise down to the close of his life."

1774 [SCOTT.] Refutation of the Misstatements and Calumnies contained in Mr. Lockhart's Life of Sir Walter Scott, Bart., respecting the Messrs. Ballantyne. By the Trustees and Son of the late Mr. James Ballantyne. *Boston: J. Monroe & Co.* 1838.

[Also:] The Ballantyne-Humbug Handled, in a Letter to Sir Adam Ferguson. By the Author of Memoirs of the Life of Sir Walter Scott. *Edinburgh: R. Cadell.* 1839.

[And:] Reply to Mr. Lockhart's Pamphlet entitled, "The Ballantyne Humbug-Handled." By the Authors of "Refutation of the Misstatements &c." *London: Longman.* 1839.

Sm. 8vo, 3 vols. bound in 1. Half calf.

The three works relating to this interesting controversy are seldom found together. They exhibit curious and minute details of Scott's connection with the Ballantynes, as a publisher, and of the events which ultimately resulted in his ruin and death.

1775 SCOTT. Rokeby, a Poem. By Sir Walter Scott, Bart. Illustrated Edition. *London: Tilt and Bogue.* 1841.

12mo, pp. (6), 303. *Green morocco, gilt sides and edges.* An Autograph Note WRITTEN and SIGNED by Sir Walter *inserted.*

1776 SCOTT. Waverly Novels. [Abbotsford Edition.] *Edinburgh: Robert Cadell. London: Houlston & Stoneman.* 1844-47.

24 *vols., imp. 8vo, half crushed green levant morocco, gilt top,* UNCUT, *by* W. MATTHEWS, in his BEST manner.

The twenty-four parts as originally issued, with the necessary ADDITIONAL TITLES, and HALF TITLES, so accurately reproduced by the photo-lithographic process, as to render it difficult to distinguish the facsimiles from the originals. The words and figures "Vol. I." etc., were EXECUTED WITH A PEN by Mr. Henry Farrar with astonishing accuracy. The series of ONE HUNDRED AND TWENTY PLATES published with the work, are MOST BRILLIANT UNLETTERED ARTIST'S PROOFS ON INDIA PAPER, one of a few sets only, struck off for presents previous to publication.

Inserted are nearly THREE HUNDRED and FIFTY additional ILLUSTRATIONS, consisting of PORTRAITS, SUBJECTS, and VIEWS; all of the most choice description and collected from the following sources. Scott's Female Characters. Complete set: UNLETTERRD INDIA PROOFS.—Illustrations to the edition of the Novels of 1829. Complete set: GENUINE PROOFS BEFORE ISSUE.—Illustrations to the edition of the Novels of 1852. Complete set: GENUINE PROOFS BEFORE ISSUE.—Finden's Landscape Illustrations. Complete set: PROOFS ON INDIA PAPER.—Scott's Historical Portraits. Complete set: PROOFS ON INDIA PAPER.—Illustrations to

Kenilworth. Complete set: PROOFS ON INDIA PAPER.—and various portraits from Lodge: PROOFS ON INDIA PAPER. SIX beautiful PORTRAITS of SCOTT in various states, and an Autograph Note WRITTEN and SIGNED by him are also inserted.

The whole work, plate for plate and leaf for leaf, is in the very finest condition, without spot or stain of any kind, and there is probably NO FINER COPY EXTANT.

This edition, the largest and handsomest in existence, has now become scarce. The illustrations comprise portraits and views from the designs of Stanfield, Nasmyth, Sir D. Wilkie, Turner, Martin, Allom, Leitch, etc., with many fac-similes of autographs.

"Single pages of these works are worth whole volumes of common inventions."—*Mrs. Brunton.*

1777 SCOTT. Marmion a Tale of Flodden Field by Sir Walter Scott, Bart. With all his Introductions, and the Editor's Notes. Illustrated by Eighty-Engravings on Wood from Drawings by Birket Foster and John Gilbert.
Edinburgh: Adam and Charles Black. MDCCCLV.

8vo, pp. 408. *Green morocco, richly gilt back and sides, gilt edges.*

1778 SCOTT. The Lord of the Isles by Sir Walter Scott, Bart. With all his Introductions, and the Editor's Notes. Illustrated by numerous Engravings on Wood from Drawings by Birket Foster and John Gilbert. *Edinburgh: Adam and Charles Black.* MDCCCLVII.

8vo, pp. 367. *Green morocco, richly gilt back and sides, gilt edges.* Uniform with the preceding No.

1779 SCOTT. The Lay of the Last Minstrel by Sir Walter Scott, Bart. With all his Introductions, and the Editor's Notes. Illustrated by One Hundred Engravings on Wood from drawings by Birket Foster and John Gilbert. *Edinburgh: Adam and Charles Black.* MDCCCLIX.

8vo, pp. 354. *Green morocco, richly gilt back and sides, gilt edges.* Uniform with the preceding No.

1780 [SCOTT.] The Scott Exhibition, 1871. Catalogue of the Exhibition held at Edinburgh, in July and August, 1871, on occasion of the commemoration of the Centenary of the Birth of Sir Walter Scott. *Edinburgh:* 1872.

4to, pp. xiv., 206. *Half crushed green levant morocco, gilt top,* UNCUT, *by* BRADSTREET.

Prepared for publication by Sir William Stirling Maxwell, Bart., David Laing, LL.D., and James Drummond, R.S.A., and illustrated with thirty-two fine photo-lithographs of portraits and busts of Sir Walter Scott, by the Woodbury process, and numerous facsimiles of original manuscripts and autographs.

This elegant and handsome work (the impression of which was limited to 250 copies) forms a most desirable volume, peculiarly valuable to all who feel interested in the Life and Writings of the great novelist.

1781 SCOTT [(Winfield.)] Memoirs of Lieut.-General Scott, LL.D. Written by Himself. *New York: Sheldon & Company.* 1864.

Roy. 8vo, pp. xxii., 653. *Half blue morocco, gilt top,* UNCUT. TWENTY FINE ILLUSTRATIONS *inserted.* LARGE PAPER. 250 *copies printed.*

1782 SCOTTISH PASQUILS. A Book of Scottish Pasquils. [With prefatory Remarks and copious Notes, edited by J. Maidment.] *Edinburgh:* 1827–28.

Sm. 8vo, 3 parts bound in 1 vol. pp. xxx. 80; *xxi.*, 102; *xiv.*, 93. *Half blue morocco, gilt top,* UNCUT. ORIGINAL EDITION. *Sixty copies only printed.* VERY RARE.

Priced in a recent London catalogue at £4. 15. 0.

The *first* and *genuine edition* of the above collection of Scottish Pasquils and Lampoons, now very scarce: they serve to explain many personal allusions and minor historical events referred to by historical writers, and illustrate in a marked degree the habits and morals of the people of Scotland, during the reigns of Charles I. and his descendants.

1783 SEARSON (J.) Mount Vernon; A Poem. Being the seat of his Excellency George Washington, in the State of Virginia: Lieutenant-General and Commander-in-Chief of the Land Forces of the United States of America. By John Searson, formerly of Philadelphia, Merchant. *Philadelphia: Printed for the Author by Folwell.* [1799.]

8vo, pp. 83, 4. *Portrait. Half green morocco.* FINE COPY. VERY SCARCE. The *portrait* is wanting in many copies.

"This rural, romantic and descriptive Poem of the seat of so great a character, it is hoped may please — with a copper-plate likeness of the General; it was taken from an actual view on the spot by the author, 15th May, 1799. Also, a cursory view of Georgetown, City of Washington and the Capitol."— *Extract.*

1784 SEAVER (J. E.) Deh-he-wa-mis; or A Narrative of the Life of Mary Jemison: otherwise called the White Woman, Who was taken Captive by the Indians in MDCCLV; and who continued with them Seventy-Eight Years. Containing an Account of the Murder of her Father and his Family; her Marriages and Sufferings; Indian Barbarities, Customs and Traditions. Carefully taken from her Own Words. By James E. Seaver. Also The Life of Hiokatoo and Ebenezer Allen; and Historical Sketches of the Six Nations, the Genesee Country, and other Interesting Facts connected with the Narrative; By Ebenezer Mix. *Devon,* ... *London,* ... 1847.

18mo, pp. 184. *Books* 18, 18. *Half red morocco, gilt top,* UNCUT, *by* BRADSTREET. RARE.

1785 SEAVER. The Life of Mary Jemison, Deh-he-wä-mis. By James E. Seaver. Fourth Edition. With Geographical and Explanatory Notes. *New York and Auburn:* 1856.

12mo, pp. 312. *Half blue morocco, gilt top,* UNCUT.

"This well written narrative, purporting to be only the biography of a captive among the Senecas, is really the best *resumé* we have of incidents in the history and common life of the Seneca Indians. Its truthfulness is vouched for by such veracious testimony as that of Eli Parker, an educated chief of that nation, though its authenticity can scarcely have greater corroboration than the fact that Mr. Seaver received almost the whole mass of incidents narrated in his book, directly from the lips of the aged captive herself. A portion of the book which future ethnologists will highly prize, is contained on pp. 300 to 312, where the Indian names of nearly 400 localities, in the State of New York, are given, with their English significations."— *Field.*

1786 SECRET Proceedings and Debates of the Convention assembled at Philadelphia in the year 1787, for the purpose of forming the Constitution of the United States of America. From notes taken by the late Robert Yates, Esq. Chief Justice of New York, and copied by John Lansing, Esq. late Chancellor of that State, Members of that Convention. Including "The Genuine Information" laid before the Legislature of Maryland by Luther Martin, Esq. then Attorney General of that State, and a member of the same Convention. Also other Historical Documents relative to the Federal Compact of the North American Union. *Albany: Websters and Skinners.* 1821.

8vo, pp. 308. *Half gray calf, carmine edges.* Fine copy of the SCARCE original edition. PORTRAIT *inserted.*

1787 SECRET Proceedings and Debates, &c. [Reprint of the preceding.] *Richmond: Va. Wilbur Curtis.* 1839.

Sm. 8vo, pp. xi., 335. *Half morocco.*

1788 SEDGWICK (T. Jun.) A Memoir of the Life of William Livingston, Member of Congress, in 1774, 1775, and 1776, Delegate to the Federal Convention in 1777, and Governor of the State of New Jersey, from 1776 to 1790. With Extracts from his Correspondence, and notices of various members of his family. By Theodore Sedgwick, Jun. *New York: J. & J. Harper.* 1833.

8vo, pp. 456. *Portrait. Half maroon morocco, gilt top,* UNCUT.

1789 SENTER (I.) The Journal of Isaac Senter, Physician and Surgeon to the Troops Detached from the American Army Encamped at Cambridge, Mass., On a Secret Expedition against Quebec, under the Command of Colonel Benedict Arnold, in September, 1775. [Edited by Edward D. Ingraham.] *Philadelphia:* 1846.

8vo, pp. 40. *Half calf,* UNCUT. *Privately Printed.* VERY SCARCE. The editor's own copy with TWO SCARCE PORTRAITS *inserted;* together with Two Autograph Letters of JARED SPARKS, and one each of GEORGE BANCROFT, and JOHN P. KENNEDY, all relating to the work.

The preface was written by Henry Penington.

1790 [SERLE (Ambrose.)] Americans against Liberty: or an Essay on the Nature and Principles of True Freedom, showing that the designs and conduct of the Americans tend only to Tyranny and Slavery. *London: J. Mathews.* MDCCLXXV.

8vo, pp. 64. *Half morocco.*

"The author is an able advocate for the British claims."— *M.R.* LIII. 51.

1791 SETTLE (D.) A true reporte of the laste voyage into the West and Northwest regions, &c. 1577. worthily atchieued by Capteine Frobisher of the sayde voyage the first finder and Generall. With a description of the people there inhabiting, and other circumstances notable. Written by Dionyse Settle, one of the companie in the sayde voyage, and seruant to the Right Honourable the Earle of Cumberland. ... *Imprinted at London by Henrie Middleton. Anno,* 1577. [*Providence: Reprinted.* 1868.]

Sm. 4to, pp. 63. *Half red morocco, gilt top,* UNCUT, *by* W. MATTHEWS. *Fifty copies only* PRIVATELY PRINTED *for* Mr. John R. Bartlett. VERY SCARCE.

1792 SEWALL (D.) An Eulogy Occasioned by the Death of General Washington, Pronounced at the Middle Parish, in Kittery, February 22d, 1800. By Daniel Sewall, Esq. *Portsmouth:* 1800.

8vo, pp. 20. UNCUT and RARE.

1793 SEWALL (J. M.) Eulogy on the Late General Washington, Pronounced at St. John's Church in Portsmouth, New Hampshire, on Tuesday, 31st December, 1799, at the Request of the Inhabitants. By Jonathan M. Sewall, Esq. *Portsmouth:* (1800.)

4to, pp. 28. UNCUT and SCARCE.

1794 SEWALL (S.) Phænomena quædam | Apocalyptica | Ad Aspectum Novi Orbis configurata. | Or, some few Lines towards a description of the New | Heaven. | As It makes to those who stand upon the | New Earth. | By Samuel Sewall, A.M. and sometime Fellow of Harvard | College at Cambridge in New-England. | The Second Edition. | ... | [Followed by:] The | Fountain Opened: | or | The Admirable Blessings plentifully to | be Dispensed at the National | Conversion of the Jews. | By ... Samuel Willard. M.A. ... | The Third Edition. | [With Appendix by Samuel Sewall.] *Massachvset: | Boston, Printed by Bartholomew Green: ...* 1727.

The two works above described are usually found together; this volume contains an addition as follows:

Proposals | Touching the Accomplishment | of | Prophesies | Humbly Offered. | By Samuel Sewall. M.A. and sometime | Fellow of Harvard College at Cambridge | in New-England. | *Massachvset; | Boston, Printed by Bartholomew Green.* 1713.

Sm. 4to, pp. (8), 64; 24. *Title* 1 *l., pp.* 12, *Verses* 1 *l.* *Crushed green levant morocco, gilt edges, by* W. PRATT. LARGE and FINE COPY. EXCESSIVELY RARE.

"Mr. Sewall inclines to the opinion that the Indians are descendants of the Israelites; and he adopts, after the learned Mr. Nicholas Fuller, the name of *Columbiana* for the continent of America."— *N.A.R.* XI. *p.* 107.

1795 [SEWALL.] A | Versification | of | President Washington's | Excellent | Farewell-Address, | to the | Citizens of the | United States. | By a Gentleman of Portsmouth, N. H. | *Portsmouth, New-Hampshire: | Printed and Sold by Charles Pierce, at the | Columbian Bookstore.* 1798.

Roy. 8vo, pp. 54. *Polished calf, yellow edges, by* F. BEDFORD. Large and clean copy. VERY SCARCE.

1796 SEWARD [(Anna.)] Monody | on | Major André. | By Miss Seward. | (Author of the Elegy on Capt. Cook.) | To which are added | Letters Addressed to her | by Major André, | in the year 1769. | The Second Edition. | *Litchfield: | Printed and Sold by J. Jackson, for the Author.* | ... M.DCC.LXXXI.

4to, pp. vi., 47. *Half morocco.* Fine copy, with Miss Seward's AUTOGRAPH SIGNATURE at the end of the Monody.

The Letters are said to have been the creation of Miss Seward's own imagination.

1797 SEWARD. Monody | on | Major André.| By Miss Seward. | (Author of the Elegy on Capt. Cook.)| To which are added,| Letters Addressed to her | by Major André |in the year 1769. | *New-York*,| *Printed by James Rivington.*| M.DCC.LXXXI.

Sm. 8vo, pp. iv., 35. *Scarlet morocco, gilt edges.* PORTRAIT of the AUTHOR *inserted.* EXCEEDINGLY RARE.

1798 SEVENTY SIX SOCIETY. [The Publications of the Seventy Six Society, consisting of the following works.] *Philadelphia:* 1855-57.

I. Papers in relation to the Case of Silas Deane. Now first published from the Original Manuscripts. Two PORTRAITS *inserted.*

II. The Examination of Joseph Galloway, Esq., by a Committee of the House of Commons. Edited by Thomas Balch. PORTRAIT *inserted.*

III. Papers relating to Public Events in Massachusetts preceding the American Revolution. Two PORTRAITS *inserted.*

IV. Papers relating chiefly to the Maryland Line during the Revolution. Edited by Thomas Balch. Two ILLUSTRATIONS *inserted.*

Together, 4 *vols., 8vo, half blue morocco, gilt top,* UNCUT. *Only* 150 *sets printed.*

This series, the editions of which were originally limited to 150 copies, owing to the fact that many sets and parts of sets have been destroyed, is extremely scarce. Single volumes have sold as high as $35. *Uncut* sets, like the present, are very seldom met with.

1799 SHAKESPEARE (W.) Mr. William Shakespeare's Comedies, Histories, & Tragedies. Published according to the True Original Copies. *London Printed by Isaac Iaggard, and Ed. Blount.* 1623. [*London: Reprinted.* 1808.]

Imp. folio, half red levant morocco, gilt top, UNCUT. LARGE and ELEGANT copy, measuring 9¼ inches by 15 inches on the leaf. RARE in this condition.

An exact reprint of the first folio, with a fine impression of the portrait after Droeshout's engraving.

"This uncastrated reprint of 1808, is much more coveted than the later attempts at facsimile, and will fast rise in value. The original, from which it is reprinted, is continually increasing in value. Mr. Daniel's copy produced £716 2s., and the competition, whenever a copy occurs, is so strong, that, probably, what our ancestors deemed dear at £100, will be regarded as cheap at £1,000 by our successors."

1800 SHAKESPEARE. The Plays of Shakespeare. In Nine Volumes. *London: William Pickering.* MDCCCXXV.

9 *vols.,* 48*mo, crimson morocco, gilt edges.* A *few copies only* printed on INDIA PAPER; and the SMALLEST COMPLETE EDITION ever issued. RARE.

This beautiful edition of Shakespeare was published under the patronage of George John, Earl Spencer; and is one of the finest specimens of typography ever produced. It is illustrated with 38 engravings from drawings by Stothard, and is further adorned with charming woodcut headings and tail pieces, portrait of the Bard after Droeshout, &c. The text is from the best edition of Shakespeare, 15 vols., by Johnson and Stevens; with a Glossary.

1801 SHAKESPEARE. The Shakespearian Dictionary; forming a General Index to all the Popular Expressions, and Most Striking Passages in the Works of Shakespeare; from a few words to fifty or more lines:

an Appropriate Synonym being affixed to each Extract, with a Reference to the Context. ... By Thomas Dolby.
London: Smith, Elder, & Co. 1832.

12mo, pp. vi., 367. Portrait. Half calf.

1802 SHAKSPERE. The Pictorial Edition of the Works of Shakspere. Edited by Charles Knight. 7 vols. [Also:] William Shakspere; a Biography. By Charles Knight.
London: Charles Knight and Co. 1838–43.

8 vols., roy. 8vo, extended to 9 vols., by the division of the Biography into two parts as published. Half crushed red levant morocco, gilt top, UNCUT, *by* W. MATTHEWS.

This SPLENDID SET bound from parts as originally issued, without admixture of any kind, and with BRILLIANT and PERFECT IMPRESSIONS of the TWELVE HUNDRED ENGRAVINGS on wood, contains FIVE HUNDRED AND THIRTY *inserted* PORTRAITS, SUBJECTS AND VIEWS of the finest description; nearly ALL of which are PROOFS, INDIA PROOFS, and INDIA PROOFS BEFORE LETTERS; forming a perfect galaxy of the beautiful in art. The plates from the HARDING SERIES are a selection from a complete LARGE PAPER PROOF SET, the BEST of which only were taken. Those of the "Heroines of Shakspere," are also GENUINE PROOFS, imported expressly for use in this set. RUBRICATED TITLE PAGES were printed specially for the Biography, with a beautifully ENGRAVED INDIA PROOF VIGNETTE mounted in each.

These elegant volumes, together with "CLARKE'S CONCORDANCE," and FAIRHOLT'S HOME," (which follow), all uniformly bound, and ranging in size, form a truly MAGNIFICENT and probably UNRIVALLED SET of the works of him "who was not of an age, but for all time."

"In this Splendid Edition the text is derived from a most laborious and careful collation of the early editions, with all that the best and most extensive modern Shaksperian criticism has discovered. The notes are copious and thoroughly elucidatory of obscure words and phrases, and of the sources of the plays, the historical characters, &c. The engravings are mostly from actual things, and are not mere fancy pictures. The biography of Shakspere is the best yet written of him, and the studies of the characters of the plays and the accounts of the plots are written with feeling as well as with critical acumen."

1803 SHAKSPERE. The Complete Concordance to Shakspere: being a Verbal Index to all the passages in the Dramatic Works of the Poet. By Mrs. Cowden Clarke. *London: Charles Knight & Co.* M.DCCC.XLV.

Roy. 8vo. Uniform in size and binding with the preceding No.

1804 SHAKSPERE. The Home of Shakspere Illustrated and Described. By F. W. Fairholt, F.S.A. Thirty-three Engravings.
London: Chapman and Hall. MDCCCXLVII.

Roy. 8vo. Uniform in size and binding with the preceding No.

Inlaid from a 12mo, in MR. TRENT'S best manner to match and range with the "Works" and the "Concordance." FOUR FINE PORTRAITS of SHAKSPERE *inserted.*

1805 SHAKESPEARE'S SCHOLAR; being Historical and Critical Studies of his Text, Characters, and Commentators, with an Examination of Mr. Collier's Folio of 1632. By Richard Grant White.
New York: D. Appleton and Co. 1854.

8vo, pp. xliii., 504. Half olive morocco, gilt top, UNCUT. PORTRAIT of SHAKESPEARE *inserted.*

1806 SHAKESPEARE. The Works of William Shakespeare, The plays edited from the Folio of MDCXXIII., with Various Readings from all

the Editions and all the Commentators, Notes, Introductory Remarks, A Historical Sketch of the Text, An Account of the Rise and Progress of the English Drama, A Memoir of the Poet, and An Essay upon his Genius. By Richard Grant White.
Boston: Little, Brown and Company. 1857–66.

12 *vols.*, 8*vo*, *half olive morocco, gilt top*, UNCUT, *by* W. MATTHEWS. PORTRAITS AND WOODCUTS; LARGE PAPER; *only* 48 *copies printed;* EXCESSIVELY SCARCE.

"After such conscientious examination of his work as the importance of it demands; after a painful comparison, note by note, and reading by reading, of his edition with those of Messrs. Knight, Collier, and Dyce, our opinion of his ability and fitness for his task has been heightened and confirmed. Not that we always agree with him;— but Mr. White has generally shown so just a discrimination, that there are few instances where we dissent. We have subjected his volumes to a laborious examination, such as few books receive, because the text of Shakespeare is a matter of common and great concern, and they have borne the trial, except in a few impertinent particulars, admirably. Mr. Dyce and Mr. Singer are only dry commonplace-books of illustrative quotations; Mr. Collier has not wholly recovered from his 'corr. fo.' madness; Mr. Knight (with many eminent advantages as an editor) is too diffuse; and we repeat our honest persuasion, that Mr. White has thus far given us the best extant text, while the fullness of his notes gives his edition almost the value of a *variorum;* and we think that a careful collation justifies us in saying that in acute discrimination of æsthetic shades of expression, and often of textual niceties, Mr. White is superior to any previous editor."—*J. R. Lowell.*

1807 SHAKESPEARE. An Essay on the Authorship of the Three Parts of King Henry the Sixth. By Richard Grant White.
Riverside Press: Cambridge. 1859.

8*vo*, *pp.* (4), 100. *Half olive morocco, gilt top*, UNCUT, *by* W. MATTHEWS. TWENTY-FIVE COPIES only printed, TWELVE of which were for sale, and the remainder for PRIVATE DISTRIBUTION. VERY SCARCE.

1808 SHAKESPEARE. Memoirs of the Life of William Shakespeare, with an Essay towards the Expression of his Genius, and an Account of the Rise and Progress of the English Drama. By Richard Grant White. *Boston: Little, Brown, and Company.* 1866.

8*vo*, *pp. xi.*, 425. *Portrait. Half olive morocco, gilt top*, UNCUT, *by* W. MATTHEWS. No. 5 of *one hundred copies only printed* on LARGE PAPER to match "The Works &c."

All of these Shakespearian productions of Mr. White are uniformly bound, and in the finest condition.

1809 SHARP (J.) A| Sermon | Preached At | Trinity Church in New-York | in America, August 13. 1706.| At the Funeral of | The Right Honourable Katharine Lady | Cornbury,| Barroness Clifton of Leighton Bromswold, &c | Heiress to the most Noble Charles Duke of | Richmond and Lenox :| and | Wife to his Excellency Edward Lord Viscount | Cornbury, Her Majesties Captain General and | Governor in chief of the Provinces of New-York,| New Jersey, and Territories depending there-| on in America, &c.| By John Sharp, A.M. Chaplin to the Queen's Forces | in the Province of New-York.| *Printed and Sold by* WILLIAM BRADFORD *at the Bible in* | *New-York*, 1706.

Sm. 4*to*, *pp.* 20. *Calf, gilt edges, by* HAYDAY. Not in any of the Bibliographical Catalogues, and probably UNIQUE.

It is said that the General Assembly of New York in reply to Lord Cornbury's request of a grant for a public funeral for Lady Cornbury, declined, but at the same time assured his Excellency that they would at any time readily respond to a similar request for himself.

1810 SHAW (*Major* S.) The Journals of Major Samuel Shaw, the First American Consul at Canton. With a Life of the Author, by Josiah Quincy. *Boston: Crosby and Nichols.* 1847.

8vo, pp. xiii., 360. *Portrait. Half green levant morocco, gilt top,* UNCUT, *by* W. MATTHEWS. Beautiful copy. VERY SCARCE.

The narrative of the military life of Major Shaw, is composed chiefly of letters written to his nearest relatives and friends, from his enlistment in the American Army, at Cambridge, in December, 1775, to its final disbandment, at West Point, in January, 1784, and describes almost every important event in the War of the American Revolution.

1811 [SHEA (J. G.) Cramoisy Series of Jesuit Memoirs, Relations, Etc., relating to the French Colonies in North America. Edited by John Gilmary Shea, LL.D.] *New York:* 1858–66.

21 *vols., 8vo. Portraits and Maps. Half crushed red levant morocco, gilt top,* UNCUT, *by* W. MATTHEWS. LARGE PAPER. FIVE SETS ONLY PRINTED. A SPLENDID SET of these RARE REPRINTS and the ONLY ONE ever offered at public sale. It was Mr. Shea's own copy and contains some Maps and Plates not usually found in the Series which is now out of print. Complete sets, whether on large or small paper, can no longer be obtained.
The Series consists of the following works:

1. BIGOT (J.) Copie d'vne Lettre escrite par Le Père Jacques Bigot de la Compagnie de Jésus, l' An 1684, pour accompagner un collier de pourcelaine envoiée par les Abnaquis de la Mission de Sainct François de Sales dans la Nouvelle France au tombeau de leur Sainct Patron à Annecy. *Manate:* M.DCCC.LVIII.

2. BIGOT. Relation de ce qvi s'est passé de plus remarqvable dans la Mission Abnaquise de Sainct Joseph de Sillery et de Sainct François de Sales, l' Année 1685, par le R. Père Jacques Bigot, de la Compagnie de Jésus. *A Manate:* M.DCCC.LVIII.

3. BIGOT (V.) Relation de ce qvi s'est passé de plus remarqvable dans la Mission des Abnaquis à L' Acadie, l'Année 1701. Par le Père Vincent Bigot, de la Compagnie de Jésus. *A Manate:* M.DCCC.LVIII.

4. CAVELIER (M.) Relation du Voyage Entrepris par feu M. Robert Cavelier, Sieur de la Salle, pour découvrir dans le golfe du Mexique l'embouchure du Fleuve de Missisipy. Par son Frère M. Cavelier, prêtre de St. Sulpice, l'un des compagnons de ce voyage. *A Manate:* M.DCCC.LVIII.

5. CHAUMONOT (P. J. M.) La Vie du R. P. Pierre Joseph Marie Chaumonot, de la Compagnie de Jesus, Missionnaire dans la Nouvelle France, Ecrite par lui-même par ordre de son Supérieur, l'an 1688. *Nouvelle York, Isle de Manate.* M.DCCC.LVIII.

6. CHAUMONOT. Suite de la Vie du R. P. Pierre Joseph Marie Chaumonot, de la Compagnie de Jesus, par un Pére de la même Compagnie avec la manière d'oraison du vénérable Père, écrite par lui-même. *Nouvelle York, Isle de Manate:* M.DCCC.LVIII.

7. TRANCHEPAIN (St. A. de) Relation du Voyage des premières Ursulines à la Nouvelle Orléans et de leur établissement en cette ville. Par la Rev. Mère St. Augustin de Tranchepain, Supérieure. Avec les lettres circulaires de quelques unes des Sœurs, et de la dite Mère. *Nouvelle York, Isle de Manate:* M.DCCC.LIX.

8. REGISTRES des Baptesmes et Sepultures qui se sont faits au Fort Duquesne pendant les Années 1753, 1754, 1755, & 1756. *Nouvelle York, Isle de Manate:* M.DCCC.LIX.

9. JOURNAL de la Guerre du Micissippi contre les Chicachas, en 1739 et finie en 1740, le 1 er d' Avril. Par un Officier de l' Armee de M. de Nouaille.
Nouvelle York, Isle de Manate. M.DCCC.LIX.

10. GRAVIER (J.) Relation ou Journal du Voyage du R. P. Jacques Gravier, de la Compagnie de Jésus, en 1700 depuis le pays des Illinois jusqu' à l'embouchure du Mississipi. *Nouvelle York, Isle de Manate.* M.DCCC.LIX.

11. DABLON (C.) Relation de ce qui s'est passe' de Plus Remarquable aux Missions des Peres de la Compagnie de Jesus en la Nouvelle France les années 1672 à 1673 par le R. P. Claude Dablon Recteur du College de Quebec. ...
A la Nouvelle York, De la Presse Cramoisy. M.DCCC.LXI.

12. DABLON. Relation de ce qui s'est passe' de Plus Remarquable aux Missions des Peres de la Compagnie de Jesus en la Nouvelle France les années 1673 à 1679 par le R. P. Claude Dablon &c. ... . *Quebec a la Presse Cramoisy.* M.DCCC.LX.

13. RELATIONS diverses sur la Bataille du Malangueulé. Gagné le 9 Juillet, 1755, par les François sous M. de Beaujeu, Commandant du Fort du Quesne sur les Anglois sous M. Braddock, Général en Chef des troupes Anglois. Recueillies par Jean Marie Shea. *Nouvelle York: De la Presse Cramoisy* M DCCC LX.

14. RELATION de la Mission du Missisipi du Seminaire de Québec en 1700. Par MM. De Montigny, De St. Cosme, et Thaumur de la Source.
Nouvelle York: a la Presse Cramoisy. M DCCC LXI.

15. JOGUES (I.) Novum Belgium, Description de Nieuw Netherland et Notice sur René Goupil. Par le R. P. Isaac Jogues, de la Compagnie de Jésus.
A New York, dans l' Ancien Niew Netherland, Presse Cramoisy. 1862.

16. SÂGEAN (M.) Extrait de la Relation des Avantures et Voyage de Mathieu Sâgean.
Nouvelle York: a la Presse Cramoisy. 1863.

17. MILET (P.) Relation de sa Captivité parmi les Onneiouts en 1690–1. Par le R. P. Pierre Milet de la Compagnie de Jésus.
Nouvelle York: Presse Cramoisy. M.DCCC.LXIV.

18. RELATION des Affaires du Canada, en 1696. Avec des Lettres des Pères de la Compagnie de Jésus depuis 1696 jusqu' en 1702.
Nouvelle York: de la Presse Cramoisy. M DCCC LXV.

19. GRAVIER (J.) Lettre du Père Jacques Gravier, de la Compagniè de Jésus, le 23 Fevriér 1708, sur les Affaires de la Louisiane.
Nouvelle York: de la Presse Cramoisy. MDCCCLXV.

20. BIGOT (J.) Relation de la Mission Abnaquise de St. François de Sales l'Année 1702. Par le Père Jacques Bigot, de la Compagnie de Jésus.
Nouvelle-York: Presse Cramoisy. M.DCCC.LXV.

21. RECUEIL de Pièces sur la Negociation entre la Nouvelle France et la Nouvelle Angleterre, ès années 1648 et suivantes.
Nouvelle York: de la Presse Cramoisy. M.DCCC.LXVI.

1812 SHEBBEARE (J.) An Essay on the Origin, Progress and Establishment of National Society; in which the principles of government, the definitions of physical, moral, civil and religious liberty contained in Dr. Price's Observations, &c. are fairly examined and fully refuted. By John Shebbeare, M.D. With an Appendix on the excellent and admirable in Mr. Burke's second printed speech of March 22, 1775. *London: J. Bew.* MDCCLXXVI.

8vo, pp. 212. *Half morocco. Presentation copy* from the AUTHOR, with his PORTRAIT *inserted.*

Dr. Shebbeare's Essay was severely censured by the *Monthly Review;* it is alleged by the reviewer that beside the objectionable character of his tenets, and his reasoning on them, that his "language is frequently intemperate, foul, opprobrious; and humour, often coarse, low, and indelicate."

1813 SHELDON (F.) The Minstrelsy of the English Border. Being a Collection of Ballads, Ancient, Remodeled, and Original, founded on Well Known Border Legends. With Illustrative Notes by Frederick Sheldon. *London: Longman.* 1847.

Sm. 4to, pp. xx., 432. Half olive morocco, gilt top, UNCUT.

The Book of Books for Legends, Border-reiving, and Battle-loving times of old.

1814 SHELVOCKE (G.) A Voyage Round the World By the Way of the Great South Sea, Perform'd in the Years 1719, 20, 21, 22, in the Speedwell of London, of 24 Guns and 100 Men, (under His Majesty's Commission to cruize on the Spaniards in the late War with the Spanish Crown) till she was cast away on the Island of Juan Fernandez, in May 1720; and afterwards continu'd in the Recovery, the Jesus Maria and Sacra Familia, &c. By Captain George Shelvocke, ... *London: J. Senex.* MDCCXXVI.

8vo, pp. (12), *xxxii.,* 468. *Map and* 3 *Plates. Paneled calf, red edges.* LARGE and FINE COPY.

Two histories were published of this voyage. This was intended by the author as a vindication of his conduct, he having been accused of piracy and embezzlement. The other was written by William Betagh who was roughly treated in Shelvocke's narrative, and, in return, wrote with the design of exposing Shelvocke.

The author's relation of the discovery of gold is remarkable. "The soil about Puerto Seguro (and very likely in most parts of the valleys), is a rich black mould, which, as you turn it up fresh to the sun, appears as if intermingled with gold dust, some of which we endeavoured to wash and purify from the dust; but though we were a little prejudiced against the thoughts that it could be possible that this metal should be so promiscuously and universally mingled with common earth, yet we endeavoured to cleanse and wash the earth from some of it, and the more we did, the more it appeared like gold; but in order to be further satisfied, I brought away some of it which we lost in our confusions in China."—*Pages* 400, 401.

1815 [SHEPARD (Thomas.)] The | Day-Breaking, | If Not | The Sun-Rising | Of The | Gospell | With the | Indians in New-England. | ... | *London,* | *Printed by Rich. Cotes, for Fulke Clifton, and are to bee* | *sold at his shop under Saint Margarets Church on* | *New-fish-street Hill,* 1647.

Sm. 4to, pp. 25. *Red morocco, gilt edges, by* W. MATTHEWS. A BEAUTIFUL COPY of this EXCESSIVELY RARE TRACT.

The second of the series of Reports to the "Society for the Propagation of the Gospel among the Indians." It is one of the most curious, interesting and valuable of the series; containing Relations of four meetings with the Indians, and describing their habitations, manner of living, language, laws, and some of the productions of the country, &c.

1816 SHEPARD (T.) The | Clear Sunshine of the Gospel | Breaking forth | upon the | Indians | in | New-England. | Or, | An Historicall Narration of Gods | Wonderfull Workings upon sundry of the | Indians, both chief Governors and Common-people, | in bringing them to a willing and desired submission to | the Ordinances of the Gospel; and framing their | hearts to an earnest inquirie after the knowledge | of God the Father, and of Jesus Christ | the Saviour of the World. | By Mr. Thomas Shepard Minister of the Gospel of | Jesus Christ at Cambridge in New-England. | *London, Printed by R. Cotes for John Bellamy at the three golden | Lions in Cornhill near the Royall Exchange*, 1648.

Sm. 4to, pp. (14), 38. *Crushed green levant morocco, richly gilt and filleted sides, the inside lined with polished red morocco beautifully tooled and gilt after an elegant original design, morocco joints, gilt edges, by* W. MATTHEWS. A desirable example of the perfection to which American book-binding has arrived. EXTREMELY RARE.

The *third* of the series of books giving an account of the results of the English missions among the natives. Small specimens of the Indian language are included. The work also includes a long letter from Eliot, the Apostle of the Indians, who is described as already so skilled in the Indian tongue that he preached regularly in it to the natives. It is otherwise very interesting, because of the details which go to make up Eliot's biography, and to shew the nature of his work among the Indians and their feelings with regard to him.

1817 SHEPARD. Eye-Salve, | Or A | Watch-Word | From our Lord Jesus Christ unto his Churches : | Especially those within the Colony of the Massachusets | In New-England. | To take heed of Apostacy : | or | A Treatise of Remembrance of what God hath been to us, as also | what we ought, and what we ought not to be to him, as we de- | sire the prolonging of our Prosperous Dayes in the Land which | the Lord our God hath given us. | By Thomas Shepard, Teacher of the Church of Christ in | Charlstown : | Who was appointed by the Magistrates, to Preach on the day of | Election | at Boston, May 15, 1672. | *Cambridge, Printed by Samuel Green*, 1673.

Sm. 4to, pp. (4), 52. *Crushed red levant morocco, gilt edges by* W. PRATT. A BEAUTIFUL COPY of this VERY RARE EARLY NEW ENGLAND IMPRINT.

An address headed "Christian Reader," pp. 2, is signed "Thomas Thacher."

1818 SHEPHERD (T. H.) Modern Athens! Displayed in a Series of Views : or Edinburgh in the Nineteenth Century : exhibiting the whole of the New Buildings, Modern Improvements, Antiquities, and Picturesque Scenery, of the Scottish Metropolis and its Environs, from Original Drawings, by Mr. Thomas H. Shepherd. With Historical, Topographical, and Critical Illustrations. *London : Jones & Co.* 1829.

4to, half green morocco, gilt top, UNCUT. FINE COPY, FIRST EDITION, with INDIA PROOF IMPRESSIONS of the ONE HUNDRED most accurate and beautifully engraved views. INDIA PROOF PORTRAIT of SIR WALTER SCOTT *inserted*.

1819 SHERBURNE (A.) Memoirs of Andrew Sherburne : a Pensioner of the Navy of the Revolution. Written by Himself. *Utica : William Williams*. 1828.

12mo, pp. 262, (2). *Half morocco.*

The author was born in Rye, New Hampshire, in 1765, shipped from Portsmouth on board the Congress ship of war, the *Ranger*, in 1779, and afterwards served in other public and private war ships until he was taken prisoner in 1781, and carried to Portsmouth, in England, where he was tried and committed to prison, "for rebellion, piracy, and high treason, on his Majesty's high seas," etc.

1820 [SHIPLEY (Jonathan.) Bishop of St. Asaph.] A Speech intended to have been Spoken on the Bill for altering the Charters of the Colony of Massachusetts Bay. The Second Edition.
London: T. Cadell. 1774.

8vo, pp. vii., 36. *Half morocco.*

"A golden speech unspoken, which illustrates the wisdom, justice, foresight, and eloquence of the good bishop. It will not be unpleasant for Americans to hear his opinion — 'My Lords, I look upon North America as the only great nursery of freemen now left upon the face of the earth.'"

1821 [SHIPLEY.] A Speech never intended to be Spoken, in Answer to a Speech intended to have been Spoken on the Bill for altering the Charter of the Colony of Massachusetts Bay. Dedicated to the Lord Bishop of St. Asaph. *London: J. Knox.* MDCCLXXIV.

8vo, pp. iv., 35. *Half blue morocco.*

"The writer of this speech declaims with some spirit and plausibility. He maintains that there are more people in England unrepresented and yet taxed, than there are inhabitants in British America. He also states that as the Parliament represents the whole body and realm of England and dominions of the same, the Americans are also represented therein."— *Rich.*

1822 [SHIRLEY (William.)] The Conduct of Major General Shirley, late General and Commander in Chief of his Majesty's Forces in North America briefly stated. *London: R. and J. Dodsley.* 1758.

8vo, pp. (6), 124. *Half morocco.* A good copy, but unfortunately wanting the Appendix containing six pages. VERY SCARCE.

Full of curious information respecting the war on the New York frontier, the attack on Niagara, &c.

"Written by William Alexander, Earl of Stirling."— *Tudor's Otis.* Ch. iv.

1823 SHURTLEFF (N. B.) A Decimal System, for the Arrangement and Administration of Libraries. By N. B. Shurtleff.
Boston: Privately Printed. MDCCCLVI.

4to, pp. 80. *Cloth extra, gilt top,* UNCUT. *Privately Printed.* EXCEEDINGLY SCARCE. *Presentation copy* from the Author to Henry Stevens, Esq.

Copies have been sold as high as $16.

SIGNERS OF THE CONSTITUTION OF THE UNITED STATES.

1824 Original Autograph Letters, Notes, Circulars, and Documents, with some Portraits of the Signers of the Constitution of the United States. September 17th, 1787.

Roy. 4to, green morocco, gilt edges, by F. BEDFORD.

This ELEGANT VOLUME contains a COMPLETE SET of AUTOGRAPH LETTERS written and signed by the signers of the Constitution of the United States; embracing FORTY-FOUR MANUSCRIPT LETTERS &c., and TWENTY-NINE PORTRAITS of the patriotic men who affixed their names to that famous instrument. The letters, which are uniformly in the finest possible condition, were arranged and mounted, and the portraits inlaid and inserted, in the most approved manner by MR. BEDFORD. A RUBRICATED TITLE PAGE, and a TABLE OF

CONTENTS printed by MR. MUNSELL, expressly for the volume, precede the letters, many of which are of a very interesting character, and some relating directly to the event which this volume is designed to commemorate. A BEAUTIFUL, HIGHLY INTERESTING, AND MOST VALUABLE COLLECTION.

1825 SIMCOE (J. G.) A Journal of the Operations of the Queen's Rangers, from the End of the Year 1777, to the Conclusion of the late American War, by Lieutenant-Colonel Simcoe, Commander of that Corps. *Exeter: Printed for the Author.* [1787.]

4to, *pp.* (8), 184, (48). 10 *Maps. Green morocco, gold filleted sides, broad inside gilt borders, gilt edges.* A SUPERB COPY of the EXCESSIVELY RARE ORIGINAL EDITION, clean and fresh as when published, and the LARGEST COPY yet heard from, measuring 8¾ inches by 10½ inches on the leaf.

"First printed soon after the termination of the War of Independence, but apparently not published, and was almost unknown to exist, until a few years ago, whon a copy turned up in a sale (I believe of Mr. Chalmers' Library) and from that copy the New York edition of 1844 was printed."— *Rich.*

1826 SIMCOE'S MILITARY JOURNAL. A History of the Operations of a Partisan Corps, called the Queen's Rangers, Commanded by Lieut. Col. J. G. Simcoe, during the War of the American Revolution; Illustrated by Ten Engraved Plans of Actions, &c., now first published, with a Memoir of the Author and other Additions. *New York: Bartlett & Welford.* 1844.

8vo, *pp.* xvii., 11–328. 10 *Plans. Half levant morocco, gilt top,* UNCUT.

"The operations detailed occurred in the vicinity of New York city, in West-Chester County, Long Island, Staten Island, in various parts of New Jersey, the neighbourhood of Philadelphia, Germantown, &c., in North and South Carolina, in Virginia, at the time of Arnold's invasion, and through the whole subsequent movements in that state, till Cornwallis' surrender at Yorktown. The memoir of the author, and some other additions as appendix, increase the attraction, interest and value of the whole volume."

827 SIMEON (*Sir* John.) Books and Libraries. A Lecture delivered before the Members of the Ryde Literary and Scientific Institute, at the Town Hall, Ryde, October 28, 1859. By Sir John Simeon, Bart., M.A. *London: John W. Parker and Son.* 1860.

8vo, *pp.* 75. *Flexible cloth.* VERY SCARCE.

A treasury of curious and interesting information relative to the origin and progress of printing, books, book-lovers, libraries, &c.

1828 SIMMS (J. R.) History of Schoharie County, and Border Wars of New York; containing also a Sketch of the Causes which led to the American Revolution; and interesting Memoranda of the Mohawk Valley .... Illustrated with more than Thirty Engravings. By Jeptha R. Simms. *Albany: Munsell & Tanner, Printers.* 1845.

8vo, *pp.* xix–672. *Half calf. Frontispiece inserted.* Long since out of print, and VERY SCARCE. Beautiful copy.

"Mr. Simms' book is one of that limited class of historical works, for which the reader will feel from youth to age, that he owes a debt of gratitude to its author. It is the very model of a local history. Crowded with details of the adventures of the early settlers of the Mohawk Valley, in their conflicts with their savage neighbors, we do not stop to question their authenticity. The midnight massacres, the long and weary captivities, the surprises of

Indian camps, the bloody encounters between the scouts and their savage foes, are all narrated with an artless style that wins and preserves the reader's attention."— *Field.*

1829 SIMMS. The American Spy, or Freedom's early Sacrifice: a Tale of the Revolution, Founded upon Fact. By J. R. Simms. ... *Albany: J. Munsell.* 1857.

Roy. 8vo, pp. 116. *Plate. Half green morocco, gilt top,* UNCUT. LARGE PAPER. *Twenty-eight copies only printed.* VERY SCARCE.

1830 [SIMMS (W. G.)] A Succinct Memoir of the Life and Public Services of Colonel John Laurens, Aid de Camp to General Washington and Special Envoy to the French Court during the War of the American Revolution. Together with a Series of Interesting Letters Written by Him, relating to that Eventful Epoch, and addressed to his Father, Henry Laurens, President of Congress. *Williamstadt:* MDCCCLXVII.

Roy. 8vo, pp. 250. *Half crushed green levant morocco, gilt top,* UNCUT, *by* W. MATTHEWS. ONE COPY ONLY printed on this paper, with RUBRICATED TITLE. THIRTY-THREE PORTRAITS inlaid in oval form by MR. TRENT *inserted.*

1831 [SIMMS.] South-Carolina in the Revolutionary War: being a Reply to certain Misrepresentations and Mistakes of recent writers, in relation to the Course and Conduct of this State, by a Southron. [William Gilmore Simms.] *Charleston: Walker and James.* 1853.

12*mo, pp.* (4), 177. *Half calf. Fine copy.* SCARCE.

1832 SIMON (*Mrs.* [Barbara Anne.]) The Ten Tribes of Israel historically identified with the Aborigines of the Western Hemisphere. By Mrs. Simon. *London: Seeley.* 1836.

8vo, pp. xl., 370. *Plate of Mexican Antiquities. Half olive morocco, gilt top,* UNCUT.
This singular work includes a copious analysis of Lord Kingsborough's Antiquities.

1833 SIMPKINSON (J. N.) The Washingtons, a Tale of a Country Parish in the Seventeenth Century. Based on Authentic Documents. By John Nassau Simpkinson. *London: Longman.* 1860.

Crown 8vo, pp. xvi., 326, *lxxxix. Plate. Half green morocco, gilt top,* UNCUT. SCARCE.
An elegant book, which contains a valuable historical account of the Ancestors of George Washington.

Dr. Stiles' copy sold for $9.

1834 SIMPLE COBBLER OF CLERKENWELL (The) willing to help to mend his Native Country, (lamentably tattered both in the upper leather and soles), with all the honest stitches he can take.

"It is his Trade to patch all the year long, gratis.
When Boots and Shoes are torn up to the lefts,
Coblers must thrust their awls up to the Hefts."

Printed in the year 1776.

8vo, pp. 19. *Half blue morocco, gilt top,* UNCUT, *by* BRADSTREET. FINE COPY. VERY SCARCE.

"A remarkably scarce and curious Tract relating to the American War of Independence. Vide the following extracts, 'We are directed by a recent Proclamation to keep a solemn Fast, a Day of Humiliation .... in order to deprecate Heaven against our brave and virtuous Brethren in North America, who have been drove by multiform Acts of Deceit, Oppression, Injustice, Violence, Despotism, and Tyranny, to take up Arms in Defence of their Lives, Laws, Liberties and Properties!' (*page* 1.) 'Your Majesty's subjects in general are so fully convinced of the injustice of the American war .... that it is apprehended very few persons will celebrate the approaching Fast,' (*page* 18.) This Tract is unmentioned by Rich, Stevens, ('Nuggets') and Lowndes, nor can we find it noticed by any other bibliographer."— *Stevens.*

1835 SIMPSON (H.) The Lives of Eminent Philadelphians, now Deceased. Collected from Original and Most Authentic Sources, by Henry Simpson. ... Illustrated with Forty-four Fine Engravings. *Philadelphia: W. Brotherhead.* 1859.

2 *vols., roy. 8vo, half green morocco, gilt top,* UNCUT. One volume extended to TWO, with RUBRICATED TITLES printed expressly for the set, and THIRTY-SIX PORTRAITS *inserted.* A UNIQUE and BEAUTIFUL COPY.

1836 SIMS (C. S.) The Origin and Signification of Scottish Surnames. With a Vocabulary of Christian Names. By Clifford Stanley Sims. *Albany: J. Munsell.* 1862.

Roy. 8vo, pp. xi.–125. Half green morocco, gilt top, UNCUT. *One hundred and fifty copies only* PRINTED FOR SUBSCRIBERS.

1837 [SINGER (S. W.)] Some Account of the Book Printed at Oxford in MCCCCLXVIII, under the title of "Exposicio Sancti Jeronimi in Simbolo Apostolorum;" in which is examined its claim to be considered the First Book printed in England. *London:* 1812.

8vo, pp. ii., 44. 3 *Facsimiles. Half blue morocco, gilt top,* UNCUT. PRIVATELY PRINTED and 50 *copies only.* VERY RARE in uncut condition.

1838 SKETCH of a Discourse, occasioned by the Death of the late General George Washington. *Dublin: P. Byrne.* 1800.

8vo, pp. 20. EXCEEDINGLY RARE. *Not noticed* in Dr. Hough's List.

1839 [SMEETON (George.)] Historical and Biographical Tracts. *London: George Smeeton.* 1820.

2 *vols., sm. 4to, embossed calf, marbled edges.* 250 *copies only printed,* most of which were destroyed by fire. VERY SCARCE.

The work embraces 16 of the most curious and rare English Historical Tracts, with upwards of 30 fine portraits, including copies of the 18 very rare portraits in "Vicars' England's Worthies," and "Cromwell between the Pillars."

1840 SMITH (C. J.) Historical and Literary Curiosities, consisting of Fac-similes of Original Documents; Scenes of Remarkable Events and Interesting Localities; and the Birth-places, Residences, Portraits, and Monuments of Eminent Literary Characters; ... Selected and Engraved by the late Charles John Smith, F.S.A. *London: H. G. Bohn.* MDCCCLII.

4to, pp. viii., 100 *Plates. Half olive morocco, gilt top,* UNCUT.

1841 SMITH (C.) The American War, from 1775 to 1783. With Plans. By Charles Smith. *New York: Printed for C. Smith.* 1797.

8vo, pp. 183. *Blue morocco, gilt edges.*

A FINE COPY of this EXTREMELY RARE work which contains a curious PORTRAIT OF WASHINGTON engraved by TISDALE, a VIEW OF QUEBEC, and SEVEN FOLDED PLANS of the leading battles of the Revolution.

We have never met with another copy.

1842 [SMITH (Buckingham.)] Copies in seven sheets from Documents in Spanish and two of the Languages [Apalachian and Timuquan] spoken by the early Indians in Florida. [*New-York:* 1864. ?]

Folio, boards. 3 *pages of facsimile manuscript.* 50 *copies only printed,* ALL FOR PRESENTATION. EXTREMELY RARE. The above is the *manuscript title,* in Mr. Smith's handwriting, on a blank leaf.

Priced in one of Trübner's recent catalogues at £5.5.0.

1843 SMITH (B.) An Inquiry into the Authenticity of Documents concerning a Discovery in North America claimed to have been made by Verazzano. Read before the New York Historical Society, Tuesday, October 4th, 1864. By Buckingham Smith. *New-York: John F. Trow.* MDCCCLXIV.

4to, pp. 31. *Map. Half blue morocco, gilt top,* UNCUT. LARGE PAPER. *One hundred and twenty copies printed.* VERY SCARCE.

1844 SMITH (J.) An Oration on the Death of George Washington, Delivered at Exeter, February 22, 1800. By Jeremiah Smith. *Exeter:* 1800.

8vo, pp. 31. UNCUT.

1845 SMITH (J.) A Trve Relation of such occurrences and accidents of noate as hath hapned in Virginia since the first planting of that Collony, which is now resident in the South part thereof, till the last returne from thence. Written by Captaine Smith Coronell of the said Collony, to a worshipfull friend of his in England. *London Printed for Iohn Tappe, and are to bee solde at the Grey-hound in Paules-Church-yard, by W. W.* 1608.

[Reprinted] *Boston: Thirty Copies Printed for the Editor.* MDCCCLXVI.

Sm. 4to, pp. xlvii., v., 88. *Map. Half red morocco, gilt top,* UNCUT. EXCEEDINGLY SCARCE.

Reprinted from the original black letter volume, the earliest published work relative to the colony at Jamestown, Virginia (the first permanent English settlement in North America), and the first printed work of Captain Smith. The Introduction, by Charles Deane, gives full bibliographical details of the early editions of this work which have heretofore formed a subject of much perplexity to collectors; some copies having the name of "Thomas Watson Gent." as the author, while Mr. Lenox's copy reads "By a Gentleman."

1846 SMITH. A Description of New-England: or The Observations, And Discoueries of Captain Iohn Smith (Admirall of that Country) in the North of America, in the year of our Lord 1614: with the success of sixe Ships, that went the next yeare 1615; and the accidents befell him among the French men of Warre: With the proofe of the present benefit this Countrey affoords: whither this present yeare, 1616, eight voluntary ships are gone to make further tryall. *At London Printed by Humfrey Lownes, for Robert Clerke; and are to be sould at his house called the Lodge, in Chancery lane, over against Lincolnes Inne.* 1616.

[Reprinted] *Boston: William Veazie.* M DCCC LXV.

4to, pp. vii., 89. Map. Half crushed blue levant morocco, gilt top, UNCUT, *by* BRADSTREET. VERY SCARCE. LARGE PAPER, *Twenty-five copies only printed,* with a Fac-simile of the Original Map.

"This is the first book published, which speaks of NEW ENGLAND, previously called North Virginia."—*Rich.*

1847 SMITH. New Englands Trials. Declaring the successe of 80 ships employed thither within these eight yeares; and the benefit of that Countrey by Sea and Land. With the present estate of that happie Plantation, begun by but 60 Weake men in the yeare 1620. And how to build a Fleete of good Shippes to make a little Nauie Royall. Written by Captaine Iohn Smith, sometimes Gouernour of Virginia, and Admirall of New England. The Second Edition. *London, Printed by William Iones.* 1622. [*Reprinted, Providence:* 1867.]

Imp. 8vo, 16 unpaged leaves. Crushed blue levant morocco, gilt top, UNCUT, *by* W. MATTHEWS. LARGE PAPER. EXTREMELY SCARCE. A "few copies" only printed for Mr. John Carter Brown, "for distribution among the collectors of books relating to America."

1848 SMITH. The | Generall Historie | of | Virginia, New-England, and the Summer | Isles: with the names of the Adventurers, | Planters, and Governours from their | first beginning An°: 1584. to this | Present 1626. | With the Procedings of those Severall Colonies | and the Accidents that befell them in all their | Journyes and Discoveries. | Also the Maps and Descriptions of all those | Countryes, their Commodities, people, | Government, Customes, and Religion | yet knowne. | Divided into sixe Bookes. | By Captaine Iohn Smith sometymes Governour | in those Countryes & Admirall. | of New England. |

London. | *Printed by I. D. and* | *I. H. for Michael* | *Sparks.* | 1627.

Folio, engraved title, pp. (12), 96, 105-248, *and errata.* 4 *Maps,* 2 *Portraits. Crushed red levant morocco, paneled and ornamented sides, broad inside gilt borders, gilt edges, by* F. BEDFORD. AN ELEGANT COPY with beautiful impressions of ALL the ORIGINAL MAPS and PLATES, and the ERRATA which is wanting in many copies. The first edition in which the portrait of Prince Charles was changed to Charles Rex.

Smith's Virginia needs no commendation; it will always be regarded as one of the most interesting of the numerous works relative to that "Colonie;" but should our reader wish to peruse a lively description of this curious work we refer him to Dibdin's "Library Companion." Lest the authorship might be disputed the valiant captain has in several parts of the work stated, "Iohn Smith writ this with his own hand."

1849 SMITH. The | Trve Travels, | Adventvres, | and | Observations | Of | Captaine Iohn Smith, | In Europe, Asia, Affrica, and America, from Anno | Domini 1593. to 1629. | His Accidents and Sea-fights in the Straights; his Service | and Stratagems of warre in Hungaria, Transilvania, Wallachia, and | Moldavia, against the Turks, and Tartars; his three single combats | betwixt the Christian Armie and the Turkes. | After how he was taken prisoner by the Turks, sold for a Slave, sent into | Tartaria; his description of the Tartars, their strange manners and customes of | Religions, Diets, Buildings, Warres, Feasts, Ceremonies, and | Living; how hee slew the Bashaw of Nalbrits in Cambia, | and escaped from the Turkes and Tartars. | Together with a continuation of his generall History of Virginia, | Summer-Iles, New England, and their proceedings, since 1624. to this | present 1629; as also of the new Plantations of the great | River of the Amazons, the Iles of St. Christopher, Mevis, | and Barbados in the West Indies. | All written by actuall Authours, whose names | you shall finde along the History. | *London, Printed by J. H. for Thomas Slater, and are to bee | sold at the Blew Bible in Greene Arbour.* 1630.

Folio, pp. (12), 60. *Crushed red levant morocco, filleted sides, corner ornaments, gilt edges, by* F. BEDFORD. LARGE and SPLENDID COPY. The several compartments in the large folded plate, generally placed at the beginning of the work, have been separated in this copy, skillfully split and mounted upon matched paper like INDIA PROOFS by MR. BEDFORD, and placed where they respectively belong in the text.

1850 SMITH. Advertisements For the unexperienced Planters of New England, or any where. Or The Path-way to experience to erect a Plantation. With the yearely proceedings of this Country in Fishing and Planting, since the year 1614. to the year 1630. and their present estate. Also how to prevent the greatest inconveniences, by their proceedings in Virginia, and other Plantations, by approved examples. With the Countries Armes, a description of the Coast, Harbours, Habitations, Land-markes, Latitude and Longitude: with the Map, allowed by our Royall King Charles. By Captaine Iohn Smith, sometimes Governour of Virginia, and Admirall of Nevv-England. *London, Printed by Iohn Haviland, and are to be sold by Robert Milbovrne, at the Grey-hound in Pauls Churchyard.* 1631.

[Reprinted] *Boston: William Veazie.* MDCCCLXV.

4to, pp. viii., 72. *Map. Half crushed blue levant morocco, gilt top,* UNCUT, *by* BRADSTREET. VERY SCARCE. LARGE PAPER. *Twenty-five copies only printed,* with a Fac-simile of the Original Map.

1851 SMITH. The | Generall Historie | of | Virginia, New-England, and the Summer | Isles: with the names of the Adventurers, | Planters, and Governours from their | first beginning An°: 1584. to this | present 1626. | With the Proceedings of those Severall Colonies | and the Accidents that befell them in all their | Journyes and Discoveries. | Also the Maps and Descriptions of all those | Countryes, their Commodities, people, | Government, Customes, and Religion | yet knowne. | Divided into sixe Bookes. | By Captaine Iohn Smith sometymes

Governour | in those Countryes & Admirall | of New England. | *London.* | *Printed by I. D. and* | *I. H. for Edward* | *Blackmore* | *Anno* 1632.

Folio, engraved title, pp. (12), 96, 105 *to* 248. 4 *Maps*, 2 *Portraits*. *Purple levant morocco, broad inside gilt borders, gilt edges.*

An unusually large copy, measuring 7½ inches by 11¼ inches on the leaf. The portrait of MATOAKA is a *facsimile;* that of the DUTCHESS *inserted*, opposite the dedication, is also a *fac-simile;* the one facing the title is an ORIGINAL impression, as also are ALL the other engravings in the volume. The title and the maps have been mounted on cloth in order to ensure their preservation.

In this edition the Portrait of Charles Rex was altered to represent a man of more mature years, and the Map includes the names of places in New-England not given in the former issues.

An exact account of the various editions, by Mr. James Lenox, and Mr. Charles Deane, may be found in *Norton's Literary Gazette*, N. S. I. 134a — 135a, 218c — 219b. There were distinct issues in 1624, 1626, 1627, and two in 1632. The printed portion is identical in them all, and all want the sheet O, pp. 97 — 104. The variations are in the frontispiece, printed title, maps, and plates.

1852 SMITH. The Trve Travels, Adventvres, and Observations of Captaine John Smith, in Europe, Asia, Africke, and America: Beginning about the yeare . 1593 . and continued to this present . 1629. Vol. I. From the London Edition of 1619.

The Generall Historie of Virginia, New-England, and the Summer Isles, with the Names of the Adventurers, Planters, and Governours from their first beginning in 1584. To this present 1626. With the Proceedings of those Severall Colonies and the Accidents that befel them in all their Iournyes and Discoveries. Also the Maps and Descriptions of Countries, their Commodities, People, Government, Customes, and Religion yet knowne. Divided into Sixe Bookes. By Captaine Iohn Smith, sometymes Governour of those Countryes and Admirall of New-England. Vol. II. From the London Edition of 1629. *Richmond: Franklin Press.* 1819.

2 *vols.*, 8*vo*, *pp.* (14), 247; *xi.*, 282. *Portrait*, 3 *Plates, and Map. Half red morocco, gilt top*, UNCUT, *by* BRADSTREET. VERY SCARCE in *uncut* condition. BEAUTIFUL COPY. FOUR PORTRAITS *inserted;* that of Captain John Smith, opposite the title in volume I., is an ORIGINAL IMPRESSION cut from the map in the edition of 1632.

1853 SMITH. The Last Will and Testament of Captain John Smith; with some additional Memoranda relating to him. [By Charles Deane.] *Cambridge: I. Wilson and Son.* 1867.

Sm. 4*to, half red morocco, gilt top*, UNCUT, *by* BRADSTREET. *Fifty copies only* PRIVATELY PRINTED from the "Proceedings of the Mass. Hist. Soc.," for January, 1867.

1854 SMITH (J. H.) An Authentic Narrative of the Causes which led to the Death of Major Andrè, Adjutant-General of His Majesty's Forces in North America. By Joshua Hett Smith Esq. ... To which is added a Monody on the Death of Major Andrè. By Miss Seward. *London: Matthews and Leigh.* 1808.

8*vo*, *pp. vii.*, 357. *Portrait, Map and Plate. Half crimson morocco, gilt top*, UNCUT. SCARCE in this condition. A BEAUTIFUL COPY with TWENTY-EIGHT ILLUSTRATIONS, some of which are VERY RARE, *inserted.*

1855 SMITH (J. J.) *and* WATSON (J. F.) American Historical and Literary Curiosities. Consisting of Fac-Similes of Original Documents relating to the Events of the Revolution, &c., &c. With a Variety of Reliques, Antiquities and Modern Autographs. Collected and Edited by J. Jay Smith ... and John F. Watson. ... Fourth Edition with Additions. *New York: G. P. Putnam.* 1850.

Folio, half morocco, gilt edges. Sixty-six plates. Fine clean copy.

1856 SMITH (J. R.) Bibliotheca Americana. A Catalogue of a Valuable Collection of Books and Pamphlets relating to the History and Geography of North and South America and the West Indies. *London: J. Russell Smith.* 1853.

8vo, pp. 196. *Half crimson morocco, gilt top,* UNCUT.
A sale Catalogue with prices affixed.

1857 SMITH. Bibliotheca Americana. A Catalogue of a Valuable Collection of Books, Pamphlets, &c., illustrating the History and Geography of North and South America. *London: J. Russell Smith.* 1865.

8vo, pp. 308, (6). *Half crimson morocco, gilt top,* UNCUT.
A sale Catalogue with prices affixed.

1858 SMITH (J. T.) The Discovery of America by the Northmen in the Tenth Century. Comprising Translations of all the most Important Narratives of this Event. ... By Joshua Toulmin Smith. ... With Maps and Plates. Second Edition. *London: W. S. Orr & Co.* 1842.

Crown 8vo, pp. xii., 348. 2 *Maps, and* 2 *Plates. Half olive morocco, gilt top,* UNCUT.

1859 SMITH (S.) The | History | of | the Colony | of | Nova-Cæsaria, or New-Jersey; | Containing, | an Account of its First Settlement, | Progressive Improvements, | the Original and Present Constitution, | and other Events, | to the Year 1721. | With | Some Particulars Since; | and | a Short View of its present state. | By Samuel Smith. | *Burlington, in New-Jersey: | Printed and sold by James Parker: Sold also by | David Hall, in Philadelphia.* MDCCLXV.

Roy. 8vo, pp. x., 574. *Crushed green levant morocco, gilt paneled sides, corner ornaments, broad inside gilt borders, gilt top,* UNCUT, *by* F. BEDFORD. An UNEQUALLED COPY almost UNIQUE.

Inserted is an AUTOGRAPH LETTER written and signed by the Earl of Bath, dated April 16th, 1681, and addressed to Lord Norreys, containing a PROPOSAL FOR THE SALE OF EAST NEW JERSEY "With all Royalltys, Priviledges & Advantages thereto belonging as Sole Proprietor; and a Country almost as big as England planted already wth several Towns and many inhabitants and likely very much to increase being a very healthy place with good rivers and harbours and the price will be betwixt 5 and 6000 £." *See Work. p.* 156.

This identical copy sold for $200, at the Rice sale, before it was bound by Bedford, and previous to the insertion of the curious, interesting and valuable autograph letter. We know of ONLY ONE OTHER uncut copy.

"A judicious and authentic compilation; never having been reprinted, it has become very scarce and difficult to be met with."—*Rich.*

1860 SMITH (S.) The Works of the Rev. Sydney Smith. Second Edition. *London: Longman.* 1840.

3 vols., 8vo, half olive morocco, gilt top, UNCUT. *Fine Copy.*

"The greatest and most brilliant of wits."—*Sir H. Holland.*

1861 SMITH (S. S.) An Oration upon the Death of General George Washington, delivered in the State-House at Trenton, on the 14th of January, 1800, by the Rev. Samuel Stanhope Smith, D.D., President of the College of New Jersey .... *Trenton:* M.DCCC.

8vo, pp. 46. UNCUT.

1862 SMITH. LIJKREDE op den Generaal George Washington, door S. Stanhope Smith. [*n.p. n.d.*]

8vo, UNCUT. A Dutch edition of the preceding No. EXCEEDINGLY RARE. *Unnoticed* by Dr. Hough.

1863 SMITH (W.) The History Of the Province of New-York, from the First Discovery to the Year M.DCC.XXXII. To which is annexed, A Description of the Country, with a short Account of the Inhabitants, their Trade, Religious and Political State, and the Constitution of the Courts of Justice in that Colony. By William Smith, A.M. *London: Thomas Wilcox.* M.DCC.LVII.

Roy. 4to, pp. xii., 255. *Folded Plate. Crushed green levant morocco extra, elegantly tooled and gilt sides, gilt edges, by* W. MATTHEWS. SPLENDID LARGE PAPER COPY, believed to be UNIQUE. It is UNKNOWN TO ALL BIBLIOGRAPHERS, and is the identical copy which produced THREE HUNDRED DOLLARS at the Rice sale.

The author was a distinguished lawyer of New York. He graduated at Yale College in 1745, and, after a successful practice, became Chief Justice of the province. When the Revolution broke out he adhered to the mother country, and was one of Gen. Clinton's deputies for receiving acknowledgments of allegiance from the colonies. Subsequently he became Chief Justice of Canada.

1864 SMITH. The History of the Province of New-York. [Another copy.] *London: Thomas Wilcox.* M.DCC.LVII.

4to, pp. xii., 255. *Folded Plate. Bright purple morocco, paneled and gilt sides, broad inside gilt borders, gilt edges.* A VERY LARGE and FINE COPY of the ORIGINAL EDITION. VERY SCARCE.

"Smith gives us important details of the wars between the French and English in America. He also gives the best account of the confederation of the Iroquois."—*De Tocqueville.*

1865 SMITH. The History of the late Province of New-York, from its Discovery to the Appointment of Governor Colden in 1762. By the Hon. William Smith .... *New York: Published under the direction of the New York Historical Society.* 1830.

2 vols., 8vo, pp. xvi., 390; *iii.,* 390. *Half maroon morocco, gilt top,* UNCUT. FOUR PORTRAITS, and FACSIMILE of the folded plate of "The South View of Oswego." *inserted.*

This was edited by the author's son, and forms the most complete edition of a highly esteemed and standard work.

1866 SMITH (W.) Discourses on Public Occasions in America. By William Smith, D.D., Provost of the College and Academy of Philadelphia. Second Edition. *London: A. Miller.* 1762.

8vo, pp. xvi., vi., 7–224, 160. Half maroon morocco, gilt top, UNCUT. BEAUTIFUL COPY of the second and BEST EDITION, containing Four Discourses not in the first.

This scarce and interesting work relates to the stirring events of the immediate pre-revolutionary period; Braddock's defeat; ravages of the French and Indians; reduction of Louisbourg; opening of the campaign of 1758; &c.

1867 [SMITH.] An Historical Account of the Expedition against the Ohio Indians, in the Year 1764. Under the Command of Henry Bouquet, Esq.: Colonel of Foot, and now Brigadier General in America. Including His Transactions with the Indians, relative to the delivery of their prisoners, and the preliminaries of Peace. With an Introductory Account of the Preceeding Campaign, and Battle at Bushy-Run. To which are annexed Military Papers, containing Reflections on the war with the Savages; a method of forming frontier settlements; some account of the Indian country, with a list of nations, fighting men, towns, distances, and different routs. The whole illustrated with a Map and Copper-plates. Published from authentic Documents, by a Lover of his Country. *Philadelphia: William Bradford.* M.DCC.LXV.

4to, pp. xiii., 71. 3 Maps. Claret morocco, paneled and gilt sides, gilt edges, by W. MATTHEWS. AN ELEGANT COPY of the ORIGINAL EDITION. EXCESSIVELY RARE.

The authorship of this work has been ascribed to Thomas Hutchins who made the maps, and with more propriety to Bouquet himself: the following extract, however, from a letter from Dr. Smith, to Sir William Johnson, dated Philadelphia, 13th January, 1776, now in the Library of Congress, seems to decide the question. "I proposed sending you a copy of Boquet's Expedition to Muskingam, which I drew up from some papers he favored me with, and which is reprinted in England, and has had a very favorable reception."

1868 [SMITH.] An Historical Account of the Expedition against the Ohio Indians. [Same Title as above.] *London: Re-printed for T. Jeffries.* M.DCC.LXVI.

4to, pp. xiii., 71. Map, 2 Plans, and 2 Plates. Crushed maroon levant morocco, elegantly paneled and gilt sides, gilt top, UNCUT, *by* W. MATTHEWS. SPLENDID COPY, and VERY RARE in *uncut* condition.

In this edition the plans are on a reduced scale, but it contains in addition, two fine historical plates engraved by Grignon, from the earliest drawings of Benjamin West, to one of which his AUTOGRAPH SIGNATURE is attached.

"The work narrates the details of the first victory, gained over Indian forces by English troops, after the savages had been taught the use of fire-arms. Nearly twenty years elapsed before the whites gained another, during which period they suffered dreadful defeats in thirteen battles at the hands of the Indians. Colonel Bouquet by his judicious arrangements first laid down the plan, in following which General Wayne secured the same result."—*Field.*

1869 SMITH. A Sermon on the Present Situation of American Affairs. Preached in Christ-Church, June 23, 1775, at the Request of the

Officers of the Third Battalion of the City of Philadelphia, and District of Southwark. By William Smith, D.D. ...
London: E. and C. Dilly. M.DCC.LXXV.

8vo, pp. (4), *iv.*, 32. *Half morocco.*

Published to "promote the Cause of Liberty and Virtue."— *Col. John Cadwallader.*

1870 [SMITH.] Relation Historique de l'Expédition contre Les Indiens de l'Ohio en MDCCLXIV. ... Traduit de l'Anglois. Par C. G. F. Dumas. *Amsterdam: Marc-Michel Rey.* M.DCC.LXIX.

8vo, pp. (4), *xvi.*, 147, (10). *Map, 3 Plans, 2 Plates. Half red morocco, gilt top,* UNCUT.

This French edition contains a preface, and some biographical notices of Bouquet by the translator, not to be found in any of the editions in English.

1871 SMITH (W.) History of Canada; from its first Discovery, to the Peace of 1763. By William Smith, Esquire; Clerk of the Parliament and Master in Chancery of the Province of Lower Canada. Vol. II. From the Establishment of the Civil Government in 1764, to the Establishment of the Constitution in 1792.
Quebec: Printed for the Author; by John Neilson. 1815.

2 vols., roy. 8vo, pp. (6), *iii.*, 383; (1), 235, 72. *Crushed red levant morocco, paneled and gilt sides, corner ornaments, broad inside gilt borders, gilt top* UNCUT, *by* F. BEDFORD. SPLENDID COPY, PRIVATELY PRINTED, and EXTREMELY SCARCE. We have never sold but *one copy* of this valuable historical work.

Mr. Quaritch recently described a copy as on large paper, which we believe to be an error. We have seen all the known copies in the United States, and invariably found them on the same sized paper, and with remarkably large margins.

1872 SMITH (W. R.) The Uses of Solitude. By William R. Smith.
Albany: Munsell & Rowland. 1860.

Roy. 8vo, pp. 64. *Half orange morocco, gilt top,* UNCUT.

1873 SMYTH (J. F. D.) A Tour in the United States of America: Containing An Account of the Present Situation of that Country: The Population, Agriculture, Commerce, Customs and Manners of the Inhabitants; Anecdotes of several Members of the Congress, and General Officers in the American Army; and Many other very singular and interesting Occurrences. With A Description of the Indian Nations, the General Face of the Country, Mountains, Forests, Rivers, and the most beautiful, grand and picturesque Views throughout that vast Continent. ... By J. F. D. Smyth, Esq.
London: G. Robinson. MDCCLXXXIV.

2 vols., 8vo, pp. (24), 400; (12), 456. *Half crushed red levant morocco, gilt top,* UNCUT, *by* W. MATTHEWS. BEAUTIFUL COPY. VERY SCARCE. The *only uncut copy* we have ever met with.

The author, who was a zealous loyalist, lost his property during the war; and his work is said to have been written to gain favour with the Government, by abusing the Americans and magnifying his own losses. He narrowly escaped hanging by the Whigs on more than one occasion, but lived to record many interesting particulars of the first days of the Revolution, together with many scandalous anecdotes relating to the public men of the time.

1874 SMYTH (W.) Lectures on Modern History, from the Irruption of the Northern Nations to the Close of the American Revolution. By William Smyth. ... *London: William Pickering.* 1848.

2 *vols.*, 8*vo*, *pp. xx.*, 433; (6), 494. *Half calf, gilt top*, UNCUT.
No historical works have ever given more enlightened and perspicuous views of the course of great events than these celebrated lectures.

1875 SNOWDEN (J. R.) A Description of the Medals of Washington; of National and Miscellaneous Medals; and of other Objects of Interest in the Museum of the Mint. Illustrated by Seventy-nine Facsimile Engravings. ... By James Ross Snowden, the Director of the Mint. *Philadelphia: J. B. Lippincott & Co.* 1861.

4*to*, *pp.* 203. *Half green levant morocco, gilt top*, UNCUT. INDIA PROOF PORTRAIT *of* GEN. SCOTT *inserted.*

1876 [SNOWDEN (Richard.)] The American Revolution; Written in the Style of Ancient History. ...
Philadelphia: Printed by Jones, Hoff & Derrick. M,DCC,XCIII-IV.

2 *vols.*, 12*mo*, *pp. xii.*, 226; *xii.*, 216. *Half gray calf, carmine edges.* VERY SCARCE in such fine condition.

1877 SOLIS (A. de) The History of the Conquest of Mexico by the Spaniards. Translated from the original Spanish of Don Antonio de Solis. ... By Thomas Townsend, Esq. The whole Translation Revised and Corrected By Nathaniel Hooke, Esq. The Third Edition. *London: H. Lintot.* 1753.

2 *vols.*, 8*vo*, *pp. xvi.*, 384, 6 *Plates*; *x.*, 386, 3 *Plates.* *Half maroon morocco, gilt top*, UNCUT. Beautiful copy. RARE in *uncut* condition.

1878 SOTHEBY (S. L.) The Typography of the Fifteenth Century; being Specimens of the Productions of the Early Continental Printers, Exemplified in a Collection of Facsimiles from one hundred Works, together with their Water Marks. Arranged and Edited from the Bibliographical Collections of the Late Samuel Sotheby by his son, S. Leigh Sotheby. *London: Thomas Rodd.* 1845.

Folio, half vellum, UNCUT. *One hundred copies only printed.* VERY SCARCE. Uniform in size with the "Principia Typographica." It contains 100 FACSIMILE PLATES of the productions of the EARLY PRINTERS, with the initials COLOURED, and ILLUMINATED in GOLD, in imitation of the Originals, besides nearly 100 cuts on wood of paper marks, &c.

1879 SOTHEBY. Principia Typographica. The Block-Books, or Xylographic Delineations of Scripture History, Issued in Holland, Flanders, and Germany, during the Fifteenth Century, Exemplified and Considered in Connection with the origin of Printing. To which is Added an Attempt to Elucidate the character of the Paper-Marks of the Period. A work contemplated by Samuel Sotheby, and carried out by his son Samuel Leigh Sotheby.
London: Printed for the Author. 1858.

3 *vols.*, *folio*, *half red morocco*, UNCUT. PRIVATELY PRINTED: and 250 *copies only*, 30 of which were presented to Public Libraries.

This copy contains the two leaves, subsequently printed, giving an account of the sale of the edition at Auction, at the upset price of £9. per set, "a result" says Mr. Sotheby, "unparalleled in the annals of literature."

One of the most important works ever produced upon the history of early printing, on which it throws great additional light. It contains an extended examination of the various editions of the block books (or books printed from wooden blocks), the earliest productions of the art, issued in Holland, Flanders, and Germany, such as the Apocalypsis S. Johannis, Biblia Pauperum, Ars Moriendi, Cantica Canticorum, Liber Regum, Temptationes Dæmonum, Ars Memorandi, Endkrist, Quindecim Signa, De Generatione Christi, Miribilia Romæ, etc.

It is not, however, confined to a history of block books, for it gives minute accounts, accompanied by exact fac-similes, of some of the most interesting and rare works printed with movable type in the infancy of the art, such as the Donatuses, Doctrinale, Catonis Disticha, Horarium, Facetiæ Morales, Speculum Humanæ Salvationis, Bartolomæus van de Proprietaten der Dinghen, Exhortatio contra Turcos, Literæ Indulgentiarum, etc. An essay upon early paper marks, illustrated by numerous cuts, concludes the work, which contains upwards of 120 plates, many of them coloured, and more than 200 engravings on wood.

1880 SOTHEBY. Memoranda relating to the Block-Books preserved in the Bibliothèque Impèriale, Paris, made October M.DCCC.LVIII., by Samuel Leigh Sotheby. *London: Printed for the Author.* M.DCCC.LIX.

Folio, half French red morocco, gilt top, UNCUT. PRIVATELY PRINTED, and "NOT FOR SALE." EXCEEDINGLY SCARCE. Uniform in size and binding with the "Principia," to which it forms an indispensable supplement.

1881 SOTO (H. de) Letter of Hernando de Soto, and Memoir of Hernando de Escalante Fontaneda. Translated from the Spanish, by Buckingham Smith. *Washington:* 1854.

Folio, pp. 67. *Map. Half green morocco, gilt top,* UNCUT. An UNLETTERED INDIA PROOF PORTRAIT of DE SOTO *inserted.* PRIVATELY PRINTED. VERY RARE.

"These translations are made from MSS. in the Original Spanish, belonging to the Historical Collection of James Lenox, Esq. One Hundred Copies have been printed for G. W. R [iggs]". *Note by Mr. Smith.*

"Soto conquered the native tribes of Indians of Florida in 1539, and this letter, dated July 9th, 1539, addressed to the Justice and Board of Magistrates of Santiago de Cuba, is the official account of the expedition. The Memoir of Hernando de Escalente Fontaneda was written in Spain about the year 1575, and is endorsed in Spanish: 'Memoir of the things, the shore, and the Indians of Florida, to describe which none of the many persons who have coasted that country have had sufficient knowledge.' These translations are followed by Notes by Mr. Buckingham Smith, who adds a narrative in paragraphs under the head of 'Espiritu Santo Bay,' compiled from both Letter and Memoir, in a consecutive form; and gives a bibliographical list of books and other original writings that treat of the expedition of Soto."—*Trübner.*

Priced in one of Trübner's recent catalogues at £5.5.0.

1882 SOUTH CAROLINA. Extracts from the Journals of the Provincial Congress of South Carolina, held at Charles-Town, June 1st to 22d, 1775. Published by order of the Congress. *South Carolina: Charles-Town, Printed by Peter Timothy.* [1775.]

Sm. 4*to, pp.* 62. *Half brown calf, gilt top,* UNCUT. EXTREMELY RARE in this size. There is an 8vo edition.

1883 SOUTH CAROLINA. Documents connected with the History of South Carolina. Edited by Plowden Charles Jennett Weston. *London: Chiswick Press.* 1856.

Sm. 4*to, pp.* 227. *Facsimile. Half olive morocco, gilt top,* UNCUT. *One hundred copies only printed for* PRIVATE DISTRIBUTION. VERY SCARCE.

Consisting of unpublished documents, beginning with the year 1568, and ending in the last century.

Priced in a recent sale catalogue £ 4.4.0.

1884 SOUTHWICK (F. M.) An Oration, delivered, by Appointment before the Albany and Troy City Guards, and the Common Council of the City of Albany, on the 23d February, 1818. In Commemoration of the Birth of Washington. By Francis M. Southwick. *Albany:* 1818.

8vo, pp. 11. *Half green morocco, gilt top.*

1885 SPARKS (J.) The Life of Gouverneur Morris, with Selections from his Correspondence and Miscellaneous Papers; Detailing Events in the American Revolution, the French Revolution, and in the Political History of the United States. By Jared Sparks. *Boston: Gray & Bowen.* 1832.

3 *vols.*, *8vo, pp. xii.*, 517; *iv.*, 531; *iv.*, 520. *Portrait. Half blue morocco, gilt top,* UNCUT. THREE PORTRAITS *inserted.*

1886 SPARKS. The Library of American Biography. Conducted by Jared Sparks. [First Series. 10 vols.] *New York: Harper & Brothers.* 1854. [Second Series. 15 vols.] *Boston: Little and Brown.* 1844.

25 *vols.*, 12*mo, half olive morocco, gilt top,* UNCUT. THIRTY PORTRAITS *inserted.*

"This work is one of the most interesting in historical literature. It is second, in importance and value, to no series of original works ever printed in this country. Mr. Sparks's labors can not be too highly estimated. His researches have been prosecuted with untiring diligence, and with such success that almost every question within their scope has been definitively settled. The great merits of Mr. Sparks are reverence for truth, soundness of judgment in regard to evidence, and exhausting fullness of detail and illustration."— *Griswold's Prose Writers.*

1887 SPARKS *and* MAHON (*Lord.*) [A complete series of the Pamphlets relating to the Controversy between Jared Sparks and Lord Mahon, respecting Mr. Sparks' Mode of Editing the Writings of Washington. 1852–53.]

6 *vols.*, *8vo, half green morocco;* numbered in their respective order at the bottom of the back of each volume, and consisting of the following:

I. SPARKS. A Reply to the Strictures of Lord Mahon and Others, on the mode of Editing the Writings of Washington. By Jared Sparks. Also, A Review of Lord Mahon's History of the American Revolution. From the North American Review for July, 1852. [By John Gorham Palfrey.] *Boston:* 1852.

pp. 89.

II. SPARKS. A Reply to the Strictures of Lord Mahon and others, on the Mode of Editing the Writings of Washington. By Jared Sparks. *Cambridge:* 1852.

8vo, *pp.* 35.

III. MAHON. Letter to Jared Sparks, Esq.; being a Rejoinder to his "Reply to the Strictures of Lord Mahon and Others on the Mode of Editing the Writings of Washington." By Lord Mahon. *London:* 1852.

pp. 32. Autograph Note written and signed by the AUTHOR *inserted.*

IV. SPARKS. Letter to Lord Mahon, being an Answer to his Letter addressed to the Editor of Washington's Writings. By Jared Sparks. *Boston:* 1852.

pp. 48. Presentation copy with the AUTHOR'S inscription.

V. REED (W. B.) Reprint of the Original Letters from Washington to Joseph Reed, during the American Revolutio- Referred to in the Pamphlets of Lord Mahon and Mr. Sparks. By W iam B. Reed. *Philadelphia:* 1852.

pp 55.

VI. SPARKS. Remarks on a "Reprint of the Original letters from Washington to Joseph Reed, During the American Revolution, referred to in the Pamphlets of Lord Mahon and Mr. Sparks." By Jared Sparks. *Boston:* 1853.

pp. 43.

AN EXCEEDINGLY SCARCE COLLECTION.

See "Washington's Correspondence with Reed." No. 2051.

1888 SPARKS. Catalogue of the Library of Jared Sparks; With a List of bound Historical Manuscripts collected by him, Conditionally Bequeathed to Harvard College, and now deposited in its Library. *Cambridge: Riverside Press.* 1871.

8vo, pp. iv., (2), 230. *Boards,* UNCUT.

Referring to this collection Dr. Cogswell remarked, "in the department of American History, so rich a collection could not now be brought together in a life time, even were a *carte-blanche* order given to an agent." It was sold by private contract to the Cornell University in January, 1872.

1889 [SPECIMEN (A) of the Best Description of Paper, Printing, Engraving and Binding, possible to be obtained in the United States in the year 1818. *New York:* 1818.]

8vo, morocco, gilt edges.

The upper cover is in French red wrinkled morocco, richly gilt and blank tooled; the under one in blue, filleted and blank tooled after a different pattern. A specimen back in red morocco, richly tooled and gilt, is attached to the inside of the upper cover. The plates are proofs, and fine examples of pure line engraving, now become, almost, a lost art.

FROM GABRIEL FURMAN'S COLLECTION.

1890 SPENCE [(Joseph.)] A Parallel; in the Manner of Plutarch: between a most celebrated Man of Florence; and One scarce ever heard of, in England. By the Rev. Mr. Spence. *Printed at Strawberry-Hill, by William Robinson: and Sold by Messieurs Dodsley, for the Benefit of Mr. Hill.* M DCC LVIII.

Sm. 8vo, pp. 104. *Maroon morocco, gilt edges.* FINE COPY. VERY SCARCE.

"A beautiful and curious little volume of which only 700 copies were printed. It was reprinted by Dodsley, but the curious seek only the present edition."—*Dibdin.*

1891 SPENCE. Anecdotes, Observations, and Characters, of Books and Men. Collected from the Conversation of Mr. Pope, and other Eminent Persons of his Time. By the Rev. Joseph Spence. Now first published from the Original Papers, with Notes, and a Life of the Author. By Samuel Weller Singer.

London: W. H. Carpenter. MD.CCC.XX.

8vo, pp. xxxix., (1), 501. *Portrait. Half blue calf.*

"One of the most entertaining volumes of Literary Anecdote imaginable; the materials of which furnished Johnson with much of the Biography of Pope and his Contemporaries."—*Dibdin.*

1892 SPRAGUE (W. B.) Memorials of Mrs. John V. L. Pruyn. By Rev. William B. Sprague, D.D. [And others.] *Albany:* 1859.

4to, half brown morocco, gilt edges. A few copies only printed FOR PRIVATE DISTRIBUTION.

1893 SPRING (S.) God the Author of Human Greatness. A Discourse on the Death of General George Washington; delivered at the North Congregational Church in Newburyport, December 29, 1799, by Samuel Spring, Pastor. *Newburyport:* [1800.]

8vo, pp. 28. SCARCE.

1894 STAPLES (W. R.) The Documentary History of the Destruction of the Gaspee. ... Compiled for the Providence Journal. By Hon. William Staples. *Providence: Knowles, Vose & Co.* 1845.

Roy. 8vo, pp. 56. *Half green morocco, gilt top,* UNCUT. Plate of the "Destruction of the Gaspee" *inserted.*

1895 STARK (C.) Memoir and Official Correspondence of Gen. John Stark, with Notices of several other Officers of the Revolution. Also, a Biography of Capt. Phinehas Stevens, and of Col. Robert Rogers, with an Account of his services in America during the "Seven Years' War." By Caleb Stark. *Concord: G. Parker Lyon.* 1860.

Roy. 8vo, pp. 495. *Portrait. Half green morocco, gilt top, uncut.*

1896 STEARNS (E.) An Eulogium on General George Washington; Spoken at Tolland, on the 22d of February, 1800, at the request of the Inhabitants. By Elisha Stearns Esq. *East Windsor: July* 29, 1800.

12mo, pp. 24. UNCUT *and* VERY RARE.

1897 STEDMAN (C.) History of the Origin, Progress, and Termination of the American War. By C. Stedman, who served under Sir W. Howe, Sir H. Clinton, and the Marquis Cornwallis. *London: Printed for the Author.* 1794.

2 *vols., 4to, pp. xv.,* 399; *xv.,* 449, (13). 15 *Plans. Half blue morocco, gilt top,* UNCUT. An ELEGANT COPY, FRESH and CLEAN as when issued.

Particularly valuable on account of the *large and splendid* MILITARY MAPS and SURVEYS, from the *official originals* by the British engineering staff, with which it is adorned. Fisher's copy sold for $38; Morrell's, $38.

See Clinton (Henry.) No. 404.

1898 [STEDMAN (E. C.)] A Reconstruction Letter. [In Verse.] *New York: Privately Printed.* 1866.

8vo, pp. 13. *Half blue morocco, gilt top,* UNCUT. 130 *copies only printed* FOR PRIVATE DISTRIBUTION.

"Now speaking of Gr—nt I'm sometimes uncertain
As to all he's concealing behind that thick curtain
Of smoke, and in doubt, as we speak from the car,
What he'll say when at last he puts out his cigar."— *Page* 8.

1899 [STEPHEN (James.)] War in Disguise; or, the Frauds of the Neutral Flags. *New York: Hopkins & Seymour.* 1806.

[Also:] An Answer to War in Disguise; or, Remarks on the New Doctrine of England, concerning Neutral Trade. *New York: Hopkins & Seymour.* 1806.

Rich attributes this to Gouverneur Morris.

[And:] An Examination of the British Doctrine, which subjects to Capture a Neutral Trade, not open in Time of Peace. [*n.p. n.d.*]

8vo, 3 pieces in 1 vol., pp. vii., 215; 76; 204. *Half green morocco. Fine copies.*

1900 STEPHENS (J. L.) Incidents of Travel in Central America, Chiapas, and Yucatan. By John L. Stevens. ... Illustrated by Numerous Engravings. *New York: Harper & Brothers.* 1841.

2 *vols., 8vo, pp.* 424; 474. 78 *Plates. Half olive morocco.* LARGE and FINE COPY of the first edition, NOW SCARCE, with BRILLIANT IMPRESSIONS of the plates which are much defaced and worn in the later issues.

"It is difficult to believe that two individuals were capable of such an astonishing amount of labor, as is evidenced in these volumes. The wonderful structures of the race of Indians which once inhabited the peninsula of Central America, are here described by pen and pencil, with great clearness and minuteness. The temples, structures, idols, utensils, builddings and architecture, of that active, intelligent, and almost mythical people, are illustrated by more than seventy large engravings, from drawings by Mr. Catherwood."—*Field.*

1901 STEPHENS. Incidents of Travel in Yucatan. By John L. Stephens. Illustrated by 120 Engravings. *New York: Harper & Brothers.* 1843.

2 *vols., 8vo, pp. xii.,* 9–459; *xvi.,* 9–478. *Half olive morocco.* LARGE and FINE COPY of the first edition, uniform with the preceding No., and with equally fine impressions of the plates.

"One year after the termination of his first explorations, the author set out upon the one, the incidents of which are here narrated. So far from exhausting the antiquities of the peninsula in his first two volumes, these add to our astonishment by portraying the gigantic ruins of still more imposing structures, erected by the vanished race of peninsular aborigines.—" *Field.*

1902 STEPHENS (J.) New Essayes and Characters. With a new Satyre in defence of the Common Law, and Lawyers: Mixt with reproofe against their Enemy Ignoramus. Written by John Stephens the younger, of Lincolnes Inne, Gent. *London: Luke Faune.* 1631.

Sm. 8vo, pp. (17), 434. *Russia, gilt edges, by* ROGER PAYNE. VERY SCARCE. A FINE COPY from Miss Currer's Collection with her book-plate.

Best Edition; comprising besides the Poetical and Prose Essays, Forty-eight Characters, including a Player, Poet, Gamester, Coxcomb, Humorist, Jailor, Witch, Pander, Country Bride and Bridegroom, Falconer, Huntsman, Crafty Scrivener, Tapster, &c.

1903 STEPHENSON (M.) A Call | from | Death to Life, | and | Out of the Dark wayes and Worſhips of the World where | the Seed is held in

Bondage under the Merchants of | Babylon, Written by Marmaduke Stephenſon ;| Who (together with another dear Servant of the Lord called | William Robinſon) hath (ſince the Writing hereof) ſuffer- | ed Death, for bearing Witneſſe to the ſame Truth ,| amongſt the Proffeſ- ſors of Boſtons Juriſdiction | in New England.| With a True Copy of Two Letters, which they Writ to the Lords | People a little before their Death.| And alſo the True Copy of a Letter as it came to our hands, from | a Friend in New England, which gives a brief Relation of the | manner of their Martyrdom, with ſome of the Words which they | expreſt at the time of their ſuffering.| *London, Printed for Thomas Simmons, at the Sign of the | Bull and Mouth near Alderſgate.* 1660.

Sm. 4to, pp. 32. *Crushed red levant morocco, gilt edges, by* F. BEDFORD. An EXCEEDINGLY FINE COPY of this CURIOUS and VERY RARE WORK.

Stephenson was a quaker who came to New England in 1659. He, together with William Robinson and Mrs. Mary Dyer, were arrested for preaching in Boston, and banished thence under pain of death. Returning, they were again arrested; tried before John Endicott, and by him sentenced to death. Stephenson and Robinson suffered the penalty; Mrs. Dyer was reprieved while on the ladder with the halter on her neck. The two men were refused the rites of burial, their bodies being stripped and thrown into a hole, even the privilege of enclosing their grave being denied to their friends. It is difficult to rise from a perusal of this tract without a feeling of intense indignation at the intolerant bigotry and cruelty of the early puritans of New England.

The following is a reprint.

1904 STEPHENSON. A Call from Death to Life, being an account of the sufferings of Marmaduke Stephenson, William Robinson and Mary Dyer, in New England, in the year 1659. *Providence : R. I.* 1865.

Sm. 4to, pp. x., 47. *Half olive morocco, gilt top,* UNCUT. *One hundred copies only* PRIVATELY REPRINTED.

"The following Tract or series of letters takes rank, among literary men, as of the highest rarity, no mention being made of it by the English Prince of Bibliographers, and its existence being utterly ignored by our early writers on the subject of religious persecution in America, unless Besse form an exception."—*Introduction.*

1905 STEVENS (Henry.) American Bibliographer. Parts I. and II. [All published.] *Chiswick :* 1854.

Roy. 8vo, pp. vii., 96. 3 *Plates. Half green morocco, gilt top,* UNCUT. 100 *copies only printed for subscribers.* VERY SCARCE.

Contains large folded facsimiles of the "Earliest known Zylographic Leaf respecting America," believed to be unique; and of the "Plan of the City of Mexico as it existed before the Conquest."

1906 STEVENS. Bibliotheca Americana. American Nuggets, or a Catalogue of Rare and Valuable Books in various Languages relating to the History of America. The Titles Alphabetically Arranged and Carefully Collated. By Henry Stevens. *London : Printed by C. Whittingham for H. Stephani et Amicorum.* 1858.

2 *vols., sm. 8vo, pp.* 805. *Half green morocco, gilt top,* UNCUT.

A UNIQUE COPY of this valuable work; issued without the preface, and with RUBRICATED TITLES entirely different from, and dated four years earlier, than those usually found in the work.

"Printed in the best style of the Chiswick Press, regardless of time, it comprises 2934 Titles given in full, with the collation and price of each work. It was intended as far as it went to be a manual for collectors of this expensive class of books. But it did not go very far, containing as it does, not a selection, but only such books as the author happened to possess at that time. It was intended to supply the deficiencies by additional volumes, but these have never appeared, and probably never will in this form."—*Author.*

1907 [STEVENS.] Bibliotheca Americana. A Catalogue of Books relating to the History and Literature of America. *London:* 1861.

8vo, pp. vi., 273. Half green morocco, gilt top, UNCUT. LARGE PAPER; 250 *copies only* printed.

This, one of the most carefully prepared auction Catalogues ever issued in London, contains 2415 lots with full collations of every work from the "Nuggets," of which indeed it seems to be an abridgment. It forms an almost indispensable aid to the Collector of *Americana.*

1908 STEVENS. Historical and Geographical Notes on the earliest Discoveries in America 1453–1530 with Comments on the earliest Charts and Maps; the Mistakes of the early Navigators and the blunders of the Geographers; the Asiatic Origin of the Atlantic coast line of North America how it crept in and how it crept out of the Maps the whole Illustrated by the Tehuantepec Railway Company's Map of the World on Mercator's Projection and Photo-Lithographic facsimiles of many of the earliest Maps and Charts of America. By Henry Stevens, G.M.B. M.A. &c. *New Haven:* 1869.

8vo, cloth extra, UNCUT. *Seventy-five copies only* printed for sale on Whatman's best hand-made paper; with *frontispiece, one new map of the World,* and photo-lithographic facsimiles of *sixteen* of the *very earliest known maps of America,* arranged on five large sheets of bond paper.

1909 STEVENS. Bibliotheca Historica; or, a Catalogue of Books and Manuscripts relating chiefly to the History and Literature of North and South America; among which is included the larger proportion of the extraordinary Library of the late Henry Stevens, Sr., of Barnet, Vt. Edited, with Introduction and Notes, by Henry Stevens. G.M.B. F.S.A., etc. *Boston:* 1870.

8vo, pp. xvi., 234. Half red morocco, gilt top, UNCUT.

Beautifully printed, and profusely annotated. One of the few bibliographical works which may be read throughout with profit and instruction combined with amusement.

1910 STEVENS. Sebastian Cabot — John Cabot = O Endeavoured by Henry Stevens, G.M.B. etc. ... *Boston:* 1870.

32mo, cloth, UNCUT. *Twenty copies only* PRIVATELY PRINTED *on Whatman's paper.* VERY SCARCE.

See Nicholls (J. F.) No. 1503.

1911 STEVENS. Schedule of 2000 American Historical Nuggets taken from the Stevens Diggings in September, 1870, and set down in chronological order of printing from 1490 to 1800, Described and

Recommended as a Supplement to any Printed Bibliotheca Americana. By Henry Stevens, G.M.B., F.S.A. etc.
Privately Printed: London: Stevens's Bibliographical Nuggetory, Oct. 1, 1870.

4to, pp. (4), 20. *Blue cloth* UNCUT. EXCEEDINGLY SCARCE.

"For five years ... he had scouted through several States during his vacations, prospecting in out of the way places for historical nuggets, mousing through town libraries and country garrets in search of anything old that was historically new for Peter Force and his American Archives. For himself and others he had tramped over many of the scenes of the Old French War and the Revolution, at one time exploring Rogers' Slide, and at another descending, torch in hand, into the wolf-den of Old Put. From Vermont to Delaware many an antiquated churn, sequestered hen-coop, and dilapidated flour barrel had yielded to him rich harvests of old papers, musty books and golden pamphlets." [Author's Account of Himself.] *See Preface.*

1912 STEVENS (J. A.) Colonial Records of the New York Chamber of Commerce, 1768–1784. With Historical and Biographical Sketches by John Austin Stevens, Jr.
New York: J. F. Trow & Co. 1867.

Imp. 8vo, pp. 404, 172. 12 *Portraits,* 2 *Plans, and* 2 *Facsimiles. Half crushed green levant morocco, gilt top,* UNCUT, *by* BRADSTREET. LARGE PAPER. A *few copies only* printed, with the plates on INDIA PAPER, and including FIVE PORTRAITS not in the small paper copies.

1913 STEWART (D.) The Collected Works of Dugald Stewart, Esq., F.R.S.S. Edited by Sir William Hamilton, Bart.
Edinburgh: Thomas Constable and Co. 1854.

10 *vols., 8vo, calf antique.* An elegant copy of the ONLY COMPLETE COLLECTED EDITION, beautifully printed on toned paper.

1914 STILES (E.) A History of three of the Judges of King Charles I. Major-General Whalley, Major-General Goffe, and Colonel Dixwell: Who, at the Restoration, 1660, Fled to America; and were secreted and concealed, in Massachusetts and Connecticut, for near thirty years. With an Account of Mr. Theophilus Whale, of Narragansett, Supposed to have been also one of the Judges. By President Stiles. *Hartford: Printed by Elisha Babcock.* 1794.

12mo, pp. 357. 9 *Plates. Half gray calf, red edges.* An unusually LARGE, FINE and CLEAN COPY of this VERY SCARCE WORK.

1915 STILLMAN (S.) A Sermon Occasioned by the Death of George Washington, late Commander-in Chief, of the Armies of the United States of America, who Died December 14, 1799, Aged 68. By Samuel Stillman, D.D., Minister of the First Baptist Church in Boston. *Boston:* [1800.]

8vo, pp. 26. UNCUT.

1916 STITH (W.) The | History | of the | First Discovery | and | Settlement | of | Virginia: | Being | An Essay towards a General | History of this Colony. | By William Stith A.M. | Rector of Henrico Parish, and one of the Governors of | William and Mary College. | *Williamsburg:* | *Printed by William Paris.* M,DCC,XLVII.

8vo, pp. viii., 331, *v.,* (1), 34. *Crushed green levant morocco, paneled and gilt sides, corner ornaments, edges gilt in the round, by* F. BEDFORD. A remarkably LARGE, FINE and COMPLETE COPY of the FIRST and BEST edition. EXCEEDINGLY SCARCE.

The valuable original documents from which this history was compiled have recently been destroyed by fire. The appendix contains a collection of charters relating to the period comprised in the volume. Besides the copious materials of Stith, the author derived assistance from the manuscripts of his uncle, Sir John Randolph, and from the records of the London Company, put into his hands by Colonel William Byrd, President of the Council.

Notwithstanding the recent efforts of American bibliographers, the bibliography of this subject remains in as much doubt and obscurity as ever. We briefly remark, that, there are two varieties of the first edition, one on *coarse*, the other on *fine* paper, except signature x which is more or less poor in both. Then we have another Williamsburgh edition of the same date, but differing in several particulars. Lastly comes the London edition of 1753, which is precisely like the second Williamsburgh issue. It is not at all unlikely that the so-called London edition is the second Williamsburgh one with an English title page.

1917 STOBO (*Major* R.) Memoirs of Major Robert Stobo of the Virginia Regiment. [Edited by Neville B. Craig.] *Pittsburgh: John S. Davidson.* 1854.

18mo, pp. 92. *Plan. Half morocco.*

Stobo was held as a hostage for many years by the French at Quebec. The Plan of Fort Du Quesne was made from the original manuscript drawing by Stobo, in the possession of Mr. W. M. Darlington.

1918 STOKES (A.) A Narrative of the Official Conduct of Anthony Stokes, of the Inner Temple, London, Barrister at Law, His Majesty's Chief Justice, and one of his Council of Georgia; and of the Dangers and Distresses he underwent in the cause of Government: some Copies of which are Printed for the Information of his Friends. [*London:* 1784.]

8vo, pp. 112. *Half red morocco, gilt top.* Fine copy. RARE.

The author of this rare and curious work was the Last Royal Chief Justice of Georgia. When he arrived in the Colony many of the first settlers were alive, and in conversation with them he gleaned many interesting historical facts. In 1778 his estate was confiscated.— See *Sabine's Loyalists.*

1919 STONE (E. M.) The invasion of Canada in 1775: including the Journal of Capt. Simeon Thayer, describing the Perils and Sufferings of the Army under Col. Benedict Arnold, in its March through the Wilderness to Quebec. With Notes and Appendix. By Edward M. Stone. *Providence: Knowles Anthony & Co.* 1867.

4to, pp. xxiv., 104. *Map, and* 2 *Portraits. Half green morocco, gilt top,* UNCUT, *by* BRADSTREET. PRIVATELY PRINTED. One of *a few copies only* on LARGE PAPER. TWO PORTRAITS *inserted.*

1920 STONE (W. L.) The Poetry and History of Wyoming; containing Campbell's Gertrude, with a Biographical Sketch of the Author, by Washington Irving; and the History of Wyoming, from its Discovery to the beginning of the present Century. By William L. Stone. *New York: Wiley and Putnam.* 1841.

12mo, pp. xxiv., 324. 9 *Engravings. Half calf.* An Autograph Note written and signed by THOMAS CAMPBELL, respecting the use of the woodcuts for this edition *inserted.*

1921 STONE. Uncas and Miantonomoh. A Historical Discourse delivered at Norwich, Conn., on the fourth day of July, 1842, on the occasion of the erection of a Monument to the memory of Uncas, the white man's friend, and first Chief of the Mohegans. By William L. Stone. *New York: Dayton & Newman.* 1842.

18mo, pp. 209. *Cloth.* SCARCE.

1922 STONE. Life of Joseph Brant (Thayendanegea), including the Border Wars of the American Revolution, and Sketches of the Indian Campaigns of General Harmer, St. Clair, and Wayne, and other matters connected with the Indian Relations of the United States and Great Britain, from the Peace of 1783 to the Indian Peace of 1795. By William L. Stone. *Albany: J. Munsell.* 1864.

2 *vols., roy. 8vo, pp. xxxi.,* 500; *vii.,* 630. 2 *Portraits. Half purple morocco, gilt top,* UNCUT. LARGE PAPER, *fifty copies only printed,* with the portraits on INDIA PAPER.

1923 STONE. The Life and Times of Sir William Johnson, Bart. By William L. Stone. *Albany: J. Munsell.* 1865.

2 *vols., roy. 8vo, pp. xxxi.,* 555; *xv.,* 544. *Portrait. Half blue morocco, gilt top,* UNCUT. One of *fifty copies only* on LARGE PAPER, with the portrait on INDIA PAPER.

"The life of the celebrated royal superintendent of Indian affairs, for a period of forty years, beginning in 1738, is full of material for Indian history. By far the most valuable contributions to it are contained in the Appendix, in which are printed for the first time, and from the original MSS., two Journals, kept by Sir William, of expeditions to Niagara, Oswego, and Detroit, through the cantonments of the Six Nations, and the Ottawa Confederacy, &c."—*Field.*

1924 STONE. The Life and Times of Sa-Go-Ye-Wat-Ha, or Red Jacket. By the late William L. Stone. With a Memoir of the Author, by his Son. *Albany: J. Munsell.* 1866.

Roy. 8vo, pp. viii., 509. 2 *Portraits. Half red morocco, gilt top,* UNCUT. *One of fifty copies on* LARGE PAPER, with the Portraits on INDIA PAPER.

The "Life of Red Jacket," is in fact a portion—the concluding one—of the history of the Six Nations. The volume has therefore a general historical as well as a personal biographical interest.

1925 STONINGTON. The Defence of Stonington (Connecticut) against a British Squadron, August 9th to 12th, 1814. *Hartford:* 1864.

Sm. 4to, pp. 54. *Half blue morocco, gilt top,* UNCUT. 125 *copies only* printed for PRIVATE DISTRIBUTION.

1926 STORK (William.) An Account of East Florida, with a Journal, kept by John Bartram of Philadelphia, Botanist to His Majesty for the Floridas; Upon A Journey from St. Augustine up the River St. Johns. *London: W. Nicoll.* [1766.]

8vo, pp. 70. *Half olive morocco, gilt top,* UNCUT. SCARCE.

1927 STORY (J.) An Eulogy on General Washington, written at the request of the inhabitants of Marblehead, and delivered before them on the Second day of January, 1800, by Joseph Story, A.B.
Salem : 1800.

8vo, pp. 24. *Elegy* 8. UNCUT.

1928 STRACHEY (W.) The Historie of Travaille into Virginia Britannia; expressing the Cosmographie and Comodities of the Country, together with the Manners and Customes of the People. Gathered and observed as well by those who went first thither as collected by William Strachey, Gent., the first Secretary of the Colony. Now first Edited from the original Manuscript in the British Museum, by R. H. Major, Esq.
London : Printed for the Hakluyt Society. M.DCCC.XLIX.

8vo, pp. viii., xxxvi., (4), 203. *Map, and* 6 *Plates. Half purple morocco, gilt top,* UNCUT.

The preface gives an historical account of early English Navigators to America, and their colonizations, particularly in Virginia. It includes a "Letter from Lord Delawarr, Governor of Virginia," giving an account of his voyage out, and of his proceedings since his arrival in Virginia. (He left Plymouth 1st of April, and dates his letter July 7th, 1610.) The History has a 2nd book, "Entreating of the first discoveries of the Colony, and of the first Colonie upon the Island of Roanoak. As also of the Northern Colonie, seated upon the River of Sachadehoc, anno 1585."

"Book I. was written probably some years before Captain John Smith's *General History of Virginia*, and is more especially remarkable as having afforded Mr. Deane and Mr. Niel the data upon which to charge the name of Pocahontas with infamy."—*Field.*

1929 STORY. (J.) An Eulogy on the Glorious Virtues of the Illustrious Gen. George Washington, who Died at Mount Vernon, December 14th, 1799, in the 68th year of his age, ripe in Honor and full of Glory. Written at the Request of the Inhabitants of Sterling, and delivered before them on Saturday, the 22d of February, 1800. By Isaac Story, M.A. *Worcester :* 1800.

8vo, pp. 23. UNCUT. VERY RARE.

1930 [STRICKLAND (W.)] The Tomb of Washington, at Mount Vernon. *Philadelphia : Carey and Hart.* 1840.

8vo, pp. 76. 4 *Plates. Half green morocco.* FIVE ILLUSTRATIONS *inserted.*

1931 STRONG (J.) A Sermon, Preached at Norwich, on Hearing of the Death of General George Washington, who died Dec. 14th, 1799. Ætat 68. By Joseph Strong, Pastor of the First Church in Norwich. *Norwich :* 1800.

8vo, pp. (4), 17. RARE.

1932 STRONG (N.) A Discourse Delivered on Friday, December 27, 1799, the Day set apart by the Citizens of Hartford to Lament before God the Death of Gen. George Washington, who Died Dec. 14, 1799. By Nathan Strong. ... *Hartford:* 1800.

8vo, pp. 31. UNCUT.

1933 STUART (I. W.) Life of Captain Nathan Hale the Martyr-Spy of the American Revolution. By I. W. Stuart. With Illustrations. *Hartford: F. A. Brown.* 1856.

12mo, pp. 230, (2). *Half green morocco, gilt top.*

Hale's Diary, in the Appendix, is a valuable contribution to our literature of the Revolution.

1934 SULLIVAN (James.) The History of the District of Maine. By James Sullivan. Illustrated by a New and Correct Map of the District. *Boston: I. Thomas and E. T. Andrews.* 1795.

8vo, pp. vii., 421. *Map. Half crushed green levant morocco, gilt top,* UNCUT, *by* F. BEDFORD. PORTRAIT of HUMPHREY GILBERT *inserted.* A very superior copy, and MOST RARE in this fine *uncut* state.

1935 SULLIVAN (W.) The Public Men of the Revolution. Including Events from the Peace of 1783 to the Peace of 1815. In a Series of Letters. By the late Hon. William Sullivan, LL.D. With a Biographical Sketch of the Author, and Additional Notes and References, by his Son, John T. S. Sullivan. *Philadelphia: Carey and Hart.* 1847.

8vo, pp. 463. *Portrait. Half green morocco, gilt top,* UNCUT. A UNIQUE COPY with SIXTY-TWO ILLUSTRATIONS (mostly portraits) *inserted.*

1936 SUMNER (C. P.) Eulogy on the Illustrious George Washington, Pronounced at Milton, Twenty-Second February, 1800. By Charles Pinckney Sumner. *Dedham:* 1800.

8vo, pp. 24. *First Edition.*

1937 SWETT (S.) History of Bunker Hill Battle. With a Plan. By S. Swett. Third Edition. With Notes, and Likenesses of the Principal Officers. *Boston: Munroe and Francis.* 1827.

8vo, pp. 58, 34. *Plan. Half crimson morocco, gilt top,* UNCUT. VERY SCARCE in this condition. The *Likenesses* promised in the title never appeared in any edition.

1938 SWETT. Who was the Commander at Bunker Hill? With remarks on Frothingham's History of the Battle. With an Appendix. By S. Swett. *Boston: John Wilson.* 1850.

8vo, pp. 39. *Half crimson morocco, gilt top,* UNCUT. PORTRAIT *inserted.* PRIVATELY PRINTED. RARE.

1939 **Syllacius (Nicolaus.) De Insulis Meridiani atque Indici Maris nuper inventis.** With a Translation into English by the Rev. John Mulligan, A.M. *New York:* 1859.

Roy. 4to, pp. xviii., 105, *lxiii. Engraved bust of Columbus. Red morocco, rich gold filleted sides, broad inside gilt borders, morocco joints, gilt edges. One hundred and sixty copies* PRIVATELY PRINTED for Mr. James Lenox *strictly for presentation.* EXCEEDINGLY RARE.

The original edition of this letter of Syllacius, relating to the second voyage of Columbus, was printed in 1494 or 1495, and only two copies are known, one of which is in the possession of Mr. James Lenox. The translation is preceded by an Introduction by Mr. Lenox, and followed by the Notes of the translator; together with a letter of Dr. Chanca, physician of Sevilla, and companion of Columbus on this voyage, first published in Spanish by Navarrete in 1837. The volume concludes with a copious and interesting bibliographical notice of the early accounts of Columbus' voyages, by Mr. Lenox, illustrated by numerous large engravings and facsimiles. In this VERY BEAUTIFUL PRODUCTION the original text of the letter of Syllacius is printed in Gothic type on one page, with the translation on the opposite.

1940 SYMMES (T.) Historical Memoirs | Of the Late Fight at | Piggwacket, | with a | Sermon | Occasion'd by the Fall of the Brave | Capt. John Lovewell | And Several of his Valiant Company, | in the Late | Heroic Action there. | Pronounc'd at Bradford, May 16, 1725. | By Thomas Symmes, V.D.M. | The Second Edition Corrected. | *Boston in New England: | Printed by B. Green, Jun. for S. Gerrish, near the | Brick Meeting-House in Cornhill.* 1725.

Sm. 8vo, half title, title, pp. xii., 32. Crushed red levant morocco, gilt edges, by F. BEDFORD. EXCESSIVELY RARE, and ONE OF THE FINEST COPIES EXTANT.

This is the same copy which produced $165 at Mr. Morrell's sale, and $175 at the disposal of Mr. Roche's collection, the highest price known to have been paid for any volume of its size at an American sale.

1941 SYMMES. The Original Account of Capt. John Lovewell's "Great Fight" with the Indians at Pequawket, May 8, 1725; by Rev. Thomas Symmes, of Bradford, Mass. A New Edition with Notes, by Nathaniel Bouton. ... *Concord: N. H. P. B. Cogswell.* 1861.

Sm. 4to, pp. 48. Map. Half red morocco, gilt top, by BRADSTREET. The Editor's own copy, with an Autograph Note written and signed by him *inserted.*

"The very rare tract of which this is a reprint, entitled, 'Lovewell Lamented; or a Sermon occasioned by the fall of the brave Capt. John Lovewell,' is a favorite object of competition among book collectors. Only one perfect copy, and that of the second edition, has been sold at public auction for many years, it has been three times offered in that manner, and at the last public bidding was bought for $175."—*Field.*

1942 TAILFER (P.) A True and Historical | Narrative | of the Colony of | Georgia | In America, | From the first Settlement thereof until | this present Period: | Containing | The most authentick Facts, Matters and Trans- | actions therein; | Together with | His Majesty's Charter, Representations of the | People, Letters, &c. | And | a Dedi-cation to his Excellency General Oglethorpe. | By | Pat. Tailfer, M.D. | Hugh Anderson, M.A. | Dr. Douglass, and others, | Landholders in Georgia, at Present in Charles-Town in South- | Carolina. | ... | *Charles-Town, South Carolina: | Printed by P. Timothy, for the Authors,* M.DCC.XLI.

8vo, pp. xviii., 118. Mottled calf, yellow edges, by F. BEDFORD. *An elegant copy.* VERY SCARCE.

"Reprinted in London, without a date, but probably in the same year. It places the conduct of General Oglethorpe in a very different light from that in which it has generally been represented. It has been said that it shows him in his true colours."—*Rich.*

The work contains some curious and remarkable particulars relating to the conduct of Rev. John Wesley during his mission to Georgia.—*See pp.* 41–48.

1943 TALBOT (S.) An Historical Sketch, to the end of the Revolutionary War, of the Life of Silas Talbot, Esq. of the State of Rhode-Island, lately Commander of the United States Frigate, the Constitution, and of an American Squadron in the West Indies. *New York: H. Caritat.* 1803.

12*mo, pp.* (8), 147. *Half green morocco, gilt top,* UNCUT. An AUTOGRAPH LETTER written and signed by TALBOT, with his PORTRAIT and those of two others *inserted.* RARE in any condition, especially so in this *fine uncut state.*

1944 TALMADGE (B.) Memoir of Col. Benjamin Talmadge, prepared by Himself, at the request of his Children. *New York:* 1858.

8*vo, pp.* 70. *Portrait. Half blue morocco, gilt top,* UNCUT. A UNIQUE COPY with upwards of SIXTY PORTRAITS, VIEWS, &c. *inserted.* PRIVATELY PRINTED. VERY SCARCE, not half a dozen copies having been offered at public sale since its issue, and it is unattainable in any other way.

1945 TARLETON (B.) A History of the Campaigns of 1780 and 1781, in the Southern Provinces of North America. By Major-General Tarleton, Commandant of the late British Legion. The Second Edition. *London: T. Cadell, Jun.* M.DCC.XCVI.

4*to, pp.* 17, (1), *vii.,* (1), 518. *Map and* 5 *Plans. Half green morocco, gilt top,* UNCUT. Fine full length PORTRAIT of the AUTHOR *inserted.* A SPLENDID COPY.

Second and BEST EDITION, which embraces much matter not included in the first, together with an exposition of the motives which prompted the production of the work.

"Colonel Tarleton's History gives a minute detail of all the military operations in both Carolinas, and part of Virginia, until the surrender of Lord Cornwallis with his whole army at Yorktown, Oct. 19, 1781."—*Rich.*

See Mackenzie (R.) No. 1306.

1946 [TAYLOR (George.)] Martyrs to the Revolution in the British Prison-Ships in the Wallabout Bay. *New York: W. H. Arthur & Co.* 1855.

8*vo, pp.* 64. *Map. Half green morocco, gilt top.* SCARCE. "The Dungeons of the Revolution," and "The Martyr's Burial," by J. A. Patten, mounted and inlaid on eight leaves by TRENT, and four engravings *inserted.*

For other works relating to this subject *see* Nos. 1484, 1485, and 1721.

1947 TAYLOR (I.) History of the Transmission of Ancient Books to Modern Times; or, a concise Account of the Means by which the Genuineness and Authenticity of Ancient Historical Works are ascertained: with an Estimate of the comparative value of the Evidence usually adduced in Support of the Claims of the Jewish and Christian Scriptures. By Isaac Taylor. *London: J. B. Holdsworth.* 1827.

8*vo, pp. vi.,* 266. *Half green morocco, gilt top,* UNCUT. FINE COPY. SCARCE.

1948 TERNAUX (H.) Bibliothèque Américaine ou Catalogue des Ouvrages relatifs à l' Amérique qui ont paru depuis sa découverte jusqu'à l' an 1700. Par H. Ternuax.
Paris: Arthus-Bertrand. M.DCCC.XXXVIII.

4to, pp. viii., 191. Half green morocco, gilt top, UNCUT. LARGE PAPER. *A few copies only printed.* VERY SCARCE.

"This catalogue contains 1153 articles: the few notes added by Mr. Ternaux, cause a regret that he has been so sparing of them." — *Rich.*

1949 THACHER (J.) A Military Journal during the American Revolutionary War, from 1775 to 1783, describing Interesting Events and Transactions of this Period, with numerous Historical Facts and Anecdotes, from the Original Manuscript. To which is added, An Appendix, containing Biographical Sketches of several General Officers. By James Thacher, M.D. ...
Boston: Richardson and Lord. 1823.

8vo, pp. 603. Half calf, gilt top, UNCUT. TWO PORTRAITS *inserted.* FINE COPY. SCARCE.

1950 THACHER. An Essay on Demonology, Ghosts and Apparitions, and Popular Superstitions. Also, An Account of the Witchcraft Delusion at Salem, in 1692. By James Thacher, M.D. ...
Boston: Carter and Hendee. M DCCC XXXI.

12mo, pp. v., 234. Crimson morocco, gilt top, UNCUT, *by* W. MATTHEWS. *An elegant copy.* SCARCE.

More than half of the volume is occupied by a description of the Salem Witchcraft Fraud.

1951 THACHER (P.) An Oration Delivered at Watertown, March 5, 1776. To Commemorate The Bloody Massacre at Boston: Perpetrated March 5, 1770. By Peter Thacher, A.M.
Watertown: Benjamin Edes. MDCCLXXVI.

4to, pp. 15. Half red morocco, gilt top, UNCUT, *by* W. PRATT. RARE.

Of all the Thirteen *Boston Massacre Orations*, this one at Watertown, while Boston was in the hands of the Enemy, is the rarest.

1952 THACHER. A Sermon, Occasioned by the Death of General George Washington, and preached February 22, 1800, By their direction, Before His Honor Moses Gill, Esq. Commander in Chief, the Honorable Council, the Honorable Senate and House of Representatives of the Commonwealth of Massachusetts. By Peter Thacher, D.D. ... *Boston:* [1800.]

8vo, pp. 21. UNCUT. SCARCE.

1953 THACHER (T.) An Eulogy on George Washington, First President of the United States, and late Commander in Chief of the American Army, who Died December 14, 1799. Delivered at Dedham, February 22, 1800, at the Request of the Inhabitants of said Town. By Thomas Thacher, A.M. *Dedham:* 1800.

8vo, pp. 22. UNCUT. SCARCE.

1954 THACHER (T. C.) An Eulogy on the memory of Gen. George Washington, who died December 14, 1799, aged 68. Pronounced at the request of the citizens of Lynn, Jan. 13, 1800. By Thomas Cushing Thacher, A.M. *Boston:* [1800.]

8vo, pp. 12. UNCUT.

1955 THATCHER (B. B.) Memoir of Phillis Wheatley, a Native African and a Slave, By B. B. Thatcher. *Boston: Geo. W. Light.* 1834.

18*mo, pp.* 36. *Portrait. Half green morocco, gilt top.*

1956 [THATCHER (B. B.)] Traits of the Tea Party; being a Memoir of George R. T. Hewes, one of the last of its Survivors; with a History of that Transaction; Reminiscences of the Massacre, and the Siege, and other Stories of Old Times. By a Bostonian. *New York: Harper & Brothers.* 1835.

12*mo, pp.* 265. *Portrait. Half calf. Numerous wood-cuts inserted.*

"What furies raged, when you in sea,
In shape of Indians, drowned the Tea."— *McFingal.*

1957 THOMAS (G.) An Hiftorical and Geographical Account | of the | Province and Country | of | Penfilvania; | and of | Weft-New-Jerfey | in | America. | The Richnefs of the Soil, the Sweetnefs of the Situation | the Wholefomnefs of the Air, the Navigable Rivers, and | others, the prodigious Encreafe of Corn, the flourifhing | Condition of the City of Philadelphia, with the ftately | Buildings, and other Improvements there. The ftrange | Creatures, as Birds, Beafts, Fifhes, and Fowls, with the | feveral forts of Minerals, Purging Waters, and Stones, | lately difcovered. The Natives, Aborigines, their Lang | uage, Religion, Laws, and Cuftoms; The firft Planters, | the Dutch, Sweeds, and Englifh, with the number of | its Inhabitants; As alfo a Touch upon George Keith's | New Religion, in his fecond Change fince he left the | Quakers. | With a Map of both Countries. | By Gabriel Thomas, who refided there about Fifteen Years. | *London, Printed for, and Sold by A. Baldwin, at | the Oxon Arms in Warwick Lane.* 1698.

[Followed by:] An Historical Description | of the | Province and Country | of | West-New-Jersey | in | America. | ... | Never made Publick till now. | By Gabriel Thomas. | *London:* | *Printed in the Year* 1698.

Sm. 8vo, pp. (8), 55; (12), 34. *Map. Crushed purple levant morocco, edges gilt on carmine, by* F. BEDFORD. LARGE and BEAUTIFUL COPY. EXTREMELY RARE.

The writer paid $300, for a copy at Auction in New York, in March, 1873, and has since sold another for a similar sum.— The author was a "friend" concerning whom little is known. He remarks "I have endeavour'd to persuade the poor, the idle and the lazy, and the vagabonds of these kingdoms and of Wales, to hasten thither, that they may live plentifully and happily, and I doubt not but they will harkin to it."

1958 THOMAS. An Historical and Geographical Account of the Province and Country of Pensilvania; and of West-New-Jersey, in

America. *New York: Reprinted for Henry Austin Brady.* 1848.

Folio, pp. (8), 55. *Map.* (12), 34. *Half brown morocco, gilt top,* UNCUT. LARGE PAPER.

Of this rare facsimile reprint TEN COPIES ONLY were issued on large paper.

1959 THOMAS. An Historical and Geographical Account, &c. [Another copy.] *New York:* ... 1848.

Sm. 8vo, pp. (8), 55. *Map.* (12), 34. *Cloth.* This copy has the MAP frequently wanting in the small paper copies.

1960 THOMAS (I.) A Specimen of Isaiah Thomas's Printing Types. Being as large and complete an Assortment as is to be met with in any one Printing-Office in America. Chiefly Manufactured by that great Artist William Caslon, Esq.; of London. *Printed at Worcester, Massachusetts: by Isaiah Thomas.* MDCCLXXXV.

8vo, pp. 42. *Half brown morocco, carmine edges.* Printed on one side only. CURIOUS and VERY RARE.

A striking illustration of the progress of the art of printing in America, may be obtained by a comparison of this specimen book of the Historian of the American press, and the printer *par excellence* of his day, with those of Messrs. Rand and Avery, [No. 1669.] and J. F. Trow, [No. 1989.] in this Collection.

1961 THOMAS. The History of Printing in America. With a Biography of Printers, and an Account of Newspapers. To which is prefixed a Concise View of the Discovery and Progress of the Art in other parts of the World. In Two Volumes. By Isaiah Thomas, Printer, Worcester, Massachusetts.
Worcester: From the Press of Isaiah Thomas Jun. 1810.

2 vols., 8vo, pp. 487; 576. *Half blue morocco, gilt top,* UNCUT. TWO FINE PORTRAITS of the AUTHOR *inserted.*

This valuable work, written and published in advance of the time, met with no favour, and was quickly forgotten. Shortly after its issue the remainder of the edition was purchased, on a venture, by the late W. Gowans and an associate, at twenty-five cents per volume in the sheets, and an arrangement made with a bookbinder to put the stock into boards, the whole of which, with the exception of a copy that Mr. Gowans had retained for himself, was returned *cut down* almost to the head-lines; an incident to which Mr. Gowans never referred without an emphatic expression of indignation. *This copy* was bound from the sheets so reserved, and which, for many years Mr. Gowans refused to exhibit, or to part with, at any price. It is clean and fresh as when published, and there is no finer copy extant.

1962 THOMPSON (B. F.) The History of Long Island; from its Discovery and Settlement, to the Present Time. With many Important and Interesting Matters. ... By Benjamin F. Thompson. Second Edition: Revised and greatly Enlarged.
New York: Gould, Banks & Co. 1843.

2 vols., 8vo, pp. 511; 554. *Portrait, Map, and* 14 *Plates. Half green morocco, gilt top,* UNCUT, *by* BRADSTREET.

1963 THOMSON (*Mrs.* [A. T.]) Memoirs of the Jacobites of 1715 and 1745. By Mrs. Thomson. *London: Richard Bentley.* 1845.

2 vols., 8vo, pp. xxv., 390; 388. 4 *Portraits. Half green morocco, gilt top,* UNCUT. Uniform with Jesse's Works, *supra.*

1964 [THOMSON (Charles.)] An Enquiry into the Causes of the Alienation of the Delaware and Shawanese Indians from the British Interest, And into the Measures taken for recovering their Friendship. Extracted from the Public Treaties, and other Authentic Papers relating to the Transactions of the Government of Pensilvania and the said Indians, for near Forty Years; and explained by a Map of the Country. Together with the remarkable Journal of Christian Frederic Post, by whose Negotiations, among the Indians on the Ohio, they were withdrawn from the Interest of the French, who thereupon abandoned the Fort and Country. With Notes by the Editor explaining sundry Indian Customs, &c. Written in Pensylvania. *London: J. Wilkie.* MDCCLIX.

8vo, pp. 184. *Map. Half red morocco, gilt top, by* BRADSTREET. FINE COPY. VERY SCARCE.

Concerning the work *see* Field's *Indian Bibliography*, No. 1548.

See Post (C. F.) No. 1619.

1965 THOMSON (J. L.) Historical Sketches of the Late War, between the United States and Great Britain; blended with Anecdotes illustrative of the Individual Bravery of the American Sailors, Soldiers, and Citizens, Embellished with Portraits of the most Distinguished Naval and Military Officers; and accompanied by Views of several Sieges and Engagements. By John Lewis Thomson. Third Edition. *Philadelphia: Thomas Desilver.* 1816.

12mo, pp. 368. 9 *Portraits,* 4 *Views. Blue morocco, gilt edges.* FINE COPY of one of the RAREST and BEST BOOKS relating to the war of 1812.

1966 [THOMSON (William.)] Memoirs of the Life and Gallant Exploits of the Old Highlander, Serjeant Donald Macleod, who, having returned, wounded, with the Corpse of General Wolfe, from Quebec, was admitted an outpensioner of Chelsea Hospital, in 1759; and is now in the CIII.d Year of his Age. *London:* MDCCXCI.

8vo, pp. 90. *Portrait. Half blue levant morocco, gilt top,* UNCUT, *by* W. MATTHEWS. *Beautiful copy.* VERY SCARCE.

1967 [THOMSON.] Memoirs of Sergeant Donald Macleod. Third Edition. *London:* MDCCXCI.

Sm. 8vo, pp. 96. *Half red morocco, gilt top,* UNCUT. FINE COPY. VERY SCARCE.

1968 THORBURN (G.) Forty Years' Residence in America: or the Doctrine of a Particular Providence exemplified in the Life of Grant Thorburn, Seedsman, New York. Written by Himself. *Boston: Russell, Odiorne & Metcalf.* 1834.

12mo, pp. 264. *Half green morocco.* PORTRAIT *inserted.*

1969 THORBURN. Fifty Years' Reminisences of New York, or Flowers from the Garden of Laurie Todd: ... Including Tales of the Sugar-

House [Prison] in Liberty-street; the Yellow Fever in New York, from 1798 to 1822; Traditions and Anecdotes of the War of the Revolution, etc. Obtained from Actors in the Scenes.
New York: Daniel Fanshaw: [1845.]

12mo, pp. 287. *Half green morocco.* AUTOGRAPH *of the* AUTHOR *inserted.*

1970 THORBURN. Life and Writings of Grant Thorburn: Prepared by Himself. *New York: Edward Walker.* 1852.

12mo, pp. 276. *Portrait. Half green morocco.* An AUTOGRAPH LETTER, written by the AUTHOR on three pages of foolscap, in which he gives some characteristic and very curious particulars of his life *inserted.*

1971 THOROVVGOOD (T.) | Jevvs In America, | or, | Probabilities | That the Americans are of | that Race. | With the Removall of some | contrary reasonings and earnest de- | sires for effectuall endeavours to | make them Christian. | Proposed by Tho: Thorovvgood, B.D. one of the | Assembly of Divines. | .... | *London, Printed by W. H. for Tho. Slater, and are to be Sold | at his Shop at the Signe of the Angel in Duck Lane,* 1650.

Sm. 4*to, pp.* (40), 136, (3). *Bright olive morocco, gilt edges.* LARGE and FINE COPY. VERY RARE.

Mr. Field remarks: "This is the first dissertation in English, on that fertile subject of controversy and hypothesis, the origin of the American Indians. The Puritans of New England awoke to it with a zeal, untempered by the knowledge that keener intellects and higher scholarship, had been stimulated by its attractive mystery a century before. They seem to have been unaware that Las Casas, Torquemada, Garcia, and Herrera, Grotius, Horn, and De Laet, had wrought the vein until all the metal was exhausted. But a new cycle of disputation now commenced, and in 1652, Thorowgood's treatise was answered by Harmon L'Estrange, in a tract entitled *Americans no Jews.* London, 1652." Thorowgood made his replication in the following work.

1972 THOROWGOOD. | Jews | In | America, | Or | Probabilities, that those Indians are | Judaical, made more probable by some Ad- | ditionals to the former Conjectures. | An Accurate Discourse is premised of | Mr. John Elliot, (who first preached the Gospel | to the Natives in their own Language) touching | their Origination, and his Vindication of the | Planters. | .... | Tho. Thorowgood S.T.B. Norfolciencis. |
London, | Printed for Henry Brome at the Gun in Ivie-lane. 1660.

Sm. 4*to, pp.* (10), 33, (4), 22, 67. *Bright olive morocco, gilt edges.* LARGE and FINE COPY. VERY RARE. *Uniform with the preceding No.* The title to this volume has, by some, been thought to be a *facsimile*, it will therefore be sold without reference to the genuineness of the title-page.

"The first work of Thorowgood printed in 1650, was sharply answered by Harmon L'Estrange. To recover the ground from which he had been driven, Thorowgood brought to his aid the Indian apostle Eliot, and their essays are joined in this replication."—*Field.*

1973 THOUGHTS on the Cause of the Present Discontents. ... The Fifth Edition. *London: J. Dodsley.* 1775.

First published in 1770.

[Also :] Observations on a Pamphlet, entitled, Thoughts on the Cause of the Present Discontents. By Catherine Macaulay. The Third Edition Corrected. *London: E. and C. Dilly.* 1770.

8vo, 2 pieces in 1 vol., pp. 118; 31. *Half olive morocco.* VERY SCARCE.

1974 [TICKELL (Richard.)] Anticipation: Containing the Substance of His M——y's Most Gracious Speech to both H——s of P——l——t, on the Opening of the approaching Session, together with a full and authentic Account of the Debate which Will take Place in the H——e of C——s, on the Motion for the Address, and the Amendment. With Notes. (First published three days before the opening of the Session.) The Third Edition Corrected. *London: T. Becket.* 1778.

8vo, pp. (8), 74. *Half blue morocco, carmine edges. Fine copy.* SCARCE.

"That which raised him (Tickell) to immediate celebrity was his admirable political pamphlet, called *Anticipation*; in which, with the most successful humour, he imitated the manner of the principal speakers in parliament, and defeated the force of the arguments of the opposition by pre-occupying them."—*Chalmers' Biog. Dict.*

It may not be uninteresting to add that Tickell believed in anticipation; he committed suicide.

1975 [TICKELL.] The Green Box of Monsieur De Sartine, found at Mademoiselle Du The's Lodgings. From the French of the Hague Edition. Revised and Corrected by those of Leipsic and Amsterdam. The Fifth Edition. *London: A. Becket.* 1779.

8vo, pp. 71. *Half green morocco, gilt top, by* BRADSTREET. *Elegant copy.* VERY SCARCE.

A curious satirical work bearing upon the prominent French and American actors in the American Revolution; Franklin, Arnold, Deane, Maurepas, de Estaing, &c.

1976 TICKNOR (G.) The Life of William Hickling Prescott. By George Ticknor. *Boston: Ticknor and Fields.* 1864.

4to, pp. x., 491. 19 *Plates. Half green levant morocco, gilt top,* UNCUT. LARGEST PAPER; a *few copies only* printed. A UNIQUE and BEAUTIFUL VOLUME, with an Autograph Note written and signed by the AUTHOR, and upwards of TWENTY FINE ILLUSTRATIONS *inserted.*

1977 TIMBERLAKE (H.) The Memoirs of Lieut. Henry Timberlake, (who accompanied the Three Cherokee Indians to England in the Year 1762,) containing Whatever he observed remarkable, or worthy of public Notice, during his Travels to and from that Nation; wherein the Country, Government, Genius, and Customs of the Inhabitants, are authentically described. Also the Principal Occurrences during their Residence in London. Illustrated with an accurate Map of their Over-hill Settlement, and a curious Secret Journal, taken by the Indians out of the Pocket of a Frenchman they had killed. *London: Printed for the Author.* MDCCLXV.

8vo, pp. viii., 160. *Map, and Plate. Half maroon morocco, gilt top,* UNCUT. FINE COPY, and VERY RARE in *uncut* state. One or the other of the engravings is wanting in many copies.

" Poor Lieut. Timberlake and his Indians, met with an inhospitable reception in England, where he got himself into debt for their expenses. After undergoing a variety of disappointments, vexations, arrests and imprisonments, he died in the flower of his age, and, we much fear, of a broken heart."— *Monthly Review.*

1978 TIMPERLEY (C. H.) Encyclopædia of Literary and Typographical Anecdote; being a digest of the most interesting Facts illustrative of the History of Literature and Printing ... with Biographical Sketches of Eminent Booksellers, Printers, Type-founders, Engravers, Bookbinders, and Paper Makers, of all Ages and Countries. Including curious particulars of the First Introduction of Printing ... and of the Books then Printed. Notices of Early Bibles ... A History of all the Newspapers ... and an Account of the Origin and Progress of Language, Writing and Writing Materials, the Invention of Paper, &c. Second Edition. *London: Henry G. Bohn.* 1842.

Imp. 8vo, pp. vi., 996, 12, 116. 11 Plates. Half crushed green levant morocco, gilt top, UNCUT. SCARCE PORTRAIT of JOHN GUTENBERG *inserted.*

A comprehensive, instructive and entertaining *omnium gatherum* of whatever could be collected from known and authentic sources.

1979 [TIMPERLEY.] Songs of the Press and other Poems relative to the Art of Printers and Printing; also of Authors, Books, Booksellers, Bookbinders, Editors, Critics, Newspapers, Etc. Original and Selected. With Notes, Biographical and Literary.
London: Fisher, Son, & Co. 1845.

12mo, pp. 208. Half olive morocco, gilt top. SCARCE.

1980 TOCQUEVILLE (A. de) Democracy in America. By Alexis de Tocqueville. Translated by Henry Reeve, Esq. Edited with Notes. The Translation Revised and in great part Rewritten, ... by Francis Bowen. *Cambridge: Sever and Francis.* 1864.

2 vols., roy. 8vo, pp. xxiii., 559; xiv., 499. Half purple morocco, gilt top, UNCUT. LARGE PAPER; *one hundred copies only printed.*

" Let me earnestly advise your perusal of M. de Tocqueville's work. His testimony, as well from actual personal experience, as on account of freedom from prejudice, is above exception."— *Sir Robert Peel's Speech.*

1981 TOMB (S.) An Oration on the Auspicious Birth, Sublime Virtues, and Triumphant Death of General George Washington. Pronounced Feb. 22, 1800, in Newbury, Second Parish, by Rev. Samuel Tomb. To which are Annexed, Two Odes and an Acrostic, Commemorative of the Birth and Death of that Illustrious Personage, composed by the same hand. *Newburyport:* 1800.

8vo, pp. 20. UNCUT *and scarce.*

1982 TORREY (S.) An | Exhortation | unto | Reformation, | Amplified, | By a Discourse concerning the Parts and Progress of that | Work, according to the Word of God. | Delivered in a Sermon Preached in the Audience of | the General Assembly of the Massachusets Colony, | at Boston in New-England, May 27, 1674. | Being the | Day of Election | there. | By Samuel Torrey, Pastor of the Church of | Christ in Waymouth. | *Cambridge: Printed by Marmaduke Johnson.* 1674.

Sm. 4to, pp. (10), 44. *Crushed red levant morocco, gilt edges, by* W. PRATT. EXTREMELY SCARCE.

"To the Reader." 6 pp., is signed by Increase Mather. An interesting example of the earliest New-England press. Marmaduke Johnson was the printer who assisted John Eliot in the production of the Indian Bible.

1983 [TOULMIN (H.)] A Description of Kentucky, in North America: To which are prefixed Miscellaneous Observations respecting the United States. [*London:*] *Printed in November*, 1792.

8vo, pp. 124. *Map. Half calf, yellow edges, by* W. MATTHEWS. BEAUTIFUL COPY. VERY SCARCE.

"It contains more full and more accurate information of the country which it describes, than any other work, and it possesses the singular advantage of being written, not by a hasty traveller, but by a man who, had lived till he was more than twenty-five years old, in the back parts of America."—*Advertisement.*

1984 Tower (F. B.) Illustrations of the Croton Aqueduct: [being an historical description of this celebrated undertaking, with an account of other similar works, ancient and modern.] By F. B. Tower, of the Engineer Department. *New York: Wiley and Putnam.* 1843.

4to, pp. 152. 22 *Plates. Half maroon morocco, gilt top,* UNCUT.

The best account of the construction of the Croton Aqueduct, with Views of all the important points along its line. NOW VERY SCARCE.

1985 TOWNSEND (J.) Some Account of the British Army, under the command of General Howe, and of the Battle of Brandywine, on The Memorable September 11th, 1777, and the Adventures of that Day, which came to the Knowledge and Observation of Joseph Townsend, late of Baltimore, Md. Accompanied by a Notice of the Life of Joseph Townsend, and an Historical Sketch of the Battle. *Philadelphia: Townsend Ward.* 1846.

8vo, pp. ii., 63. *Plan and* 2 *Views. Half calf, gilt top,* UNCUT.

1986 TRANSACTIONS of the Albany Institute. *Albany:* 1830.–64.

4 *vols., 8vo, half calf, gilt top,* UNCUT. VERY SCARCE.

1987 TRIAL (The) of William Wemms, James Hartegan, William McCauley, Hugh White, Matthew Killroy, William Warren, John Carrol, and Hugh Montgomery, Soldiers in his Majesty's 29th Regiment of Foot, for the Murder of Crispus Attucks, Samuel Gray, Samuel Maverick, James Caldwell, and Patrick Carr, on Monday Evening, the 5th of March, 1770, at the Superior Court of Judicature, Court of Assize, and General Gaol Delivery, held at Boston.

The 27th Day of November, 1770, by Adjournment. Before the Hon. Benjamin Lynde, John Cushing, Peter Oliver, and Edmund Trowbridge, Esquires, Justices of said Court. Published by Permission of the Court. Taken in Short-Hand by John Hodgson. *Boston: J. Fleming.* M,DCC,LXX.

Sm. 8vo, pp. 217. *Half blue morocco, gilt top, almost* UNCUT. BEAUTIFUL COPY of the ORIGINAL EDITION of this famous Trial, and of the GREATEST RARITY. The following is a reprint.

1988 TRIAL (The) of the British Soldiers, of the 29th Regiment of Foot, for the Murder of Crispus Attucks, ... March 5, 1770, before the Hon. Benjamin Lynde, [and others] Justices of the Superior Court of Judicature, Court of Assize, and General Gaol Delivery, held at Boston, ... November 27, 1770. *Boston: William Emmons.* 1824.

Sm. 8vo, pp. 146. *Half red morocco, carmine edges.* SCARCE.

1989 TROW (J. F.) Specimen Book of the Letterpress, Stereotype, Electrotype, and Wood-Cut Printing Establishment of John F. Trow, New York. *New York:* 1856.

Roy. 8vo, half red morocco.

See Rand (G. C.) *and* Avery. No. 1669. Also, Thomas (I.) No. 1960.

1990 TRUMBULL (B.) A Complete History of Connecticut, Civil and Ecclesiastical, from the Emigration of its First Planters from England in the year 1630, to the year 1764; and to the close of the Indian Wars. By Benjamin Trumbull, D.D. with an Appendix, containing the original Patent of New-England never before published in America. *New Haven: Maltby, Goldsmith and Co.* 1818.

2 *vols.*, 8*vo, pp.* 567; 548. *Portrait. Half blue morocco.* LARGE and CLEAN COPY. SCARCE.

1991 TRUMBULL. The Majesty and Mortality of created Gods Illustrated and Improved. A Funeral Discourse, Delivered at North Haven, December 29, 1799. On the Death of General George Washington; who Died December 14, 1799. By Benjamin Trumbull, D.D. ... . *New Haven:* 1800.

8*vo, pp.* 31. UNCUT.

One of the copies with the EXCEEDINGLY RARE PORTRAIT of WASHINGTON engraved by DOOLITTLE. It is a profile, facing to the right, with a laurel wreath suspended by an eagle surmounting the head. The discourse was sold both with, and without the portrait.

1992 [TRUMBULL (John.)] The Progress of Dullness, or, the Rare Adventures of Tom Brainless. By the celebrated author of McFingal. *Exeter: Henry Ranlet.* MDCCXCIV.

12*mo, pp.* 72. *Half green calf, carmine edges. Second Edition.* RARE.

1993 TRUMBULL. The Poetical Works of John Trumbull, LL.D. Containing McFingal, a Modern Epic Poem, Revised and Corrected, with copious Explanatory Notes; The Progress of Dullness; and a Collection of Poems on various subjects written before and during the Revolutionary War. *Hartford: Samuel G. Goodrich.* 1820.

2 vols., 8vo, pp. 177; 235. *Portrait and Plates. Half green calf, gilt top,* UNCUT. PORTRAIT of the AUTHOR *inserted.* An ELEGANT COPY, and SCARCE in this *clean* and *uncut* condition.

1994 TRUMBULL. McFingal: An Epic Poem. By John Trumbull. With Introduction and Notes, by Benson J. Lossing. *New York: G. P. Putnam.* 1860.

Imp. 8vo, pp. 322. *Portrait. Half green morocco, gilt top,* UNCUT. LARGE PAPER. *One hundred copies only printed.* An impression of the CANCELLED PORTRAIT of the AUTHOR, and a set of the ILLUSTRATIONS drawn by TISDALE, and engraved by WILLARD for an early edition of the work, and now very scarce, *inserted.*

1995 TRUMBULL (J.) Autobiography, Reminiscences and Letters of John Trumbull, from 1756 to 1841. [With an Appendix, etc.] *New York: Wiley & Putnam.* 1841.

8vo, pp. xvi., 439. 23 *Plates. Half olive morocco, gilt top,* UNCUT. An AUTOGRAPH LETTER written and signed by the AUTHOR *inserted.*

The venerable and distinguished author was an aid-de-camp and friend of Washington. The work contains many interesting details of the times, both in Europe and America.

1996 TUCKER (G.) The Life of Thomas Jefferson, third President of the United States; with Parts of his Correspondence never before published, and Notices of his Opinions on Questions of Civil Government, National Policy, and Constitutional Law. By George Tucker. *London: Charles Knight and Co.* 1837.

2 vols., 8vo, pp. xx., 612; *xii.,* 587. *Half green moroco, gilt top,* UNCUT. AN ILLUSTRATED COPY, with an AUTOGRAPH LETTER of MR. JEFFERSON, and nearly FIFTY PORTRAITS and VIEWS, many of which are SCARCE and FINE, *inserted.*

1997 TUCKER (Josiah, D.D., Dean of Gloucester.) [A Complete Series of his Celebrated Tracts relating to the American Revolution.]

7 vols., 8vo, half olive morocco, carmine edges; respectively numbered in the order of their publication, at the bottom of the back of each.

"During the Revolutionary War, Dr. Tucker, attracted much attention by his pamphlets, in which he asserted the policy of granting independence to the colonies, rather than to attempt to subdue them by arms; and, though he was abused by the friends of the ministry his deductions proved proverbially true."— *Blake's Biog. Dic.*

The Tracts are entitled as follows:

I. Letter from a Merchant in London to his Nephew in North America, relating to the Present Posture of Affairs in the Colonies. ... *London: J. Walter.* 1766.

pp. 55. PORTRAIT *of the* AUTHOR *inserted.*

Maintains the rights of Parliament over the colonies.

II. Four Tracts on Political and Commercial Subjects. The Third Edition. *Glocester: R. Raikes.* 1776.

pp. 224.

The second tract is entitled, "The Case of going to War." The third, "A Letter from a Merchant in London to his Nephew in America." The fourth, "The True Interest of Great Britain set forth in regard to her Colonies; and the only means of living in Peace and Harmony with them." The third tract was first printed in the year 1766.

III. Tract V. The Respective Pleas and Arguments of the Mother Country, and of the Colonies, distinctly set forth; and the Impossibility of a Compromise of Differences, or a Mutual Concession of Rights, plainly demonstrated. With a Prefatory Epistle, to the Plenipotentiaries of the late Congress at Philadelphia Second Edition. *Glocester: R. Raikes.* 1776.

pp. 60.

"The contents of this tract are so evidently the effusion of ill temper, that did they not proceed from so respectable a character as the Dean of Glocester, we should have imagined them solely intended as the vehicle of insinuations against the colonies, unjust in their nature and malevolent in their design."—*M. R.*

IV. A Letter to Edmund Burke, Esq.; Member of Parliament for the City of Bristol, and agent for the Colony of New York, &c. In answer to his printed Speech, said to be spoken in the House of Commons on 22d of March, 1775. Second Edition, Corrected. *Glocester: R. Raikes.* 1775.

pp. 58.

"Dr. Tucker here controverts many of Mr. Burke's arguments, and almost all his conclusions; and labours to support the expediency of his favorite plan of a separation between Great Britain and the colonies in America; and the better to dispose the public to it, he represents the colonists themselves as the most unprincipled, worthless, and detestable part of mankind."—*M. R.*

V. An Humble Address and Earnest Appeal to those respectable personages in Great-Britain and Ireland, who by their great and permanent interest in Landed Property, their Liberal Education, Elevated Rank, and Enlarged Views, are the ablest to Judge, and the fittest to Decide, whether a connection with, or a separation from the Continental Colonies of America, be most for the National Advantage, and the lasting benefit of these Kingdoms. *Glocester: R. Raikes.* 1775.

pp. 93.

In this Tract the Dean counsels the abandonment of the Colonists to themselves, they being unworthy of the protection of the mother country, and calls the Monthly Reviewers the agents and confederates of Dr. Franklin.

VI. A Series of Answers to certain Popular Objections, against Separating from the Rebellious Colonies, and Discarding them Entirely: being the Concluding Tract of the Dean of Glocester on the Subject of American Affairs. *Glocester: R. Raikes.* 1776.

pp. xxii., 16–113.

"In this tract the Dean endeavours, apparently without effect, to prove some former aspersions on the character of Dr. Franklin."—*Rich.*

VII. Cui Bono? Or Inquiry, what Benefits can arise either to the English or the Americans, the French, Spaniards, or Dutch, from the greatest Victories or Successes in the Present War, being a Series of Letters addressed to Monsieur Necker, late Comptroller General of the Finances of France. Second Edition, Corrected. With a Plan for a General Pacification. *Glocester: R. Raikes.* 1782.

pp. 139.

"A most interesting and curious volume. The Dean says, that no sooner shall the Americans have established their independency, than they will be enslaved by their present rulers — the members of Congress — who will govern them with a rod of iron; the moment they are at peace with England they will quarrel among themselves, and, with the fury of famished wolves, they will endeavor to tear each other in pieces."

1998 TUCKERMAN (J.) A Funeral Oration. Occasioned by the Death of General George Washington. Written at the Request of the Boston Mechanic Association and delivered before them, on the 22d of Feb. 1800. By Joseph Tuckerman. *Boston:* [1800.]

8*vo*, *pp.* 24. UNCUT.

1999 TUCKERMAN (H. T.) The Life of Silas Talbot, A Commodore in the Navy of the United States. By Henry T. Tuckerman.
New York: J. C. Riker. 1850.

16mo, pp. 137. *Half green morocco, carmine edges.*

2000 TUDOR (W.) The Life of James Otis, of Massachusetts: containing also, Notices of some Contemporary Characters and Events from the Year 1760 to 1775. By William Tudor.
Boston: Wells and Lilly. 1823.

8vo, pp. xx., 508. *Portrait and Plate. Half blue morocco, gilt top,* UNCUT. An AUTOGRAPH LETTER of the AUTHOR, relating to the work, *inserted.* This fine copy has the "View of Osgood Farm," which is often wanting.

2001 TUFTS (C.) An Oration in Honour to the Memory of General George Washington, ... Delivered before the Inhabitants of the Town of Weymouth, ... On the 22d day of February, 1800. By Cotton Tufts, M.D. *Boston:* 1800.

8vo, pp. 19. UNCUT. RARE.

2002 TURNBULL (W. P.) The Birds of East Pennsylvania and New Jersey. By William P. Turnbull, LL.D.
Glasgow: Printed for Private Circulation. 1869.

Roy. 8vo, pp. 62. *Wrinkled green morocco, gilt edges, by* HENDERSON *and* BISSETT. PRIVATELY PRINTED, and one of TWO COPIES ONLY on thirty-four leaves of PURE VELLUM.

Contains *twenty* beautifully executed figures, in the manner of pencil drawings, of the birds referred to in the work, including several from drawings by Alexander Wilson, the celebrated ornithologist, whose grave forms the vignette to the Memorial Dedication.

An ELEGANT VOLUME, PRESQUE UNIQUE. The only other copy in existence belongs to Mr. J. Carson Brevoort.

2003 UNITED STATES Magazine: (The) A Repository of History, Politics and Literature. For the Year 1779. Vol. I. [All published.] *Philadelphia: Francis Bailey.* 1779.

8vo, pp. 506. *Half blue morocco, carmine top,* UNCUT. EXCESSIVELY RARE in uncut and PERFECT CONDITION.

"This copy," writes Mr. George H. Moore, "is the only perfect one I have met with." It was edited by Hugh Henry Brackenridge, and abounds in curious and interesting original matter relative to the American Revolution.

See *Franklin's Corr.* 1751–90. p. 114. Also *Duyckinck's Cyclopædia.* I.–290.

2004 UPHAM (C. W.) Lectures on Witchcraft, Comprising a History of the Delusion in Salem, in 1692. By Charles W. Upham. ...
Boston: Carter, Hendee & Babcock. M.DCCC.XXXI.

12mo., pp. vii., 280. *Half olive morocco, gilt top,* UNCUT. VERY SCARCE.

2005 UPHAM. The Life of Washington in the form of An Autobiography; The Narrative being, to a great extent, conducted by himself, in Extracts and Selections from His Own Writings. With Portraits and other Engravings. By Rev. Charles W. Upham. *Boston: Marsh, Capen, Lyon, and Webb.* 1840.

2 *vols., sm. 8vo, pp.* 443; 423. *Half green morocco, gilt top,* UNCUT, *by* BRADSTREET. EXCEEDINGLY SCARCE. PORTRAITS of GENERAL, and MRS. WASHINGTON *inserted.*

Neither portraits nor engravings were published with this work, the edition having been suppressed by the Circuit Court of the United States as an invasion of the copyright of Sparks' Life of Washington. The stereotype plates were then sent to England and the work was there published under a somewhat different title.

2006 UPHAM. Salem Witchcraft, with an Account of Salem Village, and a History of Opinions on Witchcraft and Kindred Subjects. By Charles W. Upham. *Boston: Wiggin and Lunt.* 1867.

4 *vols., sm. 4to, pp. lx.,* 216; 217–469; 272; 273–553. *Map, Plates, and Facsimiles. Half crushed blue levant morocco, gilt top,* UNCUT, *by* W. MATTHEWS. *One hundred copies only* printed on this paper.

2007 UPHAM. Salem Witchcraft and Cotton Mather. A Reply. By Charles W. Upham. ... *Morrisania: N. Y.* 1869.

Roy. 8vo, pp. viii., 91. *Half blue morocco, gilt top,* UNCUT. PORTRAIT of WILLIAM STOUGHTON *inserted.*

Written in reply to a sharp criticism on Mr. Upham's "Salem Witchcraft," by W. F. Poole, published in the North American Review for April, 1869, and reprinted at Boston in the same year.

See Poole (W. F.) No. 1616.

2008 VAN DRIESSEN (P.) The Adorable | Ways of God | in His | Sovereign Government, | Particularly over | The | Powers of this World, | Explained and Applied | in | Three Sermons. | By Petrus Van Driessen, V.D.M. | At New-Albany. | *New-York:* | *Printed by* JOHN PETER ZENGER. MDCCXXVI.

Sm. 4to, pp. (10), 75. *Blue morocco, gilt edges.* ELEGANT COPY. VERY RARE. PORTRAIT of Gov. BURNETT *inserted.*

The first sermon is "On the Occasion of his Majesty King George's Accession to the Throne and Crown of Great Britain." The second is entitled "The Scaffold of Felonious Traitors against their Lawful Sovereign Lord George, King of Great Britain, erected and exposed to View." The third "On the Occasion of his Excellency William Burnet's Treating with the Five Nations of Indians."

Thomas, "*Hist. of Printing.*" II. 95, states that Zenger began to print as early as 1726; this work may therefore be assumed to be one of the first, if not the very first issued from his press. WE HAVE NEVER MET WITH ANOTHER COPY.

2009 [VAN NESS (W. C.)] A Correct Statement of the late Melancholy Affair of Honor, between General Hamilton and Col. Burr, in which the Former Unfortunately Fell, July 11, 1804. Containing the Whole of the Correspondence between the Parties and the Seconds; the Particulars of the Interview; the Death of Gen. Hamilton, his Will; and an Account of the Funeral Honors paid to his Memory, etc. To which is added, a Candid Examination of the Whole Affair, in a Letter to a Friend. By Lysander. [William C. Van Ness.] *New-York: Printed and Published for the Author.* 1804.

8vo, pp. 78. *Half olive morocco,* UNCUT. VERY RARE. SCARCE PORTRAIT *of* HAMILTON *inserted.*

From Mr. Van Ness, who acted as Burr's second, we obtain an accurate, circumstantial and interesting account of all that relates to the causes and consequences of the disastrous meeting between Hamilton and Burr.

2010 VAN RENSSELAER (S.) A Narrative of the Affair of Queenston: in the War of 1812. With a Review of the Strictures on that Event in a Book entitled "Notices of the War of 1812." By Solomon Van Rensselaer. *New York: Leavitt, Lord, & Co.* 1836.

12mo, pp. 41, 95. *Map. Half blue levant morocco, gilt top.* LARGE and FINE COPY with an AUTOGRAPH LETTER and PORTRAIT of STEPHEN VAN RENSSELAER the "Hero of Queenston" *inserted.*

2011 VAN SCHAACK (H. C.) The Life of Peter Van Schaack, LL.D., embracing Selections from his Correspondence and other Writings, during the American Revolution and his exile in England. By his Son, Henry C. Van Schaack. *New York: D. Appleton & Co.* MDCCCXLII.

8vo, pp. xii., 490. *Portrait. Half red levant morocco, gilt top,* UNCUT, *by* W. SMITH.

2012 VAN SCHAACK. Henry Cruger; the Colleague of Edmund Burke in the British Parliament. A Paper read before the New York Historical Society, January 4th, 1859. By Henry C. Van Schaack. *New York: C. B. Richardson.* 1859.

8vo, pp. 67. *Half red morocco.* SCARCE and FINE PORTRAITS of CRUGER and BURKE *inserted.*

2013 VARNUM (J. M.) The Case of Trevett against Weeden; On Information and complaint, for refusing Paper Bills in Payment for Butcher's Meat in Market, at Par with Specie. Tried before the Honorable Superior Court, in the County of Newport, September Term, 1786. Also, The Case of the Judges of said Court, before the Honorable General Assembly at Providence, October Session, 1786, on Citation, for dismissing said Complaint. Wherein the Rights of the People to Trial by Jury, etc., are stated and maintained, and the Legislative, Judiciary and Executive Powers of Government examined and defined. By James M. Varnum, Esq., Major General of the State of Rhode Island, etc., Counsellor at Law, and Member of Congress for said State. *Providence: John Carter.* 1787.

Sm. 4to, pp. iv., 60. *Half blue morocco.* FINE, LARGE and CLEAN COPY. VERY SCARCE.

"This was a case of very great importance at the time it took place. The plaintiff bought meat of the defendant, a butcher, and tendered to him certain paper money issued by act of the General Assembly of Rhode Island, which was refused. The defendant pleaded, 'that it appears that the act had expired, and hath no force;' 'that the matters of complaint are made triable before special courts uncontrollable by the supreme judicial court of the State,' &c.

'If the complaint was sustained by the judgment of the court, the creditor, merchant, farmer and every vendor was prostrated in utter ruin.' 'The whole community' says Mr. Updike, 'was stirred to its very foundation. Upon its issue was involved the destiny of thousands. Public feeling was intense upon its result. The crisis arose, and the experiment was on trial, whether the people were capable of self-government; and upon its issue depended the fate of the nation.'"—*John Carter Brown's Cat.* IV. 267.

2014 [VAUGHAN (William.)] The | Golden | Fleece | Divided into three Parts, | Vnder which are discoured the Errours | of Religion, the Vices and Decayes of the King- | dome, and lastly the wayes to get wealth, and to | restore Trading so much com- | playned of. | Transported from | Cambrioll Colchos, out of the Souther-most | Part of the Iland, commonly called the | Newfovndland, | By Orpheus Iunior, | For the generall and perpetuall Good of | Great Britaine. | *London,* | *Printed for Francis Williams,* ... 1626.

4to, pp. (28), 149, 105, 96. *Map. Polished red levant morocco, filleted sides, corner ornaments, edges gilt on carmine by* F. BEDFORD. A LARGE and SPLENDID COPY with the MAP nearly always wanting. VERY RARE.

Vaughan endeavoured to establish a colony in Newfoundland. The map of the country is by Capt. Mason. For an extended note relating to this quaint and very curious work, see *Rich. Cat.* No. 177.

2015 VESPUCCI (A.) Amerigo Vespucci, son caractère, ses écrits, sa Vie et ses Navigations, par Varnhagen. *Map and 2 facsimiles. Lima:* 1865.—Le Premier Voyage de Vespucci définitivement expliqué dans ses Détails. *Vienne:* 1869.—Nouvelles Recherches sur les derniers Voyages du Navigateur Florentin, et le reste des documents et éclaircissements sur lui, avec les textes. (Et une postface). *Map from the* 1513 *Ptolemy, and a facsimile of Vespucci's Letter. Vienne:* 1870.

Sm. folio, half red morocco, gilt top, UNCUT, *by* BRADSTREET.

"These valuable publications, which are the entire result of Varnhagen's studies on Vespucci, contain all the letters of Vespucci, both authentic and doubtful, exactly reproduced from the originals. These are illustrated with literary and bibliographical notes, a critical analysis of his life, extracts from rare books and unpublished documents, &c.; which the Editor, as Brazilian Minister in Peru and Chili, had favourable opportunities of examining. Everything that could be desired by any one who wishes to examine the matter thoroughly will be found in Varnhagen's treatises, by which it appears conclusive that Vespucci saw the American *Continent* in 1497–8, while Columbus did not see it till August, 1498."—*B. Quaritch.*

2016 VESPUCIUS. Fac-Simile of the "Dutch Vespucius." Being the celebrated Letter of Americus Vespucius to Laurentius de Medicis. Describing his Third Voyage to America, in the year 1501, for the King of Portugal. Translated from the Italian into Latin, and from Latin into Dutch. From the Unique Copy printed at Antwerp, 1506–10, in the possession of John Carter Brown, of Providence. *Providence:* 1874.

8vo, pp. (11). *Wood-cuts. Half red morocco, gilt top,* UNCUT, *by* BRADSTREET. No. 5 of TWENTY-FIVE COPIES printed for PRIVATE DISTRIBUTION. MOST RARE.

2017 VESPUCTIUS (Albericus.) Von der new gefundē Region die wol ein welt genennt mag werden. Durch den Cristenlichen Künig von Portugall wunnderbarlich erfunden. [Colophon.] Gedruckt yn Nuremberg durch Wolffganng Hueber. [1506.] [*Paris:* 1861.]

4to, pp. (11). *Wood-cuts. Half olive morocco, gilt top,* UNCUT.

An Account of the third voyage of Vespucius. Reprinted in Facsimile, on old paper, by the *Pilinsky process,* and so exactly reproducing the RARE ORIGINAL, that few eyes could detect any difference. TWENTY COPIES ONLY were reprinted. VERY RARE.

See Harrisse, Bib. Am. Vet. No. 33.

2018 VIEW (A) of the Evidence relative to the Conduct of the American War under Sir William Howe, Lord Viscount Howe, and General Burgoyne; as given before a Committee of the House of Commons last Session of Parliament. To which is added a Collection of the Celebrated Fugitive Pieces that are said to have given rise to that Important Enquiry. *London: Richardson and Urquhart.* [1779.]
[Followed by:] Strictures on the Philadelphia Mischianza or Triumph upon leaving America Unconquered. With Extracts, containing the principal Part of a Letter, published in the "American Crisis," in order to shew how far the King's Enemies think his General deserving of Public Honours. ... *London: J. Bew.* M.DCC.LXXIX.

8vo, 2 pieces in one vol., pp. 154; 42. *Half red morocco, gilt top, by* BRADSTREET. FINE COPIES. *Very scarce.*

2019 VIEW (A) of the Evidence relative to the Conduct of the American War. ... The Second Edition.
London: Richardson and Urquhart. 1779.

8vo, pp. 154. *Half red morocco, gilt top,* UNCUT, *by* W. MATTHEWS. VERY SCARCE in this FINE and *uncut* condition.

"It is a melancholy retrospect which is here given of our military exploits in attempting to reduce the revolted colonies."—*M. R.*

2020 VINING (J.) Eulogium; delivered ... at the State House, in the Town of Dover, on the Twenty-second of February Eighteen Hundred. In commemoration of the Death of General George Washington. By John Vining, Esquire. ... *Philadelphia:* 1800.

8vo, pp. 20. UNCUT. *Very Scarce.*

2021 VIRGINIA. Debates and other Proceedings of the Convention of Virginia, Convened at Richmond, on Monday the 2d day of June, 1788, for the purpose of deliberating on the Constitution recommended by the Grand Federal Convention. To which is prefixed the Federal Constitution. *Petersburg: Printed by Hunter & Prentis.*
M,DCC,LXXXVIII–IX.

8vo, 2 vols. bound in one, pp. 194; 195. *Crushed blue levant morocco, gilt top,* UNCUT, *by* F. BEDFORD. *Scarce* PORTRAIT of WASHINGTON *inserted.* VERY RARE.

A work of great interest, containing the most important debates on the adoption of the Federal Constitution. Rich refers to the first volume, but makes no mention of the second.

2022 VIRGINIA HISTORICAL REGISTER (The) and Literary Advertiser. Edited by William Maxwell. *Richmond: Printed for the Proprietor.* 1848–53.

6 *vols., sm. 8vo, half green morocco, gilt top.* PORTRAIT of WASHINGTON *inserted.* A BEAUTIFUL SET of the COMPLETE WORK. EXCEEDINGLY SCARCE, the greater portion of the edition having been destroyed by fire on the evacuation of Richmond, in 1865.

The work was issued as a serial, published quarterly, and completed in 24 numbers. It abounds in valuable historical, biographical, bibliographical, and narratory matter relative to the Colonial Period, and the Revolution. It includes, "The Narrative of the Destruction and Captivity of James Moore's Family." "The Expedition against the Shawnee Indians." "Braddock's Defeat." "The Battle of Point Pleasant." "Capt. Stobo's Narrative of Captivity." &c.

2023 **[Voragine (Jacobus. de)] Legenda Aurea.** [Colophon.] **Thus endeth the legende, named in latyn Legēda aurea that is to saye in englysshe the golden legende. For lyke as golde passeth all other metalles, so this boke exceedeth all other bokes, wherin ben conteyned all the hygh and grete feestes of our lorde, the feestes of our blyssed lady, the lyues, passyons, and myracles of many other Sayntes Hystoryes and Actes, as all alonge here afore is made mencyon. whiche werke hath ben diligētly amended in diuers places where as grete nede was. Finysshed the xxvii. daye of August, the yere of our lord. m.ccccc.xxvii. the xix. yere of the regne of our souerayne lorde kynge Henry the eyght. Imprynted at London in Flete strete at the sygne of the sonne, by Wynkyn de Worde.**

Folio, dark morocco super extra, profusely blind tooled after an old English pattern, entirely over the covers, and in exact facsimile of an early Caxton binding, gilt edges, by CHARLES LEWIS. EXTREMELY RARE.

COLLATION. Title, consisting of a large cut printed on both sides; Lyues and Historyes shortly taken out of the Byble, ii. to liiii., ending with a Table of the Saints; then folio primo to ccclxxxiiii; numerous cuts; and the large device of the printer on the final page. Size of leaf 7 inches by 11 inches.

The upper and lower margins of the title, and a portion of the fore margins of signature A have been restored by Mr. Lewis. In every other respect the volume is in the finest state of preservation.

Dibdin and Lowndes, together, refer to but four perfect copies, one of which is in the British Museum. There is no copy of this edition, either in the Spencer or in the Grenville collections. Of the forty-one known copies remaining of the three editions printed by Caxton, and recorded by Mr. Blades, all are imperfect, two copies only excepted.

"This translation from Voragine was made by the venerable father of English typography, William Caxton, at the command of William Earl of Arundel. The first portion of the work, containing the lives of the Old Testament saints, may be termed an abridged Bible, and is extremely curious and interesting, as it may be considered the earliest English version of the Bible allowed to be printed. The Genevan version, printed in 1560, from the peculiar translation of Genesis iii. 7, is commonly called the 'Breeches Bible,' but Caxton, nearly a century before, had rendered that verse thus: 'They toke figge leves and sowed them togyder for to cover their membres in maner of breches.' It may further be remarked that Caxton made considerable alterations in, and additions to the work, in the lives of the English saints, particularly in the life of Thomas à Becket Archbishop of Canterbury, &c."

MR. CORSER'S COPY SOLD FOR £130.

2024 VRIES (D. P. de) Voyages from Holland to America, A.D. 1632 to 1644. By David Peterson de Vries. Translated from the Dutch by Henry C. Murphy. *New York:* 1853.

4to, pp. 199. *Portrait. Half green levant morocco, gilt top,* UNCUT. *Two hundred and fifty copies* PRIVATELY PRINTED for Mr. James Lenox *exclusively for presentation.* EXCEEDINGLY SCARCE.

For an extended and interesting notice of this work see Field's *Bibliography*, No. 1615. A companion volume to "New Netherland &c." No. 1481.

2025 WAFER (L.) A New | Voyage | and | Description | of the | Isthmus of America, | Giving an Account of the | Author's Abode there, | The Form and Make of the Country, | the Coasts, Hills, Rivers, &c. Woods, | Soil, Weather, &c. Trees, Fruit, Beasts, | Birds, Fish, &c: | The Indian Inhabitants, their Features, | Complexions, &c. their Manners, Cu- | stoms, Employments, Marriages, Feasts, | Hunting, Computation, Language, &c. | With Remarkable Occurrences in the South | Sea, and elsewhere. | By Lionel Wafer. | Illustrated with several Copper Plates. | *London: | Printed for James Knapton, at the Crown in | St. Pauls Church-yard.* 1699.

Sm. 8vo, pp. (8), 224, (14). *Map, and 3 folded Plates. Polished calf, gilt edges, by* W. PRATT. LARGE and FINE COPY. VERY SCARCE.

Wafer was a surgeon to Dampier's expedition across the Isthmus, and was left among the Indians on being disabled by a wound. It is a most valuable book in reference to that country.

2026 WALKER (H.) A Journal: or Full Account of the late Expedition to Canada. With an Appendix containing Commissions, Orders, Instructions, Letters, Memorials, Courts-Martial, Councils of War, &c., relating thereto. By Sir Hovenden Walker, Kt. *London.: D. Browne.* 1720.

8vo, pp. (2), 304. *Half gray calf, carmine edges.* LARGE and FINE COPY. SCARCE.

"Sir Hovenden Walker was the naval commander of the Great Expedition against Canada, which sailed from Boston, N.E., 1710, but which proved a complete failure, owing, it was said, to the unskilfulness of the pilots, by which eight ships and nearly a thousand men were lost in the St. Lawrence. Great blame was attached to Sir Hovenden, and he published this account in his own defence."—*Nichol's Lit. Anec.* I. 178.

2027 WALLACE (J. W.) An Address Delivered at the Celebration of the New York Historical Society, May 20, 1863, of the Two Hundredth Birthday of Mr. William Bradford, who introduced the Art of Printing into the Middle Colonies of British America. By John William Wallace. ... *Albany: J. Munsell.* 1863.

Roy. 8vo, pp. (2), 114. 3 *Facsimiles. Green morocco extra, gilt top,* UNCUT. A beautiful and UNIQUE COPY, containing SEVENTEEN *inserted* ILLUSTRATIONS, embracing two AUTOGRAPH LETTERS of the AUTHOR respecting the work, original Notices of Committee Meetings, Cards of Admission for the Address, and for the Reception, &c., all prepared in MR. TRENT's best manner.

2028 WALLACE. An Address. [Another copy.] *Albany: J. Munsell.* 1863.

Roy. 8vo, pp. (2), 114. 3 *Facsimiles. Cloth extra, gilt top,* UNCUT. AUTOGRAPH of the AUTHOR on fly leaf. The facsimiles are only found in *presentation copies* such as this is.

2029 [WALLACE (*Sir* W.)] The Acts and Deeds of the Most Famous and Valiant Champion Sir William Wallace, Knight of Ellerslie. Written by Blind Harry in the year 1361. Together with Arnaldi Blair Relationes. *Edinburgh : Printed in the Year.* MDCCLVIII.

Black Letter. *4to, pp.* 403, 79. *Calf antique, gauffered carmine edges.* VERY RARE.
Uniform with "The Life and Acts of Robert Bruce." No. 120.

Blind Harry's poem was composed about a hundred years after that of Barbour. The fact is that John Blair, who was a contemporary of Wallace, wrote a chronicle in Latin, which Blind Harry is supposed to have made use of.

2030 WALPOLE (H.) Anecdotes of Painting in England; with some account of the Principal Artists; and incidental Notes on other Arts; collected by the late George Vertue; digested and published from his original MSS. by the Hon. Horace Walpole; with considerable additions by the Rev. James Dallaway.
London : John Major, and Robert Jennings. 1828.

5 *vols., roy. 8vo, Half crushed red levant morocco, gilt top,* UNCUT, *by* W. MATTHEWS.

This MOST ELEGANT and UNSPOTTED COPY of Major's LARGE and SPLENDID EDITION contains, in addition to the series of beautiful INDIA PROOF ENGRAVINGS which accompanies the work, a complete DUPLICATE SET of the same, embracing ONE HUNDRED AND SEVENTY PIECES, all ARTIST'S UNLETTERED INDIA PROOFS of the most BRILLIANT DESCRIPTION. EVERY ENGRAVING throughout the work, however small, whether on steel or on wood is represented. SIX SETS ONLY were taken, and ALL FOR PRESENTATION. We are unable to record the sale of another such copy in the United States, and so FINE and DESIRABLE a set would form a CONSPICUOUS ORNAMENT to the library of the most fastidious and exacting collector.

"In the good old times of the Bibliomania, this work would have walked of its own accord into the mahogany book-cases of half the collectors in London."— *Dibdin.*

2031 WALPOLE. Journal of the Reign of King George the Third, from the year 1771 to 1783. By Horace Walpole. Now first published from the Original MSS. Edited, with Notes; by Dr. Doran.
London : Richard Bentley. 1859.

2 *vols., 8vo, pp. xxvi.,* 537; *xxxiv.,* 639. *Half blue morocco, gilt top,* UNCUT.

"Contains a large amount of very interesting and important information concerning the American Revolution, and is written in Walpole's liveliest manner. An account of the treason of 'Gen. Arnold, the butcher's son,' and of the capture and execution of Major André, will be found in vol. II. p. 431. Twenty thousand pounds was the price of Arnold's treachery."

2032 WALN (R. J.) Life of the Marquis De La Fayette; Major-General in the Service of the United States of America, in the War of the Revolution. By Robert Waln, Jr.
Philadelphia : J. P. Ayres. 1825.

8vo, pp. iv., 9–505. *Half crushed green levant morocco, gilt top,* UNCUT, *by* W. MATTHEWS. Fine clean copy with an AUTOGRAPH LETTER of LAFAYETTE, written in English, *inserted.*

2033 [WALSH (Robert. Jr.)] The American Register; or Summary Review of History, Politics, and Literature.
Philadelphia : T. Dobson and Son. 1817.

2 *vols., 8vo, pp. xxxix.,* 450; *xxxvi.,* 464. *Half calf,* UNCUT.

Contains the only translation of Barbe Marbois' "Conspiracy of Arnold," Count Rochambeau's "Operations of the French Army in America during the Revolution," Papers relating to the captors of André, Biographies of Dallas, Dexter, Dwight, Burton, Bayard, Gouv. Morris and other eminent Americans, &c.

2034 WALSH. An Appeal from the Judgments of Great Britain respecting the United States of America. Part First, containing an Historical Outline of their Merits and Wrongs as Colonies; and Strictures upon the Calumnies of the British Writers. By Robert Walsh, Jr. *Philadelphia: Mitchell, Ames, and White.* 1819.

8vo, pp. lvi., 512. *Half blue morocco, gilt top,* UNCUT.

For this work the author received the thanks of the Legislature of Pennsylvania.

2035 WALSH (R.) Notices of Brazil in 1828 and 1829. By Rev. R. Walsh. *London: Frederick Westley.* 1830.

2 *vols., 8vo, pp. xv.,* 528; *xii.,* 541. *Map, Plan and* 19 *Plates. Half calf.*

"A complete picture of the actual state of Brazil."—*M. R.*

2036 WANSEY (H.) The Journal of an Excursion to the United States of North America, in the summer of 1794. Embellished with the profile of General Washington, and an Aqua-tinta view of the State House at Philadelphia. By Henry Wansey, F.A.S. A Wiltshire Clothier. *Salisbury: J. Easton.* 1796.

8vo, pp. xiii., 290, (13). 2 *Plates. Half green morocco, gilt top,* UNCUT. VERY SCARCE in this fine *uncut* state.

Particularly interesting from its personal description of Washington, whom the author visited, and for its chapter on literature, in which are given lists of English books which it has answered to reprint, and of Original publications since the Declaration of Independence.

2037 WARBURTON (E.) Memoirs of Horace Walpole and his Contemporaries; including numerous Original Letters chiefly from Strawberry Hill. Edited by Elliot Warburton, Esq. *London: Colburn & Co.* 1852.

2 *vols., 8vo, pp. xi.,* (3), 506; (2), 577. 2 *Portraits. Half crimson morocco, gilt top,* UNCUT.

2038 [WARD (Nathaniel.)] The | Simple Cobler | of | Aggavvam in America. | Willing | To help 'mend his Native Country, la-| mentably tattered, both in the upper-Leather|and sole, with all the honest stitches he can take. | And as willing never to bee paid for his work, | by Old English wonted pay.| It is his Trade to patch all the year long, gratis.| Therefore I pray Gentlemen keep your purses. | By Theodore de la Guard. | *London,* | *Printed by John Dever & Robert Ibbitson, for Stephen Bowtell, at the* | *signe of the Bible in Popes Head-Alley.* 1647.

Sm. 4to, pp. (4), 80. *Crushed green levant morocco, paneled sides, edges gilt in the round, by* F. BEDFORD.

A LARGE and FINE COPY of the RARE FIRST EDITION ending with a verse entitled "The Clench" (some copies have this verse before the *Errata*, and the heading "Sutor ultra crepidam," at p. 1.)

This rare and curious work, which abounds in quaint imagery and doggrel rhyme, was published under the assumed name of Theodore de la Guard. An account of the Author (Rev. Nathaniel Ward) will be found in Mather's Magnalia.

"This is another of the gentle Puritan souls. On page 73 he cries out, 'Cursed be he that maketh not his sword starke drunk with Irish blood ... and let him be accursed that curseth not them bitterly!' This is Christian mercy with a vengeance. Poor Charles I. is not spared in the Rhymes:

'He cannot rule a Land as Lands should ruled been,
That lets himself be ruled by a ruling Romish Queen.
No earthly man can be true subject to this state,
Who makes the Pope his Christ, an Heretique his mate.'"—*Stevens.*

Aggawam is the ancient name of Ipswich, Mass.

2039 [WARD.] The | Simple Cobler | of | Aggavvam in America. | ... | [Another Copy. The Second Edition.] *London: Printed by J. D. & R. I. for Stephen Bowtell, at the Signe of the* | *Bible in Pope's Head-Alley.* 1647.

Sm. 4*to*, *pp.* (4), 80. *Crushed green levant morocco, paneled and gilt sides, corner ornaments, gilt edges, by* F. BEDFORD. An UNUSUALLY LARGE and FINE COPY of the SECOND EDITION with many rough leaves.

In this edition "Sutor Ultra Crepidam," stands at the head of page 1, instead of "The Simple Cobbler of Aggawam in America," and "The Clench" *precedes*, instead of following the errata, as in the first edition. There were four editions of this curious work published during the year 1647, each differing in some way from the others, all of them are rare; this, perhaps, the most so. *See* John Ward Dean's Memoir of the Author, pp. 168–9, for an extended and interesting account of the work, and particulars respecting the several editions.

2040 WARDEN (D. B.) A Statistical, Political, and Historical Account of the United States of North America; from the Period of their first Colonization to the Present Day. By D. B. Warden. *Edinburgh: Archibald Constable & Co.* 1819.

3 *vols.*, 8*vo*, *pp. lxiv.*, 552; *xii.*, 571; *xii.*, 558. *Map and Plan. Half blue morocco, gilt top*, UNCUT.

"At the end of the description of each State the author has placed a catalogue of books and maps relating to it, and in his possession. He printed in 1820 a catalogue of his remarkable library and offered it in one lot, but without result; a renewed offer was made with a new catalogue in 1831, but also in vain; a third catalogue, with the addition of only 8 books, was printed in 1840. I have seen in other reports that Mr. Warden had formed 3 different collections of books and sold one after the other, but this applies to this one collection described in these 3 catalogues."—*F. Muller.*

The above statement is made on the authority of Mr. Ludewig in the *Serapeum*, 1845, pp. 209–24. It is incorrect: there *were* two collections — described in three catalogues — one sold to Harvard College, the other to the New York State Library.

See James (W.) No. 1060; also, the two Nos. next following.

2041 [WARDEN.] Bibliotheca Americo-Septentrionalis; being a choice collection of Books in various Languages, Relating to the History, Climate, Geography, Produce, Population, Agriculture, Commerce, Arts, Sciences, &c., of North America, from its first discovery to its present existing Government; among which are many valuable Articles and rare, together with all the important official Documents published from time to time by the Authority of Congress. [Collected by D. B. Warden.] *Paris: de Nouzou.* 1820.

8*vo*, *pp.* 147. *Half purple levant morocco, gilt top*, UNCUT. A RARE and valuable catalogue.

The books were purchased by Mr. Samuel E. Elliot who gave them to Harvard College in 1823.

2042 [WARDEN.] Bibliotheca Americana, being a choice collection of Books relating to North and South America and the West Indies, including Voyages to the Southern Hemisphere, Maps, Engravings and Medals. [Collected by D. B. Warden.] *Paris:* 1840.

8vo, pp. 124. *Half blue morocco.* VERY SCARCE.

Mr. Warden was well known for his researches in American History. This catalogue was first printed at Paris in 1831; it describes 1118 works, and was bought for the New York State Library at Albany.

2043 WARDEN (W.) Letters written on board his Majesty's Ship the Northumberland, and at St. Helena: in which the Conduct and Conversations of Napoleon Buonaparte, and his Suite, during the Voyage, and the first months of his Residence in that Island, are faithfully described and related. By William Warden. Third Edition. *London: Published for the Author.* 1816.

[Also:] Narrative of the Surrender of Buonaparte and of his Residence on board H. M. S. Bellerophon; with a detail of the Principal Events that occurred in that ship, between the 24th of May and the 8th of August 1815. By Captain F. L. Maitland, C.B. *London: Henry Colburn.* 1826.

8vo, 2 vols. bound in one, pp. viii., 215. *Portrait, Plate and Facsimile. xvi.,* 248. *Map. Half green morocco, gilt top,* UNCUT. PORTRAIT *inserted.*

2044 WARE (H.) A Sermon, Occasioned by the Death of George Washington, Supreme Commander of the American Forces during the Revolutionary War; ... who departed this life at Mount Vernon, December 14, 1799, in the 68th year of his age. Delivered in Hingham, by Request of the Inhabitants, January 6, 1800. *Boston:* 1800.

8vo, pp. 27. UNCUT.

2045 WARREN (J.) An Oration delivered March 5th, 1772. At the Request of the Inhabitants of the Town of Boston: to commemorate the Bloody Tragedy of the Fifth of March, 1770. By Dr. Joseph Warren. *Boston: Printed by Edes and Gill, by Order of the Town of Boston.* 1772.

4to, pp. 18. *Half green morocco, gilt top.* VERY SCARCE.

2046 WARREN. An Oration; delivered March Sixth, 1775. At the Request of the Inhabitants of the Town of Boston; to Commemorate the Bloody Tragedy of the Fifth of March, 1770. By Dr. Joseph Warren. *Boston: Edes and Gill.* M.DCC.LXXV.

4to, pp. 23. *Half green morocco, gilt top.* VERY SCARCE.

2047 WARREN (*Mrs.* M.) Poems, Dramatic and Miscellaneous. By Mrs. M. Warren. *Boston: I. Thomas and E. T. Andrews.* MDCCXC.

12mo, pp. 252. *Half calf antique. Fine copy.* VERY SCARCE. PORTRAIT of MRS. WARREN *inserted.*

Dedicated to General Washington. The author, claims his acquaintance, states that the volume is under his patronage, and that it has been written when every active member of society was in the field to resist the strong hand of foreign domination.

2048 WARREN. History of the Rise, Progress and Termination of the American Revolution. Interspersed with Biographical, Political and Moral Observations. ... By Mrs. Mercy Warren.
Boston: E. Larkin. 1805.

3 *vols., 8vo, pp. xii.,* 477; *vii.,* 412; *vi.,* 475. *Half green morocco, gilt top,* UNCUT. A UNIQUE and EXTENSIVELY ILLUSTRATED COPY, clean as when published, and VERY SCARCE in uncut condition.

This beautiful copy contains upwards of ONE HUNDRED AND FORTY INSERTED ILLUSTRATIONS, nearly all CONTEMPORARY PORTRAITS, SUBJECTS, and VIEWS, many of which are SCARCE, and some RARE, with uniformly fine impressions throughout.

A MOST DESIRABLE COPY.

2049 WARTON (T.) The History of English Poetry, from the Close of the Eleventh to the Commencement of the Eighteenth Century. ... By Thomas Warton, B.D. A New Edition Carefully Revised, with numerous additional Notes by the late Mr. Ritson, the late Dr. Ashby, Mr. Douce, Mr. Park, and other Eminent Antiquaries, and by the Editor. *London: Thomas Tegg.* 1824.

4 *vols., 8vo, pp.* (6), 123, *cclxix.,* 203; (8), 520; (8), 470; (8), 482. *Half green morocco, gilt top,* UNCUT. An AUTOGRAPH LETTER and duplicate PORTRAIT of the AUTHOR; and a FRONTISPIECE to each volume *inserted.* A BEAUTIFUL COPY. VERY SCARCE in uncut condition.

2050 WASHINGTON (G.) The | Journal | of | Major George Washington, | Sent by the | Hon. Robert Dinwiddie, Esq; | His Majesty's Lieutenant-Governor, and | Commander in Chief of Virginia, | To the | Commandant of the French Forces | on | Ohio. | To which are added, the | Governor's Letter: | and a | Translation of the French Officer's Answer. | With | a New Map of the Country as far as the | Mississippi. | *Williamsburg Printed,* | *London, Reprinted for T. Jeffries, the Corner* | *of St. Martin's Lane.* | MDCCLIV.

S*m.* 8*vo, pp.* 32. MAP. *Green morocco, paneled and gilt sides, gilt inside borders and edges.* A LARGE AND FINE COPY of THE FIRST LITERARY PRODUCTION OF WASHINGTON. EXTREMELY RARE.

Prefixed is the following: "ADVERTISEMENT. As it was thought advisable by his Honour the Governor to have the following account of my proceedings to and from the French on Ohio committed to print, I think I can do no less than apologize, in some measure, for the numberless imperfections of it. There intervened but one day between my arrival in Williamsburg and the time for the Council's meeting, for me to prepare and transcribe, from the rough minutes I had taken in my travels, this Journal."

"The original edition printed at Williamsburgh, Va., in the same year, is so rare that but two copies are known to exist. This with the London imprint, is only less rare than the other; and is sufficiently curious, as being the first of Washington's official actions recorded in print. It is principally occupied with a relation of his councils with the Indians, west of the Alleghanies."— *Field.*

2051

A MAGNIFICENT RELIC OF THE FATHER OF HIS COUNTRY.

WASHINGTON'S CORRESPONDENCE

WITH

GENERAL JOSEPH REED OF PENNSYLVANIA

DURING THE AMERICAN REVOLUTION.

Comprising FIFTY-FOUR ORIGINAL AUTOGRAPH LETTERS written and signed by GENERAL WASHINGTON ; seven excepted, which are in the handwriting of his secretaries, HAMILTON, TILGHMAN, and others, but signed by himself ; commencing at the time of his taking the command of the army at Cambridge, and extending nearly throughout the whole period of the war of the Revolution. They were written to Gen. Joseph Reed of Pennsylvania, and wholly refer to the momentous events of that time ; the successes and reverses of the army, Arnold's Treason, Lee's Defection, Reed's Collusion with Lee, &c., and include the WHOLE of the CELEBRATED CAMBRIDGE LETTERS, twenty in number, written between October 30th, 1775, and April 15th, 1776, in which, by his own hand, Gen. Washington has noted every occurrence of interest which happened in his command during that eventful period ; including an extended JOURNAL OF THE SIEGE OF BOSTON from the commencement of the American works on Lechmere's Point, until the evacuation of the town by the British.

The letters, mostly written on foolscap paper, occupy upwards of two hundred pages of an imperial quarto volume, elegantly bound in green Levant morocco, gilt edges, by F. BEDFORD, with an inserted UNLETTERED INDIA PROOF IMPRESSION of the full length portrait of WASHINGTON, painted by Stuart, in the possession of, and PRIVATELY ENGRAVED for Mr. James Lenox, by A. H. Ritchie. They are arranged, and mounted on guards, in the best and most approved manner, by Mr. Bedford, are in the finest possible state of preservation, and preceded by a TITLE PAGE and a BRIEF SYNOPTICAL DESCRIPTION of the contents of each of them respectively, printed by Mr. Munsell, expressly for the collection. The signatures, to four of the least important letters, which had been abstracted while in Mr. Reed's possession, have been replaced with others obtained from original documents.

This invaluable collection remained with the Reed family for nearly a century. It descended to the late Mr. William B. Reed, who, in consequence of some embarrassment in his affairs during the late civil war, sent it to New York to be sold. An effort made to secure it for a public institution failed to succeed, upon which it passed into the possession of its present owner.

In his "Reprint of the Original Letters of Washington to Joseph Reed," Mr. Reed remarks: "The letters in question were part[1] of a private correspondence, the most friendly and unreserved. Hence, in my opinion, their value. Their true interest depends on being the exact transcript of what the writers thought and wrote. It was the hearty, familiar letter writing of two friends, between whom there had grown up, in the daily and hourly intercourse of the same quarters in the 'Rebel' Camp, the most implicit, unsuspecting confidence. Mr. Reed was not exactly, at the age of thirty-three, of that class of thoughtless young men with whom it has been intimated Washington, himself but little over forty, was surrounded.[2] From June to October, 1775, Washington and his 'First Secretary' had occupied the same house, lived at the same table, shared the same dangers and responsibilities, watched and counselled together as two men of affectionate unreserve are apt to do; and when they were separated, the confidence was not interrupted, the unreserve not broken; and Washington writing to Reed in Philadelphia, was as if Washington were talking to Reed, in the anxious seclusion of the head-quarters at Cambridge. Such are these letters in their original form."

Referring to the CAMBRIDGE LETTERS, it is observed by Washington Irving. "How precious are these letters, and how fortunate that the absence of Mr. Reed from camp should have procured for us such confidential outpourings of Washington's heart at this time of his great trial." [3]

Thirty-three letters from this collection, were wholly or partially introduced by Mr. Sparks into the "Writings of Washington," with such unimportant verbal alterations in style and composition as, actuated by the best and purest motives, he was led to make upon them, and such others, as passed through his hands for insertion in that work. Hence arose the unfounded charge of Lord Mahon that Mr. Sparks had "tampered with the truth of history," a remark which led to an extended, animated and interesting discussion on the subject, an event which would seem to have been in some degree anticipated by Mr. Sparks, for in an ORIGINAL AUTOGRAPH LETTER written by him to Mr. W. B. Reed, and which will be found in this collection, he intimates that in case Mr. Reed should design to print Washington's Letters to his grandfather, "it would be desirable that our texts should be alike."

The following "Brief Synoptical Description," of these letters was principally prepared by Mr. Reed. It conveys a very inadequate idea of their varied and deeply interesting contents, a knowledge of which can only be obtained from a perusal of the letters themselves, as nearly twenty of them are believed not to have been published.

---

[1] Referring to the *thirty-three* letters which form the "Reprint."

[2] North American Review, July, 1852. p. 203.

[3] Irving's Life of Washington. II. 178.

It rarely happens that an opportunity is presented to acquire the possession of an autographic collection so absolutely UNIQUE in its character, so connected and complete in itself, exclusively treating of the important events attendant upon the advent of a nation, written to one address, and by an individual so prominent in the history of his country as is GEN. WASHINGTON; and it is questionable, whether any other series of his correspondence possessing the same PRE-EMINENT HISTORICAL INTEREST and VALUE which this collection will readily be acknowledged to possess, exists outside of the Department of State at Washington.

See Sparks *and* Mahon. No. 1887.

SYNOPSIS OF PRELIMINARY AUTOGRAPH LETTERS, ETC.

1. ORIGINAL HEADS OF WASHINGTON'S FIRST OFFICIAL LETTER TO THE PRESIDENT OF CONGRESS ON TAKING COMMAND AT CAMBRIDGE. . . 2 pp. octavo.

Cambridge: [July 10th, 1775.]

[*In the Hand-writing of Washington.*]

The Enemy on Bunker Hill. American Lines within Gunshot. Want of Tents. Grateful to Congress for its readiness to make everything agreeable. Want of Money, Clothing, and Powder. Spencer declines to serve in consequence of Putnam's Appointment over him. Spencer gone home without leave.

2. QUESTIONS FOR COMMITTEE OF CONGRESS, IN WASHINGTON'S AND ANSWERS IN REED'S HAND-WRITING. . . . . . . 4 pp. folio.

Cambridge: 1775.

[*In the Hand-writing of Washington.*]

Shall the British Troops in Boston be Destroyed at the risk of Destroying the Town? Indian Chiefs of the St. Francis, Penobscot, Stockbridge and St. John's Tribes have offered their Services. How shall Tory Property be treated? What shall be done with Dr. Church? Ought not Negroes, especially such as are Slaves, to be Excluded from the Service? How are Prisoners to be treated?

3. ORIGINAL DRAFT OF WASHINGTON'S LETTER TO HIS GENERAL OFFICERS. 3 pp. folio.

Cambridge: September 8th, 1775.

[*Written and Signed by Washington.*]

Plan of a Boat Attack on Boston discussed at length. Their Views solicited. The Success of the Measure must depend upon the Suddenness of the Stroke. Soldiers already impatient to get home. Desires a Speedy Finish of the Dispute.

4. JARED SPARKS TO WILLIAM B. REED. . . . . . . 2 pp. quarto.

Cambridge: February 21st, 1838.

"All Washington's papers which were in my possession, are now deposited in the Department of State at Washington. The letters from Washington to your grandfather, in 1775 and 1776, copies of which you where so kind as to send me, I recollect seemed to me the most imperfect (*in style and construction*) that I had ever seen from his pen. They were evidently written in great haste, in perfect confidence and without any thought that they would ever be published."

SYNOPSIS OF THE LETTERS OF WASHINGTON TO REED.

THE Letters not specially noted are all in Washington's Hand-writing.

I. WASHINGTON TO REED. . . . . 2 pp. quarto.

Cambridge: October 30th, 1775.

Views on Courts Martial. The Mails. Choice of a Private Secretary.

[*Not in Reed's Reprint.*]

II. WASHINGTON TO REED. SIGNED TWICE. . . . . . 3 pp. folio.

Cambridge: November 8th, 1775.

Arnold's Journal. Thinks Arnold is in Quebec. Philadelphians Supplying the Enemy. Plan for an Attack on the Enemy's Naval Forces. New Arrangement of Officers. Difficulties among the New England States. Connecticut wants no Massachusetts men in its Corps. "A blundering Lieutenant of the blundering Captain Coit, who has just blundered upon two vessels, etc."

III. WASHINGTON TO REED. . . . . 4 pp. folio.

Cambridge: November 20th, 1775.

Anxiety for his Return. Baylor not in the smallest degree a penman. Harrison sensible, clever, and confidential but not sufficiently comprehensive. Moylan very obliging but cannot retain him. Cramped state of the Treasury. The Best of Kings. Necessity of Medical Assistance in the Army. Connecticut Officers. Dr. Church in a Connecticut Jail without the use of pen, ink, or paper and to be conversed with only in English and in the presence of a Magistrate. Our Rascally Privateers-men. Arnold at Chaudiere Pond. *The Noble* Col. Enos. Mrs. Washington's Journey to Camp. Knox dispatched to Ticonderoga for Cannon.

IV. WASHINGTON TO REED. . . . . 3 pp. quarto.

Cambridge: November 27th, 1775.

Takes Possession of Cobble Hill without a Shot from the Enemy. Details of the Progress of the Siege of Boston. Sufferings of its Inhabitants.

[*Not in Reed's Reprint.*]

V. WASHINGTON TO REED. . . . . 7 pp. quarto.

Cambridge: November 28th, 1775.

The Private Secretaryship. Continental Bills. Want of Public Virtue and Patriotism. "I tremble at the prospect." "Could I have foreseen what I have and am like to experience, no consideration upon earth should have induced me to accept this command." The Siege of Boston continued. Difficulties with the Provincial Troops. Knox and the Artillery. Capitulation of Montreal. "Poor Arnold, I wonder where he is." Enos under Arrest. Obliged to *give in* to the whimsies of the People or get no Army.

VI. WASHINGTON TO REED. . . . . 4 pp. quarto.

Cambridge: November 30th, 1775.

Capture of the Nancy Store Ship. Scoundrelly Spy from Marblehead. The Affair at Lichmore's Point. Movements of the Enemy.

VII. WASHINGTON TO REED. SIGNED TWICE. . . . . . 4 pp. folio.

Cambridge: December 15th, 1775.

Mrs. Washington at Philadelphia. The Congress. Difficulties with Massachusetts. Mr. Reed's Return. Flattering Sentiments of the People respecting his Conduct. "Pray God I may continue to deserve them." Denunciation of Lord Dunmore, "that arch traitor to the rights of humanity."

That Villain Connolly. Impatient to hear from Arnold. "Would to God we may hear he is in Quebec." The Small Pox in every part of Boston.

VIII. WASHINGTON TO REED. . . . . . . 4 pp. quarto.

Cambridge: December 25th, 1775.

The Works at Lichmore's Point. The New England Governments. The Connecticut Troops. "The Inconceivable Want of Powder and no Supply administers a gloomy prospect." Mrs. Washington's visit to Philadelphia. Gratitude for the civilities shown her.

IX. WASHINGTON TO REED. . . . . 4 pp. folio.

Cambridge: January 4th, 1776.

Things wear a better face in Virginia. "Lord Dunmore's resentments and villainies." The King's Speech. Lord North. New Hampshire, Massachusetts and Rhode Island Troops desirous of "retiring into a Chimney-Corner." Ludicrous mistake of the "Red Coats." Shuldham is arrived at Boston. His own Despondency. "I wish this month was over our heads . . . how it will end God in his great goodness will direct." Movements of the British Fleet.

X. WASHINGTON TO REED. SIGNED THUS —— . . . . . 8 pp. folio.

Cambridge: January 14th, 1776.

Difficulties with the Massachusetts Government. Gloomy Prospects. Failure of Inlistments. Scarcity of Arms. Not 100 Guns in the Stores. Regrets that he had not Shouldered a Musket and Entered the Ranks instead of accepting the Command. General Despondency. "Could I have foreseen the difficulties which have come upon us, ... all the Generals upon earth should not have convinced me of the propriety of delaying an attack upon Boston till this time." Lee dispatched to secure New York. Duke of Grafton.

XI. WASHINGTON TO REED. . . . . 4 pp. folio.

Cambridge: January 23d, 1776.

Continued Anxiety for Mr. Reed's Return. His Distress and Embarrassments increased. The Unfortunate Repulse at Quebec. Death of the Brave and Lamented "Montgomerie." Arnold at Quebec. Gen. Schuyler. Enthusiasm of Governor Trumbull. The British pulling down the Houses at Boston.

XII. WASHINGTON TO REED. . . . . 4 pp. folio.

Cambridge, January 31st, 1776.

Renewed Anxiety for Mr. Reed's Services. Clinton leaving Boston. Tryon and the New York Tories. "My Countrymen of Virginia." Affairs in Canada. Capture of two Supply Vessels. Campbell's "very formidable" Portrait of the Commander in Chief with a "sufficient portion of terror in his countenance." Mrs. Washington.

XIII. WASHINGTON TO REED. . . . . 4 pp. folio.

Cambridge: February 1st, 1776.

Behaviour of the Men under Gen. Montgomerie. Want of Discipline in Raw Troops. "They will not march boldly up to a Work." "The Men must be brought to Face Danger." Gen. Arnold Wounded. Gen. Prescott.

XIV. WASHINGTON TO REED. SIGNED G. W. . . . . 7 pp. folio.

Cambridge: February 10th, 1776.

Expressions of Personal Regard. Difficulties of his Position. His Situation irksome. Has less than Ten Thousand Men Insufficiently Armed and Clothed. Sailing of the British Fleet. The King's Speech. Never entertained an idea of an Accommodation with the Ministry. "A Tyrant and his Diabolical Ministry." "Ardour of Chimney-Corner Heroes." Admiralty Courts. Bunker Hill. Narrow Escape of Commodore Manly. Receives a Letter and Poem from Miss Phillis Wheatley. Inclined to Publish the Poem. Refrains from Motives of Delicacy. Miss Wheatley's "Great Poetical Genius."

XV. WASHINGTON TO REED. SIGNED G. W—— N. . . . 16 pp. quarto.

Journal of the Siege of Boston.

Cambridge: February 26th, 1776; Continued on the 3d, 7th, and 9th, of March.

Completion of Works on Lichmore's Point. Mounting Heavy Ordinance thereon. Every thing, "*but the thing*" ready for Operation. Proposes to Cross on the Ice to Assault Boston. Overruled. Preparing to take Post on Dorchester Heights, "to try if the enemy will be so kind as to come out to us." Want of Powder. Lee's Expedition to New York. Governor Trumbull. The Long Island Tories. The Command of the North River. Sir Henry Clinton's friend Mr. Tryon. Personal Camp Equipage. The Expected "Rumpus" in Boston. Occupation of Dorchester Heights. Bombardment of Boston. "Dreadful apprehension" of the Selectmen for the Town. Want of Powder again. Questions of Rank. Merits and Claims of several Officers discussed. Ill News from the Fleet. The English Commissioners. Gen. Howe proposes to Evacuate Boston. The Selectmen again. They are in "great consternation for the Town."

XVI. WASHINGTON TO REED. . . . . 2 pp. folio.

Cambridge: March 19th, 1776.

The British Evacuate Boston. The "Inconceivable Hurry" of their Embarkation described. Capture of Artillery. Thirty Thousand Pounds worth of His Majesty's Property Abandoned. Boston found to be almost Impregnable. Troops sent to New York. Impatience for Mr. Reed's Return.

XVII. WASHINGTON TO REED. . . . . 4 pp. quarto.

Cambridge: March 25th, 1776.

The enemy's knack at puzzling. The British Fleet fitting for sea in Nantasket Roads. Speculation as to its Destination and Plans. Six Regiments detached to New York. Apprehends Danger from Expiration of Term of Service of Troops. Has "People to deal with who will not fear danger until the bayonet is at their breast." Fortifies Boston.

XVIII. WASHINGTON TO REED. . . . . 1 p. folio.

Cambridge: March 28th, 1776.

Gen. Howe makes an Inglorious Retreat. The British Fleet leaves Nantasket Roads. Six more Regiments dispatched to New York. Two others to follow. His own Immediate Departure thence.

[*Not in Reed's Reprint.*]

XIX. WASHINGTON TO REED. SIGNED TWICE. . . . 6 pp. folio.

Cambridge: April 1st, 1776.

Dispatch of the Army to New York. Resignation of General Officers. "That wonderful man General Fry." Ludicrous account of his "wonderful Services." Unfavorable account of the Carolinas. "Those universal instruments of Tyranny, the Scotch." "The first blow half the battle." Mr. Temple arrives with News from England. More about the British Commissioners. Independence must soon come. Tom Paine's "Common Sense" is working a powerful change in Virginia. "*Old Put.*" Miseries and Hardships of the Boston Tories. When the Order issued for the Embarkation of the British Troops "no electric shock, no sudden flash of lightning, not even the last trump could have struck them with greater consternation." Sullivan's and Greene's Brigades ordered to Providence.

XX. WASHINGTON TO REED. . . . . 2 pp. quarto.

Cambridge: April 15th, 1776.

Deplores Party Divisions in Pennsylvania. Still Desirous for Mr. Reed's Return. Fears he may "have a difficult card to play" and wishes for Reed's Assistance and Advice.

[END OF THE CAMBRIDGE LETTERS.]

XXI. WASHINGTON TO REED. . . . . 2 pp. folio.

New York: April 23rd, 1776.

Arrival at New York. Alarming Dissentions in Congress. "If the house is divided the fabric must fall."

[*Not in Reed's Reprint.*]

XXII. WASHINGTON TO JOSEPH REED, ESQ., OR IN HIS ABSENCE TO JOHN CADWALLADER, ESQ. ONLY, AT BRISTOL. . . . . . . 2 pp. folio.

Camp Above Trenton Falls: December 23rd, 1776.

Details at Length his Plans for the Attack on Trenton, and the Movements below. "Christmas day at night, one hour before day, is the time fixed upon." "For Heaven's sake keep this to yourself as the discovery of it might prove fatal to us." "Necessity, dire necessity will, nay must, justify an attack." Gen. Gates. Gen. Sullivan. "Heaven grant we are successful."

[This letter is of great interest and value. It was recovered, comparatively within a few years, from a gentleman to whom it had been lent.]

XXIII. WASHINGTON TO REED. . . . . 2 pp. quarto.

[*In the writing of a Secretary. Signed by Washington.*]

Morristown: January 12th, 1777.

Sullivan and Maxwell. Capture of Van Horne. His noted Character. No Dependence to be placed upon his Parole. Putnam at Princeton. Movements of Heath.

[*Not in Reed's Reprint.*]

XXIV. WASHINGTON TO REED. . . . . 3 pp. folio.

Morristown: January 14th, 1777.

Putnam at Fault. Movements in New Jersey. Cornwallis sends a British Surgeon to attend the Wounded. The Peculiar kind of attention he is to receive. Anxiety for Intelligence. The Rangers — did they Run Away? — if so, Punish or Shame them.

[*Not in Reed's Reprint.*]

XXV. WASHINGTON TO REED. . . . . 2 pp. folio.

Morristown: January 15th, 1777.

Complains of Putnam. "What in the name of Heaven can he be doing." Defects of the Militia. Anxious for Intelligence. Sends his Congratulations to General Mercer of whose Death he was then ignorant.

[*Not in Reed's Reprint.*]

XXVI. WASHINGTON TO REED. . . . . 4 pp. folio.

Morristown: February 23rd, 1777.

Reed's Resignation as Adjutant General. General Conway's Cartel. The Quarter-Master-Generalship. Command of the Horse offered to Reed. Generals Greene and Mifflin. Plan for the Prevention of Desertion. New-fangled Schemes of Congress. It ought not to Return to Philadelphia. "We are now in one of the most critical periods America ever saw." Wishes Col. Cox to accept the Appointment of Commissary of Prisoners. "If he will, I wish to God he would repair hither immediately."

[*Not in Reed's Reprint.*]

XXVII. WASHINGTON TO REED. . . . . 1 p. folio.

Middle Brook: May 29th, 1777.

[*In Writing of a Secretary. Signed by Washington.*]

Offers Reed the Command of the Light Horse, with the Rank of General.

XXVIII. WASHINGTON TO REED. . . . . 2 pp. folio.

Camp at Middle Brook: June 11th, 1777.

Refers to Reed's Letter to Gen. Charles Lee. Feels himself Hurt thereby. Intimates in Eloquent and Feeling terms that "it mortified him not a little." Overlooks it. Desirous that Reed should accept the Command of the Light Horse.

XXIX. WASHINGTON TO REED. . . . . 1 p. folio.

Whitemarsh: December 2nd, 1777.

Exceedingly Embarrassed respecting the Location of Winter Quarters. Wishes to see Mr. Reed at Camp that he may have his Sentiments and Assistance.

[*Not in Reed's Reprint.*]

XXX. WASHINGTON TO REED. . . . . 1 p. folio.

Valley Forge: June 15th, 1778.

More about the British Commissioners. Reed's Letter to Gov. Johnson. An Alteration suggested. Congress deliberating upon an Answer to the Address of the Commissioners.

XXXI. WASHINGTON TO REED. . . . . 4 pp. quarto.

Fredericksburgh: in the State of New York: November 27th, 1778.

Winter Quarters. Baylor's Dragoons. Discredited Paper Money. Infamous practice of Forestalling. Laments Faction and Party Views. Expression of Devout Submission to Providence. Mysterious Conduct of the Enemy at New York and Rhode Island.

XXXII. WASHINGTON TO REED. . . . . 6 pp. folio.

Middlebrook: December 12th, 1778.

Congratulates Reed on his Election as President of Pennsylvania. Sir Harry's Extra Manœuvre up the North River. Consequent Marches and Countermarches. The Convention Troops safe in the hands of Gen. McDougall. The "Extra Manœuvre" results in the Destruction of two or three log houses and nine barrels of spoiled herrings. Pennsylvania Politics. Monopolizers and Forestallers the Pests of Society. "Would to God that one of the most atrocious in each State was hung in gibbets upon a gallows five times as high as the one prepared for Haman." Denounces the man "who can build his greatness upon his country's ruin." Gen. Chas. Lee's Publication and Conduct. Facts barefacedly Misrepresented. Despises the Publication from his "inmost soul" and Defies Lee to Produce a Single Proof of his Assertions. Lee's Character, Temper and Plans. The Venom of his Tongue and Pen. Invited to make Philadelphia his Head Quarters for the Winter. Declines in consequence of the Care and Address required "to keep the army from crumbling." Will reconcile himself to any Place and all Circumstances while he Remains in the Army. Gratitude of the Army to Reed.

XXXIII. WASHINGTON TO REED AS PRESIDENT OF PENNSYLVANIA. 5 pp. folio.

Head Quarters: March 21, 1779.

[*In the writing of a Secretary.*]

Secret Plan of an Indian Campaign.

[*Not in Reed's Reprint.*]

XXXIV. WASHINGTON TO REED. . . . . 3 pp. folio.

Middlebrook: March 28th, 1779.

Plans of the Enemy. Fears an Attack on New London. Suspects some Vigorous Attack to Plunder or Destroy Annapolis, Baltimore, or perhaps Philadelphia. Clinton and Erskine on Long Island. Admiral Gambier gone to Rhode Island. "The fears of the people are up for New London." Necessity of Vigilance. Defensive Measures suggested.

XXXV. WASHINGTON TO REED. . . . . 2 pp. quarto.

Middlebrook: March 29th, 1779.

Plans for Assembling the Militia. The numerous Tribe of Speculators and Stock-jobbers.

[*Not in Reed's Reprint.*]

XXXVI. WASHINGTON TO REED. SIGNED TWICE. . . . . 4 pp. folio.

Middlebrook: April 8th, 1779.

The Indian Campaign. Distrusts the so-called Col. Patterson. Movements on Northern New Jersey. Recruits. Land Bounties. Party Spirit in Pennsylvania. Negociations for Peace. Col. Patterson's case Explained.

[*Not in Reed's Reprint.*]

XXXVII. WASHINGTON TO REED. . . . . 4 pp folio

Middlebrook: April 19th, 1799.

[*In Writing of Col. Tilghman. Signed by Washington.*]

Aid required from Pennsylvania. The Wyoming Expedition. Desires that Gen. Potter should Command it. Takes Measures to Prevent Mischief from Col. Patterson. The Army Distressed for Bread. Fort Pitt. Fort Laurens.

[*Not in Reed's Reprint.*]

XXXVIII. WASHINGTON TO REED. . . . . 2 pp. folio.

Middlebrook: May 8th, 1799.

Mr. Reed's Personal Explanation. Impartial Attention to the Security of each of the States avowed. Arnold's Trial. Arnold anxious to have it brought on. The Date of it fixed. Will *order* the Attendance of Military Witnesses.

XXXIX. WASHINGTON TO THE EXECUTIVE COUNCIL OF PENNSYLVANIA. 2 pp. folio.

Middlebrook: May 20th, 1779.

[*In Writing of Alexander Hamilton. Signed by Washington.*]

Attention to the Interests of the several States again Declared. Sensibly Affected by the Slightest Appearance of Distrust. Exertions of the State of Pennsylvania acknowledged. Inlistments. Arnold's Trial. Will "endeavour to have it conducted with unexceptionable propriety."

[*Not in Reed's Reprint.*]

XL. WASHINGTON TO REED. . . . . 7 pp. folio.

West Point: July 29th, 1779.

Secret Slanderers. Lee's "Queries Political and Military." The "*dark and hidden* motives, gross misrepresentations and *self known* falsehoods, of its malevolent author." Eloquent and Touching Self-Justification. The Command of the Army Forced upon him. Anxious to Return to the "Peaceful retirement, domestic ease and happiness" from whence he came. Has been for more than four years "a perfect slave." His Motives as Pure as ever man was Influenced by. Favourable Negociation with Spain. Discouraging Prospects of the Campaign. Movements of the Enemy. Arrival of Lord Cornwallis.

XLI. WASHINGTON TO REED. . . . . 7 pp. folio.

West Point: August 22nd, 1779.

The Loss of Fort Washington in 1776. Exposition of the Causes of the Disaster. Gen. Greene's Non-Compliance with Orders. Emphatic Resolve of Congress to Obstruct the Navigation of the North River. "A fine theme for the pen of a malignant writer." Valley Forge. Inlistments. The Currency. "The Spunge." The Affair at Powles Hook. 160 Prisoners and the Colours of the Garrison brought off.

XLII. WASHINGTON TO REED. . . . . 6 pp. folio.

West Point: October 22nd, 1779.

Reed to Lead the Pennsylvania Militia. His Example, Abilities, Activity and Bravery. Confidence in his Friendship and Zeal. Discontents and Jealousies in the Army. Questions of Rank. Delicate Situation of the Officers. Patriotism and Love of Honor their only Motives for Remaining in the Service. Amazing Depreciation of Money.

XLIII. WASHINGTON TO REED. . . . . . . 8 pp. folio.

Morristown: May 28th, 1780.

Surrounded by Difficulties. "Unable to administer the most ordinary calls of the Service." "We have almost ceased to hope" "This is a decisive moment, one of the most, I will go further, and say *the most*, America has seen." Relations with Foreign Powers. Glorious Effort of France for the Deliverance of America. Superiority of Great Britain to France and Spain combined. The French Fleet. Modern Wars Determined by the Longest Purse. Earnest Appeal to Pennsylvania. Can Undertake Nothing without her Aid. She "is our chief dependence." Wish for Plenipotentiary Powers in the Executive.

XLIV. WASHINGTON TO REED. . . . . 4 pp. folio.

Head Quarters: Bergen County, July 4th, 1780.

President Reed Vested with the Power to Proclaim Martial Law in Pennsylvania. Europe and America look to him to do his Part. His Situation Extremely Delicate and Critical. Advised to Exercise the Power with Boldness and Vigor. Extensive Power Insufficiently Exercised sure to Ruin the Possessor. The Bank. "Pennsylvania must do its part fully" or "we shall fail of success." Expression of Earnest Friendship.

XLV. WASHINGTON TO MRS. REED. . . . . 2 pp. folio.

Head Quarters: July 20th, 1780.

The Female Patriots. Contributions for the Relief of Soldiers. Suggestions respecting their Disposition. [*Not in Reed's Reprint.*]

XLVI. WASHINGTON TO MRS. REED. . . . . 2 pp. folio.

Head Quarters: Orangetown, August 10th, 1780.

The same Subject. The Soldiers paid in Depreciated Paper. Fears that "a taste of hard money" may produce Discontent and promote Desertion. A Supply of Shirts recommended instead. Continued Sufferings of the Troops.

[*Not in Reed's Reprint.*]

XLVII. WASHINGTON TO REED. . . . . 4 pp. folio.

Head Quarters: Orangetown, August 20th, 1780.

[*In Writing of Col. Tilghman. Signed by Washington.*]

Movements of the Pennsylvania Militia. Can scarcely Feed the Army from day to day. Assurances of Reinforcements from the French Land and Sea Commanders. Stirring Appeal to Reed to make the most of the Present Opportunity.

[*Not in Reed's Reprint.*]

XLVIII. WASHINGTON TO REED. . . . . 4 pp. folio.

Head Quarters: Passaic Falls, October 18th, 1780.

Arnold's Treason. His Conduct "is so villainously perfidious that there are no terms that can describe the baseness of his heart." His "horrid intention to surrender the Post and Garrison of West Point." Expresses a doubt whether Arnold really intended to involve *his* fate with that of the Garrison. Folly of Arnold's Subsequent Conduct. The Reasons why he was placed in Command of West Point. Regard for and Confidence in Gen. Schuyler. Exchange of Prisoners.

XLIX. WASHINGTON TO REED. . . . . 3 pp. quarto.

Head Quarters: November 20th, 1780.

Arnold's Slanders on Reed. Disclaims having treated Arnold with "the greatest politeness." Arnold's Assertion thereof "an absolute falsehood." "He *self*-invited some civilities I never meant to show him." Falsity of his Statements Repeated and Declared.

L. WASHINGTON TO REED. . . . . 1 p. folio.

Mount Vernon: November 15th, 1781.

[*In the Writing of a Secretary. Signed by Washington.*]

Answer to Congratulations on the Surrender of Cornwallis.

[*Not in Reed's Reprint.*]

LI. WASHINGTON TO REED. . . . . 3 pp quarto.

Verplank's Point: September 15th, 1782.

Answer as to Gen. Cadwallader's Pamphlet. Reed's Appeal Unexpected and Surprising. Not Suspected of Infidelity or Want of Integrity in 1776. Appeared Solicitous for the Public Good while in Delaware. His Conduct at Princeton appeared Zealous and Laudable. Disagreeable to have Hastily Written Private Letters made matter of Public Discussion.

2052 WASHINGTON. A Circular Letter, from his Excellency George Washington, Commander in Chief of the Armies of the United States of America; Addressed to the Governors of the Several States, on his resigning the Command of the Army, and retiring from public Business. *Philadelphia: Printed by Robert Smith, Jun.* [1783.]

Sm. 8vo, pp. 51. *Green morocco, paneled and gilt sides, gilt edges.* EXCEEDINGLY SCARCE. MINIATURE FULL LENGTH PORTRAIT of WASHINGTON *inserted.* From Mr. Morrell's Collection.

"Excessively rare. After considerable inquiry, I can learn of no other private library containing a copy of this ... book."—*Morrell's Catalogue.*

The London *Monthly Review* thus speaks of this Letter: "An exposition of the motives of this American Cincinnatus for returning again to the plough. His reasons do honor to his good understanding and amiable disposition; and his parting advice to the United States, is such as they ought to write in letters of gold on the front of their State house, if they had enough of that precious metal to spare from more pressing demands."

2053 WASHINGTON. The Last Official Address, of his Excellency General Washington, to the Legislatures of the United States. To which is annexed a Collection of Papers relative to Half-Pay, and Commutation of Half-Pay, Granted by Congress to the Officers of the Army. *Hartford: Printed by Hudson and Goodwin.* M.DCC.LXXXIII.

8vo, pp. 48. *Half green morocco, gilt top,* UNCUT. A fine impression of the SCARCE PLUMBEOTYPED PORTRAIT of WASHINGTON *inserted.* Includes the celebrated "Newburgh Letters," and is so VERY RARE that we have never seen a copy sold.

2054 WASHINGTON. Official Letters to the Honorable American Congress, Written, during the War between the United Colonies and Great Britain, By his Excellency George Washington. ... Copied by Special Permission, from the Original Papers preserved in the Office of the Secretary of State, Philadelphia.
London: Cadell Junior, and Davis. 1795.

2 *vols., 8vo, pp. viii.,* 364; 384. *Half green morocco, gilt top,* UNCUT. VERY SCARCE in such fine condition. Edited by John Carey, with his receipt for a portion of the proceeds of the sales, and TWO RARE PORTRAITS of WASHINGTON *inserted.*

"They cast light on the history of the American War which could not be derived from any other source."—*M.R.*

2055 WASHINGTON. Letters from General Washington to Several of his Friends, in June and July, 1776. In which is set Forth, an Interesting View of American Politics, at that All-Important Period.
Philadelphia: Republished at the Federal Press. 1795.

8vo, pp. 44. *Half green morocco.* SCARCE. SCARCE PORTRAIT of WASHINGTON *inserted.*

"These are the seven spurious letters said to have been found in the portmanteau of Washington's negro man Billy. Two volumes of Washington's Official Letters had this year been published in Boston. Some enemy of the General caused these to be reprinted as a supplement to that edition, knowing them to be forgeries, but giving no such intimation. In 1797, Washington was forced to publicly proclaim them forgeries."

2056 WASHINGTON. A Collection of the Speeches of the President of the United States to both Houses of Congress at the opening of every Session, with their answers. Also, the Addresses to the President, with his Answers, from the time of his Election: with an Appendix, containing The Circular Letter of General Washington to the Governors of the several States, and his Farewell Orders to the Armies of America, and the Answer. Dedicated to the Citizens of the United States of America. *Boston: Solomon Cotton, Jun. July*, 1796.

12mo, pp. 282. *Half green morocco.* VERY SCARCE. RARE PORTRAIT of WASHINGTON *inserted.*

2057 WASHINGTON. Epistles Domestic, Confidential, and Official, from General Washington. Written about the Commencement of the American Contest, when he entered on the Command of the Army of the United States. With an Interesting Series of his Letters, particularly to the British Admirals, Arbuthnot and Digby, to Gen. Sir Henry Clinton, Lord Cornwallis, Sir Guy Carleton, Marquis de la Fayette, &c., &c. ... None of which have been Printed in the Two Volumes published a few months ago. *New-York: G. Robinson, and J. Bull.* M.DCC.XCVI.

8vo, pp. xiv., 303. *Portrait. Half green morocco, gilt top,* UNCUT. A BEAUTIFUL COPY, with the VERY RARE and curious PORTRAIT of WASHINGTON engraved by ROLLINSON. RARE in such fine and *uncut* condition.

All the letters in this volume to p. 66 are spurious, not having been written by Washington. See *Washington's Writings.* XI. 184, 192.

2058 WASHINGTON. Epistles Domestic, Confidential, and Official from General Washington. Written about the Commencement of the American Contest. ... *New York: Printed. London: Re-printed for F. and C. Rivington.* 1796.

8vo, pp. xvi., 303. *Half blue morocco, gilt top,* UNCUT. *Fine copy. Exceedingly Scarce.*

On the 3d of March, 1797, when General Washington was about to retire to private life, in a letter to the Secretary of State, he declared these letters to be a base forgery, and that he never saw or heard of them until they appeared in print. They are said to have been written by a Mr. V——, a young Episcopal clergyman of New York.

2059 WASHINGTON. George Washington to the People of the United States, Announcing his Intention of Retiring from Public Life. *Philadelphia: A. Dickens, and H. Maxwell.* 1800.

Roy. 8vo, pp. 40. *Portrait. Half green morocco, gilt top.* VERY SCARCE. LARGE and FINE COPY, with the PORTRAIT engraved by EDWIN, one of his best efforts, and wanting in many copies.

2060 WASHINGTON'S Monuments of Patriotism. Being a Collection of the Most Interesting Documents, connected with the Military Command and Civil Administration of the American Hero and Patriot. To which is annexed, an Eulogium on the Character of General Washington. By Major William Jackson. *Philadelphia: J. Ormrod.* 1800.

8vo, pp. 338, 44. *Portrait. Half green morocco.* VERY SCARCE. VIEW *inserted.* Contains an excellent impression of the RARE PORTRAIT of WASHINGTON in military costume, PAINTED and ENGRAVED by SAVAGE.

2061 WASHINGTON'S Political Legacies. To which is Annexed an Appendix, Containing an Account of his Illness, Death, and the National Tributes of Respect paid to his Memory, with a Biographical Outline of his Life and Character.
Boston: John Russell and John West. 1800.

8vo, pp. 208, *xiv. Half green morocco.* PORTRAITS of GEN. and MRS. WASHINGTON *inserted.* FINE COPY. Contains 14 pages of the names of Subscribers.

2062 WASHINGTON. The Last Will and Testament of General George Washington, with a Schedule of his Property Directed to be Sold.
Philadelphia: A. Dickins. 1800.

8vo, pp. 26. *Half green morocco, carmine edges.*

2063 WASHINGTON. The Will of General George Washington ... Also, The Oration delivered by Major General Lee, at the request of Congress, at a Funeral Solemnity in Philadelphia, in Honour of the Memory of General Washington.
London: West and Hughes. 1800.

8vo, pp. 42. *Half blue morocco, gilt top,* UNCUT, *by* BRADSTREET.

2064 WASHINGTON. The Will of General George Washington; to which is annexed, a Schedule of his Property, directed to be sold.
Alexandria: Printed from the Record of the County Court of Fairfax. M.DCCC.

12mo, pp. 32. *Half green morocco, gilt edges.* VERY SCARCE. RARE PORTRAIT of WASHINGTON *inserted.*

"In this last will and testament of the great and good Washington, every line discovers the heart which conceived it, and the hand which drew it up. It is, on every account, a curiosity worthy of preservation."

2065 WASHINGTON. Selections from the Correspondence of George Washington and James Anderson, LL.D. ...
Charlestown: Samuel Etheridge. 1800.

8vo, pp. 76. *Half green morocco, gilt top,* UNCUT. PORTRAITS of WASHINGTON, and ANDERSON *inserted.* FINE COPY. VERY SCARCE.

2066 WASHINGTON. Letters from His Excellency George Washington, President of the United States of America, to Sir John Sinclair, Bart., M.P., on Agriculture and other Interesting Topics. Engraved from the Original Letters, so as to be an Exact Facsimile of the Hand Writing of that Illustrious Character. *London: G. and W. Nicol.* 1800.

4to, pp. 56. *Half green morocco, gilt top.* PORTRAITS of GEN. WASHINGTON, and SIR JOHN SINCLAIR *inserted.*

2067 WASHINGTON. Memory of Washington: Comprising a sketch of his Life and Character; and the National Testimonials of Respect.

Also, a collection of Eulogies and Orations. With a copious Appendix. *Newport: R. I. Printed by Oliver Farnsworth.* 1800.

12mo, pp. 246, (6). *Portrait. Half green morocco.* EXTREMELY SCARCE. Contains the VERY RARE PORTRAIT of WASHINGTON engraved by HAMLIN after SAVAGE. TWO ILLUSTRATIONS *inserted.*

2068 WASHINGTONIANA. A Collection of Papers relative to the Death and Character of General George Washington, with a Correct Copy of his last Will and Testament. To which are added his Legacy to the People of America, &c. &c. *From the Blandford Press, and Sold by Ross, and Douglass, Petersburgh, and by all the Booksellers in Virginia.* 1800.

8vo, pp. xvi., 95. *Half green morocco, gilt top,* UNCUT. SCARCE PORTRAIT of WASHINGTON engraved by EDWIN *inserted.* FINE COPY, and SO RARE that the present is the ONLY ONE we have ever seen or heard of.

2069 WASHINGTONIANA: (The) Containing a Biographical Sketch of the late Gen. George Washington, with various Outlines of his Character, From the pens of different eminent writers, both in Europe and America; and An Account of the various Funeral Honors devoted to his Memory. To which are annexed his Will and Schedule of his Property. Embellished with a good Likeness. *Baltimore: Samuel Sower.* M,DCCC.

12mo, pp. viii., 7–298. *Portrait. Half green morocco.* PORTRAIT *and numerous Cuts inserted.* EXTREMELY SCARCE.

2070 WASHINGTONIANA. [The same work.] Privately Reprinted. *New York: E. Dexter & Son.* 1865.

Roy. 4to, pp. 399, (7). *Portrait. Half green morocco, gilt top,* UNCUT. LARGE PAPER. FIFTY COPIES *only printed.* INDIA PROOF PORTRAIT in *three different states.*

2071 WASHINGTONIANA: (The) containing A Sketch of the Life and Death of the late Gen. George Washington; with a Collection of elegant Eulogies, Orations, Poems, &c., Sacred to his Memory. Also, an Appendix comprising all his most Valuable Public Papers, and his last Will and Testament. *Lancaster: William Hamilton.* 1802.

8vo, pp. 411. *Portrait. Half green morocco, gilt edges, by* BRADSTREET. AN ELEGANT COPY, VERY SCARCE, and the ONLY ONE we ever met with having the PORTRAIT of WASHINGTON engraved by TANNER after SAVAGE with an engraved head-line reading "Engraved for the Washingtoniana." PORTRAIT of WASHINGTON engraved by EDWIN *inserted.*

F. Johnson and W. Hamilton were the editors of this work. *See Historical Magazine.* Vol. II. April, 1858.

2072 WASHINGTONIANA; (The) [Another Copy.] *Lancaster: William Hamilton.* 1802.

8vo, pp. 411. *Portrait engraved by* EDWIN. *Half green morocco.* PORTRAIT *inserted.* FINE COPY.

2073 WASHINGTONIANA: or, Memorials of the Death of George Washington, giving an Account of the Funeral Honors paid to his Memory, with a List of Tracts and Volumes printed upon the Occasion; and a Catalogue of Medals Commemorating the Event. By Franklin B. Hough. *Printed for W. Elliot Woodward, Roxbury, Mass.* 1865.

2 *vols.*, 4*to*, *pp.* 272; 304. 2 *Portraits, Map and Facsimiles. Half green morocco, gilt top*, UNCUT. LARGE PAPER. 91 *Copies printed.* TWO UNLETTERED INDIA PROOF PORTRAITS of WASHINGTON, one from a PRIVATE PLATE, *inserted.*

2074 WASHINGTON. Letters from his Excellency George Washington, to Arthur Young, Esq., F.R.S. Containing An Account of his Husbandry, with a Map of his Farm; his Opinions on various Questions in Agriculture; and many Particulars of the Rural Economy of the United States. *London: J. and J. Richardson.* 1801.

8*vo*, *pp. vi.*, 172. *Map. Half green morocco, gilt top*, UNCUT. PORTRAITS of WASHINGTON, and YOUNG *inserted.*

2075 WASHINGTON. The Writings of George Washington; being his Correspondence, Addresses, Messages, and Other Papers, Official and Private, selected and published from the Original Manuscripts, with a Life of the Author, Notes and Illustrations. By Jared Sparks. *Boston: American Stationer's Company, John B. Russel.* 1837.

12 *vols.*, *imp.* 8*vo*, *half green morocco, gilt top*, UNCUT. Uniform with the works of Adams, Franklin, Webster, and Bancroft, &c.

A UNIQUE, ELEGANT, and MOST DESIRABLE LARGE PAPER COPY, containing EIGHTY-FOUR *inserted* ILLUSTRATIONS, nearly all of which are GENUINE INDIA PROOF IMPRESSIONS of the PLATES employed in the quarto edition of IRVING'S WASHINGTON, received from the late MR. PUTNAM from time to time in advance of their publication in that work.

The Fowle copy, *cut*, and *without additional plates*, brought $300.

"Aside from its intrinsic value and interest, as the production of the greatest and noblest hero whom the world has yet known, and to whom our country owes its existence, it is the most copious and by far the most reliable source for a history of the revolution."— *Courier and Enquirer.*

"The literature of the revolution was bold, direct, and without affectation. If you take the orders and proclamations of Washington, the letters written by him in the exigencies of the moment, there will be found that strength and felicity of expression that is supposed to be the offspring of care and leisure."— *Chambers.*

2076 [WASHINGTON.] Correspondence of the American Revolution; being Letters of Eminent Men to George Washington, from the time of his taking Command of the Army to the end of his Presidency. Edited from the Original Manuscripts by Jared Sparks. *Boston: Little, Brown and Company.* 1853.

4 *vols.*, *imp.* 8*vo*, *half crimson morocco, gilt top*, UNCUT.

A fine LARGE PAPER COPY, uniform in size with the preceding No., and containing *inserted* PORTRAITS of nearly FIFTY of WASHINGTON'S CORRESPONDENTS.

2077 WASHINGTON. Monuments of Washington's Patriotism: containing a Fac-Simile of his Publick Accounts kept during the Revo-

lutionary War; and some of the most interesting Documents connected with his Military Command and Civil Administration; embracing, among others, the Farewell Address to the People of the United States, and an Eulogium on the Character of Washington, by Major William Jackson, one of his aids-de-camp.
Washington: Peter Force. 1838.

Folio. Half green morocco. Portrait and Facsimiles.

"It will be recollected that Washington received no pecuniary compensation for his services during the Revolutionary War. He kept, however, himself, an account of his expenses, which, at the close of that eventful period, he presented to, and was admitted by the Government."— *Note.*

2078 WASHINGTON. Revolutionary Orders of General Washington, issued during the years 1778, '80, '81, & '82, selected from the MSS. of John Whiting, ... and edited by his Son, Henry Whiting, Lieut. Col. U. S. Army. *New York: Wiley and Putnam.* 1844.

8vo, pp. 255. *Half green morocco.* PORTRAIT of WASHINGTON *inserted.*

2079 WASHINGTON. Letters on Agriculture from His Excellency George Washington President of the United States to Arthur Young, Esq., F.R.S. and Sir John Sinclair, Bart., M.P. With Statistical Tables and Remarks, by Thomas Jefferson, Richard Peters, and other Gentlemen, on the Economy and Management of Farms in the United States. Edited by Franklin Knight. *Washington:* 1847.

4to, pp. 198. *Portrait, Map,* 4 *Plates, and* 18 *leaves in Facsimile. Half green morocco.* PORTRAITS of WASHINGTON, YOUNG, and SINCLAIR *inserted.*

The Letters to Sir John Sinclair are *engraved* from the *originals,* so as to present an exact facsimile of the hand-writing of Washington.

2080 WASHINGTON. Farewell Address to the People of the United States of America. *New York: John Wiley.* 1850.

4to, pp. (6), 56, *xlviii. Green morocco, gilt edges.* FOUR PORTRAITS, three of which are INDIA PROOFS, *inserted.* RARE.

Printed from the original MS. for Mr. Lenox, who caused a few copies of the Address to be issued for presents, with notes showing the various alterations and corrections, accompanied by letters from Chief Justice Jay, Mr. Jared Sparks, and others, throwing light on the history of this interesting document.

2081 WASHINGTON. Diary of Washington: from the first day of October, 1789, to the tenth day of March, 1790. From the Original Manuscript, now first printed. *New York:* 1858.

Imp. 8vo, pp. 89. *Half green morocco, gilt top,* UNCUT. PORTRAIT *inserted.* One of *fifty copies only* printed on *white paper* for Mr. J. Carson Brevoort for PRIVATE DISTRIBUTION. This copy has the title page in DUPLICATE, with and without the MONOGRAM of the Bradford Club, and is the ONLY ONE so printed.

"The preceding diary has been printed from the original manuscript now in my possession, for the Bradford Club of New York. One hundred copies, with rubricated title-pages, were printed for the Club, and one hundred on thinner paper, with black title-pages, for my own use."— *J. Carson Brevoort.*

2082 WASHINGTON at Valley Forge, together with the Duché Correspondence. *Philadelphia: J. M. Butler.* [1858.]

8vo, pp. 91. 5 *Engravings. Half green morocco, gilt top,* UNCUT. LARGE PAPER. A *few copies only printed.*

Contains PLATE of "Washington and the Duché letter," PORTRAIT of Dr. Duché, VIEWS of Christ's and St. Peter's Churches, and Washington's Headquarters at Valley Forge.

2083 WASHINGTON. Farewell Address to the People of the United States. Embellished with Arabesque Designs and Illuminations. *Philadelphia: Devereaux.* [1859.]

4to, half green morocco, gilt edges. FOUR ILLUSTRATIONS *inserted,* including the fine head of WASHINGTON after STUART, IN COLOURS, published by GOUPIL; and an UNLETTERED INDIA PROOF of the PIERREPONT PORTRAIT.

2084 [WASHINGTON.] An Inquiry into the Formation of Washington's Farewell Address ... [By Horace Binney.] *Philadelphia:* 1859.

8vo, pp. 250. *Half blue morocco,* FOUR PORTRAITS *inserted.*

2085 WASHINGTON. Diary of George Washington, from 1789 to 1791; embracing the opening of the First Congress, and his Tours through New England, Long Island, and the Southern States. Together with his Journal of a Tour to the Ohio in 1753. Edited by Benson J. Lossing. *New York: Charles B. Richardson & Co.* 1860.

12mo, pp. 248. *Half green morocco, gilt top,* UNCUT. PORTRAITS of GENERAL, and MRS. WASHINGTON *inserted.*

2086 WASHINGTON. Diary of George Washington, from 1789 to 1791. ... Edited by Benson J. Lossing. *Richmond: Press of the Historical Society.* 1861.

8vo, pp. 248. *Half green morocco, gilt top,* UNCUT. LARGE PAPER. A *few copies only* printed. PORTRAIT *of* WASHINGTON *inserted.*

2087 [WASHINGTON.] Addresses of the City of New York to George Washington, with his Replies. *New York:* 1867.

Imp. 8vo, pp. viii., 14. *Facsimile. Half green morocco, gilt top,* UNCUT. TWO INDIA PROOF PORTRAITS, *one from a* PRIVATE PLATE, *inserted.* SEVENTY-FIVE COPIES ONLY *printed for* PRIVATE DISTRIBUTION, *of which this is No.* 1.

2088 WATCH (The) An Ode, Humbly inscribed to the Rt. Hon. the Earl of M—F—D. To which is added The Genius of America to General Carleton, an Ode. *London: J. Bew.* 1778.

4to, pp. 39. *Half blue morocco, gilt top,* UNCUT. RARE. PORTRAIT of EARL MANSFIELD *inserted.*

2089 [WATERHOUSE (Benjamin.)] A Journal, of a Young Man of Massachusetts, late a Surgeon on board an American Privateer, who was captured at sea by the British, in May Eighteen Hundred and

Thirteen, and was confined first, at Melville Island, ... and last at Dartmoor Prison. Interspersed with Observations, Anecdotes, and Remarks, tending to Illustrate the Moral and Political Characters of Three Nations. To which is added, a Correct Engraving of Dartmoor Prison, representing the Massacre of American Prisoners. Written by Himself. The Second Edition. ...

Boston: Rowe & Hooper. 1816.

12mo, pp. 240. *Folded Plate. Half red morocco, carmine edges.* Fine clean copy. *Scarce.*

Dedicated to "the Common Sense and Humane Feeling of the People of America."

2090 WATSON (E.) Men and Times of the Revolution; or, Memoirs of Elkanah Watson, including Journals of Travels in Europe and America, from 1777 to 1842, with his Correspondence with Public Men, and Reminiscences and Incidents of the Revolution. Edited by his Son, Winslow C. Watson.

New York: Dana and Company. 1856.

8vo, pp. 460. *Half olive morocco, gilt top. Large and Fine Copy.* TWO PORTRAITS of the AUTHOR *inserted.*

2091 WATSON (J. F.) Annals and Occurrences of New York City and State, in the Olden Time; being a Collection of Memoirs, Anecdotes, and Incidents concerning the City, Country, and Inhabit ants, from the Days of the Founders. Intended to preserve the recollections of Olden Time, and to exhibit Society in its Changes of Manners and Customs, and the City and Country in their local Changes and Improvements. ... By John F. Watson.

Philadelphia: Henry F. Anners. 1846.

8vo, pp. 390. *Numerous Engravings. Half purple morocco, gilt top,* UNCUT. A UNIQUE and BEAUTIFUL COPY, with SIXTY-EIGHT ILLUSTRATIONS *inserted.*

2092 WATSON. Annals of Philadelphia and Pennsylvania, in the Olden Time; being a Collection of Memoirs, Anecdotes, and Incidents of the City and its Inhabitants, and of the Earliest Settlements of the Inland Part of Pennsylvania, from the Days of the Founders. ... By John F. Watson. [*Philadelphia:*] *Parry and M'Millan.* 1855.

2 *vols., 8vo, pp. xv.,* (1), 609; *vi.,* (1), 591. 51 *Engravings. Half purple morocco, gilt top.* UNIQUE and ELEGANT COPY with ONE HUNDRED AND TWENTY-FOUR ILLUSTRATIONS *inserted,* many of which are SCARCE, and some RARE.

Uniform in size and binding with the preceding No.

2093 WATSON (J. T.) A Dictionary of Poetical Quotations: consisting of Elegant Extracts on Every Subject. Compiled from various Authors, and arranged under Appropriate Heads.

Philadelphia: Lindsay & Blakiston. 1848.

Sm. 8vo, pp. 506. *Maroon morocco, gilt back, sides, and edges.*

2094 WATT (R.) Bibliotheca Britannica; or, a General Index to British and Foreign Literature. By Robert Watt, M.D.

Edinburgh: Archibald Constable and Company. 1824.

4 *vols., 4to, half purple levant morocco, gilt top.* LARGE and FINE COPY.

In the first part of the work the authors are arranged in alphabetical order, and under each is given a chronological list of his works, their various editions, sizes, and prices. In the second part, the same materials are digested under the names of the various subjects to which they refer, and under each the titles of works are again arranged chronologically. The first part is a full and comprehensive Catalogue of authors and their works; the second is an equally complete and extensive Encyclopædia of all manner of subjects on which books have been written.

2095 [WAYNE (ANTHONY.) THE ORIGINAL MANUSCRIPT ORDERLY BOOK, KEPT BY GENERAL WAYNE during the REVOLUTIONARY WAR, while encamped at LANCASTER and VALLEY FORGE, from Feb. 26th, 1778, to May 27th, 1778, containing some of the MOST IMPORTANT ORDERS issued during the War.]

Sm. 4to, 91 leaves, original boards, in a blue morocco pull-off case, lettered.

A considerable portion of the MS. is believed to be in the hand-writing of GEN. ANTHONY WAYNE, the Hero of Stony Point. The volume has been used as a Book of Reference by Irving, Bancroft and others. The following Letter speaks for itself.

SUNNYSIDE, June 28, '57.

DEAR SIR:—I have this day sent the Valley Forge Orderly Book to your address, ... according to your advice, and beg you to accept my grateful thanks for the loan of this interesting relic of the Revolution, which I have detained for a rather unreasonable time.

Very respectfully, yours obliged, &c.,

WASHINGTON IRVING.

Other Letters, by Jared Sparks, and George Bancroft, are equally conclusive as to the value and genuineness of this HIGHLY IMPORTANT REVOLUTIONARY RELIC, which would form a desirable acquisition to any Revolutionary Collection. An autograph signature of GEN. WAYNE, and the original autograph letters of MESSRS. IRVING, SPARKS, and BANCROFT accompany the volume.

FROM THE WIGHT COLLECTION.

2096 WEBBER (H.) Metrical Romances of the Thirteenth, Fourteenth, and Fifteenth Centuries: published from Ancient Manuscripts. With an Introduction, Notes, and a Glossary. By Henry Webber, Esq.
Edinburgh: Constable and Co. 1810.

3 *vols., sm. 8vo, pp. lxxxvii.*, 381; 479; 459, (2). *Half olive morocco, gilt top*, UNCUT. Beautiful copy. SCARCE.

This Collection forms a desirable sequel to those of Ritson, Percy, and Ellis.

2097 WEBSTER (D.) The Works of Daniel Webster.
Boston: Charles C. Little, and James Brown. 1851.

6 *vols., imp. 8vo, French green morocco antique, gilt edges.* LARGE PAPER. *Fifty copies only printed.* With autograph signature of DANIEL WEBSTER.

2098 WEBSTER. The Private Correspondence of Daniel Webster. Edited by Fletcher Webster.
Boston: Little, Brown and Company, 1857.

2 *vols., impl. 8vo, French green morocco antique, gilt edges.* LARGE PAPER. *Only fifty copies printed.* An autograph note signed of MR. WEBSTER, and TWENTY-EIGHT FINE ILLUSTRATIONS *inserted.*

Uniform with the preceding No., together with which it forms a SPLENDID and COMPLETE SET of the writings of Daniel Webster, ranging in size with the works of Adams, Franklin, Washington and Bancroft, &c.

2099 WEBSTER (N.) A Letter to the Honorable John Pickering, on the subject of his Vocabulary; or Collection of Words and Phrases, supposed to be Peculiar to the United States of America. By Noah Webster. *Boston: West, and Richardson.* 1817.

[Also:] A Key to the Indian Language of New England, in the Etchemin, or Passamaquoddy Language, Spoken in Maine and St. Johns New Brunswick. Derived and written from the Indian (Nicola Teneslas.) By Joseph Barratt, M.D. *Middletown, Conn.* 1850.

8vo, 2 pieces in 1 vol., pp. 60; 8. *Half brown morocco, gilt top,* UNCUT. SCARCE.

2100 WEEMS (M. L.) A History of the Life and Death, Virtues and Exploits, of General George Washington. Faithfully taken from Authentic Documents, and, now, in a Third Edition, improved, respectfully offered to the perusal of his countrymen; as also, all others who wish to see human nature in its most finished form. By the Rev. M. L. Weems, of Lodge No. 50 — Dumfries.
Philadelphia: Re-printed by John Bioren, for the Author. [1800.]

Roy. 8vo, pp. 84. *Half green morocco, gilt top,* UNCUT. SCARCE PORTRAIT *of* WASHINGTON *inserted.* A VERY RARE edition.

2101 WEEMS. A History of the Life and Death, Virtues and Exploits of General George Washington, faithfully taken from Authentic Documents. ... Third Edition. *Elizabethtown: Printed by Shepard Kollock, for the Author.* [1800.]

Roy. 8vo, pp. 61. *Portrait engraved by* TANNER. *Half green morocco, gilt top,* UNCUT. *Fine copy.* VERY SCARCE. The portrait is seldom found in the work.

2102 WEEMS. [A Collection of Tracts, Written by, Printed for, and Sold by that Eccentric Divine.] *Philadelphia:* 1818–23.

8vo, half gray calf, carmine edges. Very fine copies. SCARCE.

The Volume contains: "God's Revenge against Adultery." pp. 48.—"The Drunkard's Looking Glass." pp. 63.—"God's Revenge against Duelling." pp. 48.—God's Revenge against Gambling." pp. 47.—"God's Revenge against Murder." pp. 40.—With Numerous curious copper-plates, and wood-cuts.

2103 WEEMS. Life of George Washington: with Curious Anecdotes, equally Honourable to himself, and Exemplary to his young Countrymen. Embellished with Six Engravings. By M. L. Weems.
Philadelphia: Joseph Allen. 1834.

12mo, pp. 228. 6 *Wood-cuts. Half green morocco.* A duplicate, but different, set of the curious and *very original* engravings from another edition *inserted.*

2104 WELD (I.) Travels through the States of North America, and the Provinces of Upper and Lower Canada, during the years 1795, 1796, and 1797. By Isaac Weld, Junior. Second Edition. Illustrated and Embellished with Sixteen Plates.
London: John Stockdale. 1799.

2 *vols., 8vo, pp. xxiii.,* (1), 427; *xii.,* 376. 16 *Plates. Half calf.* LARGE and CLEAN COPY with many rough leaves.

"Accompanied by a faithful servant, Mr. Weld, sometimes on horseback, sometimes on foot, or in canoe, made his way through vast forests, or along rivers or lakes; narrowly escaped shipwreck on Lake Erie, and experienced all the adventure incident to passing through an unsettled country, while in the cities and towns he mixed in the best society, and had the honour and pleasure of knowing Washington."

2105 [WELDE (Thomas.)] A Short | Story | of the Rise, Reign and Ruin of the | Antinomians, Familists, and Libertines | That Infected the Churches | Of New-England: | And how they were Confuted by | The Assembly of Ministers there: | As also of the Magistrates | Proceedings in Court against them. | Together with God's Strange, Remarkable Judge- | ments from Heaven upon some of the Chief Fomenters of | these Opinions; and the Lamentable Death of Mrs. Hutchison. | Very fit for these Times; here being the same Errors amongst us, | and Acted by the same Spirit. | Published at the Instant Request of Sundry, by one that was an | Eye and Ear-Witness of the carriage of Matters there. | *London: Printed for Tho. Parkhurst, at the Bible and three Crowns at the | lower end of Cheapside, near Mercer's Chappel.* 1692.

4to, pp. (18), 64. *Polished calf, gilt edges, by* F. BEDFORD. LARGE and FINE COPY of this VERY SCARCE WORK.

In this curious work is a marvellous account of the birth of a *female monster*, the father and mother of whom were (according to the narrator) Familists, and opposed to the views of their community; the midwife being one "notorious for familiarity with the Devill, and now a prime Familist."

2106 WELLS (W. V.) The Life and Public Services of Samuel Adams, being a Narrative of his Acts and Opinions, and of his Agency in producing and forwarding the American Revolution. With extracts from his Correspondence, State Papers, and Political Essays. By William V. Wells. *Boston: Little, Brown & Co.* 1866.

3 vols., imp. 8vo, pp. xxi., 512; *x.,* 512; *v.,* 460. *Portraits and Facsimiles. Half green morocco, gilt top,* UNCUT. LARGE PAPER. *One hundred copies printed,* with PROOF PORTRAITS on INDIA PAPER.

Uniform with the writings of Washington, Franklin, Bancroft, and Webster, &c.

2107 WELSH (T.) An Oration, delivered March 5th, 1783, at the Request of the Inhabitants of the Town of Boston; to Commemorate the Bloody Tragedy of the Fifth of March, 1770. By Doctor Thomas Welsh. *Boston: John Gill.* [1783.]

4to, pp. 18. *Half green morocco, gilt top,* UNCUT. VERY SCARCE. *Presentation copy* from the AUTHOR, with his inscription on the half title.

2108 WELSH. An Oration. [Another Copy.] *Boston: John Gill.* [1783.]

4to, pp. 18. *Half red morocco, gilt top.* FINE COPY.

2109 WESLEY (John.) [A series of the Tracts relative to the Vehement and Acrimonious Controversy resulting from the publication of the

Rev. John Wesley's Celebrated Tract entitled "A Calm Address to the American Colonies."]

13 *vols.*, 12*mo*, *uniformly bound in half blue morocco*, and numbered respectively at the bottom of the back of each in the following order:

I. A Calm Address to our American Colonies. By John Wesley, M.A. A New Edition, Corrected, and Enlarged. *London: Robert Hawes.* [1775.]

12*mo*, *pp.* 22. *Gilt top*, UNCUT. PORTRAIT *inserted.*

"In the beginning of the war in America, Wesley's character imbibed a strong tincture of politics: and two sermons he preached at this juncture, in the Foundry, and West Street Chapel, from the views they contained of the conduct of the Government, and the anti-ministerial spirit which they breathed, were very remarkable. A gentleman happening to ask what he then thought of the public measures, was answered, 'What should I think? Oppression will make a wise man mad.' This is sufficient to show that at that period, he was decidedly averse to the war. Presently after, he changed his sentiments. His conversion was instantaneous; and what is most remarkable, in the history of this event, is, that sudden as it was, it was absolute and complete. Converted himself, his next care was to convert his brethren; and in this office, his zeal was indefatigable. He not only carried his sentiments into all companies, and made them the subject of almost every conversation, but he eagerly displayed them in public; and the pulpit finished what the table began. When Mr. Wesley changed his politics, and published his 'Calm Address to the American Colonies,' many copies were shipped for New York; a gentleman of that country, alarmed for the safety of a people with whom he was connected, and trembling for the probable consequences, should a pamphlet of such a tendency pass into general circulation, laid violent hands upon it, and destroyed or returned the whole impression; so that till a considerable time after this transaction, scarcely any one had heard that such a piece had been published. This incident was the salvation of Methodism in America."— *Hampson's Life of Wesley.* II. 145–148. III. 134–140.

"Perhaps no two pamphlets did more good to the American cause than Dr. Johnson's "Taxation no Tyranny," and Mr. Wesley's "Calm Address," both intended to have quite a contrary effect from that which was produced by them."— *Rich.*

II. An Old Fox Tarred and Feather'd. Occasioned by what is called Mr. John Wesley's Calm Address to our American Colonys ... By an Hanoverian. The Second Edition Corrected. *London: M. Lewis.* 1775.

12*mo*, *pp.* 24.

The Hanoverian was the celebrated Baptist preacher Dr. A. M. Toplady who proves Wesley to be a plagiarist. See *Rich.* I. 221.

III. A Constitutional Answer to the Rev. Mr. John Wesley's 'Calm Address to the American Colonies.' *London: E. and C. Dilly.* 1775.

12*mo*, *pp.* 23. *Gilt top*, UNCUT.

"Mr. Wesley is here charged with acting the part of a political incendiary."— *Rich.*

IV. A Cool Reply to a Calm Address, lately published by Mr. John Wesley; The Second Edition. By T. S. ... *London: Printed for the Author.* 1775.

12*mo*, *pp.* 33.

V. A Letter to the Rev. Mr. John Wesley, Occasioned by his Calm Address to the American Colonies. [By Caleb Evans. D.D.]
London: Printed for Edward and Charles Dilly. M.DCC.LXXV.

12*mo*, *pp.* 24.

Signed "Americanus: Bristol, Oct. 2. 1775." "Wrote," says Wesley, "by two Anabaptist ministers, assisted by a gentleman and a tradesman of the Church of England." A clever piece, in favor of America.

VI. A Full Defence of the Rev. John Wesley, in answer to the several Personal Reflections cast on that Gentleman by the Rev. Caleb Evans, in his Observations on Mr. Wesley's late Reply prefixed to his Calm Address: By Thomas Olivers.
London: Printed in the Year. 1776.

12*mo*, *pp.* 24.

VII. A Vindication of the Rev. Mr. Wesley's "Calm Address to our American Colonies:" In some Letters to Mr. Caleb Evans. By John Fletcher, Vicar of Madeley, Salop. *London: Printed and sold at the Foundry.* [1776.]

12mo, pp. 70. *Gilt top,* UNCUT.

The author claims that the doctrine of taxation maintained by Mr. Wesley "is rational, Scriptural, and constitutional," while that of Mr. Evans "is highly unconstitutional, and draws after it a long train of absurd consequences." *See M. Rev.* LIV. 325.

VIII. A Reply to the Rev. Mr. Fletcher's Vindication of Mr. Wesley's Calm Address to our American Colonies. By Caleb Evans, M.A. *Bristol: W. Pine.* [1776.]

12mo, pp. 103.

"Mr. Evans is a lively and sensible advocate for the freedom of the colonies, a spirited controvertist, and a zealous asserter of those liberal and noble principles to which we are indebted for the glorious revolution."—*M. Rev.* LIV. 326.

IX. American Patriotism Farther confronted with Reason, Scripture, and the Constitution: Being Observations on the Dangerous Politicks Taught by the Rev. Mr. Evans, M.A. And the Rev. Dr. Price. With a Scriptural Plea for the Revolted Colonies. By J. Fletcher, Vicar of Madeley, Salop. *Shrewsbury: J. Eddowes.* MDCCLXXVI.

12mo, pp. viii., 130. *Gilt top,* UNCUT.

The writer takes issue against Evans and Price, and defends the right of Great Britain to tax the colonies.

X. Political Sophistry Detected, or Brief Remarks on the Rev. Mr. Fletcher's late Tract entitled "American Patriotism." In a Letter to a Friend. By Caleb Evans, A.M. *Bristol: W. Pine.* 1776.

12mo, pp. 36. *Gilt top,* UNCUT.

XI. Observations on the Nature of Civil Liberty, the Principles of Government, and the Justice and Policy of the War with America. To which are added an Appendix and Postscript,... By Richard Price, D.D. F.R.S. A New Edition, corrected by the Author. *London: T. Cadell.* M.DCC.LXXVI.

12mo, pp. 76.

"The author of these observations must be ranked among the most respectable writers on the affairs of America."—*M.R. See Rich.* I. 233.

XII. Some Observations on Liberty: Occasioned by a late Tract. By John Wesley, M.A. *London: R. Hawes.* 1776.

12mo, pp. 36. *Gilt top,* UNCUT.

In answer to Dr. Price's Observations.

XIII. A Calm Address to the Inhabitants of England. By John Wesley. *London: J. Fry and Co.* 1777.

12mo, pp. 23. *Gilt top,* UNCUT.

"Mr. Wesley's calmness is only to be found in his title-pages; he is far from being a dispassionate writer; and the Americans have great reason to complain of him as a *fomenter*, rather than a composer of national discord."—*M. R.*

2110 WEST (S.) Greatness the Result of Goodness. A Sermon occasioned by the Death of George Washington, late Commander in Chief of the Armies, ... of the United States. ... who Died December 14, 1799, aged 68. By Samuel West, D.D. ... *Boston:* [1800.]

8vo, pp. 40. UNCUT.

2111 WETMORE (W.) An Oration on the death of General George Washington, delivered at the request of the Citizens of Castine, on the 22d February, A.D. 1800. Pursuant to the Recommendations of Congress, and the General Court of Massachusetts. By William Wetmore, Barrister at Law. *Castine:* [1800.]

8vo, pp. 30.

2112 [WHARTON (Charles Henry.)] A | Poetical Epistle | to his Excellency | George Washington, Esq. | Commander in chief of the Armies of the | United States of America, | from | An Inhabitant of the State of Maryland. | To which is annexed, | a Short Sketch of | General Washington's Life and Character. | *Annapolis, Printed*, 1779; | *London, Reprinted, for C. Dilly.* MDCCLXXX.

Sm. 4to, pp. 24. *Portrait. Crushed green levant morocco, blank tooled sides, gilt edges, by* W. MATTHEWS. A beautiful copy of this RARE WORK, with a remarkably fine impression of the very scarce "DONT TREAD ON ME," portrait of Washington, engraved by Sharp, with a black neckerchief, an article of dress which Washington never, at any time, wore.

Reprinted in London, "for the charitable purpose of raising a few guineas to relieve in a small measure the distresses of some hundreds of American prisoners, now suffering confinement in the gaols of England."— *Preface.*

2113 [WHARTON.] A Poetical Epistle. [Another Edition.] *New York: Reprinted.* 1865.

Sm. 4to, pp. 24. *Half green morocco, gilt top,* UNCUT. PRIVATELY PRINTED, and *fifty copies only* on this size. SCARCE PORTRAIT of WASHINGTON *inserted.*

2114 WHEATLEY (P.) Poems | on | Various Subjects, | Religious and Moral. | By | Phillis Wheatley, | Negro Servant to Mr. John Wheatley, | of Boston, in New England. | *London: | Printed for A. Bell, Bookseller, Aldgate; and sold by | Messrs. Cox and Berry, King Street, Boston.* | MDCCLXXIII.

Sm. 8vo, pp. 124, (4). *Portrait. Half brown morocco, gilt top,* UNCUT. A FINE COPY of the RARE FIRST EDITION, and THE ONLY ONE we have ever seen in *uncut* condition.

"Phillis was a native of Africa, whence she was brought to Boston in 1761, when between seven and eight years of age. She was sold in the slave-market at Boston and bought by Mrs. Wheatley. She was taught to read and write by one of this lady's daughters and became the pet of the family. Her biographer states that in sixteen months after her arrival at Boston she had not only learned to speak the English language but to read the most difficult parts of the Bible. She visited London with her master's family, where she received much attention, and there printed her Poems, which are dedicated to the Countess of Huntingdon."— *John R. Bartlett.*

2115 WHEATLY. Letters of Phillis Wheatley, the Negro-Slave Poet of Boston. *Boston: Privately Printed.* 1864.

8vo, pp. 19. *Half green morocco, gilt edges. One hundred copies only* PRIVATELY PRINTED on a separate form, from the "Proceedings of the Mass. Hist. Society." VERY SCARCE.

2116 WHEATON (H.) History of the Northmen, or Danes and Normans, from the Earliest Time to the Conquest of England by William of Normandy. By Henry Wheaton. *London: John Murray.* MDCCCXXXI.

8vo, pp. xv., 367. *Half red morocco, gilt top,* UNCUT. Presentation copy from the Author.

Chapter II. relates to the Discovery of America by the Northmen.

2117 WHEELWRIGHT (J.) A Sermon Preached at Boston in New England, upon a Fast Day the 19th of January, 1636–37. By the Rev. John Wheelwright. *Cambridge: John Wilson and Son.* 1867.

8vo, pp. 22. *Half blue morocco, gilt top,* UNCUT, *by* BRADSTREET. *Twenty-five copies only* PRIVATELY RE-PRINTED from the "Proceedings of the Mass. Hist. Society," for 1866–67. EXCEEDINGLY SCARCE.

2118 WHITBOURNE (R.) A | Discovrse | And Discovery | Of Nevv-Found-Land, With | many reasons to prooue how worthy and bene- | ficiall a Plantation may there be made, after a far | better manner than now it is. | Together With The Laying | Open Of Certaine Enormities | and abuses committed by some that trade to that | Countrey, and the meanes laid downe for | reformation thereof. | Written by Captaine Richard Whitbourne of | Exmouth, in the County of Deuon, and pub- | lished by Authority. | As also, an Inuitation: and likewise certaine Letters sent | from that Countrey; which are printed in the | latter part of this Booke. | *Imprinted at London by Felix Kingston.* | 1622.

Sm. 4to, pp. (18), 107, (5), 15. *Gray calf, paneled sides, carmine edges.* A FINE COPY of this EXCEEDINGLY SCARCE BOOK.

This work comprises Capt. Whitbourne's Discourse as published in 1620, with alterations and 15 pages of letters from Newfoundland, dated in 1622, giving remarkable accounts of its productions, Mermaids, Mermen, &c. It also contains the only account of Avalon, the colony founded by Sir Geo. Calvert, and abandoned in favour of Maryland.

Capt. Whitbourne was the Father of Newfoundland. He says, that, that Island was as familiar to him as his own country, having made voyages to and from for over 40 years.

2119 WHITE (D. A.) A Eulogy on George Washington, ... delivered at the request of the Inhabitants of Methuen in the Meeting House of the First Parish of that Town. By Daniel Appleton White, A.B. *Haverhill:* 1800.

8vo, pp. 18. UNCUT. VERY SCARCE.

2120 WHITEFIELD (George.) [A Collection of the American Journals of this Distinguished Divine, together with Other Works relative thereto.]

7 vols., 8vo, uniformly bound, half blue morocco, carmine edges; and numbered respectively at the bottom of the back of each volume in the order of their publication.

The Collection consists of the following Works:

I. Journal of a Voyage from London to Savannah in Georgia. In Two Parts. Part I. From London to Gibraltar. Part II. From Gibraltar to Savannah. By George Whitefield A.B. of Pembroke College, Oxford. With a Short Preface, shewing the Reasons of its Publication. *London: James Hutton.* MDCCXXXVIII.

"The following Journal would never have been published, had not a surreptitious copy of part of it been printed without the author's knowledge or consent: he knows himself too well to obtrude his little private concerns upon the world." — *Preface.*

[Also:] Remarks on the Reverend Mr. Whitefield's Journal. Wherein his many Inconsistencies are Pointed out, and his Tenets Consider'd. The Whole shewing the Dangerous Tendency of his Doctrine ... . *London: Printed for the Author.* [1738.]

pp. iv., 58; 32.

II. Thankfulness for Mercies Received, a Necessary Duty. A Farewel (*sic*) Sermon Preached on board the Whitaker, at anchor near Savannah in Georgia, on Sunday, May the 17th, 1738. By George Whitefield. *London: J. Hutton.* 1738.

pp. 19.

III. A Continuation of the Reverend Mr. Whitefield's Journal, from his Arrival at Savannah, to his Return to London. The Second Edition. *London: W Strahan.* 1739.

pp. (4), 38.

IV. A Continuation of the Reverend Mr. Whitefield's Journal, from his Arrival at London, to his Departure from thence on his way to Georgia. The Third Edition. *London: James Hutton.* 1739.

pp. iv., 114.

V. A Continuation of the Rev. Mr. Whitefield's Journal, During the Time he was detained in England by the Embargo. Second Edition. *London: W. Strahan.* MDCCXXXIX.

pp. iv., 40.

VI. A Compleat Account of the Conduct of that eminent Enthusiast Mr. Whitefield. To which is annexed, I. A true Character of him, attested by himself. II. A most useful and entertaining Catechism for the use of Female Methodists. III. Some Queries sent to Mr. W. at Bristol, by the Rev. Mr. Tucker of that City. IV. An Answer to them, supposed to be written by Mr. John Wesley. V. Some general Remarks on the Answer by the Publisher of this Account. And VI. A more particular Reply by Mr. Tucker, the Author of the Queries. Together with some Remarks on Mr. W.'s Journal. *London: C. Corbett.* 1739.

8vo, pp. 38.

VII. The True Character of the Rev. Mr. Whitefield: in a Letter from a Deist in London to his Friend in the Country. With some Observations on the Gestures of Dr. Trapp and Mr. Whitefield .... The Second Edition. *London: C. Corbett.* 1740.

A CURIOUS AND VERY SCARCE COLLECTION.

2121 WHITEFIELD. The Marks of the New Birth.| A | Sermon | Preached at the Parish-Church of | St, Mary, White-Chapel,| By George Whitefield, A.B. of Pembroke-College,| Oxford.| To which is added,| A Prayer for one desiring to be awakened | to an Experience of the New Birth | and another | For one newly awakened to a Sense of the | Divine Life.| The Sixth Edition.| *London Printed, and Re-printed and Sold by* | W. BRADFORD *in New-York.* 1739.

Sm. 12mo, pp. 28. *Half brown morocco, gilt top.* EXTREMELY RARE. The ONLY COPY we have ever seen.

2122 WHITEFIELD. The | Rev. Mr. Whitefield's | Answer. | To the | Bishop of London's | last | Pastoral Letter.| *London Printed, and Reprinted by* WILLIAM | BRADFORD *In New York,* 1739.

Sm. 12mo, pp. 21, (1). *Half brown morocco, gilt top.* Uniform in size and binding with the preceding No.

One of the RAREST productions of BRADFORD's press.

2123 WHITEFIELD. Three Letters from the Reverend Mr. G. Whitefield: viz. Letter I. To a Friend in London, concerning Archbishop Tillotson. Letter II. To the same on the same subject.

Letter III. To the Inhabitants of Maryland, Virginia, North and South Carolina, concerning their Negroes.
Philadelphia: Printed and Sold by B. FRANKLIN, *at the New Printing Office near the Market.* M.DCC.XL.

12*mo*, *pp.* 16. *Polished calf, gilt edges, by* W. PRATT.

An EARLY, VERY RARE and PECULIAR production from Franklin's Office. Printed without signatures, and with the first page of the text commencing on the verso of the title. BEAUTIFUL COPY. The ONLY ONE we have ever met with.

2124 WHITFIELD (H.) The Light appearing more and more to- | wards the perfect Day. | Or, | A farther Discovery of the present state | of the Indians | In | New-England, | Concerning the Progresse of the Gospel | amongst them | Manifested by Letters from such as preacht | to them there. | Published by H. Whitfield, late Pastor to the Chuch [*sic*] | of Christ at Gilford in New-England, who came | late thence. |
London: Printed by T. R. & E. M. for John Bartlet, and are to be | sold at the Gilt Cup, neer St. Austins gate in Paul's | Churchyard. 1651.

Sm. 4*to*, *pp.* (8), 46. *Polished calf, gilt edges, by* F. BEDFORD. A VERY LARGE *and* FINE COPY of this EXTREMELY RARE BOOK.

The fifth in order of publication of the Eliot Tracts. It contains five letters from Eliot, and one from Mayhew in continuation of "The Glorious Progress of the Gospel." In the first of Eliot's, dated 8 July, 1649, he announces his intention to translate the Scriptures into the Indian tongue.

2125 WHITFIELD. Strength | ovt of | Weaknesse ; | Or a Glorious | Manifestation | of the further Progresse of | the Gospel amongst the Indians | in Nevv-England. | Held forth in Sundry Letters | from divers Ministers and others to the | Corporation established by Parliament for | promoting the Gospel among the Hea- | then in New-England ; and to particular | Members thereof since the late Trea- | tise to that effect, pulished (*sic*) by | Mr. Henry Whitfield late Pastor | of Gilford in New-England. ... *London; | Printed by M. Simmons for John Blague and | Samuel Howes, and are to be sold at their | shop in Popes-Head-Alley.* 1652.

Sm. 4*to*, *pp.* (16), 40. *Red morocco, gilt edges.*

Of this VERY RARE WORK, the sixth in order of the series, three editions were issued in 1652. This has STRENGTH in capitals, the first address to the reader signed by 14 names, and the second dated 28th of February, 1651. It contains two letters by Eliot, one from the Rev. John Wilson of Boston with interesting accounts of Eliot's house and mode of life, one from William Leverich of Sandwich, one from A. Bessey, one from Mayhew, one from Governor Endecott of Massachusetts, and one from Thomas Allen. It is dedicated "To the Parliament of the Commonwealth of England."

2126 WHITEHEAD (W. A.) A Biographical Sketch of William Franklin, Governor [of New Jersey] from 1763 to 1776, by William A. Whitehead. Read before the New Jersey Historical Society, September 27th, 1848. [*New York:* 1848?]

8*vo*, *half red morocco. Only a few copies printed.* PORTRAIT of GOVERNOR FRANKLIN *inserted.*

2127 WHITEHEAD. Contributions to the Early History of Perth Amboy and Adjoining Country, with Sketches of Men and Events in New Jersey during the Provincial Era. By William A. Whitehead. With Maps and Engravings. *New York: D. Appleton and Co.* 1856.

8vo, pp. viii., 428. 2 *Maps,* 4 *Portraits and* 17 *Views. Half olive morocco, gilt top.*

2128 WHITMORE (H.) Catalogue of the Private Library of Henry Whitmore. Prepared by T. H. Morrell. *New York:* 1865.

4to, pp. (6), 99. *Half crimson morocco, gilt top,* UNCUT. *With Prices.* LARGE PAPER. *Thirty copies only printed.*

2129 WHITMORE (W. H.) A Handbook of American Genealogy, being a Catalogue of Family Histories and Publications containing Genealogical Information, Chronologically arranged. By William H. Whitmore. *Albany: J. Munsell.* 1862.

Sm. 4to, pp. 272. *Half purple morocco, gilt top,* UNCUT. *One hundred copies only* printed for subscribers.

2130 [WHITTIER (James G.)] The Supernaturalism of New England. *New York: Wiley & Putnam.* 1847.

8vo, pp. ix., 71. *Half crimson morocco, gilt top,* UNCUT.

"There be no beggars in this country, but witches too many."— *Josselyn.*

2131 WHITWELL (B.) An Eulogy, on the virtues of General George Washington, who Died December 14, 1799. Delivered before the Inhabitants of the Town of Augusta, at the Request of their Committee, by Benjamin Whitwell, Esq. *Hallowell: (District of Maine). Peter Edes.* 1800.

Sm. 4to, pp. 18. VERY RARE.

2132 **Whytinton (R.) The thre bookes of Tullyes offyces, bothe in latyne tonge & in englysshe, lately translated by Roberte Whytinton poete laureate.** [Colophon] **Imprinted at London in Flete Strete, by Wynkyn de Worde. The yere of our lorde god m.d.xxxiiii. the xxx. day of September.**

194 leaves, without pagination, or catchwords, with the picturesque design of the printer under the colophon. *Sm. sq. 8vo, olive morocco, broad inside gilt borders, dull gilt edges.* The FIRST ENGLISH TRANSLATION of CICERO'S OFFICES and EXTREMELY RARE.

A beautifully printed volume from the press of WYNKYN DE WORDE, with the Latin text in Italic on one page, and the English translation in black letter on the opposite. With the exception that a single worm-hole extends through the first six leaves the volume is in fine preservation, and affords an excellent and very desirable example of the press of England's second printer, the son-in-law and successor of WILLIAM CAXTON.

See *Dibdin's Typ. Ant.* II. 293.

2133 WIGHT (A.) Catalogue of the Library of Andrew Wight, of Philadelphia. ... Prepared by Joseph Sabin. *New York: J. E. Cooley.* 1864.

Imp. 8vo, pp. 315. *Half olive morocco, gilt top,* UNCUT. *Ruled* and *Priced.* LARGE PAPER. A *few copies only* printed for PRIVATE DISTRIBUTION. Particularly rich in Americana and books printed by Benjamin Franklin.

2134 WIGHT (P. B.) National Academy of Design. Photographs of the New Building, with an Introductory Essay and Description. By Peter B. Wight, Architect. *New York: S. P. Avery.* 1866.

Square folio, half brown morocco, gilt edges.

Contains FIFTEEN photographic views of the ELEVATION, with EXTERIOR and INTERIOR SECTIONS of the Academy.

2135 WILKES (C.) Narrative of the United States Exploring Expedition. During the Years 1838, 1839, 1840, 1841, and 1842. By Charles Wilkes, U. S. N. Commander of the Expedition. ... *Philadelphia: Lea & Blanchard.* 1845.

6 *vols., imp. 8vo, pp. lx.,* 434; *xv.,* 476; *xv.,* 438; *xvi.,* 539; *xv.,* 538. 64 *large and highly finished Line Engravings comprising Scenery, Portraits, Manners, Customs, &c.;* 47 *large and fine Vignettes engraved on Steel;* 248 *choice Engravings on Wood; and* 9 *Maps. Half blue morocco, gilt top,* UNCUT. The 5 large Maps which form the Atlas, are lined with fine linen and folded and bound to represent Vol. VI. AN ORIGINAL SUBSCRIBER'S COPY.

This GREAT and truly NATIONAL WORK will compare favorably with the best English editions of similar works.

2136 WILKINSON (E.) Letters of Eliza Wilkinson, during the Invasion and Possession of Charleston, S. C., by the British in the Revolutionary War. Arranged from the Original Manuscripts, by Caroline Gilman. *New York: Samuel Colman.* 1839.

12mo, pp. 108. *Half purple calf.*

2137 WILKINSON (J.) [A Series of Works by, and Relating to General James Wilkinson.]

9 *vols., 8vo. Atlas* 1 *vol. 4to. Half purple morocco, gilt top,* UNCUT.

Together 10 volumes, all in the finest state and absolutely perfect; a condition to which many copies of Wilkinson's Memoirs and such other volumes as sometimes accompany them, cannot lay claim. The present is the most complete, and best conditioned set that has ever come under our observation, and would form an admirable adjunct to the Burr Series No. 295.

The Contents of the Series are as follows:

I. Further Information and Papers laid before the House of Representatives of the United States, relative to Brigadier General Wilkinson. April 25, 1808. Ordered to be transmitted to the President of the United States. *Washington City:* 1808.

pp. 15.

In corroboration of a statement previously made by Daniel Clark, that Wilkinson had corruptly received money from the Spanish government at New Orleans, while in the service and pay of the United States.

II. Proofs of the Corruption of Gen. James Wilkinson, and of his Connexion with Aaron Burr, with a Full Refutation of his Slanderous Allegations in relation to the Character of the Principal Witness against him. By Daniel Clark, of the City of New Orleans. ... *Philadelphia:* 1809.

pp. 150, 199. PORTRAIT of BURR *inserted.* VERY SCARCE.

III. Report of the Committee who were instructed, on the thirteenth ultimo, to Inquire into the Cause or Causes of the Great Mortality in that detachment of the Army of the United States, ordered for the Defence of New Orleans. April 27, 1810. Read and ordered to lie on the table. *City of Washington:* 1810.

pp. 130. *Numerous Tabular Statements.*

The detachment of the Army referred to was under the command of Wilkinson, from which he was recalled under circumstances of disgrace.

IV. Report of the Committee, appointed to Inquire into the Conduct of Brigadier General Wilkinson. May 1st, 1810. Read, and printed by order of the House of Representatives. *Washington City:* 1810.

pp. 217.

Respecting Wilkinson's having corruptly received money from the Spanish government; and of his being concerned, as an accomplice, with Burr, in a project to dismember the United States.

V. Report of the Committee appointed to Inquire into the Conduct of General Wilkinson. February 26, 1811. Read, and ordered to be transmitted to the President of the United States. *Washington:* 1811.

pp. 582. EXTREMELY SCARCE.

In continuation of the inquiry into the charges specified in No. IV. This copy contains the two Sheets of Ciphers and Hieroglyphics made use of in Wilkinson's treasonable correspondence with Burr, one or the other of which is nearly always wanting. Most copies end on p. 522.

VI. Memoirs of General Wilkinson. Volume II.
Washington City: Printed for the Author. 1811.

[Also a second title.] Burr's Conspiracy Exposed; and General Wilkinson Vindicated against the Slanders of his Enemies on that Important Occasion. 1811.

pp. 18, 99, 136. PRIVATELY PRINTED and EXTREMELY RARE. PORTRAIT OF WILKINSON, and an AUTOGRAPH NOTE written and signed by him *inserted.*

"Persecuted to the verge of destruction, without a dawn of relief, his humble fortune ruined and his domestic happiness blasted," Wilkinson anticipated the publication of this much of his Memoirs by way of vindicating his "aspersed honor."—See "*Advertisement.*"

We know of *two other copies only* in existence. The late Peter Force was in the habit of showing his copy of this volume as one of the modern rarities of his immense collection.

VII. Memoirs of My Own Times. By General James Wilkinson. *Philadelphia:* 1816.

3 *vols.*, 8*vo*, *pp. xv.*, 855, (44); 578, (260); 496, (54); 3 *facsimiles*, 8 *folded sheets. Atlas of* 20 *Diagrams and Plans, with Title and Explanations.* A VERY FINE COPY, quite free from the stains which disfigure most sets of the work.

Inserted in this UNIQUE COPY are three curious and interesting letters of GENERAL WILKINSON, one in the first volume, dated at Philadelphia, April 15th, 1817, 2 pages quarto, relating almost exclusively to these Memoirs. The following is an extract. "The subscription has very far exceeded the impression of 1500 copies struck off ... I am barely able to send a dozen copies to Savannah and the same number for Charleston. Another edition will be issued with a continuation with which all subscribers will be supplied. ... The copies of delinquent subscribers have been sold at $15 and sought for with great avidity. ... You will find the book written with perfect freedom, regardful only of truth, ... here it is approved by all parties and persons except official sycophants. I have from General Dearborn, who has read it, a highly approbatory & complimentary letter — he insists I must go on and tell truth to our country of which they have been kept in the dark."

Another, in the second volume, dated at Fort Washington, June 24th, 1798, 4 pages quarto, describes an interview with four nations of Indians headed by LITTLE TURTLE. "They charged us with the murder of seven of their people on grounds too strong to be controverted."

That in the third volume dated at New Orleans September 9th, 1812, 2 pages quarto, is addressed to Governor Holmes respecting the organization of the militia. "I find a great error has occurred. Out of 1500 stand of arms reported at Baton Rouge Colonel Purdy informs me only 176 could be found fit for use."

Wilkinson's Memoirs comprehend many incidents and anecdotes of the Revolution little known, with a more interesting and authentic account of the battle of Breed's Hill, the siege of Boston, and the campaigns of 1776–77 than is elsewhere extant.

2138 WILLARD (J.) *and* TAPPAN (D.) An Address in Latin, by Joseph Willard, LL.D., President; and a Discourse in English, by David Tappan, S.T.D. Hollis Professor of Divinity; delivered before the University in Cambridge, Feb. 21, 1800, in Solemn Commemoration of Gen. George Washington. [*Boston:*] MDCCC.

8vo, pp. 44. UNCUT.

2139 WILLARD *and* TAPPAN. An Address in Latin, &c. [Another copy.] [*Boston:*] M,DCCC.

4to, pp. 31. LARGE PAPER. EXCEEDINGLY RARE. *Unnoticed by* Dr. Hough.

2140 [WILLARD (Samuel.)] Some Miscellany Observations On our present Debates respecting Witchcrafts, in a Dialogue Between S. & B. By P. E. and J. A. *Philadelphia: Printed by William Bradford, for Hezekiah Usher.* 1692. *Boston:* "*Congregational Quarterly*" *Reprint.—No.* 1. 1869.

Sm. 4to, pp. 24. *Half blue morocco, gilt top,* UNCUT, *by* BRADSTREET. *One hundred copies only printed.* PORTRAIT *inserted.*

Respecting the difference of opinion, relative to Witchcraft, which existed between the pulpit and the bar of the period, the editor remarks, "Mr. Poole in his paper on 'Cotton Mather and Salem Witchcraft' [*See* No. 1616 in this Catalogue] has presented the subject in a new light by furnishing Contemporaneous Documents hitherto neglected. One of them is a rare and anonymous Tract written by Reverend Samuel Willard, of the Old South Church, entitled 'Some Miscellany Observations &c.' 'Its Reproduction' says Mr. Poole 'would at this time throw more light upon the Opinions of the New England Clergy respecting Witchcraft than any other Document that has not been republished.' The S and B who carry on the Dialogue may have been intended for Stoughton and Brattle, or Salem and Boston."—*Introductory Note.*

2141 WILLETT (W. M.) A Narrative of the Military Actions of Colonel Marinus Willett, taken chiefly from his own Manuscript. Prepared by his Son, Wm. M. Willett. *New York: G. & C. & H. Carvill.* 1831.

8vo, pp. 162. *Half green morocco, gilt top,* UNCUT. An EXTENSIVELY ILLUSTRATED COPY, with a DOCUMENT signed by WILLETT, as Sheriff, and upwards of NINETY ILLUSTRATIONS, many of which are RARE, *inserted.*

2142 WILLIAMS (*Mrs.* [C. R.]) Biography of Revolutionary Heroes; containing the Life of Brigadier Gen. William Barton, and also, of Captain Stephen Olney. By Mrs. Williams. *Providence: Published by the Author.* 1839.

12mo, pp. 312. *Engraving. Half gray calf, red edges.*

2143 [WILLIAMS (Edward.)] Virginia's | Discovery of | Silke-VVormes, | with their benefit. | And | The Implanting of Mulberry Trees. | Also | The dressing and keeping of Vines, for the rich trade | of making Wines there. | Together with | The making of the Saw-mill, very ufefull in Virginia, | for cutting of Timber and Clapbord to build with- | all, and its Converſion to other as profitable Uſes. | *London* | *Printed by T. H. for John Stephenſon, at the Signe of* | *the Sun below Ludgate.* 1650.

Sm. 4to, pp. (8), 75, (3). 5 *Engravings. Polished red morocco, gilt edges,* UNCUT, *by* F. BEDFORD. AN ELEGANT COPY of one of the SCARCEST BOOKS relating to Virginia.

2144 WILLIAMS (E.) Life of Te-ho-ra-gwa-ne-gen, alias Thomas Williams, A Chief of the Caughnawaga Tribe of Indians in Canada. By the Rev. Eleazer Williams, Reputed Son of Thomas Williams, and by many believed to be Louis XVII, son of the last reigning monarch of France, previous to the Revolution of 1789. [Edited by F. B. Hough.] *Albany: J. Munsell.* 1859.

Roy. 8vo, pp. 91. *Half red morocco, gilt top,* UNCUT. INDIA PROOF PORTRAIT of the Editor, and VIEW of St. Regis *inserted.* 200 copies only printed.

"Eleazer Williams, the reputed Louis the XVII, was the son of Maria Antoinette, and shortly after his birth was committed to the care of some unknown person who either carried or had him sent to North America, where he was consigned to a certain tribe of Indians residing in the western part of New York, who adopted him as a son, and by whom he was brought up to their wild habits and customs."—*Field.*

2145 [WILLIAMS (John.)] A Brief | Discourse | Concerning the | Lawfulness of Worshipping God | By The | Common Prayer. | Being in | Answer | To a Book Entituled, | A Brief Discourse concerning the Unlawfulness of the | Common-Prayer Worship. | Lately Printed in New England and Re-printed | in London. | In which the Chief Things Objected against | the Liturgy are consider'd. | The Second edition corrected. | ... | *London:* | *Printed for Ri. Chiswell, at the Rose and Crown in* | *St. Paul's Church-Yard.* MDCXCIV.

Sm. 4to, pp. (2), 36. *Polished calf, gilt edges, by* F. BEDFORD. LARGE and FINE COPY. RARE.

In answer to Increase Mather's "Brief Discourse concerning the Unlawfulness of the Common-Prayer Worship."

2146 WILLIAMS (J.) The Redeemed Captive returning to Zion. A Faithful History of Remarkable Occurrences in the Captivity and Deliverance of Mr. John Williams, Minister of the Gospel in Deerfield, who, in the Desolation which befel that Plantation, by an incursion of the French and Indians, was by them carried away, with his Family, and his Neighbourhood, into Canada. Drawn up by Himself. Whereunto there is annexed, a Sermon preached by him, upon his Return, at the Lecture in Boston, December 5, 1706. ... The Fifth Edition. As also an Appendix, containing an Account of those taken Captive at Deerfield, Feb. 29, 1703-4; of those killed after they went out of Town; those who returned; and of those still absent from their native Country; of those who were slain at that time in or near the Town; and of the Mischief done by the Enemy in Deerfield, from the beginning of its Settlement to the Death of the

Rev. Mr. Williams in 1779. With a Conclusion to the Whole, by the Rev. Mr. Williams of Springfield, and the Rev. Mr. Prince of Boston. *Boston: Printed and Sold by John Boyle next Door to the Three Doves in Marlborough Street.* 1774.

8vo, pp. 70. *Half calf, gilt top,* UNCUT. FINE COPY. VERY RARE in *uncut* condition.

2147 WILLIAMS. The Redeemed Captive Returning to Zion. ... With an Appendix by the Rev. John Taylor, the present Minister of the Gospel at Deerfield. The Sixth Edition. [Containing some account of the mischief done by the enemy, in Deerfield, and its vicinity from the death of the Rev. Mr. Williams, to the conclusion of the last French war. Together with a circumstantial account of the FALL FIGHT which happened in May, 1676. Taken principally from an attested copy of a manuscript, written by some gentlemen who were in the action.] *Boston: Printed by Samuel Hall.* 1795.

12mo, pp. 132. *Half red morocco, gilt top,* UNCUT, *by* BRADSTREET. BEAUTIFUL COPY. VERY SCARCE. Mr. Taylor's interesting appendix extends to 18 pages. PORTRAIT of JOSEPH DUDLEY *inserted.*

2148 WILLIAMS. The Redeemed Captive Returning to Zion. ... [Another Edition.] *New-Haven.* 1802.

16mo, pp. 188. *Polished calf, yellow edges, by* F. BEDFORD. VERY SCARCE.

2149 WILLIAMS. The Redeemed Captive Returning to Zion: ... . To which is added a Biographical Memoir of the Reverend Author, with an Appendix and Notes, by Stephen M. Williams, A.M. M.D. ... *Northampton: Hopkins, Bridgeman, and Company.* 1853.

Sm. 8vo, pp. 192. *Portrait and View. Half olive morocco.* Mr. Williams' Memoir covers 40 pp.

2150 WILLIAMS (J.) An Enquiry into the Truth of the Tradition, concerning the Discovery of America, by Prince Madog ab Owen Gwynedd, about the year, 1170. By John Williams, LL.D. ... *London: J. Brown.* M.DCC.XCI.

[Also:] Farther Observations on the Discovery of America, by Prince Madog ab Owen Gwynedd, about the year 1170. Containing the account given by General Bowles, the Creek or Cherokee Indian, lately in London, and by several others, of a Welsh Tribe or Tribes of Indians, now living in the Western parts of North-America. By John Williams, LL.D. ... *London: J. Brown.* M,DCC,XCII.

8vo, 2 works in 1 vol., pp. viii., 82, (6); *ix.,* 51. *Half crimson morocco, carmine edges.* LARGE and FINE COPY. VERY RARE.

"The propositions of the learned author in favor of the existence of a tribe of Welsh Indians, are so well sustained by veritable evidence, and yet so positively known to be untrue, that it makes us doubt the value of all ratiocination. He adduces the positive testimony of more than twenty persons who had visited, or spoken with them in that language. Of all the conjectures regarding the origin of the Indians, not one has been fortified by a tithe of the absolute evidence of respectable authorities and witnesses Mr. Williams obtained, and yet not a single scholar has been convinced. If such a cordon of impregnable proofs can be thrown around a totally improbable hypothesis, there will be little we cannot doubt and nothing we may not believe."— *Field.*

See Burder (G.) No. 262.

2151 [WILLIAMS (John.)] The Hamiltoniad: or, an Extinguisher for the Royal Faction of New England. With Copious Notes, Illustrative, Biographical, Philosophical, Critical, Admonitory, and Political: Being intended as a High-Heeled Shoe for all Limping Republicans. By Anthony Pasquin, Esq. ... *Boston: Sold for the Author.* [1804.]

Roy. 8vo, pp. 104. *Half blue morocco, gilt top,* UNCUT. FINE COPY. VERY SCARCE, nearly the whole edition having been secured and destroyed by the friends of Hamilton.

Williams was an Englishman employed by a newspaper hostile to Cobbett. By a curious blunder in Lowndes' "Bibliographers' Manual," he is credited with writing most of the Federalist.

2152 WILLIAMS (R.) The | Blovdy Tenent, | of Persecution, for cause of | Conscience, discussed, in | A Conference betweene | Trvth and Peace. | VVho, | In all tender affection, present to the High | Court of Parliament, (as the Result of | their Discourse) | these, (amongst other | Passages) of highest consideration. | *London: Printed in the Year* 1644.

Sm. 4to, pp. (24), 247. *Crushed olive levant morocco, paneled and gilt sides, gilt edges.* A VERY FINE, LARGE and CLEAN COPY of this EXTREMELY RARE VOLUME, with the *Errata* usually wanting.

2153 WILLIAMS. Experiments of Spiritual Life and Health, and their Preservatives in which the weakest Child of God may get Assurance of his Spirituall Life and Blessedness and the Strongest may finde proportionable Discoveries of his Christian Growth, and the means of it. By Roger Williams of Providence in New-England. *London, Printed, in the Second Month,* 1652. *Reprinted by Sidney S. Rider, Providence.* 1863.

Sm. 4to, pp. x., 59. *Half crimson morocco, gilt top,* UNCUT.

Edited by Dr. Francis Wayland. A *small edition* only printed for Stephen Randall, Esq. nearly in EXACT FACSIMILE of the original, of which but TWO COPIES are known to exist.

2154 WILLIAMS (S.) The Natural and Civil History of Vermont. By Samuel Williams, LL.D. Published according to Act of Congress. *Printed at Walpole, New Hampshire, By Isaiah Thomas and David Carlisle, Jun.* MDCCXCIV.

8vo, pp. 416. *Map. Half green morocco.* Some signatures spotted, as in all copies. VERY SCARCE.

2155 WILLIAMSON (H.) Observations on the Climate in Different Parts of America, compared with the Climate in Corresponding parts of the other continent. To which are added, remarks on the Different Complexions of the Human Race; with some account of the Abo-

rigines of America. Being an Introductory Discourse to the History of North-Carolina. By Hugh Williamson, M.D. LL.D.
New York: T. & J. Swords. 1811.

Roy. 8vo, pp. viii., 199. Half blue morocco, gilt top, UNCUT. PORTRAIT of the AUTHOR *inserted.* VERY SCARCE.

2156 WILLIAMSON. The History of North Carolina. By Hugh Williamson, M.D. LL.D. ... *Philadelphia: Thomas Dobson.* 1812.

2 vols., 8vo, pp. xix., 289; viii., 289. Map. Half purple morocco, gilt top. LARGE and FINE COPY. VERY SCARCE.

2157 WILLIAMSON (P.) French and Indian Cruelty: Exemplified in the Life and various Vicissitudes of Fortune, of Peter Williamson. Containing a Particular Account of the Manners, Customs, and dress of the Savages: of their scalping, burning, and other Barbarities, committed on the English in North America, during his Residence among them: Being at eight Years of Age stolen from his Parents, and sent to Pennsylvania, where he was sold as a Slave: Afterwards married and settled as a Planter, till the Indians destroyed his House, and every Thing he had, and carried him off a Captive; from whom, after several Months Captivity, he made his Escape, and served as a Volunteer and Soldier in many Expeditions against them. Comprehending in the whole, A Summary of the Transactions of the several Provinces in America, particularly those relative to the intended attack on Crown Point and Niagara. And An accurate and succinct Detail of the Operations of the French and English Forces at the Siege of Oswego, where the Author was wounded and taken Prisoner. Also a curious Discourse on Kidnapping. Written by Himself. The Fourth Edition, with Considerable Improvements.
London: Printed for the Unfortunate Author. 1759.

12mo, pp. 120. Half red morocco, gilt top, UNCUT. SCARCE PORTRAIT of the AUTHOR *inserted.* PARTICULARLY FINE COPY. VERY SCARCE.

The Work is dedicated to the "Right Hon. William Pitt, Esq." The first edition was ordered to be burnt in Edinburgh where Williamson had established a Coffee-House, and introduced the useful plan of the Penny-Post. He died at Edinburgh in 1797.

2158 WILLIAMSON (W. D.) The History of the State of Maine; from its first Discovery, A.D. 1602, to the Separation, A.D. 1820, inclusive. By William D. Williamson.
Hallowell: Glazier, Masters & Co. 1832.

2 vols., roy. 8vo, pp. xii., 9–696; 729. Portrait. Half olive morocco, gilt top, UNCUT. FINE COPY. Rarely found *uncut.*

2159 WILLIS (W.) The History of Portland, from 1632 to 1864: with a Notice of Previous Settlements, Colonial Grants, and Changes of Government in Maine. By William Willis. Second Edition. Revised and Enlarged. *Portland: Bailey & Noyes.* 1865.

Roy. 8vo, pp. xv., 9–928. 7 Plates. 17 Facsimiles. Half olive morocco, gilt top, UNCUT. One of TWENTY-FIVE COPIES only printed on TINTED PAPER. The edition was nearly all destroyed in the great fire at Portland, in 1866.

2160 WILLISTON (S.) The Agency of God, in raising up Important Characters, and rendering them useful; Illustrated in a Discourse, delivered at Scipio, on the twenty-second day of February, 1800; being the day set apart by the Government of the United States, for the People to testify, in some suitable manner, their grief at the Death of General Washington. By Seth Williston.
Geneva: New York. [1800.]

8vo, pp. 14. VERY SCARCE.

2161 WILMOT (J. E-.] Historical View of the Commission for enquiring into the Losses, Services, and Claims, of the American Loyalists, at the close of the War between Great Britain and her Colonies, in 1783: with an Account of the Compensation granted to them by parliament in 1785 and 1788. ... By John Eardley-Wilmot, Esq.
London: J. Nichols, Son, and Bentley. 1815.

8vo, pp. viii., 203. *Plate. Half green morocco, gilt top,* UNCUT. VERY FINE COPY. SCARCE.

Contains a fine Outline Engraving, by H. Moses, from a Design by Benjamin West, of the Reception of the American Loyalists by Great Britain in 1783; into which Mr. West has introduced full length figures of himself, Mrs. West, and other members of his family.

2162 WILSON (B.) Memoir of the Life of the Right Rev. William White, D.D., Bishop of the Protestant Episcopal Church in the State of Pennsylvania. By Bird Wilson, D.D. ...
Philadelphia: James Kay, Jun. and Brother. 1839.

8vo, pp. 430. *Portrait, Plate and Facsimile. Half purple levant morocco, gilt top,* UNCUT. *Frontispiece* on *India paper.* THREE PORTRAITS of the BISHOP *inserted,* one of which is after the picture by Otis, in tint, and VERY RARE.

2163 WILSON (D.) The Life of Jane McCrea, with an Account of Burgoyne's Expedition in 1777. By D. Wilson. *New York:* 1853.

12mo, pp. 145. *Half green morocco, red edges.* PRIVATELY PRINTED. SCARCE.

2164 WILSON (D.) Prehistoric Man. Researches into the Origin of Civilization in the Old and the New World. By Daniel Wilson, LL.D. ... Second Edition. *London: Macmillan and Co.* 1865.

8vo, pp. xxvi., 635. 69 *Illustrations. Half red morocco, gilt top,* UNCUT, *by* BRADSTREET. Some of the illustrations are COLOURED.

2165 WILSON (J.) Substance of a Discourse; on Divine Providence, in special reference to the Memory, Character and Death of the late Gen. George Washington, delivered extempore, February 9th, 1800, before the Military Officers of Providence. By James Wilson. ... Published by Request. *Providence:* 1800.

8vo, pp. 16. UNCUT. VERY SCARCE.

2166 [WILSON (John.)] The Bibliographical and Retrospective Miscellany, containing Notices of Rare, Curious, and Useful Books, in

all languages; Original Matter illustrative of the History and Antiquities of Great Britain and Ireland; Abstracts from valuable Manuscripts; ... and Notices of Book Sales.
London: Printed for John Wilson. 1830.

Sm. 8vo, pp. iv., 160. Half red morocco, gilt top, UNCUT.

The author of this interesting bibliographical work was for several years a bookseller in Great May's Buildings, London.

2167 WILSON (R. A.) A New History of the Conquest of Mexico, in which Las Casas' Denunciations of the popular Historians of that War are fully Vindicated. By Robert Anderson Wilson.
London: Trubner & Company. 1859.

Roy. 8vo, pp. 539. Numerous Engravings. Half crushed red levant morocco, gilt top, UNCUT, *by* W. MATTHEWS. Fine INDIA PROOF PORTRAIT of DE SOTO, and PROOF BEFORE LETTER PORTRAIT of GEN. CASS *inserted.*

Really published at Philadelphia, though this copy has an English imprint.

"This work, written with a zeal which often degenerates into vehemence, is an arraignment of the Spanish historians, from whom all the current notions of the Spanish invaders have been acquired. With much show of reason, he maintains the unworthiness of their accounts."— *Field.*

2168 [WILSON (Samuel.)] An | account | of the | Province | of | Carolina | in | America. | Together with | An Abstract of the Patent, | and several other Necessary and Useful Par- | ticulars, to such as have thoughts of Tran- | sporting themselves thither. | Published for their information. *London: | Printed by G. Larkin for Francis Smith, at the Elephant | and Castle in Cornhil.* 1682.

Sm. 4to, pp. 27. Map. Crushed red levant morocco, gilt edges, by F. BEDFORD. LARGE and FINE COPY of one of the EARLIEST and RAREST books relating to Carolina.

The dedication to "William Earl of Craven Pallatine, and the rest of the true and absolute Lords and Proprietors of the Province of Carolina," is signed Samuel Wilson.

2169 WINGFIELD (E. M.) "A Discourse of Virginia." | By Edward Maria Wingfield, | The First President of the Colony. | Now first printed from the Original Manuscript in the Lambeth Library. | Edited, with Notes and an Introduction, | By Charles Deane. | *Boston: | Privately printed.* | 1859.

8vo, pp. 44. Half blue morocco, gilt top. One hundred copies PRIVATELY PRINTED. EXCESSIVELY RARE. This edition was SUPPRESSED, and the following issued in its stead.

2170 WINGFIELD. "A Discourse of Virginia." | By | Edward Maria Wingfield, | The First President of the Colony. | Now first printed from the Original Manuscript in the Lambeth Library. | Edited, with Notes and an Introduction, | By Charles Deane, | Member of the American Antiquarian Society, and of the Massachusetts | Historical Society. | *Boston: | Privately Printed.* 1860.

Imp. 8vo, pp. 45. Half blue morocco, gilt top, UNCUT. *One hundred copies* PRIVATELY PRINTED from the *American Antiquarian Society's Transactions.* Vol. IV. EXCEEDINGLY SCARCE.

Mr. Fowle's unbound copy sold for $45.

2171 WINTHROP (B. R.) The Washington Chair, presented to the New York Historical Society, ... 1857. [Also:] The Washington Chair presented to the Massachusetts Historical Society, by Benjamin R. Winthrop, Esq. *New York: Charles B. Richardson.* [1857.]

8vo, pp. 10, 7. 3 *Engravings. Half green morocco, gilt top,* UNCUT. *A few copies only* PRIVATELY PRINTED.

2172 WINTHROP (J.) A Journal of the Transactions and Occurrences in the settlement of Massachusetts and the other New England Colonies, from the year 1630 to 1644: Written by John Winthrop, Esq., First Governor of Massachusetts: and now first published from a correct copy of the original Manuscript. *Hartford: Elisha Babcock.* MDCCXC.

8vo, pp. (6), 364, (4). *Half blue morocco, carmine edges.* Some signatures a little spotted, and a corner of one leaf mended. VERY SCARCE.

"Mr. Winthrop kept a Journal of every important occurrence from his first embarking for America in 1630, to the year 1644. This Maunscript, as appears by some passages, was originally designed for publication; and it was formerly consulted by the first compilers of New England History, particularly by Hubbard, Mather, and Prince. On reading the work, the editor (N. Webster) found it to contain many curious and interesting facts relating to the settlement of Massachusetts and the other New England Colonies, and highly descriptive of the character and views of the first inhabitants. By consent of the descendants of Gov. Winthrop, proposals were issued for publishing *a small number of copies*."— *Editor's Preface.*

2173 WINTHROP. The History of New England, from 1630 to 1649. By John Winthrop, Esq. ... from his Original Manuscript, with Notes ... By James Savage. A New Edition, with Additions. ... *Boston: Little, Brown & Co.* MDCCCLIII.

2 *vols., 8vo, pp. xviii.,* (2), 514; 504. *Portrait and Facsimile. Half blue morocco, gilt top,* UNCUT. PORTRAIT *inserted.* A Review of the work pp. 23, [by S. G. Drake] is bound in with the second volume.

"The elder Winthrop has left an imperishable monument in his annals, and the laborious and learned annotations of Mr. Savage have rendered that work, as published in 1825–6, and still more in the new edition of 1853, a complete storehouse of our early New England History."

2174 WINTHROP. Life and Letters of John Winthrop, Governor of the Massachusetts-Bay Company at their Emigration to New England 1630. By Robert C. Winthrop. *Boston: Ticknor and Fields.* 1864.

[Also:] Life and Letters of John Winthrop, from his Embarkation for New England in 1630, with the Charter and Company of the Massachusetts Bay, to his Death in 1649. By Robert C. Winthrop. *Boston: Ticknor and Fields.* 1867.

2 *vols., 8vo, pp. xii.,* 452; *xv.,* 483. 4 *Plates. Facsimiles. Half green morocco, gilt top,* UNCUT.

"Mr. Winthrop has connected the letters and other documents with which his volumes are abundantly enriched, by a very clear and admirably written narrative, and has further illustrated them by short explanatory notes, wherever such elucidation is required."— *N. A. Review.*

2175 WINTHROP (R. C.) Oration Pronounced by the Hon. Robert C. Winthrop, ... on the Fourth of July, 1848, on the occasion of Laying the Corner Stone of the National Monument to the Memory of Washington. With an Introduction and an Appendix. Published by order of the National Monument Society. *Washington:* 1848.

8vo, pp. 68. *Half green morocco.* PORTRAIT *of* WASHINGTON *inserted.*

2176 WIRT (W.) Sketches of the Life and Character of Patrick Henry. By William Wirt. Sixth Edition, corrected by the Author. *New-York; M'Elrath & Bangs.* 1833.

8vo, pp. 443, 19. *Sheep, gilt back. Some signatures slightly spotted as in all copies of this edition.* PORTRAIT of the AUTHOR, and an AUTOGRAPH LETTER written and signed by him *inserted.*

2177 WISE (J.) The | Churches Quarrel | Espoused; | or a | Reply | in Satyre, to certain Proposals made, in | Answer to this Question, What further Steps are to be taken, that | the Councils may have due Constitution | and Efficacy in Supporting, Preserving, | and Well-Ordering the Interest of the | Churches in the Country? | By John Wise, Pastor to a Church | in Ipswich. | ... | The Second Edition | *Boston, Reprinted: Sold by Nicholas Boone, at the* | *Sign of the Bible in Cornhill.* 1715.

12mo, pp. (2), 116. *Polished calf, yellow edges, by* F. BEDFORD. FINE COPY. VERY SCARCE.

"This is perhaps the pertest, keenest, wittiest, stingingest little literary production that New-England ever produced, and, we venture further to say, that no American document of the kind, the Declaration of Independence alone excepted, (and we guess that Jefferson had studied Wise,) so completely covers its field and engrapes its foe. The occasion was a grand one. Certain New England Ministers, looking out with eyes too single upon their own line of business, met in Boston as self-elected Delegates in an Association, on the 5th of November, 1705, and issued sundry proposals for amending the New England Platform, so as to give more efficiency to the *Sacred Order of Men*, as well as to improve the supplies of loaves and fishes, but all put into plausible and proper ecclesiastical phrase. These Proposals were printed and well circulated throughout the country, and were well nigh swallowed whole by the hungry Fishers-of-men. The poor fish were not consulted. But the Wise old man of Ipswich kept the watch-tower and fell not asleep, so that the Camp was not surprised. Taking for his motto, *Titus* I. 13, *Wherefore rebuke them sharply, that they may be sound in the faith*, in 1710 he came out with the first edition of this little book. ... The book is very little known, but must ever stand out as a beacon of warning to aspiring ministers."— *Stevens.*

2178 WITHERS (A. S.) Chronicles of Border Warfare, or A History of the Settlement by the Whites, of North-western Virginia: and of the Indian Wars and Massacres, in that Section of the State; with Reflections, Anecdotes, &c. By Alexander S. Withers. *Clarksburg: Va. Joseph Israel.* 1831.

12mo, pp. iv., 319, (1). *Half gray calf antique.* FINE COPY. VERY SCARCE. This copy has the "Table of Contents," subsequently printed, and nearly always wanting.

"Of this scarce book, very few copies are complete or in good condition. Having been issued in a remote corner of Northwestern Virginia, and designed principally for a local circulation, almost every copy was read by a country fire-side until scarcely legible. Most of the copies lack the table of contents. The author took much pains to be authentic, and his chronicles are considered by Western antiquarians, to form the best collection of frontier life and Indian warfare, that has been printed."— *Field.*

2179 WOLCOTT (O.) Memoirs of the Administrations of Washington and John Adams, edited from the Papers of Oliver Wolcott, Secretary of the Treasury. By George Gibbs. ... *New York: Printed for the Subscribers.* 1846.

Roy. 8vo, pp. xvi., 574; viii., 556. Portrait. Half calf, gilt top, UNCUT. PORTRAITS of WASHINGTON and ADAMS *inserted.*

2180 WOLFE (James.) General Wolfe's Instructions to Young Officers, also his Orders for a Battalion and an Army. Together with the Orders and Signals used in Embarking and Debarking an Army by Flat-bottom'd Boats, &c. And a Placart to the Canadians. To which is prefixed, the Resolution of the House of Commons for his Monument; and his Character, and the dates of all his Commissions. Also the Duty of an Adjutant and Quarter Master. The Second Edition. *London: J. Millan.* MDCCLXXX.

12mo, pp. ix., (3), 106. Half red morocco.

Contains the daily General Orders and directions of Gen. Wolfe during the American Campaign, and is MOST RARE.

2181 W[OLLEY] (C[harles.]) A two Years | Journal | in | New-York: | And part of its | Territories | in | America. | By *C. W.* A.M. | *London, Printed for John Wyat at the Rose in | St. Paul's Church-Yard: and Eben Tracy, | at the three Bibles on London Bridge.* | MDCCI.

Sm. 8vo, pp. (8), 99, (5). Brown levant morocco, broad inside borders, gilt edges. A BEAUTIFUL COPY, in the finest state of preservation, and EXCESSIVELY RARE. We are unable to trace the sale of ANY COPY.

The author was an English clergyman, who went to New York with Governor Andros in 1678, in the capacity of chaplain to the garrison at Fort James. He commences the volume with the following "address to the reader:"— "The materials of this Journal have laid by me several years, expecting that some *Landlooper* or other in those parts would have done it more methodically; but neither hearing nor reading of any such as yet, and I being taken off from the proper studies and offices of my function, for my unprofitableness, I concluded that when I could not do what I ought, I ought to do what I could, which I shall further endeavour in a second part; in the meanwhile, adieu."

"Three copies known."— *Allibone.*

The following is a Reprint.

2182 WOLLEY. A Two Years Journal in New York, and part of its Territories in America. By Charles Wooley (*sic*), A.M. A New Edition with an Introduction and copious Historical Notes by E. B. O'Callaghan, M.D. ... *New York: William Gowans.* 1860.

4to, pp. 97. Catalogue 20. Half calf, gilt top, UNCUT. LARGE PAPER. *Fifty copies only printed.* A UNIQUE COPY, with the Title to the Journal printed in RED and BLACK. The ONLY ONE so done.

Forms No. II. of Gowans' "Bibliotheca Americana."

2183 WOOD (J.) The History of the Administration of John Adams, Esq., late President of the United States. By John Wood .... *New York:* 1802.

8vo, pp. 506. *Half red morocco, gilt top,* UNCUT, *by* BRADSTREET. VERY SCARCE. PORTRAITS of ADAMS and BURR *inserted.* A fine and clean copy of the ORIGINAL EDITION, rarely found *uncut.* The title page is mutilated in many copies.

This history, so full of scandal and untruth, was rigidly suppressed by Aaron Burr. The author himself wrote to his publishers thus:—"Should it not be suppressed, you will be prosecuted for the libels it contains."

See [Burriana.] No. 295. Nos. VI. and VIII.

2184 WOOD. The Suppressed History of the Administration of John Adams, (from 1797 to 1801), as printed and suppressed in 1802, by John Wood. Now republished with Notes, and an Appendix, by John Henry Sherburne. *Philadelphia:* 1846.

Sm. 8vo, pp. 392. *Portrait. Half morocco, carmine edges.*

2185 WOOD (S.) A Sketch of the First Settlement of the several Towns on Long Island; with their Political Condition to the end of the American Revolution. By Silas Wood. *Brooklyn: N. Y. Alden Spooner.* 1824.

8vo, pp. 66. *Polished calf, yellow edges, by* W. MATTHEWS. FINE COPY of the RARE FIRST EDITION, of which *one hundred copies only* were printed.

This is the EARLIEST Long-Island treatise ever published, which claims much breadth as a History.— *R. W. Bleeker.*

2186 WOOD. A Sketch of the First Settlement of the several Towns on Long Island; &c. By Silas Wood. A New Edition. *Brooklyn: N. Y. Alden Spooner.* 1828.

8vo, pp. 181, (2). *Half maroon morocco, gilt top,* UNCUT. MAP, VIEW, and APPENDIX of 60 pages *inserted.* SCARCE.

2187 WOOD (W.) Nevv | Englands | Prospect. | A true, lively and experimen- | tall description of that part of America | commonly called Nevv-England: | discovering the state of that Coun- | trie, both as it stands to our new-come | English Planters; and to the old | Native Inhabitants. | Laying downe that which may both enrich the | knowledge of the mind-travelling Reader, | or benefit the future Voyager. | By William Wood. | *Printed at London by Tho. Cotes for Iohn Bellamie, and are to be sold* | *at his shop, at the three Golden Lyons in Cornhill, neere the* | *Royal Exchange.* 1635.

Sm. 4to, 4 p. l. and 83 pp. text: Nomenclatures of the Natives' Language, etc., 5 pp. With *Map of the South part of Nevv-England, as it is Planted this yeare,* 1635. *Crushed green levant morocco, paneled and gilt sides, gilt edges, by* F. BEDFORD. AN ELEGANT COPY of this VERY RARE BOOK; the EARLIEST PRINTED ACCOUNT OF MASSACHUSETTS. Mr. Rice's copy, no better than this, sold for $200.

"The Second Part is 'Of the Indians, their persons, cloathing, diet, natures, Customes, Lawes, Marriages, Worships, Conjurations, wars, games, huntings, fishings, sports, Language, death, and burials.' It contains several short Vocabularies. The writer speaks of having resided in New England for four years, which seem to correspond to 1631–34. He mentions 'one of the English Preachers' who 'hath spent much time in attaining to their language,' and for whom the Indians entertained particular love and respect. John Eliot went out in 1631, so it is likely that the statement refers to him."— *Stevens.*

2188 WOOD. New-England's Prospect, Being A true, lively, and experimental Description of that part of America, commonly called New-England: ... The Third Edition. By William Wood. *London, Printed* 1639. *Boston, New-England, Reprinted, By Thomas and John Fleet, in Cornhill* ... 1764.

8vo, pp. xviii., 128. Half brown morocco, carmine edges. A FINE and CLEAN copy of this edition which is said to be MUCH MORE RARE than the original.

The editor appears to have been a person of learning, and though his notes do not run much in the historical or antiquarian line, they are yet judicious, and to this day of considerable value. He tells us nothing about William Wood, the author, nor has anybody else since told us much.

2189 WOOLMAN (J.) Considerations on Keeping Negroes; Recommended to the Professors of Christianity, of every Denomination. Part Second, By John Woolman ... . *Philadelphia: Printed by* B. FRANKLIN, *and* D. HALL. 1762.

8vo, pp. 52. Half gray calf, carmine edges. FINE COPY.

2190 WOODRUFF (H.) A Sermon occasioned by the Death of Gen. George Washington, Commander in Chief of the Armies of the United States of America. ... Preached December 29, 1799. By Rev. Hezekiah Woodruff, A.M. ... To which is added, an Appendix, giving a particular Account of the behaviour of Gen. Washington, during his distressing illness, also, of the nature of the complaint of which he died. By Doctors James Craik and Elisha C. Dick, attending Physicians. *Stoningtonport:* 1800.

8vo, pp. 16. UNCUT. EXCESSIVELY RARE. The ONLY COPY noticed by Dr. Hough.

2191 WOODWARD (W.) An Oration, pronounced at Hanover, New Hampshire, January 9, 1800; at request of Franklin Lodge, No. 6, in Memory of their Illustrious Brother, the Beloved George Washington. ... By Brother William Woodward. *Hanover: (N. H.) Jan.* 1800.

8vo, pp. 17. EXCEEDINGLY RARE.

2192 WOODWARD'S HISTORICAL SERIES. *Roxbury: Mass.* 1864–66.

7 vols., roy. 4to, half crushed red levant morocco, gilt top, UNCUT, *by* BRADSTREET. A SPLENDID LARGE PAPER COPY. FIFTEEN COMPLETE SETS only printed.

The Series consists of the following:

I. & II. Records of Salem Witchcraft, copied from the Original Documents. [*pp.* 279; 287.]

A full and complete transcript of the records and documents relating to the Salem Witchcraft Affair, and never before published.

III. & IV. The History of the Indian Wars in New England from the First Settlement to the Termination of the War with King Philip in 1677. From the Original Work, by the Rev. William Hubbard. Carefully revised, and accompanied with an Historical Preface, Life and Pedigree of the Author, with Extensive Notes, By Samuel G. Drake. [*pp. xxxii.,* 292; 303. *Map.*]

"The most valuable edition of Hubbard is that of Mr. Samuel G. Drake, well known as one of the most diligent of our antiquarians and historians in all that appertains to New England history in general, and to the Indians in particular."— *J. R. Bartlett.*

V. — VII. The Witchcraft Delusion in New England: Its Rise, Progress, and Termination, as exhibited by Dr. Cotton Mather, in the Wonders of the Invisible World; and by Mr. Robert Calef, in his More Wonders of the Invisible World. With a Preface, Introduction, and Notes, by Samuel G. Drake. [*pp. xcviii.*, (4), 247; *xxix.*, 212; 244.]

These volumes together with the first two of this series, contain a thoroughly exhaustive account of the beginning, progress and termination of the famous Salem Witchcraft Fraud, an event, which forms one of the most curious, interesting and remarkable episodes in the early history of New England.

2193 WOODWORTH (J.) Reminiscences of Troy, from its Settlement in 1790 to 1807, with Remarks on its Commerce, Enterprise, Improvements, State of Political Parties, and Sketches of Individual Character. ... By John Woodworth. Second Edition, with Notes, Explanatory, Biographical, Historical, and Antiquarian. *Albany: J. Munsell.* M.D.CCC.LX.

Sm. 4to, pp. iv., 112. *Half purple morocco, gilt top,* UNCUT.

2194 WYATT (T.) Memoirs of the Generals, Commodores, and other Commanders, who distinguished themselves in the American Army and Navy during the Wars of the Revolution and 1812, and who were presented with Medals by Congress, for their Gallant Services. By Thomas Wyatt, A.M. Illustrated by eighty-two Engravings on Steel, from the original Medals. *Philadelphia: Cary & Hart.* 1848.

Imp. 8vo, pp. 315. *Half blue morocco, gilt top,* UNCUT. TWENTY-FOUR PORTRAITS of the GENERALS, COMMODORES, &c., *inserted.*

2195 WYNNE (James.) Private Libraries of New York. [The Series of Articles on that Subject as they Originally appeared in the New York Evening Post; mounted on 173 leaves of Tinted paper, with a Composite Titlepage, and Ruled throughout in Mr. Trent's best style.] *New York:* 1856–57.

Imp. 8vo, half purple morocco, gilt top, UNCUT.

2196 WYNNE. Private Libraries of New York. By James Wynne, M.D. *New York: E. French.* MDCCCLX.

8vo, pp. viii., 472. *Half maroon morocco, gilt top,* UNCUT.

2197 WYNNE. Private Libraries of New York. By James Wynne, M.D. *New York: E. French.* MDCCCLX.

Imp. 8vo, pp. viii., 472. *Half purple levant morocco, gilt top,* UNCUT. LARGE PAPER; *one hundred copies printed.* TWELVE FINE PORTRAITS of persons whose collections are noticed in the work, PROOFS, INDIA PROOFS, and INDIA PROOFS BEFORE LETTERS *inserted.* The Engraving of the INTERIOR OF Mr. NOYES' LIBRARY is in two different states.

Among the principal libraries mentioned in this work, are those of John Allan, George Bancroft, Thomas P. Barton, J. Carson Brevoort, Rev. Dr. Chapin, Almon W. Griswold, William Menzies, William Curtis Noyes, Dr. Purple, Geo. T. Strong, R. L. Stuart, and Richard Grant White.

2198 YATES (J. V. N.) and MOULTON (J. W.) History of the State of New York, including its Aboriginal and Colonial Annals. By John V. N. Yates, and Joseph W. Moulton. *New York: A. T. Goodrich.* 1824.

[Also:] A History of the State of New York. By Joseph W. Moulton. Part II. Novum Belgium. *New York: E. Bliss & E. White.* 1826.

2 *vols.*, 8*vo*, *pp. xi.*, 9–325; *viii.*, 333–428. *Map.* *Half maroon morocco, gilt top*, UNCUT. THREE ENGRAVINGS and a MAP *inserted.* A fine set, RARE in any condition, particularly so *uncut.*

"The aboriginal history of New York is very ably treated, these divisions of the work being almost entirely devoted to an examination of the various questions, which have so vexed ethnologists regarding the 'origin of the savages,' the pre-Columbian history, and discovery of America, and a narrative of events connected with Indian history, to the year 1633."—*Field.*

See Moulton (J. W.) Nos. 1443, and 1444.

2199 YATES (R.) Secret Proceedings and Debates of the Convention assembled at Philadelphia, in the year 1787, for the purpose of Forming the Constitution of the United States of America. From the Notes taken by the late Robert Yates, Esq. ... and copied by John Lansing, Jun. Esq. ... Including "The Genuine Information," laid before the Legislature of Maryland, by Luther Martin, Esq. ... Also, other Historical Documents relative to the Federal Compact of the North American Union. *Albany: Websters, and Skinners.* 1821.

8*vo*, *pp.* 308. *Half gray calf.* PORTRAIT *of* LUTHER MARTIN *inserted.* LARGE and FINE COPY of this SCARCE WORK.

2200 YOUNG (A.) Chronicles of the Pilgrim Fathers of the Colony of Plymouth, from 1602 to 1625. Now first Collected from Original Records and Contemporaneous Printed Documents, and illustrated with Notes. By Alexander Young. Second Edition. *Boston: Little and Brown.* MDCCCXLIV.

8*vo*, *pp. xvi.*, 502. 8 *Plates.* *Half blue morocco, gilt top*, UNCUT.

2201 YOUNG. Chronicles of the First Planters of the Colony of Massachusetts Bay, from 1623 to 1636. Now first collected from Original Records and Contemporaneous Manuscripts, and Illustrated with Notes. By Alexander Young. *Boston: Little and Brown.* MDCCCXLVI.

8*vo*, *pp. viii.*, 571. *Portrait and Map.* *Half blue morocco, gilt top*, UNCUT. Uniform with the preceding No.

2202 [ZENGER (J. P.)] The | Tryal | of | John Peter Zenger, | of | New-York, Printer, | Who was lately Try'd and Acquitted for Printing and | Publishing a Libel against the Government. | With the Pleadings and Arguments on both Sides. |...| *London: Printed for J. Wilford, behind the Chapter-House, St. Pauls | Church-Yard.* 1738.

4to, pp. 32. *Green levant morocco, gilt top,* UNCUT. An ELEGANT COPY of the FIRST ENGLISH EDITION. VERY SCARCE.

This trial presents the first instance on record where truth was admitted as justification of a libel, a doctrine since admitted in American jurisprudence.

"The counsel for the defendant was Andrew Hamilton, of Philadelphia, who, for the able defense he made upon the occasion, was rewarded, by order of the Common Council of New York, with the freedom of the city in a splendid gold box. The trial took place in 1735."— *Rich.*

2203 [ZENGER.] The Trial of John Peter Zenger, of New York, Printer: Who was charged with having printed and published a Libel against the Government; and acquitted. With a Narrative of his Case. To which is now added being never printed before, the Trial of Mr. William Owen, Bookseller, near Temple Bar, Who was also Charged with the Publication of a Libel against the Government; of which he was honourably acquitted by a Jury of Free-born Englishmen. *London: J. Almon.* MDCCLXV.

8vo, pp. 59. *Half blue morocco, carmine edges.* FINE COPY. VERY SCARCE.

On the back of the title-page is the following sentiment: "In an age of persecution, when few people dare to write, and fewer still to print, these trials ought to be universally read by every true friend to English Liberty, who will here see two of the most noble stands, since the Revolution, in defence of Constitutional Freedom."

See *M. R.* XXXII. 238.

2204 [ZINZENDORF (*Count.*)] The | Remarks, | which | The Author of the | Compendious Extract, &c. | In the Preface to his Book, | Has friendly desired of | The Rev. of Thurenstein, | For the Time Pastor of the Lutheran Congregation | of J. C. in Philadelphia. | *Philadelphia: | Printed and sold by* B. FRANKLIN. | M,DCC,XLII.

12mo, pp. 24. *Polished olive morocco, paneled sides, centre and corner ornaments, broad inside gilt borders, gilt top,* UNCUT. An ELEGANT LITTLE VOLUME, and one of the EARLIEST and SCARCEST of Franklin's imprints.

2205 ZUBLY (J. J.) The Law of Liberty. A Sermon on American Affairs, preached at the Opening of the Provincial Congress of Georgia. ... With an Appendix giving a Concise Account of the struggles of Swisserland to recover their Liberty. By John J. Zubly, D.D. *London: John Almon.* MDCCLXXV.

8vo, pp. 73. *Half green morocco.*

"Warm for the Congress but sensible, Dr. Zubly is a man of abilities, and a good writer; witness also his rational and pathetic Address to Lord Dartmouth prefixed to this Discourse."— *Monthly Review.*

Dr. Zubly was a delegate from Georgia to the Constitutional Congress in 1775–6, and notwithstanding his "warmth for the Congress," he opposed separation from England, and returned to Savannah, which his unpopularity soon forced him to leave.

PORTRAITS.

2206 Foreign. From "Le Bibliophile Francais." 8vo. 17.

2207 American. From the "National Portrait Gallery." 8vo. 25.

2208 American. Some very scarce. 8vo. . . . . 20.

2209 American. Some scarce and fine. 4to. . . . . 19.

2210 American. "National Portrait Gallery" Series. Original impressions. 4to. . . . . 28.

2211 English. 8vo, and 4to. . . . . 19.

2212 Washington. Some very scarce. 8vo, and 4to. . . 13.

2213 American. India Proofs. 8vo, 4to, and folio. A very choice lot. . . . . 13.

2214 American. India Proofs. 8vo, 4to, and folio. Very choice and fine. . . . . 13.

2215 American. India Proofs. 8vo, 4to, and folio. Very fine and desirable. . . . . 13.

2216 American. Beautiful unlettered India Proofs. 8vo, 4to, and folio. . . . . 10.

2217 American. Beautiful unlettered India Proofs. 8vo, 4to, and folio. . . . . 10.

2218 American. Beautiful unlettered India Proofs. 4to, and folio. . . . . 9.

2219 American. Lettered and unlettered India Proofs. All from Private Plates. A most choice parcel. 4to, and folio. 15.

All the above portraits are suitable to be used either in an octavo or larger volume, and no lot contains any duplicates.

2220 Washington. Full length, leaning on a gun, with one arm resting on his horse. Mezzotint. Engraved by Valentine Green, from a painting by Peel. London, 1785. Size of plate 13½ by 19½ inches. Black Walnut and gilt frame.

2221 GREENE (*General.*) Full length, with horse. Mezzotint. Engraved by Valentine Green, from a painting by Peel. London, 1785. Same size, with similar frame, as the preceding No. to which this is a companion, and with which it forms a FINE and VERY RARE pair of portraits.

2222 WASHINGTON. Three quarter length, civil costume, with map on knee. Mezzotint. Painted and Engraved by E. Savage. London, 1793. Size of plate 13¾ by 17¾ inches. Black Walnut and gilt frame. VERY SCARCE.

2223 WASHINGTON. Same figure, in same posture, but from a different sized metal, with different accessories, and many variations in the work. It is wholly unlettered, does not appear ever to have been published, and is of the GREATEST RARITY. Framed to match the preceding No., with which it forms a VERY FINE and probably UNIQUE pair.

2224 LAFAYETTE. Full length. Engraved by Le Mire from the Picture by Le Paon. Proof before Title. Size of plate. 12½ by 16½ inches. Black Walnut and gilt frame.

2225 WASHINGTON. Full length. Engraved by Le Mire from the picture by Le Paon. Proof before Title. Same size, with similar frame as the preceding No., with which it forms a VERY RARE pair.

2226 HANCOCK. The Honble. John Hancock, of Boston in New-England, President of the American Congress. Mezzotint. 4to size. London, 1775. Gilt bead frame. SCARCE and FINE.

2227 WASHINGTON. General and Commander-in-Chief of the Continental Army in America. Done from an Original drawn from the life by Alex. Campbell of Williamsburgh, Virginia. Published at London, 1775. Full length, on horseback. Mezzotint. Size of plate 9½ by 12 inches. Blue and gold frame. Of MUCH RARITY.

THE FIRST PORTRAIT OF WASHINGTON EVER ENGRAVED.

"Mrs. Washington desires I will thank you for the picture sent her. Mr. Campbell, whom I never saw to my knowledge, has made a very formidable figure of the Commander-in-Chief, giving him a sufficient portion of terror in his countenance."— *Washington to Joseph Reed. Jan.* 31st, 1776.

2228 ROGER PAYNE. The celebrated Bookbinder, at work in his garret. Full length. Etched by S. Harding. VERY RARE. Black Walnut and Gold frame.

2229 JOHN PAUL JONES. Drawn by Notté, Engraved by Guttenberg. Half length. During the engagement between Le Bon Homme Richard, and the Serapis. Gilt bead frame.

LIBRARY FURNITURE.

2230 Solid Black Walnut Bookcase, four feet wide, double doors, each glazed with a single sheet of plate glass, two drawers underneath.

2231 Solid Black Walnut Bookcase, same size, and exactly similar to the above, but with a low press, in place of the drawers.

2232 Solid Black Walnut Bookcase. Same size, and precisely similar to the preceding one.

2233 Solid Black Walnut Bookcase. Four feet and one inch wide, with high press underneath suitable for folios. Glazed with plate glass in same manner as the doors.

2234 Solid Black Walnut Bookcase. Four feet and four inches wide, exactly similar to the preceding one.

2235 Large Solid Black Walnut Bookcase. In three compartments. Centre compartment five feet, and each wing four feet and six inches wide. Double doors, each glazed with a single sheet of plate glass. Drawers underneath.

The above bookcases were made for their present owner by Messrs. Kimbal & Cabus. They are all of uniform height, of the same style and character, and in fine preservation.

2236 Solid Black Walnut Library Table. Three feet six inches by five feet four inches. Six drawers.

2237 Solid Black Walnut Library Chairs. Covered with green leather. 4

2238 Solid Black Walnut Engraving Rack. Suitable for engravings of large size, and when open, forms a table for their exhibition.

2239 Letter Press. Black Walnut stand with drawer &c.

www.ingramcontent.com/pod-product-compliance
Lightning Source LLC
LaVergne TN
LVHW020919110826
845150LV00004B/722

* 9 7 8 1 4 2 5 5 5 5 2 4 5 *